"MY OLD CARPETBAGGER"

"MY OLD CARPETBAGGER"

How a Yankee Saved the Capital from Rebel Invaders, Led Virginia Republicans during Reconstruction and Fought Government Fraud

Taylor Matthews Chamberlin

"My Old Carpetbagger"

By Taylor Matthews Chamberlin

Copyright © 2024 by Taylor Matthews Chamberlin

All rights reserved. This book may not be reproduced in any form without permission of the copyright holders, except as permitted under Sections 107 or 108 of the 1976 United States Copyright Act.

ISBN: 978-1-942695-41-7

Cover & book design by: Hannah W. McLaughlin

Cover images: front cover: American flag sewn by Edith Matthews and sisters in 1863 (TCC), accompanied by GAR (TCC) and MOLLUS medals (JCC); back cover: Lt. S. E. Chamberlin in 118th N.Y. Inf. uniform (USAMHI); wife Edith when living in Baltimore (TCC); "Custer Badge," official emblem of Sickles's Cavalry Veterans' Association (JCC); and 19th Century Customs Special Agent Badge. (National U.S. Customs Museum, Hobe Sound, Fl.).

Mason Publishing provides support and resources to the George Mason University community for creating, curating, and disseminating scholarly, creative, and educational works.

Mason Publishing
George Mason University Libraries
4400 University Drive, MS 2FL
Fairfax, VA 22030
publishing.gmu.edu

Printed in the United States of America
Second Printing

Foreword and Acknowledgments

Almost thirty years ago, my mother dropped off a box of note cards and old documents—all that remained of my father's attempt to trace the Civil War career of his grandfather, Simon Elliot Chamberlin. As a boy, I fought mock battles with his cavalry saber and carbine, and now welcomed a chance to learn more about this mythic figure, whom we boys believed barely escaped death at Little Big Horn. Having just retired from the CIA to devote more time to our farm outside Waterford and launch an antiques business with my wife Cordelia, some historical research seemed a good way to fill the void left after a decade unmasking enemy spies as a counterintelligence specialist.

Unlike my father, an American history major at Harvard, my knowledge was mostly limited to visits to local battlefields and stories about my Quaker ancestors' devotion to Abe Lincoln's cause. I once proudly displayed the Union flag made by my great-grandmother, Edith Matthews, which twice escaped searches conducted at the family farm (Clifton) by John Mosby's Rebel partisans. However, attendance at Cornell and Columbia, followed by lengthy tours overseas, deprived me of chances to learn more before my father's unexpected death in 1977. Furthermore, I was not able to query local Civil War historian John Divine before his passing in 1996, and so was left on my own to reconstruct the lives of Elliot and his Quaker bride. What I did not foresee was the possibility that a simple exercise in tracing my roots would morph into a complex narrative that cried out to be shared with a wider audience.

Preliminary research quickly fleshed out Elliot's service in two New York regiments, as well as a later stint in the U.S. Cavalry out West, but the accompanying corruption, political intrigue, criminality and poor leadership that stalked his Civil War career presented a compelling tale of their own. In particular, I felt obligated to provide the first detailed account of the 25th N.Y. Cavalry, a regiment heretofore consigned to history's dustbin. His fellow veterans had tasked my great-granddad with documenting their accomplishments, but other than penning several published articles on their pivotal role in preventing the Confederates from invading Washington in July 1864, Elliot failed to go any further. But what a story he left for me to uncover, one so far removed from romanticized accounts found in most regimental histories, it could only be pieced together from court martial records of its officers. Yet, these same cavalrymen, recruited from Upstate farms and New York tenements, fought as well as any—when they had to.

A trip Upstate and to New England filled in Elliot's early years, including his life-long association with Vermont's powerful Republican Senator Justin Morrill, a previously unknown first marriage, and early career as a jeweler in Tennessee. To balance out his story, I turned to the Quaker girl he met at the end of the war, intending a chapter or two on what Edith's extended pro-Union family suffered at the hands of the Rebels. Anticipating an equally cursory account of their married lives on the Matthews family farm, I expected to have a compact book focusing on Elliot's Civil War experiences soon ready for publication.

This had to be shelved once preliminary findings on Edith's family showed an obvious need for a new account of the war in northern Loudoun County. As a first step in documenting the local conflict, I arranged for the Waterford Foundation to publish three primary source books: a reprint of Waterford's underground Unionist newspaper, a list of how Loudouners voted on secession, and an account of trade and travel across the Potomac border separating the warring North and South. This effort culminated in 2012 with the publication of *Between Reb and Yank*, a lengthy history of the Civil War in "North" Loudoun that I coauthored with John Souders. Great-granddad remained in limbo during the decade it took to bring this project to fruition, a period in which I was also absorbed in chairing the Foundation's Civil War Sesquicentennial Committee and editing the *Loudoun County Historical Society Bulletin*.

While these publications somewhat relieved the need to detail the wartime exploits of Edie's relatives, the discovery of a suitcase of old documents while renovating my mother's home added to my realization that Elliot's postwar career was much more significant than I had first assumed. Far from settling down to a bucolic existence at Clifton, Colonel Chamberlin found himself thrust into the political and social maelstrom that followed the war. His skill as a political activist, first demonstrated in organizing Union veterans for the Republicans, would propel this Yankee carpetbagger to that party's state chairmanship during Virginia's Reconstruction. Yet, his headstrong championship of reformist causes, including the rights of the formerly enslaved, brought him into conflict with John Mosby, the old foe of Loudoun Unionists who had improbably become President Grant's guru on Southern politics. When Elliot's behind-the-scenes support for an anti-corruption candidate to replace Grant was discovered, he was fired from his position as a special agent in the Treasury Department to make room for Mosby's brother. Reinstated under President Hayes, he would uncover massive corruption in New York's customhouse that led to the ouster of future President Chester Arthur, and he later received national attention for his role in exposing a corrupt sugar cartel that was depriving the federal government of millions of dollars in revenue. His fortunes further rose under the abbreviated presidency of James Garfield, with whom Elliot had worked closely in rallying veterans to the Republican cause, but that same high profile led to his being among the first fired during Cleveland's Democratic administrations. Although able to ride triumphally at the head of the Civil War Veterans' Division during both of McKinley's inaugural parades, he was now too old to return to his anti-corruption work as a special agent, although a less demanding Treasury position left more time for veterans' issues and other civic affairs.

Edith's story as wife of an embattled bureaucrat and political operative is no less compelling. After struggling to save their farm from foreclosure, she and their six children followed him to Baltimore and Washington. Left alone while he ran a special agency office in Savannah, Edith sought solace in the company of another. Their marriage mended after a difficult reconciliation, the couple spent their final years back on their Waterford farm, where Elliot passed away in 1908. Edith died a year later, satisfied with knowing their children were established on paths of their own. Another important figure in this story is Edith's "ultra-radical" sister Annie, whom we see pioneer the education of Waterford's Black citizens, join the first wave of women in the federal workforce and take up the cause of female suffrage. Like her brother-in-law, her Unionist heritage and reformist zeal frequently led to loss of employment.

Completion of what had become a much longer biography was further delayed by injury to my good eye in 2013 and restoration of my mother's home prior to our move there in 2016. While unable to conduct outside research without Cordelia's help, computer software and magnifiers allowed me to continue to write and read printed matter, albeit at a slower pace. Based on conversations with longtime friend Wally Grotophorst, whose duties at the George Mason University Library include oversight of the university press, I submitted my manuscript and received preliminary agreement in 2019 for its publication by Mason Publishing. Unfortunately, disruption of operations during COVID caused further delays, but as this is being written, I am pleased to be working with them to finally bring this project to a close.

It is impossible to name the many hands that aided this effort over the past quarter century, but none of this could have taken place without the aid and encouragement of my wife. From the beginning, Cordelia accompanied me on research trips and shared the task of locating relevant material in dusty files and data bases. Once my eyesight failed, her participation became even more essential, as it now included transcribing handwritten material, internet searches and communications, countless readings of the manuscript, and acting as my chauffeur.

Of the numerous repositories contributing to this work, I want to especially cite personnel at the National Archives, U.S. Army Heritage and Education Center, Strafford, Vermont Historical Society, and Leesburg's Thomas Balch Library, as being particularly knowledgeable and helpful. Although unable to visit the National Customs Service Museum in Florida, their staff was extremely forthcoming in sharing information, images and rare manuscripts pertaining to Elliot's profession. Finally, I owe a special debt to Loudoun County research librarian Anita Barrett, who has a remarkable knack for locating obscure publications and images.

As to family members, my mother Kathryn Taylor Chamberlin deserves a shout-out for getting me started on this quest, and for not throwing anything out. Bruce Clendenin, a direct descendant of Elliot's eldest daughter and current owner of Clifton, provided a trove of old letters and photographs. My cousins Robert and John Chamberlin shared useful anecdotes told by their father Wellman and grandfather Roy, as well as artifacts once belonging to our great-granddad. Their younger brother David and his wife Carolee provided access to the archives of the Goose Creek Quaker Meeting, to which they belonged, as well as documents about Edith's maternal ancestors. My nephew John C. Chamberlin, Jr., was able to locate and copy some unique newspaper articles in the New York Public Library. A more distant relative, Ellen McFann, provided very helpful information and photographs of Edith's Gover side of the family.

The acknowledged guardians of Waterford history, my former coauthor John Souders and his wife Bronwen, shared freely what was in their database and Waterford Foundation Archives. John was particularly helpful in providing high-resolution scans of images from the Foundation's and my own collections. He also provided helpful suggestions on a late version of the manuscript.

After my eyesight failed, I employed Lovettsville historian Edward Spannaus to conduct research, primarily on the internet. His tenacity in ferreting out obscure details amazed me, although I sometimes disappointed him when I pruned back some of the vast quantity uncovered.

David Nelson, who resides in the old Taylorstown mill, shared his extensive research on the Taylor side of Edith's family. Equally helpful was Pepper Scotto, founder of the Point of Rocks Historical Society, who provided images and information on Elliot's posting in that Maryland border town, as well as Taylor family residences nearby. Sharp Swan unselfishly shared detailed information that he has compiled for use in a future history of the 118th N.Y. Infantry. Finally, Phil Ehrenkranz made many useful suggestions after reading the manuscript.

Shannondale Farm
Hillsboro, Virginia
Fall 2023

Contents

Foreword and Acknowledgments i
Prologue 1

Part I: Simon Elliot Goes to War

Chapter 1: A Vermonter by Birth, 1834-1862 6
Chapter 2: Lieutenant, 118th N.Y. Infantry, July 1862-April 1863.........................13
Chapter 3: Service in Dixie, April-July 1863 23
Chapter 4: Draft Rendezvous, New York, July 1863-April 1864 31
Chapter 5: Captain, 25th N. Y. Cavalry, April-June 1864 40
Chapter 6: "Saving" the Capital, July-August 1864 47
Chapter 7: Dissension in the Ranks, August-October 1864 58
Chapter 8: Riding with Sheridan and Custer, August-October 1864 67
Chapter 9: Chasing Mosby's Partisans, October-November 1864 78
Chapter 10: Clearing Out the Valley, December 1864-March 1865 88
Chapter 11: Provost Marshal, Point of Rocks, Md., March-June 1865 98

Part II: Borderlands—Borderlines
Loudoun County, Virginia

Chapter 12: Edith's Quaker Roots 110
Chapter 13: Secession, 1859-61 122
Chapter 14: Quakers Go to War, 1862-63 134
Chapter 15: Mosby Comes to Town, 1864-65 143
Chapter 16: Horsing Around, May-September 1865 155
Chapter 17: A Long-Distance Romance, October 1865-June 1866 168
Chapter 18: The Veterans Descend on Washington, 1866 177
Chapter 19: Married to a "Boni Fido" Soldier, 1867 186

Part III: "My Old Carpetbagger"

Chapter 20: A Bureaucratic Farmer, 1868-1875 198
Chapter 21: And a Virginia Republican, 1868-1875 210
Chapter 22: Politics Derail Debut as Treasury Special Agent, 1876 220
Chapter 23: Fighting the Mosby Brothers for a Job, 1877 234
Chapter 24: Sugar Fraud and Customhouse Corruption, 1877-1881 244
Chapter 25: Clifton is Saved—at a Price, 1878-1887 260
Chapter 26: Special-Agent-in-Charge, Baltimore, 1880-1885 268
Chapter 27: On the Move, 1885-1892 278

Chapter 28: Domestic and Professional Turmoil, 1892-1894 291
Chapter 29: Happier Times, 1894-1900 302
Chapter 30: Old Soldiers in a New Century, 1900-1909 312
Epilogue 324

Appendices 326
Endnotes 330
Abbreviations and Bibliography 358
Index 369

Prologue

"LOVE AMONG THE RUINS"

As the sun rose on 25 April 1865, a sense of hope and renewal seemed palpable among the foothills of Virginia's northern Piedmont. The soft morning light streaming across the Catoctin ridgeline illuminated the rich, rolling farmland of Loudoun Valley and the Blue Ridge Mountains beyond. Mist still shrouded Catoctin Creek as it flowed north into the Potomac River, and the natural beauty and tranquility at this hour helped mask the ravages of war. The prosperous farms and thriving mills that once made Loudoun the most productive county in the state now lay in ruins—victims of four years of partisan strife and depredations by armies from both sides in a civil war local residents had sought to avert. The valley's location on the border with Maryland and the existence of a sizable pro-Union minority exacerbated tensions throughout this conflict. But the greatest blow occurred the previous November, when Gen. Philip Sheridan ordered the valley's systematic destruction in an attempt to halt the Confederacy's master of guerrilla warfare, Col. John S. Mosby.

Dawn that spring day brought unaccustomed excitement at Clifton, a 153-acre farm on the Catoctin Mountain's western slope. Although not an early riser, seventeen-year-old Edie Matthews had scarcely slept in anticipation of her pending trip to Point of Rocks. "The Point" lay only ten miles away on the far side of the Potomac, but Maryland had been a foreign and largely forbidden land for the previous four years. Even after Lee's surrender at Appomattox, federal authorities in Harpers Ferry maintained a blockade along the river until two days ago, when word was received that Mosby had finally disbanded his elusive battalion of partisan rangers, long the scourge of Union troops and sympathizers. Like most of their neighbors, the Matthews family remained loyal to the North throughout the war. This allegiance brought isolation and ostracism from the rest of the county, but an even more bitter pill to swallow had been the forced separation from loved ones and needed supplies across the river occasioned by the Union blockade. Now that the border was open to all, Secessionists and Unionists alike seized the opportunity to replenish their larders.

An accomplished horsewoman, Edie convinced her sixty-year-old father, Edward Young ("E. Y.") Matthews, to let her help him negotiate the muddy road leading to the Point. Her sisters, Marie and Annie, were jealous, but their mother Sarah needed them at home. As she dressed that morning, Edie was painfully aware of her depleted wardrobe. Her religion's plain dress code still left latitude for a young girl to look her best, but she would have to content herself with patched hand-me-downs on her first significant outing in nearly a year. She realized they could only afford the barest necessities; still, the teenager hoped she might persuade her father to buy material for a dress, or at least a hat to wear to First-day Meeting. Moreover, the prospect of celebrating the war's end with long-absent friends and perhaps meeting some of the handsome Union officers rumored to be stationed at the Point stoked her excitement.

Edith Matthews, age 18. (1866 tintype, TCC)

Kissing her mother good-bye, Edie went to the barnyard to round up an old nag whose sorry appearance had saved it from "conscription" by raiding parties. As she helped hitch up the wagon, she winced at the charred remains of their barn—a victim of Sheridan's notorious "Burning Raid." The Yankee general had ordered this devastation in hopes of denying supplies to Mosby's guerrillas, but to Edie the real victims had been the loyal farmers who supported the Northern cause. She ruefully remembered how the hand-sewn Union flag, which she and her sisters frantically waved that day had failed to dissuade the soldiers from their grim task.

As they drove away, Edie turned for a last look at their white stuccoed house. Its green shutters and comfortable porch were framed by shade trees on a hillside that rose towards the ridgeline behind. Although a Union supporter, she loved her home and surroundings above all, and never once considered abandoning Virginia for the North which, like most Southerners, she considered materialistic and ill-mannered. At the front gate they turned right on a small dirt road that ran northward past Talbott, the adjoining farm belonging to their cousins, the Walkers. Although it too had suffered during the "Burning Raid," E. Y. noted that his neighbor had already begun spring planting and wondered how much longer he could keep up Clifton without sons to help him.

Beyond Talbott, they entered the town of Waterford, a once-bustling community of 400 inhabitants on the banks of the Catoctin Creek. Quakers from Pennsylvania, drawn to its rich soil and abundant waterpower, had arrived in the area by 1733. Along with infusions of Scots-Irish and Germans from the north, the Loudoun Valley was soon populated by small farmers who relied less on slave labor than elsewhere in the county whose arrivals from Tidewater Virginia established large plantations. These differences were exacerbated during the Civil War, when the eastern and southern parts of the county solidly supported the Confederacy, while "North Loudoun" remained loyal to the Union. These Virginia loyalists would pay a heavy price for their convictions, and by war's end, Waterford resembled a ghost town, with few males present and its once busy shops and mills boarded shut.

Skirting the center of town, Edie and her father continued up High Street past the Baptist Church, still badly scarred from a skirmish that had taken place there in 1862 between Confederate partisans and the Independent Loudoun Rangers, North Loudoun's own Union cavalry unit. It had been organized by Capt. Samuel Means, a prominent miller who forsook Waterford's Quaker heritage to wage war against the Confederacy. At the far end of the village, the wagon passed the Fairfax Meetinghouse and the small Quaker school, both well known to Edie and her sisters. War had sorely tested their faith, just as it had that of other members of Loudoun's Quaker community. Unlike their brethren in the North, or

Matthews Family Home (Clifton), c.1866. (BCC)

even further to the south, their location on the front line had brought hardship and agonizing choices. The Friends' pacifist views and declarations of neutrality had offered little refuge, as they and other Unionists of draft age were imprisoned or pressed into labor gangs for failure to support the South. These actions caused an exodus of Waterford's draft-age males who, depending on their personal beliefs, either joined the military (mostly on the Union side), or sought refuge in Maryland. Likewise, the women left behind found themselves drawn directly into the war in ways that conflicted with their religious and social upbringing.

As their wagon rolled northward, Edie and her father discussed the many surprising events that had transpired since the fall of Richmond three weeks earlier. The news reaching Waterford had brought both rejoicing and sorrow. On 5 April, the Loudoun Rangers, the town's "protectors" for the past three years, received one of their most humiliating defeats at the hands of Mosby's partisans; yet, at the same time, other Rangers succeeded in killing John W. Mobberly, North Loudoun's most notorious guerrilla chieftain. Unionists barely had a chance to savor Grant's victory at Appomattox before receiving the devastating news of President Lincoln's assassination. Nor were they inclined to believe that Andrew Johnson could fill Abe's shoes in the troubled times ahead, even though the recent opening of the border brought renewed expectation they might at long last be allowed to enjoy the fruits of peace.

As father and daughter negotiated the winding road along the west flank of the Catoctin range, they could observe the war's effects on farms along the way. Near the outskirts of Taylorstown they glimpsed Downey's Loudoun Mills on the far side of the creek. It was owned by James M. Downey, North Loudoun's representative to the pro-Union "Restored Government of Virginia" in Alexandria. His wife had continued to run the mill after her husband was forced to flee, and it was said that only the quality of the corn liquor made on the premises kept the building standing, despite Mosby's vow to destroy the enterprise. At the center of Taylorstown stood a venerable stone dwelling and gristmill that had been purchased in 1784 by Edie's great-great-grandfather, Thomas Taylor, for whom the settlement was named. Here she and E. Y. took Furnace Mountain Road, which climbed over the mountain and afforded a magnificent view of Catoctin Creek's confluence with the Potomac far below and the nearby iron works, abandoned since the war's onset.

Descending to the Virginia shore brought into view the outcrop on the Maryland side that gave Point of Rocks its name and marked the spot where the Potomac carved a narrow passage through the mountain range. At the foot of this escarpment lay the Chesapeake and Ohio Canal and the Baltimore and Ohio Railroad tracks, both squeezed into a strip of land beside the river. The strategic importance of this section of Loudoun's border, second only to Harpers Ferry fifteen miles upriver, had been safeguarded by a Union encampment on the Maryland side since the beginning of the war. After Confederates burned the bridge leading to the Point, a small ferry provided the only means of crossing the river.

The settlement at the Point was a hodgepodge of tents, makeshift warehouses and stores, a railroad depot, telegraph station, and huts that served as residence for its greatly expanded wartime population. Mosby's raiders had ransacked the town the year before, adding to its ramshackle appearance. Upon arrival, Edie and her father made their way through the throng to a store owned by her mother's brother, Sam Gover, where the hard-pressed farmer tried to fill some of the family's most urgent needs, accumulated since the latest blockade had been in effect. E. Y., however, was more interested in checking a claim for losses suffered during the Burning Raid. As a Union sympathizer, he had been assured of reimbursement and the money was sorely needed to rebuild the barn and restock the heavily mortgaged farm. To check the claim's status, he and his daughter sought out the provost marshal.

Capt. Simon Elliot Chamberlin had arrived a month earlier with two companies from the 25th N.Y. Cavalry, assigned to guard railroad and canal installations along this section of the Potomac. In addition, he served as provost marshal in charge of border crossings and civilian affairs. Captain Chamberlin was thirty years old, a widower, and very much at a loss about what to do after the war. He had left his native Vermont as a young man to pursue a career as a jeweler in Nashville, Tennessee, but moved back to Glens Falls, New York, at the outset of hostilities. In 1862, he enlisted as a lieutenant in the 118th N.Y. Infantry and saw service in Virginia the following year. Two years later, he became a captain in

Capt. S. E. Chamberlin, age 30. (Boston Studio photograph, TCC)

the Twenty-fifth, which, after fending off Jubal Early's raid on Washington, participated in General Sheridan's Shenandoah Valley campaign. After the excitement and varied experiences of wartime, return to the jeweler's trade held little appeal, and the deaths of his wife and two young children three years earlier left him with no real place to call home.

Though unable to offer E. Y. Matthews much encouragement about his claim, the Union captain's attention was drawn to his daughter, who appeared to reciprocate his interest. After four years of repressive Rebel rule, the teenager viewed the dashing cavalry officer with barely disguised admiration. Edie was not the only Quaker girl with such fantasies—three of her friends had put out an underground Unionist newspaper, the *Waterford News*, that openly decried the lack of marriageable men in their village. The invitation that the editors extended for more Union soldiers to visit Waterford had not gone unnoticed at the Point.

That afternoon, Edie and E. Y. retraced their route back to Clifton. Whether her father noted anything more than a polite interest between his daughter and the handsome Yankee captain is not known, but he did not stop her from returning to the Point three days later with several girlfriends. Edie had a good excuse—the need to purchase more essentials for the family—and actually bought more than her father had. The second visit allowed for another conversation with Chamberlin, whom she invited to Quaker Meeting the following Sunday. Despite standing orders not to go into Virginia without prior permission, he risked the trip and dined with the Matthews family after the service.

What follows is the story of Edith and Elliot, who met as a great war ended and a longer period of socio-political upheaval started. That it began on the border separating North and South presaged difficulties that awaited the couple, he a New England Yankee, she a Virginia Unionist. Their refusal to shed these identities would complicate their lives and threaten his career. But it also thrust them into the midst of events that shaped America during the last third of the nineteenth century when, among his achievements, he would help mold the ex-soldiers into a potent political force, become chairman of Virginia's Republican Party, and as Treasury special agent lead a fight against corruption and fraud. As survivors of a war that almost destroyed the country and then as participants in its turbulent reunification, Edith and Elliot remind us that history can often be best appreciated through accounts of ordinary people caught up in extraordinary circumstances.

PART I
Simon Elliot Goes to War

Chapter 1

A VERMONTER BY BIRTH: 1834-1862

Even though Simon Elliot Chamberlin left his native Vermont at an early age, he never completely severed his ties to that region. For two centuries, his Puritan ancestors had cleared and tilled New England's rocky soil, with periodic interruptions to answer their country's call to arms. The first Chamberlin in his line, "Richard of Braintree" (c. 1624-c. 1673), came to Massachusetts from England prior to 1642, when his name appears in the records of Braintree, a liberal Puritan community south of Boston. Around 1655, Richard moved to nearby Roxbury, where he tended a small plot of land. Five of his children were baptized by John Eliot, known as the "Apostle to the Indians" for his pioneering work in converting the indigenous population. (Eliot's many accomplishments include the *Bay Psalm Book*, the first book printed in New England, and a translation of the Bible into Algonquin.) In 1668, Richard and his family followed the colony's westward expansion to Sudbury, where he purchased a sixty-acre farm.[1]

Richard's second son, Joseph Chamberlin (c. 1656-1721), served in the militia during King Philip's War (1675-76), a bloody Native American uprising that marked the end of the Puritans' amicable relationship with the Native American population. Afterwards, Joseph returned to Sudbury to marry and raise a family, probably on his father's farm. Around 1713, he and an older brother helped found the town of Oxford in Worcester County. Joseph's son, Benjamin Chamberlin (c. 1694-c. 1745) was sufficiently well-established to purchase 255 acres of uncleared land from William Dudley in "Keekamoochuag," near the Connecticut border. (Later renamed Dudley, the original settlement was situated on a hill belonging to Christianized Native Americans, who sold the land in return for rights, still exercised, to maintain pews in the town church.)

Ichabod Chamberlin (c. 1741-c. 1789) was only four when his father Benjamin died. After his mother remarried, the boy was raised by Samuel Newell of Dudley. Newell left his entire estate to his ward, who found himself a relatively prosperous landholder while still a young man. In addition to inherited land, Ichabod purchased a 100-acre farm after marrying Sarah Gale in 1767. A public-spirited man, he served as an official in Dudley, and his portrait hung in the town hall for many years. During the American Revolution, Ichabod belonged to two different infantry companies, and his name appears on a monument in the center of Dudley honoring veterans of that war. He is said to have sold his farm to help finance the colonist cause during the Revolution's darkest hours. (Existing records confirm his sale of several sizable pieces of property to aid Boston's poor during the British occupation of that city.) Despite this generosity, Ichabod's estate was worth 600 pounds when he died in 1789, although the individual shares inherited by his widow and ten children were small. Soon after settlement of the estate and their mother's remarriage, four sons and at least one daughter left Dudley to seek their fortunes in

---

1 The spelling Chamber<u>lin</u> is employed herein for Simon Elliot's immediate line, although the variant "<u>lain</u>" appears in many records relating to his family. Tradition holds that the first to drop the second "a" was a miller who could only fit ten stenciled letters on his barrels.

the Connecticut River Valley separating Vermont and New Hampshire.[2]

Ichabod had named his eldest son, Samuel Newell Chamberlin (1769-1844), to honor his guardian, and a year after his father's death, Samuel married Abigail White of nearby Pomfret, Conn., a descendant of Peregrine White, the first Pilgrim born in the New World. Samuel and Abigail moved from Dudley to Cheshire County, New Hampshire, after the birth of their first child, Samuel Chamberlin (1794-1855). Here near the Connecticut River in the town of Unity, three more children (Henry, Mary and Artemas White) were born, before the family moved to nearby Charlestown, where another son, George Olcott, was born in 1800. Sometime before the birth of their last child (Healy) in 1807, Samuel and Abigail crossed the Connecticut River to settle on a farm near Chelsea, Vermont.[3]

Vermonters are an independent lot, a heritage of the state's rugged topography and climate. Fearful of division between New Hampshire and New York, Vermont declared itself an independent republic during the Revolution, and did not join the Union until 1791, when its existence as a separate state was assured. The settlement of its boundary disputes at the end of the eighteenth century opened up one of New England's last frontiers, and the prospect of open land attracted many to Vermont's interior. Yet, as is often the case in such booms, the best valley land was soon snapped up, leaving many settlers to scratch out a living on the rocky slopes. Such seems to have been the fate of Samuel N. Chamberlin, who arrived in Chelsea late, and never achieved the stature his father had enjoyed in Dudley. His problems were compounded in 1808, when his wife died at age forty-one, leaving him to raise six children under the age of fifteen.

Chelsea lies in a narrow valley of the White River, surrounded by rugged foothills of the Green Mountains. Although the town has served as the seat of Orange County since 1796, its isolation limited growth, and it remains today an agricultural community of less than 600 inhabitants. Samuel Jr. was only fourteen when his mother died, and it is likely that his formal education ended at that point so he could help his father on the farm and take care of five younger siblings. The War of 1812 was not popular in Vermont, where it disrupted the state's extensive trade with Canada, but it offered a welcome diversion for a teenager. Young Samuel joined the local militia in early 1813, and subsequently enlisted for one year as a private in Captain Dickenson's company. After assembling at Burlington, the company was sent to Plattsburgh, on the New York side of Lake Champlain, to be integrated into the 31st U.S. Infantry. The American troops were successful in tying up the British in that region for over a year, before decisively defeating a superior force in September 1814, thus helping to end the war a short time later. Samuel, however, chose not to extend his enlistment, and was honorably discharged in May 1814. He received less than twenty-five dollars for his service.[4]

Whatever thoughts the young veteran had about remaining on the family farm died the following year, when his father remarried, sold the land and moved back to Charlestown, where he had six more children. The remarriage proved disruptive to his original family, and within a short time most dispersed to start separate lives. Healy, Mary and George migrated to Saratoga County, New York, while Artemas moved to Boston. Only the two oldest brothers, Samuel and Henry, remained in Vermont to work in the leather trade.[5]

While no confirmation has been found, it is likely that Samuel Chamberlin learned to make saddles and harness while working in the shop of Moses Sanborn (1757-1842), located in Strafford, Vermont, about ten miles from Chelsea. Unlike the latter, it was then a thriving agricultural center with 1900 inhabitants. Moses had three sons who served in the War of 1812, so Samuel may have forged a connection to the Sanborn family through them.

Whatever the case, in February 1817 Samuel (age twenty-three) was married to Moses's daughter Betsey Sanborn (twenty-five) by Jebidiah H. Harris, one of Strafford's leading citizens and a justice of the peace. Whether the wedding included a religious ceremony is unclear, although Betsey's parents belonged to the Universalist Church[6], a religious sect that believed in universal salvation based on the essential goodness of mankind. (Betsey's upbringing as a Universalist no doubt contributed to a strong sense of religious tolerance among her children. Moreover, the Sanborns were descended from Stephen Bachiler (c. 1561-1656), an independent-minded clergyman and early proponent of the separation of church and state after his arrival in New England in 1632. After he incurred the hostility of Boston's Puritan theocracy by casting the only vote against the expulsion of Roger Williams, Bachiler had to finish his ministerial career in Maine before returning to England. There, infidelity by the octogenarian's fourth wife was the inspiration for Nathaniel Hawthorne's *The Scarlet Letter*.[7]

Soon after their marriage, Samuel and his bride moved to Sharon, a small town in Windsor County some ten miles south of Strafford. They would have thirteen children over the next nineteen years, six of whom died in infancy. Their first child to survive, Charles Henry, was born in Sharon in 1820. The following year, Samuel's brother, Henry, paid fifty dollars for a half-interest in a tanyard, bark mill and surrounding land in Strafford Township. This development prompted Samuel to move back to Strafford and establish a business making saddles and harness from leather produced in Henry's tannery. During this period, he and Betsey had three more children, Elijah Witherell, Lucia Maria and Louisa Elizabeth.[8]

Strafford Meeting House Dominates Picturesque Vermont Town Elliot Called Home. (LC)

After Henry sold the tannery in 1827, Samuel took his family to Northfield. Located south of the state capital Montpelier, it was an agricultural and commercial center that promised a good market for a saddler, and the family remained there for over a decade, although little record of their stay has been found. After losing three daughters in infancy, Betsey gave birth on 8 June 1834 to twins, Simon Elliot and Susan Ellen, both of whom survived. Simon Elliot was named after his mother's oldest brother, Simon Sanborn (c. 1794-1855), a prosperous Strafford farmer. (Although Simon Elliot kept an engraving of his namesake, he preferred his middle name Elliot, and is so referred to in this book.) Samuel and Betsey's last child, William Sanborn Chamberlin, was born in December 1836, named after another maternal uncle. The parents remained in Northfield until at least October 1839, when their eldest daughter Lucia married Charles K. Crawford, a harness maker who may have worked at Samuel's shop.[9]

Samuel and Betsey have not been located in the 1840 Vermont census, and their whereabouts during the next decade remain unclear. Strafford probably held less attraction for Betsey after her father, Moses Sanborn, remarried shorty after her mother's death in 1832. When Moses died in 1842, he left Betsey only a third share of his furniture, which did little to help the Chamberlins financially. (Moses named Steven Morrill as his executor—an early indication of a close tie between the Sanborn and Morrill families that would prove critical in Elliot's later life.) While their parents' location is not known, some of their children spent part of this period in upstate New York with their uncle, George Olcott Chamberlin, who owned a successful farm near Galway in Saratoga County. (Elliot's fondest childhood memories were associated with vacations spent there, and in all probability this experience influenced his determination in later life to hold on to his wife's family farm in Virginia.) In 1843 Elliot's oldest sister Lucia Crawford gave birth to a son in Balston Spa, and in 1849 his sister Louisa married Duncan Cameron at West Milton, also in Saratoga County. Elliot's grandfather, Samuel N. Chamberlin, apparently reestablished ties with his first family late in life, as he died in Glens Falls and is buried in Galway Township, Saratoga County.[10]

The 1850 census found Elliot's parents living in Norwich, Vermont, a large town on the Connecticut River about twenty miles southeast of Strafford. Samuel was still working as a saddler, and he and Betsey lived in a rented house with only their youngest child William (thirteen). By this time, four of their children had married. Their oldest son, Charles, lived with his wife Susan in Montpelier, where he worked as a tailor. Lucia Crawford and her two children resided in St. Johnsbury, Vermont, where her husband ran a saddlery. Louisa resided with her husband Duncan Cameron's family in Warren County, New York, where he and his brother ran a hotel. Elijah married nineteen-year-old Mary Jane Lynch in 1850 and lived with her family in Danville, Vermont, where he too worked as a saddler.[11]

Unfortunately, Elliot's early years remain a mystery, with only glimpses of his passage into manhood. Despite his parents' peripatetic life and limited financial resources, he managed to pick up a sound secondary education through sheer perseverance. Surviving correspondence suggests that everyone in the family could read and write, but Elliot's letters were the most literate and show an uncommon skill in penmanship. Many years later, he wrote that his formal education consisted of "Common Schools and Academy, Montpelier & St. Johnsbury, Vt." Since his brother Charles lived in Montpelier, and his sister Louisa lived in St. Johnsbury, Elliot probably stayed with them during his early teens to take advantage of better schools in both locations. St. Johnsbury Academy was founded circa 1840 and remains a respected private school. His presence there has not been confirmed, but two of Elliot's best friends from Strafford, Jebediah and Myron Baxter, attended this academy.[12]

In another brief reference to his early life, Elliot stated that he moved to Boston in 1850, when he would have turned sixteen, and did not return to Vermont until three years later. Both Elliot and his twin sister appear to have spent most of their adolescence with relatives, in large part because their parents could not afford to keep them at home. In Boston, Elliot probably stayed with his uncle, Artemas, who ran a tavern in Cambridge, although there were several other close relatives living in that area who could have provided him lodging.[13] The move ended his formal education, but it would have been here that he trained as an apprentice watchmaker/jeweler, a trade he practiced during the next decade. A set of six coin-silver spoons with Boston hallmarks on which he practiced inscribing the initials S. E. C. attest to his skill. Artemas's oldest son, Nathan H. Chamberlain (as he spelled his name in later life), was then a scholarship student at Harvard College and later became a successful author, and their early association helped stimulate Elliot's intellectual interests, even after his formal schooling ended.[14]

Elliot's return to Vermont coincided with his father's decision to retire from the saddlery business in Norwich and move to Strafford. In January 1854, Samuel purchased a house and six acres of land for $300 from his wife's brother, William Sanborn. The house, which no longer stands, was located a half mile north of town on Old City Falls Road and was the only property that Samuel and Betsey ever owned. It is unclear whether Elliot ever resided with them, but by November 1854 he had already left Vermont to work in the Midwest. Not one to waste words, Samuel proffered the following advice to his twenty-year-old son on starting a new career: "I have nothing worthy to write you, only that I hope and pray that you will save your money that you earn, for there will be a day when you may need it more than at the present time." It was probably the last communication Elliot received from his father.[15]

Samuel was quite sick that fall, but his health improved sufficiently in the spring to accept an appointment from the Strafford town council to serve as surveyor of the highway. In return for a small stipend, he assumed responsibility for maintenance of the township's roads and made sure that citizens paid their road taxes. However, his stint as a public servant was short-lived, and he died of dysentery in September 1855 at age sixty-one. He was buried in the Strafford Cemetery beside Betsey's parents, Moses and Sarah Sanborn, and her brother Simon, who died later that year. No will has been found, but his estate was mostly limited to the house in Strafford, which his widow later sold for $425. Soon after her husband's death, Betsey and daughter Ellen moved to Glens Falls, New York, to stay with Louisa Cameron. In June 1858, Ellen married William Henry Martin at the First Presbyterian Church in Glens Falls.[16]

The sale of Samuel's house marked the end of any Chamberlin presence in Strafford, and Elijah was probably the only immediate family member still left in Vermont. (William's location is unknown, but he later resurfaced in New York.) Despite Elliot's departure from Vermont for Boston at age sixteen and having lived in Strafford for a few months at most, he later fostered the impression that his childhood had been spent in this scenic town. He left almost no record of his early life, and what he did write down was in response to requirements to obtain employment. One might therefore conclude that he either found his early years too unpleasant to dwell on, or, as seems more likely, at odds with an image he wished to portray of himself. His own children and their descendants grew up believing that he had been raised on a middle-class farm outside Strafford and were apparently unaware their paternal grandfather had been an itinerant saddler. As we shall see, Elliot was a typical Victorian male who kept his life strictly compartmented and frequently declined to share what he deemed inappropriate, even with his most intimate acquaintances. That his parents had been too poor to own property until the very end, that they had been constantly on the move in search of better economic opportunities, and that their children had to cut short their education and leave home to support themselves were matters he thought best forgotten.

Over the years, Elliot's descendants have made pilgrimages to his "birthplace" in Strafford and have not been disappointed by the picturesque village nestled in the Vermont hills. Strafford is little changed from when the Chamberlins left in 1855, with the exception that it has even fewer inhabitants and businesses. The most striking feature is the Town House, which sits atop a hill overlooking the common and is one of the most photographed buildings in the state. This all-white structure with its commanding steeple was built by the Universalists in 1798 as a combined non-denominational place of worship and assembly hall. On a steep slope behind the building one can glimpse the graveyard where Samuel Chamberlin is buried, and to the right is the Greek Revival house where Betsey Sanborn was raised. Another popular attraction is the Justin Morrill Homestead, a National Historic Landmark opened to the public in 1969. Located in the south end of town, the Homestead features the Gothic Revival house that Morrill designed and occupied until his death. Elliot's later claims to having a close affiliation with Strafford had much to do with it also being Morrill's hometown.[17]

Justin Smith Morrill (1810-1898) was born in Strafford and worked in his father's blacksmith shop as a boy. Forced to leave school at age fifteen, young Morrill was so successful as a merchant that he was able to retire in 1848 at age thirty-eight and devote himself to the study of architecture and landscaping, avocations put to good use in designing the house and grounds that comprise his Homestead. Tiring of life as a country squire, Morrill successfully ran for Congress in 1854. Among the last members of the Whig Party to be elected to national office, Morrill switched to the newly-formed Republican Party soon after his arrival in Washington and became one of its most influential members, first in the House and later in the Senate. Despite his national prominence, Morrill always returned to Strafford when Congress was not in session and played an active role in the local community.

Because of his own background, Morrill was particularly desirous of providing a means for farmers, mechanics and artisans to attain a combined liberal and practical education. His efforts culminated in the Land Grant College Act, which President Abraham Lincoln signed into law in 1862. It formed the basis for this country's public college system and is the legislation for which Morrill is best remembered today. Less well-known is his authorship of a bill that played a critical role in helping the North win the Civil War. After Southern Democratic congressmen abandoned Washington to join the Confederacy in early 1861, the Morrill Tariff Act passed the Senate just days before the outbreak of hostilities. By mandating a twenty-eight to thirty-five percent tax on imports, it had the immediate effect of restoring confidence in the government's ability to carry out a sustained military campaign. While this act literally financed the war and later retired the resulting debt, its author's principal motivation was the promotion of American manufactures. Morrill remained a champion of high tariffs until his death, as did the Republican Party through the McKinley administration, and his stance would have a significant influence on Elliot's later career in the Treasury Department.[18]

An intriguing aspect of this story is the origin of the close relationship Elliot enjoyed with Justin Morrill, who would serve as his mentor and protector from the Civil War era until the end of the century. A partial explanation lies in the close ties between the Morrill and Sanborn families. Justin Morrill's uncle had served as executor for the estate of Betsey's father, while her brother, William, was Justin's business partner and managed his affairs when the congressman was in Washington. However, the support Justin Morrill provided Elliot was not extended to other members of the Chamberlin family. Perhaps Morrill saw in his protégé the type of individual his Land Grant Act was designed to benefit. Both he and Elliot were sons of artisans, whose formal education had been cut short by economic necessity. They also shared practical and intellectual interests, including gardening, politics, history and scientific agriculture. While no record has been found to document when they became acquainted, a window of opportunity occurred between 1853, when Elliot returned to Vermont from Boston, and late 1854, when they both left the state to start new careers. Most likely their initial association was a fleeting one, though Elliot could have worked for Morrill during this period. Aside from a letter from his father, a set of spoons and the engraving of Simon Sanborn, the only item Elliot preserved from his youth was an honorary membership cer-

Vt. Congressman Justin S, Morrill, c. 1865, Elliot's Lifelong Ally. (LC)

tificate from the American Historical Society, dated May 1854. Elliot had a life-long interest in history, but one wonders whether Justin Morrill might have encouraged his young friend to join as a means of stimulating his intellectual curiosity. In any case, Morrill would favorably remember him when the Civil War brought them together a decade later.[19]

Like most twenty-year-olds eager to prove themselves, Elliot apparently gave little thought to leaving his aging parents behind as he set off for Chicago in late 1854. He had already come a long way on his own, having gotten a sound education and start in the jeweler's trade. Most likely, he continued apprenticeship in this field during the two years he spent in the "Windy City." While there, he met Margaret ("Maggie") G. Hobson, and in 1858 they were married in her hometown of La Porte, Indiana, about fifty miles east of Chicago.[20] Elliot took his nineteen-year-old bride to Rochester, a small city in the southeast corner of Minnesota, where he had already started employment as a watchmaker/jeweler. Their first child, Charles W., was born there in October 1859.[21]

Soon after Charlie's birth, Elliot and his wife moved to Nashville, Tennessee, along with her mother and younger brother. The move may have reflected the Panic of 1857, which ushered in a prolonged economic depression that dried up the market for watches and jewelry in newly established towns like Rochester. In Nashville, Elliot found employment with W. H. Calhoun & Co., a "purveyor of fine imported watches and quality jewelry" on the main square. A set of jeweler's tools and a gold scale from that period have been passed down in the family. A plaque with Elliot's name and Nashville address is fastened to the scale and confirms his skill as an engraver, a talent reflected in his penmanship. Elliot listed himself in the 1860 census as a professional jeweler with a net worth of $400.[22]

Yet, what appeared a promising start soon faded, as war clouds gathered over the nation, and Tennessee found itself sharply divided over the issue of secession. Although voters overwhelmingly rejected a break from the Union by a four to one margin in January 1861, the governor and state legislature favored the Southern cause, and maneuvered Tennessee into a military alliance with the Confederacy after Fort Sumter fell in April. Elliot, however, did not wait that long to investigate the possibility of relocating to avoid being trapped in the South. In February 1861 he traveled to Glens Falls, where he met with his mother and signed a quitclaim for his share in the Strafford house in return for one hundred dollars. Since it had been sold two years earlier, the delay in signing this document suggests he and his mother were not in regular contact. After surveying the job market in "the Glens," Elliot returned to Tennessee to bring Maggie and their son back to New York. She was again pregnant, and their daughter, also called Maggie, was born later that year.

Glens Falls is located halfway between Albany and Lake Champlain on the site of an old Native American portage trail around a fifty-foot waterfall in the Hudson River. Its strategic location was first recognized by the Native Americans, and the area played a vital role during both the French and Indian War and the American Revolution. The portage and cave at the base of the falls (known as Cooper's Cave) are central elements in James Fennimore Cooper's *The Last of the Mohicans*. In 1762, a group of Quakers led by Abraham Wing established the first permanent settlement, which they called Queensbury, and by the early nineteenth century, the town was the lumber capital of the United States. Logs cut in the nearby Adirondacks were floated down the Hudson to the falls, where they were cut into lumber and pulp wood for transport by barge to New York City. A feeder canal was completed around the falls in 1832, facilitating transportation on the upper Hudson and contributing to the area's prosperity. In 1839 Glens Falls was incorporated as a separate town and soon eclipsed neighboring Queensbury, which remained the seat of Warren County. Its prosperity was directly linked to power generated by the falls, which ran sawmills and factories along the river and canal. By 1860, the town had 3,400 inhabitants, nine churches, three newspapers, two banks, various inns and hotels, and several "manufactories," including four large sawmills. "The Glen" was one of the most prosperous communities in the region and a propitious spot for Elliot and his family to call home.[23]

Two of Elliot's sisters were already living in the Glen. His mother Betsey resided with his twin sister Ellen and her husband, William Martin, in a small frame house in a blue-collar neighborhood close to the factories along the river. The Martins had no children, and William was variously described as a laborer, carpenter, mechanic and lumberman. Elliot's other sister, Louisa, was better off, and she and her husband, Duncan Cameron, owned a brick house in a better neighborhood. They had moved to the Glen in 1857, when Duncan obtained a license to run the American Hotel. (He and his brother had previously managed a hotel in nearby Thurman.) Two years later, Duncan received licenses to run a hotel and tavern at the Mansion House, a well-known hotel in the center of Glens Falls. (It burned during a disastrous fire that swept through downtown in 1864.)[24]

Elliot and Maggie purchased their own home in July 1861, a modest brick residence that cost $1050 and still stands on the north side of Notre Dame Street, opposite a Catholic church. Although Elliot took out a mortgage to buy the house, he had saved enough by the following year to jointly purchase with a neighbor a vacant lot between their two homes. The details of Elliot's employment are not known, but he undoubtedly worked at one of the jewelry stores that benefited from the Glen's booming lumber business. Increasingly, however, the demand for personalized lockets and other mementos to give to loved ones heading off to war would occupy his time as a jeweler, especially one with his skill as an engraver.[25]

Chapter 2

LIEUTENANT, 118th N. Y. INFANTRY: July 1862-April 1863

Although Elliot Chamberlin later claimed he returned north to join the Union Army, over a year elapsed before he enlisted. Having lived in Tennessee, he knew well the South's determination to defend the Confederate cause, whereas most Northerners assumed the rebellion could be put down quickly. Rather than rashly answer President Abraham Lincoln's call for 75,000 volunteers after the fall of Fort Sumter in April 1861, Elliot opted to first establish his family in its new abode. He also had his sights set on becoming an officer, but this required establishing a base of support in Glens Falls, as officers in the Volunteer Army were generally selected by community leaders. The first regiment raised in the area was the 22nd N.Y. Infantry, which included Elliot's brother-in-law Duncan Cameron. "Dunc," as he was popularly known, joined in June 1861 as a first lieutenant, and would win promotion to captain within a year. The Twenty-second left the Glen in July but did not arrive in Virginia in time for the First Battle of Bull Run.

Elliot's oldest brother, Charles Chamberlin, was an even earlier volunteer, having enlisted as a private in the 1st Mass. Infantry in May. Charles (then forty-one) was a clothier in Cambridge, Massachusetts, and may have viewed military service as a way to cope with the loss of his wife and children several years earlier. His regiment, cobbled together from militia units and raw recruits, left for Washington in June amidst clamor from the press and Congress for the Union Army to march on Richmond. Their optimism was not shared by most Federal commanders, who were acutely aware their troops were poorly trained and equipped. But further delay to correct these deficiencies was not feasible, as many Northerners had enlisted for only sixty to ninety days and would soon be eligible to return to their homes. Thus, on 16 July, the Union generals reluctantly launched an invasion of Virginia.

The Confederates had entrenched themselves on the far side of Bull Run at Manassas, a railroad junction twenty-five miles southwest of Washington. When the Union vanguard neared Manassas on 18 July, Charles's regiment was sent forward to probe Southern defenses at Blackburn's Ford. After a fierce firefight, the 1st Mass. retreated amid considerable confusion, compounded by the resemblance of its grey uniforms to those of their opponents. Charles was among the casualties and taken back to Washington, where he was diagnosed with a hernia and discharged "for disabilities."[1] The engagement at Blackburn's Ford proved but a prelude to the main Battle of Bull Run on 21 July, when Union forces were decisively defeated and fled in disarray back to the capital. For the first time, the Northern public realized victory would not come easily, or quickly.[2]

Even relatively isolated communities like Glens Falls soon experienced the horrors of war as bodies of their young men, or more frequently the sick and wounded, were returned to loved ones. Disease killed many more soldiers than bullets during the war, and it is quite possible that a microbe brought back from the front was the culprit in tragedies that beset Elliot's family in 1862. His son Charlie died in March, and the loss was compounded in July when his wife and infant daughter also succumbed to illness. All three lie in the Bay Street Cemetery, under a large gravestone inscribed: *Maggie G., wife of S. E. Chamberlin, died July 23, 1862, aged 24 years./ Charles W., died Mar. 22, 1862, age 2 yrs., 4 mos., 23 days./ Maggie, died July 30, 1862./ Only children of S. E. and M. G. Chamberlin.* Elliot left no record of his grief during this period, nor did he discuss his first family's fate with his later children. Although he enlisted before Maggie died, he was not mustered into service until several weeks later and by then must have welcomed a chance to leave the scene of his recent bereavement.[3]

Gravestone for Elliot's First Wife and Children, Glens Falls, N.Y. (TCC)

During the first year of the war, both sides relied on haphazard recruitment systems. But the failure of Maj. Gen. George B. McClellan's Peninsula Campaign to take Richmond and President Lincoln's consequent call for 300,000 volunteers on 3 July 1862 forced Northern states to implement more effective procedures to fill their ranks. To meet New York's quota and administer the recruitment process, the governor established a "war committee" in each state senatorial district. Glens Falls was located in the 16th District, made up of Warren, Essex and Clinton Counties in the state's northeastern corner. The district committee selected Col. Samuel T. Richards of Warren County, Lt. Col. Oliver Keese, Jr., of Essex, and Maj. George F. Nichols of Clinton to raise a three-year regiment that became the 118th N.Y. Infantry, or "Adirondack Regiment." Selection of officers for each company in the regiment was left to committees in each county. Once chosen, company officers recruited the men who would serve under them.[4]

The organization of the Union Army reflected the need to mobilize an enormous body of men in a short period of time. At the beginning of the war, the Regular U.S. Army consisted of only 1,100 officers, many of whom resigned to join the Confederacy, and 15,000 enlisted men (most of whom remained in the Regular Army). Although two million men would eventually fight for the North, the Regular Army did not substantially increase in size. Instead, Northern states assumed responsibility for creating a separate Volunteer Army, which formed the bulk of the Union forces. The basic unit in this army was the regiment, which consisted of roughly 1,000 men divided into ten companies (lettered A-K, no J) of one hundred men each. (Cavalry regiments typically had twelve companies of eighty men each.) Regiments were led by <u>field-grade</u> officers—usually a colonel assisted by a lieutenant colonel and one or more majors. In addition, there was a small cadre of regimental <u>staff</u> officers, including a surgeon, chaplain, adjutant, and quartermaster. Companies were grouped into two or more battalions within the regiment, each commanded by a major. Individual companies were led by their <u>line</u> officers—a captain assisted by first and second lieutenants. Companies were subdivided into two squadrons, each led by one of the lieutenants.

The regiment, normally composed of men from the same geographic area, was the wartime home of the Union soldier. States designated their regiments in numerical sequence as they were formed, i. e., 1st, 2nd, and 3rd N.Y. Infantry Regiment, etc., although most also had informal names as well. State governments were responsible for recruiting, organizing, and any rudimentary training the men received before going to the field. Once there, regiments were grouped into larger components: typically, five to a brigade, three brigades to a division, three divisions to a corps, and two or more corps to an army. In reality regiments were seldom at full strength, and exceptions in the composition of the larger components were common. Length of service changed over time, early volunteers typically enlisting for periods ranging from three to nine months. This soon increased to one year, and by the time Elliot joined, the norm was three years, or the duration of the war.[5]

Halsey R. Wing, a descendant of Queensbury's Quaker founder, headed the committee of eleven prominent citizens who selected officers for Company A of the 118th. (Co. A would have taken precedence on parade and in line of battle over the other two companies raised in Warren County, D and G.) Josiah H. Norris, the popular foreman of the Glens Falls Fire Department, was chosen to be captain, Edward Riggs as first lieutenant, and S. E. Chamberlin as second lieutenant. His selection showed not only having achieved some standing in the community, but also that he must have lobbied for the position. His appointment was approved by the Adjutant General's office in Albany on 17 July, enabling him to begin enrolling volunteers into Company A. Lieutenant Chamberlin later recalled recruiting twenty-six men, or roughly one-quarter of his company. Since his wife died on 23 July, and his daughter a week later, it is difficult to imagine how he managed to function during this trying period, let alone participate in a successful recruitment drive.[6]

In a scene duplicated in thousands of towns across the country, North and South, the Glens Falls press reported the departure of the first batch of men destined to form the Adirondack Regiment:

> Fifty-one Volunteers from the company being raised in this village, left for the rendezvous at Plattsburgh [on Lake Champlain near the Canadian border] on Thursday last [31 July, the day after Elliot's daughter died], in charge of Lieut. Chamberlin, there to be examined and mustered into the U.S. service. They were taken to the cars at Fort Edward in wagons, accompanied by a band of music. Crowds of people congregated in our streets to see the brave fellows off, and many a blanched cheek and tearful eye told of the struggle to suppress that grief of parting with brothers, husbands and sons too holy and pure for public gaze...Many proudly carried little tokens of affection or remembrance...and all were followed by the blessings of those left behind.[7]

Capt. Josiah H. Norris, Co. A, 118th N. Y. Inf. (TCC)

At Fort Edward the recruits caught the train to Whitehall on the south end of Lake Champlain, where they boarded a steamer for Plattsburgh. After delivering his charges to the site where his father had served during the War of 1812, Chamberlin returned to Glens Falls and was present with Captain Norris and Lieutenant Riggs when the remaining forty-seven men in Company A left town on 8 August. On that occasion, firemen presented their former chief with a sword, which Norris promised to put to good use in the field. Chamberlin was formally mustered into the 118th at the Plattsburgh Barracks on 10 August.

Since the record shows that he was re-mustered ten days later, he may have been given compassionate leave to attend to personal affairs after the deaths in his family.[8]

With little more than two weeks to organize and train, the 118th was officially designated a regiment on 27 August, although subsequent events revealed that discipline remained lax. Volunteer regiments in the Civil War reflected their commanding officer to a large degree, and even his supporters admitted Col. Samuel Richards was not a "disciplinarian." In fact, the regiment might have been better served if he had stuck to his job as treasurer of Warren County, since chronic rheumatism frequently kept him absent from his command. As a result, the organization and training of the 118th at Plattsburgh fell to its twenty-one-year-old adjutant, Lt. Charles Pruyn, whose prior experience was limited to some militia service and a brief stint in Virginia with the 96th N.Y. Infantry. The situation confronting the Adirondack Regiment, however, was all too typical of other Northern volunteer units, with officers selected for political reasons, rather than prior military experience and leadership skills.

Lt. S. E. Chamberlin, Co. A, 118th N.Y. Inf. (1862 NYC carte de visite, USAMHI)

As the date for departure from Plattsburgh approached, there were last-minute visits with loved ones and a round of farewell celebrations. Congressman-elect Orlando Kellogg, dubbed "father" of the 118th, gave a rousing farewell speech to the regiment, in which his son also served. The soldiers broke camp on 1 September to board a steamer in a drizzling rain. After an overnight voyage down Lake Champlain to Whitehall, the men were herded into boxcars for the trip to Albany. Considerable damage was done to the cars along the way, as enlisted men broke out siding to improve ventilation and enjoy the view. When the train stopped at Saratoga Springs, inhabitants staged a celebration that turned into a "joy riot," as young girls rushed to collect uniform buttons and bestow kisses on the soldiers. Word had just arrived of the outcome of the Second Battle of Bull Run, which had been fought two days earlier "without checking the northward march of Lee's Army." As the regiment's chronicler would recall: "Fear, apprehension and anxiety prevailed, and not since the very commencement of the war were men moving towards conflict so thoroughly appreciated, and never before was the seriousness of their mission so fully understood; and so it was that our journey south was a continuous ovation."[9]

In Albany, Adjutant Pruyn's mother arranged lunch for the troops, who were then transferred into cattle cars, causing widespread complaints about arriving as "freight" and leaving as "live stock." The soldiers finally arrived in New York City at midnight and were marched to temporary barracks in City Hall Park. The next day, the men stole so much from souvenir vendors in the park the police had to be summoned. Later, the soldiers broke ranks to see the widely advertised wonders in P. T. Barnum's nearby museum. Others used the confusion to sample different pleasures in the big city, and at least sixty men were missing when the regiment left to catch the ferry to New Jersey. After a night on the train, the 118th arrived in Philadelphia in time to wash and eat breakfast at a canteen staffed by ladies from Philadelphia's Union League. Many of the stragglers caught up with the regiment here, having taken a later train from New York. Another train ride brought them to Baltimore on the evening of 4 September.

Maryland was sharply divided over the war, and the Adirondack Regiment had its first encounter with civilians vocally hostile to Union soldiers while marching through Baltimore's dim streets. At the headquarters of Gen. John E. Wool[10], a fellow Upstater who commanded the Middle Military Department, the 118th received orders to entrain immediately for Harpers Ferry. At that moment, Robert E. Lee had assembled a large Confederate force in Loudoun County, Virginia, with the obvious intention of crossing into Maryland. However, since Chamberlin's regiment had not yet received arms, and there were no railroad cars available, the New Yorkers spent the night sleeping on the sidewalks. The following day, they learned their orders had "very fortuitously" been changed to an assignment guarding the "Relay House," an important railroad junction ten miles south of Baltimore. (Had the 118th gone to Harpers Ferry as originally planned, it would have been involved in either the surrender of the garrison there, the largest capitulation of U.S. troops until the Second World War, or the Battle of Antietam several days later.)

At their new destination, the New Yorkers began the task of setting up their headquarters, christened "Camp Wool" in honor of their district commander. After sleeping on the ground that first night, orders were given for each company to set up tents, which included a walled officer's tent for the captain and a similar one to be shared by its two lieutenants, while the enlisted men each had shelter tents. Under the direction of 1st Sgt. James S. Garrett, Company A's tents were the first to be properly erected, and the sergeant proudly wrote home that the other companies were directed to follow the "pattern" he had established. Garrett also praised the generosity of Captain Norris, who agreed to allow 1st Lieutenant Riggs to share the captain's own tent, thus permitting Garrett to move into the unoccupied half of Chamberlin's tent. Several nights later, as Garrett sat writing home, Chamberlin was described as "snoring loud enough to raise the tent off the foundation." Garrett, a Glens Falls dentist, had enlisted as a private in August, but had already won promotion to first sergeant and seemed intent on making himself an indispensable part of Company A. While his roommate may not yet have realized it, the officious sergeant would become an implacable rival for Chamberlin's own position.[11]

The Relay House was located at the junction where the B&O tracks running between Baltimore and Washington met those headed west through Frederick, Point of Rocks, Harpers Ferry and beyond. Nearby stood the Thomas Viaduct over the Patapsco River, at that time the largest masonry railroad bridge in the country. The likelihood of an attack on this structure subsided after Lee's southward-bound army re-crossed the Potomac in late September, but the threat from sabotage or a raid remained. During the weeks that followed, the soldiers kept busy constructing fortifications to protect the tracks and viaduct.

Soon after their arrival, the men watched a trainload of paroled prisoners from the 115th N.Y. Infantry pass by. They had surrendered at Harpers Ferry and were on their way to a "prison camp" outside Chicago.[12] The 115th had departed New York just before the 118th and taken the last train to Harpers Ferry that might otherwise have transported Chamberlin's regiment to a similar fate. Another consequence of the Antietam Campaign was that Lee's defeat gave President Lincoln the political support necessary to announce his plans to free the slaves. On 24 September the regiment was called out on dress parade to hear Lt. Col. Oliver Keese read Lincoln's Emancipation Proclamation. Lt. John Cunningham, who later became the regiment's historian, recalled that many were upset to discover they would now be "fighting for the niggers" rather than just to preserve the Union.[13]

During a stay of over six weeks at the Relay House, the regiment lost six men to disease, including two to typhoid fever. The soldiers were kept busy with drills and preparations for winter. During their spare time, they wrote home, with over 3,000 letters mailed in just one week. A regimental band formed during this lull to replace the hopelessly untalented drum corps. The Relay House's rail station facilitated visits from friends and enabled the men to talk with returnees from the front, including members of the 22nd N.Y. Infantry, then on their way back to Glens Falls to recover from casualties suffered at the Second Battle of Bull Run. Chamberlin learned his brother-in-law, Duncan Cameron, had been hit by shrapnel and had to have his right arm amputated at the shoulder. Louisa joined her husband at a military hospital in Alexandria to nurse him through the ordeal and accompany him back to the Glen, where "the jovial, fun-loving, generous 'Dunc'" was given a hero's reception.[14]

The 118th's stay at the Relay House was unexpectedly cut short on 23 October, when General Wool ordered its immediate transfer to the Defenses of Washington Department. In doing so, Wool advised the War Department that a picket from this regiment had "killed an engineer of the Washington train, and threats were made that other injuries might be done to passing trains." He added: "The man who murdered the engineer is in jail. I therefore deemed it best to send the regiment where it would do no harm." Cunningham attempted to minimize this incident in his history, claiming the picket's gun had accidentally discharged when he jumped to attention. Cunningham, however, had a personal interest in the case, as the man came from his company (F), and he participated in the soldier's legal defense against murder charges. A letter written by another officer reported that the picket guards that evening had been drinking so heavily their captain had been afraid to make his rounds. According to this version, the man who discharged his weapon deliberately shot the engineer when the latter failed to heed his drunken challenge to "halt" the train. This writer was upset that this "wanton act" had forced them to leave their comfortable camp in Maryland and establish new quarters in Virginia at the onset of winter, but the shooting had provoked an outcry among Baltimore's citizenry, already ill-disposed to the presence of Yankees in their midst. The case went to trial, where the soldier responsible was convicted of manslaughter, although he was later pardoned and rejoined his regiment.[15]

To minimize further public reaction to the killing, the 118th boarded a train at the Relay House after dark on the 23rd and arrived in Washington before dawn the next day. The following morning, the New Yorkers marched along Pennsylvania Avenue to Georgetown, where they reported to the headquarters of Brig. Gen. John J. Abercrombie, commanding a brigade in the Defenses of Washington. That afternoon, they continued upstream along the Potomac to Chain Bridge, where they crossed the river and ascended the palisades on the Virginia side, reaching their new post at nightfall.[16]

Here the Adirondack Regiment would share the relatively undemanding task of guarding the approaches to Chain Bridge as part of Abercrombie's Brigade in Silas Casey's Division. For its regular administration, the 118th was assigned to a provisional brigade commanded by Col. Clarence Buell of the 169th N.Y. Infantry, which in addition to Buell's regiment also included the 152nd N.Y. and an artillery battery. When the Adirondack men arrived at Chain Bridge on 24 October, they found the two earthworks commanding the heights, Forts Marcy and Ethan Allen, already occupied by the 152nd and 169th, leaving the newcomers to construct their quarters from scratch beside Buell's headquarters at Fort Ethan Allen. The 118th could not have asked for a more scenic setting, as Company A's wagoneer wrote home: "We are in a very fine situation, our camp is situated on a very high hill and commands a very fine view of the country around; Washington, Georgetown and Alexandria are in sight of our camp – and over 30,000 troops are visible...."[17]

An early sign of Lieutenant Chamberlin's skill in manipulating military bureaucracy occurred soon after arrival, when he went on a mission to liberate two "care packages" destined for his company. The boxes, stuffed with provisions and clothing by friends and relatives back home, weighed 206 and 411 pounds. One of the beneficiaries wrote the following account to his mother:

> [Capt. Norris's] mess chest and boot box have both arrived here safe and sound. The boxes lay in Washington some days before the Capt. knew they were there. Yesterday Lieut. Chamberlin went down to Washington to see Capt. Dunc Cameron [who had returned to service after only a month's recuperation from his amputation], and whilst there made search for the boxes. After much inquiry he found them and by dint of hard labor, some coaxing, and paying out nearly all his money, he managed to get the boxes as far as Georgetown, and, this afternoon [19 Nov.], they were brought here to the Company, by the team which goes to Georgetown for bread to supply our Regiment. [The writer then described his comrades' delight with their gifts, in particular one soldier who received his favorite clay pipe, which everyone wanted to smoke.][18]

During the winter of 1862-63, the Adirondack Regiment settled into a routine, which for the enlisted men consisted primarily of "fatigue work" (manual labor) improving the forts, batteries and rifle pits that comprised the Ethan Allen/Marcy complex. This was interspersed with guard duty on the

Ft. Ethan Allen, Defenses of Washington. (stationery printed for fort commander, TCC)

picket line and occasional expeditions to scout and forage in the surrounding countryside. Unusually cold weather and illness were the soldiers' chief enemies, although at least one was accidentally shot on picket duty. While a direct attack was unlikely, isolated pickets had to remain alert for spies, saboteurs, or small raiding parties. Their biggest fear was that "snipers" among the local populace might seek "the glory of killing a Yankee." Cunningham described picket duty as "an anxious, trying and nervous business, this standing out in the open of nights as a target." There were lighter moments, however, when the men engaged in snowball fights and athletic events.[19]

The situation of line officers such as Chamberlin was somewhat more comfortable. In addition to running their companies, they took weekly turns serving as regimental "officer of the guard," when they commanded the pickets, and "officer of the day," when they handled administrative duties. The three officers in each company typically shared a small wooden hut, which in addition to their cots had a makeshift table and chairs. One lieutenant wrote that he and his captain had recently added to "their stock of personal property," a cat and a "niger boy" named Andrew Jackson, who slept in the supply tent. "We did have a kind of partnership in the darkie; but the little scamp snatched an oyster which I had roasted & ran away." This so infuriated the lieutenant he gave up his right to use the services of the "contraband,"[20] as former slaves were called by their Union liberators.[21]

In December, Chamberlin learned he would be promoted to first lieutenant, replacing Edward Riggs who would become captain of Company D. Receiving an increase in rank within four months of enlistment was an auspicious start to his military career, one he proudly announced on the title page of a new diary begun on 1 January 1863 to record his increased responsibilities as Company A's second-in-command. Unfortunately, most entries are limited to noting the weather and daily assignments. He and his twin sister Ellen exchanged occasional letters that winter, and she sent him a valise filled with warm clothes. (Their mother Betsey found writing difficult and communicated with her son via Ellen.) He also corresponded with his mother-in-law, Mrs. Emily Hobson, who sent him a "care package" from Janesville, Wis.[22]

Some evenings Chamberlin dined at nearby homes in Fairfax County, as Virginia housewives often earned scarce cash by serving meals to Union officers. Not a few of these women channeled information gained from their patrons back through the lines via Mosby's Rangers, the only Confederate unit operating in the area that winter. John S. Mosby, the Civil War's most famous and successful guerrilla leader, had only just begun to form his band of partisans. From bases in Fauquier and Loudoun Counties, Mosby honed his skills by conducting raids against Union forces stationed in western Fairfax County, and also ran probes as far as the defense line around Washington.

In a January letter home, a private from the 118th complained that their acting commander, Lt. Colonel Keese, "is a good deal harder on the men than the Col. and is disliked by most of the Regiment." Colonel Richards had spent the past two months in Glens Falls due to poor health, but had recently returned to Washington, and the writer expected him to resume his duties shortly. "He will receive a cordial welcome. He is deservedly popular and does the best he can for the health and comfort of his men." The soldier had heard the regiment would soon be transferred to provost guard duty in the D.C., which he preferred to camping in the Virginia woods. Still, he proudly described their present camp as "far superior in appearance and neatness to most of the camps in this or any other place," adding that his regiment had been cited as a "model of cleanliness and good order."[23]

In mid-January, Chamberlin was granted two days leave in Washington. The first night he attended a play at the East Lyceum, and the following day visited the Capitol building, where he spoke with Vermont Representatives Justin Morrill and Portus Baxter, both personal acquaintances. His decision to meet the Vermont congressmen rather than the New York delegation is significant in light of subsequent developments and was the first indication he was still in contact with Morrill. Afterwards, the lieutenant stopped by the Navy Yard and that evening saw "Lady Gay Spanker" at a theater. (Spanker was a character in a popular British comedy entitled *London Assurance*, "a rich study in sexual equivocation.") The following morning he took time to view exhibits at the Smithsonian Institution before returning to camp. During another trip to town, he had a photograph taken to send to his mother.[24]

At the end of January, the soldiers received their first salaries since enlistment. The arrival of the paymaster was initially greeted with enthusiasm but was soon followed by "demonstrations" against the sutler, Lot Chamberlain. Lot (no known relative of Elliot) was a civilian who worked with the quartermaster to procure and transport food and supplies for the 118th. Sutlers earned extra income by selling personal items to the men from their wagons, or a hut erected for that purpose. Lot had teamed up with a moneylender from Washington, who advanced funds so that the soldiers could buy items from the sutler's store on credit. The sutler, paymaster and money lender worked together to see that these loans, plus interest, were deducted from the soldiers' pay, hence the latter's dissatisfaction upon finding how little they actually received.[25]

Chamberlin's promotion opened the position of 2nd lieutenant to Sgt. James Garrett. The morning of 3 February found the prospective lieutenant enjoying his first taste of company command, as Norris and Chamberlin were both out on picket duty. In a letter to his wife, Garrett expounded on his newfound status, and whether it would be made permanent. He felt entitled to the promotion, but feared others plotted against him.

> I do not expect the promotion for Colonel Keese has got it in for me and had issued an order that all candidates for promotion shall be examined by a board of three commissioned officers…If I am ordered before the board and recommended for promotion I shall accomplish what no other man in the regiment has the ability to do. Lieutenant Chamberlain has done his best or worst to make me unpopular in the regiment. The powers-that-be seek to have a son [Edgar] of Judge Halsey R. Wing appointed. There is not a man in the company less qualified for the position or more universally disliked by the company. He knows that I am competent to drill the company far better than he ever could. All the officers of the regiment know it and admit it. Chamberlain knows that I neither love, respect nor fear him. Let him do his worst. If I live, a day will come when he will be my inferior in rank as he is in brain.[26]

That same night, Garrett was unexpectedly called before an officers' examination board, and given questions on tactics and Army regulations to answer. Informed that he had passed, he claimed to his wife that no other officer in the regiment could have done as well, something the board itself had confirmed to him. Not just content with his new status, Garrett went on to reveal his inner feelings for yet further advancement: "How I wish fortune would favor me once and place me one peg higher[27] than Lieutenant Chamberlain so that I could repay some of his insults with interest."[28]

Garrett's promotion was finalized by 21 January, the date on which Chamberlin noted that his second lieutenant had purchased a new uniform to reflect his status as an officer. The only other mention of him in Chamberlin's diary is an entry a month later that he had sold Garrett his old uniform. There is, however, no indication in either this diary, or a second one begun in April, that he was aware of the animosity that Garrett bore towards him, or to Norris and Keese. Since Chamberlin was a personal friend of Judge Wing, the charge that he favored the judge's son for promotion over Garrett is probably accurate and was perhaps a reason for the falling out between the two lieutenants. Unfortunately, the problem did not go away.[29]

Implicit in Garrett's letters is his assumption that he was more popular within the company than the first lieutenant. This is hard to substantiate, but of twelve photographs Chamberlin kept of members of the 118th, four were of immediate superiors (Lt. Riggs, Capt. Norris, Maj. George Nichols and Col. Richards), and five were staff members (two surgeons, the chaplain, quartermaster, and adjutant). There were also *cartes de visite* of fellow officers: 1st Lt. John Cunningham (F), Capt. William Bailey (H) and 1st Lt. John Carter (B). Notably absent are any of enlisted men or NCOs in his company.[30]

In early February, Brig. Gen. Nathaniel J. Jackson, then commanding the Army of the Potomac's XII Corps, headed a delegation to Forts Marcy and Ethan Allen. Chamberlin accompanied this group during its rounds, and the acquaintance he made with Jackson helped land a position on the general's staff later that year. On 9 February, Chamberlin temporarily took command of Company D in the absence of Captain Riggs, who spent the day with Lieutenants Cunningham and Kellogg in the Senate and House galleries, where they met with New York's Senator Ira Harris and Representative William Wheeler. (Frequent contact between Union officers and their Congressional representatives was typical in the highly politicized Volunteer Army.)

On 11 February, Chamberlin's brigade received orders to move to Washington, and the following day all three regiments set up headquarters about a mile north of the Capitol Building near Findley Hospital. Individual companies from the 118th were dispersed to serve guard duty at public buildings throughout the city, including the train station, supply depots and Old Capitol Prison. (During this period, the Adirondack Regiment was under the overall command of Gen. John Martindale, the city's military governor.) Companies A and B were detailed to guard the Soldiers' Retreat, a canteen near the train station, and did not have time to pitch their tents until the following day. It was Chamberlin's first exposure to the unglamorous but important work of the provost marshal and his attendant guard. Several days later he, Captain Norris and a lieutenant from Company B were transferred to special duty at the train station. Chamberlin's orders specified that he:

> 1st. ...assume command of all guards at Rail R. Depot and those furnished from that Post for regular Guard duty. He will see that good order and obedience to orders is enforced.
>
> 2nd. It is also directed that Guards be furnished to Captain Ware 10 NY Vols. and Lieut. Quimby (who are detailed to examine passes, & etc. at the Gates leading to the cars) in such numbers as shall be absolutely necessary for the purpose of arresting and detaining deserters or other persons who may be arrested.
>
> 3rd. Lieut. Chamberlin will also assist to examine passes & etc. at the gates and will also furnish one *Corpl. and six Privates* to Lieut. Kellogg for patrol duty daily.// by command of Wm. F. Garrett, Major [2nd D.C. Inf.], Comdg. Post.[31]

The following day, he received supplementary orders directing him to deliver a detachment of recruits to the provost marshal at Fortress Monroe for assignment to their permanent regiments. Chamberlin accompanied the men by train to Baltimore, where they caught a steamer to their destination at the juncture of the James River and Chesapeake Bay. The assignment gave him his first glimpse of Hampton Roads, an area he would come to know well after the war. Fortress Monroe guarded the entrance to Norfolk's harbor and, along with other parts of Virginia's Eastern Shore, never fell into Confederate hands. Throughout the war, it served as a vital staging and communications center for Union forces in southern Virginia.[32]

Upon returning to Washington on 20 February, Chamberlin learned that State Senator R. M. Little of New York's 16th District had arrived with word that Governor Horatio Seymour had finally signed his commission as first lieutenant. The next day he sold his old uniform to 2nd Lieutenant Garrett and borrowed forty-five dollars to purchase a new one. (His diary reveals a pattern of making and receiving loans that continued long after the war.) He then celebrated his official promotion at a dinner with his younger brother William[33] and Major Garrett, the post commander who had assigned him to the railroad depot.[34]

In late February, the soldiers received a second visit from the paymaster, who paid them through December. Of the $270 Chamberlin received, $150 was forwarded to his mother (probably for mortgage payments on his house), and another sixty dollars was given to Captains Riggs and Norris to pay off loans. After lending ten dollars to a corporal and paying another ten dollars owed for meals at a nearby boarding house, he had only forty dollars to last him for the next several months. In March, his routine at the train depot was interrupted to allow him to escort recruits by steamer down the Potomac to Belle Plain, a port about fifteen miles east of Fredericksburg, Virginia. The sole diary entry for 2 April was "Maggie's birthday," a poignant reference to his late wife.[35]

In early April, Republican Congressman Orlando Kellogg paid a visit to regimental headquarters at "Camp Adirondack." He was accompanied by a delegation from Clinton County that had come to Washington to protest the closing of the customhouse in Plattsburgh. (The well-connected Cunningham later accompanied the delegates to an audience with the President and Treasury Secretary.) For some time, rumors were rife that the 118th would be sent south to fight in Tidewater Virginia, and as the anticipated departure date neared, Kellogg and another New York politician hosted dinners for the officers. Although Kellogg had a personal stake with a son in the regiment, Northern politicians increasingly found it in their interests to support soldiers from their districts.[36]

On 12 April, the 118th was told to prepare to leave for the front within two days, although over a week would elapse before the actual departure. Much of the regiment's equipment was hastily put in storage, or abandoned, including such amenities as tables and chairs. Enlisted men carried all their own equipment, plus seven days' rations, in their knapsacks. Officers' baggage was limited to blankets, a small valise or carpetbag, and a "reasonable" mess kit. The stay in the capital, which one sergeant termed a "filthy city," had not been as enjoyable as anticipated; at least six men had died of disease, and nine others were sent home to recuperate. The regiment had been split up since leaving Fort Ethan Allen, and the week before departure was devoted to drill in a last-minute effort to improve discipline and morale. Colonel Richards presided over a final dress parade on 19 April, but rheumatism prevented him from joining his command at the front. The following day, the men boarded the steamer *Utica* and were soon treated to a view of Mount Vernon as they passed down the Potomac. That evening they anchored in the Chesapeake Bay at the mouth of the river.[37]

Chapter 3

SERVICE IN DIXIE: April-July 1863

The transport carrying the 118th N.Y. Infantry encountered heavy swells entering the Chesapeake Bay on the morning of 21 April 1863, causing many to spend the remainder of the voyage leaning over the rails. After arrival at Fortress Monroe, Lt. Col. Oliver Keese went ashore to receive orders from Maj. Gen. John A. Dix,[1] commanding the Department of Virginia, who directed the New Yorkers to proceed immediately to Suffolk, a small city twenty-five miles southwest of Norfolk. For ten days prior a sizable Confederate force under command of Gen. James Longstreet had been probing Union defenses around Suffolk, and the 118th was one of several regiments rushed to defend the city. Returning to the *Utica*, Keese and his men crossed Hampton Roads to Norfolk, where they boarded flatcars for the ride to Suffolk.

In the evening, as their train passed Great Dismal Swamp, the Yanks watched "the arched paths of the burning fuses of bombs and shells, and the flash of their explosion. It was our first experience with hostile artillery and most of us remembered our homes and 'bitterly thought of the morrow'." After a few hours of fitful sleep beside the Suffolk railway station, the Adirondack Regiment marched to the city's outskirts and pitched camp in a wheat field. A lucky few found pig pens and abandoned hovels that offered greater protection from mud and rain than their "dog tents." The "city" proved little more than a sleepy rural town, whose male population had long since departed. In fact, the only civilians in evidence were the ever-present "Yankee peddlers," selling their wares to the soldiers.[2]

On a rainy 24 April, Chamberlin deployed with forty men on picket duty along the Dismal Swamp Canal, where they were attacked by Rebel snipers, but suffered no casualties. The next day, the 118th was sent to occupy "Fort Dix," which, despite its imposing name, consisted of some low earthworks thrown up along the Nansemond River's east bank. "Old Glory" was raised above the fort in plain sight of Rebel sharpshooters on the far side of the narrow channel, and several New Yorkers were wounded while working on the fortifications. From these hastily erected defenses, Keese's men directed sufficient fire across the river to allow a small steamboat to escape downstream. A few days later, the 118th was transferred to "Fort McClellan," an equally squalid camp situated in a swamp. Only the paymaster's arrival brightened the soldiers' otherwise muddy existence.

Chamberlin's diary confirms that their stay was marred by constant rain, while he kept occupied filling out the April muster roll. There is no mention, however, of an incident that occurred there, which resulted in charges written up against him by 2nd Lt. James Garrett. In a document that has come down through Garrett's family, the lieutenant charged his immediate superior with: (1) Using insulting and abusive language, specifically calling Garrett a "Damned Coward," "Liar," and a "God damned stinking lying son of a Bitch"; (2) Assault and battery, by grabbing him by the hair and jamming his head into the ground; (3) Conduct prejudicial to good order and military discipline, by challenging Garrett to a duel, and when he refused to fight, taunting him as a coward who "had not the spunk of a Louse"; and (4) Conduct unbecoming an officer and a gentleman, by all of the above actions. The allegations, written in a legalistic format, ended with a demand for a court martial against the accused, and named as witnesses for the prosecution: Capt. Edward Riggs, 1st Lt. R. C. Kellogg, and 2nd Lt. Sam Sherman, all from Co. D, and 1st Lt. J. L. Cunningham and 2nd Lt. William Stephenson of Co. F. (If Chamberlin wanted to know who his enemies were, he did not have to look far from this group.)[3]

Since no mention of this incident appears in either Chamberlin's private correspondence, or in the regimental record, Garrett either dropped the charges, or was persuaded not to formally file them. It should be noted that the witnesses named in this document were not necessarily present at the alleged assault, only that these were fellow officers whom Garrett felt would support his side in any dispute with Chamberlin. While the latter could still count on the support of Captain Norris and Colonel Keese, there was clearly a group of young line officers who were not on Chamberlin's side. Even though this is the only known instance he resorted to physical violence against a fellow officer, a similar incident would cost him a federal position after the war. Chamberlin had a hot temper and an elevated sense of honor, which Garrett would have known about and may have deliberately used to provoke a confrontation, perhaps by disobeying a direct order. We do know that Garrett, on the day his promotion to second lieutenant was confirmed, expressed frustration over still having to answer to Chamberlin, and wished that this situation could be altered. But even after he had apparent grounds to bring his immediate superior before a court martial, Garrett apparently found he still lacked the necessary support needed to pursue this action, specifically from Norris and Keese, who by then were preoccupied with leading the regiment on successive expeditions against the enemy.

No doubt Chamberlin was relieved to put this whole matter aside, when the 118th moved its camp to Fort Union on 1 May. The expected Rebel offensive never materialized, so two days later the Federals launched their own attack on the Southerners, who promptly "skedaddled." The following day, the "Siege of Suffolk" was declared over, after the Rebs were found to have slipped westward behind the Blackwater River. "Our troops advanced after the enemy and followed them across the Blackwater," reads Chamberlin's entry for 4 May, but the next day the Yanks were ordered back to camp. After several days of inactivity, the soldiers began to chafe at their commanders' caution and longed for a chance to show what New York "mudsills" (privates) could do when they got their "grit up."[4]

After being assigned to several different brigades since arriving in Suffolk, the 118th was placed in the Reserve Brigade under Col. David Wardrop of the 99th N.Y. Infantry. The brigade headquarters at "Camp Union" proved more satisfactory than previous camps occupied by the 118th, which was fortunate as Wardrop's forces remained there while other units crossed the Nansemond in pursuit of the enemy. While in camp, Chamberlin answered letters from his mother, sister Ellen and his mother-in-law, as well as attending church twice. A visit from the paymaster on 7 June enabled him to send $180 to his mother.[5]

Their turn "to bag a few greybacks" came a short time later, when the Reserve Brigade participated in a reconnaissance to the Blackwater River to search for Rebels and protect work crews tearing up track west of Suffolk. The Adirondack Regiment took the lead during these operations, with Companies A and F deployed in front as skirmishers. Most of the Confederates had already withdrawn, however, and casualties from enemy sharpshooters were light. But after a few pickets were "bushwhacked," the Yankees set fire to several buildings in retaliation. At the onset, the soldiers had been under strict orders not to pillage or forage, although these restrictions ceased after their rations ran out.[6]

On 14 June, General Dix received orders from the Army's General-in-Chief, Henry Halleck, to employ all available troops in a concerted effort to threaten Richmond and cut off its supply lines by destroying railroad bridges across the South and North Anna Rivers. Halleck's orders were issued in the expectation that an offensive by Dix's army against the Confederate capital would divert troops from a large force that had been detected marching northward in the Shenandoah Valley under Robert E. Lee. It was feared the Southerners were again planning to invade the North—and Lee would in fact get as far as Gettysburg. Dix's concurrent advance towards Richmond has been called "Gettysburg's Second Front," but its more common name, "the Blackberry Raid," better reflects its meager results. [7]

In response to Halleck's directive, the expeditionary forces to the Blackwater received urgent orders on 17 June to return to Suffolk, necessitating a forced march of twenty-five miles. Near the town Carrsville, Wardrop's Brigade stopped to rest at the "Deserted House," site of a fierce skirmish on 30 January 1863. With no time to spare after their return to Camp Union, the weary soldiers broke camp at 9 AM and boarded a train to Norfolk. Despite their fatigue, they enthusiastically discussed rumors their brigade would soon march on Richmond. While the 118th had had little opportunity to prove itself at Suffolk, reports filed by its various brigade commanders reflect that Keese's regiment had faithfully performed all assigned tasks, and thus seemingly weathered its baptism under enemy fire.

Cunningham relates one incident towards the end of their stay in Suffolk that further points to a rift within his regiment's leadership. One night Colonel Keese observed lights in a tent after taps had been blown, in contravention of his standing orders. Keese charged the officer on duty, Capt. Edward Riggs, with "dereliction of duty," and ordered him to stand watch a second night. Riggs, a lawyer, refused to accept the punishment, and was backed by four other officers, who also were attorneys. The matter caused considerable controversy within the 118th and was kicked up the chain of command, which finally decided in Riggs's favor on the basis that he had not been brought before a court martial. Cunningham was one of those who supported Riggs and later declared: "It took 'grit' for the Captain to stand upon his rights and dare a quarrel with his Colonel, but Captain Riggs was equal to the occasion and the incident was helpful in many ways; especially in proving that there is a limit to the authority of even Colonels in command." (Riggs, who was one of Garrett's "witnesses," was discharged from the regiment for disability two months later.)[8]

On 18 June, the Adirondack Regiment reboarded the *Utica* at Norfolk and, after a brief stop at Fortress Monroe and rounding Old Point Comfort, steamed up the York River. At one spot the ship ran aground, allowing the soldiers to amuse themselves by swimming in the river and taunting some comrades who had rowed ashore to procure milk from a cow that turned out to be a bull. After the tide floated them off the sandbar, they reached Yorktown the following day. Here, Keese's men were placed with the 99th N.Y. Infantry to form a small Provisional Brigade, again led by Colonel Wardrop, which was attached to the VII Army Corps under the command of Maj. Gen. George W. Getty. The VII and IV Corps, the latter led by Maj. Gen. Erasmus Keyes, comprised the bulk of Dix's forces in the Department of Virginia.

During a stay of almost two weeks in Yorktown, the men were under orders to hold themselves "in readiness as marching orders were expected at any moment." They continued to drill with an occasional dip in the river to cool off. On one occasion, the regiment's sutler was forced to spend a day astride the "wooden horse," a narrow board suspended twelve feet off the ground, as punishment for selling whiskey to the men. On 26 June, the 118th and 99th were rousted at 2 AM and marched aboard the transports *Kennebec* and *Kueka* to be ferried up the York River. This time, they left their tents behind and carried only raincoats in their rucksacks for shelter.[9]

At West Point the transports entered the Pamunkey, the York's southern branch, and by evening reached their destination at White House Landing. Their arrival interrupted Confederate efforts to construct a turntable on a railroad spur along the opposite bank which, had it been completed, would have allowed the positioning of artillery pieces mounted on flat-cars to prevent the landing. After coming ashore, the Union troops bivouacked amid the ruins of the White House, the mansion where George Washington once courted the wealthy widow Martha Custis. At the start of the war, it had been the home of Robert E. Lee's son, Gen. William H. F. ("Rooney") Lee, but after the main house was destroyed in 1862, Union forces often used the plantation as a depot for operations against Richmond.

The 118th was but a small part of a 16,000-man expeditionary force that Dix ordered Getty and Keyes to assemble on the York Peninsula. For a variety of reasons, including the location of many of Dix's forces in remote Suffolk, it took until late June for his troops to reach White House Landing. (In retrospect, the Confederate siege of Suffolk can be seen as a successful feint to lure Dix's forces into an area where they could not easily hinder Lee's campaign plans.) From the Pamunkey landing, Dix planned to send Keyes's IV Corps directly up the peninsula to destroy railroad installations around

Bottoms Bridge (thirteen miles east of Richmond), while Getty was to lead the VII Corps fifteen miles north of Richmond to burn two key railroad bridges across the South Anna, a tributary of the Pamunkey.

Wardrop's Provisional Brigade, which, in addition to two infantry regiments, included an artillery battery and Col. Samuel Spear's 11th Pa. Cavalry, was chosen by Getty to lead the South Anna expedition. On 27 June, a portion of the 118th, including Company A, crossed the river from the White House to guard spoils taken during a raid by Spear's Cavalry. The previous day, the Pennsylvania troopers had attacked the Central Railroad Bridge on the South Anna, in what would turn out to be the most successful operation of the entire campaign. Spear's men burned the bridge and captured a wagon train, mules, horses, $20,000 in Confederate currency, and 108 prisoners (mostly from the 44th N.C. Infantry, part of Pettigrew's Brigade), as well as the aforementioned Confederate general, "Rooney" Lee. Strategically, however, the destruction of the Central Line bridge had little effect as long as the Richmond and Fredericksburg Railroad Bridge remained intact, since the two rail lines intersected north of the river and could be used interchangeably.

On 30 June, the rest of Wardrop's Brigade marched across the Pamunkey on the railroad bridge at White House Landing, only to stop for the night at Lanesville, about two miles from the river. The following morning (Wednesday, 1 July) Wardrop's men took their assigned position at the head of the column, but covered less than ten miles before heat forced a halt on the far side of King William Court House. That morning, as the soldiers passed "magnificent" fields of wheat, corn and oats ripening under the summer sun, they reflected on the futility of a widespread belief that the South could be starved into submission. That evening, according to one account, "was one of beauty, and as the full moon rose, several bands discoursed enchanting strains of music, causing us to forget the vexations of the day and loose ourselves in sleep."[10]

On Thursday, the men turned out at 2:30 AM, but covered only eight miles before stopping at Brandywine in the early afternoon. Better progress was made on Friday, but a delay ensued when a court-martial was hastily convened to try soldiers who had looted a mansion along the way. By the time a halt was finally called at 10 PM at Taylor's Farm, many had dropped by the wayside from heat exhaustion. (Cunningham described his regiment as completely "fagged" after covering twenty-five miles, although the actual distance was closer to sixteen.) After dark, Keese's men sang "John Brown's Body" to revive their spirits.

"Hurrah for the Fourth" began Chamberlin's diary entry for the day that would mark his regiment's most important engagement to date. The significance of Wardrop's Brigade location in the column's vanguard became apparent early that day when General Getty left his entire Second Brigade, along with two artillery batteries and some cavalry, at Taylor's Farm, which he later explained were needed to guard the "sick, exhausted, and foot-sore from the other commands, and all the wagons and baggage." The reduced column left Taylor's Farm at 6 AM on Saturday and advanced a few miles to Littlepage's Bridge, where the Union forces re-crossed the Pamunkey River. The men had expected the Rebels to make a stand at this crossing, but no opposition was encountered, spoiling hopes of celebrating the Fourth "in a manner befitting the present perilous state of the country." Getty next ordered his entire Third Brigade to remain behind to guard this bridge, while the remnant of the column moved on to Hanover Court House. Here, Getty established his headquarters, keeping the First Brigade with him "to secure my withdrawal," and "sent forward Spear's cavalry, Davis's battery and Foster's and Wardrop's infantry brigades, all under the command of Brig. Gen. [Robert S.] Foster, to destroy the railroad bridge over the South Anna and tear up the track."[11]

It was already 7 PM when Wardrop's Brigade, now practically all that was left of the 10,000 men who had set out from White House Landing, finally reached the Richmond and Fredericksburg tracks, just over a mile south of the South Anna bridge, and about three miles west of the Central Railroad Bridge that Spear's Cavalry had destroyed a week earlier. By this time, Union cavalrymen had ascertained from local citizens that the enemy was concentrated around the remaining bridge, but the troopers failed to obtain an adequate picture of its defenses, or number of Rebels manning them. (In fact, there were approximately 2,500 men defending the bridge, consisting of Brig. Gen. John R. Cooke's N. C. Infantry Brigade, the 3rd N.C. Cavalry and some field artillery.)[12]

Cunningham's recollection that the 118th and 99th were the only Union regiments to reach the tracks was no exaggeration. The brigade's artillery battery did not participate in the subsequent action, and the cavalry was diverted south along the tracks after its initial scout of the immediate area. Furthermore, the twelve-hour march had taken its toll on the foot soldiers, many of whom had fallen back to Taylor's Farm to recover from the oppressive heat. Getty's puzzling failure to utilize more of his forces must have been painfully obvious as the tired New Yorkers peered through the growing shadows towards their still unseen objective down the tracks.

Soon after their arrival, Colonel Wardrop ordered Companies A and F of the 118th to proceed along both sides of the rail line towards the bridge. Hearing artillery and musketry fire, Wardrop "ascertained" from his post in the rear that those in advance had met resistance and at 11 PM sent two more companies as reinforcements. This time, Wardrop could hear "some smart skirmishes [taking] place, and we discovered that the enemy was there in strong force. Accordingly, about 2:30 AM, by direction of General Foster, these companies were called in...and at 3 AM, the whole column fell back to Taylor's farm, arriving at 1 PM [on 5 July]." The colonel described the conduct of all four companies that participated as "most satisfactory," noting that his brigade lost two killed, ten wounded and four missing, while managing to capture twelve prisoners. On Monday, the entire expeditionary force returned from Taylor's Farm to King William Court House, a distance of twenty-three miles, and reached White House Landing by early afternoon on Tuesday, making noticeably better time than on the way out. Thus ended what the expedition's leaders undoubtedly assumed was a minor engagement soon to be forgotten.[13]

Clearly failing to appreciate the scope and significance of the battle that had taken place on 1-3 July at Gettysburg, General Dix telegraphed a brief, but positive, assessment of the South Anna affair to the War Department on 7 July. In it, Dix stressed that Getty's forces had found the bridge guarded by a force of 8,000 men and fourteen artillery pieces,[14] and therefore opted to tear up track south of the bridge and burn a railroad depot at Ashland. The terse reply from the War Department showed it was not impressed: "Sir: We feel a good deal chagrined at the slight results of the late operations in your department. General Getty in all probability multiplied the enemy's force two or three times, for his representations do not accord with the conditions of things shown in [CSA President Jefferson] Davis's [intercepted] letter to Lee."[15]

Reporting from the Confederate side confirmed Washington's skepticism about the meager results of Dix's Peninsula Campaign, including the number of defenders at the South Anna Bridge, which did not exceed 2,500 on the night of 4-5 July. As might be expected, the Southerners also exaggerated the size of the Federal attacking force at the bridge from the four companies that actually advanced up the tracks. Confederate Brig. Gen. John R. Cooke reported on 5 July that he had been attacked by three brigades of infantry, 1,500 cavalry, and three batteries of artillery, but failed to add most of these forces never came near his line. Cooke's defenses at the bridge consisted of the 15th and 46th N.C. Infantry and a regiment of cavalry, which, he proclaimed, "repulsed [the enemy] repeatedly in handsome style." But his superior, Maj. Gen. Daniel H. Hill, provided a more accurate assessment in a report to CSA Secretary of War James Seddon on 5 July that termed the engagement "a mere skirmish with cavalry," in which the Yankees "surprised and captured a dozen of our men," before being repulsed. Accounts in the Richmond press substantiate an estimate of only 2,500 defenders at the railroad bridge, and also confirm that the Federal offensive, both at Bottoms Bridge and against the two South Anna bridges, had only minimal effect on the Confederate capital.[16]

Military and civilian authorities in the North demanded to know why an operation designed to hinder Lee's northward march had been so patently unsuccessful. Not only had Dix failed to threaten Richmond in a timely manner, but the combined IV and VII Corps had managed to avoid any significant engagement with the small force the Confederates had left behind to guard their capital. In fact, General Keyes's portion of the operation had fared even worse at Bottoms Bridge, where on 1 July he abruptly withdrew his entire IV Corps (6,000 men and fourteen artillery pieces) without firing a shot against a vastly inferior enemy force. (His precipitous retreat allowed the Confederates to augment their defenses at South Anna Bridge before the arrival of Getty's VII Corps.)

Within two weeks, Dix was transferred to New York City to head the Department of the East, an administrative position he would occupy for the remainder of the war. Keyes was removed from command and eventually resigned. (He maintained he had only been ordered to make a "demonstration" against Richmond that did not include engaging the enemy in combat, but Dix blocked his request for an investigation.) Getty, on the other hand, did not suffer significantly for his failure at South Anna, since he was able to plausibly blame Keyes for allowing the Confederates to concentrate their meager resources around the bridge. (As he later proved to be a capable infantry commander, Getty's cautious tactics at South Anna probably reflected Dix's prior instructions.) The IV and VII Corps were soon abolished, and their components scattered among other commands. For a minor engagement, the "affair" at South Anna Bridge had far-reaching consequences.

* * * * *

The scrutiny afforded the Blackberry Raid resulted in detailed reports from the commanding officers involved, including Lt. Col. Keese, Captain Norris, and Lieutenants Riggs and Cunningham. Their accounts of the night of 4-5 July sharply contrast with the failure of the expedition as a whole. Not only did the 118th reach its target, but three of its companies acquitted themselves well, fighting in the dark on unfamiliar terrain against an enemy whose size and position were essentially unknown. Given that it was the most significant engagement during Chamberlin's stay with the Adirondack Regiment and may have contributed to his decision to leave it, a detailed look at that night follows.

When Wardrop's Brigade arrived at the rail bed Saturday evening, the men were greeted "by volleys of musketry" from Rebel pickets, who had been monitoring their approach, but who then pulled back into the gathering gloom. As the rest of the brigade stacked arms and rested, Colonel Keese was asked to detach two companies from the 118th and turn them over to Colonel Wardrop for use in probing the enemy's position. For this task, Keese selected the same two companies (A and F) that had served him well as advance skirmishers during the Blackwater Expedition. Captain Norris (A) had overall command of both companies, while Lieutenant Cunningham led Company F in the absence of its captain, then on sick leave. On receipt of Wardrop's orders to proceed down the tracks and destroy the bridge "at all hazard," Norris had both companies divided into forward and reserve platoons. While he led Company A's forward platoon down the right side of the track, that of Company F advanced on the left side "under command of Lieutenants Chamberlin and Cunningham." (Shared command of a platoon was unusual, suggesting that Norris wanted his own man present to assist Cunningham, who undoubtedly resented the intrusion.)[17]

As Norris's men set off towards the bridge, thought to be almost two miles distant, clouds "overspread the sky. Not one glimmering star [lent] its kindly light to cheer them on their way…and no sound [was] heard save the returning echoes of their measured tread. They [turned] neither to the right or left, but [expected] at every step to receive the murderous fire of the enemy's concealed artillery, or that superior numbers [might] spring from ambush upon them with resistless fury."

Soon, they began to draw scattered musket fire, which, after Norris ordered it returned, brought the first response from Southern artillery, at first still off-target. Followed by their respective reserves, the two advance platoons now had to contest "every step of ground, and in addition to a murderous [musket] fire…, a battery on the left with shot and shell, which burst over and around them; but, nothing daunted, they [pressed] on…[until] the enemy [got] accurate range and also [unmasked] a heavy battery." At this point, Cunningham signaled Norris that the Rebels were trying to flank his position. After consultation between the two officers, they decided to fall back until reinforcements could be obtained, with the reserve platoons, led by Lieutenants Garrett (A) and William Stevenson (F), now posted closest to the enemy to ensure they were not followed. As they withdrew, Cunningham was struck in the hip by a spent bullet but did not leave the field.[18]

A short time later, Maj. George Nichols arrived with Companies D of the 118th and E of the 99th. As senior officer, Nichols took command from Norris, although the major remained at the rear, content to pass orders to those in front. At 11 PM, Captain Norris ordered Company A forward again, noting later that: "each man was instantly on his feet, ready to give them another trial. Lieutenant Garrett had command of the platoon deployed and Lieutenant Chamberlin of the reserve." Company D of the 118th was deployed on the left of F, and Company E of the 99th was to the right of A. During this second advance, the New Yorkers encountered stiff opposition, including "galling" artillery fire that "horribly mutilated" Pvt. Martin Sherman (A). Sgt. Edgar Wing (A) described to his father how the men had lain on the ground for almost two hours under heavy fire, while Norris coolly walked back and forth along the line, giving direction and encouragement to his troops. Just when the captain ordered them to fix bayonets in preparation to charge the Rebel breastworks, Nichols signaled them to fall back once again.

The growing rift among the officers of the 118th was evident in their after-action reports. That of Captain Riggs (D) made no mention of Norris or Company A, although he cited Cunningham and Company F on several occasions. After arriving with Major Nichols, Riggs had led his forward platoon up the tracks to join the others. Once there, he claimed his men clamored for an opportunity to charge the enemy, but this action "had not been contemplated in the orders given me from the major commanding." This assertion was a far cry from Norris's initial orders to destroy the bridge "at all hazard," and suggests that a decision had already been made not to try and take the bridge.

While Cunningham remained with Company F's reserve platoon, it was 2nd Lt. William Stevenson, leading the deployed platoon, who gained the most glory that night. Acting on his own initiative with five volunteers, Stevenson overran a fortified Confederate position—killing one and capturing twelve. (He was subsequently promoted to first lieutenant for "gallantry in action.") Not unexpectedly, Cunningham did not mention sharing command with Chamberlin during the first advance, either in his official report of night's action, or in his regimental history. His failure in the latter to make more than one passing reference to Norris in recounting this skirmish is more surprising, especially when others roundly praised the captain's performance. (Apparently, Cunningham's differences with Norris still lingered when he wrote his history fifty years later.) In contrast, Sergeant Wing compared Norris's "coolness and courage" to his earlier daring as Glens Falls fire chief, and clearly wanted Judge Wing to use his influence to have his captain promoted to major.[19]

Once the signal to retreat was fired at 2:30 AM, the four companies moved back in good order to rejoin their respective regiments, and a withdrawal toward Hanover Court House commenced at daybreak. "Much dissatisfaction and chagrin [was] manifest," wrote one disappointed participant, "and all we [could] do [was] keep marching and wondering why?" Unfortunately, Chamberlin's diary sheds little light on events that night. Despite beginning that day with an exuberant, "Hurrah for the Fourth," his perfunctory account of the next twenty-four hours suggests disappointment in both his assigned role and the futility of the whole "affair": "A and F sent out to attack Bridge...the fight advanced close to Batteries, and fell back for assistance. Co. D and Co. of the 99th sent to us. Renewed attack and fell back. Sherman killed and 5 wounded." His next entry only recorded that they buried Pvt. Sherman when the 118th reached Taylor's Farm in the early morning hours of 5 July. (Casualties in Norris's company were actually higher than Chamberlin indicated: one killed, one mortally wounded, six less severely wounded and two missing. Company D suffered one slightly wounded, and F had two wounded that night; the 99th lost one killed and six missing.)[20]

After their return to White House Landing on 7 July, Keese's men were heartened to learn of the Union victory at Gettysburg and, according to Cunningham, pleased to think their actions in making a feint towards Richmond had prevented Lee from leading even more troops into Pennsylvania. However, another member of the 118th, writing to his hometown paper shortly after the expedition's return, was less charitable about the scanty results of what he satirically dubbed "the Great Peninsular Campaign of '63...with which the 118th had the honor (?) of being connected." As for the "masterly retreat" back to White House Landing, this soldier felt the expeditionary force must have set a "record" covering the same ground that had taken so much time on the way out. Yet, despite what appears to have been widespread disappointment among the enlisted men over their perceived failure to have made any significant strategic impact on the war, these hardy men from the Adirondacks could take considerable satisfaction from their performance that night, having coolly operated under fire in a difficult and exposed position while inflicting equivalent losses (at least one killed, twelve captured) on a much larger enemy force. Regrettably, the promise these men showed in their first real test was lost in the overall failure of the expedition; nor was it acknowledged up the chain of command, which was too busy trying to consign the entire operation to the dustbin.[21]

Without a troop transport waiting at the Landing to carry them, the regiment continued on foot towards Yorktown in heavy rain, camping along the way on wet ground. As the soldiers passed through Williamsburg, they observed the damage this historic town had suffered during the 1862 Peninsula Campaign. Arriving at their former camp in Yorktown at sundown on 10 July, Keese's men received two days rest before crossing the York River to garrison Fort Keyes on Gloucester Point. Here the regiment would remain for four long months, much to the dismay of many, who found its climate unhealthy and felt it served little strategic purpose. Lieutenant Chamberlin's future, however, would take a different turn, propelled by events taking place far to the north.[22]

Chapter 4

DRAFT RENDEZVOUS, NEW YORK: July 1863-April 1864

To keep the Union Army ranks filled after patriotic fervor began to wane in the North, President Lincoln reluctantly signed the nation's first conscription law in March 1863. (The Confederate Government had mandated its draft a year earlier.) The "Enrollment Act," as it was euphemistically called, made liable for military service all able-bodied male U. S. citizens aged twenty to fifty-six, as well as foreigners who declared their intention to become citizens. It also listed exemptions to general conscription, allowed for the purchase of substitutes, and defined procedures for allocating quotas among Congressional districts. The draft would be conducted by provost marshals in the various Northern states, and the position of Provost Marshal General was established to oversee these activities. The act also made reference to "draft rendezvous" where new recruits would be gathered before being sent to the field.

Fueled by the high casualty rate at Gettysburg, opposition to conscription peaked in the North that summer, and for a while, threatened to alter the course of the war. The draft was particularly unpopular in New York's large cities, where the Democratic political machine, led by Governor Horatio Seymour, seized upon this discontent to undermine Lincoln's administration, by telling constituents, particularly Irish-American laborers, they would be drafted to free slaves who would then come North and take their jobs. Moreover, many New Yorkers already harbored sympathy for the South, particularly on economic and states-rights issues. (Seymour viewed conscription as unconstitutional, along with emancipation and the President's suspension of *habeas corpus*. By positioning himself as a leader of states-rights Democrats, he was maneuvering for a possible run in the 1864 presidential election and would become the Democratic presidential nominee in 1868.)[1]

Federal authorities seemed unaware of the extent of this opposition when they picked New York City as the site for the Empire State's first draft lottery. To make matters worse, the provost marshal published the list of resulting draftees in the press rather than notifying them individually. The intervening weekend passed without incident, but on Monday (13 July) rioters, including many Irish workers, surged through the streets, clashing with police and looting shops. Although newspaper accounts exaggerated what followed, at least seventy-four persons, many of whom were Black, were killed by the mob. Over three days, rioters caused an estimated $1.5 million in damages, including setting fire to the provost marshal's residence, draft headquarters and a "colored" orphanage. Federal authorities blamed city and state officials for not stopping the agitators, while others accused Confederate agents and radical Democrats of inciting the unrest. The rioting was abruptly quelled on 16 July, when Union troops were rushed to the scene from Gettysburg. The battle-weary soldiers had little

New York City Draft Riots. Angered over conscription and fearful Blacks will take their jobs, White workers burn "colored orphan asylum." (*Harpers Weekly*, 1Aug63, LC)

sympathy for civilian agitators, and in the clash that followed, over 1,000 demonstrators were killed or wounded.

Two days later, an equally determined John Dix, criticism of his failure on the York Peninsula still ringing in the major general's ears, arrived in New York to assume command of the Army's Department of the East. The War Department had chosen well in kicking Dix "upstairs," as he proved a far better politician than warrior. Above all, he served effectively as Lincoln's foil to the wily Democratic governor in Albany. (In evaluating Dix's authority in dealing with Seymour, one should keep in mind that the whole country was technically under military rule. Northern states were grouped into large departments that were in turn subdivided into military districts, whose commanders relied on provost marshals to carry out military directives aimed at the civilian population.) Dix did not get all of the 10,000 troops he initially requested to reinstate the draft, but his command was augmented considerably. Although secretly pleased by the discomfiture that the riots had caused the federal government, Governor Seymour realized any increase in Dix's command threatened his own autonomy. In the days that followed, Seymour maneuvered frantically to abolish the draft in New York and arm the state militia. Lincoln's aide John G. Nicolay characterized the governor's conduct thusly: "Seymour gave but little help in the disorder, and left a stain on his record by addressing a portion of the mob as 'my friends.'" By early August, however, the governor was forced to comply with the new draft laws or risk the imposition of martial law and a direct confrontation with an increasingly hostile federal government.[2]

To augment the force needed to conduct the draft and manage the expected influx of draftees, the War Department sent a circular order to the field on 3 July that requested each three-year regiment to select a detail composed of three officers and six enlisted men, each of whom "must be judicious and reliable." These details were to be immediately sent to the rendezvous nearest to where the regiment was recruited and organized, for the "purpose of receiving and conducting to their several regiments the men of the draft assigned to fill them up." (The rendezvous for the 118th N.Y. Infantry was on Riker's Island, located in New York City's harbor at the intersection of the East River and western end of Long Island Sound.)[3]

The 118th received this notice after reaching Fort Keyes on Gloucester Point, and it was not until 17 July that Colonel Keese appointed Capt. Henry Ransom (I), 1st Lt. S. E. Chamberlin (A), and 2nd Lt. William Stevenson (F) to represent the regiment at Riker's Island. The chance to visit New York represented a plum assignment, and, at least in Stevenson's case, a reward for gallantry at South Anna. In a later summary of his military career, Chamberlin pointed with pride to his selection, and he probably lobbied to be included. (Captain Norris undoubtedly influenced Keese's decision as a way to separate his two feuding lieutenants, as well as allowing Chamberlin to go north and lobby for both their promotions.) Even though Ransom and Stevenson rejoined the 118th later that summer, Chamberlin opted to remain in New York in various staff positions for the next ten months. Two NCOs and four privates accompanied the officers to Riker's Island, and this detail stayed under Chamberlin's supervision, performing various duties at the Draft Rendezvous.[4]

Chamberlin left Fort Keyes on 20 July by steamer to Fortress Monroe, where he overnighted at the nearby Hygeia Hotel. The next day he visited fellow soldiers in the hospital, before boarding a boat to Baltimore, where he continued on to New York City by train. After spending a night at the Howard House in Brooklyn, he reported for duty at the Rendezvous on 24 July. Soon after his arrival, he received a letter from his mother urging him to come home to discuss urgent family matters, and on 4 August he obtained permission to travel Upstate, arriving at Glens Falls the following day.[5]

His journey coincided with the draft's resumption, and he found the atmosphere Upstate tense. Only three weeks had elapsed since the New York City riots, and authorities feared similar unrest might break out elsewhere in the state. On 21 July, the assistant provost marshal in Auburn had warned the Provost Marshal General in Washington, Col. James B. Fry, about possible unrest in Syracuse, describing precautions being taken there and in other cities. On the same day, E. F. Bullard, a prominent Upstate citizen, wrote an alarmed letter to U. S. Senator Henry Wilson, warning that restarting the draft would be a much bigger problem than Washington realized: "Our State Militia is mainly officered by open secessionists recently appointed by the Governor. They will lead the mob in these counties." Bullard requested local provost marshals be authorized to appoint an armed guard to meet the threat. His letter was forwarded to the Albany office of Maj. Frederick Townsend, acting Assistant Provost Marshal for the state's Northern Division, and then to Capt. J. P. Butler, provost marshal in Schenectady. In response, Butler requested a force of 200 men be sent. After re-starting the draft in Oswego without serious difficulties, Townsend asked Fry to inform Governor Seymour of his intention to send ninety "regulars" to oversee conscription in Schenectady on 7 August, which Fry agreed to do.[6]

Chamberlin arrived in Glens Falls on 5 August, and after discussions with his family (described later), he traveled to Albany to brief the governor about developments in the Adirondack Regiment. While in the state capital, he took the opportunity to visit Provost Marshal Townsend, who asked him to join the force being sent the following day to Schenectady "in anticipation of a Riot." Once there, Chamberlin helped staff the local provost marshal's office when conscription began on the 10th. Despite widespread fears of unrest, the draft in Schenectady went smoothly, allowing Townsend, in a report to Dix, to credit the troops he had sent there with preventing a "bloody riot." On 12 August, the draft having been completed Upstate, Chamberlin returned to New York City in time for the resumption of the draft there. (Informing Fry that he planned to re-start the draft in New York City on the 19th, Dix included a request for more troops to ensure its success. As it turned out, there were no serious problems.)[7]

Meanwhile, on 13 August, Judge Halsey Wing, head of the "war committee" in Glens Falls, had written to acknowledge two letters Chamberlin had sent him earlier that month from Albany and Schenectady. Wing was "glad to learn that [his] Schenectady trip was occasioned by a causeless 'scare.' It would have grieved me to know that you had *gratuitously* aided in enforcing the unjust and unequal draft, which really seems to have been more aimed at the Democracy of our State, than at the Rebels." (Despite what he may have told Wing, Chamberlin did not share the judge's negative opinion on military conscription.) Continuing, Wing expressed his pleasure on learning from Chamberlin's Albany letter that the Governor "had consented to hold the Major questions of the 118th [a reference to Norris's possible promotion to major] under advisement until Capt. Norris and his friends have an opportunity to be heard." Wing had taken the liberty of forwarding Chamberlin's letter to Norris (who was still at Gloucester Point), advising that "no *undue* advantage would be allowed to prevail against him [Norris] by the Governor, and telling him that the whole matter now seemed to rest with himself." Fearing the captain might have already left for New York and, not knowing how to reach him, Wing proposed a discreet meeting with Chamberlin in Albany to plan how best to promote Norris' candidacy.[8]

While Seymour had probably listened politely as Chamberlin pressed the case for Norris' promotion during their 5 August meeting, the Governor was likely more interested in questioning the lieutenant about the South Anna to gain ammunition for use against General Dix. Both Chamberlin and Wing were apparently unaware Seymour had already been persuaded to appoint another officer to fill the position of major. In his book, Cunningham explained that, when Col. Samuel Richards finally resigned his command for health reasons in early July, all the officers agreed Lt. Colonel Keese should succeed him and that Major Nichols should move up to Keese's slot. Differences of opinion arose as to who would replace Nichols:

> ....The field officers [majors and above] and a few of the line officers had in mind one of our Captains [clearly Norris] for Major, and he would make a good one, but when our regiment was in course of organization at Plattsburgh under Lieutenant Pruyn, representing the Governor, he rendered such satisfactory service...that he was persuaded to accept the Adjutancy of the regiment with our promise that he would be made Major when a vacancy came. Most of the line officers felt the obligation of this promise. A meeting of our officers was held and a vote taken, Pruyn receiving a majority of several votes. But as the field officers favored the Captain, Colonel Keese, securing a short leave of absence, went to Albany to recommend the Captain's appointment.
>
> Those who favored Pruyn made up a statement of the officers' vote, setting forth the promise made to him. This document, signed by the officers voting for Pruyn, was sent to his mother, an influential Albany lady, and she promptly took it to Governor Seymour, who at once made the appointment of Pruyn. When Colonel Keese reached Albany and presented his recommendation, he was advised that the appointment had already been made. Naturally this division of opinion and its result caused some regimental friction; but be it said to the credit of the defeated officers, it was finally pleasantly accepted and all was forgotten in a few weeks.[9]

In fact, neither Chamberlin nor Norris forgot this *fait accompli* as readily as Cunningham claimed. Chamberlin's promotion to Company A's captaincy was now blocked, and his efforts to lobby for Norris further strained his relationship with the Pruyn faction. Norris would resign from the service four months later, and one must assume this was related to being passed over for promotion. The incident provides further evidence of a well-connected group of officers in the 118th, who included Cunningham, Capt. Edward Riggs, Pruyn (whose father was a lifelong friend and advisor to Governor Seymour), and Lt. Rowland Kellogg (son of a congressman). (It was mostly the same group that had blocked Keese from disciplining Riggs, and which 2nd Lt. James Garrett cited as witnesses for a possible court martial against Chamberlin.) Their ability to manipulate the selection of Pruyn raises questions about who actually ran the regiment, something rendered moot the following year when Nichols replaced Keese as commander of the 118th. It should therefore come as no surprise that Chamberlin, whose tenuous ties to Glens Falls effectively precluded inclusion in this dominant clique, and whose ongoing feud with Lieutenant Garrett further hampered his prospects, never returned to active duty with the Adirondack Regiment.[10]

* * * * *

As noted earlier, Chamberlin's travel Upstate was initially prompted by a letter from his mother urging him to come back to discuss family matters. In part, Betsey was upset that the wife of her son Elijah had just died from giving birth. Elliot's twin sister Ellen had gone to Elijah's home in Danville, Vermont, to bring back the baby to be raised at Glens Falls, as the mother had requested on her deathbed. (Ellen and William Martin later adopted the child, named Henry.) Betsey also revealed her daughter Lucia had spent four weeks in the Glen before going back to Vermont with her husband, Don Stone. Both Don and Charlie Crawford (Lucia's son by her first marriage) had recently been drafted in their home state of Vermont, and Betsey commiserated with Lucia's plight, as she had already "buried her youngest child last winter," and did not know what she would do, if both her husband and son had to go into the army.[11]

Earlier that summer, Betsey's son-in-law, Duncan Cameron, had returned to the Glens, much to the delight of his wife Louisa. Although not mentioned in the letter, Duncan had completed two years of service in the 22nd N.Y. Infantry and, despite the loss of his arm, had re-enlisted as a major in the 2nd N.Y. Veterans Cavalry, then being assembled in Saratoga Springs. Rather than let Don Stone and Charlie Crawford face the uncertainties of serving as draftees in Vermont, Duncan persuaded them to enlist in his cavalry regiment in early August. Now that Elliot worked at a Draft Rendezvous, Betsey hoped her son could help Major Cameron avoid the consequences of having recruited two already conscripted Vermonters into a New York regiment. Her fears were warranted, as Cameron was arrested the following month by Vermont's provost marshal on charges of helping conscripts evade the draft. His release a short time later may well have reflected Chamberlin's behind-the-scenes help. Cameron would arrange for Charlie to serve as his orderly and thus keep Lucia's son out of harm's way. (Lieutenant Stone was not so fortunate, dying the following year of yellow fever in Louisiana.)[12]

When Chamberlin returned to Riker's Island on 13 August, he found "considerable dissatisfaction" among the officers serving there under Col. Marshall S. Howe. This abruptly changed four days later with the arrival of a new commander, Brig. Gen. Nathaniel Jackson,[13] who would be greatly favored by his officers. Chamberlin already had a positive impression of Jackson from the time the general visited Fort Ethan Allen the previous winter, and this experience may have influenced his decision to delay returning to the 118th. The lieutenant had a knack for getting assignments that meshed with his personal agenda, and this propensity seemed the case when Jackson authorized him on 21 August "to proceed without delay to Plattsburgh… to arrest deserters from this command and confer with the Provost Marshal there." The travel Upstate allowed him to overnight at the Glen, before reporting to the provost marshal in Plattsburgh.[14]

He already had some experience looking for deserters while posted at the Washington train station, and one senses he was not displeased at this latest opportunity to root out disloyal citizens. If so, it was early evidence of a moral and political fervor that would characterize his adherence to the Union cause long after the war. While most Southern soldiers entered the war with deep-seated convictions, a strong sense of purpose took longer to form in Northern volunteer ranks. As the conflict dragged on, however, these same Northern soldiers became increasingly impatient with corruption and a lack of patriotism back home. Much of this sentiment found expression in the emergent Republican Party and from 1864 until the end of the century, Union soldiers and veterans would dominate the GOP. While Chamberlin's earlier political orientation is unclear, he emerged from the war an ardent Republican and supporter of veterans' rights.

After his trip to Plattsburg, and instead of returning to Virginia with the other two officers from the 118th, Chamberlin managed to extend his stay at Riker's by securing an appointment in September as First Battalion adjutant at Draft Rendezvous Headquarters. The position was a significant step towards his new goal of becoming a career officer and provided direct access to General Jackson's personal staff. More importantly, he was seen to possess the varied administrative, social and political skills required of a staff officer in a large metropolitan post. An adjutant serves as the right-hand man to the commanding officer of a military unit, in this case a battalion, and all routine contact with that commander is usually made through him. Adjutants are also responsible for the administration of personnel, general supervision of quarters, and preparation, distribution and posting of official correspondence.[15]

In early October, Chamberlin received fifteen days leave to travel to Janesville, Wisconsin and "attend to business of great importance relative to the decease of my wife, whose death has occurred since I have been in the service." Maggie's mother had moved to Janesville at the start of the war, and he wanted to return some of his wife's effects and otherwise commiserate with his mother-in-law over their mutual loss.[16]

Chamberlin must have enjoyed his experience working with Albany Provost Marshal Frederick Townsend, because soon after his return from the Midwest, he wrote the major requesting "to be assigned to service under your command in performance of duties connected with the recruiting service." Although he did not get the assignment, the letter reflected his goal of joining the regular Army, Townsend being a major in the 18th U.S. Infantry.[17]

His decision to seek a position in the regular Army rather than return to the 118th was further influenced by news about the deteriorating situation in his former company. An indication of this unrest is contained in a letter his old adversary, James Garrett, wrote to his wife on 2 November. The second lieutenant had returned from the hospital to find himself unexpectedly in command of Company A, since Captain Norris was on sick leave and Chamberlin was "still north." Yet, his long-held dream of running the company was shattered a day later, when a second lieutenant from another company arrived with orders relieving Garrett of command. "There never was a more beastly outrage in command over me," Garrett fumed, before launching into the following diatribe:

> I would not stand such an outrage and wrote a request for immediate discharge… [But] headquarters returned my application disapproved, thus compelling me to remain… [and] be the laughingstock for the entire regiment. All of the officers say I did perfectly right in tendering my resignation. I have sent to the adjutant general's office at Washington today giving him all the facts and asking him for a decision. I will follow it up if I have to visit "Uncle Abe" in person. Colonel Keese has always done all he can to injure me and make me unpopular in the regiment. He is a black-hearted scoundrel and doesn't deserve to live….[18][19]

In early December, Chamberlin, who now rated a personal staff of three privates, traveled on the Steamer *Thorn* as "commissary of the command" to the Department of North Carolina and Virginia. ("Commissary" is here used in its older sense of the "representative" of the command, *i.e.* General Jackson.) After the brief trip south, he returned to find he had been appointed aide-de-camp (ADC) on Jackson's personal staff and was to "be obeyed and respected accordingly."[20]

He still remained responsible for the detachment of enlisted men from the 118th—a sergeant, corporal, and four privates. These men were primarily deployed as provost guards to accompany recruits to their assigned regiments. As such, they spent a good deal of time away from Riker's and later Hart Island, often on troop transports. For example, Sgt. Peter Hewitt, Cpl. Samuel Emory, and Pvt. Wilbur Abare were on duty on the steamer *John Romer* when Chamberlin filled out their detachment muster roll at the end of February. Pvts. Reuben J. Davis and George Danforth were deployed to the Albany Draft Rendezvous during the first part of 1864. Only Chamberlin and Pvt. Henry Covil spent most of their time at their home post.[21]

Despite less than ideal living conditions on Riker's Island, and the depot's limited career opportunities, Chamberlin enjoyed working on Jackson's staff. Among his mementos is a *carte de visite* inscribed "Yours truly, N. J. Jackson, Brig Gen Vols," and a group picture showing the general and his staff. His promotion to ADC in December, while similar to his earlier duties as adjutant, carried the added authority of the post commander. The perennially cash-strapped lieutenant may have been less thrilled to learn he was now expected to contribute towards the purchase of an engraved watch, chain and seals, which Jackson's staff gave their boss during an elaborate Christmas party. He saved a clipping of this affair which reported the "magnificent" watch cost $800—an enormous sum at the time, but perhaps the former jeweler had gotten it wholesale and engraved it himself.[22]

A letter in early December from 1st Sgt. Andrew J. Weeks to his uncle would seem to confirm the comfortable existence of those posted on the Island, at least compared to life on the front lines. "We have very little excitement of any kind. Sometimes a few Conscripts gets dissatisfied with Uncle Sam, and succeed in getting off the Island. Then we have to hunt them up. That is about the only change

Gen. Nathaniel Jackson and Draft Rendezvous Staff, New York Harbor, Winter 1862-3. Jackson, seated center and inset; Chamberlin, 2nd row, far left. (group photo and *carte de visite*, TCC)

we have from our usual round of Guard duty." He explained that all "volunteers and Conscripts...have to pass through our hands before they get to the Army. We receive about One hundred daily...[mostly] volunteers from New York and Brooklyn City. The large bountys they receive is bringing them out pretty fast. If they keep it up, there will be no danger of another draft riot in New York."[23]

Despite Sergeant Weeks's upbeat tone, the reality for draftees on Riker's was far from ideal, and the provost guards were little more than prison wardens keeping the new recruits in check until they could be shipped by steamer or train to the front. Just three weeks later, in a letter written to his sister, Weeks's attitude about his post had drastically changed, and he now referred to it as a "detestable rat hole of an Island." His description was quite literal: "...in the lonely midnight hour with [the rats'] infernal squealing & knawing...[we] sleep in dread of being carried off bodily... A great many of the recruits that comes here with 3 or 500 dollars...gets robbed. They say their pockets are picked. But it's my opinion that the Rats Cart it off, they are big enough." Weeks had charge of one of the "Company Streets" at the Rendezvous, making him responsible for between seventy-five and 300 recruits. In addition to the paperwork this entailed, he complained about the food, which consisted of over-salted mackerel and barely cooked potatoes. When he could not stand this fare, he purchased meals at the officers' mess.[24]

Problems at the Rendezvous were exacerbated by the quality of recruits and draftees being received during the late stages of the war, something that was particularly evident in large metropolitan areas such as New York City. Here the staff and guards had to contend with a confusing system of quotas and bounties that individual boroughs and surrounding communities used to fill their share of recruits. Not infrequently, this "system" included kidnappings, abduction of foreigners, and sending in criminals, drunkards, fugitives and others unfit for service—leading Jackson's successor to estimate that no more than half of the recruits became effective soldiers.[25]

Their quality aside, the recruits' living conditions on Riker's were abysmal, a situation rendered worse on a low-lying island in the middle of winter. This situation came to a head in early 1864 when Generals Dix and Jackson were compelled to respond to inquiries from the New York State Assembly about the treatment of draftees. A depiction of the Island's "disgraceful" conditions had surfaced in a mid-January article in a Brooklyn newspaper, which was soon reprinted around the country. The account described how new arrivals were lined up on the parade ground and stripped naked, no matter what the weather, so they could be searched for concealed civilian clothing, and then sent to their tents with only their flimsy issued uniforms "to freeze, sicken, and perchance die" from exposure. The article also brought to light a system of extortion and price-gouging, by which recruits were grossly overcharged for water, heating stoves, and other necessities.[26]

New York Democrats pounced on the revelations as a means of getting back at the Lincoln Administration for its imposition of the draft. In late January, the chairman of the Assembly's Committee on Federal Relations, William Dewey, forwarded a resolution to General Dix regarding allegations of abuse against volunteers in military depots across the state. Dix immediately replied that the statements made in the press and elsewhere were gross misrepresentations, but promised a fuller response at a later date. Dix then asked Jackson to report back to him about allegations about ill-treatment of recruits on Riker's.[27]

Responding to Dewey on 30 January, Dix provided his own refutation of the charges, as well as reports from Jackson and the surgeon on Riker's, who both maintained that no one had frozen to death and only one individual had suffered severe frostbite, due to his own negligence after becoming drunk. Dix further maintained the number of sick was not large, and the number of deaths was remarkably small—only twenty-four in six months, out of 15,000 men passing through the Island. Furthermore, Riker's was never intended as a permanent depot for recruits and was only being used until new barracks could be constructed on Hart Island. In the meantime, both the troops and their officers on the Island lived in tents just like the recruits, so Dix said, and all were as comfortable as could be expected. The general also strongly denied allegations that volunteers were ill-clothed, or covered with filth and vermin, noting that Governor Seymour had recently conducted his own survey of the Island.[28]

Dix's report, along with that of Jackson and the surgeon, was presented to the Assembly on 5 February, and the state legislature debated the issue "with a good deal of political skirmishing," before finally deciding to print 4,000 copies of Dix's exculpatory report for public distribution. Regardless of the accuracy on either side of this debate, the Draft Rendezvous was shortly moved to more suitable quarters on Hart Island at the end of Long Island Sound.[29]

At about the same time as the move to Hart Island, Chamberlin was appointed acting assistant adjutant general (AAAG) on Jackson's staff, a senior position for a lieutenant. (An adjutant general is primarily responsible for the administration of personnel and miscellaneous records, and for providing general administrative services. Jackson had several AAAGs, one of whom would have always been on duty to draft and sign routine correspondence, as well as handle day-to-day affairs.)[30]

One of Chamberlin's less pleasant duties and a further indication of unhealthy conditions at the Draft Rendezvous was to head the honor guard that accompanied the remains of a colleague back to Glens Falls. Capt. Hiram Wilson of the 93rd N.Y. Infantry was bitten by a rat on Hart Island and suddenly died from the resulting infection. A brass band played as Chamberlin and the honor guard carried Wilson's body through the streets of the Glen on the way to a local cemetery.[31]

"The Little Minette." Chamberlin kept this image of a favorite actress. (Brooklyn studio photo, TCC)

As AAAG, Chamberlin would have known that Jackson's present tour of duty was coming to an end when he penned a letter in early April to Rep. Justin Morrill at the beginning of April. With no mention of his prior service in the 118th, the lieutenant outlined his current staff duties and indicated his desire to obtain "a position in the Regular Army...Knowing you to be a friend of my family, I feel justified in addressing you and asking that you may give me some assistance in the matter." The Vermont congressman forwarded the letter to Secretary of War Edwin Stanton with a note that "Lt. Chamberlin is a bold, strong and intelligent young man and will, I have no question, prove a valuable man anywhere, but he should have a chance to have at least a company. There is not a drop of the blood of cowards in his veins." As it turned out, Chamberlin did not have to wait for a response to Morrill's endorsement before resigning from the 118th later that month to accept a captaincy in the 25th N.Y. Cavalry.[32]

After he left, the men in Chamberlin's old regiment would overcome their growing pains and personnel disputes to serve with distinction under Colonel Nichols for the remainder of the war, suffering some 500 total casualties, including the battles of Cold Harbor, the

Siege of Petersburg, Fort Harrison and Fair Oaks. Their most significant contribution came at the Battle of Drewry's Bluff on 16 May 1864. This action was highlighted in a letter to New York Governor Reuben E. Fenton by Maj. Gen. Charles Devens, written to mark the muster out of the regiment: "[The 118th] distinguished itself for great valor and pertinacity, and won the reputation it has since enjoyed, of being one of the most resolute Regiments in the service. Out of about three hundred and fifty men engaged, it lost in this conflict, in casualties, one hundred and ninety-eight men and thirteen officers, and it is a most noteworthy fact that, having taken two hundred prisoners from the enemy, *the Regiment had considerably more prisoners at the close of the action than it had men fit for duty.*"[33]

Chapter 5

CAPTAIN, 25TH N. Y. CAVALRY: April-June 1864

Elliot Chamberlin's military service continued with a regiment about which little has been written. Long after the war, he agreed to compile a history of the 25th N.Y. Cavalry, but neither he nor anyone else completed the task. The following chapters attempt to fill this gap by chronicling the Twenty-Fifth's principal operations, as well as resurrect from obscurity its remarkable cast of characters, good and bad. Even though published accounts, including the War Department's massive *Official Records* only mention the regiment in passing, much remains in the National Archives to flesh out the story. Fortunately, Chamberlin saved orders and other material, including a diary, that help document his own service. As the regiment's designated historian, he also received information from other veterans.[1]

Yet, this story could not have been written without the input of the Twenty-Fifth's contemporary chronicler—a soldier who sent at least twenty-three letters from the field for publication in the *New York Sunday Mercury*. Signing himself only as "B.O.B." (hereinafter BOB), this correspondent has been identified as Quartermaster Sgt. Robert M. Clark. His often-acerbic observations suggest prior military service, probably as a lieutenant in the 79th N.Y. Infantry. An indication of his outsize personality can be gleaned from his role as the Twenty-Fifth's flag-bearer, despite standing only five foot five inches tall. At the time of his re-enrollment, the thirty-three-year-old native of Glasgow listed himself as a "printer," which helps account for the readability and wit of a correspondence that is replete with details and vitality lacking in other sources.[2]

Having made up his mind not to return to the 118th, Chamberlin's position at the Draft Rendezvous allowed him to monitor openings in regiments being formed throughout the Empire State. Since the 25th N.Y. Cavalry was initially raised around Saratoga Springs, it is possible his relatives in that area played a part in his acceptance of a captaincy in it. More likely, he already knew some of its future officers through their work as recruiters in New York City. One of these men was Aaron Seeley, who ran the Army Recruitment Center on Broadway before assuming command of the Twenty-Fifth.

After tendering his resignation to the 118th, and being relieved from duty on Gen. Nathaniel Jackson's staff, Chamberlin was on 16 May mustered into the Twenty-Fifth as captain of Company K. Undoubtedly aware of problems his new regiment had had in getting off the ground, he was nevertheless proud of a chance to have his own command in the glamorous cavalry corps. Aided by contacts at the Draft Rendezvous, Chamberlin found capable junior officers for his company—1st Lt. Archibald ("Arch") Wilson and 2nd Lt. George J. Underwood. Both proved good choices and received promotions during the coming year. Two days after Chamberlin's enrollment, Lt. Col. Aaron Seeley put him in charge of all members of the Twenty-Fifth still on Hart Island—a promising sign that he enjoyed the confidence of his new commander.[3]

The Twenty-Fifth was one of the last cavalry regiments raised in the Empire State, and many questioned whether it would ever see service in the field. In early September 1863, Col. Henry F. Liebenau was granted authority by Gov. Horatio Seymour to recruit a regiment from around Saratoga Springs that was initially called the Daniel Sickles[4] Cavalry in honor of the New York general who lost a leg at Gettysburg. The fifty-two-year-old Liebenau evidently was given this task as a political favor, since he did not come from Upstate or have prior cavalry experience. Instead, his background had been in staff and recruiting officer positions in several New York City regiments prior to their going to the field. In mid-1862, he served as lieutenant in the short-lived 53rd N.Y. Infantry, and concurrently as quartermaster (with rank of sergeant major) for the 71st N.Y. Militia, then part of Sickles's Brigade. Late that year, while still carried on the books of the other two regiments, Liebenau, using the title "colonel," began recruiting volunteers for the 1st Seymour Light Infantry. During this period he developed a lucrative sideline selling commissions to prospective officers, which continued after he began to raise the Sickles Cavalry. (BOB alludes to the sale of commissions in several of his letters.) The colonel's wrong-doing must have been discovered around March 1864, when he remained behind in Saratoga Springs on prolonged sick leave rather than accompany the Twenty-Fifth for muster on Hart Island. While his court martial has not been found, his trial evidently did not take place until early 1865, when President Lincoln declined to overturn a verdict that "excluded [Liebenau] from mustering in a regiment on charges of having received considerations for appointment granted to applicants for commissions." It is not possible to positively identify which officers destined for Sickles Cavalry purchased positions, but those who joined before it moved to New York City must be considered suspect.[5]

Capt. S. E. Chamberlin, Co. K, 25th N.Y. Cav. (1864 *carte de visite*, TCC)

Considering these circumstances, the delay in the regiment's formation is not surprising, and it probably was exactly what Liebenau had in mind, as he had no intention of going to the front himself. Even though additional enrollment stations were opened Upstate at Hancock and Elmira, the colonel had only succeeded in filling Companies A and B by early 1864, while Companies C through F remained in varying stages of completion. Matters were further delayed when a measles epidemic swept through the Sickles Cavalry encampment on the Saratoga Springs Fairground, causing several deaths. Finally in March the companies raised Upstate were sent to Hart Island to await their regiment's completion. Those companies that had not been filled Upstate, as well as all later companies, were completed at the Draft Rendezvous from a heterogeneous mix of volunteers, draftees and substitutes (hired by draftees to take their place) from all over the state. This practice differed from the preferred method of raising companies from a specific locality, and its hodgepodge composition contributed to the Twenty-Fifth's inconsistent record and high desertion rate. Beginning in late April, individual companies were sent south to serve on detached duty in Washington, D.C. and Virginia. Captain Chamberlin's company (K) was only filled in late May and was the last to be added until the final three companies (I, L and M) were completed that fall.[6]

Beyond difficulties in filling its ranks, the Twenty-Fifth would be hampered by bitter rivalries, absenteeism, and self-promotion among its officers. After Liebenau's fall from grace and the individual whom the colonel picked to take his place declined the position, command of the regiment fell by default to Aaron Seeley, who was offered the position of lieutenant colonel in April 1864. He had been a New York City fireman before the war, and subsequently served as quartermaster in the 10th N.Y. Infantry (the "National Guard Zouaves"). The reason for his early departure from that regiment is unclear, but he was with the New York Militia at the time of the August 1863 draft riots. The following month his militia commander, Maj. Gen. Charles W. Sandford, wrote President Lincoln describing Seeley as currently in the national guard, but with a reputation of having earlier been an "able and competent officer" in the volunteer army, and who wanted "again to enter the service of the United States." On 15 September Lincoln forwarded the letter to Secretary of War Edwin Stanton with his endorsement of Sandford's recommendation to give Seeley a staff appointment. Soon afterwards, Seeley took over the Army Recruitment Center on Broadway in New York City. No doubt, the prior endorsements by Sanford and the President also helped to secure his later appointment as lieutenant colonel in the Twenty-Fifth, although it is possible he too purchased the position from Liebenau. In any case, Seeley was in no hurry to give up his comfortable post in the city and was not mustered into the Twenty-Fifth until September, shortly before finally joining his regiment in the field. Yet despite his late appearance on the front, BOB's letters and other sources indicate the former fireman was popular among the enlisted ranks and with most of his subordinate officers. On the other hand, he would receive severe criticism from his superiors for failure to instill discipline among his men.[7]

Maj. Samuel W. McPherson served as the Twenty-Fifth's interim commander for the period preceding Seeley's assumption of his role that fall. At the start of the war, he enlisted as first lieutenant in the short-lived "Depineuil Zouaves," and later with the 174th N.Y. Infantry. In the fall of 1863, during the early organization of the Twenty-Fifth, McPherson became Colonel Liebenau's adjutant before being promoted to captain of Company A. In what appears to have been one of Libenau's last personnel decisions, McPherson was given the brevet rank of major on 16 March and placed in command of the 1st Battalion (Companies A-D) which shortly thereafter was sent to Washington. McPherson was thus not present when the later companies were completed on Hart Island and consequently enjoyed less support among officers recruited after Seeley assumed nominal command. Nevertheless, McPherson's rapid rise in the Twenty-Fifth seemed assured, when on 6 June, the twenty-four-year-old was formally mustered as major. It was, however, the same date that the regiment's other major, Charles J. Seymour, was also mustered, and ambiguities about who had seniority contributed to Seymour's decision to return to New York, leaving McPherson as the Twenty-Fifth's acting commander for the remainder of the summer.[8]

Charles Seymour's rise through the ranks appears at every turn to have been the result of political pull. Like Seeley, he enlisted at the start of the war in New York's National Guard Zouaves, but served only four months before leaving to accept a promotion to second lieutenant on General Sickles's staff. (President Lincoln personally endorsed the recommendation for his lieutenancy.) Seymour remained on Sickles's staff until November 1862, when he enrolled as lieutenant in the 2nd Pa. Heavy Artillery— apparently arranged through his mother's connections to an influential Pennsylvania congressman. His battery (L) was deployed around Washington, where in April 1863 he was arrested and charged with staying out overnight without permission and lying about it when he returned. Seymour was allowed to resign rather than face charges, after his commander advised the Adjutant General that it would be a "death blow" to his "respectable" family, if he were to be convicted. Five months later, Liebenau provisionally appointed him a major to take over recruiting for the Sickles Cavalry in New York City—where he apparently worked with his old comrade from the Zouaves, Aaron Seeley. Like McPherson, Seymour was mustered as major on 6 June at Camp Stoneman in Washington but returned to New York rather than accompany the Twenty-Fifth into Virginia. (While McPherson's case is less clear, all evidence suggests Seymour purchased his rank as a major.)[9]

In his first letter to the *Sunday Mercury* on 9 May, BOB described the pleasant surroundings the first companies from the Twenty-Fifth found upon arrival at Camp Stoneman. The enormous cavalry depot was situated in D.C. on Giesboro Point at the mouth of the Anacostia River. Established the year before, the huge camp was equipped to care for over 10,000 horses and served as administrative and logistical headquarters for cavalry operations in the East. Newly assigned troopers stopped here to receive equipment, mounts, and onward orders before proceeding to the front. BOB was less complimentary about the quality of the would-be troopers from the Twenty-Fifth who had accompanied him there but was understandably silent about the role their two most senior officers, Seeley and Seymour, played in recruiting them.

> The numerous desertions which have taken place from our ranks have almost endangered our existence as a regiment. I understand that over 1,500 men have enlisted..., and yet now, with seven companies here, we do not number 500. Where is our boasted detective system, when so many rascals are allowed to go at large? Many of those who have deserted are professional bounty jumpers, and I have heard one of them boast that he had taken seventeen bounties...It is amusing, sometimes, when the roll is being called, to see a fellow start suddenly and answer to a name the sergeant has called perhaps two or three times without getting the expected response of "Here." In fact, I am convinced that one-third of the names on the roll are assumed and having been taken by their bearers to assist them in contemplated desertion.[10] [11]

Since the widely dispersed Twenty-Fifth remained unmounted, and therefore required little cavalry training, companies stayed at Camp Stoneman only long enough to receive equipment, including Burnside carbines. The companies that accompanied BOB (C, E and G) boarded a steamer on 16 May that took them down the Potomac to Belle Plain Landing on Aquia Creek. They were roughly following in the wake of General-in-Chief Ulysses S. Grant's bloody overland campaign towards Richmond, and Belle Plain was an important depot for supplying Grant's troops in the Fredericksburg area.

While the Twenty-Fifth as a whole kept very poor records, details about its early service in the field, when the regiment was widely scattered, are particularly hard to come by. After the war, Pvt. William D. Campbell (E) recalled that about one hundred men from his and other companies were detailed to the command of Col. Louis Palma di Cesnola of the 4th N.Y. Mounted Rifles. One night they "were ordered out to repel an attack by Mosby on our pickets and wagon trains. The detail succeeded in bringing in 250 Rebel prisoners," including a major who asked Cesnola that he be given better accommodations than his enlisted men. Cesnola, who had been captured and sent to Libby Prison the year before, replied in very salty language that the Confederate major and his men were being afforded the same tents his own soldiers used, which he emphatically stated were "too good for you."[12]

Most of the regiment spent their time at Belle Plain bringing in casualties and prisoners from the front. After the number of prisoners grew to 6,000, the "greater part" of the Twenty-Fifth present there (including Capt. James Smith (E) and fifty of his men) was detailed to escort the captives by boat to Fort Delaware, a prison camp on an island in the river below Philadelphia. The remainder accompanied Cesnola's column into southern Virginia on 23 May. After a skirmish with "Wheelers Cavalry" outside Bowling Green, they "found some burning U.S. wagons [and] a teamster lying dead with skull split open and otherwise mutilated." Having acquired a horse, Private Campbell rode back to inform the colonel, who, upon arriving on the scene, spotted a "Johnnie wandering around the place," evidently the husband of a woman standing in the door of a nearby house with a "babe" in her arms. Brought over for questioning, the man admitted he had been in the house the night before, but only replied "nothing" when asked what he knew about the teamster's death. When the "Johnnie" became even more insolent after Cesnola threatened to kill him if he did not cooperate, the colonel had him shot.[13]

Closely followed by the Confederates, Cesnola's column engaged in further skirmishes at Port Royal, Hanover Court House (reached on 31 May) and North Anna, before reaching its destination at White House Landing on the Pamunkey River in early June. On 13 June during a skirmish outside the Landing, Privates Campbell and James Clark (also E) were captured and subsequently taken to a number of prisons throughout the South, including Andersonville. Campbell, who had enlisted at age sixteen, weighed just seventy-four pounds when he finally arrived at Camp Parole in Annapolis in April 1865. There he learned that his companion Clark had reached there two months earlier, but died before he could be sent home.[14]

White House Landing served as a principal supply site for the Army of the Potomac as Grant pushed south that spring, but by mid-June its utility had declined after the Federals crossed the York Peninsula and reached City Point on the far side of the James. With its deep water access and proximity to Richmond, City Point became the new headquarters for the siege of Petersburg and thus allowed closure of the depot at White House. Grant left Brig. Gen. John J. Abercrombie behind to guard the facility with a small force that included a 3rd N.J. Artillery battery. The arrival of Cesnola's column proved a welcome addition when Abercrombie's troops were attacked on 20 June by Maj. Gen. Wade Hampton's cavalry division, which hoped to capture Federal supplies and equipment still at the depot. Grant must have had warning of a possible attack, as he sent two gunboats the day before, as well as alerted his cavalry commander, Maj. Gen. Philip H. Sheridan, to divert troopers to Abercrombie's defense.[15]

In the engagement that followed for most of 20 into 21 June, the Twenty-Fifth was caught in a brisk firefight as described below by Sgt. James Coutant (D):

> I thought we would be in Yorktown before this, but we have been kept here with other forces, to protect this place falling into the hands of the Enemy. Before daylight, Monday June 20, our pickets were driven in by Rebel skirmishers, and we were ordered into the rifle pits in a hurry. We were supported by the 3rd New Jersey Battery, and the artillery on each side kept up a steady fire for hours. At first the Rebel guns were placed out of range, but presently, they advanced them, and their missiles fell within our lines doing considerable damage. We had two gunboats in the river, and after a while they got into position and began to drop their heavy shells into the Enemy's backs and we could see wide gaps open after every fire. The shells passed over our heads, and they sounded like heavy railroad trains passing through the air at the rate of a mile a minute. [Pvt. Harry Lane, Co. B, voluntarily crawled out between the lines and held up his carbine to give the Union gunners something to set their sights on. He would demonstrate similar gallantry less than a month later at Fort Stevens.] The Rebels outnumbered us four to one, and the day would have proved disastrous to our cause, if Sheridan had not arrived with his cavalry at an early hour in the morning. As soon as the Enemy became aware of our reinforcements they retreated, and left us masters of the field. We were in the rifle pits from 3 o'clock Monday morning until eleven o'clock on the morning of the following day, with no sleep and nothing to eat but hard tack.[16]

A few days later, Sergeant Coutant recounted how 1st Lt. Charles N. Howard (G) was killed in this engagement. Howard would be the only officer in the regiment to die in action, and his fate may have had a cautionary effect on other officers, as BOB would later allude to the absence of "shoulder straps" whenever the enemy drew near.

> Howard is dead. I have to shed tears as I write his name. He was very popular, and is mourned by the whole Regt. He arrived here on the 9th of June and had held his commission as Lieut. just four months. About 9 o'clock on the morning of the battle he was sent, with ten of his men, to occupy an encampment just inside the picket lines. When he reached his position, his ambition would not allow him to remain there, and he asked his men if they would follow him to the advanced outposts. They went forward as he desired, but when they reached the picket and were informed that the wood in front of them was filled with 'bushwhackers,' they refused to go any further. Just then, the Lieut. saw two mounted men come out of the wood and stop to cross the railroad track. He seized a rifle from one of the pickets, and fired at them. As he did so, he was shot in the abdomen and fell to the ground. The Enemy appeared in force and Howard begged his men to leave him and take care of themselves, but they refused to do so, and carried him to a place of safety within our lines, where he died a few hours afterward.[17]

While these actions were taking place in Virginia, members of the Twenty-Fifth still at the Draft Rendezvous finally boarded the steamer *Admiral Dupont* in late May and were already *en route* to Washington, when Chamberlin received orders on 1 June to "proceed without delay" to join his company. He left by train the following day and caught up with his men two days later at Camp Stoneman. Since their regiment had not yet been issued horses, he and his subordinates used the next two weeks to provide basic training for the raw recruits in Company K. On 22 June, Chamberlin's company, along with other detached elements of the Twenty-Fifth that still remained in Washington, boarded a steamer at Alexandria to join the rest of their regiment at a spot their captain knew all too well—White House Landing. (In a harbinger of things to come, two lieutenants from other companies in the Twenty-Fifth were not onboard, both having been dishonorably discharged days earlier by order of the President for "having tendered their resignations for frivolous reasons, while their commands were in front of the enemy." One can presume they[18] were among those who had purchased commissions from Liebenau in order to receive an officer's pay, but with no intention of going to the front and fight.)[19]

Their arrival united the Twenty-Fifth for the first time, but there would be little time for Chamberlin and the others to hear about the recent attack, or otherwise get acquainted with their comrades before the regiment set off across the York Peninsula for City Point. The New Yorkers were to be part of an escort for a wagon train carrying ordinance and other supplies from the Landing to Grant's new headquarters. To keep the Rebels from learning of this mission and avoid the heat, they departed from White House on the night of 24 June. The five-day march under a blistering sun proved more difficult than expected, and one skirmish fought on the 26th near Charles City Court House resulted in two killed and one wounded from the Twenty-Fifth. Another veteran recalled they were "harassed" by Hampton's cavalry nearly all the way.[20]

The New Yorkers narrowly lost a chance to see President Lincoln, who had arrived at City Point on 21 June to confer with Grant. Just a few days before, the general had selected this site to serve as his headquarters for a projected siege of Petersburg and Richmond. Strategically located less than twenty miles east of both cities, the camp sat on a low bluff overlooking the juncture of the James and Appomattox Rivers. Its deep-water port, now part of the city of Hopewell, was accessible to large vessels and served as the hub of a logistical network that ultimately enabled Grant to overrun the Confederate defenses around Richmond.

Upon arrival at City Point on 29 June, the unmounted Twenty-Fifth was assigned to provost guard duty under the command of Brig. Gen. Marsena R. Patrick, the Army's Provost Marshal General. (Provost Guards combined the present-day roles of military police, counterintelligence officers and civilian liaison.) The following day, Chamberlin was detached to a Board of Inquiry to investigate problems relating to a shipment of quartermaster supplies. (His writing and administrative skills often landed him on courts martial, boards of inquiry, and provost duties.) After the board was adjourned two days later, he was ordered to report with his company to guard the "Camp of Prisoners, Convalescents, Stragglers and Civilians" at City Point. (Other companies from his regiment were charged with escorting Rebel prisoners and Union deserters to and from the prison.) Serving at the notorious "Bull Pen," as the squalid open-air prison was known, was a far cry from the glamorous life of cavalry officer that Chamberlin envisioned when he joined the regiment. In addition to the unpleasant surroundings, he would be expected to keep detailed lists of prisoners, file daily reports, and closely supervise the guards.[21]

In a letter to the *Sunday Mercury* written on 3 July, BOB was of the opinion that provost duty was "about the wisest disposition which could have been made with the regiment in its present, depleted and undrilled condition." Although the erstwhile cavalrymen remained without mounts, a surprising number had already obtained horses outside official channels—a propensity that would come back to haunt the regiment.

> [A]bout sixty or seventy of the men have mounted themselves on horses which had been abandoned by the various raiding parties as broken down and unfit for service. Some of these had sore backs, others sprained joints, and more were merely ridden and starved almost to death. By good and careful treatment and feeding, and, in some instances, by judicious "swapping," quite a passable lot of horses were mustered out of the unpromising material, and are now doing good service here, in guarding conscripts, skedadlers, substitutes, [etc.]...to the front.

This letter committed a potentially serious security breach by revealing that Union troops were digging a mine under the defenses around Petersburg, "and from all accounts there will be such an exhibition of fireworks on the morning of some day in July, as Petersburg has never before witnessed." The tunnel was completed on 23 July and an explosive charge was detonated on the 30th, setting the stage for the ill-fated Battle of the Crater. Rebel spies scanned the Northern press for exactly this sort of information, and the Southerners were expecting the explosion when it occurred. In the resulting melee, the Confederates easily picked off the Federals, many of them Black troops, as they rushed into the resulting crater and became easy targets.[22]

Chapter 6

"SAVING" THE CAPITAL: July-August 1864

The Twenty-Fifth's stay at City Point lasted barely a week before it was ordered on 7 July to embark for Baltimore. Grant had just learned a large Confederate force under Lt. Gen. Jubal Early had crossed the Potomac above Harpers Ferry and was headed eastward through Maryland. Although he initially believed the invasion was a feint to relieve pressure on Richmond, the Union commander reluctantly agreed to send some units north to defend the capital, including the unmounted 25th N. Y. Cavalry. Chamberlin's regiment reached Baltimore by steamboat on Friday afternoon (the 8th) but had to wait until 2 AM the next day to board cattle cars that deposited them in Washington at daybreak. (During the layover in Baltimore, BOB archly noted some officers spent time "horse-trading and whiskey-drinking.") After catching naps on sidewalks outside the train station, the men marched to Camp Stoneman, reaching it about noon on Saturday, fully expecting they were finally to receive their horses.[1]

While the Twenty-Fifth was *en route*, Early's army exacted ransoms from Marylanders in Hagerstown and Frederick in return for sparing their towns from the torch. The Rebels were now poised at Frederick, apparently ready to move either towards Baltimore, or south to Washington. Their only obstacle was a small force Gen. Lew Wallace had hastily assembled on the banks of the Monocacy River, three miles southeast of Frederick. Although greatly outnumbered, the Union soldiers held back Early's forces throughout most of Saturday (9th), before withdrawing late that afternoon. The Battle of Monocacy—one of the less vaunted engagements of the war—witnessed heroics on both sides, particularly by the 10th Vt. Infantry. The Vermonters had left City Point just before the Twenty-Fifth, but on arrival at Baltimore were ordered to join Wallace's command rather than proceed to Washington. (Fate had again intervened on Chamberlin's behalf at Baltimore, just as it had two years earlier, when the 118th came close to be sent to Antietam. Had the Twenty-Fifth arrived a bit sooner, it almost certainly would have been sent on a westbound train to Frederick and suffered heavy casualties at Monocacy.)[2]

After Wallace withdrew towards Baltimore, the way lay open to the capital—Early's objective all along. There were, however, more impediments to overcome. Not only had a day been lost and with it the element of surprise, but Early's troops had suffered losses at Monocacy estimated as high as 1,500 killed or wounded. In addition, his infantrymen had been on the move since leaving Staunton on 28 May and were close to exhaustion, having fought four significant battles in Virginia and Maryland. Early knew Washington's impressive ring of forts was little more than a façade, now that Grant had stripped its veteran defenders to augment his forces at City Point. Left behind to defend the capital were convalescents, untested units and military bureaucrats, who could not hope to withstand Early's seasoned veterans. Even if he could not hold the city for long, the Rebel commander was convinced a spectacular raid, accompanied by burning public buildings and the looting of the Treasury, would give a tremendous psychological boost to the South and strengthen Confederate diplomatic initiatives abroad. Furthermore, sacking Washington would devastate morale in the North and almost certainly doom Lincoln's re-election, paving the way for a negotiated peace settlement that would guarantee the South's continued independence.[3]

On Sunday morning (10th), General Wallace wired: "I have been defeated...the enemy are not pursuing me [towards Baltimore] from which I infer they are marching on Washington." Only then did the gravity of their situation dawn on the White House and War Department, which up to then seemed hypnotized by Early's approach. Army Chief of Staff Henry Halleck telegraphed Grant that "the boldness of the movement would indicate [Early] is stronger than we supposed." Finally convinced an attack on the capital was imminent, Grant ordered Gen. Horatio Wright's veteran VI Corps to embark for Washington, the only question being whether it could reach it in time.

Early's battle-weary men spent Sunday on a forced march they would never forget. The road from Monocacy Station to Rockville, some 12 miles north of the D.C. line, was narrow and dusty, the soldiers inevitably becoming strung out along the way. The Rebels' most positive memory that day was the reception accorded them by sympathetic civilians, who stood along their route offering sustenance to the weary men. (This token support by Maryland "Copperheads" was a far cry from the armed uprising Early had hoped for.) Still, the chimera of an undefended Yankee capital beckoned only a few miles away, and as late as Sunday afternoon, Washington's northern perimeter was held by just two regiments of raw militia, who could "scarcely fire a gun." If the Rebels could move fast enough, a chance to alter the outcome of the war seemed within their grasp.[4]

Symptomatic of the paralysis gripping the capital,[5] the Twenty-Fifth stood by idly at Camp Stoneman throughout Sunday afternoon and evening, unaware of the impending danger. It was only after midnight on Monday (the 11th) that the New Yorkers were awakened by a bugle call and told to get ready to march into the city, some seven miles distant. Before dawn, Maj. Samuel McPherson had his men on the move, arriving downtown shortly after daybreak. There, the major learned he was to report with his men to Maj. Gen. Alexander McCook, who only the day before had assumed command of Washington's northern defenses, which he ran from hastily-established headquarters in a tavern on 7th Street (now Georgia Avenue), not far from Fort Stevens.[6]

Early's troops also roused themselves from camps around Rockville and were underway before dawn. But after reports were received from Brig. Gen. John McCausland's cavalry scouts that the direct road into the capital was heavily defended, Early turned his infantry east along present-day Viers Mill Road on a longer course that would bring it directly in front of Fort Stevens, a part of the defenses that was still lightly manned. Once again, the stifling heat and dusty road forced the Confederates to reduce their pace, and it was around noon before Early's vanguard arrived at the northern end of 7th Street road, which led directly downtown past Fort Stevens, the latter still almost two miles farther south. The area was dominated by several Blair family estates, including Silver Spring, home of patriarch Francis P. Blair, and nearby Falkland, belonging to his son, U.S. Postmaster General Montgomery Blair. According to one source, "Old Jube" was angered to find his advance scouts had spent precious time looting these mansions and their wine cellars rather than gathering information on the Yankee fortifications. While his foot soldiers were catching up, Early and his lead infantry commander, Maj. Gen. Robert E. Rodes, went forward to reconnoiter the defenses for themselves, and found, as Early would explain to Lee, the forts more formidable and better manned than anticipated. Before riding farther east to look for more promising spots to launch an attack, Early instructed Rodes to put out sharpshooters and skirmishers to probe the area around Fort Stevens.[7]

As the 25th N.Y. Cavalry left Pennsylvania Avenue Monday morning and hastened up 7th Street towards the front, still five miles away, they passed the Patent Office where elderly clerks were seen shouldering ancient muskets to guard against an imminent attack. As BOB recalled: "All was confusion, and white lips and pale cheeks were announcing that 'the Rebels were right at hand in great force'." For the first time, the New Yorkers realized they had not been sent to Washington to be mounted, but for a more serious purpose. Even then they found it difficult to believe Early had gotten so near, that was until they heard the heavy guns in the forts begin to fire. Further along, "couriers dashed back and forth, frightened men and women flying from their homes and crowding into the city, and everything betokened the complete surprise which the Rebels had succeeded in making." Closer to the front, the unmounted cavalrymen found their way impeded by convalescent soldiers and government workers rushing to man the defenses, as well as curiosity seekers hoping to glimpse the impending clash. Headed in the opposite direction, civilians hurried their families and prized possessions out of harm's way. At McCook's headquarters, McPherson was directed to take his regiment to Fort Stevens, but only after each man was issued forty rounds of ammunition.[8]

While accounts of when the regiment arrived at the fort vary widely, most indicate it was late morning before McPherson reported to Lt. Col. John N. Frazee, whose 150th Ohio Infantry had occupied this sector of the defenses since early summer. (The 150th was composed of Ohio militiamen who had enlisted for one hundred days, and its Company K, composed of students from Oberlin College, garrisoned Fort Stevens.) Frazee also had nominal command over a 13th Mich. Light Artillery Battery, as well as convalescents and members of the Veteran Reserve Corps, who continued to arrive from their normal assignments around the city. The troopers from the Twenty-Fifth took little comfort when they discovered the small size and questionable experience of the garrison that was expected to hold off Early's army. As one recalled: "[W]e found a few men that...belonged to some 100-day regiment, as their clothing looked quite new and fit pretty well." Stepping inside the fort, he observed an "old wounded sergeant trying to teach the new men how to man the big guns." (As the fort's permanent garrison, the Ohioans maintained picket posts as far out as the Blair mansions, but their primary role was to help operate the guns, a task they would perform well, despite the New Yorkers' initial concerns.) McPherson established his command post inside the fort, where he was assisted by Capts. Stephen W. Wheeler (B) and Nicolas D. Moffett (C), while the men and other officers took their places in the rifle pits in front.[9]

By the time McPherson's regiment was in place, there were already ominous signs this sector might bear the brunt of any attack. McCook later wrote that scouts from the 8th Ill. Cavalry advised him at 10 AM of the enemy's approach on the road to Silver Spring. These same cavalry scouts also alerted members of the 150th Ohio manning picket posts out along the 7th Street road of the enemy's proximity. It was the Ohioans' first indication of the Rebel vanguard's approach, and one was mortally wounded before he could reach the safety of the fort. At this point, McCook wired that the enemy was about 2.5 miles away, adding "My force is small, but will do my best." (The Twenty-Fifth apparently arrived as the Ohioan pickets were being driven in.) By 12:30, the situation had grown dire, leading McCook to wire tersely: "The enemy is advancing on my front with cavalry, artillery and infantry." Benjamin Cooling, a life-long student of Early's raid and Washington's defenses, has called the noon hour of 11 July "the moment of greatest danger to the national capital—at any point during the four years of war." It was also the hour the Twenty-Fifth took to the field.[10]

In the midst of this turmoil, Abraham Lincoln arrived to personally assess the danger, becoming the only sitting President to come under enemy fire. On entering the fort, he impressed upon those present, including McPherson, the importance of holding their position. "Upon you and your men depend the safety of the Capital; but should any of your command be captured, say nothing about the situation in Washington, and if they ask whose command you belong to, say the advance of the Sixth Corps." (This visit should not be confused with Lincoln's better known return to Fort Stevens the following day. On that occasion Confederate sharpshooters wounded a man standing next to the President, who was observing the action from the parapet, causing future Supreme Court Justice Oliver Wendell Holmes, Jr. to shout, "Get down, you fool!" Lincoln meekly complied.)[11]

News of Lincoln's presence spread rapidly among the New Yorkers in the rifle pits. As Sgt. Henry M. Nevius (E) recalled: "The President went about cheering the men, and cautioning them to be careful. Every man of us determined to die before the enemy should pass us and get within reach of the Capital and our President...we preferred death rather than turn our backs upon the enemy in the face of the President." Long after the war, Pvt. John H. Wolf (B) vividly recalled the "enthusiasm and pride" the Twenty-Fifth felt on learning Lincoln had come out to witness them risk their lives. "Word seemed to pass quickly from man to man that he had said: 'We must hold this position at any price. Every man who takes up his gun in defense of the National Capital today is worth his weight in gold...' It made a great impression on us, that we were skirmishing right there under the eyes of...the 'Soldier's Friend'." [12]

Shortly after the President's arrival, McPherson was directed to form his command into a skirmish line to intercept the enemy's advance force, which could now be seen in front of the fort. The New Yorkers' line stretched from the 7th Street road on the right flank westward toward Rock Creek, where it was anchored by Chamberlin's Company K. Rebel skirmishers and sharpshooters had already advanced to within 150 yards of the fort and were posing a threat to the defenders within, when the order was given for the Twenty-Fifth to advance and drive them back. As they moved out, the Rebels fired their first volley and the fighting began in earnest. Sgt. Daniel McLean, whose Company A was on the right end of the line, remembered: "Giving the rebs a volley from our Burnside carbines, we started on the double quick; halting every 20 or 30 rods, would drop, fire and load, and then on we went under a terrific fire from the enemy, until we took the position they had occupied in the morning. This was 10 a.m. [too early by most accounts] and we held that ground until 3 in the afternoon, when we were relieved by the Thirteen Corps."[13]

Lack of a detailed contemporary account of the Twenty-Fifth's actions, plus confusion among the diverse groups of men and officers on the field that day, make reconstruction of events difficult. What seems clear is that the Twenty-Fifth fought with unaccustomed determination, pushing back Early's vanguard a mile or more before being relieved by the arrival of fresh troops. Their decisive role was cited a day later in the *Alexandria Gazette:* "About two o'clock yesterday there was some very severe skirmishing...on the 7th St. road, ...the Confederate sharpshooters, under cover of the houses in the vicinity, having advanced to within thirty or forty rods of the fort. The 25th regiment New York cavalry advanced as skirmishers, dismounted, and drove them from the houses, which were then committed to the flames." Chamberlin's diary entry for 11 July adds but few details: "Manned the rifle pits on the west side of Fort Stevens about noon. The regiment received orders to move out of the defenses and deploy as skirmishers. The enemy were within rifle shot of the fort, when the regiment deployed as skirmishers and drove the enemy from the houses, burning several by order, and held the skirmish line until night, when they were relieved by a part of the 6th corps. Lost, 5 killed [including Pvt. Jeremiah Maloney (K)] and 13 wounded."[14]

That afternoon, medic Richard Coutant was kept busy tending to casualties and getting them to a field hospital set up in the Ohioans' barracks behind the fort. He recalled the men filed out of the fortifications about 1 PM, and soon ran into stiff resistance. "For half an hour the bullets flew as thick as hail." The Rebels held a strong position in the rear of several houses and barns from which they were only dislodged "when the forts opened fire." The New Yorkers then occupied these same positions until the buildings were ordered burned and darkness brought an end to the fighting.[15]

Although BOB composed a letter less than a week after the fighting, the *Sunday Mercury* correspondent for once seemed at a loss for words, perhaps because, as regimental standard bearer, he likely remained with McPherson inside the fort:

> The regiment was now pushed out to the front of Fort Stevens, and hardly had it taken position when the Rebels were soon coming down the opposite hill, a perfect cloud of skirmishers. The Twenty-fifth was immediately deployed in skirmish-lines, and ordered forward to check the advance of the Rebels, which they did in gallant style, and after two hours' hard fighting drove them over the crest of the second range of hills, and held this advanced position until they were relieved, the fire of the enemy being by this time completely silenced. The handsome manner in which the regiment behaved itself elicited the warmest commendations from all who witnessed it... The few officers of the regiment who went on the field behaved themselves in most excellent style, but on the line, where shoulder-straps should have been, there were many, many vacancies. Major McPherson has raised himself considerably in the estimation of the men by his conduct during these few days, as they had supposed he was too much of a martinet in camp to show much

fight in the field, but I am happy to say that he has belied this opinion.[16]

Pvt. Harry Lane (Company B, later promoted to sergeant) would provide the most detailed account of the day's action. While veterans' memories are often unreliable, he was clearly in the thick of the fighting, and his dramatic account deserves repetition here.

> Immediately [after the President's arrival] the command was given, "Form the center to right and left, take skirmishing distance, march." We deployed and moved steadily down the sloping ground. The enemy at once opened fire upon us and before we could return it we had to advance a considerable distance, exposed to a severe dropping fire. We flushed our first game, a skirmish line of the enemy..., at a point a little more than midway between [Ft. Stevens and] Justice Blair's blue-stone mansion, and what a grueling they gave us..., but... we took it without a grimace and returned their hospitality into the bargain. We... pushed them back till we gained a fair position, a couple of small houses with their outbuildings..., those commanding the more open ground, which lay to the right of and beyond Judge Blair's house. [Pvt. Albert] Giddings [B], myself and some six or eight others selected the best points of resistance here and made it as warm as we could for Early's people. The owners of the houses had evidently fled just as they were sitting down to breakfast, for it was on the tables. We ate the breakfast for them, fighting the while. Giddings called out: "They are getting around our flank." At the same instant, they advanced rapidly against our immediate front and our entire line was forced back. The guns from Fort Stevens then opened a tremendous fire on them and after a little we again advanced, reoccupying the ground from which we had just been driven. Here I heard the slap of a bullet striking someone and looking over my shoulder I saw [Pvt. Jonathan W.] Byrnes, one of our company with a very dazed expression. I said, "Byrnes, you're hit." He called to Giddings, saying, "Giddings, I'm hit!" "Well, then, skedaddle to the rear. What do you stand grinning there for?" said Giddings.... Byrnes was struck on the throat [but survived]. There were very few of us at this spot now and Giddings was saying to me, "This is getting very hot here, Lane," when the order came to set fire to houses and move a little to our left. We did so, and I took cover from a small manure heap, from which we had a good sight of some gray coats. Sergt. [Thomas] Richardson [B] was standing on the first rail of the fence and I said to him, "Keep low, Richardson, or you'll get hit." He had hardly replied, "They can't fire straight enough to hit me," when he was shot through the head and fell off the fence. [Richardson is one of five members of the Twenty-fifth buried in Fort Stevens's Battleground Cemetery.]
>
> The owner of one of the houses just now returned and was sitting, dressed only in his shirt and pantaloons, on a box very close to me and in the middle of the yard, and I drew his attention to the risk he ran. He said, "I don't care. I've lost everything I have in the world," when another idea seized him, and picking up a carbine and pouch he, from that moment, fired and fought like a Trojan. Again we were driven back, but again advanced and got possession of Judge Blair's house and grounds, which afforded a grand position for defense. I got into the house somehow and from the library I took the loan of a handsome volume of 'Moore's Melodies' and the 'Arabian Nights Tales.' I met almost immediately after with our surgeon major... [James D.] Jones, who promised to take care of them for me.... Had the judge known that I had borrowed his books, I am certain he would have overlooked my having done so, for shortly after we committed arson by setting fire to his house so as to give better sight to our guns on Fort Stevens. Once more we were driven out of our position and our ammunition running low we were served out with a fresh supply on the line. I was one of those who went back and helped to carry down a box to the line. After some sharp fighting we again pushed forward and drove the enemy

"Confederate Assault on the Works near Washington Repulsed by Dismounted Cavalry and Militia." Somewhat fanciful sketch of Early's vanguard approaching Fort Stevens prior to the Twenty-fifth's advance to meet them.

"Night [sic] Attack on Fort Stevens, July 11th, While President Lincoln Was There." Only known depiction of Lincoln's first visit shows houses set on fire to prevent use by snipers. (both illustrations from Mottelay, Paul F., and T. Campbell-Copeland, eds., *The Soldier in Our Civil War*, v. II, (New York: Stanley Bradley:.297)

back from the judge's house and grounds and held them all the time after. Capts. [Clinton G.] Townsley [D], [Edward W.] Woodward [A] and [Stephen W.] Wheeler [B] were standing in the yard around the pump. Townsley was taking a drink of water and I asked him to let me have one. He handed me the glass and pumped it full for me. As I replaced the glass on the spout of the pump a bullet glanced therefrom and struck Townsley in the groin, giving him, however, only a skin wound.

Wheeler then gave me instructions to take five men to go down to the iron gate that opened on to the wood from Judge Blair's grounds and keep a hot fire up that road. I took with me [Pvt. Patrick] Cannon [D], [Pvt. James] Quinn [C], [Pvt. John] Tierney [A], a man whose name I did not know and little [Pvt.] Dan Dibble of Company A. We had hardly got to the gate before the man I did not know was shot through the heart. Cannon got a bullet through his left breast and arm, the same bullet... must have been passing into Quinn immediately above his right hip and killing him. Tierney had his arm shattered above the elbow, and only Dibble and myself were left. I noticed a puff of smoke coming out from a large palm [pine?] tree about fifty yards in front of me, and I said to Dibble... "There is a man there; fire at him." He fired and... must have hit the man, as no more smoke came from the tree. When Cannon, who was an Irishman, was struck, he danced about, poor fellow, calling out in accents racy of his native soil, "Oim kilt, oim murthered; what is it for, at all?" and thus affording a good mark, the bullets came on us fast and thick. I said to him, "For God's sake dance somewhere else or you will have us all killed." Dibble and I then crept across the road, where Orderly Sergeant [Alfred C.] Starbird of Company A and some of his fellows were. I had but reached this spot when Starb[i]rd was shot through the head and carried to the rear. [He is buried in Battleground Cemetery.] The enemy now made a determined advance on us, but covered by the guns from both forts we stubbornly held our ground. It was now well on in the afternoon and there appeared on the field what I always understood to be the thirteenth army corps, under Gen. Merritt. How he did cheer and pour in volley after volley. This corps took up exactly the same ground as we did in the morning, and we were moved across to a position in front of Fort de Russey.... We lay there during the night and on the [12th] had a small edition of the [fighting on the 11th]....[17]

"Judge Blair's house" appears in several other accounts, including that of Lane's companion, Dan Dibble, who claimed their initial sally from the fort forced the Southerners back beyond "the Blair house at Silver Spring." There, some Germans in the regiment found a keg of beer and refused to fire another round until it had been consumed. John Wolf similarly wrote: "We slowly but surely advanced our line towards Judge Blair's house, which is about a mile or more north of the fort. The Blair house is where Early ate his breakfast that morning." Elsewhere, Wolf claimed he finished off Early's meal. (If so, it was more likely the remains left by the Ohio picket.) In another account, Wolf more realistically has the Twenty-Fifth advancing to what later became Walter Reed Hospital, where the enemy "made a long stand. But finally they went on back to the Blair place." He did not claim to have followed them there.[18]

Could 400 dismounted New York troopers have driven Early's vanguard some two miles back to Silver Spring and then occupied these same premises? Only if a relatively small number of Confederate scouts and sharpshooters were on the field. In any case, it is more likely the dwellings Lane and the others entered were on what became the Walter Reed complex, or roughly a mile north of the fort and well within range of its guns. (Local historian William Cox also noted possible confusion among Union soldiers over the location of the Blair estates.) Buildings on the low rise at Walter Reed that were used by Rebel sharpshooters before being burned included the Carberry and McChesney homes. Sgt. Henry Nevius (E) was hit in his arm "about 2 o'clock" during fighting around the McChesney house but stayed with his men for several more hours. Once, after fainting from loss of blood, he was taken to have his wound dressed. While in the rear, Lincoln tried to shake his hand, leading Nevius to protest that he did not want to get blood on the President's proffered hand. "Never mind," Lincoln replied, "it is the blood of a hero." Later the President fulfilled a promise made that day to have the sergeant promoted to lieutenant. Unfortunately, Nevius's arm could not be saved, and he was unable to return to active service.[19]

Since Major McPherson never filed a report on his command's performance in the battle, we must turn to General McCook's overview of the first day's action along Washington's northern defenses. Written two weeks later, it varies significantly from those given by participants from the Twenty-Fifth, especially with regard to the duration of their engagement with the enemy and their location on the field when reinforcements came to their relief. Of course, McCook, veteran of battles out West and scion of the "fighting McCooks," had a different perspective than did the relatively green members of Chamberlin's regiment and, given his responsibilities for the entire front, he may have been unaware of the extent of the Twenty-Fifth's actions that day.

> ....At 12 p.m. a strong line of the enemy's skirmishers came in view, advancing upon our position. The picket line...was composed of 100 days' men [150th Ohio]...and a portion of the Twenty-fifth New York Cavalry (dismounted). Being satisfied that they could not contend favorably against the enemy's line, were ordered to fall back slowly, fighting, until they reached the rifle-pits... [T]he enemy was held in check until the dismounted of the Second Division of the Cavalry Corps...600 strong...were made ready to go out, drive the enemy back, and re-establish our picket line. This was handsomely done about 1:30 p.m., the enemy's skirmishers being forced back, and our line well established at 1,100 yards in front of the works.... [and] affairs remained in this condition until evening.[20]

The detachment that McCook describes as arriving to relieve the Twenty-Fifth in front of the fort was led by Maj. George H. Briggs of the 7th Mich. Cavalry. Briggs had been charged with rounding up all available troopers at Camp Stoneman and rushing them to the front. The resulting force of 400-600 dismounted cavalrymen included many from Brig. Gen. George A. Custer's Michigan Brigade, who were then at the camp for refitting after an engagement at Trevilian Station. While Briggs may have arrived at McCook's headquarters at 1:30 PM, the accounts of Lane and others put the arrival on the field of their relief, whom they tentatively identified as belonging to the XIII Corps, at mid-afternoon. These same sources show the New Yorkers' skirmish line far out in front of the fort at the time of Briggs's arrival.[21]

At the end of his previously quoted letter, Harry Lane raised two questions that had puzzled him over the years. One was why, when the capital was at its greatest peril, did the Federal authorities leave the Twenty-Fifth alone to face Early's army, "for hour after hour" against such "appalling odds." The answer is probably quite simple, until the arrival of Briggs's detachment, McCook did not have fighters to spare to hold a line that stretched from Rock Creek east to Fort Slocum. The situation improved throughout the day, as a steady stream of reinforcements began to arrive. Mostly convalescents, clerks and grizzled veterans, they were, if not suitable as skirmishers, quite capable of manning the earthworks. After Briggs's men replaced the Twenty-Fifth on the skirmish line far out in front of the fort, the New Yorkers fell back to closer-in earthworks, where, as John Wolf recalled: "We kept up our firing until 5 PM, then a portion of our line was relieved by the Reserve Corp."[22] Pvt. Rufus Lord (A) remembered being relieved by a Veteran Reserve regiment about 6 PM, but never saw anyone from the VI Corps take the field before the Twenty-Fifth was shifted to Fort DeRussy later that evening. (Despite being frequently credited with saving the capital, the first troops from the VI Corps, the 98th Pa. Infantry, did not arrive at Fort Stevens until after 5 PM and was the only part of Wright's command to engage the enemy that evening.)[23]

Like many others, Lane also wondered why a capable and aggressive general such as Early did not recognize that only a skeleton force stood in his way and simply push into the city before the VI Corps arrived. Chamberlin thought he had found the answer when he read an 1871 article in which Early described how, during the early afternoon of 11 July, while his lead infantry brigades were still being brought up, he and General Rodes went forward to inspect the Federal defenses. Their attention was soon drawn to a regiment that was just then filing out of Fort Stevens to form a skirmish line with such "precision" that Rodes exclaimed: "They are not hundred-day' men; they are old soldiers." At least in Early's version of events, Rodes became convinced that what they saw were veteran fighters from Grant's army, not the militia and convalescents they had expected. Concluding the VI Corps had already arrived, Rodes convinced Early that seizure of the capital was no longer possible.[24]

Positive the "old soldiers," who had caused the two generals to hesitate and ultimately discard plans to invade Washington were from his regiment, Chamberlin published his theory in an unsigned 1871 newspaper article (reprinted in Appendix A) that challenged the then widespread belief that the VI Corps deserved sole credit for saving the capital. As proof, the article's author cited a "diary in my possession" and pointed out that the only graves in the Fort Stevens cemetery marked as killed on 11 July were those of five members of the Twenty-Fifth. Chamberlin, the only officer named in the article, was described as the "plucky" captain of a battalion of skirmishers in front of the fort. He would expand his argument in an 1877 magazine article (excerpted in Appendix B) that further inflated his role to being the regiment's acting commander in front of the fort. Self-promotion aside, his basic argument about the Twenty-Fifth's part in deceiving Early was a theme he repeated in speeches and interviews for the rest of his life, and, in doing so, gave the veterans of his oft ill-starred regiment something positive they could point to—the realization that, for a few hours, they had made a difference in the war.[25]

The fighting on the second day was more intense and occasioned greater casualties, but anticlimactic (a "smaller edition" as Lane put it) for the Twenty-Fifth, which played a secondary role after the arrival of the VI Corps the night before. Early by then recognized raiding Washington was no longer possible, but still had to mount a convincing diversionary attack throughout Tuesday to keep the Yankees pinned down behind their defenses and thus disguise his intention to withdraw. The most serious fighting took place between 5 PM and sunset as the Federals attempted to clear nests of Rebel snipers that had harassed their lines all day, including almost hitting President Lincoln during a second visit to Fort Stevens.[26]

The Twenty-Fifth was deployed early Tuesday on the left flank (near Fort DeRussy) where the New Yorkers replaced a Veteran Reserve detachment. Chamberlin's diary entry for 12 July reads: "Early in the morning again ordered out on the skirmish line and relieved regiment of Invalid corps exchanging shots with enemy until evening, when they advanced a strong line of battle. Sharp fighting by the 6th corps; and the enemy driven back." John Wolf recalled that "shortly" after being relieved by the VI Corps on Monday, "word came that a portion of the [Veteran' Reserve Corps] was getting cut to pieces. A detail of men…under Capt. S. E. Chamberlin started in the direction where it was said the Reserve Corps men were, and through this false rumor some of our squad were wounded." Coutant recalled driving back a Rebel force while posted near Fort DeRussy, only to have it return after being reinforced. "Finally our forces made a resolute stand, and the battle continued fiercely from 5 o'clock until 9. The Rebels made ten different charges, but our columns remained unbroken."[27]

BOB adds some details, but like Coutant, does not clarify the degree to which the Twenty-Fifth contributed to driving back the Confederates at the end of the second day:

> [We] were marched toward Fort DeRussy, and pushed out in front of it on the skirmish-line, and hardly had we taken position when the music opened again in lively style, and the effectiveness of our Burnside rifles began to be apparent in the number of stretchers which the Rebs began to bring into requisition on their side of the field. We kept up an incessant fire until about six o'clock in the afternoon, when our lines of battle advanced, and attacked the Rebs in their chosen position, and after about three hours' hard fighting we drove them over three miles, the Rebels burning the farmhouses as they retreated.[28]

As dawn broke on Wednesday, everyone in the Union lines was astonished to discover Early's forces had slipped away during the night and were already on their way back to safety on the Virginia side of the Potomac. BOB's account of this unexpected development follows:

> When daylight broke we advanced to the hills which the enemy had occupied in our front, and found their dead lying around in great numbers. The party detailed for that purpose buried about two hundred of them, and we have taken about four hundred prisoners, inclusive of 163 wounded, who were left in a house in charge of two of their own surgeons.
>
> What they mean to do with this regiment, the Lord only knows. We have very few men; very, very few officers, and very d___d few of those who are with us will be found on the battle-field, although the regiment has some noble exceptions, but, as a whole, the line of shoulder-straps is exceedingly of the "dead beat" order. This will always be the case where money, not merit, is the keystone of the arch that leads to preferment. [An apparent allusion to Colonel Liebenau's sale of commissions.][29]

Pursuit of Early's army fell to the VI Corps, but even with the addition of the XXII Corps, the Federals' desultory response allowed the Southerners to escape into Loudoun County with barely a shot being fired. The Twenty-Fifth remained near Fort Stevens, where it bivouacked for the next five nights, giving the men ample chance to discuss the climactic events of the past week. With no inkling of what lay ahead, they would not have known they would look back on their role in defending the capital as their most significant contribution to the Union cause. Yet, without a senior officer to make their case to the Army high command, their accomplishment received little notice. Nor did the Twenty-Fifth have prominent patrons back home, or even a hometown paper, to trumpet their exploits—the *Sunday Mercury* published soldier letters from all across the Empire State. Absent any specific accolade, we are left with McCook's valedictory to all who manned the defenses on 11 July. "I cannot...recall the names of the commanders of detachments who reported to me, but I may hazard the remark, there never was before a command so heterogeneous yet so orderly. The hale and hearty soldier, the invalid, the convalescent, the wounded, and the quartermaster's employees, side by side, each working with a singleness of purpose and willing to discharge any duty imposed upon him."[30]

If BOB's account is representative, one topic among the New Yorkers was the absence of many officers from the battlefield. As previously noted, McPherson, along with two of his captains, set up headquarters inside the fort and remained there throughout the fighting, as his adversaries would later point out. His decision was, however, not inappropriate for a regiment's senior officer. Chamberlin, on the other hand, was on the field both days, first as battalion leader on the skirmish line's left flank and then in charge of a squad sent out the second day. Unfortunately, there are no detailed accounts from members of his end of the skirmish line, making it hard to reconstruct events in that sector, other than the fighting was apparently less intense there than closer to the 7th Street road. What he did not want to dwell on in later years was having to leave the field due to sunstroke. The source for this absence is a letter from a soldier in Company K seeking help obtaining a pension. The writer had served under an alias, and to help Chamberlin identify him added: "Captain, do you know when we went into the fight at Ft. Stevens I was on your right side in battle line together. You was overcome with the heat and you fell to the ground and William Smith of our Co. came along and picked you up and took you back to the rear and then the next day I seen Williams I asked him how you was and he said you was overcome with the heat." Given temperatures in the mid-nineties and the wool uniforms worn by Union soldiers, it was not unusual for them to succumb to heat, but if true, Chamberlin recovered sufficiently to lead another sortie early the next morning.[31]

Whatever the case, Company K's captain was clearly proud of both his and his men's performance at Fort Stevens. It was a feeling that grew through the years, and as time went on, he began to see the hand of Divine Providence guiding the Twenty-Fifth to the exact spot where it could make a difference. An early indication of this pride was a diary he bought to record the momentous events of the preceding days, most likely purchased on 14 July, when he received a pass to go into Washington. He also mailed two letters recounting his company's exploits to former colleagues at Hart Island. Several days later, they wrote back congratulating him and his lieutenant, Arch Wilson, on their performance at Fort Stevens.[32]

As early as 1877, Chamberlin, the first known member of his regiment to do so, began calling for a monument to honor those of the Twenty-Fifth who gave their lives in Washington's defense ("a grateful nation should inscribe their names in granite"). It was a cause that his fellow veterans came to embrace and would eventually bring to fruition. The losses at Fort Stevens were significantly greater than the five buried at Battlefield Cemetery and cited in Chamberlin's published accounts. Days after the fight, BOB put the number at nine killed and seventeen wounded. Based on letters written by a member of the regiment right after the battle, historian William Cox concluded that the New Yorkers "suffered severely," incurring losses of "17 killed and 23 wounded out of 400 engaged." In 1901, Henry Nevius found records of four burials at the Soldiers' Home and fourteen at Arlington Cemetery, which with the five at Fort Stevens brought the total killed, or mortally wounded, to twenty-three. Aside from an Ohioan mortally wounded in the morning and a member of the 98th Pennsylvania killed that evening, the only casualties on 11 July were those of the Twenty-Fifth—perhaps the most persuasive argument that these untested cavalrymen from the Empire State did "save" the capital for a few critical hours.[33]

Chapter 7

DISSENSION IN THE RANKS:
August-October 1864

On 17 July, the Twenty-Fifth decamped to Soldier's Home in northwest D.C., before returning to Camp Stoneman several days later. Plans to transfer the regiment back to City Point were dropped, and the regiment was instead temporarily attached to the XXII Corps for the defense of Washington. The prospect of an undemanding assignment caused a number of officers to return from sick leave, prompting the *Sunday Mercury*'s acerbic correspondent to suppose that "with a return to active service in the field, we shall have a recurrence of the direful sickness with which they were before afflicted." BOB also complained that, while the officers had been paid, none of the enlisted men had received any money, even though some had been in the regiment since the start of the year. With no prospect of wiping out existing debts, the regiment's sutler left for parts unknown, leaving the soldiers with no way to obtain items for their personal use. "When faith is thus broken with men, are deserters to be so blamed? Hardly." To help fill his shrinking regiment, Major McPherson planned a recruiting trip to New York.[1]

The Twenty-Fifth began its transformation into an actual cavalry unit on 25 July, when the First Battalion received horses, but no saddles. Undaunted, the delighted recipients rode their "steeds" bareback, resulting in a number of humorous mishaps. The fun was short-lived, as the battalion was awoken two nights later and told to turn the horses over to another regiment headed to the front. Within a few days, saddles and sabers were issued to everyone, but it was not until 14 August that the regiment finally received its permanent mounts. There would be less than a week to practice rudimentary cavalry drill before leaving Camp Stoneman.[2]

The following description of new recruits learning to ride at the cavalry depot was written by a trooper from the 15th N.Y. Cavalry, but could just as easily have applied to the Twenty-Fifth:

> [T]hey received their horses and equipment, and then commenced the fun...Scarcely one out of a hundred of the men composing the regiment had ever rode a horse to any great extent while at home, and to witness their attempts to mount and go through the evolutions was amusing to say the least. They were first put through a course of drill bareback for several days. After becoming used to that, a blanket was given them, which afforded them some relief. Next came saddles without stirrups, and the agony was increased tenfold. But we had enlisted to be soldiers, and must take the bitter with the sweet. Finally stirrups were put on and our troubles were over...
>
> A cavalryman's life is not an easy one by any means. The first thing in the morning he has

to feed his horse. The horse eats his grain out of a nose bag which is held on by a strap... While he is eating the men groom him, which usually occupies an hour. After that the men get their breakfast and then go and water their horses. Guard mounting follows, then drill; next comes dinner, to be followed by more drilling; then dress parade, feeding and watering horses again, supper, and in a little while to bed. On a march or a scout, no matter how tired you are, your horse has to be taken care of when you halt for the night, whether you have anything to eat or not; for if neglected they would soon give out and become worthless.[3]

Other than not ordering the Twenty-Fifth back to perform dismounted guard duty at City Point, there is little indication the Cavalry Corps was aware of the Twenty-Fifth's gritty performance at Fort Stevens. Instead, the month the regiment spent cooling its heels at Camp Stoneman suggests greater official concern over its leadership and lack of readiness. Fortunately, everyone benefited from the opportunity for drill, even if horses were lacking for most of this period.

Unfortunately, this inactivity also heightened tension between Major McPherson and his subordinate officers, especially those who owed their allegiance to Lt. Col. Aaron Seeley. This friction came to a head on 9 August, when a petition was circulated among the line officers protesting the assignment of 1st Lt. Thomas R. Scott to the regiment. Scott's commission had already been signed by Governor Seymour, and he had probably been handpicked by McPherson during the latter's recent recruiting trip. Ignoring the obvious wishes of their acting commander, the fifteen petitioners requested the lieutenant not be mustered into any existing company, since this would ignore "the claims of those officers who had served with the regiment since it has been in the field." The body of the petition, which appears to be in Chamberlin's handwriting, was addressed to regimental adjutant, William Brusle, and the first four signatures were those of Capts. James M. Smith (E), Chamberlin (K), Henry Louis Lazarus (G) and Richard Hudnut (F). Arch Wilson (K) was one of eleven lieutenants to sign the document.[4,5]

McPherson flew into a rage when he learned of the petition, and, on confronting the instigators, accused them of insubordination and demanded their resignations. One of the first to comply was 2nd Lt. Frederick J. Eaton (F). However, instead of writing a simple letter of resignation, Eaton included a lengthy account of why the line officers "unanimously" opposed Scott's appointment. McPherson accepted his resignation on 10 August, but felt compelled to write a long rebuttal on the back, in which he tried to justify his own actions and denigrate the charges made by Eaton. The major's conclusion was particularly revealing: "I am satisfied that this matter is brought up as a test to compel me to give up my manhood and submit to a set of officers, who, having formed a clique, think by this united action to bend me to their will, and this I have determined to resist to the last of my ability." Camp Stoneman's commander, Col. William Gamble, signed off on the letter the following day, recommending acceptance of Eaton's resignation. The colonel apparently concluded that Eaton's rebuttal was sufficient evidence of insubordination, although at this point he may not have been fully aware of the crisis brewing in McPherson's regiment.[6]

Capt. Richard Hudnut also submitted his resignation on 9 August. Since it contained only a simple request to leave the service, McPherson merely signed the back as approved, before forwarding it to Colonel Gamble. This time, however, the camp commandant refused to accept the resignation and returned it to McPherson. By now Gamble would have discovered the split in the Twenty-Fifth between those men and officers recruited in Upstate New York and those added at Hart Island after Seeley assumed nominal command. In addition to belonging to the latter faction, Chamberlin had his own motives stemming from his experiences in the 118th, where he witnessed how a "clique" of officers could influence their superiors regarding promotions and discipline of its members. This time, Chamberlin evidently resolved to be an active participant among the protesting line officers, perhaps with a long-range goal of laying the groundwork for further promotion.[7]

In the meantime, McPherson resorted to staging a series of unannounced drills and inspections to ensnare other protest leaders. On 11 August, Capt. James Smith was arrested on charges of insubordination and failure to obey orders. (The latter involved minor infractions, most of which occurred after the petition had been circulated. There can be little doubt about Smith's loyalty to Seeley, as both served together in 10th N.Y. Infantry, or "National Guard Zouaves.") A court martial was hastily convened on 18 August to try the captain. However, when two of the prosecution's witnesses failed to appear and Adjutant Brusle's testimony contradicted McPherson's allegations, the court absolved Smith on all charges. The judges also took the unusual step of censuring McPherson for having pressed charges in the first place, characterizing the major as having acted out of malicious intent rather than in the best interests of the service. (It was also noted he had to be forcibly ejected from the court when he tried to disrupt the proceedings.) Colonel Gamble added his endorsement to Smith's acquittal, but declined to second the accusations against McPherson. Instead, he attributed the affair to "a very bad state of discipline in the 25th N.Y. Cav. caused by incompetency, inefficiency and want of harmony among its officers."[8]

Although not necessary for his defense, Smith had an emotional response to McPherson's charges entered into the court record. In it, the defendant stated that the court was aware he had had nothing to do with the petition, except to sign it, and, furthermore, the officers' decision to protest was sanctioned by military law. Smith went on to depict the major as a petty tyrant, who continued to seek revenge against everyone involved by withholding approval of passes and leave requests. The captain ended his version of events by "pronouncing the whole of these charges a piece of willful malice & an underhanded device to get an officer dismissed [from] the service who has done his duties for him on the field of battle, while he, the Major Com'd'g, was shielding himself behind breastworks [at Fort Stevens] out of range of the enemy's fire."[9]

On 11 August, the same day McPherson ordered Smith's arrest, Chamberlin wrote the Adjutant General of the Cavalry Department to tender his resignation. His only explanation was that he wanted to resign "on account of having left my business unexpectedly and in an unsettled state to join the service. I have served faithfully two years as a commissioned officer and now desire to leave the service to attend to business affairs which require my personal attention." He ended with a declaration that he was not indebted to the U.S. Government and was prepared to turn over all official property. McPherson countersigned the letter as "approved and forwarded," but Gamble sent it back with the following note: "Respectfully returned. Every tender of resignation must be accompanied with a certificate of non-indebtedness to the government from the 2nd Auditor before being considered."[10]

As one of the ringleaders, if not the author of the original protest, Chamberlin also must have been offered by McPherson the choice of resignation or facing charges similar to those brought against Smith. His decision to not openly contest the major, as Smith had done, may have reflected a genuine desire to leave the regiment, but more likely, it was a calculated assessment that the major had already overplayed his hand, and therefore the resignation would not be accepted by McPherson's superiors. Having witnessed his old company commander passed over for promotion in the 118th also must have played a part in his strong reaction to bringing an outside officer into his current regiment. (He would take valuable lessons from both incidents that would later help him overcome attempts to remove him from government office.)

By this time, Gamble had decided to reject all resignations coming from the Twenty-Fifth (including Captain Easton's) to give both sides a chance to cool down. Above all, the depot's veteran commander did not want the regiment's internal squabbles to escalate to the point where the Cavalry Corps lost men and officers needed in the field. On 15 August, as McPherson's troopers prepared to head for the front, Gamble offered their acting commander some sage advice, tailored to the problems that had beset the Twenty-Fifth in recent weeks:

> Your Regt. will be mounted and prepared for active service in two or three days hence. See that your command is supplied with everything necessary.... Exact, require and enforce strict, healthy discipline among the men & officers; be sure that your orders are lawful and necessary, then enforce prompt obedience from all without exception, at all hazard; do not tolerate insubordination or mutinous symptoms...Administer discipline with a cool head and firm steady hand..., because the true interests of your Regt. and the Public

service demand and require it...This can only be accomplished by a cheerful harmonious Cooperation on the part of the officers..., each one performing his own duty faithfully, never allowing private feelings to interfere with official duty. No one can be a good and efficient officer or soldier who does not make private feelings subservient and submissive to public duty...[11]

The Cavalry Corps took other steps to promote harmony within the regiment, including plans to remove McPherson as acting commander at the first opportunity. In the interim, Smith was allowed to remain at Camp Stoneman and did not rejoin the Twenty-Fifth until McPherson's removal took effect. Although for ostensibly different reasons, Chamberlin, too, ended up being away from the regiment for an extended period. He may have already been suffering from the onset of pleurisy, a particularly serious lung disease in the days before antibiotics, when he had his confrontation with McPherson. In any case, on 19 August, a week after he submitted his resignation, the chief surgeon at Camp Stoneman ordered the captain to report to the Army Medical Director for treatment, and he was admitted to the Seminary Hospital in Georgetown the following day. After his release from the hospital on 8 September, he was placed on convalescent leave. On 19 September, Myron L. Baxter, an army doctor and boyhood friend from Strafford, recommended he be given an additional fifteen days to fully recover. In his note, Doctor Baxter stated that he was personally acquainted with the captain and could vouch that he was a "gentleman in every respect and no *dead beat*." The recommendation was accepted, and Chamberlin spent his leave in New York. Like Smith, he was in no hurry to return while McPherson remained in command, and records show other officers from the Twenty-Fifth taking extended leave after disputes with their superiors When Chamberlin finally returned to Camp Stoneman in early October, he would find much change had taken place in the Union army.[12]

* * * * *

Abraham Lincoln called August 1864 "the darkest month of the war." Beset by relentless attacks in the press and growing impatience with the war, the President feared his Democratic opponent, Gen. George McClellan, was likely to win the fall election. McClellan was running on a peace platform, and Lincoln worried, if elected, his rival would seek an accommodation with the South that would permanently divide the country. The raid on the capital, followed by the burning of Chambersburg, Pennsylvania, by Jubal Early's cavalry, and the enormous casualties in Ulysses Grant's seemingly stalled drive on Richmond, had further eroded public confidence in the President and his general-in-chief. Both realized bold steps were needed on the battlefield to reverse their sagging public support, if the Union was to be preserved. In early August, Lincoln conferred with Secretary of War Edwin Stanton over a proposal put forth by Grant to consolidate the Middle, Washington, Susquehanna and West Virginia Departments into a single Middle Division. By putting the four "fiefdoms" under one commander, Grant hoped to eliminate duplication and old rivalries, which would then enable him to use their combined resources to end Early's hold over the Shenandoah Valley, the "breadbasket of the Confederacy." His choice for heading this new division was Maj. Gen. Philip H. Sheridan, an aggressive young cavalry commander with exceptional charisma on the field. Lincoln and Stanton were reluctant to place so much power in the hands of a thirty-four-year-old, particularly one who owed his allegiance solely to Grant and was far younger than the department heads who would serve under him. Nevertheless, when better alternatives failed to emerge, Grant's proposal was provisionally approved on 7 August.[13]

Pleased he would remain responsible only to Grant, Sheridan hurried to Harpers Ferry the same day to take command of what would become the Army of the Shenandoah. Warfare in the Valley of Virginia would henceforth be conducted quite differently from earlier days when prisoners were routinely paroled and civilian losses minimized. Grant's first instructions to Sheridan read: "In pushing up the Shenandoah Valley...it is desirable that nothing should be left to invite the enemy to return. Take all provisions, forage, and stock wanted for the use of your command. Such as cannot be consumed, destroy." Sheridan fully endorsed Grant's harsh "programme" and was resolutely convinced that destruction of property was a necessary adjunct to achieving victory. "Death is popularly considered the maximum of punishment in war, but it is not; reduction to poverty brings prayers for peace more surely and more quickly."[14]

Within days of his arrival, Sheridan hastened up the Valley, hoping to catch Early unprepared. As the Federals neared Strasburg (fifty miles south of Harpers Ferry), reports of Confederate reinforcements *en route* to the Valley caused him to halt at Cedar Creek and await the arrival of his supply train. Lt. Col. John S. Mosby's scouts had been observing these developments closely and, as the Federal supply convoy neared Berryville on 13 August, the partisans struck. The guards were mostly "100-days troops," who fled before the first salvos from Mosby's horse artillery and the sight of Rebel riders bearing down on them. The Southerners took 200 prisoners, nearly one hundred loaded wagons, and 700 mules, horses and head of beef. Sheridan tried to shrug off the loss, writing Grant that "Mosby has annoyed me and captured a few wagons," but the raid persuaded him to act more cautiously. During the following week, the Yanks pulled back to where they had started on the outskirts of Harpers Ferry, as "Little Phil" and "Old Jube" engaged in a prolonged period of thrust and parry, each looking for an opportunity to deliver a telling blow.[15]

Grant, however, made no attempt to hide his anger at the reverse, and his initial instructions to Sheridan were to round up the families of Mosby's raiders as hostages, and to hang without trial any captured guerrilla. A somewhat more temperate, but still strong, message followed that focused on Mosby's sanctuaries in Loudoun County (Chamberlin's future home). Lying just east of the Blue Ridge, this area offered the partisans a convenient platform from which to harass Sheridan's troops in the Valley, leading Grant to urge: "If you can possibly spare a division of cavalry, send them through Loudoun County, to destroy and carry off the crops, animals, negroes, and all men under fifty years of age capable of bearing arms. All male citizens under fifty can fairly be held as prisoners of war..."[16]

Alarmed by Grant's harsh dicta, Asst. Secretary of War Charles Dana pointed out that Loudoun had a large Quaker population "favorable to the Union," and opined they "would be very willing to have their produce and animals impressed" by the Federals but should be exempt from Grant's blanket arrest order. The following day (21 August), Grant heeded Dana's advice by instructing Sheridan to spare Quakers and, stipulating that property belonging to loyal Loudouners be impressed, not destroyed, so owners would be eligible for reimbursement.[17]

Unwilling to divert his own cavalry into Loudoun, Sheridan passed the task to Maj. Gen. Christopher C. Augur's Department of Washington. In response, Augur sent the 8th Ill. Cavalry across the

"Mosby Destroying Sheridan's Supply Train at Berryville." August 1864 raid forced Federals to adopt more cautious tactics. (*Taylor Sketchbook*, Western Reserve Hist. Soc.)

Potomac from their camp in Maryland. After passing through the county seat of Leesburg on Saturday (20th), the Illinois riders turned south. Near Aldie they clashed with a small party of Mosby's 43rd Va. Cavalry, the only encounter with guerillas during the three-day sweep.[18]

The Yanks pushed west as far as Snickers Gap on the Blue Ridge, before turning back east to spend their second night near Purcellville. Along the way they picked up many civilians, including several Friends returning home from First Day services at Goose Creek Meetinghouse, located in a village renamed "Lincoln" after the war. Their arrests were of immediate concern to Goose Creek's minister, Samuel M. Janney, Loudoun's most influential Quaker leader. Early Monday morning, Janney arrived at the Federal camp and spoke with its commander, Maj. John M. Waite. The latter had by then received the amended orders exempting Friends from arrest and agreed to their release, but Janney was unable to persuade him to free more civilians before the soldiers broke camp.[19]

After passing through Waterford, the Federals crossed the Potomac at Point of Rocks late Monday afternoon. There, Waite fired off a telegram announcing the successful completion of his raid. Augur later informed Sheridan the Illinoisans had brought out sixty-two "rebel sympathizers," as well as all horses fit for cavalry service. His Washington commander added that, as a great deal of green corn, unthreshed wheat, and hay remained, he planned to send Waite out again to gather this forage. But given a reported shortage of wagons in Loudoun, Augur wanted guidance on whether it was still necessary to destroy crops that could not be brought over to Maryland. Sheridan responded unequivocally that all forage should be either "carried off or destroyed."[20]

Colonel Mosby was so concerned by the threat that continued Federal raids posed to the ability of his partisan rangers to obtain food and shelter that he sent two of his men to call on Samuel Janney shortly after the minister's return from Waite's camp. They informed the Quaker he had fifteen days to secure the release of a doctor taken by the Federals or be arrested and sent to Richmond's notorious Libby Prison. They also warned that "other Union men would be held responsible for the return of such of the prisoners as were secessionists." Janney replied he had already asked Waite to release the Aldie physician and planned a trip to Washington to pursue the matter further.

Armed with a passport given him by President Lincoln, Janney set off the next day for the capital, where he met with General Augur on 24 August. The department commander agreed mass arrests of civilians "would lead to unpleasant consequences," and so provided an endorsement to deliver to Assistant Secretary Dana, who received the minister "kindly." But since the orders originated with Grant, Dana was not willing to authorize any prisoner release on his own authority, and instead suggested Janney discuss the matter directly with Sheridan.

The following day, carrying letters of introduction from Augur and Dana, Janney rode the train to Harpers Ferry, then walked to Sheridan's headquarters at Halltown, where he was received in the general's tent. The latter's initial response gave the minister little cause for optimism: "We must all bear the burdens imposed by this war. I and my soldiers have to bear our burdens...; and you people of Loudoun must not complain if you have to bear your share." Yet, when the Quaker persisted, reiterating the likely consequences for the Unionists, Sheridan softened and agreed to the release of physicians and prisoners over fifty.[21]

Acutely aware that Mosby's threat to seize other Unionists remained likely to be carried out as long as Waite's other prisoners stayed locked up, Janney returned to Washington on the 27th, accompanied by two other Friends, including William Williams, a Waterford Quaker who the year before had been held captive three months in Libby Prison for the return of secessionist prisoners. Both General Augur and Secretary Dana agreed that continuance of Grant's arrest orders would result in Unionists being carried off to Richmond, a fate Williams was able to describe in great detail. Janney also opposed any extension to Loudoun of the crop burning then being carried out by Sheridan in the Valley, a practice he believed would "inflict great suffering without any equivalent advantage." Dana suggested he include these points in a letter to Grant. The following day, a Sunday, Janney spoke at a widely attended service in Alexandria that helped broaden support for a milder policy regarding Loudoun Unionists. More concrete progress was made the following week, when Augur consented to parole prisoners on a list submitted by Janney, after each took a loyalty oath to the Union. By early September, only a few of the original sixty-two captives remained in confinement.²²

Yet Grant's orders still remained in effect, and even as Janney and his companions worked to secure release of prisoners from the first sweep, a second batch of thirty-two "Mosbyites in farmer's garb" was delivered to Washington, the result of a joint raid into Loudoun by the 8th Ill. and 16th N.Y. Cavalry on 30 August. Augur had ordered this second foray after learning from the earlier prisoners that Mosby's command was far larger than previously estimated. Those in the second group of prisoners who failed to win parole were held hostage for twenty-six Pennsylvania civilians seized by Confederates during the Gettysburg campaign.²³

Janney's *Memoirs* do not reveal the content of his letter to Grant, but its call for restraint apparently influenced the following message the lieutenant general sent Sheridan on 4 September: "In clearing out the arms-bearing community of Loudoun County, and the subsistence for armies, exercise your own judgment as to who should be exempt from arrest, and as to who should receive pay for their stock, grain, &c. It is our interest that the county should not be capable of subsisting a hostile army, and at the same time we want to inflict as little hardship upon Union men as possible." The following day, Sheridan forwarded Grant's latest dispatch to Augur, confirming that the Washington commander could henceforth use his own discretion in carrying out the original order. Sheridan made it clear, however, that he still thought "it best to clean out that section of country, leaving [only] a bare subsistence to those who are undoubtedly Union, and paying for what may be destroyed belonging to such Union people."²⁴

The arrest of nearly one hundred citizens during the two August raids would be the largest such action in Loudoun by either side during the war, evidence that the swift intervention of Janney and his fellow Quakers had forestalled further escalation of the targeting of civilians. Loudouners breathed a collective sigh of relief as these arrests all but ceased in the following months. As they turned later that fall to gather in the harvest, most were unaware that neither Grant nor Sheridan had foresworn their original determination to keep Loudoun's produce out of Rebel hands.

* * * * *

After his convalescent leave ended in early October, Chamberlin returned to Camp Stoneman to await departure of the next cavalry detachment for the Shenandoah Valley so that he could rejoin his regiment. Instead, he found himself destined for the heart of "Mosby's Confederacy" to participate in an ultimately unsuccessful effort to reopen the Manassas Gap Railroad, which, before being destroyed early in the war, had linked Alexandria with the Shenandoah Valley. After entering Fauquier County through Thoroughfare Gap in the Bull Run Mountain, the rail line continued westward through The Plains, Salem (now Marshall) and Rectortown, before crossing the Blue Ridge at Manassas Gap and descending into Front Royal on the Shenandoah River. Union military engineers surveyed the roadbed in late September, concluding it could be reopened with little difficulty to provide a supply line for Sheridan's army that winter.

Keenly aware that the railroad ran through an area controlled by Mosby's partisans, General Sheridan opposed the project, which he feared would require a large permanent force to guard the tracks against sabotage. Grant and the War Department thought otherwise and were determined to create a direct rail link into the mid-Shenandoah Valley, which could supply Sheridan's army and thereby override the latter's objections to establishing his winter quarters nearer to Richmond. The task of reopening the railroad was assigned to Augur's Department of Washington, but its commander, too, was dubious about his new assignment after having tried unsuccessfully to contain the partisans in that region for over a year.²⁵

Railroad repair crews, guarded by a brigade of Federal troops under Col. George Gallupe, started to clear the tracks in late September, and their work proceeded smoothly until they neared Salem on 4 October. Although Mosby's 43rd Battalion Va. Cavalry, as his partisan rangers were formally known, was drawn from a broad area, including Loudoun and Fauquier Counties, Salem was its primary assembly point. In this instance, wishful thinking must have persuaded the War Department that the "Grey Ghost" would stand idly by and allow Yankees to operate a railroad that literally ran through his "backyard." Having just returned to his command after recuperating from a bullet wound, Mosby summoned 250 of his Rangers to stop the work crews as they neared Salem. The Federals scattered at the first attack and the next day, Gallupe moved his headquarters several miles west to a more secure location near Rectortown.

Directed by the War Department to personally take charge of the operation, Augur arrived at Rectortown on 8 October with authority to remove Rebel sympathizers living near the tracks but found most had already left the area. Then, after several trains were derailed by saboteurs, orders were given for prominent local Secessionists to be placed onboard the trains to deter further attacks. This strategy failed after Mosby, who always had good intelligence about Federal intentions, warned everyone in the vicinity to flee. On 12 October, Secretary of War Stanton proposed leveling every house within five miles of the tracks but rescinded the order several hours later. The reason for this reversal is not known, although Stanton may have decided to await a pending meeting with Sheridan before carrying out such draconian measures, and Augur, usually a moderating force with regard to the treatment of civilians, may also have voiced objections.[26]

Augur's solution instead was to order all available cavalrymen at Camp Stoneman to Fauquier County to protect the work crews. Caught up in this latest development, Captain Chamberlin was placed in command of the "Dismounted Cavalry Camp near Rectortown." A muster roll he kept shows the detachment consisted of 119 men from Custer's Michigan Brigade, including seven from the 25th N.Y. Cavalry (then with Custer's Brigade). Details are lacking about this assignment, although an order issued by Gallupe on 14 October for Chamberlin to send a detail of thirty enlisted men and non-commissioned officers to Brigade Headquarters suggests his duties were largely confined to making sure the men under his command were available for guard and escort duty.[27]

Dazzled by the Army of the Shenandoah's recent string of successes (described in the next chapter), the War Department and Grant assumed the Valley was already secured and began to pressure Sheridan to detach troops to help reopen the Manassas Gap line. Sheridan did not agree but must have gained a certain wry satisfaction from the difficulties that Augur was having in Fauquier County, since it confirmed his conviction that the rail line could not be easily defended, even if it were reopened. When Grant suggested that the VI Corps be returned to Richmond via that line, Sheridan replied he preferred to send General Wright's infantrymen on foot as far as Alexandria, explaining the soldiers could march there more quickly through Ashby's Gap and Loudoun County. By this stratagem, Sheridan precluded any possibility that the VI Corps might be diverted to guard the railroad as it passed Augur's headquarters in Fauquier. The day after the VI Corps departed, members of Custer's division spotted a sizable Confederate cavalry force south of Front Royal. This bit of luck caused Sheridan to reflect on the wisdom of letting the infantry leave on the eve of his departure for a meeting in Washington. A courier overtook the VI Corps near Ashby's Gap with orders to return immediately to Sheridan's headquarters at Cedar Creek. Without the presence of Wright's stalwart foot soldiers on the Union side, Jubal Early would have easily won the Battle of Cedar Creek five days later.[28]

In addition to pressuring Sheridan to expend his limited resources guarding railroads, Grant and the War Department wanted him to establish his winter headquarters far enough south in the Valley to serve as a base of operations to disrupt Richmond's supply lines around Charlottesville and Gordonsville. Sheridan, however, knew he could not meet these objectives without jeopardizing the security of his forces in the Valley. On 13 October, Secretary of War Stanton "invited" the general to the capital to discuss their differences. Despite at least two intercepted messages of a possible Confederate offensive, Sheridan decided to risk a quick trip to the War Department to defend his point of view, though only after first assembling his forces into a defensive position at Cedar Creek. Late on 16 October, he and a cavalry escort appeared without warning at Augur's camp in Rectortown, where he could observe first-hand the problems Mosby was causing the work crews. At dawn the next morning, he continued to ride east before boarding a train on the far side of Thoroughfare Gap (where he was less likely to be ambushed). Arriving in Washington at 8 AM the same day, Sheridan first asked for a special B&O train to take him back to the front at noon. He did not record what he said to Stanton, but subsequent events more than proved his contention that Early remained a dangerous adversary.

Sheridan's return train arrived at Martinsburg on the night of the 17th, and the next morning his party set out for Winchester on a journey slowed by two colonels sent to receive the vote of New York troops for the upcoming presidential election. One was "of enormous weight" and neither could ride well, so the group did not reach Winchester until late afternoon and, after ascertaining all was seemingly in order at Cedar Creek, Sheridan opted to remain there overnight. Meanwhile, General Early had force-marched his troops, augmented by reinforcements from further south so that they were in position to attack the Union forces at Cedar Creek before daybreak on 19 October. Aided by a heavy fog, surprise was complete, and the demoralized Yankees began to fall back in the midst of fierce combat.

The sound of artillery to the south awoke Sheridan, but he remained unconvinced a serious battle was underway and enjoyed a leisurely breakfast before setting off. Only when he heard the jeers of local women along his route and began to encounter fleeing Union troops did he realize the gravity of the situation. Setting spurs to his horse, the general left the jammed roads and began the cross-county race to rejoin his men that is memorialized in Thomas B. Read's poem, "Sheridan's Ride." Meanwhile, the Southerners' initial momentum began to flag as many of Early's hungry soldiers paused to loot the Federal camps, thereby giving General Wright and his stalwart VI Corps time to organize a defensive position near their Middletown camp and help stem the tide of retreating Union soldiers.

The arrival of "Little Phil" further revived the morale of his troops, who were regrouped into a battle line south of Middletown. At this point, one of his staff officers suggested he ride along this line so that all could see for themselves that their commander had returned. "Not even Sheridan expected what occurred as his large horse carried the diminutive general along the edge of the woods. As his soldiers saw him, they erupted in thunderous cheers that cascaded along the entire line." What followed is well known: the Federals pushed back the surprised Confederates, and regained their old campsites at Cedar Creek by day's end. Even though Union casualties were almost twice those of Early's, the latter could ill afford to lose any men, and certainly not the artillery pieces he was forced to abandon.[29]

Nevertheless, the Union army's near disaster at Cedar Creek resulted in abandonment of all plans to reopen the Manassas Gap Railroad. Before departing Fauquier County, Augur's men tore up the rails from the line and shipped them by train for use in constructing a spur linking Harpers Ferry with Winchester that could more securely supply Sheridan's forces that winter. Mosby's success in denying the Manassas Gap line to the Federals may have been his most significant accomplishment that fall, as it forced Sheridan to establish winter quarters near Winchester rather than at Cedar Creek as Grant had wanted. (Whether this consequence prolonged the war to any extent is more difficult to judge.) Their work finished in Fauquier, Augur's forces returned to Washington, accompanied by Chamberlin, who caught a B&O train to Harpers Ferry in time to rejoin his regiment at Camp Remount on 28 October, the first entry in his diary since mid-August.[30]

Chapter 8

RIDING WITH SHERIDAN AND CUSTER:
August-October 1864

During Capt. S. E. Chamberlin's absence on sick leave and detached duty, his regiment was involved in some of the pivotal engagements of the Valley Campaign. Expectation filled the air on the morning of 21 August, as the Twenty-Fifth rode out of Camp Stoneman on its way to the front. After a month of inactivity and internal strife, the regiment was being sent to join Philip Sheridan's Army of the Shenandoah. The mood among the enlisted men was unusually upbeat, in part because they had been paid for the first time, but also because, a week earlier, they had finally been issued their own mounts. As the troopers left Washington astride their new steeds, the sun glinting off their carbines and sabers, it was easy to overlook how little time they had had to master basic cavalry skills on horseback.

The mood among the officers may not have been as positive, particularly that of the regiment's acting commander, Maj. Samuel McPherson. While riding through the Maryland countryside at the head of his men, McPherson had time to reflect on his recent clash with the officers of the line. His superiors' decision not to accept the ringleaders' resignations, along with the acquittal of Capt. James Smith, had weakened his authority at a critical juncture. He now wondered whether he could effectively control his regiment in the field, or how much longer he would be left in command.

The New Yorkers arrived at Harpers Ferry (now part of the year-old state of West Virginia) at noon on 23 August, the third day of a journey that left many saddle-sore. Pausing only long enough to draw three days' rations, they proceeded to Sheridan's headquarters at Halltown, three miles further west. There, the men heard skirmishing nearby and observed fellow cavalrymen bivouacked with reins tied around their wrists, enabling them to mount at a moment's notice. Members of the regiment who had served in the Army of the Potomac under McClellan marveled at the changes that had taken place. Even though "Little Phil" had only been in the Shenandoah Valley for two weeks, Grant's former cavalry commander had already instilled aggressive tactics and a new fighting spirit in the Union troops under him.

Upon arrival at Halltown, the Twenty-Fifth was assigned to Brig. Gen. Wesley Merritt's First Cavalry Division, where it was placed in the Third Brigade under the command of Col. Charles Lowell of the 2nd Mass. Cavalry. (The nephew of poet Robert Lowell had recently been promoted to brigade commander and would win a reputation as a "superb combat officer" before his death at Cedar Creek in October.) The following day, elements of the Twenty-Fifth and the 2nd Massachusetts made a joint reconnaissance (or "scout") that netted five prisoners. On 26 August, both regiments, assisted by an infantry battalion, attacked and overran a Rebel position near Halltown, capturing over one hundred

The Men Who Secured the Valley (l. to r.): Maj. Gen Philip Sheridan; Chief of Staff George Forsyth; and generals Wesley Merritt, Thomas Devin and George Custer. (LC)

Confederates, including a lieutenant colonel and nine line officers. Under Lowell's able leadership, the Twenty-Fifth showed its potential to become an effective cavalry force. Even BOB, the heretofore critical *Sunday Mercury* correspondent, proclaimed that his regiment "behaved on this exciting occasion with the coolness of veterans; and…the Empire State will count her Twenty-fifth Cavalry a brilliant addition."[1]

The following day, the New Yorkers encountered the enemy drawn up in front of Charles Town, and the Rebels "soon let [their attackers] know that they meant to stay there." After Lowell's Brigade pushed the enemy back, a squadron was detached from the Twenty-Fifth under the command of Capt. Henry Lazarus (G) to scout in the direction of Duffield Station. "They proceeded in that direction under the guidance of a 'good Union man,' who led them directly into the jaws of [Maj. Harry] Gilmore's Rebel cavalry, and Captain Lazarus, and three sergeants and two corporals were taken prisoners."[2]

Continuing with BOB's account:

> This, the fourth night since the saddles had been off our horses' backs, was rather a gloomy one, as our forage was out, and…our own rations were also exhausted…We overtook [Gilmore] about four miles the other side of Charles Town, and made him get up and get along the Winchester Turnpike at a high old rate; when we again advanced and took up the position [Summit Point, West Virginia] which we now occupy, mid-way between Berryville [Virginia] and Smithfield [now Middleway, West Virginia]. Our first night here was an exceedingly critical one, as there was no support within five miles of us, and we were surrounded by Rebel cavalry, who would have gobbled us up but for the Yankee shrewdness of our commander, Colonel Lowell. He has with him the band of the brigade, and he sent the fifer and drummer into the woods to play infantry-calls at different points, thus leading the Johnnies to believe that our force was much larger than it really was. But, I suppose that during the night some 'good Union man,' who had lived in our neighborhood, informed them of our force; and yesterday morning [the 29th] they made a bold attack upon us, which was promptly met and audaciously repulsed with a total loss on our side of four killed and eleven wounded, while the Rebels left fifteen dead upon the field and five prisoners in our hands…During the day large supports of both cavalry and artillery came up to our advanced position, and to-day we have our saddles off for the first time since we left Harpers Ferry, and are enjoying quite a rest.[3]

During the first half of September, the Twenty-Fifth's routine varied little from that described above, as the men continued to skirmish almost daily with their Confederate foes in the area between Charles Town and Berryville. A brief lull occurred in the middle of the month, when the regiment was assigned to picket duty on the eastern bank of Opequon Creek, which divided the Union forces from the main Southern force around Winchester. The New Yorkers got "on extremely good terms" with the Rebel pickets on the other side, "exchanging newspapers, trading spurs, tobacco, etc."[4]

The Twenty-Fifth was affected by two changes in command during this period. The first was Maj. Charles J. Seymour's arrival on 31 August to replace McPherson as acting commander. (McPherson immediately departed on extended sick leave, and later served in a detached support unit before finally rejoining the Twenty-Fifth the following spring. He would claim his prolonged absence was engineered by the same officers who had conspired against him at Camp Stoneman.) The record is not clear on Seymour's whereabouts prior to arriving in the Valley, but by serving on detached duty all summer, he had escaped involvement in the regiment's recent factional disputes. On the other hand, the Twenty-Fifth's new commander had the disadvantage of being thrust into the middle of the Valley Campaign with no prior experience in leading the men under him, nor did his earlier checkered military service augur well for his new responsibilities.

On 8 September, scarcely a week after Seymour assumed command, the New Yorkers learned that Lowell's 3rd Brigade was dissolved, and they had been transferred to the 1st Brigade under the command of Brig. Gen. George A. Custer, the twenty-four-year-old "Boy General." Custer's Brigade, also known as the Michigan Brigade (or Wolverines), was one of the most effective Union cavalry units in the war, and Seymour's regiment now donned its distinctive emblem—red neckties. The Twenty-Fifth's assignment to this famed brigade reinforces the impression that it had performed well under Lowell. Custer would also have heard of the regiment's performance at Fort Stevens, as it was a detachment composed mostly of his men that had relieved the New Yorkers on that battle's first day.[5]

Although a month had by then passed since his arrival, Sheridan remained mired in a stalemate with Early, and Secretary Stanton, who had opposed his selection from the start, began to needle "Little Phil" about the meager results of his Valley Campaign. Even the Rebels had taken to calling his army the "Harpers Weekly" because of its frequent withdrawals back to Harpers Ferry. But well aware of the ignominious fate of earlier Union generals in the Valley, Sheridan had no intention of risking a direct confrontation without having a clear numerical superiority over his opponent.

An answer to this dilemma came from an unlikely source—Rebecca Wright, a Quaker schoolteacher in Winchester. On the night of 16 September, Miss Wright received a message from Sheridan asking her for any news about Confederate troop strength in her town. The query was delivered through the Southern lines to her home by a slave, who concealed it in a ball of metal foil carried in his mouth. Her reply, sent back in the same manner, contained the welcome news that a Confederate division and artillery battery had just left Winchester for Richmond. Armed with this information, Sheridan believed he could take the offensive and promptly drew up plans to attack Early's forces in Winchester, which he took to a meeting with Grant in Charles Town the next day. Grant had called the conference to present his own proposal for confronting Early but kept it in his pocket after hearing what Sheridan had in mind.[6]

The resulting clash, known as the Third Battle of Winchester, took place on 19 September. The 25th N.Y. Cavalry, along with the rest of Custer's Brigade, was awakened from their camp near Berryville at 1 AM and under way an hour later. After a circuitous route, the brigade arrived, just as dawn was breaking, at the east approach to Locke's Ford on Opequon Creek, several miles northeast of Winchester. Despite the early hour, the Yanks found the crossing well defended, and Custer's Brigade was charged with forcing a passage to the other side. As BOB described in his sanitized account of the opening events to that momentous day, the Twenty-Fifth unexpectedly found itself at the head of this attack.

> The Rebels fiercely contested the passage by a strong line of sharpshooters, and our first advance of dismounted men [from the 6th Mich.] was checked. The Twenty-fifth was then ordered to charge the position of the sharpshooters, in order to dislodge them from behind the impromptu breastworks of rails and logs, which gave them cover from our

attacking footmen, and the charge was made at a gallop through a rocky ravine which would scare many a horseman to even walk his horse over. The charge was met by a perfect hailstorm of bullets, but with a ringing cheer, which set the blood boiling and bounding through the throbbing veins, the position was ours and the brigade crossed over with but few casualties. The enemy attempted to take up another position, but we pressed him so closely that he was compelled to fall back to Bruceville [Brucetown] where he was heavily reinforced, and made a gallant rally, hurling us back in confusion in two successive charges, which the whole brigade made on his position. Here he brought some heavy fieldpieces into play, and dosed us with shell, grape and canister, while we had nothing to reply with but two small pieces of our horse-battery (six-pounders).[7]

Other accounts depict the Twenty-Fifth's performance at the start of the battle quite differently. In his after-action report, General Custer wrote that he selected the 25th N.Y. and 7th Mich. Cavalry to attempt the crossing at Locke's Ford. At the request of their senior officer, the New Yorkers were allowed to lead the initial charge on horseback. (Why the inexperienced Seymour asked for the honor of leading the charge remains a mystery, unless he saw it as the best way to ensure his own personal safety.) Everything appeared promising, but when the cavalrymen under Seymour's command entered the water, "the enemy, from a well-covered rifle pit opposite the crossing, opened a heavy fire upon our advance and succeeded in repulsing the head of the column, whose conduct induced the entire portion of the command to give way in considerable confusion." At this point, Custer turned to his favorite shock troops—the 1st Mich. Cavalry under the command of Col. Peter Stagg—to re-attempt the crossing. Stagg's regiment, using more cautious tactics, succeeded in fording the creek and overran the hidden rifle pits that had repelled the first charge, thus enabling the rest of the brigade to follow.[8]

Col. James Kidd, another Wolverine commander, was blunter in describing the Twenty-Fifth's ineffectual charge: "Custer then directed the 25th New York (attached temporarily to the Michigan Brigade) followed by the 7th Michigan, to take the ford mounted. The attempt was a failure, however, for the head of the New York regiment..., when it reached the crossing, instead of taking it, kept on and, circling to the right, came back to the point from which it started; thus, in effect, reversing the role of the French army which charged up a hill and then charged down again."[9]

3rd Battle of Winchester, Sept. 1864. Custer's final charge on exhausted Rebel artillerymen turned tide in Sheridan's favor. (Prange & Co. lithograph, LC)

Later, when Custer's forces stalled west of the creek at Brucetown, heavy artillery was called in to silence the Rebel guns, and the defenders soon withdrew. At this point, the brigade was joined by the rest of Sheridan's cavalry, presenting an unforgettable sight as the riders poured into the valley from all directions, their equipment reflecting the sun. Meanwhile, the Union infantry, which crossed the Opequon further south on the Berryville-Winchester road, found itself bogged down in a ravine on the other side. Sheridan's cavalry sought to relieve pressure on the foot soldiers through a series of skirmishes, charges and counter-charges, as the Southerners reluctantly gave ground. At one point the 25th N.Y. Cavalry, along with the 1st and 7th Michigan, "succeeded in piercing the enemy's line of infantry and reaching to within a few feet of their artillery," but they were beaten back with heavy losses on both sides. By late afternoon, Custer's command was so reduced in numbers he had to combine all four Michigan regiments with a "portion of the 25th" to make up a 500-man force, which he personally led in a final saber charge against a larger body of Confederates. The sight of the "Boy General" bearing down on them once more proved too much for the exhausted defenders, who turned and fled through the streets of Winchester.[10]

Capt. James M. Smith, 25th N.Y. Cav. Sketched after Winchester battle by James Taylor, who once served with Smith in 10th N.Y. Inf. (*Taylor Sketchbook*, Western Reserve Hist. Soc.)

Seymour's name is missing from almost every account (including BOB's) of the Twenty-Fifth's participation at Winchester, apparently for the simple reason that Custer, furious over his botched performance in the opening charge, had the major summarily placed under arrest. In an early 1865 letter to the Army's Adjutant General about whether Seymour should be retained in the service, Lt. Col. Aaron Seeley reported the following: "On the 19 September 1864, previous to the fight at Winchester, [Seymour] was ordered in arrest by General Custer and at once relieved from command of his Regiment; he remained at Winchester till our troops had advanced beyond Harrisonburg, [when] he was released from arrest by General Merritt [on] Oct. 1st and reported to...the 25th."[11]

Continuing his account of the battle, BOB proudly proclaimed: "Our brigade captured five stands of colors, three guns and six hundred prisoners—the biggest day's work ever performed by a brigade of cavalry. The Twenty-Fifth behaved in such a manner as to elicit the warmest approbation of Gen. Custer. Our losses in horses were heavy, although light in men." (The regiment lost at least seven killed or wounded, including Sgt. James Coutant (D), shot through the lungs during a charge and buried on the field.)[12] As to the horrific loss of horses, Cpl. Edward Devine (B) was searching a nearby barn to replace his mount, when he was startled to hear a small boy cry: "You can't take that horse. He's mine." (Devine commandeered another one in the barn.) Aside from its shaky performance at the beginning of the day, the Twenty-Fifth acquitted itself well in the largest battle it would ever face. Even if the New Yorkers did not equal the exploits of the battle-hardened Wolverines, they contributed to Custer's remarkable performance that day. Long after the war, veterans of the 25th N.Y. Cavalry chose to commemorate their participation in these events by having a medal[13] struck to proudly proclaim their inclusion in the Custer Brigade.[14]

Sheridan's first act on triumphantly entering Winchester was to seek out his "Quaker spy" and offer gratitude for her role in his success. Two years after the war, Sheridan sent Rebecca Wright an engraved gold watch, chain and breast pin to further express his appreciation of the service she had rendered her country. After word of the gift leaked to the press, she was forced to flee Winchester and resettle with her family in Philadelphia. President Grant later secured a position for her in the Treasury Department.[15]

The morning after his great victory, Sheridan set out with his infantry in pursuit of Early's army, which had retreated to Fisher's Hill, a previously fortified position south of Strasburg dubbed the "Gibraltar of the Valley." Although most of Custer's Brigade remained behind to recuperate from their heroics of the day before, the 25th N.Y. Cavalry and other regiments from Gen. Wesley Merritt's 1st Cavalry Division accompanied Sheridan towards Strasburg. At the same time, Gen. Alfred Torbert, Sheridan's overall chief of cavalry, led the main body of Union horsemen on the road to Front Royal with orders to punch through the narrow Luray Valley and cut off Early's retreat at the southern terminus of Massanutten Mountain. On 22 September, Federal forces under Sheridan's direction made a daring assault on Fisher's Hill that succeeded in routing its defenders. A second Union victory in four days provided a significant boost to Lincoln's re-election and seemingly foreshadowed the end of Early's hold over the Valley.

Even though the Twenty-Fifth was officially credited with participating in the Battle of Fisher's Hill, most, if not all, of the regiment was detached *en route* to Strasburg on the afternoon of 20 September and diverted to "find" Gen. James H. Wilson's 3rd Cavalry Division. After locating Wilson's cavalrymen in the vicinity of Front Royal and informing him "of the whereabouts of the First Division," the New Yorkers became informally attached to Wilson's forces. On 22 September, while Sheridan was successfully storming Fisher's Hill some ten miles to the west, Wilson's cavalry met unexpectedly strong resistance on its way south through the Luray Valley and decided to return to Front Royal for the night. The Twenty-Fifth had several casualties that day, including 1st Lt. Arch Wilson (K), who, while leading a charge as battalion commander, had his horse shot from under him and seriously injured his leg. (After spending six months convalescing in the Boston area, Lieutenant Wilson's valor would be recognized by a promotion to captain.)[16]

By reentering Front Royal, the Twenty-Fifth was present for one of the more notorious events of the Valley Campaign—the summary execution of six of Mosby's Rangers on 23 September. Earlier that day, a Union cavalry officer had been shot by Mosby's partisans after he tried to surrender. Still alive when found by his companions, the lieutenant was able to relate what had happened, and his death a short time later fanned a desire for revenge that swept through the Federal ranks, and which quickly focused on six partisans captured in the same engagement. Colonel Mosby would blame Custer for what happened next, but the Union general was miles away at the time. What might have led the guerrilla leader to this conclusion was the presence of the 25th N.Y. Cavalry, still wearing the distinctive insignia of the Custer Brigade. According to BOB's highly exaggerated account, about an hour before the Twenty-Fifth returned to Front Royal with the 3rd Division, Mosby's men "had made a dash on our pickets, and having captured fifteen [*sic*] of them, shot them in cold blood. Parties were immediately dispatched in all directions in pursuit, and we captured nineteen [*sic*] of them, seventeen of whom were immediately shot, and two hung. One of the latter was the notorious Jack Carter, one of Mosby's lieutenants [*sic*, no officer was executed], who boasted that he had recently fastened a Yankee scout to a tree and roasted him alive."[17]

Years later, a veteran of the Twenty-Fifth's Company H, William H. Gardner, provided a somewhat more accurate account:

> I saw the execution of seven [*sic,* six] of Mosby's guerrillas at Front Royal. I think that it was by orders of Gen. Torbert. Three men were hanged; one being a Mosby Lieutenant, a young man who, with the rope around his neck, said: "Tell Mosby how I died." An older man had a big scar clear across his cheek, but I do not clearly recall the appearance of the third. After the hanging two more of the captives were brought out and shot. After them, two more. These latter were brothers, not over 18 and 20 years old, respectively. They were terribly frightened. Three or four women were there, one a sister of the boys. The

women pleaded for mercy for the condemned, and said that they had been but two weeks with the guerrilla commander. One of them said to them: "Boys, I told you how it would be!" They were permitted to run the gauntlet, and were shot to death.

Apparently unaware of the killing of the Union officer earlier in the day, Gardner speculated the executions were in response to the "butchery" of nine Pennsylvania cavalrymen who had been "cut to fragments" near Berryville without being allowed to surrender, an act he attributed to Thomas Rosser's cavalrymen, whom he considered no better than Mosby's bushwhackers. Although the alleged atrocity against the Pennsylvanians has not been positively identified, Gardner was quite accurate in his recollection of the pervasive apprehension that the partisans generated among Union troops: "Our soldiers in that territory at that time had become desperate. To be caught by Mosby's men then was almost certain death. We found bodies of our men hanging in trees with all their clothes, except shirt and drawers gone; throats cut; pierced by bullets, bayonets, sabers, and knives; often with papers pinned bearing abusive messages." (Here Gardner was recalling the execution of six of Custer's men in retaliation for the Front Royal killings, an event described in the next chapter.)[18]

After learning of Sheridan's victory at Fisher's Hill, Wilson's 3rd Division made another stab at traversing the Luray Valley. This time, the Yankees met no resistance until they reached the town of Luray, near the southern end of the valley, where they easily routed the Rebel cavalry and captured over one hundred prisoners. "Their cavalry had no chance against ours, and this they candidly admit themselves." On 26 September, Wilson's forces again caught up with the Southern troopers outside Port Republic and drove their opponents back during the initial action. However, Early's infantry had had by then regrouped after its retreat from Fisher's Hill and kept the Northern riders from venturing farther south.

As the Union cavalrymen consolidated their positions north of Port Republic, they learned of significant changes in their leadership. Disappointed by the failure of the 2nd and 3rd Divisions to cut off Early's retreat from Fisher's Hill, Sheridan replaced both commanders. Custer took over Wilson's 3rd Division, allowing Col. James Kidd of the 1st Mich. Cavalry to replace Custer as commander of the Michigan Brigade, which remained in Merritt's 1st Division. Despite its participation with the 3rd Division in the Luray Valley, the 25th N.Y. Cavalry was returned to Kidd's Brigade in the 1st Division.

After establishing headquarters near Cross Keys, a small settlement between Port Republic and Harrisonburg, Colonel Kidd sent the Twenty-Fifth about ten miles northeast to a crossing on the South Branch of the Shenandoah River known variously as Conrad's Ferry, Store, or Crossing. The New Yorkers set off on 27 September and "had to fight [their] way through the woods with guerrillas—ten of whom we captured in the neighborhood of [McGaheysville]." From there, they pushed on to their destination along the river, where they would spend the following week. There, the regiment was joined by its long-absent lieutenant colonel, Aaron Seeley, who arrived from New York City to replace the still incarcerated Major Seymour. The Twenty-Fifth's primary mission at Conrad's Ferry was to keep watch over Swift Run Gap and ensure that Confederate reinforcement did not pass unnoticed over the Blue Ridge into the Shenandoah Valley. Scouting parties were sent out each day and returned "with lots of prisoners and horses." The men took considerable pride in defending this isolated outpost, which three other regiments "had previously tried [to hold]...and been driven back by the bushwhackers, who swarm in this locality."[19]

Despite receiving orders on 4 October to evacuate their camp due to the reported presence of a brigade of Rebel infantry and cavalry nearby, the Twenty-Fifth remained at Conrad's Ferry until the next morning. "[The enemy's proximity] was not sufficient to cause...Seeley to hurry off the regiment in unseemly haste, and he made up his mind that if the Johnnys did come there in the morning they would find nothing left that could be of any service." Before their departure, the New Yorkers burned a large cloth mill and destroyed a bridge. They also took time to round up and take with them between ten and thirty captured horses, the disposition of which would become an issue in Seeley's court martial the following year. According to testimony in that trial, when the regiment rejoined the rest of Kidd's Brigade at Cross Keys, the colonel was told to brand the captured animals with the "U.S." mark, and turn them over to the quartermaster corps. Before this could be done, however, the call to "Boots and Saddles" sounded, and Seeley "neglected" to pursue the matter later, with the result that the horses remained with the regiment.[20]

About noon on 5 October, Kidd's Brigade began its "retrograde march, General Sheridan having come to the conclusion to follow the enemy no further...and it was not advisable for our Army to move any further from...[our] base of supplies at Harper's Ferry or Martinsburg, the roads between these points and our position being infested by strong and active parties of guerrillas." As the Union cavalrymen withdrew (northward) down the Shenandoah Valley, they were instructed to burn all crops and barns, and seize any livestock. Seeley's regiment were carrying out this "hazardous and disagreeable duty" on the left side of the Valley Pike, when they "stumbled upon" a factory with new machinery and some 2,000 freshly completed gun stocks. After destroying the building and its contents, the regiment hurried to their rendezvous point in Edinburg, where they "found the division in line of battle, and some skirmishing had been going on previous to our arrival, the enemy having mistaken our movement for a retreat." Once the Rebels were driven back, the division encamped for the night before setting off towards Woodstock early on 8 October. Acting as the rearguard, Kidd's Brigade found the wind spreading the flames of barns set afire by the soldiers ahead of them, with the result that fire now threatened to engulf the town of Woodstock. Halting his brigade, Kidd ordered the 7th Mich. Cavalry to extinguish the flames. "This work occupied some hours, and by this time the advance-guard of the Rebels had come up, and actually fired on the men who had been working to save the town. This was not to be endured, so the rest of the brigade...pitched in, but the main body of the Rebels, under General Rosser, having by this time come up, we were overmatched, and had to fall back to where the rest of the division was halted. The skirmishing had lasted all day, so we camped for the night [near Toms Brook], expecting a big set-to in the morning."[21]

The Shenandoah Valley was Virginia's breadbasket, and the Confederates had no intention of letting its bounty be destroyed without a fight. The cavalrymen who pursued Kidd's Brigade out of Woodstock were members of Thomas Rosser's elite Laurel Brigade (formerly Turner Ashby's Cavalry), recently sent from Petersburg to aid Early. Attached to Rosser's command was Col. Elijah V. White's 35th Va. Cavalry (the "Comanches"), which had initially been raised in Loudoun County. White's second-in-command, Capt. Frank M. Myers of Waterford, left the following description of what confronted the Comanches when they entered the Valley in early October:

> The scene was horrifying, for with the infernal instincts of his worse than savage nature, the merciless fiend, Sheridan, was disgracing the humanity of any age and visiting the Valley with a baptism of fire, in which was swept away the bread of the old men and women and children of that weeping land. On every side, from mountain to mountain, the flames from all the barns, mills, grain and hay stacks, and in very many instances from dwellings, too, were blazing skyward, leaving a smoky trail of desolation to mark the footsteps of the devil's inspector-general, and show in a fiery record, that will last as long as the war is remembered, that the United States, under the government of Satan and Lincoln, sent Phil Sheridan to campaign in the Valley of Virginia. Rosser's men tried hard to overtake them, and did capture a few, who lingered to make sure work of a mill near New Market, but they were instantly shot.[22]

Despite what Myers described as the superior numbers and weapons (Spencer and Henry carbines) of the Yankee cavalry, the Confederates shadowing them failed to question why they were having so little difficulty in "driving" the Northerners back down the Valley, apparently not realizing Sheridan's cavalry was making an orderly withdrawal as it laid waste the surrounding countryside. Many in the Laurel Brigade came from nearby and, enraged by the pillaging, threw caution to the wind in their pursuit of the hated Yankees. Excess hubris, bred by too many victories against cavalrymen who did not measure up to those now with Sheridan, also played a part. (When Rosser entered the Valley, he was so sure of victory, he had his men place laurel branches on their heads and proclaimed himself "the savior of the Valley.")[23]

What appeared to be a hasty retreat soon drew Rosser's men into an exposed position, and on 9 October the 1st and 3rd Cavalry Divisions received orders at Tom's Brook to turn and drive back their outnumbered opponents. Seeley's regiment awoke with the rest of Merritt's Division and was told to proceed south along the Valley Pike in search of the enemy. The New Yorkers were deployed on the extreme right of the 1st Division, where they connected with the left of Custer's 3rd Division, centered along the Back Road on the western side of the Valley. BOB's description of what turned out to be an exhilarating day follows:

> Long before daylight the bugles blew, and we were in readiness to meet the expected attack; but the Rebels, elated by their partial success of the previous day, were too dilatory to suit General [Alfred] Torbert [Sheridan's overall cavalry commander], and we accordingly went out to look for them. We found him posted in a strong position, with two six-gun batteries, pouring shell into our advancing columns, but we marched steadily on.... [O]ur advance was not for a moment checked, and we sent their skirmish-line skedaddling on the gallop. A charge now made by our portion of the line gave us possession of five pieces of artillery and about three hundred prisoners, and this was the signal for a general stampede of the Rebels...They put, helter-skelter, every man for himself, their boasted General Rosser proving himself the fleetest. They left the balance of their artillery in our hands, their entire wagon-train, and large numbers of prisoners. We pursued them fifteen miles, and then leisurely returned to our old camping-ground of the morning, both horses and men thoroughly played out. The conduct of the Twenty-fifth on this day elicited the warmest praise from General Custer, who said that our charge of the morning, when we broke the enemy's line, "had never been surpassed." The men, encouraged by the brilliant example of Lieutenant-Colonel Seeley, and the other officers, fought with a courage and valor which could not be excelled, and, as a natural consequence, we suffered severely. Company I... which only joined the regiment the night before, suffered considerably. Toward the close of the action, Lieutenant-Colonel Seeley was wounded in the foot, and the command consequently devolved on Major Seymour [who had been released from detention on the 1st].[24]

Although the preceding account may have exaggerated the Twenty-Fifth's role in the running battle that began at Tom's Brook and ended near Woodstock, BOB's description of the Confederate defeat was accurate.[25] Both sides used the term "Woodstock races" to describe the Southern cavalry's unseemly flight, and Early himself added an unkind comment about the Laurel Brigade when he quipped Rosser's men should have worn grape leaves, since "laurel is not a running vine." Once again, however, the failure of the Union cavalry to adequately pursue the retreating Rosser cost an opportunity to completely crush the enemy, although the Confederates lost all of their supply wagons and artillery.[26]

Notably absent from the *Sunday Mercury* account was mention of the latest crisis to beset the Twenty-Fifth's leadership. Seeley had been rushed to the front to fill the vacancy left by Seymour's imprisonment, but less than two weeks later the foot wound received at Tom's Brook put him out of action, causing command to return to the recently-released Seymour.[27] But the major proved no better prepared to lead his men at Woodstock than he had been a month earlier at Winchester. Seeley's withdrawal from the field did not take place "towards the close of action," as BOB reported, but much earlier. Yet, as Seeley himself later wrote, Seymour "was not seen with his command [on the way to Woodstock] until very late in the day." Continuing, Seeley further related that the 1st Division's commander, Colonel Kidd, had Seymour re-arrested the following day (10th) "for occupying and sleeping in homes in...Woodstock, while his Regiment was on picket and he in command of same; also for allowing his horses to be unbridled in the face of the enemy...also for delay in drawing in his picket line at least one hour and a half after he was ordered to, placing his regiment in peril of being cut off by the enemy. He was released from arrest Oct. 11th or 12th."[28]

Included in charges that would be leveled against Seymour later that month by his subordinate officers were accusations that he "did shamefully misbehave himself in the presence of the enemy on the skirmish line, and did absent himself from his command...while such command was engaged with the enemy, and did not return until the Regiment had been withdrawn from the skirmish line...near Woodstock." Yet, despite the absence of Seeley and Seymour for much of the day, the Twenty-Fifth appears to have given a good account of itself, and there seems little reason to doubt that its enlisted men and junior officers could fight effectively, when they wanted to.[29]

On 11 October, the Twenty-Fifth accompanied the rest of Sheridan's victorious cavalry past Fisher's Hill and Strasburg to camp at the Army of the Shenandoah's headquarters near Cedar Creek.

> Next day there was an inspection of horses. So many of our men being dismounted entirely, and quite a number of horses which were still in the regiment being used up, General Merritt thought it most advisable to dismount the balance of the regiment, and send it [back to Maryland] to be remounted. We were accordingly furnished with condemned horses, and, in company with about two hundred men from the other regiments...were sent hither [Camp Remount]. I hardly think that our regiment will go out again this winter, as horses are scarce, the fighting season nearly over, at least in the Valley, and so I think we shall remain here and drill until spring.
>
> During our march here we saw several bands of guerrillas prowling along the road, but, owing to the quality of our horse-flesh, were unable to turn aside to purse them.[30]

The decision to send the Twenty-Fifth to the rear had as much to do with its leadership as to the condition of its horses. With no suitable replacement available in the regiment, Kidd was forced to release Seymour once again and return him to command, despite his strong reservations about keeping the major in a position where engaging with the enemy might be required. (Kidd would not have known that assigning the regiment the task of conducting condemned horses to Maryland would make it easier to take along the still-unaccounted-for animals captured at Conrad's Ferry.) The Twenty-Fifth left Cedar Creek on 13 October and arrived two days later at Camp Remount, several miles east of Harpers Ferry in Pleasant Valley, Md.

On 18 October, 1st Lt. Samuel David (F) brought formal charges against Seymour for "conduct prejudicial to good order and military discipline" and "neglect of duty." Of the ten other line officers who signed the document as witnesses to the major's misconduct, seven had previously signed the petition against Maj. Samuel McPherson in August, including Lt. David's captain, James Smith. In addition to Seymour's alleged cowardice at Woodstock, David cited his failure to maintain discipline on the way to Maryland, when he allegedly allowed "his command to straggle on the road and roam through the several towns and villages on the route, committing sundry depredations therein." At one point during this march, an officer approached the major for instructions and, within hearing of the enlisted men, was told by Seymour that he "didn't care a damn. The whole command may go to Hell!" David's accuser concluded that, since taking over the regiment on 9 October, Seymour had "neglected to care properly for his command, or to inforce proper discipline, and has otherwise given evidence of total incompetency as a commanding officer."[31]

In a response similar to that employed by McPherson at Fort Stoneman, Seymour tried to intimidate his opponents by charging Capt. James Smith with being absent from camp without permission. Seymour's superiors, however, dismissed Smith's case as "frivolous," and instead placed the major under detention to await a court martial. On 27 October, Seymour asked the Harpers Ferry district commander, Brig. Gen. John Stevenson, for permission to resume his duties pending trial. In justifying his request, the major branded the charges against him "frivolous and malicious, as well as insulting." He further claimed they originated from the same "clique" that had brought similar charges against Major McPherson that "were disapproved [sic] by the Comd's Officers of Camp Stoneman." This same group of officers continued, he charged, to oppose whoever attempts to lead the regiment and "have to be almost driven to the performance of their various duties." He further claimed his accusers' current intent was to "shackle me...by my being in arrest as to eventually place the regiment under the control of themselves or their friends."[32]

Going on to refute the charge of allowing his men to straggle on their way to Maryland, Seymour pointed to having covered the distance between Cedar Creek and Camp Remount in less than three days. Completely ignoring his two feckless appearances on the battlefield, and aware Seeley could not be easily reached for corroboration, Seymour added: "The encomiums of my comd'g officer upon my bravery and good conduct on the field upon the 9th inst. after he left the line wounded, and the evidence of officers of my com'd, who were with me under fire often upon that day—defeat and completely extirpate the charge of misbehavior made by this Lt. David—who, had just but joined the Reg't, not having participated in any of the fights, or hardships, but that of the 9th inst." Claiming to welcome a chance to clear his name in court, the major asked, in the interim, to be allowed to accompany his regiment back to the front. Stevenson, however, kept Seymour confined to quarters, while he consulted with Sheridan's cavalry corps. Finally, on 4 November, Seymour was permitted to transfer to a military hospital in Annapolis for treatment of malaria, his court martial still pending. Capt. Stephen W. Wheeler (B) had taken over as acting command of the Twenty-Fifth after Seymour's arrest, but, like his predecessors, his tenure as leader would be brief. (Wheeler had been one of McPherson's few allies but had also signed Lieutenant David's statement of charges against Seymour.)[33]

Chapter 9

CHASING MOSBY'S PARTISANS:
October-November 1864

Arriving at Camp Remount on 15 October precluded the Twenty-Fifth's participation in the Battle of Cedar Creek four days later. While leadership problems figured in the decision to send them to the rear, Sheridan was also under pressure to better protect the B&O Railroad, which had suffered several attacks from Mosby's partisans, including an embarrassing robbery on 14 October of a train carrying army paymasters. The so-called Greenback Raid had taken place near Duffields Station, several miles west of Harpers Ferry, and by sending the Twenty-Fifth back with the cavalry's worn-out horses, Sheridan was increasing Harpers Ferry's ability to defend the B&O without significantly weakening his own forces at Cedar Creek.

The men of the Twenty-Fifth were quite content to tarry at Camp Remount, located a few miles east of Harpers Ferry in Maryland's aptly named Pleasant Valley. Many, like BOB, assumed campaign season was over and hoped to remain there all winter. In doing so, they seriously underestimated Sheridan's determination to continue fighting well into the winter, but the New Yorkers would make the best of their three-week layover, "reveling in the undisturbed enjoyment of...soft-tack and fresh beef." Their daily schedule gives an idea of the relaxed lifestyle of troopers removed from the front lines:

Reveille	6:00 AM	Dinner	(right after Roll Call)
Breakfast	6:15	Afternoon Drill	2:30-4:00 PM
Sick Call	8:00	Supper	5:30
Guard Mount	8:30	Retreat	Sundown
Camp Fatigue	9:00	Tattoo	8:00
Morning Drill	10:30	Taps	8:30
Roll Call	Noon		

Once it became clear the Twenty-Fifth would return to the front, a number of malingerers "came to the conclusion that they had had enough of glory for this year, and made up their minds to pass the winter in the hospital. By the way," BOB continued, "going to the hospital is now called 'going into winter quarters.'" During this period, the regiment was finally completed with the arrival of Companies L and M. Heartened by this development and the quality of the new men, BOB became more optimistic that his regiment, and the volunteer service as a whole, would now pass from the hands of political tricksters and be managed by soldiers. We have been too long fooled by designing knaves, selling commissions to men who, if ordered before a board of examination, could not answer the simplest questions as to company or battalion drill, and whose only idea of holding a commission is that "it is a pretty good job." But do not suppose that all the officers of the Twenty-fifth are of this class. We have some as fine officers as there are in the service, but these good men have to bear the onus brought on the regiment by the incompetents.[1]

Camp Remount fell under the jurisdiction of the Harpers Ferry Military District and its commander, Brig. Gen. John D. Stevenson. Sheridan had handpicked Stevenson to safeguard his rear and oversee his army's logistical needs. As it turned out, the choice of this competent, if arrogant, Virginia native played no small part in the success of the Valley Campaign. In trying to supply a large force by wagon train, Stevenson had to contend with partisans operating in northern Virginia and the West Virginia panhandle, who were determined to sever the supply lines south from the rail depots in Martinsburg and Harpers Ferry. If there was one subject on which the cautious Stevenson and his boss disagreed, it was evident in the former's repeated requests for additional troops to guard the B&O line and wagon trains that supplied the Union forces. Sheridan, however, refused to substantially divert troops from the front, with the result that the partisans were unable to significantly alter the outcome of operations in the Valley.[2]

After a hiatus since 10 August, Capt. S. E. Chamberlin resumed signing Company K's muster rolls on 29 October, the date he rejoined his regiment. At the same time, he was appointed squadron commander for Companies G, H, I and K—part of a reorganization of the Twenty-Fifth by its interim commander, Capt. Steven Wheeler. With ambitions of his own, Chamberlin may not have been entirely disappointed to find the regiment's leadership in an even more deplorable state than when he left it in Washington. Once again, Lt. Col. Aaron Seeley was absent, this time convalescing in New York from a foot wound. Of the two majors, Samuel McPherson had been absent on extended sick leave for over two months, and Charles Seymour was, at the time of Chamberlin's arrival, under arrest pending the outcome of charges leveled against him by his subordinates. Neither was expected to resume command any time soon, and at least one captain, James Smith (F), had also been briefly under arrest pending a court martial, although the charges against him were subsequently dropped. Captain Wheeler's days as acting commander were also numbered, as he would soon be removed from command and charged with letting his regiment slip into a "deplorable state of readiness." Although Company K's captain may have viewed this situation as favorable to his own chances for promotion, his absence during the major engagements of the Valley Campaign cost him support within the regiment.[3]

Part of the delay in getting the Twenty-Fifth back to the field was the necessity of remounting and refitting Merritt's 1st and Custer's 3rd Divisions after the Battle of Cedar Creek. By the time the Twenty-Fifth received orders on 1 November to rejoin the 1st ("Michigan") Brigade in Merritt's Division, the Wolverines were under the leadership of Col. Peter Stagg, who had replaced James Kidd. Refitted and remounted, the New Yorkers left Pleasant Valley on 2 November and arrived at Martinsburg the next day, after spending a cold, rainy night on the road. Two days later, Sheridan's overall cavalry commander, Gen. Alfred Torbert, ordered Merritt and Custer to recall their scattered divisions back up the Shenandoah Valley. The Twenty-Fifth and detachments from several other regiments were assigned to guard a supply train "that numbered some seven hundred wagons." Departing Martinsburg at dawn on 5 November, the convoy reached Winchester at dusk and the next day continued south to Sheridan's headquarters at Cedar Creek. About four miles from their destination, the soldiers encountered a forage train which had recently been attacked by guerrillas, most likely a party of Mosby's 43rd Va. Cavalry that Capt. "Dolly" Richards had led in the area south of Middletown the day before. As BOB would recount, the partisans "had captured four men, wounded one, cut the throat of the negro driver of one of the wagons, and captured two of the wagons. The murdered negro lay at the roadside as we passed, and it was a sickening sight. The horrors on the battlefield are not felt so much as one cold-blooded murder."[4]

Two days after their arrival at Cedar Creek, the New Yorkers cast their ballots, most ignoring the wishes of their governor and voting instead to re-elect Abraham Lincoln. After undergoing a snap inspection, the men returned to camp, but were warned to be ready to move at a moment's notice. There, they received the unwelcome news that Maj. Manning Birge of the 6th Mich. Cavalry would replace Captain Wheeler as their interim commander. Echoing this sentiment, BOB groused that an outsider "has to-day (the 8th) been ordered to take command of the regiment. Great God! What is New York coming to? O Governor Seymour, if you have any patriotism left, give us Lieut-Colonel Aaron Seeley for Colonel and promote such men as Captain Wheeler, James Smith and [Clinton G.] Townsley, and pay no heed to those wire-pulling curs who do their campaigning in barrooms in New York."[5]

But the aforementioned inspection had evidently convinced Merritt that neither Wheeler, nor anyone else in the Twenty-Fifth, was capable of instilling the discipline required to face what was becoming a heated war with the partisans. Several days earlier, four members of the Michigan Brigade had paid scant attention to a squad of Union cavalrymen riding towards them on the Valley Pike near Newtown (now Stephens City, Va.). As the two parties drew even, the second group, actually Mosby's Rangers dressed in Federal uniforms, placed revolvers to the heads of the Wolverines and forced them to surrender. Among the prisoners was brigade Commissary Chief Charles Brewster, who later wrote they were led across the Shenandoah and up into the Blue Ridge at Ashby's Gap. There on the mountain, Brewster and his companions were personally interrogated by Mosby to confirm their affiliation with Custer's Brigade. After the earlier execution of his Rangers at Front Royal, the partisan chief had obtained permission from Richmond to put an equal number of Custer's men to death. (Mosby mistakenly believed Custer had ordered the killings, although as previously noted, this error may have been due to the presence of the Twenty-Fifth in Front Royal on the day of the executions.) Satisfied about their links to Custer, the Rebel colonel ordered the four taken to a makeshift prison near Rectortown, which Augur's railroad crews had only recently abandoned.[6]

After some twenty-five men from Custer's old brigade were captured, Mosby assembled his command on 6 November to witness the prisoners draw lots to determine who would be killed. The six condemned men were then taken into the Valley, where their executions would have greater public impact. A little west of Berryville on the road to Winchester, three of the captives were hanged and three shot, although at least two lived to tell the story. Their corpses were later brought into Winchester, where Chamberlin had a chance to view them as his regiment prepared to leave town the morning of 7 November on its way to Cedar Creek. In addition to a note left at the scene of the executions, Mosby sent a communication to Sheridan under a flag of truce, stating "Hereafter any prisoners falling into my hands will be treated with the kindness due to their condition, unless some new act of barbarity shall compel me reluctantly to adopt a course of policy repulsive to humanity." In a reply addressed to General Early, Sheridan emphasized that the killings in Front Royal were carried out without his authority, and that henceforth all captured members of Mosby's command would be treated as prisoners of war.[7]

After their arrival at Cedar Creek, troopers from the Twenty-Fifth were hopeful they would not have to move until spring, as the weather was turning cold and a light snow had already fallen. On 9 November, however, Sheridan ordered the Army of the Shenandoah to pull up stakes and fall back to Kernstown, a few miles south of Winchester. (According to Chamberlin's diary, the infantry started out that same day, and the cavalry followed the next morning.) There on the north bank of Opequon Creek, the Federals established permanent winter quarters, which they named "Camp Russell" in honor of the Union general who fell at Winchester. Sheridan had finally convinced Grant and the War Department to allow him to select a location that significantly shortened his winter supply lines.

The next day, while the rest of the regiment commenced building shelters, Chamberlin's squadron went out to patrol the Front Royal Road, ending with an overnight camp near the Shenandoah River. It was his first experience leading mounted cavalrymen in hostile territory, but little of significance occurred until they received word at dawn on the 12th to return to their regiment. On the way back, his command encountered the enemy "in force" near Newtown, and an "engagement" ensued, during which several New Yorkers were captured as they retreated through town. As Chamberlin's squadron withdrew north along the Front Royal Road, it was joined by other cavalry detachments, and so in late afternoon "moved out with strong force on Middletown Pike." There, according to his diary, they "engaged with the enemy, hard fighting, lost several killed, wounded and missing. Returned to same camping ground on Front Royal Road at midnight." The next day, the squadron participated with other cavalry units in a scout past Middletown, which confirmed Early's forces had fallen back to Strasburg. They returned to Camp Russel that night, capturing a prisoner on the way.[8]

The incident at Newtown was but the first of several "actions" and "engagements" that took place on 12 November, the most significant occurring near Ninevah Church. Having heard rumors that Early's combined forces were gathering near Strasburg in preparation for an attack, Sheridan sent Merritt's and Custer's Divisions to counter this threat. The withdrawal of much of Sheridan's cavalry into Maryland for refitting in late October had misled the Confederates into thinking the Yankees had either retired for the winter or returned home to vote in the 8 November presidential election. Despite this misinterpretation, Early's cavalry performed well during the first part of the Ninevah engagement, repulsing several charges by Custer's Division. That was until at least one Rebel commander (John McCausland) prematurely "concluded that he had finished a good day's work. As his men nonchalantly ate dinner and fed their horses, ignoring as usual the basic disciplinary and security measures necessary in disputed country, a renewed Federal surge caught and destroyed them."[9]

Sheridan's account of the various engagements that day focused almost exclusively on the role of Custer's Division in the victory at Ninevah. He dismissed the morning attack at Newtown as a "demonstration," and stated that "Merritt was but slightly engaged after dark with enemy's infantry on the pike." The Twenty-Fifth fought in the latter engagement, called the "Action at Cedar Creek," until midnight, losing four killed, sixteen wounded and two missing, including one wounded and two missing from Company K. With the exception of Fort Stevens, it was the highest number of casualties sustained by the Twenty-Fifth during any single day of the war.[10]

The group that Chamberlin's troopers encountered at Newtown on the morning of the 12th may have been part of Mosby's command, rather than an advance party of Early's cavalry. According to a post-war account, Capt. Richard Montjoy led a company of Mosby's Rangers that ambushed an unidentified Union cavalry unit near Newtown on the morning of the 16th. Other sources fail to mention any similar attack on that date, so faulty memory could account for the discrepancy in dates. According to one Ranger chronicler, the Union cavalrymen were "carelessly approaching, apparently unconscious of danger." As the Yankees rode by the concealed Southerners, the latter charged and the "astonished Federals fled in confusion, leaving a number of dead and wounded on the field, and 17 prisoners and horses in [our] hands." On their way back, however, Montjoy's men were in turn ambushed by "Blazer's Scouts," as they tried to ford the Shenandoah. In the ensuing melee, at least two of Montjoy's men were killed and several wounded before they finally got across the river. All of the Union prisoners managed to escape in the confusion.[11]

Blazer's Scouts were an elite one hundred-man counterinsurgency force led by Capt. Richard Blazer. Armed with seven-shot Spencer carbines, they operated against partisans who infested the Blue Ridge mountains between western Loudoun County and the Shenandoah River. Living off the land much like the guerrillas whom they pursued, the Scouts were effective in reducing attacks on Sheridan's supply lines during the height of the Valley Campaign. In the opinion of one Ranger, "Blazer was not only a brave man and a hard fighter, but by his humane and kindly treatment, in striking contrast with the usual conduct of our enemies, he had so disarmed our citizens that instead of fleeing on his approach and notifying our soldiers, thus giving them a chance to escape, but little notice was taken of him. Consequently, many of our men were 'gobbled up' before they were aware of his presence." After the attack on Montjoy's company, Mosby resolved to rid himself of Blazer before he did any further damage. Less than a week later, the Scouts were lured into an ambush at Myerstown, W. Va., where almost the entire unit was killed or captured.[12] The Rangers' lopsided victory over Blazer's well-trained and -equipped guerrilla fighters does much to confirm the oft-cited view that Mosby employed superior tactics. He discouraged his men from using sabers and carbines, but insisted they carry two or more loaded revolvers. They were also taught to close with their foe as quickly as possible to maximize the element of surprise and the effectiveness of their revolvers at a range where carbines became unwieldy and impossible to reload.[13]

As already noted, a day after skirmishing at Newtown and Cedar Creek, the Twenty-Fifth participated in mop-up operations around Strasburg, where they helped capture stragglers from Early's retreating army before returning to Camp Russell. The next days were devoted to renewed work on winter quarters prior to the onset of cold weather. On 19 November, the troopers were delighted to receive an extra issue of beans, onions and whiskey, termed "dainties" by the men. Their mood abruptly changed the next day when the soldiers went to draw two-days rations from the commissary for a pending march and were stupefied to receive only salt-fish and salt, or so BOB claimed.

At 1 AM on 21 November, the entire 1st Cavalry Division, commanded by Brig. Gen. Thomas C. Devin in Merritt's absence, set out in the rain for an extended scout around Front Royal. Towards morning the rain stopped, but a chill wind arose that froze man and beast. Near Front Royal, the Twenty-Fifth was "met with a flag of truce, which had been sent in by a Union soldier who had been left at Harris[on]burg, on safeguard, not having been relieved when the Army fell back from that town." Safeguards were posted in civilian homes to prevent looting by their own side. BOB explained how they often got left behind when their units departed the area. "They are always respected by either army, and sent within their own lines, although, when any of our safeguards fall into guerrilla hands, they are generally robbed of their arms and accouterments."

Although Devin's forces encountered no significant resistance, the 2nd and 3rd Divisions engaged the rear guard of Early's army further west in sharp fighting at Rude's Hill, just north of New Market. The purpose of this massive reconnaissance by the Union cavalry was to determine the disposition and intentions of Early's troops, thereby enabling Sheridan to decide when he could let the VI Corps return to Richmond for the winter.[14]

All three cavalry divisions returned to Camp Russell, heartened by the information gathered of Early's intention to withdraw his infantry from the Valley and let his cavalry disperse to find winter shelter and forage. This prospect soon dimmed for the men of the Twenty-Fifth, who had a rude surprise when they rode into camp and discovered the boards from their new shelters had been pilfered. Their spirits brightened, however, with the prospect of celebrating Thanksgiving on the 24th with a dinner of turkey and chicken, plus a whiskey ration courtesy of "Uncle Sam." The poultry had been donated by the ladies of New York, and BOB was lavish in his thanks for their generosity, which served to offset the "Copperhead effusion" that frequently appeared in the press and made the soldiers think their sacrifices were not appreciated back home. Yet, he roundly chastised one of the officers, who had tried to reserve the birds for the officer's mess. Reversing his earlier opinion of Major Birge, BOB credited him with ending the practice of pilfering food meant for the enlisted men, and claimed it was now the "unanimous wish that [their acting commander] might have a permanent position in this regiment." As the men settled around their campfires to enjoy their Thanksgiving meal, they were aroused by the sound of gunfire.[15]

Lincoln had declared the first national day of Thanksgiving a year earlier, but Mosby had his own ideas on the proper way to celebrate Yankee holidays. The day before, the Grey Ghost led a squadron of Rangers across the Shenandoah "for the purpose of extending some protection to the citizens of Warren and Clarke [Counties] against the foragers from Sheridan's army, and camped for the night in the neighborhood of White Post." The next morning, the Rangers surprised a Federal wagon train from the 21st N.Y. Cavalry, as it was "returning to the Brigade camp near Perkin's [sic—Parkin's] Mill" after foraging in the vicinity. Intoxicated by the chase, Mosby and his men pursued the fleeing guards right into their camp. "It was about 4 o'clock in the afternoon of a Yankee Thanksgiving Day, and the soldiers were having a fine time seated around their camp-fires, and did not at once discover what had burst upon them. Their consternation saved us, and the men had time to rob them of their greenbacks before they rallied. But it was soon time for us to travel. The whole camp turned out to pursue." Mosby's bravado would erase his earlier gains and almost resulted in his capture. After their initial shock, the

Yankees grabbed their carbines, leapt on their horses and chased the Rangers to Millwood, where they recovered the wagons and set free their colleagues. All returned to camp to finish their holiday dinner.[16]

The Twenty-Fifth's quarters were on Camp Russell's east side, near Parkin's Mills, but BOB played down this incident, describing the "wagon train" as having but two wagons sent out about two miles from camp to load bricks with an escort from the Twenty-Fifth. Although most of the guards were captured with the wagons, they were quickly released when the 14th Pa. Cavalry responded to Mosby's initial sally. One private from "our regiment was severely wounded in the left leg, and then severely beaten by the guerrillas when the heat of the pursuit compelled them to abandon him."[17]

* * * * *

The withdrawal of Early's forces to the southern end of the Shenandoah Valley left the partisans as the only significant threat to Sheridan's Army. These forces included Mosby's Rangers (43rd Va. Cavalry), small guerrilla groups such as John Mobberly's band in northwest Loudoun County, and members of the regular Confederate cavalry, including Elijah White's "Comanches" (35th Virginia), who chose to fight as irregulars during the winter. In all, they probably totaled no more than 700 within striking distance of Camp Russell, but their potential for embarrassing attacks and disruption to supply lines was greater than their numbers might suggest.[18]

Sheridan never allowed the partisans to distract his pursuit of Early, but there is little doubt Mosby in particular had gotten under his skin ever since the Wagon Train Raid back in August. In addition to keeping the Manassas Gap Railroad from reopening, Mosby's Rangers could easily strike the B&O Railroad, Sheridan's principal lifeline that winter. This threat had been driven home in the Greenback Raid on 14 October, when they derailed a B&O train between Harpers Ferry and Martinsburg and seized over $200,000 from two U.S. Army paymasters on board. The money was divided among the partisans, and later circulated "so freely in Loudoun that never afterwards was there a pie or blooded horse sold in that section for Confederate money."[19]

Directed to keep his troops as far south in the Valley as possible, Sheridan's most immediate concern was to devise a secure means of provisioning his troops before the onset of winter. Unless heavily guarded, wagon trains were vulnerable to disruption by the guerrillas and bad weather, nor could they carry the huge amount of forage required by his cavalry during winter. As mentioned in Chapter 7, a solution was found by using rails salvaged from the Manassas Gap line to rebuild a railroad spur between Harpers Ferry and Winchester. As this line neared completion, Sheridan warned the local populace that, if the railroad was interfered with by guerrillas or disloyal citizens, he would "arrest all male secessionists in the towns...and in the adjacent country, sending them to Fort McHenry, Maryland, there to be confined during the war; and also to burn all grain, destroy all subsistence, and drive off all stock belonging to such individuals."[20] The threat was effective, and few disruptions to rail service occurred that winter.[21]

With Early out of the way and his winter supplies assured, Sheridan could finally turn attention to partisan strongholds in Loudoun and Fauquier Counties. General Grant had been needling him on this subject since August, and two days after the bodies of Custer's men were found hanging from a tree, Grant suggested that Sheridan take retaliatory action:

> Do you not think it advisable to notify all citizens living east of the Blue Ridge to move out north of the Potomac all their stock, grain, and provisions of every description? There is no doubt about the necessity of clearing out that country so that it will not support Mosby's gang. And the question is whether it is not better that the people should save what they can. So long as the war lasts they must be prevented from raising another crop.[22]

Two days later, Sheridan informed Grant he had just sent a small cavalry division across the Blue Ridge to Rectortown. After burning all granaries and provisions in their path, the Yanks returned with 300 head of cattle, as well as numerous sheep and horses. Sheridan felt this action would "be a warning which will probably be taken advantage of by any Union citizens living in that country. I think it best, general [Grant], to settle the question of which way the people go [by leaving it up to them]." Sheridan apparently ordered the foray into Fauquier as a trial run for the much larger raid on the Loudoun Valley that followed, but, despite his assurance to Grant, it did not serve as an adequate warning to the many Union sympathizers in northern Loudoun. If anything, these loyalists were lulled into thinking Sheridan would confine his counterinsurgency efforts to "Mosby's Confederacy" in southern Loudoun and northern Fauquier. Had a public announcement been issued that gave Unionists time to sell their livestock and forage across the border in Maryland, it would have greatly reduced their losses two weeks later. But the liquidation of Blazer's Scouts on 18 November had further convinced Sheridan to abandon tactics that relied on hunting down the partisans in favor of targeting the civilians who supplied them.[23]

Moreover, the Union army was under considerable pressure to put an end to Mosby's activities. The so-called "Prince of Guerrillas" made good copy, and newspapers on both sides featured his exploits. Northern readers were particularly inflamed by two recent stories—the killing of Blazer's second-in-command after he had allegedly surrendered, and reports that Mosby's Rangers were fighting under the "black flag," i.e., not giving their foes the option to surrender. (Both allegations referred to isolated incidents not sanctioned by Mosby himself.) With the Presidential election and Thanksgiving over, Sheridan advised the War Department he would "commence work on Mosby. Heretofore I have made no attempt to break him up, as I would have employed ten men to his one, and for the reason that I have made a scape-goat of him for the destruction of private rights. Now there is going to be an intense hatred of him in that portion of this Valley which is nearly a desert. I will soon commence in Loudoun County, and let them know there is a God in Israel."[24]

The following day (Sunday, 27 November), Sheridan ordered Gen. Wesley Merritt's 1st Cavalry Division to undertake a systematic campaign of destruction on the east side of the Blue Ridge. Merritt's forces were to scour the fertile Loudoun Valley, which stretched from the Potomac River southward into Fauquier County and was bounded on the west by the Blue Ridge and on the east by the Catoctin/Bull Run mountain range. Although the troopers were to include the northern part of Fauquier as far south as the Manassas Gap Railroad, most of the targeted area fell in Loudoun County. The order further specified Snickersville (now Bluemont) as Merritt's "point of concentration," from which he should operate "in destroying towards the Potomac." Clearly, Sheridan wanted to leave the Virginia side of the river incapable of supporting a guerrilla force that could threaten the B&O Railroad, which skirted the Potomac between Harpers Ferry and Point of Rocks. But this direction also insured that much of the consequent devastation would take place north of the Snickersville Turnpike and include the pro-Union Quaker and German inhabitants of "North Loudoun" (a term used to denote the quasi-independent Unionist sector of the county).[25]

A second part of Sheridan's order was intended for publication as justification to "the people of Virginia" for the events that followed. In it, the area subject to the raid was described as a "hot-bed of lawless bands" that had "depredated" the Army's communication lines, "safe guards left at houses," and "all small parties of our troops. Their real object is plunder and highway robbery." To clear out these guerrillas, troops were being sent to "destroy and consume all forage and subsistence, burn all barns and mills with their contents, and drive off all stock in the region." Stressing no dwellings would be burned, nor "personal violence" done to citizens, Sheridan was careful to blame "the Guerrilla system of warfare" and the "the authorities" in Richmond who had authorized these partisans for the damages his Federal troops were about to carry out. "The injury done this Army by [the guerrillas] is very slight. The injury they have indirectly inflicted upon the people and upon the Rebel Army may be counted by millions."[26]

Peter Stagg's 1st and Thomas Devin's 2nd Brigades set off from Camp Russell before dawn on Monday (the 28th). After crossing the Shenandoah at Berry's Ferry, the cavalrymen ascended the Blue Ridge at Ashby's Gap, where they could gaze upon the rich farmland of Loudoun and Fauquier below. (Merritt's staff and the Reserve Brigade entered Loudoun via Snickers Gap on Tuesday and established division headquarters at the foot of the Blue Ridge at Snickersville.) As the 25th N.Y. Cavalry, still under the

November 1864 "Burning Raid" Targeted Mosby Strongholds in Loudoun. (*Taylor Sketchbook*, Western Reserve Hist. Soc.)

command of Major Birge, descended into the upper (southern) end of Loudoun Valley with the rest of Stagg's Brigade, the troopers paused in the town of Paris long enough to empty some hen houses. From there, both brigades pushed eastward along Ashby's Gap Turnpike (today's Route 50, which roughly follows the Loudoun/Fauquier boundary), until they reached Upperville, where they captured three members of Mosby's "gang." Continuing his account, BOB referred to guerrilla chieftain John Mobberly, whom he had had probably heard about while the Twenty-Fifth was at Camp Remount, as his band operated mainly in Loudoun's northwest corner, opposite Harpers Ferry.

> [Upperville] was searched, and an immense quantity of ordinance stores found and destroyed, among which were over two hundred Government saddles. Upperville is one of the great storehouses of the guerrillas, all the male inhabitants...who are able to bear arms, being attached to either Moseby or Mobly's gangs. This latter guerrilla chief, Mobly [sic, John Mobberly], lacking the dash and ingenuity of Moseby, depends on making a name by his horrible cruelties toward his prisoners. So blood-thirsty is this wretch that it was owing to his infamous deeds that this raid was ordered,[27] and thus thousands have been made to suffer by the guilt of a few.[28]

After camping on the outskirts of Upperville the first night, both brigades assembled early Tuesday morning to hear Sheridan's previously quoted order read aloud, and for the first time the men, who had only been told they were on a lengthy reconnaissance, learned the extent of the grim task that lay ahead. The brigades separated at this point, with Devin's troops continuing east past Middleburg, while the Twenty-Fifth turned south with Stagg's Brigade towards Rectortown. Members of Custer's old brigade were undoubtedly pleased with a chance to settle scores in the same area where their fellow Wolverines had been imprisoned several weeks earlier. Yet, even seasoned veterans like BOB recoiled at what they now had to do. One "could easily follow the track of each Brigade by the volumes of smoke and flame which filled the air in all directions," observed the *Sunday Mercury* correspondent. "Such work as this is the most unpleasant that can fall to the lot of a soldier. It is hard to listen to the piercing cries and entreaties of the women and children, as they see you about to fire their winter-store and drive off their last head of stock. Thoughts of our own dear ones at home often intrude themselves upon our minds at such times..."[29]

As the day wore on, the captured livestock increasingly hindered the forward progress of each regiment. To alleviate this impediment, Merritt sent supplementary orders for Stagg's Brigade to assemble

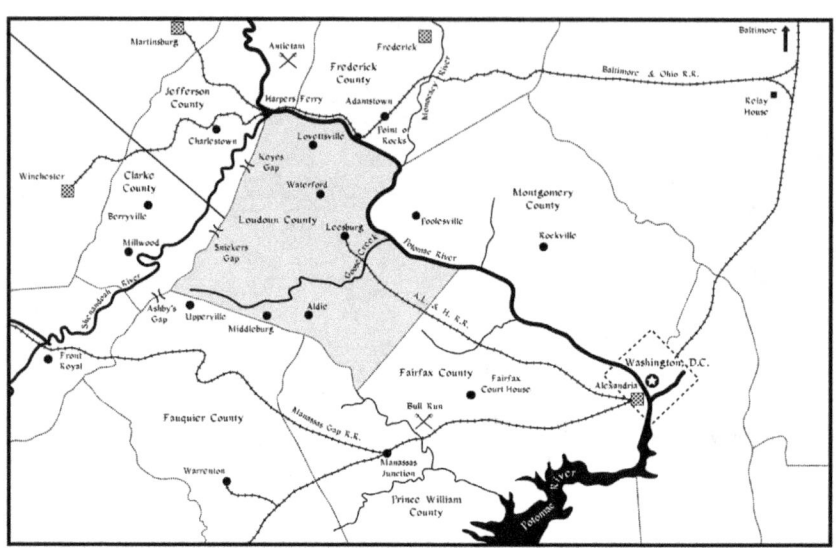

Map 1: Loudoun County and Surrounding Area, (Jennifer Belland, artist, WFA)

that night at Philomont to enable the Reserve Brigade to come and relieve it of the confiscated animals. After that was done, Stagg's forces were to set out the following morning in the direction of "Circleville Post Office [south of present-day Lincoln], Hamilton, and Waterford, and thence along the Catoctin Creek to the Potomac." As things turned out, the general had grossly underestimated the logistical demands of Sheridan's initial order, particularly the vast area to be covered and delays caused by herding the livestock. It is unclear whether Stagg's Brigade ever reached Rectorstown before heading back into Loudoun by sunset, and it certainly did not have time to cover all of northern Fauquier County. Only two regiments succeeded in reaching Philomont by ten o'clock Tuesday night. The other three were forced to camp along the way, "it being exceedingly difficult to march with the herd in the darkness." According to Chamberlin's diary, the Twenty-Fifth returned to Loudoun through Middleburg, and spent the night near Uniontown (later renamed Unison).[30]

The parties sent out from the Reserve Brigade to receive the livestock proved insufficient for the task, and both Stagg's and Devin's Brigades ended up driving their herds to Snickersville, where they spent Wednesday night with the rest of Merritt's Division. Due to a change in orders, Stagg's Brigade did not proceed towards Waterford the following day, thus sparing Captain Chamberlin the irony of participating in the despoilment of his future home. Instead, the task of destruction in North Loudoun fell mainly on Devin's troops. They were aided by part of the Reserve Brigade, which left Snickersville Wednesday to burn farms lying between the Short Hill and Blue Ridge. After reaching the Potomac opposite Harpers Ferry, the Reserve Brigade turned eastward to meet up with Devin's Brigade near Lovettsville.

Meanwhile, Stagg's men headed back east and south from Snickersville on Thursday morning (1 December). The Twenty-Fifth worked in tandem with the 6th Michigan that day in an effort to flush guerrillas hiding along the Blue Ridge south of Snickers Gap. The New Yorkers moved along the mountain's eastern slope, while the Michigan cavalrymen combed the crest as far south as Ashby's Gap.

> We captured thirteen guerrillas, and killed and wounded several of those wretches. On hand that day was about sixty horses, five hundred head of cattle, and about as many sheep. But the biggest joke of all was our discovery of a pen containing over two thousand hogs, under a Rebel guard who fled at our approach. We captured one of the guard, who informed us that the hogs were the product of the "tax in kind" which was just being levied, and of course the hogs were the property of the Confederate Government—and consequently a lawful prize. They were immediately taken charge of, and we expect a letter of thanks from Jeff Davis for the great care we took of his taxes. We found one mill, where were stored about forty thousand pounds of bacon, all barreled and addressed to

the Chief Commissary of Subsistence at Richmond. Having no means of taking it with us, and not being able to go to Richmond with it, it was burned along with the mill in which it was stored. At night we returned to Snickersville, and the sight presented by the men was a comical one, every horse being loaded with poultry, so that nothing but the heads of the horse and rider were visible above the mass of feathers in which they were imbedded.[31]

On Friday morning, Merritt's entire division began its homeward march through Snickers Gap. By the time the Twenty-Fifth reached the Shenandoah River at the foot of the mountain, the cattle had already been driven across. Getting the sheep and hogs over posed a bigger problem, and Chamberlin's regiment formed a line on horseback across the river to catch any animals that washed downstream. This was easier said than done, and the plan was abandoned after many animals drowned. The New Yorkers then slung individual sheep over their saddles and carried them across. The hogs were not so easily managed, and most had to be shot and left behind, as "the guerrillas were beginning to press the rear of the column." The Twenty-Fifth lost one man, who drowned when his horse fell into the river. After spending the night near Berryville, Merritt's Division returned to Camp Russell on Saturday afternoon (3 December).[32]

Sheridan's preliminary estimate of livestock driven off or destroyed during the "Burning Raid," as it is still known locally, was 6,000 head of cattle, 5,000 sheep, 1,000 fatted hogs and 700 horses. Damage to mills, barns and forage was estimated to run into the millions of dollars, although a full report was never completed. BOB was confident the "once flourishing county of Loudoun" had been turned into a "wilderness," its citizens suffering a "terrible retribution" for the guerrillas' crimes. He set the figure of livestock "brought in" at 8,000. As to property losses, "the damage done by [the Twenty-Fifth alone] is estimated at $500,000, and taking this as the average of each regiment in the division, shows a destruction of property to the amount of $7,500,000."[33]

If the expedition surpassed its goals in terms of destruction and confiscation, it failed to have an equal impact on the partisans. Merritt admitted "it was found next to impossible to come in contact with any guerrilla," although he thought thirty to forty might have been captured or killed, a figure certainly on the high side. Mosby's men did not confront their adversaries during the raid, but shadowed their movements, killing Yankees whenever the opportunity arose and driving off livestock before it could be seized. The Twenty-Fifth reported three men missing on 29 November around Upperville, and two the following day near Snickersville, all probably "bushwhacked" by guerrillas.[34]

Merritt's raid was an exceedingly bitter pill for local Unionists to swallow. Many felt the soldiers had singled them out, and all agreed the guerrillas were scarcely affected. The Federals left a legacy of hatred and suffering that lingered into the twentieth century. Because the raid's ostensible target—the partisans—remained behind to continue extracting their "tithe" from citizens, it was even harder for Unionists to defend what had occurred. Efforts by the Unionists to secure reimbursement for losses were only partially successful, and even then, a decade elapsed before payment was received for livestock driven off, while the much larger property losses were never repaid. Many loyalist farmers were financially ruined and simply left the county after the war. Thus, despite the sizable pro-Union sentiment that existed in the county throughout the war, the "Burning Raid" was a factor in the Republican Party's failure to make significant inroads in Loudoun after hostilities ended.[35]

Chapter 10

CLEARING OUT THE VALLEY:
December 1864-March 1865

When the Twenty-Fifth returned from Loudoun on 3 December, it was assigned a different site at Camp Russell, forcing the men to begin anew constructing winter quarters. This work was hampered by a shortage of axes, shovels and other tools, further indication the New Yorkers stood low on the Michigan Brigade pecking order. Three days later, Maj. Manning Birge ordered the regiment restructured as follows: 1st Battalion (Companies A-D) under Capt. Stephen Wheeler (B); 2nd Battalion (Companies E, F, H & I) under Capt. James Smith (F); and 3rd Battalion (Companies G, K, L, M) under Capt. S. E. Chamberlin (K). The three captains were further directed to divide their battalions into squadrons of two companies each, led by the senior officer in those companies.[1]

Work on the new huts had barely begun, when the first heavy snow fell on 9 December. (Although Vermont native Chamberlin only recorded "some" snow fell that night, the coming winter proved one of the worst in Valley history, the ground remaining snow-covered until spring.) An inspection the next day brought the regiment's miserable living conditions to the attention of division staff officers, who were irritated directives on the quartering of men and horses had been ignored in two of the Twenty-Fifth's battalions. A day later (11th) Major Birge was arrested, along with the heads of the two offending battalions, Captains Wheeler and Smith, Chamberlin's battalion having coped with the snow sufficiently to avoid censure. Another outsider, Maj. Thomas M. Howrigan of the 1st Mich. Cavalry, was brought in to briefly run the regiment.

Birge and the two captains were charged with disobedience of orders and neglect of duty in letting the Twenty-Fifth slip into "a deplorable state of readiness." At Birge's court martial, convened a day after his arrest, witnesses for the prosecution spoke of finding horses standing in snow tied to nearby trees, rather than properly corralled. Furthermore, the enlisted men were still living in tents pitched in the mud, rather than in quarters raised on logs, as specified by division policy. Birge's defense witnesses included Captains Wheeler and Smith, as well as Chamberlin. All affirmed the charges against their acting commander were exaggerated, and that the snow around the horses had been removed in a timely manner. Furthermore, the regiment had requisitioned tools needed to construct quarters almost a month earlier but did not receive them until Birge's trial was under way. After three days of hearings, the major was acquitted of all charges, although the division officer who reviewed the case only "reluctantly affirmed [the findings of the court]. It is evident from the testimony...that had the proper attendance of Maj. Birge and his officers been given to the condition of his command, proceedings would never have been obliged to be acted upon." Wheeler's hearing immediately followed that of Birge, while Smith was not tried until the end of December. Their acquittals also drew acerbic comments from division staff officers, who felt both could have found ways to improve living conditions within their battalions, despite the excuses cited in their defense.[2]

Even before this latest crisis was resolved, speculation was rife within the Twenty-Fifth as to the identity of its next commander. In a letter to the *Sunday Mercury* in early December, BOB named two officers from other regiments who were rumored to be in line for the position. Both were said to be excellent candidates but, the correspondent claimed, the Twenty-Fifth's officers and men were "unanimous" in wanting Gov. Horatio Seymour to make Lt. Col. Aaron Seeley a full colonel so he could return as their permanent commander. Anyone else "would find his seat too hot to be pleasant."

It is unlikely BOB's letter had any influence on the lame-duck Democratic governor, still smarting from his recent defeat by a Republican opponent, in large part due to the soldier vote from the field. In any case, Seeley returned from medical leave on 17 December to resume command. Although he had not been promoted to full colonel, he must have been very gratified by his reception: "Cheer upon cheer ran through the camp, the men spontaneously turning out of their tents to pay him this compliment, as soon as his arrival was known." He was still "very lame" from the wound received at Woodstock, but even this left a favorable impression on the soldiers, pleased he had not used it to prolong his absence.[3]

Virtually everyone in Merritt's division expected the recent raid into Loudoun would be their last action until spring. General Grant had other ideas, however, and ordered Sheridan to destroy railroad facilities around Gordonsville to prevent resupply of Richmond's defenders. To the dismay of his troopers, Sheridan sent out his entire cavalry corps on 19 December on a grueling ten-day raid. As BOB characteristically described the mood: "The 'muttering thunder' of which the poets speak would be but a faint echo of the growling heard through the camp; and you might almost fancy that every man had become a prospective miller, from the constant utterance of the word dam." Gen. Alfred Torbert, overall cavalry chief for the Army of the Shenandoah, led the expedition's main body (the 1st and 2nd Divisions) across the Blue Ridge, while Custer's 3rd Division carried out a diversionary raid up the Valley.

After fording the icy Shenandoah near Front Royal, Torbert's forces crossed the mountain at Chester Gap and proceeded via Little Washington to Sperryville, where the column camped for the night. It was bitterly cold, and, as BOB described the scene when reveille sounded, "there was about a foot of snow covering us all, and to see us bursting our superincumbent cerements and standing erect, would have suggested...an animated graveyard, each little hillock yielded up its quota of frozen soldiers, whose purple-tipped noses, pendant with icicles, reminded one of anything but glory. Having refreshed the inner man with hot coffee, hard tack, oaths and other delicacies," the Union troopers pushed on to Madison Court House, where heavy skirmishing took place. On 22 December, the column neared its objective at Gordonsville, but withdrew after a day of inconsequential fighting, when it was discovered Rebel reinforcements were on the way from Richmond. Some of Torbert's force returned via Fauquier and Loudoun Counties, where they unsuccessfully searched for Col. John Mosby, who had been severely wounded several days earlier. The exhausted cavalrymen finally straggled back to Camp Russell on 28 December, both men and horses having, as their commander reported, "suffered almost beyond description from the cold and bad weather." Torbert listed only twenty-eight casualties, but many more had varying degrees of frostbite, and it was clear even to Grant that further campaigning would have to wait until the weather improved.[4]

Colonel Seeley and Captain Chamberlin were among 154 dismounted and convalescent members of the Twenty-Fifth who remained at Camp Russell. (Records show Chamberlin was sick and confined to quarters two days before the raid began.) Seeley's return had been a welcome development for Company K's captain, who hoped to regain the confidence the colonel had shown towards him back in New York. Chamberlin had been absent when Seeley briefly took command of the Twenty-Fifth that fall, so their confinement together at Camp Russell provided a fortuitous chance to renew their relationship. With most of the senior officers in Stagg's Brigade on the raid, Seeley was put in charge of brigade headquarters, leaving Chamberlin in command of the Twenty-Fifth. Two days later, Seeley invited the captain to accompany him to a band concert. The evening must have gone well, as Seeley subsequently asked Chamberlin to serve as the brigade's Acting Assistant Adjutant General (AAAG), thus enabling K's captain to pass the holiday season in more comfortable surroundings. (Not every day was spent in camp; on Christmas Eve the "whole command," responding to an alarm, rode to Front Royal, but found no sign of the enemy.)[5]

For most who remained at Camp Russell, "the only notice taken of Christmas" that year was the distribution of extra whiskey rations. There was, however, a special holiday treat for enlisted men in Seeley's regiment. Based on an appeal contained in one of BOB's earlier letters, and some lobbying with New York tobacco companies by the colonel, a sizable quantity of chewing and smoking tobacco was donated for Christmas. Even more appreciated was the muster on New Year's Eve, which included a yearend bonus payment, although regular salaries were still six months behind.[6]

Seeley and Chamberlin resumed their regular positions after Torbert's raiding party returned. At the same time, Gen. Thomas Devin was ordered to move his brigade to Lovettsville in northern Loudoun County, where it could better protect local Unionists and the B&O Railroad from partisan attack. This relocation proved fortunate for the Twenty-Fifth, which was allowed to occupy the comfortable winter quarters vacated by Devin's troopers. Less pleasant was word from cavalry headquarters that, despite the winter lull, only five furloughs at a time would be granted for every hundred men. Many would be disappointed at not receiving the coveted permission to spend time with loved ones back home.[7]

An incident that occurred during the Gordonville Raid only came to Seeley's attention in early January, when Pvt. Martin O'Donovan (F) complained of being unjustly charged for the loss of his horse and equipment. After looking into the matter, Seeley decided to prefer charges against 1st Lt. Samuel David (F) for disobeying the colonel's pre-raid instructions that no one was to leave the main column, except in at least a squad accompanied by an officer. According to O'Donovan, however, on 20 December in the vicinity of Sperryville, Lieutenant David ordered him to kill and bring back a sheep visible in a field along the road. When the private demurred that he knew nothing about slaughtering sheep, the lieutenant ordered two more privates to accompany him. While O'Donovan went up to a nearby house to distract the owner by asking for food, the other two tried unsuccessfully to catch the sheep, before returning to the column. Meanwhile, O'Donovan, who had lagged behind, approached another dwelling to ask a slave for some cake. When he emerged from this cabin, he was captured by four Confederates, who eventually set him free after taking his horse and equipment. In his court martial, David argued the blame lay with the private for straggling, but the lieutenant was found guilty and sentenced to loss of a month's pay, a verdict Seeley endorsed. In all probability, it was the desired outcome for Seeley, who was fully aware of David's role in Seymour's ouster and wanted to keep his officious lieutenant on a short leash.[8]

The following melancholy poem, penned on New Year's Day by Chamberlin's "affectionate cousin, Lizzie M. Reynolds," has dubious literary merit, but its retention by the recipient suggests he shared her mood that winter:

>Another year has passed Cousin.
>What have we gained thereby?
>Are we better fitted to live Cousin,
>Or better fitted to die?
>
>How quickly the year has passed Cousin.
>How swiftly the time has sped.
>Friends are scattered here and there,
>And some perhaps are dead.
>
>We have been spared for something Cousin.
>For what? we well may ask....
>
>You are now in the army my Cousin.
>Oh, manfully do your part,
>And while you fight your Nation's battles
>Guard well your *head* and heart.
>
>You are on the field of battle Cousin,
>Fighting your fellow man,

> And while you're engaged in war Cousin,
> Oh, do what good you can....
> I wish you many "Happy New Years" Cousin,
> And when this life is o'er,
> May you be borne on angels' wings
> To that brighter, fairer shore.[9]

In early January, Chamberlin wrangled twenty days of leave that included a stay in Boston, where he had his photograph taken. Just before leaving camp, he would have witnessed the execution of two Union cavalrymen who tried to defect to the other side. Riding away from Camp Russell, the deserters encountered a group of Confederate riders to whom they told their plans and provided details of the Union defenses. At this point, the "Rebels" pulled their guns and placed both under arrest. The defectors had had the misfortune of running into Sheridan's "Jessie Scouts," a group of sixty hand-picked volunteers who habitually dressed in Confederate uniforms and spoke with Southern accents. Named after Gen. John C. Fremont's wife, who suggested the idea, Sheridan continued their use after taking over the West Virginia Department, and under the leadership of Maj. Henry Harrison Young, they had considerable success in obtaining information from unsuspecting Southern citizens and soldiers.[10]

The acquittal of Captains James Smith and Stephen Wheeler allowed Colonel Seeley in early January to republish Major Birge's order dividing the regiment into three battalions commanded by Wheeler, Smith and Chamberlin. Soon after the latter left for Boston, Seeley was appointed acting commander of the 1st Brigade during Col. Peter Stagg's absence on leave. As head of the 1st Battalion, Wheeler took over command of the Twenty-Fifth during Seeley's absence; that is, until he became so intoxicated during an overnight stay in Winchester that he was unable to resume his duties and was replaced by Captain Smith. Evidently hoping to spare his regiment further embarrassment, Seeley tried to have Wheeler removed from the service without a court martial but was overruled by General Sheridan. Set free pending resolution of his case, Wheeler was captured during operations around Staunton in early March and was not paroled until the end of the war.[11]

In mid-January, the regiment participated in a reconnaissance towards Front Royal. Unable to cross the swollen Shenandoah, the Union soldiers were met by a detachment from the 7th Va. Cavalry carrying a flag of truce and escorting a member of the 1st N.Y. Dragoons, who had been left near Front Royal as a "safeguard." The Union soldier was ferried across the river and affirmed he had been well treated by the Rebels. In fact, an officer from Mosby's Rangers had recently spoken with his escorts and impressed upon them the need to respect the rights of all safeguards, adding that not having done so in the past had cost the partisans "dearly." Sheridan's cavalrymen considered this development "very significant," since it confirmed "our severe retaliation on the counties infested by guerrillas for their former harsh treatment of safeguards has brought them to their senses." (Poor treatment of safeguards was one of the primary reasons Sheridan cited for the raid into Loudoun.)[12]

Colonel Seeley was still in charge of the brigade when Chamberlin returned from leave. Leadership of the 25th N.Y. Cavalry was now rotated among the various captains, and Chamberlin waited until he was acting commander before writing Justin Morrill to ask the Vermont Congressman's assistance in obtaining a commission in the regular Army. After summarizing his military career, he stressed having "received these commissions without the assistance of my friends, but from merit alone." Three days later, Morrill replied that he had forwarded the letter to Secretary of War Stanton with an endorsement, but warned a transfer would be difficult to arrange at this time. Instead, he advised winning a promotion to major in the Volunteer Army and then switch after the war was over.[13]

Disappointed by Morrill's response, Chamberlin may have feared continued further service with the ill-fated Twenty-Fifth might only hurt his chances to enter the regular Army. He had given considerable thought to the request, which repeated a similar petition to Morrill the year before. Despite only limited opportunity to prove himself in combat, his performance in various staff positions showed many of the skills needed in a peacetime army. In addition, he had no family to return to, and the watchmaker's trade held little allure after all that he had seen and done in the past three years. With the end of hostilities in sight, Chamberlin turned to the only other profession he knew—as a career military officer.

Seeley's return to the regiment on 2 February after a stint as acting brigade commander did little to relieve the monotony of camp life, which was broken only by occasional patrols up the Valley, and the arrival of new troops for the anticipated spring offensive. Regimental records show numerous orders designed to keep the men occupied, ranging from a directive to air blankets regularly to construction of feed troughs and corrals for the horses. On Valentine's Day Chamberlin and two others were appointed to a Board of Inquiry to inspect mounts recently received by the regiment.[14]

BOB's letters reflect growing discontent over reduced food rations and the rising cost of Government-issued clothing and other items, which were not accompanied by an increase in pay, compounded by the paymaster's failure to appear since June.

> If this is justice, I should like to see a little 'injustice,' as 'justice' certainly does not work conducively to the interests of the men who have periled...their lives for the safety of the Union they love, but which is in more jeopardy by the ill legislation of the whisky-swilling buncombe speechefyers at home, than from Rebels in the field...They say they have increased the pay of a soldier. It is a lie! A soldier is now far poorer...than he was five years ago...I, in the name of thousands of other soldiers, ask the omnipotent press to advocate our cause.

The results of the last election had shown that soldiers were a potent political force, and their growing conviction that change was needed back home would reverberate long after the war, a movement in which Chamberlin would play a key role.[15]

On 1 February, Sheridan held a grand review of his Cavalry Corps on the site of his Winchester victory the year before. Seated astride his magnificent black horse Rienzi, "now made famous in song," he galloped down the line to the blare of trumpets and the acknowledgment of each regiment as he passed. The diminutive general seemed like a centaur of old as his staff tried to keep up. The Twenty-Fifth was unable to wave its banner on this glorious occasion, because "the storms of shot and shell to which it has been exposed [had] torn it into ribbons." The old colors would soon be returned home, and BOB appealed to the ladies of New York to sew a replacement. On a more humorous note, he added: "There were a number of Northern ladies witnessing the review...Perhaps you may suppose that I am rash in saying they were Northern ladies, but we knew they were, from the fact that not one of them had a pipe in her mouth! However, all Southern ladies don't smoke pipes, the more exquisite ones...only chew snuff!"[16]

The year had scarcely begun before General-in-Chief Grant began to query Sheridan about the Army of the Shenandoah's readiness to move south for the final drive on Richmond. On 12 February Sheridan reminded his commander the winter had been the worst in memory and snow still covered the Valley. Notwithstanding, he was just as eager to get started and had no intention of missing Richmond's fall, or the glory that would attend those who forced Lee's surrender. To get a jump on Jubal Early and mask preparations for the spring campaign, Sheridan passed disinformation through two Union spies that were known to be Confederate double-agents. Both were allowed to see foxes and hounds which had been specially procured to give the impression Sheridan planned to call his officers together for a great fox chase on the last day of February. The spies were then sent south on a mission which would enable them to pass the spurious story that Sheridan would not take the field until sometime in March.[17]

The *Sunday Mercury* correspondent decried the lack of any celebration to mark Washington's Birthday. "We did hope that the Commissary of the post would...have opened his heart and a barrel of 'rot' at the same time, and invited us all to join in a toast to the founders and the saviors of this country. No, not even an onion to put a drop in our eye, not a spoonful of sourkraut to moisten our lips." Two days earlier, the guerrillas had routed a scouting party from the 12th Pa. Cavalry, capturing sixty of them. "We must do the guerrillas the justice to say that on this occasion they attacked a force double their own number, and whipped them handsomely, but they well knew the regiment they had to deal with...The sooner the regiment is disbanded, the better for the service." One hundred men from the Twenty-Fifth, under the command of Capt. Edward Woodward, were sent out in pursuit, "but the Rebs, with their prisoners, had been too lively, and we only captured two stragglers from their party."[18]

* * * * *

Sheridan hoped to have his cavalry on the move by 25 February, and orders given to the Twenty-Fifth confirm it would be expected to travel fast and light during a one-way sweep through the Valley on the way to Richmond. Each cavalryman was issued five days' rations for himself and his horse, plus a half-shelter tent and a blanket. Enlisted men carried seventy-five rounds of ammunition for their carbines and thirty for their revolvers. Each squadron, plus the regimental command, was allowed one packhorse to haul additional supplies. Only "one colored servant for each officer and no more" could accompany the column. To maximize available troopers, those on sick leave were directed to give their horses to men without mounts.[19]

Heavy rains and melting snow had washed away the pontoon bridges at Harpers Ferry, delaying the departure of Gen. Thomas Devin's troops from their winter camp at Lovettsville. As a result, Sheridan's combined cavalry, now under the command of Gen. Wesley Merritt, did not depart Camp Russell until Monday the 27th, the last day of pleasant weather for several weeks. For the first time since October, Colonel Seeley was able to accompany his regiment into the field, assisted by squadron leaders Chamberlin and Smith. The New Yorkers remained part of Stagg's Brigade in the 1st Division, with General Devin replacing Merritt as division commander.

After reveille sounded at 4 AM on Monday, a profound sigh escaped the lips of the men in Seeley's regiment as they tore down the "many little contrivances for comfort which had been put-up, in hopes of a prolonged stay. But soldiers—more especially cavalrymen—are birds of passage, and 'have no abiding city here'." Sheridan personally led the column, some 10,000 strong, along the Valley Pike, a well-maintained, macadamized highway running between Harpers Ferry and Staunton. The horses, sleek and rested after the winter, "pranced and curvetted along in fine mettle," as their riders traded insults with the "sour-looking villagers" along the way. In all, the column covered thirty miles before halting for the night at Woodstock. The troopers from the Twenty-Fifth were just getting their fires started and saddles off, when they were ordered out on picket duty. The night was made longer as squads of Rebels constantly probed the Union lines before being driven off.

As the cavalrymen prepared to resume their march on Tuesday, orders were read prohibiting foraging, yet at the same time they were told to stretch their rations to cover eight days—for many it was the first indication they might not be returning to Camp Russell. The column left Woodstock in a light snow, and by the time it reached Edinburg, large numbers of Rebels could be seen on the right flank. After the Twenty-Fifth was assigned to guard a bridge until the supply wagons got across, Colonel Seeley led a charge against a party of Confederates trying to stampede the wagon train. Several "grey-coated gentry" were captured, and the rest sent "flying into the woods as if the devil was after them." This incident had a positive effect on the teamsters, who afterwards kept their wagons close to the main column. A large skirmish took place later at the head of the column, and as many as 1,200 Rebels under the command of Gen. Thomas Rosser were driven off.

The Union cavalry pushed on through Mount Jackson to the banks of the North Fork of the Shenandoah, where a halt was called until a pontoon bridge could be constructed. "Gen. Custer with his usual impetuosity, chafed under the delay…while the insulters of the flag he loves were in front, and undertook to swim the river, as the retreating Rebels had done." Leading the way, Custer reached the other side, but his men were heavily laden with rations, and several drowned before the project was abandoned. After the bridge was completed, the column passed through New Market and camped for the night within four miles of Harrisonburg, having covered twenty-nine miles that day.[20]

At first light on Wednesday (1 March), Sheridan's forces continued to drive the Confederates before them until they reached Mount Crawford, where the Southerners made a stand, while they tried to

"Sheridan Moving Up River." Sheridan's would men ford many swollen rivers before cornering Early's army at Waynesboro. (*Harpers Weekly*, 15 Mar 65)

burn the only bridge over the swollen North River. The capture of this crossing intact was critical, as the water was too high to swim and enemy fire from defenses on the far side prevented Union engineers from erecting a pontoon bridge. "But a sabre charge drove off the burning party, and, while some of our men went to extinguish the flames, another party stormed the heights and breastworks, and sent the Johnnys to the right-about." The Yankees pressed on so quickly, they overtook Rosser's personal supply wagon near Mount Sidney. At 3 PM the column halted for the night at Cline's Mills, about nine miles north of Early's winter headquarters in Staunton.

The order against foraging having been rescinded, Stagg's Brigade enjoyed "a bully supper of Rebel mutton and poultry," and was just getting settled for the night, when "Boots and Saddles" rang out about 9 PM Wednesday. The air "turned blue" with curses, as the men learned they would not get any sleep that night. Despite the dark, Stagg led his brigade out on the left flank, thereby circling around Rosser's camp without being detected, and eventually reaching their objective, a railroad bridge on the far side of Staunton. The Yanks set the extensive trestlework on fire, the flames giving Rosser his first indication the enemy was already behind his lines. Fortunately for Stagg and his troopers (including the Twenty-Fifth), the Confederates assumed only a much larger force would have dared penetrate so far, and thus gave the intruders a wide berth as they evacuated the area.

Their mission accomplished, Stagg's cavalrymen returned to Staunton early Thursday morning in time to meet the main body of Sheridan's Army, as it passed through the city on the road to Waynesboro, about fifteen miles to the east. Custer's 3rd Division was in the lead that day in a determined race to corner Jubal Early, before the Rebel commander could cross the South Fork of the Shenandoah and escape across the Blue Ridge. Because of their exertions the night before, Stagg's men were given permission to remain in Staunton to procure breakfast and feed their horses. "Foraging commenced on a large scale, and flour, bacon, hams, and tobacco were unceremoniously appropriated in immense quantities. A few of us had breakfast in the town, and we actually sat on chairs, ate from plates set on a table, on which a snowy cloth was spread, used knives and forks, and poured our coffee into saucers without the slightest accident happening, or the faintest symptom of cramp...!"[21]

About noon, the brigade, now designated the rear-guard, set off towards Waynesboro as quickly as the extremely muddy road would allow. On the way, they "heard the great guns thundering in our front, and knew that Custer, with his usual luck, had 'struck ile,' but anxious as we were to have a hand in the game, fortune was against us, and 'the battle was over, the victory won' before we reached Fisherville [about halfway to Waynesboro]." Custer had found Early with his infantry and cavalry outside of Waynesboro, their backs drawn up to a swollen tributary of the Shenandoah. Sensing a chance for immediate victory, he ordered his men to charge without waiting for reinforcements. Exploiting a weakness in the Confederate position, the Union cavalrymen made short work of the ensuing battle. Although Early and his immediate command escaped across the flooded river into the Blue Ridge, 1,600 Confederates surrendered and all of Early's artillery and supplies were captured, including a trainload of ordnance just arrived from Richmond.[22]

Stagg's Brigade remained at Fisherville for the night in a drenching cold rain that put out campfires as soon as they were lit. After two days in the saddle and without tents, "you can picture to yourself what a forlorn-looking lot of beings we were when the welcome notes of the reveille gave the sun permission to rise." Nevertheless, the brigade was eagerly preparing to set off Friday morning in pursuit of the fleeing Rebels, when Colonel Seeley learned his regiment would be returning to Winchester. Each brigade in Devin's Division had to furnish one regiment for a guard detail to accompany Rebel prisoners and captured ordnance, as well as Federal sick and wounded, back to Winchester. The detail was placed under Lt. Col. George Nichols of the 9th N.Y. Cavalry and consisted of the 4th, 5th, 22nd, 25th N.Y. and 1st R.I. Cavalry, as well as troops without mounts. As this detachment started back towards Staunton, the rest of Sheridan's cavalry crossed the Blue Ridge to join Grant's forces near Richmond, where they played a key role in the defeat of Lee's army. Ostensibly in hot pursuit of Early, Sheridan used this pretext to ignore his original orders to continue up the Valley, until he met Gen. William T. Sherman's forces coming from North Carolina.[23]

The job of convoying their charges back to Winchester proved no easy task for the troops Sheridan left behind. The weather remained nasty, rations were lacking for both Union soldiers and their prisoners, and the horses and mules were often too weak to pull the ambulances and wagons. Adding to the urgency, General Rosser had escaped at Waynesboro and was desperately trying to assemble a cavalry force large enough to free the prisoners before they reached Winchester. BOB's account of what befell the Twenty-Fifth continues:

> When we reached Staunton, Colonel Seeley received information of a large quantity of Rebel stores being secreted at the Insane Asylum; these he immediately seized, and amongst them were a large number of shoes, which he distributed to the most needful in the command. There were also about five hundred hams, which were soon adorning the saddle-bows of our gallant troopers.[24] Quartermaster [Isaac V.] Trust, accompanied by Captain [Stephen W.] Wheeler, having gone some distance from the command to search for forage for the horses, were captured by a portion of Rosser's command. We now learned that Rosser had come back with his force to endeavor to rescue the prisoners from us, and great watchfulness on our part had therefore to be observed.[25]

The greatly reduced Federal column headed out of Staunton on Saturday afternoon, reaching a point about five miles south of Mt. Sidney before nightfall. At 2 AM on Sunday (6 March), Captains Chamberlin and Smith went ahead with two squadrons to seize and hold the bridge at Mt. Crawford, which had been captured intact on the way south. Despite constant skirmishing with the enemy near the crossing, they were able to secure the bridge until the main column arrived that afternoon. Once all were across, the Twenty-Fifth tore up the span's roadway behind them, and pushed on to Harrisonburg that afternoon.[26]

After the war, Pvt. William Gardner (K) wrote Chamberlin asking assistance in obtaining a pension. He had used an alias in the Twenty-Fifth, and, to identify himself, asked his old captain to recall an incident at Mt. Crawford, when he had "saved" the private's life. Chamberlin had come across Gardner trying to keep members of the 22nd N.Y. Cavalry from breaking into a private home. Citing orders issued before they left Camp Russell that prohibited soldiers from entering dwellings, Chamberlin sent the other troopers away. Then, after he and Gardiner had breakfast, Chamberlin left the private to guard the house, which was occupied by "three Girls thare alone," and only rejoin the regiment when he saw it start to cross the river.[27] After busying himself fixing the door latch, which the other soldiers had broken, Gardner was surprised to find the Union column already on the opposite bank, firing back across the river at the pursing Rebels.

> ....I rode right towards the Rebs until I Came to the Steepest part of the Hill and then turned towards the River and Came on the Bridge [under fire from both sides], and the fier of [our] Rear guard was very unpleasant for me, and you was thare and told them who I was and not to Shoot toward me and then They had torn up the planks from the bridge and thrown them in the River and you and thay told me to Shoot my horse and Come on. But I concluded not and got Some pieses of Boards off the Bridge and laid them in the Stringers and walked my horse over and went on.[28]

Although Rosser's men hindered the convoy's efforts to forage food from the countryside, they failed to slow the column's progress until it reached the banks of the North Fork of the Shenandoah at Mount Jackson on Sunday evening. (According to Chamberlin's diary, the Twenty-Fifth spent Sunday night near Harrisonburg and did not arrive at Mt. Jackson until noon the next day.) Sheridan had kept the pontoon bridge used at this crossing on the way south, so word was sent ahead to Winchester for a party to meet the convoy with a replacement, but the messenger was captured and shot.

> We passed rather an anxious night, as our position was really a critical one. We were encamped on a narrow peninsula, with a formidable force in our rear, an almost impassable river on three sides of us, with all its fords guarded by entrenched riflemen. About an hour before daylight next morning (the 7th), the Rebels made a desperate assault on our camp, with hope of taking us by surprise and stampeding the prisoners, but we were too wide awake for them. The Twenty-fifth were in the line and ready in one minute from the first alarm being given by our pickets. The pickets were driven in and the Rebs came along, yelling like demons, thinking they had everything their own way, but as soon as they came within good range of our line, a withering volley emptied many a saddle, and sent them skedaddling to the rear as fast as their horses would carry them. We killed eleven of them, and took nine prisoners. One of them penetrated to the outer edge of the chain of guards which encircled the prisoners, and shouted, "Break and run, boys!" But he was unceremoniously told by some of the prisoners to go to hell, and one of our guards acted on the hint and shot him dead. Had there been any inclination on the part of the prisoners to escape, many of them would have done so, but the majority of them expressed...satisfaction at having been captured.[29] Their only regret...was that we did not get General Early. No wonder the men would not fight under a leader whom they hate with such a bitter hatred...They all spoke highly of...Gen. [John] Gordon, who had been removed, they affirmed, by the machinations of Early, as his talents showed the imbecility of the latter in too strong a light. Poor Early! He's down now, and everyone wants to have a kick at him.

> Shortly after daybreak on the morning of the 8th inst., there being no sign of the expected re-enforcements...and every minute a delay making our position more precarious...it was determined to force the passage of the ford. The river had fallen considerably during the night, and the water was now about waist-deep, although the current was very strong... [T]he Twenty-second New York and First Rhode Island charged across the river, stormed the enemy's breastworks, and sent him howling in the direction of Mount Jackson. The whole of the prisoners and dismounted men were then got across, the weak and sickly being ferried over behind mounted men...The whole crossing was under the immediate

supervision of Lieutenant-Colonel Seeley. All had been got over, except the rearguard—the Fifth New York—when Rosser made a charge on the latter, expecting to overwhelm them by his vastly superior numbers, but Major [Theodore] Boice, commanding the Fifth, by an instantaneous charge of front and countercharge, cut Rosser's force completely in two, and whipped them in the handsomest style, killing about twenty and capturing about thirty. General Rosser, in this fight, rode the horse which Captain Wheeler was using when captured. Lieutenant-Colonel Seeley, seeing the precarious position in which the Fifth were placed, drew the Twenty-fifth up in line on the bluff of the north bank of the river, to cover the crossing of the former regiment, but in the unexpected daring and brilliant move of Major Boice, and its admirable execution, rendering our firing one shot unnecessary.[30]

After the crossing at Mt. Jackson was completed, the column "marched that day and night until we reached Cedar Creek, which stream we forded about 2 a.m., of the 9th instant, and lay down for the balance of the night in one of the old camps of the Eighth Corps." Chamberlin's squadron brought up the rear during the thirty-mile march to Cedar Creek, skirmishing the entire way. The convoy was back on the road at dawn on the 9th, and shortly afterwards there was a scare outside Newtown, when a scouting party from Camp Russell mistook the column's advance guard for Rebels and fired on them. Fortunately, the error was discovered "before any blood was shed." The wet and tired troopers finally reached Winchester in the early afternoon and turned over their prisoners. The Twenty-Fifth, which had lost at least nine men on the return from Staunton, was displeased to discover it had been assigned to a campground with "no wood, no water, nor anything to eat." Moreover, the rain, which had been falling for much of the previous twelve days, turned into snow that night. Spirits improved somewhat the following day, when the "untiring efforts" of Colonel Seeley succeeded in getting the regiment moved to a better campsite about a mile outside Winchester. But the best news came several days later when the paymaster finally arrived with the soldiers' wages through the end of December.[31]

A week after its return, the Twenty-Fifth learned it would not be rejoining the old Custer Brigade, but instead serve on dismounted duty in the Harpers Ferry Military District. In anticipation of this move, the New Yorkers broke camp south of Winchester on 17 March and pitched their tents beside the Stevenson Depot train station north of the city. The next day, they turned in their government horses and loaded captured ordnance on the rail cars, which later that afternoon carried a party of men led by Chamberlin to Harpers Ferry.[32]

Chapter 11

PROVOST MARSHAL, POINT OF ROCKS, Md.:
March-June 1865

Once they parted ways in the upper Shenandoah Valley, members of the 25th N.Y. Cavalry guessed they would never rejoin Sheridan around Richmond. Part of the regiment, under Capt. S. E. Chamberlin, turned in their government horses at Winchester on 18 March and rode the train to Harpers Ferry, where they overnighted at the Soldiers' Rest. The following day Harpers Ferry's commander, Brig. Gen. John Stevenson, received confirmation from the Middle Military Division the entire Twenty-Fifth would arrive on 20 March to relieve the 1st Md. Home Brigade Cavalry (Cole's Cavalry) as guards along the B&O Railroad. The message included an aviso: "You will have to keep a strict hand on the Twenty-fifth New York, as it is said to [be] in not first-rate discipline, though full of officers. The general wishes you to hold the colonel [Aaron Seeley] strictly to the mark. You may have to send him before a board [of inquiry] unless he reforms his habits."[1]

The regiment originally believed it would be posted at Duffields Station, a railroad stop ten miles west of Harpers Ferry, but, when Colonel Seeley reported to Stevenson, he learned they were being assigned as provost guards along the B&O tracks between Harpers Ferry and Point of Rocks. (Cole's Cavalry was reassigned to the Twenty-Fifth's original destination at Duffield's Station.) "This order," BOB wrote, "though extremely pleasing to us, was very distasteful to the routed Marylanders, who had made up their minds to remain at this point until the close of the war, and a good deal of unnecessary ill-feeling was exhibited by them toward our boys."[2]

Stevenson had already transferred the Loudoun Rangers, a Union cavalry command raised in Loudoun County, to the Shenandoah Valley earlier in March, and loyalists in North Loudoun wondered whether the subsequent removal of Cole's Cavalry signaled a change in policy towards their county, now that the war was about over. But in his 20 March order announcing the Twenty-Fifth's assignment, Stevenson made the point that he only considered Loudoun a part of his Department of West Virginia, "when we occupy it." This position was a disappointment to Union sympathizers, who had long advocated stationing a permanent garrison in the county, but neither Stevenson nor his predecessors had been willing to take this step. Even now that the front had shifted far to the south, Col. John Mosby's 43rd Battalion still controlled much of the countryside and had become even bolder after Gen. Thomas Devin's troops left Lovettsville to rejoin Sheridan in late February. Stevenson had no illusions that Seeley's dismounted regiment could rid Loudoun of the guerrillas but may have felt the pacification process would proceed more smoothly under the auspices of a regiment other than the locally-raised Loudoun Rangers and Cole's Cavalry. Both had long been involved in operations in Loudoun, which might pose a liability once hostilities ceased. Cole's Cavalry and the Loudoun Rangers would remain in Jefferson County, W. Va., until mustered out of the service, although at least twenty Rangers stayed behind at Point of Rocks and Berlin to serve as scouts for the Twenty-Fifth.[3]

Seeley's regiment crossed the Potomac at Harpers Ferry on 20 March and spent the night at Camp Remount, located between the Maryland towns of Sandy Hook and Knoxville. There, the New Yorkers had to turn in any remaining government horses, as well as exchange their Spencer and Sharps carbines for single-shot Burnsides. At the same time, Seeley issued orders establishing his headquarters several miles farther east in Berlin (today's Brunswick), on a low hill overlooking the Potomac and surrounding mountains. The view prompted BOB to exclaim: "If picturesqueness was the only point to be studied in a camp, we might challenge the Army to beat us." From their tents, they could gaze across the river into Loudoun, "the home of Moseby's guerrillas," and soon learned their primary task would be to "prevent those wretches" from destroying the railroad and canal. (The Chesapeake & Ohio Canal was about to resume operation after suffering damage from the Rebels.)

> The campsite occupied by Cole's Cavalry was found to be in such "filthy condition… that Colonel Seeley would not allow his men to occupy it, but had the men carry down the logs and other fixtures and erect a new camp," *i.e.,* one closer to the town. It was promptly dubbed "Camp Seeley" by the officers, reportedly "in opposition to the wishes of the Colonel." [Since BOB soon revealed he was sleeping on a "featherbed," it is evident the colonel's close cronies were allowed to quarter in town.][4]

There was, however, less harmony inside the camp than its "picturesque" surroundings might have implied. One source of contention was the return of Maj. Samuel McPherson, who still smarted from his run-in the previous summer with the junior officers. This incident had led to his removal as acting commander, and the major ended up serving the next six months on detached duty. Most recently he had charge of a dismounted detachment of the Twenty-Fifth at Camp Remount, evidently arranged to keep him out of Seeley's way. (The *Sunday Mercury* correspondent dismissed the major's unit as one composed of "[dead-]beats and hospital 'vets'."[5]

BOB had equally unkind words for the regiment's chaplain, who had remained behind at Camp Remount while the Twenty-Fifth campaigned in the Valley. "I do not think he will be scared by the immense numbers who will flock to his ministrations. Soldiers are not such darned fools as most people seem to think them. When a man dons a forage-cap, he does not necessarily doff his common sense, and muscular Christianity is a commodity that is admired in the Army. We don't believe in fellows who, like the bombast in the play, make a stirring harangue to us to fight, and conclude…'when you've won the victory—let me know'."[6]

The addition of McPherson and several other officers to the regiment's active roster forced Seeley to restructure his command with the result that Chamberlin was demoted from head of a battalion back to squadron leader. Under the new arrangement, Major McPherson would command the First Battalion with assistance from his old allies, Capts. Edward Wood-

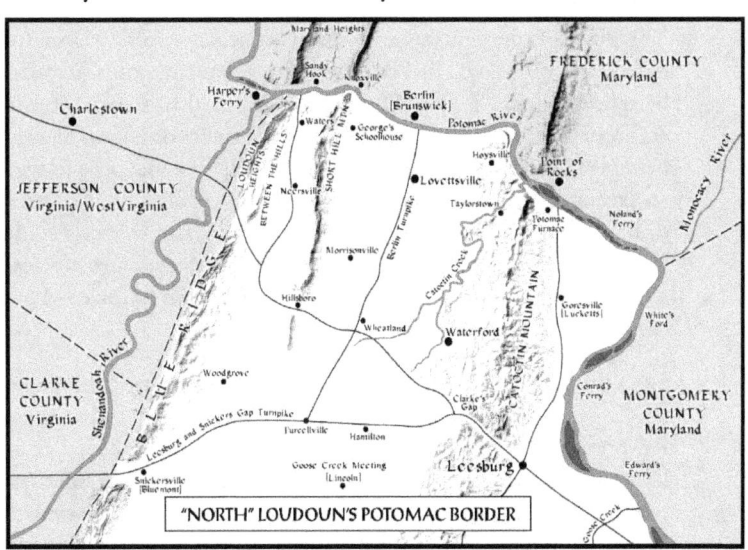

Map 2: (Jennifer Belland, artist. WFA)

ward (A) and Clinton Townsley (D), as squadron leaders. The Second Battalion was led by Capt. Nicholas Maffet (C), with Capts. Chamberlin and James Walters (M) as squadron leaders; and the Third Battalion was assigned to Capt. James Smith (E), with Capt. William Brusle (H) and another officer (to be named) as squadron leaders.[7]

The Twenty-Fifth's new assignment included supervision of civilian and commercial traffic along the Potomac border, a role previously exercised by the Loudoun Rangers and Cole's Cavalry. Battalion and squadron leaders would have little say in these matters, so Seeley's selection on 21 March of provost marshals to oversee civilian activities in the four principal towns within the Twenty-Fifth's jurisdiction provides an important indicator of the regimental pecking order. Captain Woodward was appointed provost marshal at Sandy Hook and given command over Companies A, B and L to serve as his provost guard. (McPherson's First Battalion headquarters were also located in this town.) Company D was assigned to Knoxville's provost marshal, Captain Townsley. Chamberlin was appointed provost marshal at Point of Rocks with command of Companies F and K to aid his provost duties. Captain Smith was assigned the key position of provost marshal in Berlin, where Seeley's headquarters and the rest of the companies were located.[8]

Later that afternoon, Chamberlin marched his two companies east along the C&O towpath to "the Point," where he established headquarters in a warehouse previously used by the Loudoun Rangers. It stood in a row of buildings between the canal and railroad tracks at a point where a pivot bridge allowed ferry passengers to cross the canal into town, and thus controlled civilian traffic into and out of Virginia. (The following week, Chamberlin would be joined by Arch Wilson, who was promoted to captain of Company F after a long convalescence.) Shortly after receiving their assignments, the Twenty-Fifth's four provost marshals went to Harpers Ferry to confer with Capt. E. W. Andrews. As provost marshal for the military district, Andrews had overall responsibility for the border eastward to the Monocacy River and would serve as their superior officer on all matters not directly related to the Twenty-Fifth.[9]

The myriad functions of a Civil War provost marshal are not well known today. Chamberlin already had some experience in this field from prior assignments with the 118th N.Y. Infantry and his short stay at City Point, but his responsibilities and authority at Point of Rocks would be considerably greater, particularly since it was a relatively isolated post. The office of the Harpers Ferry Provost Marshal was unique in having its own chronicler, Cpl. Charles Moulton, whose diary provides a working-level view of provost guard duties and served as the basis for the following description of the powers suddenly invested in Colonel Seeley and his officers:

> The Provost Marshal was a regular Union Army officer appointed and empowered to enforce military law. His Provost guard, a detachment of regular...soldiers, would today be called Military Police. The Provost Marshal had the authority to arrest anyone. He enforced martial law and could ignore the rights of *habeas corpus*. As a military governor he replaced civilian authority and was in effect a mayor, a judge, a jailer, and if need be an executioner. The Provost Marshal dealt with disciplinary problems in his own army, drunks, deserters, bounty jumpers, mutinous and thieving soldiers. He also dealt with local citizens, disloyal civilians, enemy sympathizers, prostitutes, whisky sellers, unruly merchants and traders, and a general line of camp followers. He regulated all trades and commerce and intercepted the mail.
>
> Since the Harpers Ferry area became one big army garrison, he had to administer the oath of allegiance to ascertain loyalty. There were guards and curfews to regulate the town. Anyone traveling here needed a pass from the Provost Marshal, and their baggage would be searched...Arresting and interrogating spies and guerrillas as well as receiving large numbers of captured prisoners from the front meant that much time was spent...processing prisoners...The Provost Marshal was even authorized to take political hostages.[10]

In a position much to his liking, Chamberlin found himself the ranking official at the Point. This included responsibility for the town's small permanent population, most of whom engaged in activities supporting the canal and rail line but was now swollen by refugees from the Virginia side, soldiers, and the usual camp followers that war begat. His duties also included oversight of civilian trade and travel across what was effectively an international border. However, cross-border activity had been severely curtailed in recent months and came to a complete halt on 25 March, when Stevenson closed the border to all non-military traffic, a ban that remained in effect for the next month. To bring him up to speed on cross-border affairs, Chamberlin relied on a small cadre of Loudoun Rangers that remained at the Point, as well as a group of Quaker exiles from Waterford, who held key positions there, including customs agent Samuel Steer and shopkeep John Dutton, who oversaw all mail crossing the border.[11]

Although Chamberlin could hardly have known it, he had reached a turning point in his life. Shortly after his arrival, he received a letter from Louise Fisher, a "sincere friend" from Boston. Nothing is known about her, except the two apparently met while he was on leave in January. She had since received two letters from him and, aside from expressing concern for his safety, seemed to be giving their relationship some encouragement, when she added: "As for myself, although our acquaintance has been so short, I am free to confess that you have won my admiration and respect. Not for your bravery alone, dear Captain, but because I believed I discovered those elements of character that ornament the *Christian gentleman*." She was particularly impressed he did not allow swearing in his command. Alluding to the horrors of war, "too little appreciated by those at home," Louise prayed he would be protected. One can only speculate whether their brief friendship might have blossomed into romance if fate had not already set him on a different path. However, the interlude with Louise signaled he was beginning to get over the loss of his wife and children three years earlier.[12]

The Twenty-Fifth's arrival coincided with an incursion into North Loudoun by Mosby's commissary, which had emerged from winter quarters to collect "the tithe" (grain and forage) from local Unionists. The partisans also scoured the countryside for young men to fill the dwindling Confederate ranks. This conscription included free Blacks, who were frequently seized and shipped south to work in labor gangs. BOB provided his own slant on this activity:

> [Our] almost monotonous duty is occasionally varied by a scouting party across the river into Loudon County, which is still infested by the gang of Moseby. This scoundrel has lately taken up a new branch of business, viz., nigger-stealing. He has already seized and run South several free negroes, where he sells at a cheap rate to some confiding fool with more Confederate script than brains. But his race is nearly run. The Loudon Rangers, an independent loyal organization, have determined on his capture, and they being all natives of that county, are as familiar with his homes and haunts as he himself.

Like many others, BOB (or his type-setter) may have confused Mosby with John Mobberly, a Loudoun native who led a small guerrilla band noted for its ill-treatment of Unionists and prisoners, as well as selling free Blacks into slavery. However, the Confederate Congress had only recently allowed the recruitment of Blacks into the Southern army, and four days later Mosby began conscripting them in Loudoun.[13]

The partisans had a secondary objective of destroying stills in the area. Like most military officers, Mosby worried about the ill effect of liquor on his troops and had already closed distilleries in Fauquier and southern Loudoun. Furthermore, the manufacture of whiskey consumed scarce grain needed to feed his men's horses until grass reappeared that spring. In particular, the Rebel leader wanted to shut down the Taylorstown distillery owned by James M. Downey, a prominent Unionist exile and Speaker of the House in Alexandria's Restored (Unionist) Government of Virginia. Downey's mill and distillery had long served as a popular rendezvous for the Loudoun Rangers, and, upon learning of Mosby's intention to destroy the still, four of them received permission from Captain Chamberlin to investigate. The scouts crossed the Potomac from Point of Rocks on 28 March and, after a short hike, found three partisans inside the still house, apparently more interested in filling their canteens than shutting the operation down.[14] Hidden in a nearby shed, they easily captured the Rebels as they emerged. BOB described the captives as "three of the most important" guerrillas ever taken in that area and, even though he garbled their names and ranks, including misidentifying one as Mosby's brother, they were a significant catch: Quartermaster J. Wright James, Pvt. John M. Bolling, and "Major" William Hibbs, the "notorious" commissary head, "chief scout, and one of the most universally-detested men in this section." According to BOB, the Rangers' main objective was to get horses for themselves, as they had had to relinquish their mounts when the rest of their command was transferred to the Shenandoah Valley. In this endeavor they were successful, as the scouts returned with "three of the most beautiful horses you could wish to look at," all taken from Mosby's men.[15]

General Stevenson was so pleased with this foray, he telegraphed Chamberlin the next day to have him authorize Sgt. David Hough and three other Rangers, "the same party who captured Rebel Officers...to scout in Loudoun for ten days, crossing at Point of Rocks. Capt. [Samuel] Means is to go with the party." (Permitting Means to accompany the scouting party was a favor to the former Ranger captain, which would allow him to take supplies to his family in Waterford now that the border was closed to civilian traffic.) This second raid under Chamberlin's direction was also successful, the scouts returning via Harpers Ferry on 31 March with four more prisoners, including the "notorious rascal and assassin" George Painter, a civilian wanted for killing a Loudoun Ranger the year before.[16]

Berlin's provost marshal had not been idle, and on 30 March Captain Smith led a party across the river to destroy "a number of boats, which the guerrillas had concealed on the other side." The skiffs more likely were used by smugglers to circumvent the blockade. As BOB would aver: "The people here declare that the blockade of the river was never before so vigilantly enforced as it is at present, and the discrimination of Colonel Seeley in selecting such able men for the position of Provost-Marshals as Captains Woodward, Smith and Chamberlin, thus reflects a high compliment." To the loyalists in Loudoun it was far too strict, and Chamberlin may have agreed with them when he wired Stevenson on 10 April for permission to allow four Unionists to cross the line to attend a "meeting of the Loyal citizens and refugees as convened by [Unionist Governor Francis] Pierpont to be held in Alexandria tomorrow." The district commander denied the request.[17]

Mosby paid a visit to Waterford with thirty followers on April Fool's Day, hoping to catch some Loudoun Rangers off-guard and commandeer wagons to carry off any corn that had escaped the "Burning Raid." Although he found no Rangers, he left a photograph of himself to taunt their commander, Capt. Daniel Keyes. This same photograph found its way back to Chamberlin.[18]

On 5 April, Seeley promoted Clinton Townsley to major, filling the vacancy created by Charles Seymour's resignation earlier in the year. The promotion "caused not a little surprise, as there were four captains in the regiment senior to him, but he was strongly recommended by Generals Merritt, Devin and others." Four days later, Seeley reorganized his provost guard, naming Major McPherson provost marshal at Knoxville and Sandy Hook. Major Townsley was transferred from Knoxville to the more important position of provost marshal at Seeley's Berlin headquarters, replacing Captain Smith. Chamberlin's position remained unaffected. Despite disappointment at not being made major, he still harbored hopes for fulfilling Justin Morrill's recommendation to win a promotion before re-

Col. John S. Mosby, 43rd Battalion, Va. Cavalry. This *carte de visite*, taken early 1865 while recuperating from wounds in Richmond, was likely left to taunt Loudoun Rangers. (Found in Capt. Chamberlin's wallet, TCC)

questing a transfer to the regular Army—not impossible given ongoing turmoil in the Twenty-Fifth.[19]

Even though Loudoun remained under Mosby's control, the war in southern Virginia was coming to an end. On 3 April Seeley announced the fall of Richmond during a dress parade punctuated by salutes fired from the regiment's howitzer. A week later, the New Yorkers were awakened at 2 AM by cannon fire at Harpers Ferry, signaling the surrender of Lee's Army the day before, and many expected to be home in a few weeks. That evening, Seeley and orderly William Maher, celebrated late into the night at a hotel bar in Knoxville. Their alleged conduct while in uniform, in particular leaving with two women of low repute sitting "man fashion" astride their saddles, would be later used to unseat the colonel. Seeley had reason to celebrate, but it is hard to fathom why he did so in the same town where arch-rival McPherson was named provost marshal the day before, who likely reported the incident to Harpers Ferry.[20]

Despite Stevenson's long-standing orders against the sale of alcohol, BOB revealed having "an abundant supply of good ale here, which Colonel Seeley, in his wisdom, allows to be sold to the boys, and I am glad to say that the privilege has not been abused. Whisky, or any other form of distilled liquor, is positively forbidden." Unstated was the colonel's arrangement for his brother to run the sutler's store where the ale was sold. When this came to light, Seeley had the store's owner, a Berlin merchant, named sutler in place of his brother. With time on their hands, the men also amused themselves racing horses. A roan belonging to Lt. George J. Underwood (K) had never been beaten, and its owner accepted a challenge with a purse of $600. Members of the Twenty-Fifth lost heavily when the roan lost, and BOB failed to explain where the dismounted regiment got its racehorses.[21]

The return of Capt. Louis Lazarus (G) after a year's captivity prompted BOB to lambast Northern peace advocates: "The account which he gives of his own and fellow prisoners' suffering is heart-rending, and I wish to God that some of the Northern Doughfaces and Copperheads, who more than any others helped to start and carry on the Rebellion, had to submit to them until they should make a full recantation of their cowardly treason; I think there would be many a sudden conversion." BOB was thinking of anti-war Democrats such as Mayor Fernando Wood, who went so far as to suggest that New York become a free city so it could continue to trade with the South. After the war Republicans would capitalize on this growing hostility among Union soldiers to the Democratic Party.[22]

A chapter in North Loudoun's internecine conflict closed on 5 April, when renegade chieftain John Mobberly was lured to a barn near Lovettsville and killed. It was carried out by a party of "civilian scouts" led by Sgt. Charles Stewart, a Loudoun Ranger whom Mobberly had viciously attacked a year earlier as he lay wounded on the ground outside Waterford. Stewart's chance for revenge came when Lovettsville farmer and sometime spy, Luther Potterfield, hatched a plan to catch the guerrilla leader. With Stevenson's approval, Provost Marshal James Smith armed Stewart's party and sent them across the river. According to BOB, who claimed other press accounts were incorrect, a member of this group (presumably Potterfield) sent word to Mobberly that he had quarreled with Captain Smith and now sought the guerrillas' protection. If interested, he was to meet him at Potterfield's barn. After Mobberly took the bait and was gunned down, his body was taken to Harpers Ferry, where souvenir hunters cut off most of his clothing. Loudoun's controversial "Robin Hood" was buried at Salem Church outside of Hillsboro, where a gravestone and poetic epitaph commemorate his wartime exploits.[23]

The sweet taste of revenge from Mobberly's death evaporated a day later, when the Loudoun Rangers suffered their most humiliating defeat. Colonel Mosby picked his newest subordinate, Capt. George Baylor, to attack the Virginia Yankees' camp at Key's Switch near Halltown, W. Va. Dressed in Union uniforms, Baylor's company crossed the Shenandoah early on 6 April and discovered the Rangers carelessly lounging around their campfires. Discipline had slipped under their new leader, Lt. Edwin R. Gover, who assumed the war over and momentarily expected news of Lee's surrender. (When the attack occurred, at least twenty Rangers were absent on special duty as scouts for the Twenty-Fifth, while others were out on a raid.) Gover's men paid little heed to the blue-coated horsemen until it was too late, and then offered only token resistance. Baylor's troopers captured thirty-eight soldiers, including Gover, and eighty-one horses. The captives, of little importance at this point, were quickly released, but the all-important animals were taken across the Blue Ridge. In reporting this fiasco, General Stevenson succinctly commented the Loudoun Rangers had been "cleaned out." Besides a blow to their pride, the Rangers had furnished their own mounts, and would be hard-pressed to find replacements before returning to their farms at war's end.[24]

Word of Lincoln's assassination on 14 April reached the Twenty-Fifth the next day with, as BOB described, devastating impact.

> It would be vain of me to attempt to depict the horror and indignation which was aroused in this camp when the news of the murder of President Lincoln was received here. At first no one would believe it, considering it one of the canards which are constantly flying around…But when full confirmation was received—when an official dispatch to Colonel Seeley placed beyond dispute that which we had looked upon as a lie, when told by the passengers on the train that first brought the news—profound sorrow became universal. The meridian of joy, in which all had been basking, at the glorious events which had crowned the nation's brow…was at once overcast by the darkest thunder-cloud…If J. Wilkes Booth—who has apparently been recognized as the murderer—receives but a little of the execrations and anathemas which were poured out upon him, hell would be a paradise for him.[25]

On 15 April Chamberlin and the other provost marshals were ordered to "arrest all persons applying at your post to cross the Potomac who are not known to be loyal and trustworthy. Give these instructions to the commanding officers of detachments guarding fords of Potomac and Monocacy River. The President and Secretary of State were both assassinated [*sic*, Secretary William Seward survived] last night, and the assassins will doubtless try to escape across the Potomac." The following day, a fifty-man squadron from the Twenty-Fifth crossed into Loudoun at Berlin in hopes of capturing the assassins, who were suspected of having links with Mosby's command. Not missing a chance to tout his commander, BOB predicted Seeley would make "that beautiful valley…too hot for the guerillas… The fruit of his efforts is shown in the fact that Mosby has sent in an offer of surrender…provided they receive the same terms as were accorded to the Army of Northern Virginia, of which he claims to be a component part."[26]

In fact, Seeley's operations in Loudoun seemed aimed more at seizing horses. On 17 April, a detachment, undoubtedly with Loudoun Rangers as guides, rode to Waterford "and gathered up about 20 sorry horses of secession farmers." Prominent Quaker farmer James Walker, already looking ahead to smoothing relations with his secessionist neighbors, demanded the lieutenant in charge show authorization for taking the animals. When he could not produce any orders, Walker called on General Stevenson, who confirmed no such orders had been given and agreed to have the lieutenant return the animals. Whether this actually took place is unclear. The Twenty-Fifth and their scouts were actively engaged in horse-trading, and the Loudoun Rangers had the additional incentive of replacing ones lost at Key's Switch.[27]

Flags were flown at half-mast and a twenty-one-gun salute fired at all military posts in observance of Lincoln's state funeral on 17 April. The following day, District Provost Marshal Andrew circulated a detailed description of the man who tried to assassinate Secretary Seward and called for his arrest, if he tried to cross the Potomac. Although no name was attached, the description was that of Louis T. Powell, alias Louis Payne, who had been a member of Mosby's command before being picked by the Confederate Secret Service to help Booth in Washington. Already aware of Payne's involvement, the U. S. Secret Service speculated he might try to cross into Loudoun, rather than follow Booth's escape route through southern Maryland. (By the time Andrew sent his message, Powell was already caught, having carelessly returned to Mary Suratt's boarding house, the same place Booth and the other conspirators used to plan their attack.) As late as 24 April, provost marshals along the B&O were advised to look out for Lincoln's assassin, paying special attention to the possibility he might be disguised as a woman. Booth was killed in Tidewater Virginia two days later.[28]

The desolation felt by North Loudoun's Unionists in the wake of Lincoln's death was partially relieved when they learned Mosby finally agreed to disband his command on 21 April, after over a week of protracted negotiations. Rather than surrender, he called his men together for an emotional farewell in Fauquier County before dismissing most of them to individually seek paroles. Mosby, however, did not resign his command, but instead led fifty men southward with the intention of joining Gen. Joseph Johnston's army in North Carolina.[29]

Although the last Confederate army did not concede defeat until May, the Federals considered the war in Loudoun over. Many along the border could begin to demobilize, but the 25th N.Y. Cavalry would remain for almost two more months, even though the blockade on the Potomac was lifted as soon as news of Mosby's "surrender" reached Harpers Ferry. Within days, the border was jammed with Virginians crossing into Maryland to purchase food and other necessities. On 24 April, Waterford farmer Edward Y. Matthews and seventeen-year-old daughter Edith joined the throng at the Point to buy supplies. Stopping at the provost marshal's office to check on claims for losses suffered during the Burning Raid gave "Edie" a chance to meet the cavalry captain in charge. As the principal Federal authority remaining on the border, the Twenty-Fifth was now directly involved in reestablishing order in Loudoun, a circumstance that facilitated further contact between Chamberlin and Edie. Despite Stevenson's prohibition of unauthorized visits into Virginia, provost marshals had valid reasons to check on the status of Unionists there. Thus, when Edie appeared in his office a few days later and invited him to attend services on 30 April at her Quaker meetinghouse and afterwards dine with her family, he accepted.[30]

The first ceremonial flag-raising of the Stars and Stripes in Loudoun took place at Lovettsville on 3 May, and was attended by authorities from Harpers Ferry, as well as Colonel Seeley and his staff. Most of the speakers were local Unionist politicians, but BOB credited the Twenty-Fifth's QM Sgt. William D. Haley with delivering "the speech of the day" and receipt of "the warmest plaudits." Continuing in his last known letter to the *Sunday Mercury,* BOB praised the entertainment and refreshments, which ended with a ball accompanied by a military band.[31]

Three days later, another milestone in Loudoun's apparent return to normalcy took place, when an assembly of local Unionists met in Waterford and passed resolutions calling for the rapid restoration of state and local governments. BOB planned to attend, but "was prevented from being present" and thus could give "no account of its proceedings." This suggests Seeley wanted his regiment to play a role at the Waterford assembly, much as it had at Lovettsville. Perhaps a military presence at a purely political event was deemed unwise by his superiors, but more likely renewed problems within the Twenty-Fifth prevented BOB and others from attending.[32]

Chamberlin's location at the Point provided some insulation from the latest upheavals in his regiment, and as provost marshal he was able to attend a flag-raising staged by the citizens of Waterford on 13 May that included dinner for "several hundred" and the reopening of the town's stores. Company K's captain termed it a "pleasant affair" in his diary and undoubtedly helped preside over the ceremony. Further signs of normalcy followed on 17 May when collection of customs duties on goods going into Virginia ceased. With the border now completely unrestricted, Chamberlin and his provost guard rejoined the regiment at Berlin at the end of May.[33]

* * * * *

Meanwhile, Seeley and five of his officers had been detained on 10 May, pending resolution of charges brought against them. (The others were Captain Smith (E) and Lieutenants Corwin Holmes (B), Frederick Eaton (E) and Samuel David (F), plus Adjutant Robert Cummings.) As he evidently intended in pressing the charges, McPherson assumed command during the time Seeley was on trial, and on the day following the colonel's arrest, he hosted a flag-raising and barbecue for the entire regiment at his Berlin headquarters, an indication he intended his new position to become permanent.[34]

Stevenson had been forewarned about the possible need to discipline Seeley when he first arrived, but testimony during the colonel's court martial indicates it was McPherson who instigated his arrest.

Bad blood between the two had festered for over a year, but a reprimand the major received from Seeley in early May brought their animosity to a head. Specifically, McPherson was charged with being absent from his post without permission, after he accompanied the Twenty-Fifth's band to the Lovettsville flag-raising on 3 May.[35]

When Seeley's court martial convened at Berlin on 11 May, some twenty separate charges were brought against the colonel, which can be summarized as follows:

- Seeley and his subordinates kept, swapped and sold horses captured during the Valley Campaign, in contravention to standing orders to mark them with a "U.S." brand and turn them over to the Quartermaster Corps.
- While the regiment wintered at Camp Russell, Seeley rigged the auction of a gold watch belonging to a deceased soldier so he could purchase it at a devalued price.
- He improperly appointed his brother, Isaac Seeley, as sutler at Berlin and allowed him to illegally sell beer to the soldiers from a store adjacent to the camp.
- On 10 April, he became drunk at a Knoxville hotel, and later that night he and his orderly departed with two women astride their saddles.[36]

The colonel pled "not guilty" to all charges and retained a lawyer. The trial's first week was devoted to testimony by prosecution witnesses, led off by Lt. Thomas Randolph Scott (D), the same officer whose appointment to the regiment sparked a protest the summer before. That McPherson promoted him to captain while Seeley's trial was in progress provided ample motive for Scott to testify against the colonel. To make space for Scott, McPherson dismissed Capt. "Arch" Wilson for allegedly having changed his orders to cover his servant's travel expenses (four dollars). The major had not forgotten that Wilson, then Chamberlin's lieutenant, signed the petition against him last summer. (Wilson was later reinstated with full honors.)[37]

When Scott and other prosecution witnesses tried to substantiate charges of "horse trading," they became bogged down by questions from the defense asking them to specify which horses were sold (or traded), and to whom. It was not long before the judges were totally confused about what was potentially the most serious allegation against the defendant. Chamberlin demolished the charge about the watch when he testified to having personally conducted the auction according to regulations and gave his professional opinion as a jeweler that Seeley overpaid for a broken watch that was plated, not solid gold. Clearly, the prosecution had expected different testimony from him. The witnesses to Seeley's intoxication were made to look petty for faulting an officer for celebrating Lee's surrender the day before. One prosecution witness, a captain no less, completely discredited himself by claiming not to understand the meaning of the terms "intoxicated" and "drunk." That Seeley's supporters brought pressure to bear on the witnesses is apparent from the court record.

The last prosecution witness, Lt. Charles Atwell of the Loudoun Rangers, was asked to identify a horse currently belonging to Seeley as one he had traded to the colonel for a captured bay mare. The defense succeeded in excluding the question on grounds it was irrelevant and not included among the original charges. The query implied, however, that some horses captured in the Shenandoah Valley may have been hastily exchanged with ones belonging to Loudoun Rangers to make it more difficult for the prosecution to prove its case. (Other horses apparently were hidden in Virginia, including some Chamberlin left at the Matthews farm, as described in a later chapter.)

After a delay to allow Seeley to testify at a separate court martial, the defense presented its case. Seeley's first witness portrayed his accusers as part of a clique that had waged a personal vendetta against their commander since the previous year. The second witness, Pvt. William Hough of the Rangers, testified that, several days earlier he had met the prosecution's lead witness, Lieutenant Scott, as the latter was leading another horse down the mountain towards Point of Rocks. The lieutenant voiced concern to Hough that Atwell's pending testimony at Seeley's trial might implicate him on the stand and result in his (Scott's) arrest. Presumably aware Hough was Atwell's father in-law, the lieutenant warned the Ranger he "knew charges enough" against Atwell to put him in prison. (Another source also once described Atwell as dealing "too much in horses") Hough's testimony undermined Scott's earlier statements by giving the impression he tried to intimidate a witness and was engaged in his own "horse business." In all likelihood, the Loudoun Rangers closed ranks behind Seeley to have the trial resolved as quickly as possible without undue prying into their own activities.[38]

After the regiment's other major, Clinton Townsley, testified on Seeley's behalf, Chamberlin had the distinction of being the only prosecution witness to also take the stand for the defense. Stating he had known Seeley since their regiment was being formed, the captain declared he had "always considered him a gentleman," and vouched that the colonel was held "in high favor with the General [Jackson] whose staff I was on." More critical to Seeley's defense was testimony by Berlin shopkeeper William H. Bush, who identified himself, not Seeley's brother, as the Twenty-Fifth's sutler. Bush explained that it was he who had hired Isaac Seeley to run his store, a technicality that served to insulate the colonel from accusations of nepotism. Finally, Knoxville hotel owner James Riley testified he observed no evidence of intoxication on Seeley's part on the night of 10 April. In the end, Seeley was acquitted on all charges on 26 May and allowed to return to his regiment two days later—an occasion marked by a spontaneous serenade from his men.[39]

The following day, the same court tried Seeley's orderly, Pvt. William Maher, who was accused of entering the colonel's personal stable in downtown Berlin on 13 May (two days after the latter's trial began) to remove five horses. Major McPherson had placed guards at the stable with orders to prevent anyone from taking the animals without his authorization, and Maher was challenged by the guards. The orderly, who had been drinking heavily, put a pistol to the head of one of the soldiers and forced his way in, but was eventually subdued. With Seeley already acquitted, the court chose to ignore the larger implications of why the colonel of a dismounted regiment kept a private "stable." Instead, the judges seemed more concerned over the orderly's blasphemy of the Army, when he exclaimed to the stable guards, "there is not a god-damned soldier in the regiment; they are all thieves, robbers and bummers." (Bummers foraged for supplies from the enemy countryside.) In the end, Maher was given a slap on the wrist and confined to quarters for thirty days under Seeley's supervision.[40]

General Stevenson's personal reaction to the outcome of both trials is not known, but the six officers from the 5th N.Y. Artillery who judged the two cases appeared more amused than shocked by antics within the Twenty-Fifth. Although the same court quickly condemned two deserters in unrelated cases, it was not anxious to pursue what seemed minor peccadilloes, now the war was over. Their sentiments were shared by many others, who preferred to bask in the glory of the great Union victory than dwell on the seamier side of the war. Corruption bred during wartime did not simply vanish, however, but would surface repeatedly in later years, most notably in Grant's administration.

Chamberlin's testimony showed loyalty to his commander without revealing anything that could be used against either of them. Why he originally appeared as a prosecution witness is intriguing and suggests McPherson might have threatened dismissal if he did not cooperate. Chamberlin, who had not forgotten the humiliating circumstances leading to his near resignation, certainly relished a chance to get back at his old antagonist, although he may first have waited until he could evaluate Seeley's chances for acquittal. (It is likely he also encouraged Private Hough, one of the Rangers who worked for him, to testify on Seeley's behalf.) His satisfaction over McPherson's failure to take over the regiment was tempered by realization retention of the status quo left no opening for a promotion.

Not long after Seeley's trial got underway, McPherson must have realized things were not going his way, both in the courtroom and in trying to run a regiment that was mostly hostile to him. On 19 May, the obviously worried major sent a message to the Harpers Ferry AAAG, requesting that the other five officers being held pending their trials "be furnished with a copy of charges preferred against them... as many of them claim their release [from arrest], by not having a copy of their charges." There is no evidence any of these officers were ever tried, an indication their cases were dropped after Seeley was acquitted, if not before. In a more trivial matter, when someone complained about soldiers from the Twenty-Fifth bathing nude in the canal where they could be seen by passing passenger trains, the major ordered his officers to restrict bathing "until after Retreat and not even then, when the usual trains are passing." The complaint and its response were symptomatic of life returning to normal, and soldiers were no longer exempt from society's norms.[41]

The Twenty-Fifth did not get to participate in the Grand Review for the victorious Union armies, which took place in the capital on 23-24 May and featured 200,000 Union soldiers marching along Pennsylvania Avenue. The Army of the Potomac, under General Grant, took up the entire first day; representatives from the armies of the West, led by General Sherman, paraded on the second day. For the participants, it was a highlight of the war, and the single most important ceremony in which the Nation formally gave thanks to its conquering heroes. One can imagine the disappointment Chamberlin and his companions felt in later years at not having marched past the Presidential reviewing stand. Instead of receiving adulation, they found themselves strung out along the Potomac, guarding a railroad and canal from an enemy that no longer existed, and suffering the humiliation of having their commander on trial.[42]

On the same day that he was released from arrest (28 May), Colonel Seeley issued sweeping orders undoing personnel changes McPherson had initiated during his absence, including restoring Chamberlin to his former position as battalion commander. Their services no longer needed at the Point, Chamberlin and his men rejoined the rest of the regiment at Berlin. While the captain was in no hurry to leave his Quaker girlfriend, most were eager to reunite with their families up north. Thus, when orders were received at the end of May for the Twenty-Fifth to report to Gen. Alfred Torbert's Cavalry Headquarters in Winchester, everyone assumed it was a final stop before heading back to New York. Leaving Harpers Ferry on 1 June, the dismounted enlisted men arrived at Stevenson Depot the next evening, only to remain there for over two weeks before being allowed to travel north by train on 20 June. After celebrating for two nights in New York City, the weary troopers proceeded to Hart Island to be mustered out on 27 June. (Chamberlin, left behind to testify in a court martial at Harpers Ferry, did not muster out until later.)[43]

And so the 25th N.Y. Cavalry passed out of existence, almost unnoticed, and certainly with little fanfare, other than two nights of partying in the city. In his last letter, BOB lamented the government's failure to issue a medal to all who served in the Union army. "The price would not be great. We ask for neither silver nor gold, just plain copper, but such a thing would be a priceless heirloom." It did not happen, and veterans of the Twenty-Fifth would have to wait a quarter-century before they arranged to have their own medal struck, the "Custer Badge."[44]

Much like the Grand Review in Washington, New York staged a ceremony to honor its returning heroes on 4 July, at which the various regiments ritually presented their flags to the governor, who was flanked by a host of notables, including Lt. Gen. Ulysses S. Grant. The Twenty-Fifth was represented by Lt. Frederic Easton, the same officer whom McPherson had tried to cashier two months earlier. Regrettably, the book published to commemorate this event, and which carried summaries on each regiment's accomplishments, contained barely a quarter-page on the Twenty-Fifth, with no mention of its engagements, leaders, or casualties. (By comparison, the summary on the 118th Infantry took up three pages.) It was a portent of things to come, as the Twenty-Fifth, without influential leaders or patrons to make its case, slipped into oblivion. There is no doubt the boys from Upstate farms and New York tenements could, despite repeated failures of leadership, fight when they had to, but they would have to wait until 1871 when Chamberlin seized on their performance at Fort Stevens to begin their resurrection from obscurity.[45]

PART II
Borderlands—Borderlines
Loudoun County, Virginia

Chapter 12

EDITH'S QUAKER ROOTS

Edith ("Edie") Dawson Matthews grew up on a farm outside of Waterford, then a thriving village in northern Virginia's Loudoun County. Her Quaker ancestors came to the New World in early Colonial times, and their faith profoundly influenced her upbringing. The Religious Society of Friends was founded in 1652 by English reformers opposed to the rituals and hierarchy of the Anglican Church. Quakers, as its adherents are often called, refused to pay tithes to support the official religion, doff their hats even before the king, or take oaths of allegiance. To emphasize their egalitarian principles, Friends wore the plain dress of working men and women and used the informal "thee" and "thou." In place of "pagan" names for weekdays and months, they employed a numerical system, *e.g.,* First-day (Sunday), Second-month (February). Their nonconformity led to persecution, and many fled to America.

The Society was founded upon the principle that God resides in everyone. Accordingly, Friends believe individuals can only discover true faith through communication with their own divine spirit, and they therefore emphasize personal meditation over instruction from a professional clergy. The Society has minimal structure and doctrine, but members meet regularly in small groups organized into Monthly Meetings. These in turn send representatives four times a year to larger Quarterly Meetings. The largest administrative body is the Yearly Meeting, and since 1790, Friends in northern Virginia have been governed by Baltimore's Yearly Meeting. There are no sacraments for baptism, communion, or confirmation, but in the past couples wishing to marry had to obtain approval from their respective meetings.

With no paid ministry, Quaker services are marked by silence until someone is moved to speak. The term "minister," however, was awarded members with a particular talent for speaking, or carrying out traditional ministerial duties, such as aiding the sick and performing missionary work. Women have always played a prominent role, often serving as ministers and elders. Friends place great emphasis on education for both sexes and established some of the first schools in Loudoun. Their general level of education, reputation for honesty, and businesslike ways gave them greater influence than their numbers might suggest. In particular, they were active in efforts to aid the underprivileged, including slaves, and were mainstays in the abolitionist movement.[1]

An equally important facet of Edie's background was her "Southern-ness." It is said the essence of being Southern stems from a love of the land and its way of life. In Edie's case, this affection was nurtured by a family which had remained in the area for over a century. Furthermore, unlike most Waterford Quakers, whose roots lay north of the Mason-Dixon Line, her ancestors had come to Virginia via Maryland. To be sure, Edie's parents sided with the rest of their Meeting in opposing Virginia's secession from the Union, nor did they own slaves, but the free Blacks employed as servants and field hands made the environment in which she was raised little different from countless other middle-class farms in Virginia's Piedmont.

The Civil War abruptly ended Edie's idyllic childhood and would, before it ended, curtail the active social life every "Southern belle" hoped to enjoy before marriage. Not surprisingly, she would look back fondly on happier times before the war, as she struggled to preserve the family farm and its way of life for her own children. Her love for Loudoun's rolling hills never waned, nor would she consent to live farther away than Baltimore and Washington. In doing so, she reflected a strong matrifocal tradition within her family that persisted throughout the nineteenth century. While marriage might change their names, a line of strong Quaker women remained in and around Waterford to preserve the extended family's identity.

Edie's descendants have accorded Thomas Taylor (c. 1725-1797) the honor of being their family's progenitor, even though he was not the first ancestor to arrive in the New World. Thomas was born into a prosperous English family, whose fleet of ships traded with the colonies. An only child, he was two years old when his parents died. Raised in London by an aunt, at age fourteen he was sent to Pennsylvania and "bound" to Zerubable Thacher, a farmer and member of Kennett Meeting in Chester County.[2]

On attaining his majority, Thomas moved to Frederick County in western Maryland, where in 1747 he received a patent for a fifty-acre tract of called "Mount Pleasant," and three years later bought an adjoining parcel, "Addition to Hazel Thicket." The properties were located on the Catoctin Mountain's eastern slope, about six miles southwest of Fredericktown, the county seat. Both purchases proved astute, as resurveys increased their size to several hundred acres apiece. Over the next thirty-five years, he and his sons made over fifty land transactions in Frederick County, leading one historian to label him an "English land speculator." Much of this land would be subdivided and resold to German settlers arriving from Pennsylvania.[3]

Thomas belonged to Monocacy Meeting in nearby Buckeystown. Established in the 1720s, it was the first organized church on Maryland's western frontier, and later fell under the jurisdiction of Fairfax Monthly Meeting, located twenty-five miles south in Waterford, Va. In 1750, Thomas married Caleb Pierpont, then a member of Baltimore's Gunpowder Meeting, but whose roots lay in the plantations of southern Maryland. Her great-grandfather, Samuel Chew, was born in Jamestown, Va., before becoming one of the earliest settlers in Calvert County, Md., where his plantation home (Maidstone) remains a well-known landmark. Caleb's upbringing was typically Southern—she inherited a slave from her father—and influenced her husband to adopt attributes of the planter class. Together she and Thomas raised eight children, of whom Edie's great-grandfather, Henry (1765-1811), was the sixth. Little is known of the Taylors' early years, although during 1754-58 Thomas served as overseer of a new road (roughly US 340) that crossed the mountain near his home. In 1767, Thomas purchased Pile Hall, a 360-acre farm on the west side of the Catoctin Mountain, a mile north of present-day Jefferson. Built some twenty-five years earlier by Richard Sprigg and named for his mother Elizabeth Pile, the dwelling served as the family's residence for the next seventeen years. Further evidence of Thomas's prosperity can be inferred from an elegant tall-case clock he had made in time for his eldest daughter's wedding in 1774.[4]

Caleb grew up with slaves, and Fairfax Monthly Meeting minutes document a lengthy dispute with her husband over this issue. Originally, Thomas hired slaves to clear and cultivate his land, a common practice among early Quakers. In 1762, however, it was disapprovingly recorded that he had purchased a "Negro" of his own. Ignoring the reprimand, he continued to buy slaves until 1776, when the Philadelphia Yearly Meeting formally prohibited the practice. Afterwards, Thomas was "much labored with on account of slaves, yet he continue[d] in the practice of keeping them in bondage." After meeting with him in 1778, elders from Waterford reported back that he "proposed releasing his slaves in two years, paying one of them wages," which gave them hope he would abandon the practice altogether. This indeed seemed the case several months later, when Thomas was persuaded to publicly denounce slavery, although the Meeting still wanted him to buy the freedom of a slave he had sold. Some compromise must have been reached, as the issue did not appear further in the minutes, even though at the time of his death in 1797, Thomas still owned two slaves, Moses and Jude.[5]

At the start of the Revolution, the two oldest Taylor sons were fined by Maryland officials for failure to enlist in the militia, although Thomas Jr. apparently later abandoned the Quaker faith and joined a local regiment. Throughout the war, the Society of Friends opposed any military involvement by its members, including payment of taxes to support the American cause, or the hiring of substitutes to fight in their places. Their stance increased animosity against the faith, and in some areas, Quakers had to flee. Tolerance for their pacifism was more widespread in Loudoun, although on one occasion a local recruiter forced several young Friends to accompany him to Valley Forge. When the recruiting officer complained to George Washington that his conscripts belonged "to a very peculiar religious sect" and "swear they will not fight," the general, who as a youth had surveyed land in Loudoun, admonished the officer: "I know these men: they neither swear nor fight." Washington then ordered them to return to Virginia, where they could best aid his cause by raising food for the soldiers.[6]

Monocacy Meeting, in decline since its house of worship burned in 1759, was "laid down" at the onset of the Revolution, when many members left for more promising Quaker settlements in Virginia. Thomas and Caleb delayed their departure until the end of the war, reflecting a need to attend to his substantial land holdings in Maryland, as well as differences with Fairfax Meeting over slavery. But in 1784, Thomas, then fifty-six, purchased a 300-acre tract in Virginia, about six miles north of Waterford. The property included a mill, and straddled Catoctin Creek, two miles from where it empties into the Potomac. The mill, the second oldest in the Loudoun Valley, was constructed of logs in 1737 by Richard Brown, and included a malt house, miller's residence, sawmill, and brew house. The Taylors' youngest son Henry was given responsibility for running the business, which was renamed "Taylor Mill." The main fieldstone dwelling, then called Millford and known today as Hunting Hill, is considered Loudoun's oldest intact Quaker home.[7]

One of Virginia's two northernmost counties, Loudoun extends eastward from the crest of the Blue Ridge to a point only twenty miles northwest of Washington, D.C. The Potomac forms its northern boundary, starting at its confluence with the Shenandoah River at Harpers Ferry and running southeast towards the capital. The low-lying Catoctin range bisects the county on a north-south axis, crossing the Potomac at Point of Rocks, Md. The western part of the county, lying between the Blue Ridge and Catoctin ranges, is known as the Loudoun Valley, and its rich soil and rolling hills attracted small farmers who typically made a living with few or no slaves. The northern half of this valley is drained by Catoctin Creek, which once provided waterpower for the mills and other industries that sprang up along its banks.

Although Loudoun was not established as a separate county until 1757, the Treaty of Albany opened the region to settlement after 1722, by prohibiting Native peoples from crossing east of the Blue Ridge. The first settlers were English land speculators from Tidewater Virginia, who arrived in the southeastern end of the county shortly before 1730. Their land patents became the basis for large slave plantations in that area. At the same time, a different migration pattern emerged to the west, where settlers of German origin from Pennsylvania established the "German Settlement" (around present-day Lovettsville) just south of the Potomac. They were followed by Quakers, also mostly from Pennsylvania, who settled along the Catoctin Creek be-

Millford, Taylorstown, Va. Reputedly oldest intact stone dwelling in Loudoun, it was purchased by Thomas Taylor in 1784. (c. 1940 photo, TCC)

tween the German and English settlements. Scots-Irish Presbyterians followed and occupied positions as skilled artisans and tradesmen.[8]

Loudoun's first Quaker settler, Amos Janney of Bucks County, Pa., established his homestead in 1733 and a short time later erected a log gristmill. The community that sprung up around "Janney's Mill" was renamed Waterford in the 1780s by an Irish joiner and cabinetmaker after his birthplace. The first permanent place of worship for the Quaker settlement was built in 1741 and named Fairfax Meeting after the county to which the area still belonged. Three years later it was upgraded to a Monthly Meeting with jurisdiction over Monocacy Meeting in Maryland.[9]

Four years after Thomas and Caleb Taylor moved to Virginia, their daughter Rachel married Abraham Griffith at the Fairfax Meetinghouse. A widower from a prominent Baltimore family, Griffith was accompanied by his daughter Ann (1771-1821). A romance ensued between Ann, then sixteen, and twenty-three-year-old Henry Taylor, but because of her age and their status as in-laws, the couple did not receive permission to marry from their respective meetings and opted instead for a civil service at Frederick in 1790. Caleb and Thomas welcomed the couple back to Millford and provided them with a residence of their own (a log dwelling, now called Whiskey Hill because of its proximity to the old distillery). Such was not the case with Fairfax Meeting, which disowned Henry "for neglecting attendance and for marrying contrary to discipline." (Ann was similarly condemned by her meeting.) Although both were readmitted to Fairfax Meeting in 1797, a dispute over the use of slave labor led them to discontinue active membership the following year.[10]

As they had in Maryland, Thomas and his sons acquired property around Millford, sometimes fueling disagreements with neighbors that ended in court, and there were other issues. In 1795, Henry's sister, Nancy (Anne) Taylor, was dismissed from Meeting for marrying a non-Quaker, and their brother Joseph was barred "after long care" and previous reprimands for drinking "to excess" and using "unbecoming language." Another brother was ousted in 1799 for "taking the Test [oath of allegiance], nonattendance & having dancing at his house." The Taylors were not the only backsliders in Waterford. In 1760, a visiting minister was shocked at "disorderly drunks" attending his service, while similar visitors the following year found cause to remonstrate against "those who are in the practice of stilling grain & using the liquor to excess." Another staid visitor in 1792 enjoyed the hospitality, but was dismayed by the music and "frolicking," noting his host's home was "crowded with most of the young people of this licentious little town." (Early visitors were more favorably impressed with the piety of Goose Creek Meeting, located ten miles southwest of Waterford in present-day Lincoln, Va.).[11]

When Thomas Taylor died in 1797, he left an estate worth over $22,000, consisting primarily of "lands and plantations in Maryland and Virginia." A small fortune in those days, it testified to the perseverance and financial acumen of the fourteen-year-old who had landed in America fifty years earlier. Eschewing luxuries in favor of real estate, his most valuable personal possessions were two slaves and the aforementioned clock. Much of his life had been spent clearing land and establishing settlements on Maryland's frontier, and even after moving to Virginia, Thomas chose relative isolation in the Catoctin foothills to a more comfortable life in town. Although he and Caleb remained Quakers, their dealings with Fairfax Meeting indicate they valued independence over conformity to the Society's dictates. In his will, Thomas left Millford, including the mill and 200 acres, to his youngest son Henry, with the stipulation that Caleb receive profits from the mill during her lifetime. The rest of his estate was divided among his heirs. Before he died, Thomas had land near the mill divided into lots for a proposed settlement, which his sons named Taylor Town (Taylorstown) in his honor.[12]

Despite Henry's generous inheritance, bad luck and poor judgment prevented him from matching his father's successes. The original log mill burned around 1803 and was replaced by a three-story frame and stone structure that still stands. The old mill was not insured, and Henry had to borrow money to cover the loss. Renamed "Taylor Town Mills," the new complex employed the latest milling technology,[13] and included a sawmill and double stills capable of making 180 gallons of whiskey. But by the time it was completed, Henry faced competition from a new mill a mile upstream, owned by John Hamilton. Establishment of the first post office in the area at "Hamilton Mills" in 1807 drew even more customers away from the Taylor business. Adding to his woes, Henry lent a large sum to a friend who later went bankrupt.[14]

Fortunately, additional income came from clover and wheat grown on the farm. Transported to Europe on ships belonging to the English side of the Taylor family, the flour brought high prices during the Napoleonic wars. Henry relied extensively on slave labor contracted from local landowners to work his farm. By not owning slaves, he hoped to avoid problems with Fairfax Meeting, although privately he felt having to hire laborers put him at a disadvantage with those who owned them outright. In 1798, Fairfax Meeting asked Baltimore for clarification on the issue, and Henry was not pleased with the Yearly Meeting's response that he must phase out all use of slaves. By then, he and Ann were so dependent on the practice they chose to distance themselves from the Meeting.[15]

Taylorstown Mill, c. 1920. Built in 1803 by Henry Taylor after original structure burned. (David A. Nelson, current owner)

They would raise six daughters and a son, beginning with the birth in 1791 of Edie's grandmother, Miriam Griffith Taylor. A useful, if not always accurate account of growing up at Millford was penned in the 1920s by Henry's grandson, also named Henry Taylor, when the author was over one hundred years old. Even though his father, Thomas Taylor, had been the only boy in the household, it was the six girls who received favored treatment. Raising seven children in a remote area forced their parents to hire a governess to provide home schooling. Later, each girl spent two years at boarding school in Baltimore, as those who did not send their daughters to finishing school were considered unrefined. Quaker women did not wear gaudy ornaments, but were nevertheless fashion-conscious. The Taylor girls, however, carried this to an extreme, dressing in the most expensive English silk and calico. Their father also took them to Washington each year when Congress was in session so they could acquire a taste for "society." The first to marry was Elizabeth, who was only fifteen when she wed the son of a local planter, an action condemned by Fairfax Meeting. Ann and Henry paid little attention to the education of their son Thomas, who spent his spare time fox hunting, or so Henry Jr. recalled being told by his father.[16]

Reportedly despondent over his financial situation, Henry died in 1811 at age forty-six, leaving five children under the age of sixteen for his widow to raise. The distillery was sold at this time, and a miller hired to run that side of the business on shares. Ann managed the farm herself, but was unable to resolve the family's financial problems, even with the help of six slaves. The strain took its toll, and she died in 1821 at age forty-nine. Her personal effects, even the family Bible, were auctioned off to pay debts. Ann's only son Thomas (then twenty-two) tried his hand at running the farm, but was ill-prepared for this endeavor. In 1822, he was dismissed from Fairfax Meeting for marrying a non-Quaker and moved to Leesburg, where his son Henry was born. When the youngest Taylor daughter reached her majority in 1830, the court ordered the remaining property sold, severing the family's direct tie to Taylorstown. Miriam and her three youngest sisters all married Quakers and ended up in Waterford, while their brother Thomas migrated with his family to Ohio in 1834.[17]

By all accounts, Edie's grandmother, Miriam Taylor, grew up in a decidedly un-Quaker atmosphere, one filled with partying, drinking and expensive frivolities. She was only six when family patriarch Thomas Sr. died, and without his restraining influence on her father and his brothers, their lavish lifestyle increased apace. As a young girl, Miriam got on well with her peers, a group that Waterford Quakers would later disapprovingly describe as "indulging in much gaiety and frivolity." As part of this circle, Miriam's "natural temperament led her to wear gay apparel and to join in the amusements of the day." While still in her teens, however, she experienced Divine visitations that prompted her to "renounce the vanities of the times," but all efforts by Miriam to adopt her faith's plain dress and speech were met with "taunts and sneers" from those around her. Unsure of what course to take, she often lay awake crying on her pillow. Finally attaining the age of eighteen in 1809, she moved to Waterford, where she joined Fairfax Meeting and rearranged her life in accordance with her religious beliefs.[18][19]

In addition to piety, Miriam had a "lively, social temperament" and quickly made new friends in Waterford. Passing over more promising suitors, she set her sights on Jesse Gover, who returned to the village in 1812 to open a saddlery, after serving an apprenticeship in nearby Leesburg. At Millford, Miriam would not have been allowed to consider an artisan as a potential spouse, but she was impressed by the young man's ambition and moral convictions. Furthermore, both shared the grief of losing a parent, as well as a determination to renew their faith after spending time in non-Quaker surroundings.[20]

Jesse's father, Samuel Gover, had labored for years as a carpenter to support his exceptionally large family. Like the Taylors, Samuel's forebears had known better times. His great-grandfather, Robert Gover, was one of southern Maryland's first Quaker settlers, arriving as a bricklayer prior to 1674. At the time of his death in 1700, Robert had amassed plantations in Calvert and Anne Arundel Counties totaling over 2,000 acres. His descendants augmented these holdings, which they farmed with slave labor, or rented out. Samuel's comfortable upbringing on one of these plantations was cut short when his father died in 1762, leaving ten children to divide his estate. By the time Samuel reached his majority, he had abandoned notions of becoming a planter. It is unclear whether this decision was influenced by growing opposition within the Society of Friends to the slavery, disruptions associated with the American Revolution, or the inadequacy of his legacy. Whatever the reason, he left southern Maryland in 1778, and transferred further inland to Pipe Creek Meeting in Carroll County.[21]

In 1784, Samuel moved again, this time into Virginia to join Waterford's Fairfax Meeting. Two months later he married Sarah Janney (*nee* Harris) at nearby Goose Creek Meeting. She was a young widow with two small children and went on to have fourteen more (ten of whom survived) with Samuel, an astounding number even in those times. Initially, the couple resided near Goose Creek, which helped cement ties with the influential Janney family, before moving in 1791 to Waterford so he could work for the Lacys, prominent local builders. In 1804, Samuel used proceeds from the sale of land inherited from his father to set up a cabinet and chair-making shop, specializing in the then popular Windsor chairs. Eight years later, he was able to purchase the workshop and adjacent house, a small brick and timber building on Main Street, which currently serves as Waterford's telephone exchange.[22]

Samuel and Sarah's son Jesse was born in 1791, shortly after their move to Waterford. Already his mother's seventh child, the subsequent addition of five more to the Gover household necessitated his being sent at an early age to be raised by Mahlon and Sarah Janney, an elderly childless couple. Mahlon, the only child of Waterford's founder, inherited the town's principal mill and had the means to arrange for his ward to receive a secondary education at a Quaker boarding school in Westtown, Pa. When Jesse reached the age of eighteen, he began an apprenticeship in Leesburg at a saddle and harness shop owned by his non-Quaker brother-in-law, George Head, Jr. After learning all he could of this trade, Jesse bought out his contract and opened a saddlery in Waterford. The business flourished, enabling him to hire his own apprentice three years later.[23]

Jesse's courtship of Miriam began soon after his return and culminated in their wedding at Fairfax Meetinghouse in 1814. Both twenty-three at the time, their union was justly said to be one of "true affection." Nevertheless, the untimely death of Jesse's mother, by her own hand, earlier that year cast a pall over the ceremony, and influenced the couple's decision to reside with Jesse's father, enabling Miriam to help care for her husband's four youngest sisters, ages nine to seventeen.[24]

A family crisis occurred in 1818, when Jesse's sister Ann gave birth to a son out of wedlock. The reputed father, Andrew Anderson, was a cabinetmaker and later a tavern keep. Ann was promptly dismissed from Fairfax Meeting, but her family supported the decision to raise the boy, named Edwin, in her father's house. When Ann married in 1833, she insisted her husband-to-be sign a prenuptial agreement that left any share in her father's estate to Edwin, a future officer in the Loudoun Rangers.[25]

Heartened by the success of his saddlery, Jesse began preparations to open a combined grocery and dry-goods store. In 1819, he borrowed $2,000 against Miriam's share of her father's estate in Taylorstown and used it to buy property on Waterford's Main Street, about a hundred yards up from the mill. The purchase included a framed-over log dwelling (known today as the Gover House) and two adjoining lots with frame buildings housing the store, as well as a separate lot with a brick residence that Jesse promptly sold to his father. When Samuel died a few months later, he left this house and its contents in trust to his four youngest daughters.[26]

Jesse and Miriam's marriage was blessed with four children. The oldest, Sarah Harris Gover (1817-1900), was named after Jesse's mother and destined to be Edie Matthews's mother. Henry Taylor Gover (1819- c. 1900) and Ann Taylor Gover (1820-96) were named for Miriam's parents, and the final addition, Samuel ("Sam") A. Gover (1824-1907), was named after his paternal grandfather. Their arrival served to blunt the loss of Jesse's father in 1820 and Miriam's mother the following year. (Jesse acted as executor for both estates, confirmation of his high standing in the extended family.)

Jesse's new enterprise, to which he added a butcher shop and hat manufactory, prospered, and, after selling Miriam's share in Millford for $1,500 in 1823 and freeing themselves from debt, in 1830 he was able to purchase a large brick home in Waterford's "New Addition" His son would recall that their new residence on Second Street was "always open to his [parents'] many friends, both members of the Society and others." Over the next decade, Jesse continued to acquire real estate, most of which was rented out.[27]

His success coincided with the zenith of Waterford's economic and political influence, which during the first half of the nineteenth century was only surpassed by the county seat of Leesburg. This prosperity derived from surrounding farms, which depended on the town for services and supplies. These same farms flourished on the valley's fertile soil, enhanced by a crop rotation system developed by local Quakers that helped make Loudoun the state's top agricultural producer. The village became an incorporated town with elected officials in 1836, a year after the following description was published:

Gover (l.) and Hollingsworth Houses, Waterford, Va. After purchasing both dwellings and adjacent store in 1819, Jesse and Miriam Gover sold the brick house to Jesse's father. When they moved to larger quarters, the clapboard dwelling served as home for sons Henry and Sam, from which they continued to run the adjacent store. (1940s postcard, TCC)

Waterford is a fine flourishing little village, situated 6 ms. N.W. of Leesburg.... The land is equal to any in the state of Virginia, admirably adapted to clover and plaister [gypsum], and is excellent wheat and corn land...the staple production of the county. Waterford contains 70 dwelling houses, two houses of public worship, 1 free for all denominations, the other a Friends meeting house, 6 mercantile stores, 2 free schools, 4 taverns, 1 manufacturing flour mill, and 1 saw, grist and plaister mill, and (in the vicinity) 2 small cotton manufactories. The mechanics are 1 tanner, 2 house joiners, 2 cabinet makers, 1 chair maker and painter, 1 boot and shoe manufacturers, 2 hatters, 1 tailor, &c. Population about 400 persons; of whom 3 are regular physicians.[28]

Both Jesse and Miriam found strength in their faith and took an active part in Fairfax Meeting. One of her first duties was to keep the Meeting's visitor log, a duty previously performed by Jesse's mother. In 1824, Jesse assumed responsibility for upkeep of the meetinghouse and graveyard, and two years later he was elevated to the rank of minister. His name continued to appear in the minutes on a regular basis, often handling disputes that arose between members. In 1834, Miriam also became a minister, and she and her husband took turns attending Quarterly Meetings in Pennsylvania, Ohio and Maryland.[29]

Mahlon Schooley House, 2nd Street. Jesse and Miriam Gover moved here in 1834, and it later passed to son Henry. (c. 1910, photo, WFA)

Their travels coincided with a period of internal discord that divided Friends into so-called Orthodox and Hicksite factions. The Govers, like the rest of their Meeting, were aligned with the Hicksites, whose members tended to come from agrarian communities, whereas Orthodox Friends were more prevalent in urban areas. The split's progenitor, Elias Hicks, accused the latter of wanting to make "the Society a more respectable body—to transform their sect into a church—by adopting mainstream Protestant orthodoxy." In line with the Society's founders, Hicks's followers argued salvation did not come through Christ's sacrifice, but through "the Spirit of Truth within." Hicksites "recognized the Bible as a valuable guide...but believed it remained secondary to the revelations of the inner light." (The Universalist Church in which Elliot Chamberlin grew up held similar views.) This dispute, which lingered into the twentieth century, was less acrimonious in Loudoun than elsewhere, largely because so few sided with the Orthodox side.[30]

Reflecting the growing importance of women in her Meeting, Miriam became its foremost spokesperson during the years leading up to the war, and second in influence only to Goose Creek's minister, Samuel Janney. Her ministerial duties were aided by a thorough knowledge of medicine, which she augmented by extensive reading. Local doctors, frequently finding her present at the homes of the sick, "would joke her and tell her she should get a diploma and practice medicine, —not thinking then that it was possible that women would ever be doctors." She studied the Bible daily, along with the lives and writings of prominent Friends, and called her family together every evening to discuss what she had learned. Her addresses during Meeting were invariably concise, well-spoken, practical rather than doctrinal, and bore evidence of "divine authority." She was said to be very accepting of other religions, "believing that all who know their Master's will, and do it, will be accepted by Him." Her home was open to all who sought advice, just as she was willing to travel afar to meet those in need. Mindful of her own youth, she advocated against what she termed the "folly of decorating the body," believing the time thus wasted could be spent in doing "much good in the world." Testifying to her ministerial talents were the many who found in her a way to awaken and comfort their own souls.[31]

Jesse involved his sons in his commercial enterprises at an early age, and both Henry and Sam became successful businessmen. When Henry turned twenty-one, his father made him a full partner in the dry-goods store, and at the same time arranged for fifteen-year-old Sam's appointment as caretaker of the meetinghouse and graveyard. This job paid forty dollars per year and gave Sam his first taste of working on his own. He also learned the saddlery trade as a young man, working in his father's harness shop before taking over the family store.

A paralyzing fever claimed Jesse Gover's life in 1842. His passing at age fifty came as a shock to his close-knit family and the community as a whole. A "large concourse of Friends and others" assembled at his home on 14 November to bear the body to the meetinghouse where Loudoun's two most eloquent Quaker ministers, Samuel Janney and the widowed Miriam, were moved to speak about the deceased and his steadfast adherence to their faith. The local press mourned the passing of "a man of great worth, beloved, respected and sincerely lamented by his numerous friends." A memorial published by his meeting emphasized how he raised his children to "live in the truth" and "seek wisdom from above." Before dying, he expressed a desire for his youngest son Sam to stay with and take care of his mother, although it would be Miriam who proved the rock around which the family and community gathered during the trying years ahead.[32]

Jesse's will specified his widow retain their residence and furnishings, plus the contents of the store. With his estate valued over $7,000, it was unnecessary to sell his other properties, which the children later divided among themselves. After his marriage in 1844, Henry took over his parents' residence on Second Street, while Sam and his mother moved into the log dwelling next to their Main Street store. Ann received the Arch House further up Main Street as her home, and Sarah, already married, rented out her legacy, a log cabin (the Collins Cottage) on the same street.[33]

During the period leading up to the Civil War, Loudouners voted overwhelming with the Whig Party in state and national elections. The county's leading Whig was John Janney, a former Quaker who was dismissed from the Society after refusing to condemn slavery. He reportedly lost a chance to become William Harrison's Vice President by one vote at the 1840 Whig convention, but their victory that year brought a bonus for the Govers. Jesse had actively campaigned for Harrison, and afterwards used his influence with Janney, a distant relative, to have his eldest son appointed Waterford's postmaster. Henry Gover was only twenty-two at the time and would hold the position until the Whigs lost their national influence in 1853. With Henry's appointment, the post office moved into the family's store, bringing a steady stream of customers. (The earlier Democratic administration of Andrew Jackson is credited with the dubious honor of introducing the "spoils system" into the Federal Government, with the result that party loyalty became a primary consideration for holding government office.)[34]

After his father's death, Henry expanded his store's product line which, in addition to "cheap groceries" and fresh meat, included patent medicines, fashionable clothing and brass candlesticks. He also increased advertising, such as a press announcement of exclusive rights to sell a new line of washing machines. Henry married Ann Eliza Gardiner of Baltimore in 1844, and the following year made his brother Sam, then twenty-one, full partner in the store. Henry was also an original investor and board member of the Loudoun Mutual Fire Insurance Company, which opened its first office above the Gover store in 1849 and still operates in Waterford. During the years that followed, the brothers seemed on track to surpass their father's accomplishments, and when Henry lost his position as postmaster, he sold his share in the store to Sam in order to devote himself to other ventures. Like his father, Henry remained active in Fairfax Meeting, serving as clerk and treasurer, in addition to winning a contract to renovate the Quaker school next to the meetinghouse.[35]

Little is known about the early lives of the two Gover sisters. Ann never married and remained in Arch House, except for a period spent on a Nebraska reservation when she and Samuel Janney were involved in Quaker efforts to improve the lot of Native Americans. A copybook prepared by her sister Sarah in 1834 has survived with orthographic exercises and original poetry. The poems show considerable talent, confirming the seventeen-year-old received a sound education at local Quaker schools. Many concern death and religion—not unusual themes for that era, but which also presage Sarah's moral severity in later life. One poem, however, was inspired by the teenager's recollections of a visit the Marquis de Lafayette and President John Quincy Adams paid to Loudoun in 1825, when she was eight. The celebrated visitors stayed at former President James Monroe's home outside Leesburg, and the festivities held in their honor are said to have been the most important social event in the county's history.

Family tradition is silent concerning Sarah's courtship by Edward Young ("E. Y.") Matthews, a Quaker farmer from Baltimore County.[36] They were married at Fairfax Meeting on 14 October 1841, when she was twenty-four and he was about to turn thirty-six. Jesse and Miriam furnished a large wedding for their daughter, and the seventy-five witnesses who signed the marriage certificate included many leaders in the community. After the ceremony, Sarah accompanied her husband to his family's farm outside Baltimore, their home for the next three years.[37]

Maryland apparently did not agree with E. Y.'s bride, who persuaded him to dispose of his share in the Matthews farm and look for land near Waterford. Aside from wanting to be near her own family, the town-raised Sarah apparently harbored dreams of owning a farm of their own, perhaps thinking of stories of Millford passed on by her mother and aunts. In February 1844, E. Y. purchased a 153-acre tract for $6,618 at an auction to settle the estate of Joseph Wood. Clifton was located a half-mile south of Waterford on the western slope of the Catoctin Mountain and was bounded on each side by farms owned by relatives. To the south lay The Willows, the home of Isaac Steer, whose only son, Samuel, was married to Sarah's aunt, Harriet Taylor Steer. Talbott, the 300-acre farm situated between Clifton and the village, had recently become home to one of E. Y.'s nieces. The original homestead of Waterford founder Amos Janney, Talbott, had been purchased by Isaac Walker, whose son James married Eliza Hunt, the daughter of E. Y.'s oldest sister. Their 1843 wedding marked the start of a close relationship between the Matthews and Walker families.[38]

To complete the sale, E. Y. and Sarah signed a promissory note for $3,400, to be repaid at the "highest legal interest." Clifton was still being rented out, so the new owners could only assume occupancy in early 1845. Their financial resources depleted, they twice borrowed money from Sarah's brother Henry to purchase livestock and farm equipment. Poor management by previous occupants forced E. Y. to

Edward Young Matthews and wife Sarah. (c. 1850 daguerreotypes, TCC)

place the farm's hilly land in pasturage to restore the soil before planting more lucrative cash crops. The barn and outbuildings were in disrepair, and the main house was a simple one-and-a-half story log cabin needing extensive renovation.

Within a few years, the Matthews family would include four daughters. The oldest, Ann ("Annie") Eliza, was born in 1844, while her parents were still living near Baltimore, and was evidently named after Henry Gover's wife. A second daughter, called Miriam in honor of Sarah's mother, arrived in 1845 after the family moved to Clifton. Auburn-haired Miriam was reputedly the prettiest, and her death in January 1853 was a severe blow that prompted a decision to renovate the drafty log cabin. Edith ("Edie") Dawson Matthews was born on 10 October 1847 and named for one of her father's sisters. The youngest child, Mary ("Marie") Ruth, arrived in 1850.[39]

E. Y. did not insure Clifton until 1850, when his brother-in-law sold him a policy with the recently formed Loudoun Mutual Insurance Co. The poor condition of the buildings is evident from the policy, which only covered the house for $150, less than its contents ($200), while the remaining barns, sheds and their contents were valued at a modest $250. A running account between 1848 and 1857 with the Schooley sawmill shows E. Y. making only small purchases of cut lumber for minor repairs until 1853, when he bought large quantities of building material to completely redo his home. The original log cabin was enlarged to a full two-and-a-half stories, and the outside was covered with lathe and stucco. Photographs taken just after the Civil War show a comfortable whitewashed home with shuttered widows, a Greek Revival front porch and white picket fence surrounding the yard. It was a tableau similar to other antebellum homes in upper Virginia.[40]

According to census data, the farm's value rose from $7,000 to $9,600 during the decade following 1850, mostly due to improvements to the house and construction of a new barn. By 1860 E. Y. estimated his personal property at $2,600, mostly attributable to farm equipment and livestock, but also reflecting acquisition of furniture and other household effects. During the same decade, production of cash crops—wheat and corn—doubled, while the value of his livestock dropped by half, as acreage was switched from pasture to cropland. Grain from Clifton was ground at Waterford Mills, one of the most prosperous enterprises in the county. This operation changed hands in 1859, when Samuel Means purchased it, and began shipping flour to market with the help of a brother who ran the train depot at Point of Rocks, Md.[41]

In fact, most farmers in the northern part of the Loudoun Valley shipped their produce into Maryland rather than south through Virginia. The period 1830-60 was marked by tremendous growth in the

Marie, Edie and Annie Matthews (l. to r.), c. 1858, when Edie was about 10. (TCC)

nation's transportation system, an initiative closely associated with the Whig Party. Like their counterparts elsewhere, Loudoun Whigs ignored social issues such as slavery to focus on ways to improve their regional economies. The almost simultaneous completion of the Chesapeake and Ohio (C&O) Canal and the Baltimore and Ohio (B&O) Railroad in the 1830s had an immediate impact. The canal began in Georgetown, D.C., and followed Maryland's Potomac shoreline west to the coal fields near Cumberland. Yet, it was soon rendered obsolete for all but heavy cargo by the arrival of the B&O rail line, which began in Baltimore but followed the same right-of-way as the canal between Point of Rocks and Harpers Ferry. To facilitate commerce via both modes of transportation, local companies were formed to build bridges across the Potomac at Point of Rocks, Berlin (Brunswick) and Harpers Ferry, and connect them with turnpikes stretching southward into the Loudoun Valley's rich farmland.[42]

As a result, inhabitants of northern Loudoun could now easily ship produce to the ports and markets in Baltimore and D.C., as well as travel the same rails to buy supplies. Faced with a decline in revenue, investors in the port of Alexandria launched several initiatives to recapture trade by building a railroad through Loudoun to the Shenandoah Valley. Early plans had the tracks going west through Leesburg to Waterford and Hillsboro before connecting to existing rail lines at Harpers Ferry. The Alexandria, Loudoun and Hampshire Railroad, under the able leadership of Alexandria businessman Lewis McKenzie, proved the most successful of these ventures, and succeeded in extending track as far as Leesburg before the war halted construction. Like other farmers in the area, E. Y. purchased stock in the company, but never saw the expected benefits.[43]

By the late 1850s, the Matthews family enjoyed a relatively comfortable existence, even if Edie's father, now in his mid-fifties, had made little headway in paying off the note on the farm, or the loans from Henry Gover. The girls could not help their father with heavy farm work, but they were expected to assist their mother and two house servants with laundry, sewing, cooking, gardening and other duties that made up the daily and seasonal round of a rural housewife, regardless of her social status. Far from resenting these chores, Edie looked back on this period as one of the happiest of her life. A small stream running through the bottom of the yard was a favorite spot to play with younger sister Marie, and the upper fields provided enticing venues to pick berries and wildflowers. All three sisters were educated at the Quaker school in Waterford, and the oldest daughter Annie later went to Springdale Academy, a boarding school run by Goose Creek's minister, Samuel Janney[44].

Chapter 13

SECESSION: 1859-61

When the Matthews family celebrated Edie's twelfth birthday on 10 October 1859, they had no reason to believe their lives were about to dramatically change, nor, six days later, did they sense anything amiss, other than note the effects of the season's first killing frost, as they made their way to First-day meeting. Yet, just fifteen miles away, abolitionist John Brown and sixteen followers were preparing to steal into Harpers Ferry that night and capture the U.S. Armory—an act which would profoundly affect not just Loudoun County, but the entire nation. While Brown's hoped-for slave insurrection never materialized, and he and most of his men were killed or captured within days, the attack galvanized both sides of the slavery issue.

Once word of the raid reached Leesburg, the local militia mobilized and hastened to the scene, albeit too late to participate in the action. Awakened to the suitability of Loudoun's mountains to harbor abolitionists intent on freeing Brown, who after a hasty trial was being held in nearby Charles Town, pending execution, local militiamen stood watch along the Potomac to repel a possible invasion. Waterford magistrate Charles Anderson empowered a vigilance committee to conduct nighttime inspections of "negro quarters and other places suspected of having...unlawful assemblies."[1]

Despite the turmoil, E. Y.'s family and others made their way to Winchester on 10 November to attend Sam Gover's marriage to Margaret (Maggie) A. Parkins at Hopewell Meeting. Sam was a favorite of the Matthews girls, who never missed a chance to visit his store. Their uncle had obeyed his father's injunction to watch over his mother, but all agreed at age thirty-five he should marry, and Maggie, also thirty-five, seemed an ideal choice. The only child of Nathan Parkins, owner of a thriving mill outside Winchester, she shared Sam's views on abolition and the need to preserve the Union.[2]

At first, Friends tried to skirt issues raised by Brown's raid, and a Northern visitor was surprised to hear no mention of it during the February 1860 Quarterly Meeting in Waterford. Indeed, Fairfax Meeting

"Harpers Ferry Insurrection," October 1859. U.S. Marines under Col. Robert E. Lee storm John Brown's fort. (*Leslie's Illustrated*, 5Nov59, LC)

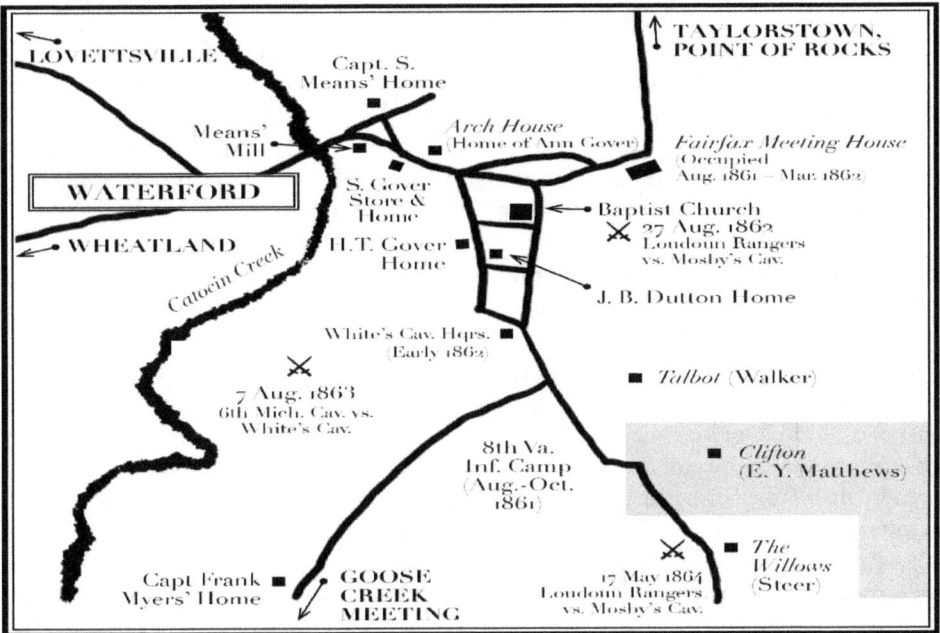

Map 3, Civil War Era Waterford. (Adapted by Electronic Ink from 1853 Yardley Taylor map)

minutes provide little indication anything unusual was afoot. Like their ancestors during the Revolution, its elders hoped by remaining neutral they would be left alone during any eventual conflict. Had Fairfax Meeting represented a cohesive majority in Waterford, this strategy might have prevailed (as it did in nearby Goose Creek) but it had only a tenuous hold on its younger members, and even apolitical Friends such as E. Y. Matthews would have to make hard choices pitting their faith against the sectional divisions sweeping the land.[3]

In the ensuing months, Loudoun's radical minority, fanned by Leesburg's *Democratic Mirror*, cited the North's failure to condemn John Brown as ample reason to revamp the county's military preparedness. Although compulsory for men under age forty, Virginia's militia had become a largely ceremonial organization, given to parades and a means for wealthy landowners to earn military titles. Edie's father was too old to serve, but Quakers paid small fines to exempt themselves from drill. Regular militiamen were not uniformed and had to provide their own arms. Better *esprit de corps* and preparedness characterized *volunteer* companies, whose members furnished their own uniforms in return for arms supplied by the state. Leesburg had two such companies, but there were no volunteer units in northern Loudoun until the Hillsboro Border Guards were organized after Brown's raid.

Infantry, however, could not easily patrol the county's lengthy Potomac border, and to address this need, Capt. Thompson Paxson, owner of a farm south of Clifton, raised a volunteer cavalry company known as Paxson's Troop. One of his lieutenants, Frank Myers, also lived nearby, and at nineteen was not much older than the Matthews girls. In the fall of 1860 the troopers were issued sabers and revolvers and outfitted in spiffy grey uniforms that made them the envy of their young friends. Their motives for joining varied, as did their allegiance to the Southern cause. One young Quaker, John W. Hough, succumbed to peer pressure and enlisted, for which he was promptly censured by Fairfax Meeting. After he refused to resign, Henry Gover and James Walker were appointed to reason with the youth. When this failed, Edie's uncles recommended Hough's dismissal, but the Meeting as a whole opted to delay any final decision, an early sign Waterford Friends were not of one mind on issues such as military service and neutrality.[4]

As summer stretched into fall, the presidential election began to worry many Loudouners. Virginia arguably had more in common with border states like Maryland than with the Deep South—something particularly true in a county situated barely thirty miles from both the Mason-Dixon Line and the U.S. Capital. Loudoun's "Old Line" Whig majority had up that point shown little interest in states' rights issues that monopolized political thinking in far-off Richmond, and instead sought to preserve the Union by sidestepping the issue of slavery. The so-called "peculiar institution" never dominated Loudoun's rural economy to the extent it did farther south. In fact, slave numbers declined slightly from 1800 until 1860, when they represented a quarter of Loudoun's 21,744 inhabitants. During this same period the number of free Blacks rose, despite slave owner opposition to their presence. By far the largest grouping of free Blacks was in Waterford, where they made up a third of the population. Most were employed as farmhands, day laborers and washerwomen. (The 1860 census listed two Black field hands and one White domestic living at Clifton.)[5]

Dissolution of the Whigs' national party in the 1850s left moderates without a political home. Many sided with the American ("Know-Nothing") Party, but it too disintegrated after carrying only Maryland in the 1856 presidential election. That same year, a few flirted with the Republican Party, which organized in Virginia for the election despite widespread opposition to its abolitionist platform. Inspired by their father's participation in Virginia's first abolitionist convention in 1827, Henry and Sam Gover dared to support the "Black Republicans" (as their Democrat opponents invariably labeled them). A Republican operative in the 1856 campaign recalled both brothers having been "conspicuous" on his party's Southern mailing lists for their well-known opposition to slaving and for having "aided many a slave to freedom."[6]

Southern radicals' rapid rise in influence finally moved Virginia moderates to make a belated effort to regain control of their state, which had almost unwittingly allowed itself to identify with the goals of the Deep South. Aided by an anti-secessionist governor and a split in the Democratic Party, which fielded two presidential candidates in 1860, former Virginia Whigs rallied behind yet another new party, the Constitutional Unionists, hoping to find a compromise that would keep the nation intact. (In Loudoun, this effort was spearheaded by its longtime political leader, John Janney.) Although Southern Democrats mounted a spirited campaign for John Breckenridge, on election day Loudouners continued to show a preference for moderation by giving Constitutional Unionist John Bell sixty-nine percent of the vote (eighty-three percent in Waterford). Statewide, however, the Southern Democrat only lost by a narrow margin to Bell. Despite efforts of party activists such as Edwin Gover, Northern Democratic candidate Stephen Douglas garnered only 120 votes in Loudoun, and Abraham Lincoln, the national winner on the Republican ticket, received just eleven votes. Lack of a secret ballot and intimidation discouraged some from picking "Old Abe," while others turned to Bell as the best way to forestall secession. Two Waterford Friends and a handful from Goose Creek risked reprisals to align themselves with the despised "Black" Republicans. Two were married to daughters of Henry Taylor: Wheatland miller David Mansfield and Samuel Steer. The latter joined the party while living in Baltimore and continued to support its abolitionist goals after returning to his family's farm next to Clifton.[7]

Lincoln's victory led South Carolina to secede in December, and other states in the Deep South followed suit in early 1861. Unable to delay any longer, Virginia held elections in early February to select delegates for a convention in Richmond to decide the issue. There, under the chairmanship of John Janney, moderates held the upper hand, voting as late as 4 April to reject secession. But the shelling of Fort Sumter, deliberately timed to influence Virginia's decision, and Lincoln's call for 75,000 volunteers to crush the rebellion, swung the tide against the moderates. Under tremendous pressure and threat of an armed coup, the convention decided on 17 April to secede, despite negative votes by both Loudoun delegates. Ignoring a requirement that the resolution be submitted to a statewide referendum, secessionists acted as if Virginia was already in the Confederacy and immediately sent armed militiamen to seize the U.S. Armory at Harpers Ferry and Norfolk Naval Yard. A short while later, Robert E. Lee accepted command of Virginia's armed forces, and Jefferson Davis was invited to move his government to Richmond.[8]

Eliza Walker, E. Y. Matthews's niece and mistress of Talbott, bemoaned the turn of events in letter to her son Elisha: "Secession, has spread like a raging epidemic...I was almost sick yesterday [20 April] at hearing [South Carolina's] Palmetto Flag was floating over the Court House in Leesburg." Noting ruefully how many erstwhile "Union men" had switched sides, she rejoiced her son was away at college, as otherwise the authorities would "order thee to muster & go to fight." There was to be a mandatory muster in town that afternoon, and Eliza's uncle had come over from Clifton to discuss the situation, now that paying a fine was no longer an option. Both agreed "*Friends* will *not* obey & likely we may have much trouble." Furthermore, E. Y. expected his brother-in-law Henry Gover and others would "go to jail rather than respond to the summons."⁹

Paxson's Troop was also struggling to prepare for war, having been ordered to guard the bridge crossing to Berlin. Despite having gotten his men handsomely equipped, the captain now had to order them to procure mounts from local farmers, who bitterly complained over what they called "stealing." The company's composition mirrored "the divided sentiment of North Loudoun," consisting of a "few hot secessionists, a few hot to fight against it, and [the rest]...waiting for events to decide for them." Paxson himself was not keen on being sent to the front, having confided to Eliza Walker "he never expected to go to war," but had gotten up his company for "parades & musters." As it turned out, their stay at the bridge, about a mile north of Lovettsville, proved little more than an abbreviated camping trip before the untried troopers were ordered to restore the horses to their owners. Dejected, Paxson and his men returned home, and a short time later his company was disbanded. The only active Quaker in the troop, John Hough, was admitted back into Meeting after acknowledging the error of his ways.¹⁰

As the 23 May referendum neared, Loudoun's political and military leaders were heartened by the dramatic shift in favor of secession throughout most of the county but were aware this sentiment was not shared closer to the Potomac border. Hoping to avoid a sizable negative, they suspended militia drills and confiscation of horses that had so infuriated north Loudouners. The May vote included election of state delegates, and among the candidates vying for these seats were two Unionists, Dr. John J. Henshaw and Rev. William F. Mercer. Deliberately ignored by the press and unable to stump outside of north Loudoun, Henshaw and Mercer ran a campaign that attempted to link local Unionists to a separatist movement already underway in western Virginia. In a last-minute bid to influence the outcome along the border, secessionists arranged a rally for their candidates at Lovettsville. During this event, Mercer managed to get on the platform and ask why small farmers should have to fight to protect plantation owners and their slaves. In its only mention of either Unionist candidate, Leesburg's *Mirror* dismissed Mercer's resort as an attempt to incite class warfare.¹¹

As expected, secession was approved in Virginia by a large margin, except in those western counties that two years later would become West Virginia. In Loudoun, secession won by 1,628 votes to 726. Majorities in only three precincts along the northern border opted to stay in the Union. Waters (Neersville) in the extreme northwest corner voted thirty-nine to twenty-six against secession, as did Lovettsville by a decisive 325 to forty-six margin. Waterford tallied a similar Unionist landslide, 220 to thirty-one. The three precincts accounted for eighty percent of the county's pro-Union total and reflected a "North Loudoun" identity that persisted long after the war. Of more immediate importance, their vote demonstrated the Confederacy's failure to gain control over the far reaches of the county before the outbreak of hostilities.

That memorable day, E. Y. Matthews joined the rest of Fairfax Meeting in voting unanimously to preserve

Henry Taylor Gover in his 40's. Support for abolition forced him to abandon successful career and flee into exile. (1860's Baltimore studio photo, TCC)

the Union. In taking this path, Waterford Friends began to exhibit a more robust embrace of Unionism than their counterparts in Goose Creek, where many including its acknowledged leaders, Samuel Janney and Yardley Taylor, stayed away from the polls, and Samuel's brother Asa Moore Janney voted to secede. By contrast, Waterford's turnout, encouraged by activists such as Samuel Steer and the Govers, was notably higher than in recent elections. Looking at these results, the *Mirror* branded Unionist voters "traitors," and singled out Waterford for actively conspiring to undermine Virginia's unity.[12]

Having shown singularity of purpose in the referendum, North Loudoun hunkered down to await the inevitable reckoning, as Rebels scrutinized poll lists to identify every vote against secession. Their farms were the first to have horses, wagons and forage taken, and active supporters of Lincoln's Administration were singled out for retribution. Losing candidates Mercer and Henshaw got out in time to attend a separatist convention in Wheeling that resulted in the creation of the Restored Government of Virginia, headed by pro-Union Governor Francis Pierpont. Although Henshaw and Mercer were warmly welcomed by the other delegates (mostly from the western counties), their bid to have Loudoun included in Unionist Virginia was rejected for the time being, on the grounds they did not represent a majority of their county.[13]

Henry Gover (forty-two) fled to Baltimore, where he enlisted his brother-in-law's help in getting employment with the Treasury Department. Despite letters to the Treasury Secretary and the President describing Henry as unable to return to his Virginia home because of his support for the Republicans, Edith's uncle failed to land a government job, and instead set up a trading company in Baltimore, Gover & Gardner, that specialized in getting produce out of Virginia for use by the Union side. His family joined him the following year, and their Waterford home was sold soon after the war.[14]

Virginia Troops on Maryland Side Prepare to Burn Point of Rocks Bridge. (*Harpers Weekly*, 29Jun61)

On 9 June, Waterford spinster Rebecca Williams exclaimed in her diary: "Great excitement and confusion this morning. The bridges at Point of Rocks & Berlin both burned by the crazy secessionists. It seems as though destruction and desolation are their only pursuit." Along with the bridges at Harpers Ferry, the Confederates hoped their destruction would deter a Yankee invasion and inhibit contact between "disloyal" Virginians and Federal troops on the opposite side. Regardless of political persuasion, everyone along the border was affected, and their outrage increased a few days later, when Rebel soldiers forded the Potomac to block the railroad tracks between Point of Rocks and western Virginia, an act that contributed to Maryland's decision to stay in the Union. Despite these belligerent moves and the proximity of the opposing forces, the first weeks after the May vote saw little military activity. Much to the dismay of Loudoun loyalists, the Federals passed up this opportunity to come to their rescue in favor of a static defense that focused on keeping Maryland out of the Confederacy. As Unionists would discover, a precedent had been established.[15]

North Loudoun's Fifty-Sixth Militia Regiment resumed drill in June and, with those opposed to the Confederacy keeping their opinions to themselves, all appeared in order. This changed when rumors spread that "the militia would be ordered [to Manassas] to aid in a grand battle." Yet, despite warnings of Unionists' intentions, local authorities were unprepared when, on the night before being mustered into service, large numbers of militiamen fled across the river. At the 14 July induction ceremony, "the answer given to many a name at roll call, was, 'gone to the United States'." Fewer than twenty of the one hundred-man Waterford company were present, and even more defected at Lovettsville and Taylorstown. In all, some 1,000 exiles left Loudoun during the war's first year, of whom an estimated 200 came from the Waterford area. Union sympathizers who remained behind were seized and taken to Leesburg. Although most were released after signing loyalty oaths, able-bodied men could be forcibly impressed into the army. The *New York Times* picked up the story, proclaiming, "The reign of terror in Loudon...is at its height." After Loudoun's three militia regiments failed to participate in the Battle of Bull Run, which began on 18 July and ended with a Yankee rout three days later, they were summarily ordered afterwards to commandeer wagons teams and forage for the victorious Confederate army. What remained of the 56th Militia assembled at Wheatland (three miles west of Waterford) on 26 July and spent the next few days pressing and hauling supplies to Manassas. It would be the militia's only contribution to the Southern cause.[16]

With early victory no longer in sight after the ignominious defeat, Northern forces along the upper Potomac adopted more cautious tactics to probe enemy lines in Virginia. Aided by exiles who served as guides, the Federals conducted small raids across the river near Lovettsville in early August. To put an end to these sorties and better deal with what he saw as widespread disloyalty in Loudoun, the Confederate commander at Manassas, Gen. Pierre Beauregard, dispatched a brigade to Leesburg under the command of Col. Nathan G. Evans, a fellow South Carolinian.[17]

On arrival at the county seat, Evans was confronted by rumors the Yankees already controlled Lovettsville. To deal with the purported threat and put a stop to further treachery, Evans led an expeditionary force into North Loudoun on 13 August., unaware his approach was being monitored by two spies from Waterford. Suspecting a Confederate offensive was imminent, the Union commander in Berlin sent Samuel Steer and Amasa Hough, Jr., to investigate. The two Quakers crossed the river after dark and, evading Rebel pickets by creeping along fence rows in a thunderstorm, reached their hometown after midnight. Learning Evans' forces were already on their way, they hurried back with the news, taking along "16 colored men," who feared being sent south and sold into slavery. Hough and Steer reached Berlin barely an hour before the Confederates arrived on the opposite shore.[18]

Despite reports to the contrary, Evans entered Lovettsville "without opposition, it having been deserted by most of the inhabitants, who unfortunately were for the most part sympathizers of Lincoln." The Quaker spies had alerted the German Settlement to the Southerners' approach, and aside from an exchange of shots across the Potomac, there was no fighting. Nevertheless, according to a Rebel artilleryman, the colonel "allowed the troops to appropriate the property of those citizens who had fled, thereby doing great wrong not only to them, but to some innocent ones."[19]

The following day, the column withdrew to Waterford, where the soldiers commandeered the front of Sam Gover's house for Evans' headquarters. The same artilleryman found this town more hospitable: "Here we halted two days, our guns being put in position near an ancient Quaker meeting-house....Our men occupied its portals two nights, and we are glad to say treated its sacred precincts with all respect. The inhabitants of this pretty village are for the most part Quakers; and whatever else may be said of this silent sect, certain it is that they treated us kindly." As in Lovettsville, Evans found many villagers had fled before his approach.[20]

Aware his "opposition to secession made him a marked man among his disloyal neighbors," Sam Gover and his wife abandoned their once thriving mercantile business before Evans occupied their home. Despite his mother remaining there, she was unable to prevent her son's adjacent store from being ransacked. Meanwhile, Sam and

Samuel A. Gover in his 30's. President Lincoln would make the loyal Unionist Waterford's next postmaster. (c. 1860 daguerreotype, TCC)

Maggie made their way to Washington, where his "services, sacrifices and condition were reported to President Lincoln, who sent [for them] to come to the Executive Mansion." After the interview, the President appointed him to become Waterford's postmaster as it was possible. In the meantime, Sam remained in the capital working at a cousin's shoe store, while Maggie went back to live with her mother-in-law.[21]

Waterford's other store owner, John B. Dutton, had four young daughters, which influenced his decision to remain in town despite being an outspoken supporter of Lincoln's administration. Nominated along with fellow Quaker Dr. Thomas Bond to represent North Loudoun in the Wheeling separatist movement, their six-man delegation failed to leave before the border closed. The shopkeeper therefore could not have been too surprised when Evans' men hauled him off to a military prison in Manassas. Fortunately, Dutton's daughter Lizzie was able to secure his release from "durance vile" two weeks later.[22]

The expedition's show of force had its desired effect, and Yankee incursions stopped for the time being, leading the *Mirror* to assure readers there were no Northern troops left on the Virginia side. In reporting the enemy prudently "vamoosed" before the Southerners arrived, the newspaper dismissed rumors that Evans' column had routed a large body of "Hessians," killing 300 and capturing 1,700. Given the exaggerated stories circulating in Leesburg, one might suppose they referred to some distant region, not one just a few miles away. As to the arrest of "several" citizens from that area, the newspaper predicted the prisoners would be afforded a fair trial and acquitted, if found innocent. But if guilty, they would have to bear "the consequences."[23]

Evans' visit convinced him the northern border could not be defended without establishing a permanent garrison in Waterford. On 18 August, officers from the Madison Cavalry rode up to Fairfax Meetinghouse during First-day services and informed worshipers they intended to commandeer the building as a barracks. Fortunately for the congregation, it had a sliding partition to permit separate men's and women's meetings, and the Quakers negotiated a compromise whereby the soldiers would occupy one half, leaving the other for worship. From their new post, the Madison troopers patrolled the border between Lovettsville and Point of Rocks, an arduous task alleviated by the arrival of the Loudoun Cavalry the following month.[24]

Taking no chances, Evans also sent the Eighth Virginia Infantry. The foot soldiers, most of whom came from Loudoun, established their encampment on high ground south of Waterford on the west side of today's Clarke's Gap Road. It was the largest body of soldiers to spend significant time in the vicinity, and, while the small contingent of local secessionists was delighted by

Fairfax Meeting House, Built c. 1760. Moveable partitions allowed Friends to continue services after Confederate occupation, and it remained in use until 1927 before being converted into a private residence. (WFA)

their presence, others were not. Within a week, Rebecca Williams complained of soldiers "raviging [sic] the country of horses, fruit and almost everything; taking people's corn, potatoes & destroying the fences..." Female visitations to the Rebel camp did not escape her jaundiced eye: "[O]ne of the sad effects [of war] is the depravity engendered by such an idle plundering life, calculated to stifle all good and kindly feelings. Even the taste of the softer sex is becoming viciated [sic], as is evident by the continual running of carriages fill'd with them to the camp."

Individual companies spilled onto adjoining farms, including Talbott, Clifton and The Willows. On top of war taxes, their owners now had to feed hungry soldiers. Sometimes they received Confederate scrip in return, sometimes poultry and livestock just disappeared along with fence rails for campfires. Free Blacks working on Quaker farms dispersed, fearful of the Rebel troops. With her brother across the border, Rachel Steer now had to run The Willows by herself. Seeing the forty-seven-year-old driving a wagon through town moved an acquaintance to comment: "What a change for her...she has to see after everything indoors and out."[25]

John Dutton's arrest signaled a campaign to intimidate local Quakers prior to their August Quarterly Meeting at Goose Creek. On the same Sunday Waterford's meetinghouse was occupied, Samuel Janney had to appear before Colonel Evans, who warned the Goose Creek minister not to oppose military rule in the county. Although Confederate cavalrymen surrounded Janney's meeting, they did not take over the building, and the quarterly assembly was allowed to take place. With so many younger members in exile, the Waterford delegation was mostly confined to a conservative group of elders. Except noting "care" being extended to several Quakers who had broken the Society's prohibition against military service, Quarterly Meeting minutes contain no allusion to the war. However, with Evans' warning fresh in his ears, Janney offered to draft a "statement of our principles." The following month the resulting document was sent to Waterford, where it was approved prior to publication in the press. In this joint communiqué, both Meetings affirmed their status as citizens of the Confederacy and willingness to obey its laws, except those requiring them to bear arms.[26]

Goose Creek Friends abided by these precepts and, in return, were allowed to practice their religion with their livelihoods relatively unmolested. The situation was different in Waterford, closer to the border, where events had overtaken the elders' ability to put the genie back in the bottle. There, the townspeople had voted overwhelmingly against secession; and from there many had already fled to Maryland, making them traitors in the eyes of state and local officials. Many were actively abetting the enemy by serving as informants; others would put country ahead of faith and take up arms against the South.

For the most part, opposition remained hidden and Rebel-occupied Waterford became a popular destination for off-duty soldiers from Leesburg. An English officer assigned there penned the following rather fanciful description:

> [A]s our camps were near the little town of Waterford, many pleasant hours were spent there among the pretty Quakeresses and widows—the latter being numerous and handsome. With their little town of one [sic] street screened by surrounding hills, the inhabitants seemed perfectly happy and contented: they possessed a fine mill, two woolen cloth factories, several tanneries; had a large meeting-house, two small chapels, a newspaper and excellent grazing land all about them. In general aspect, Waterford looks much like an English village, only that the inhabitants were prouder in step, wore better clothes, and had rosy, well-cut features that plainly indicated the best of "blood." A large number of the men had decamped into Maryland; but the women, Heaven bless them! were as true as steel, and behaved like heroines on all occasions...[Although their] creed forbade warfare, they fought amazingly well with the tongue in favor of Unionism, and had on several occasions betrayed our men to the enemy.[27]

* * * * *

Previously serving as northern Loudoun's primary commercial outlets before the war, Berlin and Point of Rocks now became home for its exile. Established to service the canal and rail line, both settlements found themselves thrust into national prominence due to their location on a front line that also served as a main artery linking Washington with the Ohio River. Belying its picturesque setting, prewar Point of Rocks was a "hard place" where fights were common, and consisted of little more than "half a dozen white washed cabins." Construction of a bridge in the 1850s made it a convenient shipping point for Waterford's farm produce, and the preferred gateway for travel to the North.[28]

On assuming command of the Army of the Potomac after the Union defeat at Manassas, Maj. Gen. George B. McClellan gave Maj. Gen. Nathaniel P. Banks' division responsibility for the sector between Harpers Ferry and Washington. Within Banks' division, Col. John W. Geary's 28th Pa. Infantry was enlarged into a brigade that guarded the Potomac from Harpers Ferry to Point of Rocks. At forty-two, Geary already had an impressive résumé, serving with distinction in the Mexican War before holding positions as San Francisco's first "Anglo" mayor, and governor of Kansas Territory. Somehow he found time to oversee a struggling iron foundry in Loudoun, across the river from Point of Rocks. Back in Pennsylvania, after selling his share in the Virginia foundry, the popular Geary had no trouble raising the "oversized" 28th Pennsylvania.

Having known the colonel before the war, local Unionists were elated when he established headquarters at the Point in mid-August, but were less enthusiastic when Geary, convinced secessionists were smuggling vital supplies into Virginia, banned all civilian travel and commerce into Loudoun, a measure that included closing several ferries established after the bridges were burned. Despite his travel ban, the colonel welcomed refugees for the information they possessed, such as the two "colored teamsters" from the 8th Virginia who escaped with an officer's diary. Aided by these exiles, Geary's soldiers resumed sporadic raids across the river. Distrusting the loyalty of the Point's inhabitants, Geary put his soldiers in charge of the railroad station, post and telegraph offices, and the ferry.[29]

Waterford miller Sam Means and his brother Noble got a head start at the Point after they rented a large warehouse there in 1858 to serve as a store and freight depot. Once Sam purchased Waterford Mills the following year, his teams hauled flour, mail and other freight to and from the Point on a regular basis before war brought a halt to the brothers' lucrative enterprise. Sam's troubles multiplied after he rebuffed Confederate efforts to have him raise a company, a decision reflecting the sentiments of his wife Rachel, a staunch Unionist and member of Fairfax Meeting. In retaliation, the Rebels sacked his mill and seized other possessions, leaving him little choice but to flee into exile. When his role in guiding a Federal attack on a Loudoun Cavalry camp was discovered, Sam was branded a traitor and the Leesburg court began proceedings to seize his mill and other real estate. (Similar legal action was opened against the absent Henry Gover.) Remembering him from his earlier days at the Point, Geary began using Sam to develop a network of informants inside Loudoun, and by late fall was lauding the miller as "one of our principal and most valuable Scouts." But Sam had set his sights higher than being a spy, hoping instead to organize Loudoun exiles into a cavalry force that could protect their families back home. Although Geary and General Banks supported this initiative, a shortage of horses led the War Department to withhold approval for the time being.[30]

The departure of the 8th Virginia and Madison Cavalry in mid-October left the Loudoun Cavalry alone in unfriendly surroundings that wore on the troopers' nerves. Suspecting Sam Means donned a disguise to visit his family, the Rebels kept close watch on his Waterford home, and thought they had caught the wily traitor when they saw a shadowy figure slip inside one night. Unaware it was a female friend on a visit, the soldiers burst in, guns firing, to conduct a fruitless search that prompted comments about "our brave cavalry's" treatment of women. The town was further shaken three nights later when a Rebel picket was shot near the Means residence. The killer was never identified but authorities in Richmond, suspecting the miller's involvement, offered a reward of $5,000 for the head of "the renegade, Sam Means." Inflamed by the killing, soldiers from Leesburg joined the Loudoun Cavalry in assaulting and arresting Unionists on "'frivolous' charges."[31]

In the midst of this harassment, Loudoun's largest single engagement of the war, the Battle of Balls Bluff, took place outside Leesburg on 21 October. It began as a reconnaissance by Northern troops, who crossed the river above the county seat before dawn. Encountering no opposition, the Federals reinforced their position throughout the morning, until Colonel Evans, finally convinced the beachhead was not a diversion, threw his combined forces at the enemy. By late afternoon, a stampede had begun as exhausted Yanks scrambled down the bluff and flung themselves into the river to escape their adversaries on the heights above. While some 1,700 soldiers participated on each side, the North counted 921 casualties and the Southerners just 155. As bodies of dead Union soldiers floated downstream past Washington, the U.S. Congress opened an investigation of the North's second major setback of the war.[32]

Promoted to brigadier general afterwards, Evan's report on the battle singled out Loudoun's militia for again failing to respond to a call to repel the enemy. A Charleston reporter, in Leesburg to interview South Carolina's latest hero, picked up Evans' views on disloyalty in the county, and his dispatch described Loudoun as "one of the foulest festers" in Virginia, one where in some neighborhoods there was hardly a family that did not include a Lincoln supporter. Citing a recent visit to Baltimore by three local Quakers, the newspaperman lamented the impossibility of keeping Yankee spies from slipping across the Potomac. In a lengthy rebuttal, Leesburg's *Mirror* enumerated the county's past contributions to the war effort and minimized disloyalty as being "almost wholly confined to Waterford and the German settlement." As to any suggestion Quakers were aiding the enemy, the paper described them as strictly neutral, an indication the Friends' joint communique had had its desired effect.[33]

Samuel Janney and another Goose Creek Quaker had in fact taken advantage of a temporary withdrawal of Southern troops from the border to attend Yearly Meeting in Baltimore. There, Janney's views on maintaining strict neutrality prevailed, and statements issued by that body contained nothing which might invite recriminations against their brethren in Dixie. Once back home, Janney was taken to Leesburg for questioning about why he had left the state without permission. As the minister would recall, when Evans exclaimed, "Don't you know that your first duty is to your country?" he replied "No, my first duty is to God." After several days of house arrest in Leesburg, Janney was allowed to return home.[34]

Arriving in Waterford in November to reinforce the Loudoun Cavalry, the Bedford Southside Dragoons (Co. F, 2nd Va. Cav.) took over the half of the meetinghouse previously reserved for worship. The Quakers initially found the arrangement "heart sickening," but warmed to the newcomers after they proved more "kindly disposed" toward their sect than the Loudoun troopers, who had left town permanently a month later. Their departure coincided with the arrival of another South Carolinian, Brig. Gen. Daniel H. Hill, to replace Evans as Loudoun's commander. Civilians soon discovered they had an even sterner taskmaster, one who also harbored doubts about their loyalty.

Where he significantly differed from Evans was in his determination to turn Leesburg into a fortress. On his first day, Hill put his soldiers to work digging earthworks, and soon ordered slaves be furnished from nearby plantations to join in. But work slowed after Southern soldiers balked at performing manual labor traditionally done by Blacks, and slave owners worried about possible loss of their "property," when Federals began shelling the work crews from across the river. Moreover, the slaves themselves took advantage of proximity to the border to slip across the river. By year's end, as many as a third of the county's slaves had fled to Maryland. Hill next turned to militia members, threatening them with detention in Richmond if they did not show up for work. The edict caused a renewed exodus from North Loudoun, fueled by rumors that, once assembled in Leesburg, they would be forced into the army. McClellan's intelligence chief, Alan Pinkerton, set up a program to debrief the refugees, who assured him many more would flee, were it not for threats to confiscate their property. What remained of North Loudoun's 56th Militia was ordered to the county seat on 23 December and quartered inside the walled courthouse grounds to prevent escape.[35]

Christmas and the approach of the new year, normally a time of celebration, brought little joy to North Loudoun, where the recent arrest of several Lovettsville citizens and their incarceration in Richmond added to the uncertainty. High prices and shortages of staples such as salt, sugar and coffee made life difficult for all, particularly in northern border towns cut off from their usual sources of supply across the river and faced with Confederate refusal to send scarce goods into a disloyal district. Winter's arrival compounded the gloom that settled over Waterford, where Rebel cavalrymen still occupied the

Waterford's Famed Quaker Minister, Miriam Gover, with Daughter Ann. (Pre-war daguerreotype, TCC)

once bustling village. Even so, there had been a good harvest, and the thrifty Quakers were well prepared to ride out the fallow season. This situation was aided by their adept cultivation of the town's occupiers, evident in a letter a Bedford corporal sent his wife in mid-December: "This is a great country up here...The Quakers are becoming quite kind to us. They send in a good many [supplies] for the sick." Two weeks later, he was even more enthusiastic: "Now we have excellent quarters, good warm houses to stay in... and plenty to eat and feed our horses...and men have dinners furnished them almost every day."[36]

Cessation of mail service to the North was keenly felt by Waterford Friends, who maintained close ties with other meetings, and now had so many members living in exile. To meet this need, a clandestine service was inaugurated under the Dragoons' noses by Temple Fouch, a handyman living on the outskirts of town who, after gathering letters and messages during the day, followed an "underground" route at night that took him to a boat hidden along the Potomac. Despite also helping Whites and Blacks escape into Maryland, Fouch was never caught by the Rebels, who dismissed him as the "town drunk." Eventually this acclaimed local hero and two sons would further aid the cause by serving in the Loudoun Rangers, while Temple, Jr., joined Coles Cavalry, a Maryland unit.[37]

With the outbreak of war, Fairfax Meeting put aside religious differences and served as a source of fellowship and assistance for the entire community. To fill in for the exiles, less active members like E. Y. and Sarah Matthews rose to the occasion and played more prominent roles in Meeting. But the person most associated with this outreach was the town's renowned minister, Miriam Gover. Belying her faith's reputation for silence, she made a deep impression upon the soldiers when, with the dignity of her years, she rose to speak during what the Rebels came to call "Mrs. Gover's meeting." Officers met her carriage and escorted her inside, their "glittering" uniforms contrasting with her "plain Friends' dress." This juxtaposition of grey and black, united in worship, became an image that resonated in prose and verse long after the war. It also influenced her grandchildren, Annie, Edie and Marie Matthews, who preserved the following account read by their cousin, Susan Walker, to her college literary society in distant Indiana:

> Almost all [the soldiers] had curiosity to be present, having heard of Quaker meetings. When the members entered, the scenes presented there were strange ones...The old ladies ascended the steps into the gallery and took their seats, though rather daintily, as arms were stacked...beneath the benches. In one corner of the room the "Stars and Bars" were unfurled. In an opposite one was a large fireplace with a blazing fire, over which was roasting a large turkey...[A]n amused whisper of some of the more mischievous soldiers... could be distinctly heard. But when all were seated it was perfectly quiet, and when an aged and feeble lady [Miriam Gover] arose, every countenance wore a thoughtful aspect and each attentively listened to her words of truth and love. When she invoked a blessing on the little band there assembled, she also prayed that the wings of peace might be spread over our once prosperous and happy land, also for the strangers that were that day gathered in their midst, until loud sobs broke from strong men and great tears forced themselves down their sunburnt cheeks.[38]

Perhaps no other scene has come to symbolize Waterford during the war than this iconic picture of Quaker and soldier praying together. Yet, it tells only part of the story. In the period following Reconstruction, when Loudoun was dominated by former Rebels, it had good reason to downplay its wartime resistance. Thus, as memories dimmed and records were lost, or deliberately destroyed, few would recall the stirring acts of bravery that her citizens would soon undertake for the Union cause.

Chapter 14

QUAKERS GO TO WAR: 1862-63

Leesburg farmer Elijah ("Lige") White so distinguished himself as a Rebel scout at Balls Bluff, he was granted authority to raise an independent cavalry company. Attracted by promises to remain in the area, many of his early recruits came from North Loudoun, including his second-in-command, Lt. Frank Myers, whose family lived on a farm outside Waterford. Ordered at the start of 1862 to reenforce the Bedford Dragoons, White established his command in a vacant blacksmith shop on Waterford's south end, close to Talbott's front gate. Not an hour had passed before the Rebels called on owner James Walker to furnish "corn, hay, straw &c," and, as his daughter Mary put it, they "have been doing it ever since. They call themselves the 'Independent Rangers' as they are not to belong to any regiment, but...stay about here and *watch the river."* Discomfited that their loyalties were so well known to White's men, Union sympathizers found the intruders "a great annoyance" and began calling them the "Loudoun Ruffians."[1]

In addition to keeping Federal spies and escaped slaves from crossing the Potomac, White's command was responsible for rounding up "delinquent" militiamen to work on Leesburg's fortifications—no easy matter as many had fled or were Quakers opposed to military service. The alternatives of paying fines or hiring substitutes exposed a rift among Friends when Samuel Janney attended Fairfax Meeting and let it be known "nearly all" Goose Creek members were paying Confederate war taxes. Although her family agreed with Janney, Eliza Walker feared civil disobedience by other Waterford Friends would bring "additional trials" to the village. Matters grew more contentious after passage of a conscription act in April that made no provision for conscientious objectors.[2]

In February the Dragoons vacated the meetinghouse for Waterford's Quarterly Meeting to take place along with representatives from Goose Creek and Hopewell Meetings. Samuel Janney was impressed with the amity between Friends and soldiers, which reminded him of the lamb lying down with the lion. While little of import took place at the meeting, a Rebel soldier from Leesburg "enjoyed it very much...The ladies were the most interesting [preachers]. Saw several very pretty young Quaker ladies. Dined in Waterford, a very fine table indeed."[3]

Yet, even as attendees savored the peaceful tableau, plans were underway to bring the war into their midst. From sources inside Loudoun, Col. John Geary learned Daniel Hill planned to withdraw his troops to meet an expected Union offensive by George McClellan in southern Virginia. Convinced Hill would no longer take a sustained stand, Geary led the 28th Pa. Infantry and part of the 1st Mich. Cavalry across the river at Harpers Ferry during the last days of February. Catching their opponents off guard, and with Sam Means showing the way, the Yanks easily occupied Lovettsville, where they were warmly received by most inhabitants. Over the next days, they consolidated their position in the German Settlement and fended off cavalry attacks meant to delay any further advance until the main Confederates could evacuate the county.

Early 7 March, Geary's men were surprised to see a woman galloping towards their camp. Having overhead White's men threaten to burn her "cursed Quaker settlement" before letting it fall into Federal hands, Maggie Gover resolved to stop them. "In the absence of any *man* who was willing to perform the perilous duty," or even lend her a horse, she had a servant steal one, then slipped Rebel pickets to the Union lines. There, after a salute "to the good old flag," she was led before Geary, whom she convinced to accelerate his advance on Leesburg, passing through Waterford on the way. Her daring ride and the information she provided earned praise not only from Geary, who was promoted to brigadier general on the basis of his successful invasion, but also from Gen. John Dix, division commander in Baltimore. Aside from considerable attention at the time, other accounts imply she was also the source of information that prompted Geary's offensive into Loudoun. In a letter to the Secretary of War, Sam Gover related how his wife had "risked her life and property to give information to Gen. Geary, upon which he immediately marched through and took possession of our county." Another writer cited Maggie's part in providing Geary with "such important information" about Rebel intentions, it "enabled him to circumvent those designs and gain a great advantage to the Union cause."[4]

That same morning, White's men headed towards Leesburg to seek instructions on the pending withdrawal. As they crested the Catoctin range, they were appalled to see "what destruction [Hill's] retiring army was inflicting…for all over the country could be seen the flames going up from the stackyards." On entering the county seat, White found the general preparing to march south and uninterested in carrying out further operations in North Loudoun. With orders to remain behind to monitor the invaders, White stationed his men "up among the Quakers" near Goose Creek for several days, before they too headed for southern Virginia.[5]

It was already dark when Maggie and Sam Means guided Geary's brigade into Waterford. The first appearance of Union soldiers in the village prompted its loyal inhabitants to stay up all night to cheer them and offer refuge from the cold. A few days later, the Yanks published an account of freeing the town "from the terror maintained…by the rebel soldiery. The residents hailed us as their deliverers…especially…the women, who immediately set about preparing coffee and eatables for us." The next morning under dim light from a quarter moon, but fortified with a "warm breakfast, spread before us at home by fair hands," the men resumed their march. The route took them past Clifton, and even at that hour, Edie and her family would have been among those lining the way. As one soldier recalled: "From the time we left, until we reached Leesburg we were welcomed with shouts of joy." From a hastily abandoned Rebel fort above the county seat, Geary later claimed to have seen retreating Confederates setting fire to mills and forage as they hastened south, although almost all Rebel troops left the day before. In contrast to their earlier reception, only sullen stares from almost all but the town's Black inhabitants greeted the Yanks' unopposed occupation of Leesburg.[6]

The Federals' departure south two weeks later was as unexpected as their arrival. Before he left, Geary recommended a permanent garrison be established in Leesburg, but the War Department did not want to divert troops from McClellan's drive on Richmond, and the county was left without a governing body for the rest of the war. With communication to the South cut, Loudouners looked elsewhere for supplies and information. Only a token military presence remained to control river crossings and ferries Geary had previously closed. Stagecoaches between Leesburg and the Point resumed carrying mail, passengers and trade goods. Prices came down as merchants restocked their shelves, facilitated by the reopening of the B&O rail line to through traffic. Perhaps most surprising was the reopening of U.S. post offices in Leesburg, Hamilton and Waterford.[7]

Believing the county permanently "liberated," exiles began to return and Unionists came out of their homes to find their "Secesh" neighbors "less defiant, less confident, and more courteous." In the heady days that followed, Sam Gover rushed back to reunite with his wife and, as Lincoln promised, a post office in their store. Convinced "the worst was over," James Walker urged his son to come back home, and blacksmith Frank Steer hurried back to marry fiancée Mollie Dutton. Others, like Samuel Steer, found themselves returning to Maryland to procure horses to replace those taken by the Rebels.[8]

To fill the void left by the collapse of civil government in newly "liberated" Virginia counties, Unionist Governor Francis Pierpont wanted to schedule elections to facilitate their integration into his Restored Government. On 6 May, Unionists gathered in Waterford to discuss the issue and choose election overseers, including Edwin Gover, Samuel Steer and Sam Means. The venue and participation of Fairfax Meeting members signaled a shift towards Waterford taking the lead in the loyalist cause. But, while elections were held in Federally-occupied Fairfax County, Loudoun's secessionist majority made this impossible without a similar military presence.[9]

In mid-May Miriam and Maggie Gover journeyed to Winchester for Quarterly Meeting. Other than to record a drop in attendance at regular services, the minutes ignored recent tumultuous events. Only two months earlier, Stonewall Jackson's army dragged off several Hopewell members during the Confederate evacuation of Winchester and at least one died during a forced march in bad weather. Maggie was eager to comfort her father, Nathan Parkins, who had been among those taken away after refusing to renounce "allegiance to the Union." He survived, but his health was "seriously impaired" by this ordeal and by the shock of finding his mill destroyed by secessionists during his absence.[10]

Any later, and the Quarterly Meeting would not have taken place, as Jackson reversed course and decisively defeated Nathanial Banks' army at Winchester on 25 May. Afterwards, the Confederates chased the Federals to Harpers Ferry and sent cavalry patrols as far east as Leesburg and Waterford, causing Unionists again to flee across the river and renew demands for protection. The War Department responded by ordering two sorties into Loudoun to arrest "Secesh" leaders and seize horses. The instructions reflected a hardening in Washington towards civilians, who were seen to hold the key to controlling occupied areas of the South. Governor Pierpont conveyed this view to John Janney, warning the influential Leesburg politician that disloyal citizens would be "arrested and sent out of the state," if Union men or their property were further disturbed.[11]

* * * * *

His services as a scout no longer needed by Geary, Sam Means took the opportunity to press his earlier proposal to raise a cavalry company. Recent events had convinced Governor Pierpont and Secretary of War Stanton something had to be done to protect Loudoun loyalists. Although the governor expected Means would come under his control, Stanton was persuaded by the would-be captain to authorize a company of partisan rangers that would remain outside the army's chain of command. (A similar template was already being tested by the Confederates in units such as White's Cavalry.) The *quid pro quo* for allowing Means to operate exclusively in or near Loudoun required his men to provide their own mounts, *i.e.*, seize them from local secessionists. On 8 June, Stanton signed an order creating the Independent Loudoun Rangers, the only Union cavalry unit raised inside Confederate Virginia.[12]

After his muster into the service at Harpers Ferry, Means filled his company with recruits from Waterford and the German Settlement. Many were "more or less of Quaker lineage," including at least two related to the Matthews family, Sgt. Edwin Gover and Cpl. Edward Taylor White. Several were active members of Fairfax Meeting, which made no apparent effort to oust them from its midst. In explaining the pacifists' presence in his company, its historian Briscoe Goodhart observed that, when war was "brought to the threshold of their own homes, the flesh grew stronger than the spirit." The Rangers' chronicler also cited the case of one Quaker facing the enemy, who raised his rifle with the remark, "Friend, it is unfortunate, but thee stands exactly where I am going to shoot."[13]

The Rangers were nominally assigned to the Harpers Ferry Military District, which also maintained infantry companies at Berlin and Point of Rocks to protect the rail, canal and telegraph lines, as well as control border crossings. Even though successive district commanders paid lip service to safeguarding Loudoun loyalists, effective Federal control seldom extended beyond the river. Intended to alleviate this situation by serving as a "home guard," the Rangers' independent status left them without a strong advocate within the army, and they never received the training or support needed to overcome their captain's lack of military experience.

McClellan's failure to capture Richmond resulted in a northward advance by Lee's forces. Chaffing at the Confederates' slow pace and anxious to put an end to the Loudoun Rangers' harassment of Southern sympathizers back home, Capt. Elijah White received permission to proceed ahead of Lee's main army. On learning Means' company was camped at Waterford's Baptist church, White was able to surprise his adversaries before dawn on 26 August. Their captain, at home on the other end of town, had left a lieutenant in charge but after he was severely wounded in the initial volley, a sergeant rallied the Rangers and led them inside the church, where they put up a fierce resistance before an ammunition shortage on both sides forced an agreement by the Rangers to surrender in return for being paroled on the spot. It had literally been a battle between neighbors, and one of White's men had to be physically restrained from shooting his brother as he emerged from the church. Although they suffered fewer casualties than their opponents, the impact of losing their first significant engagement, along with their horses and arms, weighed heavily on the Rangers and slowed future recruitments.[14]

Capt. Samuel C. Means, Loudoun Rangers. (Goodhart, Briscoe, *History of the Independent Loudoun Virginia Rangers*, Washington, D.C.: McGill and Wallace, 1885, 4)

When residents came out to survey the damage and care for the wounded, they had reason to ponder their future. Their concerns increased a few days later after the North failed to check Lee's army at the Second Battle of Bull Run. Once again, Waterford found itself cut off behind Southern lines and, even though most Confederate forces stayed east of the Catoctin range before crossing into Maryland, 400 Rebel cavalrymen descended on the village on 3 September. Demanding keys to the shuttered shops, the intruders "took what they wanted... & paid for them in Confederate money—that is not worth anything here." Sam Gover had fled to Maryland several days earlier with his stamps and postal equipment, just escaping a patrol sent to arrest the postmaster.[15]

On 17 September, Waterford residents could hear the fighting at Antietam, where Lee's advance was finally halted in the bloodiest day of the war. Much to "Lige" White's annoyance, he and his men were not allowed to participate in the invasion of Maryland and, with nothing better to do, a portion of them broke into Gover's store, the second time it had been "raided and pillaged." After the war, Sam sued White for $3,000 in damages but had to drop the suit after White was elected sheriff.[16]

McClellan's failure to exploit the advantage won at Antietam allowed Lee to slip back into Virginia without further loss, and it was not until late October that Union soldiers began crossing the Potomac. Guided by Means' Rangers, the 1st Division of the IX Corps made its way into Waterford on 29 October, and during the next five days, ten regiments camped on farms around the village. The Yanks were accorded the town's customary warm welcome and one picket, apparently stationed on Rachel Steer's farm, recalled how the mistress of The Willows plied him with food. But feeding and provisioning such a large force put a heavy strain on farmers. E. Y. Matthews provided six tons of hay during the 45th Pa. Infantry's stay at Clifton, yet when the Keystone Staters left, he only received a note from the officer in charge apologizing for not having time to repay Matthews for unspecified services. The following year, when E. Y. tried to file a claim without the necessary receipt, he was told he would have to first prove his loyalty, no easy matter during wartime.[17]

The arrival of Federal troops allowed loyal citizens to once again cross the border to buy supplies and several Quakers, including Miriam Gover, took this opportunity to attend Yearly Meeting in Baltimore. Those expecting the Society to take a stronger stance against the Rebellion were again disappointed, although the minutes did lament the earlier occupation of Waterford's meetinghouse and perhaps more importantly, failed to condemn what the August Quarterly Meeting at Goose Creek euphemistically termed a "few deviations respecting military service." As the war ground on, Waterford Quakers in particular became increasingly active partisans on the Union side, some in military units like the Loudoun Rangers, others in noncombatant roles. In October, many Southern Friends were heartened by an amendment to the Confederate conscription law exempting pacifists who paid a fine, or hired a substitute, but even so, Waterford Friends continued to prefer exile to supporting a government they so vehemently opposed.[18]

Exasperated it had taken McClellan over two weeks to advance twenty miles into Virginia, President Lincoln replaced "Little Mac" in early November with Maj. Gen. Ambrose Burnside, who would prove equally indecisive during fighting that winter. As the main armies of both sides moved farther away, refugees ventured back across the border, apparently unaware White's Cavalry remained behind. By now, his original company had grown into the 35th Battalion Va. Cavalry, its commander promoted to major.

Even as White's "Comanches" came out of the Blue Ridge to prey on their opponents, Unionists in North Loudoun faced an additional threat from paroled Confederate prisoners sent home to await formal exchange. In mid-November a prisoner less than a month earlier rode into Waterford on a horse taken from the Gover family, and a few days later, a group of young parolees came into town, stole a horse and seized a young conscript. Outraged at once more having to seek safety at the Point, an exasperated John Dutton pleaded with Harpers Ferry to do something about the "horse stealing bands," which, under White "and God knows who else," were again harassing Unionists. The Quaker shopkeeper, whose son was now serving in the Union army, emphasized his town's willingness to host Federal troops to put an end to the lawlessness. Their problems were exacerbated by the emergence of a renegade band, mostly men from White's Cavalry who, barred from returning to regular service while under parole, turned to the lucrative horse trade.[19]

There is no indication the Federals responded to Dutton's plea, and even after the Loudoun Rangers returned from guiding Burnside's army, Means' men spent much of the winter in camp at the Point. In early December, White's battalion unexpectedly entered Waterford, "frightening [its] intensely tory citizens...half out of their wits." During this foray, the Comanches cleaned out Dutton's store, forcing the owner, like his Gover competitor, to permanently close his shop and relocate to the Point. A short time later, several "stragglers" from White's command seized two horses from Talbott, prompting owner James Walker to pay a visit to the Rebel camp and get White to issue orders for the animals' return. Clearly, some prominent Quakers had an understanding with the Rebel commander not available to those of lower status, or who were less scrupulous in maintaining their neutrality.[20]

Once White's Cavalry retired to winter quarters in the Shenandoah Valley at Christmas time, North Loudoun found itself free of any organized body of soldiers during the first months of 1863. There were, however, continued depredations by Loudoun's "desperados," their numbers augmented by soldiers who returned home on leave but then decided to fight as irregulars. This activity was most pronounced in the county's northwest corner, home of Loudoun's most notorious guerrilla leader, John W. Mobberly. Familiar with every path and hiding place in the Blue Ridge and Short Hill mountains, he easily evaded patrols Harpers Ferry sent to catch him. Never more than a private in White's Cavalry and with no patience for military discipline, Mobberly brought others under his sway while not yet out of his teens with his daring and success as a guerrilla.[21]

This second winter of the war placed strains on all. Civilians who could prove their loyalty and had "greenbacks" could cross the river to buy necessities, but this privilege was subject to disruption by the weather and Federal authorities. Since Yankee money was in short supply and Confederate scrip rarely accepted, most resorted to barter within the county to fill their needs. The Quakers attempted to aid the most impoverished, including those with whom they differed politically, yet many of these thrifty and self-reliant Friends now found themselves unable to pay their annual assessment to Fairfax Meeting.

The Matthews family, with a farm to supply their table and E. Y. too old for conscription, fared better than most, even managing to send their oldest daughter Annie to boarding school in Maryland.[22]

The porous border proved a constant headache for Union commanders. Early in the war, when the Potomac was the front line, each side sought to bar the other from crossing, although refugees, smugglers and spies continued to find ways. After the front shifted farther south in early 1862, cross-border civilian traffic resumed via ferries at Berlin, Point of Rocks and Edward's Ferry (near Leesburg), and a pontoon bridge at Harpers Ferry. Provost marshals and their guards were assigned to each crossing, relying on local informants such as the Loudoun Rangers to identify Unionists eligible for a pass. Prompted by Northern business interests, Federal policy sought to expand commerce into liberated parts of the South ("trade should follow the flag"), but widespread abuse convinced Union commanders that Northern goods were only prolonging the conflict. The Treasury Department responded in early 1863 by assigning customs agents to Harpers Ferry, Berlin and Point of Rocks. These officials were empowered to permit Unionists to transport small quantities of "family supplies" into Virginia upon payment of duty on these goods. Matthews neighbor Samuel Steer won appointment customs agent at the Point.[23]

Of almost equal concern to Waterford was resumption of mail service. After wresting control of the Point of Rocks post office from the Means brothers, John Dutton had it moved to his new trade store, where he arranged for his nephew to become postmaster, while he took on the task of certifying to the provost marshal which Loudouners had the privilege of sending and receiving mail. Several months later, the P.O. Department sanctioned regular delivery via wagon between the Point and Waterford.[24]

The sudden death of Miriam Gover on 18 April 1863 at age seventy-two was a heavy blow to her family and the community she served so faithfully. As Samuel Janney's wife observed, "a general gloom... overspread the faces of all our friends. In Waterford all looked as though they had lost one of their dearest connections...We all feel that we have lost one of the strongest pillars...of our church." Philadelphia Friends lamented "the removal of so beloved a mother in Israel," while Baltimore Yearly Meeting memorialized Miriam "as a remarkable instance of the influence of one of solid deportment, silently waiting upon her God." Sarah Matthews and her family were among the "large concourse of friends and neighbors" that accompanied her mother's body to the burial ground and attended the "particularly solemn meeting" that followed. One attendee found the size of the crowd "remarkable, considering the state of affairs existing in our midst. Some Rebel soldiers were present, intent on capturing Sam Gover, who had come from Washington to pay a "last tribute of affection to his mother. But as there were few of them, they wisely desisted from the undertaking. It would not have been allowed by the friends of Sam Gover."[25]

During visits to her father in Winchester, Maggie established contact with Capt. Carrick Heiskell, a childhood friend then part of Gen. Robert Milroy's Federal occupation of that city. In gratitude for information she provided on the Rebels, the captain provided her with an endorsement to U.S. Senator Waitman Willey, Unionist Virginia's representative in that body. In recommending her for a government position, Heiskell explained how she remained separated from her husband in order to protect their few remaining possessions, despite "frequent threats of White's noted band." (The letter went on to describe her role in preventing Waterford's destruction and her father's arrest.) Maggie was back in Winchester that June, when Milroy had the misfortune of being in the path of Lee's invasion of Pennsylvania and would risk her life caring for the wounded during the ensuing battle. Since fleeing to the capital, Maggie's husband made ends meet through work at cousin Henry Janney's shoe store on Pennsylvania Avenue. There Sam had the opportunity to assist the President try on boots, and when none fit, the embarrassed clerk observed, "Mr. President those boots are too small." "No! Mr. Gover," Lincoln graciously replied, "my feet are too big." Maggie did not join him, perhaps because after his mother's unexpected death, she dared not leave their home for any extended period, lest it be confiscated.[26]

West Virginia's admission to the Union in June forced Governor Pierpont to transfer what remained of his Restored Government to Alexandria. To compensate for this territorial loss, the governor directed that Loudoun be included in elections held on 28 May to choose representatives for the state legislature. Only Unionists could vote at polls set up across the river from Berlin and Point of Rocks. John Henshaw and James Downey won seats in the House of Delegates, and William Mercer was elected to the state Senate. After two years in limbo, North Loudoun was officially part of Unionist Virginia, although few benefits would result from its new status. To commemorate their county's "restoration" and West Virginia statehood, Edie and her sisters sewed an American flag with 35 stars arranged in the concentric "Baltimore pattern." Pictured on the front cover, the Stars and Stripes were displayed whenever Northern soldiers passed by their farm—both to show support and discourage "foraging" by the Yankees. Confederates searched for the "treasonable" banner on several occasions, but never found its hiding place under a board in Clifton's attic.[27]

The major armies bypassed North Loudoun on their way to the decisive encounter at Gettysburg on 1-3 July. Afterwards, Maj. Gen. George Meade was quicker to follow the retreating Lee than McClellan the year before. Though fleeting, transit of the vast Union army through Loudoun was memorable. Led by the Loudoun Rangers, the I Corps began pouring into Waterford on 18 July and set up camps along Catoctin Creek at the town's west end. With their departure and the simultaneous arrival of the XI Corps the following day, the village was awash in blue. Rebecca Williams counted 600 wagons in the supply train, incorrectly assuming she had witnessed Meade's entire army. Most townsfolk were overjoyed to welcome the victors of the great battle and did their best to make them feel at home. To reciprocate, officers of the 24th Mich. Infantry staged a ball in the town's honor. "That evening merry maidens of the place with elastic step tripped the fantastic toe with our army officers. The streets were lined with smiles and beauty. Windows and balconies were filled with matrons, maidens, and children, who waved handkerchiefs and the starry flag, and cheered on the Union troops with many a hurrah." In all likelihood the Matthews family was present that night, waving their newly sewn flag from one of their aunts' houses, and Annie, back from school, surely attended the ball.[28]

The 7th Indiana had equally fond memories of their brief stay.

> ...as we passed through the village the street was lined with citizens—men in broad-brimmed hats and drab coats, women dressed in the modest garb of their sect, and young ladies and misses slightly more fashionably habited...Here and there...a group of... these demure young Quakeresses...[distributed] cups of cool water...It was astonishing the number of thirsty men in the line.... [One of the girls encountered that day, Lizzie Dutton, later married a member of the regiment.] It had been noticed that among our many visitors there were but few youngish men. Inquiries as to why this was, brought the answer, "Many of them are in a Maryland Union regiment." How do you reconcile that with your religious faith? was asked of one. "We do not call this war but correcting wayward children."[29]

Such celebrations were short-lived, as the Comanches also returned to harass Federal troops who tarried in the county. At midnight on 7 August, White's Cavalry attacked the 6th Mich. Cavalry's overnight camp on Walker's farm. Before the Yanks fled the scene, they managed to inflict enough casualties on their attackers that the Comanches' historian later termed it a "disaster." Another setback followed in September, when Loudoun Rangers teamed up with Cole's Cavalry to scatter a company of White's men on Catoctin Mountain. The Yanks gained entry to the camp dressed in Confederate uniforms, as both sides increasingly relied on ambush, informers and unorthodox means to gain advantage. None could match the master of such tactics, John S. Mosby, who was beginning to make his presence felt at the county's southern end but was still relatively unknown in North Loudoun.[30]

Loudoun's Quaker community is generally credited with preventing the targeting of civilians from reaching levels of savagery common in border states farther west, but the county's divided loyalties inevitably led to reprisals. Back in June 1862, James Downey complained to Senator Willey about the plight of seven Lovettsville Unionists who had languished in Richmond prison for over six months. Downey had already given Secretary of War Stanton a list of prominent Secessionists to be held hostage until their release, but having heard nothing since, sought advice on whether to approach Harpers Ferry's commander on this issue. Governor Pierpont also threatened to jail Secessionists unless mistreatment of Unionists was halted.[31]

These proposals were shelved as authorities waited to see whether the Loudoun Rangers could protect loyalists and their property. Most Unionists, particularly Quakers, opposed taking hostages, fearful retaliation would follow. Their concerns were borne out in late summer 1863, when Union soldiers arrested Henry Ball and Campbell Belt, two Loudoun residents charged with aiding the "guerrillas." Major White responded by ordering two Waterford Quakers seized: William Williams, head of the insurance company, and Asa Bond, father-in-law of Samuel Means. Williams was easily captured, but Bond managed to escape while the intrepid Rachel Means attacked her father's would be captors with broomstick, rolling-pin and eventually a revolver. For their second victim, White's men settled for schoolteacher Robert Hollingsworth.[32]

Citizens from both sides persuaded White to parole the captives for a month to give time for them to convince Federal authorities to release Ball and Belt. Agreeing to help this effort, Samuel Janney asked his cousin Henry Janney in Washington to contact Henry Gover, Frederick S. Corkran and John Underwood for assistance. (Gover's participation was limited to securing the aid of his brother-in-law Corkran, a top customs official in Baltimore and personal acquaintance of the President. Underwood had been recently appointed a Federal judge by Lincoln.) Later that month, Samuel Janney accompanied William Williams' wife and her brother, James Walker, to Washington where, armed with a letter of introduction from Corkran and escorted by Underwood, they called on the White House. After listening sympathetically, Lincoln sent them to the War Department, where Stanton made it clear he considered Ball and Belt legitimate prisoners of war and, fearful their release might encourage further hostage-taking, turned down the Quakers' request.[33]

In the midst of these negotiations, Waterford received a visit from the 1st Md. Eastern Shore Infantry, then stationed at the Point. Returning from a raid to Leesburg and prepared to escort the Quaker hostages to safety, the Marylanders were greeted on their way into the village by Edie and her sisters. As the soldiers marched by the "welcome sight" of the girls and their flag, the band struck up "When This Cruel War Is Over." Although Edie was preparing to go to boarding school in Maryland a few days later, she and her older sister would have followed the infantrymen into town. As one officer recalled: "Waterford was fairly alive. The Quakers turned out *en masse* and overwhelmed us with kindness. Every lady had a small flag it seemed, and joy was upon every countenance...I went off with the rest of the officers and I must say never had such an interesting time. The 'Thee' and 'Thou' was almost forgotten by the young Quaker ladies. I took a walk with one that evening and her conversation was very interesting... and we had a gay time..." The Marylanders returned to the Point the next day, leaving the disappointed villagers once more unprotected.[34]

Rather than accompany the Eastern Shore troops to safety, Williams and Hollingsworth honored their parole and reported to White's camp, from which they were taken to Richmond's notorious Castle Thunder Prison. That fall, Samuel Janney sent Stanton a petition signed by eighty-six Unionists calling for the Secessionists' release on humanitarian grounds, plus a request the government refrain from arresting any more civilians. When the Secretary of War still refused to budge, friends and family of the Confederate prisoners successfully petitioned their own government to release the Quakers, who made their way back home on Christmas day. Shortly thereafter, Ball and Belt were also freed.[35]

While Unionists felt unduly victimized by White's Comanches, his battalion at least provided a semblance of law and order until it was ordered later that fall to leave Loudoun and merge into the regular Confederate army. A number of White's men refused to obey, including John Mobberly. Considered Loudoun's Robin Hood by his admirers, Mobberly had already begun to operate independently, and his band of guerrillas would prey on Union soldiers and sympathizers for the rest of the war. Just as the 35th Battalion was about to depart, Mobberly and five others accosted James Downey near Taylorstown, claiming Major White had ordered his arrest. The guerrillas, however, seemed more interested in a payoff and accompanied their captive to his home, where Mrs. Downey willingly paid one hundred dollars for her husband's release "on parole." With an admonishment to report to White's camp the following day, Mobberly's men rode off. Downey instead fled to Maryland, leaving his wife and children to run their mill and distillery. (White probably did order the arrest of Loudoun's most prominent Unionist politician to increase pressure for Ball and Belt's release but failed to account for the venality of the men sent to perform the task.)[36]

* * * * *

Since early in the war, control of the Maryland side of the border rested with the Middle Department in Baltimore, where Loudoun Unionists, especially the Quakers, had developed good contacts. This changed in late 1863, when the Harpers Ferry Military District transferred Baltimore's jurisdiction to Brig. Gen. Benjamin Kelley's West Virginia Department, and Harpers Ferry was placed under the command of Kelley's son-in-law, Brig. Gen. Jeremiah Sullivan. Kelley previously worked for the B&O Railroad, and both he and Sullivan were far more concerned with guarding the rail line than protecting Unionists in Loudoun. They also took a dim view of Treasury Department efforts to boost trade into Virginia which, under the nominal supervision of its customs agents, had flourished since the passage of the Union army that summer. John Dutton, Noble Means and several others already operated officially licensed "trade stores" at Point of Rocks to serve this market, and Sam Gover opened a competing store there by year's end.

Commerce was not all one way, and that fall many Loudouners sold their harvest to buyers in Maryland, thereby earning greenbacks to purchase needed supplies. The Treasury's Customs Special Agency issued licenses for agents, including Sam Gover and Amasa Hough Jr., to go inside Loudoun and purchase produce directly from farmers. Problems arose when a competing group, with ties inside the military, attempted to corner the market on forage and grain, which they resold to the Harpers Ferry quartermaster for a substantial profit. Despite these problems, temporary crossing points were established lower down the Potomac to handle the many secessionist farmers who also preferred to sell their produce for greenbacks.

The new Harpers Ferry commander quickly became dissatisfied with the amount of goods going into Virginia, much of which Sullivan suspected of falling into Rebel hands. (A review of Point of Rocks' customs ledger confirms secessionists were among the purchasers of $30,000 in "family supplies" taken into Virginia during the last six weeks of 1863.) Unable to get the Treasury Department to modify its procedures and, annoyed by allegations linking his quartermaster to irregularities in the procurement of forage, Sullivan tried unsuccessfully to have the customs house at Berlin closed. Despite belated attempts to resolve these issues, it was clear by year's end the Treasury agents were on a collision course with the military.[37]

Nevertheless, Loudoun Unionists had good cause for optimism as 1863 drew to a close. The withdrawal of White's battalion and the hostages' return augured for better treatment of civilians by both sides. Furthermore, North Loudoun's influence in Virginia's Restored Government seemed assured after the Alexandria legislature chose James Downey as Speaker of the House and John Henshaw as state Treasurer. John Dutton reflected this upbeat mood in two letters to Governor Pierpont, one on the need to reestablish local government, the other on expansion of mail service.[38]

Chapter 15

MOSBY COMES TO TOWN: 1864-65

John Singleton Mosby began the war a scout before persuading J. E. B. Stuart in late 1862 to let him raise an independent command under the Confederate Partisan Ranger Act. Many of his followers came from the Fauquier-Loudoun borderland that would be later dubbed "Mosby's Confederacy." His first newsworthy feat occurred in March 1863, when he grabbed a Union general out of his bed in Fairfax County. Three months later, his early recruits were mustered into what would become the 43rd Battalion Va. Cavalry, a unit destined to wreak havoc on Union supply lines and tie up enemy manpower as it operated outside Confederate lines.

In January 1864, Major Mosby undertook his first significant operation in North Loudoun, a nighttime attack on the winter camp of Cole's Cavalry, located on Loudoun Heights across the Shenandoah River from Harpers Ferry. Although the raid did not go well for the attackers, the daring incursion into the most heavily defended part of Loudoun delivered a clear message that no section was safe from the partisans. Unionists and their Federal defenders, who until then paid scant attention to Mosby's influence in southern Loudoun, were about to discover his partisans were a far more formidable foe than White's Cavalry, one that would prove the greatest obstacle to Governor Pierpont's goal of integrating the county into his Restored Government.

Already fed up with the Treasury Department's role in promoting trade into Virginia, Harpers Ferry's commander, Gen. Jeremiah Sullivan, seized on Mosby's raid as an excuse to order provost marshals to halt all civilian traffic across the Potomac, in expectation this interruption would deny supplies to the Rebels, as well as induce Loudouners to turn against the "few guerrillas" in their midst. Additional regulations threatened retaliation against prominent Secessionists in the event Unionists were forced into the Rebel army, or had their property seized. But without Federal troops in Loudoun to enforce these edicts, they remained hollow threats.[1]

John Dutton spent the start of the New Year with his family in Waterford but hastened back to Maryland on learning of the pending border closure. Upon arrival, he was dismayed to discover he had been appointed to oversee a special election to choose delegates for a constitutional convention. Pierpont's government was viewed in the North as a model for how reconstruction should proceed after the war, and both the governor and President Lincoln were anxious to have a new constitution in place that included prohibition of slavery. Mosby's recent raid dampened Dutton's optimism about a rapid return to civilian rule, but despite his objections, "several hundred" cast ballots on 21 January at polling booths set up just inside North Loudoun, the turnout aided by a temporary suspension of the blockade to allow exiles to cross over from Maryland. The resulting three-man delegation, composed of Loudoun Ranger Edwin Gover and Unionists James Downey and Dr. John Henshaw, was the largest at the convention, which opened the following month in Alexandria with fourteen additional representatives from other parts of Virginia under Federal control.²

Since losing the West Virginia counties, Pierpont's government suffered additional setbacks, including the failure of the U.S. to seat its representatives and Gen. Benjamin Butler's refusal to recognize the Alexandria Government's authority inside his Norfolk military district. Pierpont therefore seized on the convention as a way to salvage his dwindling influence, and the resulting "Alexandria Constitution" would be the most lasting legacy of his tenure in that city. In one stroke, this document "destroyed much of what was old Virginia and laid the constitutional groundwork for a new society." In addition to prohibiting slavery, it barred many Confederates from voting or holding office, and mandated the state's first public schools. To help ensure Unionist control after the war, it replaced the voice vote with a paper ballot, eliminated tax benefits for plantation owners, and repudiated repayment of Confederate war bonds. To further help Northerners and returning exiles participate in state government, residency requirements were relaxed. Worried that Secessionists would vote down such a radical departure from the past, Pierpont simply declared the constitution in effect. Even though it would have little impact on wartime Virginia, the Alexandria Constitution served as the state's legal foundation afterwards, anticipating many of the changes associated with radical Reconstruction mandated elsewhere in the South.³

North Loudouners, however, were too preoccupied with the blockade to take much notice of the far-reaching changes the new constitution promised. Instead, they gave vent to frustration over Sullivan's edict in an outburst of protest directed at official Washington. In his capacity as postmaster at the Point, Waterford exile William Schooley wrote President Lincoln twice to ask for easement of border restrictions, while Lovettsville residents sent a petition imploring the War Secretary to lift the sanctions so they might at least buy clothing to cover their "nakedness."⁴

Sam Gover had just won the right to open a trade store at the Point, when the blockade cut off his clientele. Trapped on opposite sides of the river, despite both having passes to cross "at will," Sam and Maggie each wrote Secretary Stanton for reinstatement of these privileges. Sam wanted to take provisions to his pregnant wife, whom he cited for her "many good deeds for the Union cause," along with his postmaster appointment by Lincoln and financial losses to the Rebels. For confirmation of his patriotic service, he directed Stanton to contact Generals Milroy, Slough and Geary. Maggie's letter pleaded for a pass to Winchester to care for her ailing father and a dying aunt, as well as one so her husband could visit her, giving Milroy as reference for their loyalty.⁵

Both requests were denied. Undeterred, Maggie wrote Stanton again in March, this time "on behalf of the Union people of our *truly loyal* section...[to] beg the privilege of getting the necessary supplies for our families." Recognizing Rebel sympathizers abused the old trading system, she emphasized only those who could prove their loyalty should be allowed to make purchases. Her latest missive was accompanied by an endorsement from the same commissary officer who earlier wrote on her behalf to Senator Willey, who this time carried both documents to the War Department. The packet was subsequently forwarded to Gen. Max Weber in Harpers Ferry for comment. Weber, who had just replaced Sullivan as district commander, asked the Point of Rocks provost marshal for his opinion on Maggie's request. "More true and loyal people do not exist," replied this officer, who also concurred that suffering in North Loudoun could be alleviated "without aiding the Rebels." Weber, who already shared a natural affinity to the German Settlement and would prove more sympathetic towards loyalists than his predecessor, added his endorsement before returning the package to the War Department. The Army's Inspector General finally advised Maggie that even though the Secretary of War was aware of her services to the government and sympathized "with the losses sustained by you and the Union people of Loudoun County, the exigencies of the military service will not allow the granting of permanent passes to any citizen." Sensing a softening in the military's position, Maggie immediately asked Stanton to reconsider, pointing out the blockade was not being enforced consistently, as some individuals, including the Downey family, crossed into Maryland almost daily.⁶

One of the most spirited appeals was penned to Lincoln in April by nineteen-year-old Lida Dutton, right after witnessing a raid by Mosby's partisans. Despite this incursion and the many other hardships her village had endured, Lida assured the President they would "willingly suffer" even greater

Emma Eliza ("Lida") Dutton, Most Outspoken of the "Waterford Girls." (NYC photo, probably taken after marriage to a Union soldier, WFA)

adversity, "if our forces can whip the rebels any sooner with [the blockade] down." What they could not understand was the government's failure to provide them with protection. "The Rebels have been...carrying off every bit of corn, stealing every good, bad or indifferent horse...thus strengthening the *mean* commands of Moseby and White...How anxiously we have been watching and waiting for some of our soldiers to come." With her brother serving in the Union army, and her father forced into exile, she proudly proclaimed: "There are many 'Friends' [i.e., Quakers] in our neighborhood, but the organ of combativeness is pretty strongly developed in us all, particularly in my Father's daughter."[7]

As they had after Gettysburg, sixty women from Waterford worked all winter to make items for sale at the Baltimore Sanitary Fair (18 April to 2 May), proceeds of which went to aid Northern soldiers. Rather than ship their handicrafts, several younger women suggested delivering them in person would help publicize their current plight under the blockade, and in early April John Dutton and Postmaster Schooley tried unsuccessfully to persuade Secretary Stanton to authorize passes. The "Waterford girls" were not so easily put off, and on the day the Fair opened, Dutton informed General Weber his daughter Lizzie was waiting across the river, hoping to pass. Their persistence paid off, and Lizzie arrived in time for the opening ceremony. With one across, Sam Gover wired the Harpers Ferry commander that his sister Ann Gover and niece Annie Matthews were "on the River brink," ready to cross. After an exchange of messages, permission was granted a day later.

Lizzie's arrival at the Fair was a minor sensation. As one paper reported, "the ladies at the National [booth] have received a large contribution of beautiful and valuable articles from an association of loyal ladies in the very heart of Virginia...The articles, and the young Virginia lady who came with them, arrived by an 'underground railroad,' the exact location of which has not yet been made public." Two days later, the paper announced Annie and her aunt's arrival, also via an "underground railroad, in a way best known to themselves." Not only did their table sell out, but the experience would inspire a more daring expression of loyalty a month later.[8]

It is unknown whether Edie's sister and aunt took advantage of their stay in Baltimore to visit her at Fair Hill School, located outside of Olney, Md. Annie finished her secondary education there, after Samuel Janney's Springdale Academy closed in Goose Creek. Edie's chance came in the fall of 1863, when she was about to turn sixteen. Although her sister had been allowed to attend on credit in recognition of hardships facing Loudoun Quakers, the schoolmistress' largess had run out, and E. Y. had to pay the first third of Edie's tuition (fifty dollars) at the start of her term. Nothing is known of her one year at the school, other than a notebook she kept for an American history class, which required her to contrast current events (mostly about the war) with earlier U.S. history. In March 1864, E. Y. took advantage of looser restrictions at Edward's Ferry to take his wife and youngest daughter across the river to visit Edie and pay her final tuition installment. His financial situation prevented her continuing past June, something Edie would always be defensive about.[9]

* * * * *

A great deal of the isolation felt in Waterford was the result of problems facing the Loudoun Rangers and their captain after Maj. Gen. Franz Sigel took over the West Virginia Department in early March.

The former Prussian officer had little use for an "independent" unit in his command and ordered the Rangers' integration into the West Virginia Cavalry. Citing their unique status, Means and his men refused to comply and threatened to join Cole's Maryland Cavalry instead. Persistent questions about their captain's leadership, commercial dealings and erratic treatment of civilians had taken their toll, just when Means needed all the support he could muster. To make matters worse, James Walker was demanding closure of Downey's distillery, a favorite watering hole of the captain and his men, and John Dutton accused Means of tampering with the U.S. mail. Alarmed by the threatened loss of their "home guard," if not its captain, William Schooley asked Governor Pierpont to intervene. Matters were delayed until Max Weber's installation as Harpers Ferry's commander, but when Means led an unauthorized raid to Waterford, Sigel ordered his dismissal. Upon review, Secretary Stanton upheld this decision, but let the Rangers remain along the Loudoun border, as he had originally agreed.[10]

While the Rangers awaited their fate across the border, North Loudoun had its first sustained look at Mosby's Forty-Third Battalion, now grown to four companies. The same Rebel incursion that prompted Lida Dutton's letter to Lincoln led James Downey to complain to Governor Pierpont: "They have conscripted about fifty men…and are taking all horses, corn and hay they can get, impressing Union men's teams to haul it." With the Rangers' fate still undecided, he exclaimed, "it would be very wrong to take them away here. The people of Loudoun only find out now the protection they were to them and are begging for them to come over…When we organize these upper counties [politically], we must have them." He suggested two Matthews relatives, Lt. Gover and QM Sgt. Edward White, to replace Means as captain.[11]

Only with the installation of Daniel M. Keyes as the new captain of Company A and Edwin Gover as second-in-command were the Rangers ready to venture back into Loudoun in mid-May. After capturing several of Mosby's followers, high water in the Potomac forced Keyes's men to overnight in Waterford. Eager to free his comrades, Capt. Adolphus Richards approached the town with thirty partisans the next morning (17 May). At Waterford's southern edge, the Rebels spotted several pickets Keyes posted while his men procured breakfast in town. A lone Rebel rode forth and lured the pickets past Clifton into an ambush in front of Rachel Steer's home, where a hail of bullets felled the Rangers, including Sgt. Charles Stewart. Renegade chieftain John Mobberly, accompanying Richards' men that day, tarried behind, and riding over the prostrate sergeant, shot the wounded man in the face before taking his boots. Believing Stewart dead, Mobberly rejoined the other riders, who would capture several more Rangers before Keyes could regroup his forces on the far side of town. (Keyes's debut in the "Second Battle of Waterford" fared little better than that of his predecessor two years earlier, prompting potential recruits, including Postmaster Schooley, to enlist elsewhere.)

At The Willows, Rachel Steer ventured across the road to find two Ranger privates mortally wounded, and the sergeant barely clinging to life. Dr. Thomas Bond arrived with some women, including Annie Matthews, to carry the soldiers into Rachel's home, where the privates died. On learning of Mobberly's conduct, the "venerable" Quaker doctor declared "his only ambition in life was to live long enough to make another hell for the man that shot Stewart after he surrendered." In saving the sergeant's life that day, his wish would be granted, but at the time, they all felt in great danger. Even twenty years later, when Annie testified on behalf of Stewart's pension request, she still vividly recalled finding him "shot to pieces," and their fear the Rebels might return any moment. Recent renovations to Clifton's attic revealed a hidden compartment containing bloody bandages and Union army buttons, confirming family lore a wounded Union soldier was hidden there. Since The Willows was the first place Mosby's men would search for survivors, Stewart was moved there until he was able to be carried on a litter back to the Point, where he eventually returned to service and exact vengeance against his would-be killer.[12]

After driving off the "Virginia Yankees," Richards's troopers tarried to "collect the tithe," as they termed raiding Unionist larders and farms. Particular attention was paid to the Dutton home (Sunnyside on 2nd Street), then occupied by his wife Emma and their three youngest daughters: Lizzie (twenty-four), Lida (nineteen) and Anna Ellen (eleven). Lida, the family's most outspoken Unionist, ran an informal network to monitor Rebel activities. Now, a grim determination gripped the teenager, as she helplessly watched the partisans harass her hometown for the second time in a month. Inspired by her sister's reception in Baltimore, Lida hit on the idea of publishing a newspaper to let the outside world know of their travails. Sister Lizzie and neighbor Sarah (twenty-four), daughter of Samuel and Harriet Steer, agreed to help, and her father offered to get the *Baltimore American* to print the paper. Within days a draft was smuggled across the river, and the first issue of the *Waterford News* appeared on 28 May. The four-page underground paper would be published on a roughly monthly basis until the end of the war and, even though the names "Sarah, Lizzie, & Lida" appeared on its masthead, the Confederates never succeeded in stopping publication, perhaps concluding their arrest would only make them martyrs. As a mouthpiece for Union sentiment, the *News* had national impact and was the subject of an editorial in the *New York Tribune*. Copies of the first two issues were sent to President Lincoln, while Jefferson Davis was said to have denounced the "traitorous sheet." Although primarily aimed at a Northern readership, the paper's sly humor also sought to lift the spirits of local Unionists by openly espousing resistance to the Confederacy and correcting slanted reports in the Southern press.

The *News* was popular with Union troops along the border, and editorials championed military themes. The editors deliberately portrayed their town as full of young women eager to find suitable partners, which was only partly an artifice, as only one marriage had taken place since the war began. Volunteers for missions passing near Waterford skyrocketed, and several marriages with Union soldiers took place after the war. The timing and content of the first issue was intended to encourage the new Harpers Ferry commander to lift the blockade, and the editors could congratulate themselves when, a few days later, General Weber authorized loyal citizens to spend ten dollars weekly in Maryland trade stores. The second issue of the *News* applauded this development with a humorous description of a housewife trying to stay within the purchase limit during her first shopping spree in six months.

But their troubles were far from over, especially while valuable forage remained on farms. On 8 June, the partisans reappeared to spend two days collecting horses and wagons to haul grain south. After the Loudoun Rangers captured eight Rebels and recovered several wagons, Mosby himself returned with forty men, hoping to ambush Keyes's troopers. Instead, they ended up capturing Samuel Steer during an ill-advised visit to his family. The customs agent was sent to Richmond, prompting the Federals to retaliate by seizing several Secessionists. They had to post a $40,000 bond, refundable upon Steer's return, which his daughter Sarah negotiated in August. Waterfordians suffered another blow when partisans seized their mail carrier's horse and wagon, temporarily ending postal service.[13]

Matters worsen on the Fourth of July, when Mosby, now a lieutenant colonel, led 250 men on a raid to Point of Rocks that caught its defenders—two Maryland infantry companies and the Loudoun Rangers—in the midst of Independence Day celebrations. (The attack was timed to divert attention from a large force led by Gen. Jubal Early, then crossing the Potomac

Editorial Masthead, *Waterford News*. Lida and Lizzie Dutton joined Sarah Steer to publish the underground Unionist paper. This final issue was only rumored to exist until copy found among Elliot's papers. Despite the paper's notoriety at the time, it was all but forgotten by mid-20th Century, a victim of scrubbing "inconvenient truths" from Loudoun's Civil War history. When a local newspaper reported the "discovery" in 1955 of copied among Abraham Lincoln's papers, it erroneously stated no one recalled its having existed. In fact, Matthews and Steer descendants still preserved copies as treasured mementos of their ancestors' wartime resistance. (3 April 1865 issue, TCC)

on its way to the U.S. Capital.) After driving off the Federals and cutting communications between Washington and Harpers Ferry, the Rebels devoted themselves to systematic looting of the trade stores, resulting in so much merchandise being taken back into Virginia, it was dubbed the "Great Calico Raid." For a third time the hapless Sam Gover was cleaned out, and John Dutton would later unsuccessfully petitioned Harpers Ferry for $7,000 in damages to his store. (Weber rejected the merchant's argument that his loss was due to the Federals' failure to provide adequate protection.)[14]

Back at the Ferry, the combined forces of Sigel and Weber sought safety atop Maryland Heights, making no effort to impede Early's entry into Maryland. With Union forces neutralized by the Rebel advance, Waterford found itself again cut off from the North. This began to change after Early's army failed to breach Washington's defenses at Fort Stevens and slipped back into Loudoun. C.S.A. Gen. Bradley Johnson's weary cavalry brigade arrived in Waterford during the night of 14 July, escorting wagons filled with grain and booty seized in Maryland. Despite stories of pillaging and burning across the river, the Confederate intruders behaved better than expected, paying with recently purloined greenbacks for services rendered. The main Federal force assigned to pursue Early was still getting under way in Washington, but Johnson, aware other Union troops were crossing at Berlin and Harpers Ferry, hastened his brigade out of town after an anxious second night. No sooner had they left, than a Union infantry brigade entered "amidst the wildest cheers of the citizen," but the Federals only tarried a few hours to enjoy the love fest before pulling out in a futile effort to catch Early, then safely beyond the Blue Ridge.[15]

Angered over Sigel's failure to keep Early from threatening Washington, and even more frustrated his troops were then allowed to escape back into Virginia, General-in-Chief Ulysses S. Grant convinced Washington in early August to combine the region's four military departments and place them under the command Maj. Gen. Philip Sheridan, his charismatic cavalry chief. Sheridan and his Army of the Shenandoah would have one task—drive "Old Jube" out of the Valley. To protect his rear and manage his supply lines, Sheridan picked the capable Brig. Gen. John Stevenson to head the Harpers Ferry Military District. Although Loudoun loyalists were heartened to learn he was a native Virginian, Stevenson never let civilian concerns interfere with his primary responsibility of supporting operations in the Valley.

Sheridan's priorities were made clear, when, just days after taking command, he received word that Waterford citizens wanted troops sent from Harpers Ferry to protect them from continued harassment by Mosby's guerrillas. Instead, Sheridan tasked the Department of Washington to respond, with the result Lt. John Hutchinson found himself leading a patrol from the 13th N.Y. Cavalry out of Falls Church on 10 August. Two years earlier, he had been separated from his unit on a similar scout and had to seek directions from a girl he encountered in Waterford. Uncertain of his intentions, Lida Dutton evaded his questions, until the frustrated rider demanded, "What side would you like for me to be on?"; whereupon Lida burst out, "If you're a rebel I hate you; but if you're a Northerner I love you." Unbuttoning his coat to reveal Union insignia, the soldier told the flustered girl he would hold her to that promise. This time, as his squad rode through the village, the lieutenant spotted Lida on her porch and paid his respects. Passage of time had not cooled his ardor, and he told his comrades he would marry her. Returning to Falls Church without finding the enemy, Hutchinson could only repeat Lida's confirmation of the passage of 300 partisans several days earlier. In the next issue of the *News*, the editors coyly noted the New Yorkers' appearance had made them "happy."[16]

Later that month, the "Waterford girls" appeared at Quarterly Meeting in Goose Creek, determined to show they were not intimidated by their hosts' continued adherence to neutrality, which certainly did not include publication of an underground paper that openly welcomed Union soldiers and proclaimed, "the best Christian makes the best soldier." With the approval of likeminded elders from Fairfax Meeting, the assembly issued its sternest warning yet against those who strayed from the Society's precepts against military service. The three editors must have felt indignation at what they viewed as collaboration with the enemy, and the next edition of the *News* contained several pieces in support of Union soldiers. They could not have expressed more clearly their differences with the Quarterly Meeting.[17]

After Mosby's 43rd Battalion captured a Union supply train in the Valley, Grant urged Sheridan to take punitive action against partisan strongholds in Loudoun, including imprisonment of males capable of bearing arms. Once again, Sheridan ordered the Department of Washington to carry out the harsh measure, which resulted in almost 100 civilians being seized during two raids into southern Loudoun in late August. As previously described, Mosby warned Samuel Janney that Unionists would be seized unless the Quaker minister convinced the Federals to stop. After meeting with the War Department, Janney succeeded in getting most of the secessionists released, as well as making Grant and Sheridan aware of the dangers such measures posed for Loudoun's sizable loyal population. Targeting of civilians all but ceased.

In late October, Stevenson gave permission for Friends to attend Yearly Meeting in Baltimore. In addition to the usual elders, the Waterford delegation included Sarah Matthews, evidence of her increased role after her mother's death. Unlike Goose Creek, the Baltimore meeting refused to take a stand against military service, a shift welcomed by many Waterford Quakers. The most significant accomplishment was creation of a Friends Relief Committee that included Sarah Matthews, William Williams and Samuel Janney. Afterwards, Janney traveled to Washington to obtain a permit for the committee to send goods to Waterford and Winchester—at that point the Meetings most in need.[18]

Early autumn brought "a quietude unknown for several preceding months," allowing inhabitants, tired of abuse and violence, to declare Waterford a neutral zone. There, Reb and Yank could visit loved ones without fear of retaliation—as long as they respected the rights of citizens and did not draw their weapons. North Loudoun was benefiting from Mosby's preoccupation with Federal operations in the Shenandoah Valley and along the Manassas Gap Railroad. Recognizing the partisans would return once crops were in, James Downey tried to convince Washington to station troops in Loudoun to protect the fall harvest: "[The loyalists] can subsist from 1,500 to 2,000 cavalry for one or two months…Union men would rather your cavalry get their produce for nothing…than the rebels." His suggestion was ignored.[19]

Since its first issue, the *Waterford News* had exhorted readers to vote for Lincoln, and, after earlier fear that a "peace candidate" might prevail, the President's reelection was celebrated by local Unionists. Convinced a Northern victory was now assured, they had no reason to suspect, as they sat down to Thanksgiving dinner, the worst catastrophe to hit the county was only days away, nor could they imagine it would be perpetuated by their own side.[20]

While Mosby did not alter the Valley Campaign's outcome, he remained a constant irritation to Grant and Sheridan, who, with the election over, settled on a "scorched earth" strategy to destroy partisan bases of support in the Loudoun Valley. As previously related, Sheridan chose Wesley Merritt's 1st Division to carry off livestock and burn barns, mills and forage throughout this fertile region. After crossing the Blue Ridge on 28 November, Merritt's troopers began their destructive task along the Loudoun-Fauquier border before working their way towards the Potomac over the following four days. Loyal farmers in North Loudoun were hard hit by the "Burning Raid," a name seared ever after into the county's psyche.

While Captain Chamberlin's 25th N.Y. Cavalry remained in southern Loudoun with the 1st Brigade, Thomas Devin's 2nd Brigade approached Waterford on the 30th, its arrival announced by pillars of fire from burning barns and haystacks. The village itself was spared and was probably the only place where the incendiaries were greeted with cheers, as the Dutton girls urged the passing soldiers to "burn away, burn away, if it will keep Mosby from coming here." Yet even their exuberance must have paled after they joined others on the surrounding hills and saw the night sky illuminated by flames. The next edition of the *News* offered sympathy to those who lost property, but stressed Rebels, not Union soldiers, were ultimately to blame.[21]

As they approached town on the Clarkes Gap road, Devin's troopers remained unaware they were being shadowed by Colonel Mosby and his men, wearing Union uniforms and ready to "gobble up" any stragglers. Thus, only "a few moments" after the Federals left Rachel Steer's farm, the owner mistook the next group of blue-coats to call at The Willows for Yanks. Pointing to the smoking remains of her haystacks and barn, Rachel implored the newcomers to do "no further damage," adding that she had assured the earlier group of soldiers "she was a Unionist, but they would not listen." Instead, despite her entreaties, they did not even allow her to remove her "stock of killing hogs" before setting the barn afire, where they all perished, nor was she permitted to keep a single "milch cow." Rachel was therefore thoroughly surprised when told she was in the presence of the notorious Mosby. The *Richmond Sentinel*, which carried the story, speculated she might want to reconsider who her true "friends" were. (The Steers had over $2,000 in losses.)[22]

At their next stop, Clifton, neither protestations of loyalty, nor the Union flag, persuaded Devin's men to ameliorate the destruction, which amounted to an aggregate loss of over $4,000. The barn, built in 1860 and valued at $2,500, was totally destroyed, along with its contents: thirty-five bushels of wheat, fifty-five bushels of oats, eighteen tons of hay and fifteen tons of straw. Fire also consumed a wagon, carriage and other equipment. Livestock carried off included two draft horses, a bull, six milk cows and five beef cattle, at a total value of $760. It was a devastating blow from which E. Y. never recovered.

Rachel Steer, mistress of The Willows (now Greystone).). (*Carte de visite*, TCC)

Devin's men were still in town being applauded by the Dutton sisters when Mosby rode over from The Willows to commiserate with the Matthews family over their loss, which he said left nothing for his men to take in the future—scant solace when Edie and her sisters came out to talk. Mosby was getting to be a regular visitor, having searched the place a few days earlier for Ranger Quartermaster Edward White, whose parents were apparently then residing there. That the Grey Ghost would so "coolly" follow in the burners' footsteps gave little assurance the raid would succeed in ridding the county of guerrillas. When told about the partisans' visit to Clifton, neighbor Elisha Walker agreed Mosby could "subsist in this Country as long as any citizens." It was a view shared by most Unionists, who questioned the rationale for their losses.

Few Unionists were hit as hard as the Matthews family. Their prosperous neighbor, James Walker, had only $955 in losses; his barn was spared lest flames spread to the house, and he had the foresight to hide livestock in a remote field. Another relative, David Mansfield, was able to save his Wheatland mill after General Devin, who knew the miller personally, gave him time to gather containers of water before the mill was set on fire, thus enabling Mansfield to douse the flames once the soldiers were out of sight.[23]

From Waterford, Devin's Brigade proceeded to Lovettsville for the night, before returning to Snickersville on 1 December. The next day, Merritt's Division crossed back over the Blue Ridge and reached Winchester two days later. A demoralized E. Y. Matthews followed the Federals there in hopes of getting his animals back. All that he managed was a perfunctory note from Merritt certifying he was "a good Union man" who deserved "protection for his property." It proved of no use when E. Y. then took it to Harpers Ferry and was told livestock seized in the raid had already been sent to auction.[24]

Although many more Confederate sympathizers suffered losses, Unionists were proportionally harder hit by the raid, and it was not just the loyalists who thought so. The same Richmond paper that described Rachel Steer's misfortune noted pointedly that Merritt's men were "entirely indiscriminate" in their destruction, treating Secesh and Union alike. "Indeed, the heaviest blows fell upon the Unionists," which the paper attributed to their farms having been plundered less up until then, and their owners' refusal to accept Confederate money. While it was true Quaker farms around Goose Creek had received preferential treatment from the partisans, this was not the case for loyalist farms in North

Loudoun, and the *Sentinel* was only partly right on the currency issue, as everyone in Loudoun preferred greenbacks to inflationary Confederate scrip. What the paper did not admit was how many secessionist farms lost production after their slaves fled, and therefore had less on hand to destroy. While total losses ran into the millions, Union farmers later filed claims for $256,000 in damages. Of this amount, $80,000 was lost by Goose Creek Friends, and $23,000 by their Waterford counterparts.[25]

These losses were compounded in mid-December, when Stevenson prohibited all trade and travel into Loudoun, edicts that remained in effect through much of the winter. Nor was North Loudoun's inclusion in the Alexandria Government any help in dealing with the Federal military. In his annual address to the legislature, Governor Pierpont described conditions in the Commonwealth as "deplorable." Despite the Rebel army having been driven from large portions of the State, "predatory bands of guerrillas and robbers infest the rear of the Union Army...so that I have not deemed it prudent to attempt a re-organization in the Northern Counties." The Governor was blunt in his denunciation of "abuses of military power," a reference to Federal commanders' refusal to recognize his government's authority. He could, however, point with pride to the passage of a constitution abolishing slavery, the first by any Southern state. Overall, his speech previewed his tenure as Virginia's first postwar governor—too radical for Secessionists, too conciliatory for Unionists.[26]

General Devin's Brigade returned at year's end to establish winter camp in Lovettsville, and their presence significantly curbed Rebel activity during the first two months of 1865. Ironically the Union soldiers were expected to subsist in the same area they had so efficiently laid bare, but Devin may have foreseen this possibility, as his brigade had spared farms along the river during the November raid. Furthermore, the general was well-disposed towards Unionists, and set up facilities for loyal farmers to submit claims for their earlier losses. Capt. Daniel Keyes and customs agent Samuel Steer were present to certify applicants' loyalty, when E. Y. Matthews filed claims for animals carried off and property destroyed. A total of 140 Unionists submitted claims to present to Congress. Although no action was taken before it adjourned, James Walker and Samuel Janney spearheaded a sustained campaign to win reimbursement that finally met with partial success in 1873, when Congress authorized $60,000 to pay for livestock losses. Efforts to recover larger property claims continued into the twentieth century before being abandoned.[27]

Sam Gover and John Dutton took advantage of a snowy winter to slip undetected across the frozen Potomac to visit their families and, for the first time since the war began, the "Waterford girls" indulged in sleigh rides, even though the only nags available were either blind or lame. The young women also called on troops in Lovettsville where, after bringing cheer and gifts to inmates at the camp hospital, they socialized with Devin and his officers at brigadier headquarters. Recounting this activity in the *News*, the editors apologized "for our party not being more vivacious and talkative, but we can only say, if they had lived in Dixie as long as have we, away from any society but our own, they could not have talked either." It is probable E. Y. Matthews drove his daughters to Lovettsville that day, as he received a written statement, dated 24 January, ordering members of Devin's command to respect his property.[28]

Maj. Howard Smith of the New York Dragoons remembered the "Waterford girls" being more "vivacious" than they cared to admit in print. He had passed through their town during the Burning Raid and marveled at the inhabitants' willingness to endure the desolation wrought by the soldiers for the sake of helping end the rebellion. Although absent when the girls visited their camp in January, the major was told "some of them are quite 'wild' for Quakeresses, and know how to 'carry on' as well as Northern girls." Naturally, Smith was delighted to be on hand when the young women returned on Valentine's Day on a similar errand. This time the festivities included a band concert and oyster dinner.[29]

The security afforded by Devin's troops ensured a large turnout at Waterford's Quarterly Meeting on 18-20 February. Although the minutes show nothing out of the ordinary, the absence of criticism of Friends serving in, or aiding, the military showed further reluctance to censure Waterford Quakers who donned a blue uniform, not to mention at least one Goose Creek member who had chosen grey. Sunday marked the high point of the festivities, as attendees and guests gathered in homes for a round of meals and socials after service at the meetinghouse.[30]

The most important visitor that day was General Devin, who agreed to come as a way to reciprocate kindnesses shown his men by local Friends. Accompanied by two squadrons of Dragoons under Major Smith, the general's party arrived as the religious service ended. Flooded with "more than fifty invitations to dinner," Devin and Smith accepted one from "Mr. Matthews, a wealthy farmer, who lives a little way from town. He is an intelligent, well educated man and had a beautiful home. Mrs. Matthews is an excellent woman...and the daughters, of which there are three, Annie, Edith and Mary, are lovely." (Aware of the prestige his presence for dinner conferred, Devin may have accepted the invitation to Clifton in acknowledgement that his men had caused more damage there than all but one other farm in the neighborhood.) On his way back through town, the general called on John Dutton and "Major" Sam Means.[31]

Brig. Gen. Thomas Devin. He inscribed this *carte de visite* "your old friend" when he presented it to Annie Matthews, probably during a dinner at Clifton in early 1865. (TCC)

At the end of February, Devin's Brigade left Lovettsville to rejoin Sheridan's army in a final sweep through the Shenandoah Valley. Meanwhile, the Loudoun Rangers had sufficient time to regain their aplomb after being ambushed during a Christmas party near Taylorstown. Lt. Edwin Gover was now provost marshal at the Point, although the blockade and high water left little for him to do. In a letter to his wife, Gover discounted rumors they might have to relocate to the front, and instead predicted the war would be over by July. Many shared his optimism and were therefore doubly demoralized by the partisans' reappearance after Devin left. In early March, Mosby summoned 150 men from winter camps farther south to round up young boys to fill the dwindling Confederate ranks and scrounge for whatever forage the Yankees might have missed. The partisans stayed in Quaker homes around Goose Creek for nearly a month, finding their hosts both cordial and well-provisioned.[32]

Collection of the tithe in Waterford began 5 March with impressment of a team from Talbott to haul corn, bacon and other spoils south. Over the next week, "Major" Williams Hibbs and Mosby's new quartermaster, J. Wright James, directed the acquisition, pausing only to demand mid-day meals from local homes. When they called at Rachel Steer's place to claim a tenth of her bacon, she asked indignantly whether they had not read the press account of how the "Yankees had burnt up her Pork in the barn? They seemed to remember it & did not take any meat." But Rachel had had enough of running The Willows by herself, and shortly thereafter rented it out so she could move into town. More traumatic for those in the village was the arrival of a conscription detail, which entered Elisha Walker's school and dragged off Cornelius Shawen (seventeen), whose Secessionist parents owned an adjacent farm. Elisha was on lunch break at his parents' house but, not believing the partisans' assurances that "Friends were exempt," he and two other Quakers hid out at The Willows for the next few days.[33]

After the partisans left to concentrate on other parts of Loudoun, General Stevenson took the opportunity to transfer Cole's Cavalry and most of the Loudoun Rangers to Jefferson County, W. Va., replacing them with the 25th N.Y. Cavalry. The newcomers' arrival might have gone unnoticed a while longer had their new provost marshal at the Point, Capt. S. E. Chamberlin, not sent a party of four Loudoun Rangers, led by Sgt. David Hough (a Quaker), to investigate Rebel activity at Downey's distillery, as described in greater detail in Chapter 11. Repeated exposure to drunken soldiers from both sides had heightened interest in the national temperance movement, and Downey's establishment was a particular *bete noir* of James Walker, who repeatedly demanded its closure by the Federals. Whether the still sustained any damage in this incident is unclear, but the Rangers returned with three prisoners from Mosby's command, including "Major" Hibbs and Quartermaster James, the same two who directed the cleaning out of Waterford farms two weeks earlier. Pleased, Stevenson had Chamberlin send the Rangers back into Loudoun along with their old captain, Sam Means, who wanted to take supplies to his family. The scouts surprised two of Mosby's men having their pictures taken at Waterford's photography studio, and another was captured nearby, but not before the home of Clifton's eighty-year-old neighbor, Joshua Pusey, was "pillaged" by group led by the colonel's brother, William Mosby.[34]

Mosby himself came to Waterford on April Fools' Day to personally investigate the recent loss of his men. With his commissary staff captured, he put an aide in charge of pressing teams from Talbott to haul Amasa Hough's corn south. Another was dispatched to Clifton to get "a little sugar for the Colonel's coffee—about which he is very particular—drinks nothing but the genuine." That afternoon, Mosby had his picture taken in town, and then left another photograph behind to taunt Captain Keyes, apparently unaware the Ranger captain had recently resigned and been replaced by Lieutenant Gover.[35]

The last issue of the *News* was dated 3 April, just as word arrived of Richmond's fall. The editors complained of being "constantly annoyed by Mosby's band of guerrillas," especially their refusal to admit the fighting was nearly over, even after being told of the rout of Early's army at Waynesboro. One article drew an analogy between the destruction of the countryside and the moral decay that accompanied it, tacit recognition their community would never be the same.

When news of Lee's surrender to Grant on 9 April reached Waterford, local legend records the "joy was uncontrollable, and grabbing each other by the arms, these black-frocked, sedate Quakers—momentarily forgetting the tenets of their Meeting—danced a jig." Their happiness would be tempered by Lincoln's assassination and a seemingly endless wait for Mosby's surrender. When he finally dismissed his command on 21 April, the blockade was lifted the next day, allowing Edie and her father to travel to the Point on 24 April to buy supplies and check on his claims.[36]

On First-day, 30 April, Rebecca Williams was pleased to see Samuel Steer and Sam Gover once again at Meeting. She also noted the presence of Captain Chamberlin, although she may not have known he was there at Edie's request. Above all, Rebecca was happy the town had witnessed no recent incidents of violence, despite the presence of soldiers from both sides. "Returned paroled rebels walk the streets unarmed; armed Federals here, mingling together. Reminds me of the Lion & the Lamb lying down together, if we could only see anything lamb-like in either." Two days later, Sam Gover requested permission to reopen his store in town, and on 5 May he joined other merchants to complain about continued collection of duty on goods.[37]

The 25th N.Y. Cavalry's correspondent has provided the only account yet discovered of the ceremonial raising of the Stars and Stripes on 3 May at Lovettsville, the first official flag-raising in Loudoun: "The immense crowd which assembled testified to the importance attached to the event, and the enthusiasm displayed by the returned Union refugees was in marked contrast to [those who had been] either active participants in or sympathizers with the treasons of Jeff Davis and Co." A military band from Harpers Ferry "made the air resonant with sweet music. A large number of military gentlemen were present…and the assemblage of the fair sex was perfectly dazzling." Among the speakers were Samuel Janney, Unionist state senator William Mercer, Lovettsville Unionist Thomas Marsh and aspiring politician Charles Janney. After further entertainment and a meal, the event ended with a ball.

Three days later 300 attendees at a "Meeting of the Loyal Citizens of Loudoun" met in Waterford's Quaker meetinghouse and passed resolutions calling for the rapid restoration of state and local government, fair treatment of secessionists, an end to slavery and nullification of Confederate laws. The printed resolutions also expressed preference for the selection of Unionist candidates to run for public office under rules set forth in the 1864 Constitution. Internal turmoil kept the 25th N.Y. Cavalry from playing a ceremonial role at this meeting, but Provost Marshall Chamberlin was able to attend a flag-raising in Waterford on 13 May that Edie and her sisters helped prepare. The event included dinner for "several hundred" and the reopening of local shops. Chamberlin termed it a "pleasant affair" and as provost marshal would have helped preside over the ceremony.[38]

Further signs of normalcy followed quickly, and by 17 May the collection of duties on goods going into Virginia was discontinued, allowing Chamberlin and his provost guard to rejoin their regiment at Berlin by. With shops reopened and Sam Gover restored as postmaster, Waterford seemed poised to regain its past vitality. Moreover, hosting the county's first postwar mass political gathering signaled a willingness to take the lead in returning the county to the Union. Although rapid demobilization of Federal troops would make this goal far harder than the still celebratory Unionists realized, Waterford appeared up to the challenge, and an earlier description in the *News* of its resolve seemed even more relevant at war's end:

> Many threats have been made about burning our houses over our devoted heads; but Waterford is still standing, and we trust it may stand long in the future to remind other generations that in its time-honored walls once dwelt as true lovers of their country as ever breathed the breath of life—long-suffering, but *faithful* to the *end*.[39]

Chapter 16

HORSING AROUND: May-September 1865

A century later, Eleanor Chamberlin would recall her parents' romance began when her grandfather took his daughter, "a winsome girl of sixteen" [*sic* seventeen], to complain to the Provost Marshal at Point of Rocks about his wartime losses. The attending officer,

> a dashing young cavalryman, found more of interest that day than the claim of an outraged farmer. An acquaintance was formed with the young lady that drew the officer to Waterford whenever duty permitted. Often the trip was quite hazardous, for on at least three occasions he was fired on by Confederates along the way. However, it took more than a few shots from ambush to discourage the gallant suitor from making his trips. Mute evidence of the courtship is still visible today in the chiseled initials on the old stone stile at Clifton, long the home of the Matthews family.[1]

Although Edie may have heard stories about the Point's new commander when she accompanied Edward Y. Matthews to the Point on 24 April 1865, family lore that it was "love at first sight" between the "dashing cavalryman" and the "winsome" maid is apparently accurate. Three days later, Edie returned with her mother Sarah to make small purchases and, more importantly, invite the captain to attend services at their meetinghouse. He accepted, and afterwards accompanied her family to Clifton for dinner. That afternoon, or soon thereafter, he and Edie rode up the "Trough Road" (Rt. 704) to admire the view. The outing made a lasting impression on Elliot, who later sketched the scene and sent it to Edie. Whether or not he was shot at during visits to Waterford is open to speculation. The war was over, but horse thieves and disgruntled Rebels were certainly present along his route over Catoctin Mountain.[2]

Fortunately, the diary of Edie's fifteen-year-old sister Marie has survived to chronicle their budding romance and is presented below, interspersed with commentary, in slightly abridged format:

> Clifton, May 25th, 1865// I have commenced many times to keep a diary, but somehow I never kept one very long...Now...I just want something to keep fresh in my memory the "scenes of my childhood." *Thus* begins my chronicle.
>
> We have been having quite a good deal of excitement here lately. Last week we had the extreme, the unbounded pleasure of hoisting once more the "Star Spangled banner, the flag of our pride" over loyal old Waterford and Oh! the joy, the inexpressible joy of that day. From loved Clifton we can watch that flag floating to the breeze and giving evidence of release from Rebel thralldom. Since then we have had real gay times...One week ago sister and self went to town to assist in preparing the decorations for that great "gala day" on which we raised the Stars and Stripes, and now they float triumphantly vouchsafing pro-

tection to the loyal and true, and bidding defiance to the enemies of justice and liberty.

On 13 May, ten days after Lovettsville held Loudoun's first symbolic flag-raising, Waterford hosted a similar ceremony that included hoisting a flag atop a pole on the hill at the east end of Main Street.[3]

> There has also been some shadows. For instance the stealing of Captain Chamberlin's horses of which he was so fond. Indeed [they were] too bad for any use in the world. They were such sweet horses and we had all become very much attached to them. They had been here a good deal & sisters [Annie and Edie] had had delightful rides upon them.
>
> I played a splendid trick upon Captain [D. Henry] Burtnett's expense last night. I made him suppose that I had come with the horses for which he had offered a handsome reward. He declares he will have his revenge, but I do not much fear it. He is so nice. I admire him so much. Had I but one 4th of the knowledge he possesses, I would be content. He writes and speaks magnificently. Our Captains C & B left Clifton today followed by many regrets from its inmates and hopes of a speedy return.

Loudoun was renowned for its fine "blooded" horses, so the central role they play in Marie's diary is not surprising. Even a fifteen-year-old knew her horseflesh, and a man's mount was as much of an attraction to the opposite sex as a sleek car might be today. The premium placed on horses was even higher after four years of war had depleted the county's equine population. Once the border reopened, John Henshaw asked the War Department to address this shortage by allowing farmers to purchase horses in Maryland, a question that became moot after all restrictions were removed in May.[4]

The return of soldiers from the front increased demand for horses and mules needed for spring planting and transportation, dramatically driving up their value. During the war, both sides became accustomed to commandeering mounts from nearby farms. Owners had little say in the matter, although they might receive vouchers promising reimbursement. The Loudoun Rangers lost most of their horses during a skirmish with Mosby's partisans in early April. As an independent unit, they had been required to furnish their own mounts and now simply returned to their old, mostly Secessionist, sources for replacements. What the "Virginia Yankees" failed to take into account was that, with the war over, these same civilians could now seek redress from Union authorities. On 11 May, Gen. John Stevenson received a complaint about the Rangers "seizing US horses, even from funeral processions...and converting them to their own use." The Harpers Ferry commander had gotten several similar reports and assured the complainant he had already issued orders prohibiting soldiers going into Loudoun without prior permission, and then only "with express orders not to disturb any persons or property." After the Rangers were disbanded at the end of May, ex-Confederates accustomed to seizing animals from Unionists accounted for the preponderance of equine theft.[5]

As Marie's diary suggests, the horses' disappearance from Clifton created quite a stir and became an oft-told part of family lore. Colonel Seeley's lengthy trial disrupted normal activity within the Twenty-Fifth, leaving Chamberlin free to pursue his romantic interests. On the night of 22 May, when the captain and his orderly stayed at the Matthews farm while ostensibly in Loudoun to arrest a civilian, they quartered their horses near the springhouse. The orderly planned

Couple Stand beside Flagpole Used to Raise Stars and Stripes at War's End on Waterford's Upper Main Street. (C. 1870 photograph, WFA)

to spend the night nearby, but when he returned from getting supper in the house, he found them missing. The next morning Chamberlin was able to track their mounts as far as the turnpike to Snickersville and a short time later received a note from Sam Gover informing him they were spotted being ridden through Union, a small town in southwest Loudoun (soon to change its name to Unison to avoid any association with the North).[6]

Adding to the drama was discovery that one of the perpetrators was Edward S. Wright, whose family lived in Waterford and were well known to the Matthews clan. Wright, a sometime private in White's 35th Va. Cavalry, had been twice charged with desertion and thrice captured by the North—the theft at Clifton occurred just two days after his return home from prison at Point Lookout, Md. During his multiple absences from White's Cavalry, he often rode with John Mobberly's band of renegades, giving Wright ample opportunity to hone his special talent for stealing horses. This time he found little to attract him in a county under Union control and, with a companion, J. L. Taylor of Fluvanna County, resolved to seek a more congenial environment elsewhere. They needed horses, and Chamberlin's frequent visits had not gone unnoticed, so the ex-Rebels helped themselves.[7]

To catch the culprits and recover the animals, Chamberlin turned to "Captain" D. Henry Burtnette, then head of a "secret service" run by the Harpers Ferry Provost Marshal. The suave Burtnette, whom Marie described as a captain, and who favored the title "Provost Marshal of Loudoun," was then only a private in Cole's Cavalry. Given its implications for other events taking place at this time, a summary of Burtnette's checkered military record follows. In May 1861, he enrolled as a major in the 99th N.Y. Infantry at Fortress Monroe, using the name Henry B. Burtnette (age forty-five), but was discharged two months later before receiving a commission. The following October, under the name D. Henry Burtnette (then forty-four), he joined the 2nd N.Y. Heavy Artillery in Alexandria but was arrested and dismissed from the regiment before year's end. Yet, several weeks after being led away under guard, he was spotted hanging around the camp in a colonel's uniform. The regiment's commander charged the interloper with fomenting insubordination among his men, describing him as "a desperate character...indicted for various offenses, particularly forgery."

Undaunted, Burtnette managed in April 1862 to get appointed a major in the U.S. Volunteer Corps, where he served as aide-de-camp to Gen. John Frémont, then in charge of the Mountain Department in western Virginia. After the general was removed from command, Burtnette remained in New Creek, a town along the B&O tracks, where he was arrested in August for "conduct unbecoming an officer and a gentleman." His court martial included charges of demanding kickbacks from local merchants, staging a fraudulent auction of seized liquor to benefit a saloon in which he partnered with two Englishmen, stabbing an enlisted man during an altercation at this saloon, and speaking abusively of fellow officers after his arrest. He was convicted in September and sentenced to forfeiture of four months' pay and public censure. Gen. John Wool thought the sentence too lenient and had him dismissed from the Army in October.

Marie (l.) and Edie with Unidentified Civilian and Union Infantry Lieutenant. (C. 1865 photograph, TCC)

Burtnette dropped from sight until he enlisted as a private in Cole's Cavalry in early 1864. He soon won promotion to sergeant and later persuaded Maryland's governor to nominate him for captain. Alarmed by this possibility, the War Department barred him from becoming an officer "in any grade." After being detailed to the district provost marshal's office in Harpers Ferry that fall, Sergeant Burtnette served as assistant provost marshal in Berlin and Point of Rocks, where he worked closely with the Loudoun Rangers. He continued to pose as an officer, however, and his undoing came in late November, when he referred to himself as "captain" in two telegrams pertaining to the Rangers' participation in the Burning Raid. After this latest insubordination came to the attention of authorities in Washington he was demoted to private, a rank he still held when mustered out in late June 1865.[8]

> We had Mr. James Rinker to stay all night with us last night—a fact at which we marveled much as he never was here before. He came over in company with Captain Chamberlin, who returned here on the hardest old steed you ever saw. We laughed at him so much about it & he made such a quantity of odd speeches. He proposed having it shingled, which I think would have been a decided advantage. He has been used to such splendid chargers that it is hard for him to descend to "Dixie nags."
>
> ...Cousin Randolph White has returned from Hillsborough where he took dear Cousin Sarah yesterday. She will remain some time. We miss her so much when she is absent. She feels just like one of the family. Cousin Randolph came by Waterford on his return & got the mail. The "Ladies Book" came tonight. I have been looking at the fashions which I think are real ugly. Bonnets without crowns. Hats without rims. Was there ever anything so absurd? I think not.

James Rinker was a local auctioneer, who would have been particularly knowledgeable about horse trading, and likely provided the horse Chamberlin rode that day. John Randolph White's kinship with the Matthews family was through his wife (née Sarah G. Janney), the granddaughter of Sarah Harris Gover. Both were in their mid-fifties and lived on a farm outside Leesburg before the war, but Marie implies they had been staying at Clifton for some time, perhaps finding it a more congenial environment after their only child, Edward, became the Loudoun Ranger quartermaster.

> Captain Chamberlin gave sister Edie the most ridiculous photograph of [former C.S.A President] Jeff Davis in "crinoline." I really do think our costume disgraced in being worn by such a base traitor as he has ever been. Poor man, I fear his doom is a terrible one. He has "sowed the wind, he will reap the whirlwind."

After the fall of Richmond, President Davis and his cabinet tried to escape to Mexico. When they were cornered by Federal troops in rural Georgia in May, Davis hastily donned his wife's clothing in a futile attempt to avoid capture. The Northern press circulated caricatures of this incident, much to the discomfiture of Davis and his supporters.

> Some persons, Cousin R White among others, think Captain C will not get his horses, but I am confident he will. Perhaps it is because I am so anxious that he should. I always hope for the best. I do not know how such despondent folks get along—always looking on the dark side of the picture. I really pity them. Some persons thought the war would last 20 years. I never did though.
>
> I have been working on the rug today. I am awfully tired of it, but Mother wishes us to finish it as soon as possible. I fear it is my nature to tire of anything ere it is complete. I have not patience nor perseverance to a very great extent, and (speaking confidentially) I have not the reputation of being very industrious. Now sister Edie works very rapidly and sister [Annie] very neatly, and I do not work at all when I can help it. But indeed I should not be telling all these things for they are both older than I (I am only 15)...
>
> Auntie [possibly Ann Gover] and sister Edie have gone into Waterford. I commissioned the latter to purchase some articles for me which I trust she will not forget. It has not been long since we had no stores at all here and Oh! those were sorry days when we had to send 9 miles for a paper of pins. Those Dixie days are over now. How glad I am that I have lived in the South. Now I know something of war from experience and that is something those who live north do not.

> Saturday [27 May]. We are quite busy today. We always have rather more to do on this than other days and then we have company, Captain Chamberlin having come over last night to bring our carriage, which by the way was a present from some of our kind Maryland friends. It is quite a nice vehicle and we hope to have many pleasant rides therein. I think it was particularly kind of Capt. to bring it over. He had so much trouble as he had but one horse. It is real amusing to hear him relate his adventures. Oh! He is splendid! "He's gallant, graceful, gentle, tall//Noblest, bravest, best of all."
>
> Father went for the carriage a few days since and had his horse, old Buck, stripped. So instead of driving up in style in the new carriage, he was obliged to ride home without saddle or bridle. Dear, dear, what we Dixieites do have to endure. We heard that the country flag was to be hoisted at Leesburgh today and expected to go, but Cousin Eddie White has just been out and informed us it was to be postponed. I am real glad for it did not suit us very well to go today. Indeed I have quite neglected my Journal. I have not written any in it for several days.

Sarah Matthews served on the Friends Relief Committee, established at the last Yearly Meeting to coordinate donations to needy Quakers in war-torn Virginia, and helped arrange for the carriage.

> Capt. Chamberlin went away this morning. Yesterday, whilst we were at the dinner table his sergeant came with an order for him to report to Berlin today. We suppose to be mustered out. He is almost beside himself at the idea of going home. I do not wonder. We miss him very much indeed. He vows he has left his heart at Clifton...

On the day (28 May) Col. Aaron Seeley was released from arrest, he ordered Chamberlin and his guard to rejoin the regiment at Berlin, their services no longer needed on the border.

> I started to school this morning. *Such* a school. Four scholars besides myself and they scarcely know the first letter of the alphabet. Oh! It is awful. I do not know whether I can continue or not. Sister Edie tells me to stop right away, but sister [Annie] who has study on the brain advised me to go. Now I know I ought to go and learn all I can, for I feel very much behind in my studies, but it is terrible: Tis a struggle between duty and inclination. Time will prove which triumphs.

Marie was referring to a small school which Elisha Walker opened in early 1865 in a house at the end of Trough Road, opposite his parents' farm (Talbott).

> Sister Annie received a beautiful letter from Captain Burtnett. Also one of Moore's poems entitled "Loves of the Angels," which formerly belonged to Mr. [John] Cook who was hung with John Brown. We hear this morning that Uncle Sam [Gover] is very much indisposed today. I am so sorry; his constitution seems to be broken entirely. I fear he will never rally. Billie Steer came out to bring the mail. He rode up on a horrid old gray horse and shouted he was [former C.S.A. Colonel Elijah] "Lige" White. Poor fellow, he doesn't know any better. [Billie had an intellectual disability.] I tease him so much. I do feel a little conscience smitten and think I will not do it again, but I cannot help [it]. I believe it is one of my besetting sins to worry other people.
>
> I am real tired tonight in consequence of Sister [Annie?] and myself practicing some extraordinary gymnastics that we saw "Brother Elliot" (we have adopted him) perform. We concluded he should not excel us. So we really learned to clear a fence at a bound. Refined is it not? Nobody saw us though.
>
> It seems so long since I wrote any in my Journal and so many things have transpired that I scarce know which to relate first. Think I shall begin with the flag raising at Leesburgh [on 31 May] which was quite a delightful affair. Captain Chamberlin came over from Berlin (with 4 other officers whom we liked very much) and drove us down in the car-

> riage. The ride was a very pleasant one. We arrived in Leesburgh quite early and walked around until 12 o'clock. Then went to Mr. [James M.] Wallace's [hotel] and dined. Had *delightful strawberries* and cream. We then returned to the Court House yard to listen to the speaking which by the way was very poor, Mr. Downie occupying most of the time to say *worse than nothing*. We were so disappointed that Captain Burtnett was not there. We had fully expected him. He has been here this week. Oh! he is so elegant. I just love him. He gave me one of his curls. I do appreciate it so highly. Tis so pretty. He says a great many flattering things to me which he protests are true as faith, but somehow I can't think so. Indeed I know they are not. They are entirely too good to be true. He is going to teach me French and I know he will regret that he ever undertook it, for I know I will give him a lot of trouble for I am so dull.

The Leesburg flag-raising was followed the next day (1 June) by elections for county and district officers, and candidates for these offices monopolized the speaker's platform that Marie had hoped would feature Loudoun's "provost marshal." Both William B. Downey, campaigning to become Commonwealth Attorney, and his father—James M. Downey, north Loudoun's representative to Pierpont's Restored Government—spoke at the Leesburg ceremony. Marie's comment confirms the Downeys were no favorites of the Quakers. Although the day proved boring to the teenager, most were relieved that it "passed off pleasantly and in good order."[9]

> Captain C left this morning for Winchester whence he has been ordered. We will miss him so much having become very much attached to him…

The Twenty-Fifth left Berlin on 1 June for Stevenson Depot outside Winchester, where it remained until finally being sent back to New York City on the 20th to be mustered out of service.

> We feel so sad this morning on account of Darling little Nathan's illness. We think there is no hope of his recovery. Oh! my how we will miss him. He is such an idol with us all. It will almost break our hearts to lose him. He is too pure for this world. Mother is in at Uncle Sam's. We are very anxious to hear from there today although we fear too…

> Capt. Burtnett has returned. He is en route for southern Va. in search of Capt. C's horses which I trust he will find. He this evening brought with him Captains Rockwell and [Harpers Ferry Provost Marshal] Andrews of General Stevenson's staff [in Harpers Ferry]. They are just as nice as they can be…I must retire for Capt. B says he is going to have reveille at 5½ o'clock and that is terrible in my opinion.

> June 10th. Dead! Is he dead? [Nathan Gover died on June 9th.] He the sunbeam of our household who shed his brightness and happiness around him? Yes alas! and Oh! what a void has his death left in our hearts…I did not go to the grave…I know it is wrong, but every shovelfull of earth that I hear sound upon the coffin seems like 'twere thrown upon my heart, and the echo haunts me for many days. He did look so beautifully, just like a blessed angel, which he now is. Poor dear Uncle Sam and Aunt Maggie. It seems almost more than they can bear.

> Cousin Sarah [White] has returned again. It is real nice to have her back. Some days since I had the extreme pleasure of beholding Mr. N___ S___ [probably Cornelius ("Neil") Shawen, who lived across the road and was briefly impressed into the Confederate Army that spring] through the spy glass. He looked very natural as it was and had he had on his "long gray" he *would have looked more than natural*. Capt. Burtnett returned from his raid south this evening with 3 Federal deserters as prisoners. Poor fellows. I know their offense is a great one, yet I could not help feeling sorry for them, though I know he will treat them as kindly as possible. He also gave me a captured cow which I prize very highly both as a present from him and for its real value. He gave it the name of Henrietta for

himself [i.e., Henry]. He expects to return in two weeks with his son, Lieutenant Burtnett and his daughter. I want to see them so badly. If they are anything like him, I know I shall be pleased with them.

June. Coming home from school this evening I gathered the first raspberries I have seen this summer.

July. So long and so eventful has been the time since I have written any, that I know not where to commence. It has been two weeks and during that period many things have taken place. We have so much company and have visited quite a quantity. We have three ladies staying with us whose society we enjoy very much. Aunt May Wiley from Philadelphia and Mattie Gover and Anna Colbert from Baltimore…One of the greatest events of the past fortnight is the capture of the notorious horse thief Ed Wright by our friend Capt. B. He told where Captain C's horses are, so he will get them after all the despondencies folks have said…

With a squad from Harpers Ferry, Burtnette tracked the horse thieves into southern Virginia and then to Baltimore, where he arrested Wright and Taylor on 15 June. On the train back to Harpers Ferry, the "secret service" agent foiled Wright's attempt to escape from the moving car through a lavatory window. Two days later, a military commission was hastily convened to hear the case, despite the defense's objection that it had no jurisdiction over a civilian since the war was over. Chamberlin and Burtnette were both key witnesses at the trial, which dragged on until the end of June, making it impossible for the former to return to New York with his regiment. Several citizens from Loudoun, including Sam Means, stood ready to give evidence, but their services were not needed once Taylor agreed to testify against Wright in exchange for immunity. In his closing summary, the prosecutor implored the court, "in the name of the people of Waterford and Loudoun County" to make "an example" and find Wright guilty. Despite a lengthy and quite eloquent final plea by his lawyer, Ed Wright was convicted and sentenced to five years in the Wheeling penitentiary.[10]

Our servant walked off this morning without any ceremony whatever. It does make me so indignant to think of the colored people being so impudent. They have entirely forgotten their places. [Emancipation encouraged free Blacks as well to seek better employment opportunities.]

Captain B and C have been here again [after Wright's trial ended on 28 June]. The former gave us a full description of the capture and examination of Mr. Wright which was very entertaining. I would dislike very much to be a Rebel while he is Provost Marshal of Loudoun Co. He is so decided. I was just learning to speak of Henrietta as "my cow" when he asked me if I would milk her. I informed him that I could and lo! he took the cow that he had given unconditionally from me and bestowed it upon Sister Edie. I do think it was awful in [him] to do so. I did not suspect him of such a thing. Sister Edie claimed it, but I could not think he had really given it to her. Sister is so cute. She has no hope of it being hers, so she says he gave it to all the family. She said something else droll too that I will not put on paper.

Captain C came down last week and remained until this morning [probably 3 July] when [he] departed [for New York] followed by sighs and perhaps tears. He amused us so much yesterday (Sunday) by asking for an old linen coat that he might go raspberrying. He is so odd sometimes. He, Cousin [Randolph White], Father, Mr. Bond and Mr. Janney took a ride yesterday. They went to Governor Swan's country residence [Morven Park, the country estate of Maryland Governor Thomas Swann, located outside of Leesburg] and came home laden with cherries & very much delighted with their ride. We had a splendid walk "last night by the dim twilight," and I chose the star of my destiny which is a bright one. We went last evening at Aunt Nancie's [probably Ann Taylor Ratcliff's home in

Waterford]. Enjoyed it very much...[Marie would only resume her diary in September.]

According to Marie's diary, the stolen horses had been at Clifton "a good deal" before their disappearance and were frequently ridden by her sisters. Since this activity took place during Seeley's court martial, it seems likely the animals were connected to the "horse-trading" that figured so prominently in that trial, perhaps being hidden on the farm to prevent their discovery by the prosecution. Another incident involving Edie's suitor and horses was turned over to the War Department's Judge Advocate General for further investigation on 23 June. In doing so, the Baltimore Provost Marshal reported an allegation had been made that a "black mare purchased from S. E. Chamberlin, Capt. & Prov. Marshal Point of Rocks, and subsequently taken from A. S. Bunwell as bearing the brand US." (The supporting documents have not been located.)[11]

After the completion of Wright's trial, Chamberlin tarried a few more days, probably to spend the Fourth of July with Edie's family, before departing for New York City. He was among the last members of the Twenty-Fifth to muster out, and on his final day (7 July) at Hart Island, Seeley provided a letter of commendation describing him as a "most excellent officer and gentleman," one who had never received a "censure or reprimand...On the field of battle, no one was more brave, and executed his orders with coolness, and was perfectly fearless."[12]

Also at his muster-out, Chamberlin learned his final pay was being held up, pending resolution of an allegation made in a telegram sent by "C. Maxwell" of Point of Rocks to Secretary of War Stanton on 3 July. In it, Maxwell requested $150 be deducted from Chamberlin's salary to cover the cost of a horse that the Union captain sold him as "private property, since proved and taken as Government property." (Although the War Department apparently did not connect this telegram to the sale of a black mare to A. S. Bunwell, they were most likely related, if not the same.) In response to Maxwell's telegram, the Department wired Hart Island to withhold final payment until the allegation could be resolved, forcing Chamberlin to travel to Washington. There on 22 July, he swore out an affidavit affirming he had never sold "any horse whatsoever at Point of Rocks either for the government or on his own account, and that he never knew or heard of Mr. C. Maxwell. In the meantime, a military investigator was dispatched to the Point, but could not locate Maxwell, or any record that someone with that name had passed through town, nor could he find any evidence Maxwell's telegram originated there. Failure to substantiate the allegation resulted in Chamberlin's receipt of full back pay on 16 August, after which he would spend the next five weeks at Clifton.[13]

* * * * *

The war was barely over, before 300 "loyal citizens" gathered in Waterford's Quaker meetinghouse on 6 May to begin restoration of the county's civil government. Aside from calling for fair treatment of secessionists, an end to slavery and nullification of Confederate laws, their printed resolutions expressed preference for the selection of Unionist candidates to run for public office under rules set forth in the Alexandria Constitution that Governor Pierpont ratified a year before. (President Andrew Johnson would within days recognize Pierpont's Alexandria regime as Virginia's legitimate government and authorize its relocation to Richmond.) The Waterford gathering also called for a countywide convention in Hamilton on 15 May to pick candidates for local office. Quakers exerted considerable influence on this occasion, and several were nominated at Hamilton, much to the annoyance of those who had allied themselves with the Restored Government during the war, and now felt their influence waning. Under the terms of the 1864 Constitution, eligibility to vote was limited to White males over the age of twenty-one, who had resided in the state for a year (six months for local elections) and were willing to take an oath to uphold the U.S. Constitution and Pierpont's state government. Persons who actively aided the rebellion after 1 January 1864, or held Confederate national and state office, were barred from voting or holding office, until the state legislature passed additional laws to restore their political rights.[14]

Only 930 voters turned up at polls on 1 June, a far cry from the 2,900 who cast ballots in 1860. As intended, restrictions on eligibility effectively limited participation to Unionists, still about a third of

Loudoun's electorate. The turnout was highest in north Loudoun, where 280 voted in Lovettsville and 162 in Waterford, but even there, apathy and war-related attrition produced sharp declines from earlier elections. Given the lawlessness of the times, the race for sheriff drew the most attention and was won by north Loudoun merchant Samuel C. Luckett. Though he voted against secession, he had owned slaves and lost a son in the Confederate cause, giving him broader appeal than his opponent, a former Lovettsville magistrate. William Downey narrowly won his contest for commonwealth attorney over the previously unknown George A. Thatcher, a former Union officer who had opened a Leesburg law office to become, it appears, Loudoun's first carpetbagger. Downey's failure to carry Waterford and the precincts around Goose Creek showed continued dissatisfaction with his father among Quakers, rather than disapproval of the son's wartime service as a Union cavalry officer in Kentucky. William Mercer's status as Unionist state senator was not enough to ensure his election as clerk of the circuit court, a position won easily by Capt. James Grubb, Company B, Loudoun Rangers. Hillsboro lawyer Charles P. Janney was the only Quaker to win countywide office as clerk of the county court. Despite some resentment among those denied the right to vote, the overall reaction to the outcome among ex-Confederates was one of resignation, mixed with relief some form of local government was being put into place.[15]

But as local Unionists soon discovered, this would be their high-water mark. Within weeks, the same newspapers that advocated secession before the war would reopen in Leesburg and become mouthpieces for the "conservatives," as former secessionists came to be known. Furthermore, it was the judicial system, not elected officials, that actually ran the county, and by July the various district magistrates were up and running under an ex-Confederate officer.

Events taking place outside Loudoun were also working against the Unionists. Once Pierpont moved to Richmond, his government came under severe pressure to remove restrictive clauses from the new constitution. Outside of a few counties with significant loyalist populations, there were, it was claimed, not enough qualified men to restore civil government. Pierpont was persuaded, and his proposed solution was to call a rump session of the legislature to make the necessary changes. After word of the governor's intentions reached his more radical supporters in northern Virginia, Quaker abolitionist John Hawxhurst helped craft a proposal to amend the constitution by extending suffrage "without regard to color," thereby countering the expected return of former Rebels to the ballot box by allowing Blacks to also vote. Samuel Janney and Yardley Taylor, two of Loudoun's most influential Quakers, cast off their wartime neutrality to also urge Pierpont to extend the vote to "citizens of African descent." Otherwise, they argued, the state would inevitably fall back into the hands of those who had fomented the rebellion. Their analysis, correct as it turned out, went unheeded by the governor, who may well have wondered where these Goose Creek abolitionists had been when he needed their support during the war.[16]

Once the legislature met in late June, it quickly re-enfranchised many White males previously denied voting rights and expanded the number of persons eligible to hold office. In addition, provision was made to hold state and Congressional elections in October. While the "ex-Confederates could hardly have hoped for easier terms or a more lenient governor," Loudoun's Unionists who had backed Pierpont throughout the war felt betrayed, and doubly so when they learned that their three-man delegation in that legislature helped bring about this outcome. Moreover, it was Loudoun Senator William Mercer who introduced a measure to allow voters to decide whether the next General Assembly could make further changes to the constitution, primarily to remove any remaining restrictions on ex-Confederates. Mercer's bill passed, subject to voter approval that fall. When the special session adjourned, the Richmond (and Leesburg) press lavished praise on the governor and his assembly. Republicans and most Unionists were furious, particularly after House Speaker James Downey congratulated his colleagues for keeping the state out of the abolitionists' hands: "Virginia is now safe...Whatever they may do to other states, they cannot now saddle negro suffrage upon us." In fact, what had just occurred in Richmond convinced many Republicans of the impossibility of taking control of the state without the addition of Black votes, and if Mercer and Downey thought they could extend their political careers by courting the conservatives, they were mistaken.[17]

After the flurry of political excitement in June, a relative calm settled over Loudoun, broken only by occasional Federal patrols to keep order until county officials assumed office in July. Almost everyone condemned the lawlessness that persisted in the county, and the local press prematurely lauded the first civil arrests in four years as an indication that a new era was at hand.[18]

A diary kept by Frank Myers, former captain in White's Cavalry, provides insight into the difficulties former Confederate soldiers faced. He returned to his family farm, less than a mile from Clifton, much disturbed by the South's defeat, and for months Myers fantasized about killing Yankee soldiers he encountered. When he finally ventured into the Unionist stronghold of Waterford in early August, he "staid 5 minutes & swore [he] would never go again." He particularly detested Unionist stalwarts such as Samuel Steer, now an I.R.S. agent, and town magistrate John Dutton. The latter returned the enmity, calling Myers "one of the worst rebels in Va." and demanded he take the amnesty oath, or leave the country. In late August, Sheriff Luckett summoned Myers to testify in a suit Sam Gover brought against Elijah White for damages caused when the colonel's men looted his Waterford store. Despite his unruly behavior in the courtroom, where he "cursed some of the people who sued me," Myers was acquitted of any blame in the case. But for Unionists such as Gover, it was further evidence they could not prevail in a judicial system already back in ex-Rebel hands.[19]

Ed Wright had been a private in Myers's company, so it was quite natural for him to show up at his old captain's home on 18 July and spend the night. Despite having been sentenced to five years in the penitentiary three weeks earlier, and the verdict having been approved up the Federal chain of command, Wright somehow slipped out of custody, or been released. One can only imagine the unease his return caused, not only at Clifton, but throughout north Loudoun, especially as other members of John Mobberly's band also began to resurface. That fall, when Myers learned two other "Comanche" veterans were stealing horses, he speculated: "If they are, I know Ed Wright is engaged in it & is making tools of them." A few weeks later, the *Mirror* decried the theft of horses in the county, by then a near daily occurrence.[20]

That summer and fall, Loudoun's former Secessionists took further heart from conciliatory gestures President Johnson extended to the South, which included issuance of numerous pardons to prominent Confederate office-holders and military leaders. This apparent shift on the national level in favor of their old enemies did not go unnoticed by the Unionists, who became further alarmed when they read advertisements for a "Grand [Jousting] Tournament" scheduled for 17 August, in which "successful knights" would win the chance to crown Queens of Love and Beauty. Prominently featured was the planned attendance of Col. Elijah White, as Marshal of the Day, and Col. John Mosby. Such events were common in the South before the war, not just as a way for young men to impress the opposite sex with their riding ability, but as a means to hone cavalry skills as they tried to spear rings with a lance while galloping past. Postwar jousts helped sustain a sense of camaraderie among former Southern cavalrymen, and in Loudoun's case, provided a way to mobilize Secessionist support for the fall election. Unionists accordingly denounced them as efforts to perpetuate the "Lost Cause."[21]

Mosby's expected presence at the joust coincided with the opening of "August Court Days," the high point in the county's legal calendar. Perhaps no single event had demoralized Unionists throughout northern Virginia so much, or energized the former Secessionists to an equal degree, as the pardon Gen. Ulysses Grant arranged for Mosby in June. It was not long before the former partisan chieftain began testing the limits of his parole, and soon after opening a law office in Warrenton, he advertised his intention to handle cases in neighboring Loudoun. But it was his appearance at the Leesburg courthouse on 14 August to apply for permission to practice law that galvanized Commonwealth Attorney William Downey to implore Secretary of War Stanton to find a way to keep "the villain Moseby" out of the county. Particularly insulting to the loyalists was to have to witness the partisan leader return to "the scenes of his triumphs," a place where "there is not a Union family in the County who has not been made desolate by his acts." "His friends," Downey declared, "are rejoicing and laughing in their sleeves at the loyal people, and where a dispute [hinges] on the acts and doing of Moseby, they point to the Government and tell us that it has endorsed his acts, his warfare, his robberies and murders & calls it honorable warfare." Aside from satisfying Loudoun's 1,000 Unionists, Downey thought few Secessionists would protest having Mosby barred from the county, since it was his partisans who caused the destructive Burning Raid.[22]

In response, Federal soldiers descended on Leesburg and forced Mosby's return to Warrenton, as well as postponement of the "Grand Tournament." At the end of August, the War Department posted Capt. Thomas E. Allen as provost marshal in Leesburg with a detachment of fifty men from the 96th N.Y. Infantry to maintain order and carry out the work of the Freedmen's Bureau. One of Captain Allen's first acts was to order everyone with horses or mules bearing "CS" or "US" brands to register them at his office. In addition, paroled Confederate prisoners were required to report in, as well as seek authorization for travel outside their neighborhoods. The soldiers also began "taking a census of the colored population," arousing more unease among Whites. These and additional directives from the War Department reflected a widening rift between Secretary Stanton and the President over how to treat the South that would come to a head the following year.[23]

Matters reached a boiling point much sooner in Loudoun after a list of large property owners was published in the Leesburg papers, preparatory to their lands being confiscated and distributed to former slaves. A lengthy editorial in the *Mirror* argued that Johnson's Amnesty Proclamation should have put this issue to rest and appealed to the President to intervene. Bowing to the outcry, including an appeal from Governor Pierpont, the Freedmen's Bureau ordered its Loudoun agent to stand down in early September. Although no property in the county was distributed, the threat of confiscation led presiding magistrate William H. Gray to publish a statement to counter any impression that Loudoun was a hotbed of treason. The resulting document accepted a permanent union of the states and admitted slavery was "dead." It also praised President Johnson's "efforts to reconstruct the States of the late Confederacy upon conservative principles."[24]

Despite announcements touting their expected presence, neither White nor Mosby showed up for the rescheduled contest held in early September at Leesburg's fairgrounds. This time, riders had to appear before the provost marshal and take a loyalty oath before competing. Despite some knights' use of provocative names, such as "Guerrilla," the event took place without serious incident, according to the local press. A reporter from Washington saw the tournament differently, writing that it was gotten up by former Rebels solely for political purposes, and "the glorification of Mosby." William Downey, then currying favor among conservatives despite his earlier letter to Stanton, penned a scathing rebuttal in the *Mirror*, pointing out that Mosby had not been present and denying charges that Blacks had been mistreated during the event. Downey was rewarded by being allowed to give the principal speech and crown the beauty queen at a second tournament in October.[25]

* * * * *

Marie's diary resumed on 18 September:

> How varied have been the scenes enacted at Clifton since I penned these lines...[A]lmost 3 months have elapsed and each day has brought something new. A succession of lights and shadows. I have to pass over these 3 months as I cannot pretend to enumerate the ever varying events that have occurred in *our little world*.
>
> This morning Capt. C closed a visit of almost 5 weeks. We have enjoyed his society so much. It was very hard to give him up. He seems just as one of the family (which he will be some day I suppose). Sister Edie particularly feels his absence very much. She has almost subsisted upon his society since he has been here. Yesterday I found them very romantically situated on a log in the carriage house. Indeed it was real ludicrous. They seem devoted to each other and, if he is sincere in all his professions, we would not desire anyone superior for our dear Sister; and that is saying a great deal for his lordship for she deserves a very *worthy spouse*. God grant that he prove so, for it would be terrible to have

her young life blighted by he, whom she loves as the life, proving false...

[Sept.] 22ⁿᵈ. Very pleasant day. This evening Cousin Randolph [White] returned accompanied by Capt. C (whom we supposed was in N.Y.) with some very fine horses which he wishes to sell. We were so glad to see him. It is so nice to have him back. The rest of the family were very much surprised that he came, but I was not at all. I rather looked for him. We had a great time when they came. We had no bread baked—twas between 8 and 9 o'clock. Sister Edie, [cousin] Scott [Dawson] and myself went to getting them supper in earnest. The evening has been very pleasant.

The three animals Elliot brought back were purchased for $243 at an auction of surplus cavalry horses held the day before at Camp Stoneman. Elliot considered them a good investment, which in the interim could be boarded at Clifton, where they were sorely needed on the war-ravaged farm. (In addition, Edie received another horse named "Pet" that her suitor had ridden while assigned at Point of Rocks. Since it was not turned in at the end of the war, Elliot apparently considered the animal personal property.) The Yankee captain's success as a "horse trader" created some resentment in the neighborhood, at least among the ex-Confederate faction, and even years later, children in Waterford would taunt Elliot's sons by calling their father a "horse thief." [26]

Sept. 23ʳᵈ. Sister Edie took a ride on one of the Captain's horses this morning. Pronounces it splendid. We laugh very much at his turning horse dealer...We spent the afternoon at Aunt Nancie's very pleasantly. The Capt. taking us in and bringing us back with a splendid span of horses.

Sept. 24ᵗʰ. Father, Auntie [probably Ann Gover] and Sister Edie went to meeting. Uncle Sam [Gover] returned with them. Auntie and I wishing to go to the colored school held in Waterford, the Capt. hitched up and took us. I had been very much prejudiced before going, but I divested myself of all that and became Oh! so much interested in them. I hope I can get a class as I should like to so much. I think [it] is "bread cast upon the waters and in time it will return." Had a delightful ride home. After tea Sister Edie, Capt. C and Scott have gone to fulfill an engagement to spend the evening with Alice Bond [daughter of tanner Asa Bond and sister of Rachel Means]. Captain [George] Thatcher [the unsuccessful candidate for commonwealth attorney in June] and Lida Dutton called here. Did not tarry long. [The Dutton and the Matthews girls appear to have been more rivals than friends.]

Faced with a hostile environment in Loudoun, the Freedmen's Bureau initially had difficulty achieving its goal of providing education to the previously enslaved persons. Instead, this initiative was started by Quaker volunteers, and Marie's diary provides the first indication that young Friends like Sarah Steer and Annie Matthews had begun to teach Blacks by that fall. These first classes were in private homes until a "colored school" was erected on 2ⁿᵈ Street in 1867.[27]

Sept. 25ᵗʰ. Capt. C attempted to drive, but as she did not wish to be harnessed she cut some high capers. I presume she thinks "labour degrading" and shows her high spirit, but I believe I like her better for it. I glory in her spirit, though he does not admire it at all and chastised her quite severely. We all thought that was awful in the extreme. They then hitched up another team and took Mother [on] a ride which she enjoyed very much. Sister E, Scott and the Capt. called at Cousin Eliza Walker's [Talbott farm], and the result of the call was Scott became very much enamoured of Sue Janney who is visiting there. Scott and the Capt. amused us very much during the evening with some "parlour theatricals" [as] they termed them, but I should call them "monkey tricks."

Sept. 26ᵗʰ. This being a delightful morning the Capt. invited me to take a ride. I accepted the invitation and went escorted by he and Scott. We joined a party and had a delightful ride. The horse I rode was a perfect charm. I fell in love with it. I have christened him "Arab." Scott dined at Cousin James [Walker's] and came home still more desperately smitten than ever with the "beautiful Miss Janney." We laugh at him about her. She rides beautifully. Capt. Chamberlin dressed in female attire this evening. He did look too ridiculous for anything.

Marie's diary abruptly ends at this point. A notation by Edward Matthews Chamberlin, Jr., the author's father, on his transcription of the journal states: "Marie was killed in a horseback riding accident on Corbin's hill, Waterford, perhaps the day following the close of the journal, and perhaps while riding the horse 'Arab'." However, because other sources establish that Marie died of illness in 1867, it was more likely her sister Annie who suffered a serious riding accident on the hill leading into the village. In late 1865 correspondence, she is referred to as a bed-ridden "invalid," and shock over her accident could well have caused Marie to abandon her diary.[28]

Chapter 17

A LONG-DISTANCE ROMANCE:
October 1865-June 1866

Elliot's return to Clifton in September 1865 resulted in another lengthy stay with the Matthews family, allowing him to celebrate Edie's eighteenth birthday on 10 October, as well as observe the state-wide elections two days later. Despite its significance, there was surprisingly little enthusiasm over this chance to pick representatives to the state legislature and U.S. Congress, or to decide whether to adopt William Mercer's proposal to remove restrictions barring ex-Confederate officials from holding office. Whereas Loudoun Unionists had eagerly turned out in June, they had since seen the county slip towards conservative rule and felt further betrayed by actions taken by their representatives in the Pierpont government. On the other hand, many former secessionists were unwilling to take an oath of allegiance to vote, especially when it was widely believed the U.S. Congress would refuse to seat anyone who could appeal to the majority of Virginia's White voters.

Heading the Unionist ticket was Alexandria railroad magnate Lewis McKenzie, running for the U.S. House of Representatives, and Waterford's William Williams, vying with incumbent William Mercer for the state senate. Another Waterford Quaker, Dr. Thomas Bond, and Taylorstown merchant Jonas Schooley hoped to fill the two slots in the House of Delegates previously held by James Downey and John Henshaw. Leesburg papers gave little coverage to the Unionist campaigns, which started late and had little appeal beyond the Quaker community. In published statements, Bond and Williams warned of a Congressional backlash if Southerners continued to pursue their reckless course of returning ex-Confederates to power. In that case, they correctly predicted, Virginia would find readmission to the Union blocked by Congress and be forced to extend suffrage to the "colored race." Aware of this issue's paramount importance to the electorate, Williams assured voters he was opposed to grating suffrage to freedmen at that time.

As the election neared, Loudoun's conservative leaders sought to show restraint and acceptance of the war's outcome. To them, the departure in early October of the provost marshal and his guard was welcome evidence that the Federal authorities considered their county pacified, and indeed, the election "passed off most quietly." Fewer than 1,200 Loudouners went to the polls, an increase from June, but still half the normal turnout. This time, conservatives won all the races, as well as approval for ex-Confederates to hold office. Waterford and Lovettsville provided most of the votes for the losing candidates, but even there, totals were down from June, particularly in Lovettsville, where fewer than half as many bothered to go to the polls.[1]

Statewide, Unionists fared no better, failing to win almost every contested race, or block approval for constitutional changes favoring ex-Confederates. A turnout less than a third of prewar times produced a state legislature dominated by former Whigs, who, like John Janney, had initially resisted secession, only to embrace it after the war began. Led by House Speaker John Baldwin, they were confident that former Whigs in the northern Republican Party would embrace them, and thus felt empowered to ignore the need to court wartime Unionists and freedmen. In their belief that they had the support of President Johnson, the Baldwin legislature ignored Governor Pierpont's proposals for economic improvements and civil rights reforms. Instead, to improve their standing with Southern rights Democrats, who had dominated the state before and during the war, legislators called for the release of Jeff Davis and appointment of Robert E. Lee as provisional governor. While the Baldwin "moderates" desired reunification, they were surprisingly deaf to the effect their actions, and those of their colleagues elsewhere in the South, were having on northern public opinion, and were therefore caught off guard when Congress refused to seat any of the newly elected Southern representatives.[2]

It was almost Christmas before Elliot left Clifton for Glens Falls. Extended visits between the homes of young couples were common in those times, helping families judge prospective spouses. Edie, however, did not accept invitations to visit his home in New York, a sign that, at least in her mind, he would be marrying into her family, not *vice versa*. Before his departure, the couple exchanged vows, but stopped short of a formal engagement. Her parents were not informed of this development and would not have condoned a more serious commitment as long as he remained unemployed. On the other hand, E. Y. Matthews was not getting any younger, and undoubtedly hoped that, if a marriage did take place, the former captain would stay and help manage the farm.

Elliot, however, was having second thoughts about the wisdom of settling in the South. Since his arrival at the Point that spring, he had seen the Unionists briefly ascend to power, only to be supplanted by their former foes in a political process that culminated in ex-Rebels sweeping to victory at the polls. After nearly a half-year's residence in Waterford, he knew what the town had endured during the "rebellion." Likewise he had been there to share their disappointment at seeing their apparent victory slip away. Having political aspirations of his own, he could identify with the losing candidates, whom he knew personally, and must have questioned whether he, an outsider, could expect to fare any better. Nor could he overlook that a notorious Rebel renegade, whom he had personally helped put behind bars, was back at large stealing horses from loyalist farms.

Despite opposition from Edie and her family to her ever becoming a military wife, Elliot resurrected earlier plans to join the regular Army. Attaining this objective would not be easy, as the U.S. Army did not expand appreciably during the war, and there were many former volunteers like himself seeking a permanent military career. To win a commission, he would at a minimum need Congressional support and pass a stiff examination. Thus, in late November, he wrote his maternal uncle, William Sanborn, and asked him to raise his candidacy for officership with Justin Morrill, then at his home in Strafford. To this request, Elliot attached the recommendation Col. Aaron Seeley penned at the time of his discharge. Sanborn, who handled the Vermont congressman's business affairs, turned both documents over to Morrill, who in turn gave them to Secretary of War Stanton, when he returned to Washington in early December for the opening of Congress. In doing so, Morrill added his own endorsement that he knew the applicant "to be a *brave* and accomplished officer."[3]

Elliot later wrote to thank Morrill and provide a summary of his military service. Apparently realizing a letter from the thoroughly discredited Seeley was unlikely to be of much help at the War Department, he went to the opposite extreme and cited four generals as references: Nathaniel Jackson, George Stannard, Wesley Merritt and Thomas Devin, of whom only Jackson would have had much direct contact with the applicant. Stannard was a fellow Vermonter, but their paths probably only crossed in early 1863 when the general headed the Defenses of Washington. Devin was better known to the Matthews family from his days in Lovettsville, and as commander of a division, Merritt would have had little interaction with a captain not on his staff. This letter, too, was forwarded to the War Secretary by Morrill, with a short explanation that the applicant was "now of N.Y. but was born in my town [*sic*] and I feel sure the Government has not often at its disposal so fine material for an officer. If not recommended from any Cong. Dist., he desires an appointment at large." Elliot was certainly disappointed not to be nominated from Morrill's district, and his ill-defined residency contributed to his failure to win a commission at this time.[4]

Aware the Matthews's Quaker beliefs were already being put to the test by his prior military service, he did not inform Edie of his renewed efforts to win a commission, rationalizing there was no need to raise this issue until he was sure of an appointment. Like many Victorian males, Elliot kept his professional and personal lives separate, but his lifelong reluctance to share important decisions with those closest to him went deeper than this, suggesting a distrust rooted in childhood.

Beyond offering an opportunity to adjust to civilian life and ponder his future, his extended stay at Clifton gave Elliot a chance to observe the first stages of the South's reintegration into the nation. Unlike most Northern soldiers, who returned home believing the major issues had been settled on the field of battle, he could see reunification would be a long and contentious process. Having concluded that the South held little promise for a Union soldier, at least as long as President Johnson controlled Reconstruction, he returned north to seek employment in more friendly and prosperous surroundings. There, he hoped to cultivate political and military contacts who could assist him to rejoin the Army or start another career. Soon after his arrival in New York, he helped form a veterans' movement that became actively involved in pressuring Congress to safeguard the goals for which they had fought. In doing so, he was not only advancing his own agenda, but also those of the Matthews family and their Unionist neighbors.

But, if Elliot thought he could induce Edie to join him, he badly underestimated the bonds tying her to the Southland. Consequently they would be separated for long periods over the next two years. Fortunately, enough of their correspondence survives to document their courtship and show that the teenaged object of his affection was more than a match for her thirty-one-year-old suitor. Like many of her contemporaries, she was adept at manipulating her admirer's emotions through the written word, a skill all but lost since the advent of modern communications. Alternately playing the flirt, adoring paramour, practical mother and wise sage, her letters dispel any notion nineteenth century Quakers were cold and aloof. It is worth mentioning that she began every missive with the heading "Clifton, Home," a not-so-subtle reminder of her expectation that Elliot would eventually join her there. Their letters, full of passion and life itself, later achieved a certain cult status among later generations of young girls in the family, who would sneak into Clifton's attic to read them.

Leaving his horses at Clifton under the care of a Black farmhand named Jesse,[5] Elliot returned to Glens Falls in time to spend Christmas Eve at a Presbyterian festival and "hop," but left early to read a letter just received from Edie. On Christmas Day, he attended church, marveling on the way at the splendid turnout of gaily-decorated sleighs. He already had good prospects for employment and was looking forward to when he and Edie would be living there together. He referred to the house he owned in the Glen as their "future home," and revealed plans to purchase a vacant lot next door to provide space for a garden. The house had been rented since he left for the war, but for the first time, Elliot took the precaution of insuring it, something as a bachelor he had not bothered to do. In a nod to Edie's culinary skills, he expressed regret at not being present to sample her holiday delicacies, particularly mincemeat pies, a byproduct of the hog butchering that had just gotten underway when he left. In closing, Elliot sent his warmest regards to Annie, inquiring whether she could go up and down the stairs. (This and later references to her as an "invalid" seemingly confirm that Annie, not Marie, suffered a serious riding accident earlier that fall.)[6]

On New Year's Day, Edie wrote a passionate letter to "my own, my darling," in which she complained of not having heard from her suitor in two weeks. "Yet darling, numerous as are the mountains and valleys which lie between us, in spirit and memory I am ever with you. Not only in my waking moments but nightly I…dream I am with thee, and am loved by thee, and oh! how I almost mourn their departures, and feel quite provoked that our 'Day God' should so soon make his appearance." Lest he feel too smug, she reported that "gentlemen friends," whom she feared "had departed forever" while Elliot was staying with them, had resumed making social calls. She and her friends had enjoyed many good times being drawn in a sleigh by "Arch" and "Charles Augustus," two of Elliot's horses. She

Annie Matthews, age 25. A riding accident cut short pioneering efforts by Edie's "ultra-Radical" sister to teach Waterford Blacks to defend their political rights. Over a year later, her face still shows strain of lengthy recuperation from her injuries. (1867 photograph, TCC)

was particularly excited about the resurrection of Waterford's Literary Society, already beginning to assume the prominence it once held in the social lives of the village's younger set. Meetings resembled a modern-day "roast" and included witty toasts and recitations. On a somber note, she reported Sam Gover's wife, Maggie, had passed away (of "consumption").[78]

Marie enclosed a letter of her own, describing a quiet Christmas day with few visitors. She dutifully noted that Edie had declined an invitation to a party that day, not caring to go "under existing circumstances," presumably a reference to her relationship with Elliot. Marie's earlier criticism of Elisha Walker's school had vanished, and she was eager to resume classes after the holidays. A vivid account of problems she and Edie faced getting to the last Literary Society meeting followed, in which she described how Jesse had inexplicably hitched up "lazy old Barney" to make what turned into an agonizingly slow trip. To urge the horse along, the Black youth found a "stick about 6 inches long" that had no effect on the animal. They eventually made it to town, but according to Edie's postscript, Jesse's frustration produced much merriment along the way, especially from Marie, who was "just as wild and gay as ever." That experience aside, Marie observed that Jesse had celebrated the holidays by attending numerous parties, adding "the darkies are doing just as they please." The sisters returned to Waterford a few days later to hear a lecture by George Thatcher, the losing candidate for commonwealth attorney. A crowd was on hand, but the speaker, a carpetbagger like Elliot, failed to appear, or send an excuse. "Perhaps it is the way you are in the habit of doing in the 'Land of the White Rabbit' [the North], but we do not like the style much." Elliot's letters to Edith were passed around the family, and Marie softened her previous jab by praising his handwriting. ("I see that your nib is as brilliant as ever. It is indeed quite dazzling.") Closing on an affectionate note, she wrote "I love you so dearly and nothing would more highly delight me than a letter from my '*Big Brother,*' for among all your sisters you have not one more devoted than Marie."[9]

Elliot and his brother-in-law, Duncan Cameron, spent New Year's Day at the Saratoga Springs home of his uncle, George Chamberlin. A cousin came up from New York City and accompanied Elliot to the nearby town of Galway to see "the old home where we were children together." After his return to the Glen, Elliot and twin sister Ellen accompanied the Camerons to a dinner-dance at the local fire hall, where he was honored by being asked to give one of the toasts. He was then living with Ellen and her husband William Martin, and spoke fondly of their adopted son Frank, who had recently asked his uncle for a pair of skates. Having just accepted a position at $1,200 per year in a local jewelry store, Elliot no longer thought he could get back to Clifton that winter. Aware Edie might not like this development, he explained his employment was necessary for their future happiness. "Darling, you know that I have greater responsibilities now and must use my best endeavors to make you happy. I shall look forward anxiously to that time that I may call you my wife and never to be separated from you again."[10]

Edie was glad to learn he had gone back to being a jeweler but warned him not to work so hard he jeopardized his health. In her mind, the new job showed he had dropped plans to re-enter the army, a possibility she claimed not to "fear," based on his earlier promises to her. She did not, however, consider his current employment sufficient excuse to break his vow to visit Clifton in the near future. In a revealing glimpse at her expectations, she advised against purchasing the lot next to his house, as she did not want her suitor to become too tied to worldly "goods" in the Glen. In answer to his query about Annie, she informed him that her sister was still bed-ridden, and enclosed a funeral notice prepared by Marie for the burial of "Alone," a kitten Elliot and Annie had adopted that fall.[11]

In mid-January, Elliot moved in with the Camerons to make room at his sister's house for their brother Elijah Chamberlin, then recovering from encephalitis. A heavy snowfall Upstate had helped the local timber industry, promising an upturn in the jewelry trade. Referring to Edie's impatience to see him, he asked whether she feared he might "hang his harp on the willow, and go off to the wars again," before reassuring her that he had no desire to become a soldier and only wanted to please his love.[12]

Snow had also fallen in Loudoun, making it easier to travel by sleigh. Edie was caught up in a whirl of winter activities, including nighttime sleigh rides and parties at Goose Creek that kept her out until 3 or 4 AM. Sleigh riding was a popular pastime among the young, in part because it allowed them to go out in groups relatively free of chaperones, a point not lost on Elliot. At the last Literary Society meeting, it had been Edie's turn to read some of the anonymous *bon mots* and witty stories members placed in a basket, and it was abundantly clear she was making the most of the town's renewed social life. Not wanting to make him too jealous, she apologized that her busy schedule left so little time to write and assured her lover she had not forgotten "those pledged vows to be ever unbroken."[13]

Although still confined to Clifton, Annie had recovered sufficiently to resume tutoring a small class of Black students to prepare them to meet literacy requirements for voting. She wished Edie to tell Elliot "of her 'Contraband Class,' consisting of four [Black students]. Says you need not be surprised to receive a letter from Jesse, sometime soon, (excuse me for differing with her). Says she is preparing two, *to maintain their rights*. She approves highly of *negro suffrage*, oh! fy! *I don't indeed*. We tell her she is real *ultra* [radical]. She defends herself, as you know she is able." A week later, Edie's skepticism about her sister's class vanished, and she admitted the pupils "really are quite apt, particularly in forming letters... All seem so interested, and eager to learn. Jesse is real apt and *so studious*. He has grown a real *pet* with us all. Is just as good and kind as can be."

As Marie's diary established, several young Quaker women had begun to teach Black students the previous September. With funding from Philadelphia Friends, Sarah Steer would take the lead in this effort, holding classes in the basement of the *Bank House* on Main Street until a one-room "colored school" was erected on Waterford's 2nd Street in 1867. Annie's physical incapacitation limited her to instructing a few pupils at home, but never dampened her commitment to civil rights causes. Her "ultra" views were nurtured by attendance at Samuel Janney's boarding school in Goose Creek, and conversations with abolitionists like Sam Gover, who would have informed her of postwar efforts by the Union League to educate and organize Black voters in the South. In any case, Annie and Elliot would share a close bond based on their common interest in politics and social issues.

As to the gossip, Edie recounted how a married woman visiting from Boston had begun to flirt with one of the local men—typical Yankee behavior in her opinion. Changing the subject, she described a recent sleigh ride with male and female friends near Hamilton, which reminded her of a horseback ride with Elliot in the same vicinity. Edie, who could be very affectionate in her letters, complained of needing his "petting and caressing" to help recover from a cold, and insisted he come visit her for at least a few days, warning "absence can conquer love." Furthermore, she claimed indignation whenever her Quaker friends teased her about preferring to go to New York to visit Elliot rather than attend February Quarterly Meeting in Waterford.

Still not having heard whether her beau was coming, Edith proposed as added inducement that he bring his sisters along. To finance the trip, he could sell one of his horses, which her father said were bringing good prices in Washington. She assured him the animals had recovered from wartime service, but after "Pet" began rubbing his hair off on the fence, she had appropriated "Arch" for her own use. Marie had begun studies at a nearby boarding school and only came home on weekends. Recent visitors to Clifton included her cousin Ike Steer and Will Irish, a Waterford jeweler originally from the North, who frequently dropped by when Elliot was not around. With the implied threat that she could find a jeweler closer to home, Edie enclosed locks of her parents' hair for Elliot to fashion into a pin.[14]

Hotel records show Elliot overnighted in Baltimore on 13 February, allowing him to arrive at Clifton for Valentine's Day, and a receipt for a horse sold to E. Y. Matthews confirms he followed Edie's suggestion for financing the trip. During his stay, he extracted a promise for them to marry the following January. Her parents could hardly have been surprised to learn of their intentions, as even Marie had raised this possibility the year before. Yet, they hoped any decision would be delayed until their daughter was older and her fiancé more comfortably situated. The following undated letter provides Edie's version of her family's reaction to learning of their plans, as well as some second thoughts of her own:

> I will tell you what a great shock it was to my parents and sisters, when I told them of my promise to become your wife...I told them soon after you left. Ma upon hearing it, exclaimed..."Why Edith!!"—and could say no more. My father said "Oh no."—and then wept—and my darling sisters clung to me and really mourned, saying I must not...leave them.... Marie would not go to school and no one seemed to feel any interest in the things of life. You know Captain, our little band has never been broken...and the prospect of it being irretrievably so seems more than can be endured...The rest of us try to be strong on poor sick sister's account...[Annie] seems so weak—and grieves constantly—and we find it impossible to divert her at all. She has scarcely slept any since you left. I am sure dear Captain I could not be induced *under any circumstances*, or by *any power*—to leave this *house of mine and its inmates*, which seem my life almost, for *anyone—but you*.
>
> Were I to lose you, my heart would never know another emotion. *Never!* It is indeed strange how one can leave everything—this home and friends which have been idolized from childhood for one new object. It may be Captain that on account of precious sister's health we will have to postpone longer than January, the marriage ceremony—for she seems too frail to endure much crossing. She said to Ma, she "felt it would kill her to let me go from her forever." She talks to me, and says she does not wish to interfere in the slightest degree with our happiness—and that we must not let it influence us—yet it will of course. But believe me Captain, if her strength will admit—I shall keep my promise to you—as you so much desire I should—and the trial for me will be the same, six years hence, that it is today. You know you have the consent of my family to claim me as your own...They all love you as a son, and brother—and delight to have you come here to our home, yet when they think of you taking me from them, their joy is almost turned to sorrow...My heart is sad this morning, and my only comfort is in tears—Oh! how much I wish you were here to talk to me, I need you. I should be perfectly happy with you, if not for one thing, you know Captain, and this I cannot forget. I don't know why, but I think of it more than I used to. I know you love me, yet at times your love makes me unhappy and I almost shrink from your embrace—I love you as fondly, perhaps more so than ever, yet my pen refuses to write the endearing titles by which you were once addressed by me. I feel that I dare not—and why? I know not. But away with such gloom. I should not write this to you, yet 'tis natural for me to come to you, and were you here I should speak to you. Please write to me very soon. I shall feel better in a little while. Pardon this, I have written it in the fewest moments and as they are waiting to take my letter, I must leave you.   With love, Edie.[15]

Within a short time, Edie got over her blues and was back to her coquettish self, alternately trying to lure Elliot back to the balmy South and regaling him with tales of would-be suitors. Although she frequently expressed concerns over the former Secessionists' return to power, she was quick to remind her fiancé that she remained true to her Virginian heritage and had no plans to leave Loudoun. The decision by one of her cousins to give up chewing tobacco provided Edie an opportunity to beg her "dear sogier" (soldier) to do the same. As added inducement, she promised to think of a way to repay him. The reward came when Elliot reported he had stopped, and Edie took four pages to thank him for giving up the "evil weed," letting him know how much more pleasurable it would be for them to exchange kisses. Upon receiving this good news, Elliot replied he would have quit sooner had he known how much it meant to her. He was less pleased to learn Edie's "kissing cousin," Joseph Janney,[16] had spent the last week of March at Clifton, even though she assured Elliot she now much preferred him in that department.[17]

When her father was too ill to drive the carriage, Edie had to take her mother and Annie ("our invalid") into Waterford to shop and pick up mail at Sam Gover's store. (Her cousins, Jake and Elisha Walker, worked as clerks at the post office/store and helped turn the carriage around when they left.) Recently, Edie visited the Walkers' home to inspect a quilt Jake's sister, Mary Ruth, was sewing. It had a square dedicated to Elliot, which Edie could not wait to show him, as it exceeded her "most brilliant imaginations." The Walkers also showed her a stereoscope slide of Glens Falls that a friend had sent them.[18]

Elliot's brother-in-law, Duncan Cameron, had run a hotel in the Glen before it burned during the war and was now making plans to buy another in Saratoga Springs. With the prospect of losing his room at the Camerons' home, Elliot seemed unsure whether to move back with Ellen and his mother, or live in his own house, which had just become vacant. Several people had applied to rent it, but he wished Edie was there to help decide whether to rent or sell. He recognized his inability to manage the place alone and now seemed more resigned to not being able to persuade her to join him in New York. Looking over some old papers from his posting at Point of Rocks, he realized exactly a year ago (8 April), he had ridden "Pet" to Adamstown (between Frederick and the Point). Meeting Edie a short time later had completely changed his life, and he wished he could exchange places with the horse, which ironically was with his love while he was far away. "It now seems that my future, all future happiness, is centered on this one spot [Clifton]."[19]

With the arrival of spring, Edie missed her lover all the more. Taking advantage of the warm weather, she walked and rode around the farm. "Often by your side have I roamed o'er *peerless* Clifton's hill and dale, and been so happy. It seems to me that every spot is associated...so closely and intimately with you, and the pleasures we have known together." Later, on her way to Meeting, Edie too was reminded that nearly a year had passed since they first met.

After the Camerons left for Saratoga Springs in late April, Elliot abandoned any thoughts of living in his own house and moved back into cramped quarters at his sister's home. Upset by this development as well as lack of news from Edie, he accused her of trying to forget him. His mood improved markedly after receiving a letter, prompting him to quote some romantic poetry in response. He had intended to commemorate the anniversary of his first attendance at Fairfax Meeting by going to a nearby Quaker service, but bad weather forced him to stay home. For the first time, he admitted that he was considering resettling closer to Clifton. The jewelry business was not going as well as he had expected, and he had recently met an investor who might hire him to explore opportunities in Virginia. After the war, Northern speculators bought up property and businesses throughout the impoverished South for a fraction of their prewar value, taking advantage of the owners' desperate need for "greenbacks." These investors and their agents lived out of carpetbags, as their light luggage was called, and the term "carpetbagger" was soon applied to all Northerners who came south after the war.[20]

* * * * *

In early 1866, growing dissatisfaction with Andrew Johnson's lenient policies towards the South brought an effective end to so-called "Presidential Reconstruction," and ushered in a harsher, Congressionally-mandated version that would endure for another decade. That February, Dr. John Henshaw of Lovettsville was called to testify before the Joint Congressional Committee on Reconstruction about the situation facing Loudoun Unionists since the end of the war. The former delegate to Pierpont's Alexandria government described how control of his county had effectively reverted to the ex-Confederates, whom he described as hostile to both the Federal government and the county's loyalists. According to the doctor, Unionists could not expect a fair trial in any case involving a former Rebel, and it was rumored that Mosby's partisans had been told to lie in wait in case their services were needed to restore the old regime to power. Virginia's Assembly had recently proposed legislation to increase the residency requirement for voting from one to five years, which Henshaw called a blatant attempt to disenfranchise Unionists who fled the state during the war, as well as discourage immigration from the North. Attempts by northern-controlled religious bodies to assign pro-Union ministers to Loudoun churches had been blocked, including a physical attack on a Methodist minister who was given days to return to Maryland. Efforts by the Freedmen's Bureau to help formerly enslaved persons had likewise been ineffectual in the doctor's opinion, and without Federal intervention, the former slave owners would return Black individuals to a state of servitude. On a personal note, Henshaw reported being completely ostracized by his former Confederate friends.[21]

Prompted by the pending anniversary of Lincoln's assassination and recent Presidential vetoes of bills supporting civil rights and the Freedmen's Bureau, Edie gave vent to her feelings about Andrew Johnson: "Darling how do you tolerate *old rebel* Johnson? I wish I might express to you my feeling for *him*, but *language fails*—except that I entertain for him the utmost contempt and disgust—and think were it not for *dear good* Congress (with some few *democratic* exceptions) we are lost." In this vein, she expressed enthusiasm for Elliot's recent involvement in founding a veterans' association at Glens Falls. Aside from pride that its members "had manifested a great deal of taste and wisdom" in selecting him to represent them at a convention in Albany, Edie was especially pleased that he was using his first-hand knowledge of conditions in the South to help mold the nascent veterans movements into a potent political force.[22]

Just when it seemed things could not get worse, Loudoun Unionists had to face the prospect their old nemesis, Col. Elijah V. White, might become sheriff. As Edie looked out her window one morning in March, she spied "dozens of people flocking past on their way to that *old rebel court,* the thought of which makes me wish *something* real *wicked*. And what do you [Elliot] think of *horrible* old 'Lige White' for Loudoun's new sheriff? Dr. [Thomas] Bond declares if he is elected it will *kill him*." The procession Edie saw was headed to Leesburg to choose a candidate for sheriff. Although William Noland won the nomination, he withdrew in favor of Colonel White, who was elected to a four-year term in May.[23]

Unionist fears of unequal justice from the former cavalry commander were confirmed shortly thereafter, when an elderly Union man had seventeen fat cattle stolen. Not receiving assistance from local authorities, the owner traced his cattle to Alexandria and identified the thief as a former private in White's Comanches. At this point, various citizens in Leesburg, concerned this incident might derail Sheriff White's recent election, tried to discredit the victim by claiming he was a Yankee guerrilla. Concerns about the sheriff's willingness to protect Unionists intensified after he appointed Frank Myers as deputy sheriff for the Waterford district. Myers, still very much an "unreconstructed Rebel," fretted his new office would require him to swear out an oath of loyalty before Waterford's justice of the peace, John Dutton. To his diary, the former Comanche captain confided he "still hate[d] the Yankees and the U.S. more than ever" and considered Dutton "the grand high priest of the devil." Given these circumstances, it is understandable Unionists harbored suspicions that the sheriff and his deputies might be less diligent in tracking down former comrades. These concerns persisted into 1868, when Waterford residents chose William Williams and Charles Hollingsworth to head the newly-formed "Citizens' Organization for the Recovery of Stolen Horses, and the Punishment of Horse Thieves."[24]

While not all horse thieves plaguing postwar Loudoun were ex-Confederates, Unionists felt disproportionately victimized by this criminal element. At first, Ed Wright and his cronies kept a low profile after their return to the county, but the man who had stolen Elliot's horses was making no effort to hide when Edie wrote about him in March 1866: "Says he 'intends being a *peacible* citizen (something he has all his life before failed to be), 'if persons will only allow it.' He also says, he came home before with the intention of going to work quietly, but found *union men* would not permit it, so he started to walk *south*, but when they got this far [Clifton], Taylor [his companion] said they had as well take horses and ride, which *they did*,' as we are well aware. Captain I declare if he does take my sweet little 'Pet,' I do not know what I *will* do."²⁵

As Frank Myers had surmised, Wright and two other veterans of White's Cavalry were actively engaged in stealing horses by late 1865. Their luck ran out in September 1866, when the trio was arrested and charged with the theft of three horses and other property worth a total of $500. Their biggest mistake may have been that the horses belonged to another member of Sheriff White's old command. Just a month later, Edie would again have reason to worry about the safety of "Pet," when she learned Wright and one of his cellmates managed to break out of the Leesburg jail. This time, they were careful to steal horses from two Union men in Hamilton to make their getaway. Predictably, it was not Sheriff White who tracked the thieves down in the Shenandoah Valley, but the "Horse Insurance Association," an organization of Union men in the Hamilton area.²⁶

Edie excitedly recounted the pair's escape and recapture: "Ed Wright and [George] Campbell, escaped from imprisonment last Saturday night, by sawing from their links the irons—and the bars from a window—then tunneled their way under the brick walk—assisted by some kind friend on the outer side, perhaps the same who furnished the saw. [Landon] Lovett was a larger man than the others—hence his non-escape. I think E. W.'s thieving accomplishment is excelled by nothing. I trust he will meet his reward someday." She was later overjoyed when she received "the best of best news...his excellency, Ed Wright [has been] recaptured, with all his stolen horses. Is to be tried by court, very soon, and I trust sentenced to incarceration for twenty years." Wright and Campbell were sentenced to ten years each in the state penitentiary. Lovett got fourteen years plus another year tacked on for malicious wounding of a Black man, provoking him to complain, "Fourteen years for stealing a horse is all right, but it is d-----d hard luck having to serve a year for shooting a nigger." All three were sent to Richmond to serve their sentences, but Wright would escape two years later and, according to one rumor, become a missionary in England.²⁷

Chapter 18

THE VETERANS DESCEND ON WASHINGTON: 1866

Campaigning under the "National Union Party" banner in 1864, Abraham Lincoln chose "War Democrat" Andrew Johnson to be his running mate, in expectation Tennessee's Unionist governor would garner support in the Border States. But by the summer of 1866, President Johnson found his "National Unity" tag a liability among northern Republicans and Democrats alike, as he sought backing in the only constituency left, the defeated South. That summer, in response to dwindling support among Union veterans for the upcoming elections, Johnson opened more Federal jobs to the ex-soldiers. But this belated outreach failed from a political perspective, as his Radical opponents in Congress already dominated the appointments system and would see that positions went to applicants opposed to Johnson's policies. Abandoning his career as a jeweler, Elliot was one of many Union veterans who flocked to the capital in hopes of securing Federal employment.

Leaving Glens Falls in time to spend the Fourth of July at Clifton, he would use the farm as a base for his job search over the next three months. Aside from wanting to be near Edie, his decision to relocate to the Washington D.C. area reflected his involvement in the nascent veterans' movement. Helping organize ex-soldiers in Upstate New York had stimulated his political inclinations and placed him in contact with like-minded activists, many of whom were also gravitating to Washington to find jobs and influence the political process. Their activities were heavily swayed by the Congressional elections that fall, which would decide whether Radical Republicans or the President would dictate how Reconstruction was to be administered in the South. At the beginning of the Civil War, a majority of Northern officers and enlisted men identified with the Democratic Party. This situation had changed three years later, when the "soldier vote" secured Abraham Lincoln's reelection. However, the Democrats' unexpectedly strong showing in state and local elections in 1865 signaled that Republicans could not take veterans' support for granted. During the following year, both parties rushed to organize former soldiers into political blocs for their side.

These developments coincided with rising frustration among ex-soldiers in the North over their peacetime status. No longer content to simply bask in the glory of having returned home as conquering heroes, these men now faced problems common to returnees from all wars—getting a job, overcoming physical disabilities and adapting to civilian life. During wartime, many soldiers, including Elliot, had enjoyed a status and responsibilities far surpassing their earlier careers, thus making the transition to civilian life even harder. In addition, there was a perception among veterans that Northern politicians, in their haste to return the nation to normalcy, had abandoned the larger goals for which they had fought. Unlike their Rebel counterparts, who returned to a South greatly altered by war, and nostalgically

Clifton, c.1866. Elliot, behind the horse, has returned to woo Edie, seen on front porch, as family and servants look on. (TCC)

longed for the "good old days," Union veterans were more apt to demand broad social and political changes, as well as special recognition for having served. Many were dismayed to see their old foes resume political and economic control in the former Confederate states, roles they had assumed would be reserved for the victors. Although Democratic politicians initially showed greater willingness to grant Union veterans concrete benefits in the form of job preferences and disability pensions, they were unable to shed an image that linked their party to the vanquished South. Mainstream Republicans were quick to grasp the potential of the soldier vote, and, spurred by fears their Radical wing might form a third party with the veterans' support, moved to forge an alliance with veterans that endured into the next century.[1]

Among the numerous veterans groups organized after the war, the Soldiers' and Sailors' National Union League (hereafter Soldiers' Union) was the earliest to assume national prominence after its formation in Washington, D.C., in June 1865. Its first president, L. Edwin Dudley, had been a private in the 16th Mass. Infantry before becoming an IRS auditor. Both Dudley and his successor, Major C. H. Hall of the 6th N.Y. Cavalry, identified with the GOP's Radical wing, and over the next year attracted some 1,000 like-minded veterans from the Federal workforce in the capital. Local Soldiers' Unions were established elsewhere in the Northeast, particularly in New York, where they received the backing of William Bourne, editor of the influential *Soldier's Friend*, a New York City newspaper with a circulation of 25,000 and a decidedly Radical agenda. By early 1866, the national Soldiers' Union had become completely dominated by Radicals, determined to use it to mobilize veterans for the fall election.[2]

Elliot had already established contact with the Washington D.C. Soldiers' Union before returning to Glens Falls at the end of 1865 and, once there, helped found several local chapters. This led to his selection as Warren County's representative to the first state Soldiers' Union convention, held in Albany on 17-18 April. He was already acquainted with some of its organizers, including Col. William L. Bramhall and his brother Frank J. Bramhall, whom Elliot had met while serving at the Draft Rendezvous in New York City. As acting president, William Bramhall called the Albany assembly to order and both he and Frank played prominent roles throughout the convention. Elliot also would have known the convention's acting chairman, Col. James B. McKean of Saratoga Springs.

During the opening session, Elliot and Frank Bramhall were appointed to a "Committee of 7" to draft by-laws and a constitution, which were read and accepted later that day. On the second day, Elliot's motion to limit the size of delegations to future conventions was approved, as was his appointment to represent his district at a national convention to be held in Washington that fall. (The Bramhalls would represent their New York City district.)

The main body then approved an open letter urging ex-soldiers to form sub-unions throughout the state to defend their interests. In an appeal to veterans living Downstate, where Democrats predominated, the letter averred that the National Soldiers' Union was not tied to a specific party, nor was it just a "pleasant" fraternal organization, but instead an advocacy body dedicated to reminding the country that debts have been incurred by the Republic which cannot be canceled by triumphal receptions, votes of thanks, or military promotions, dear and grateful to the veterans as such tokens may be. The heroes of our struggle cannot all be rewarded or distinguished, but they may, at least, be rescued from neglect and forgetfulness. The armless sleeve, the wooden leg, the mutilation, the scar, the broken constitution, appeal to sense and heart in every walk of civil life...It is the duty of soldiers to stand by soldiers in a respectful advancement of all just claims; and to ask, as a body, from Congress and the people, a proper consideration of these claims.

The letter also listed the principal issues endorsed by the convention: 1) equalization of bounties, so soldiers who enlisted earlier when bounties were not paid, or were very low, received the same as those who enlisted later; 2) preference for veterans in filling government appointments; and 3) improved benefits for disabled veterans. Omitted from the open letter were resolutions passed in support of two (Republican) House bills on bounty equalization and pension reform, to which was added the more Radical position of asking Congress to make "no distinction...on account of color" in granting benefits to veterans. Also omitted was a direct jab at the President, which Frank Bramhall delivered by first citing Johnson's oft-repeated declaration that treason was "a crime and should be punished," then adding sarcastically, "we have been waiting most patiently for a practical application of the principle to the leaders of the late Rebellion."[3]

Within a month of the Albany convention, sixty sub-Unions were established, mostly in Republican-controlled areas Upstate. Each district was visited by a veteran speaker, who emphasized the need to place "soldiers' friends" in control at Albany and Washington. Anyone supporting the Democrats, or National Union Party, was urged to switch sides to guarantee an overwhelming Republican victory that would put a decisive end to the South's reluctance to accept defeat. With first-hand knowledge of the ex-Rebels' return to power in Virginia, Elliot was a particularly effective speaker at these rallies, thus adding to his proficiency in setting up such groups.[4]

Not chosen for permanent office at Albany, Elliot nevertheless established useful contacts there. His friend William Bramhall had been elected vice-president of the state Soldier's Union and was subsequently awarded the brevet rank of full colonel by the governor. During the war, William served in the 93rd N.Y. Infantry under Col. John Crocker, now a brevet brigadier general, and Elliot was pleased to learn that both wartime acquaintances planned to set up a law firm in Washington to handle veterans' claims. Frank Bramhall, then working for the Bureau of Military Records in New York City and also in line for brevet promotion to colonel, would have an even greater influence on Elliot's political aspirations. More "radical" than his brother, Frank advocated formation of a separate Soldiers' Party, and belonged to the Union League of America (ULA). The latter had begun as a secret society in the Border States during the war, and now openly supported a more punitive Reconstruction policy towards the South, including helping organize the Black populace to vote. The Bramhalls' views on the South were influenced by their uncle, John Bramhall, a native New Yorker who had been appointed a judge in postwar northern Virginia, where he owned an orchard in the Washington D.C. suburb of Falls Church.[5]

Elliot's efforts on behalf of the Soldiers' Union were likewise rewarded in May, when he was breveted a major in the N.Y. State Volunteers. This honorary appointment was followed in December by brevet promotion to lieutenant colonel. Both commissions were signed by Reuben Fenton, the new Republican governor, and carried the usual notation of being given for "gallant and meritorious service in the late war." However, a letter signed by Governor Fenton accompanying the second award stated that it was "a testimonial of the *Zeal, Fidelity and Courage* with which you have maintained the honor of the State of New York in her effort to enforce the Laws of the United States, the supremacy of the Constitution and a Republican form of Government"—a clear reference to his role in politicizing the veterans' movement. Brevet promotions were common after the war and reflected political connections as much as valor. Nevertheless, Elliot was immensely proud of the title "colonel," which he favored for the rest of his life.[6]

Not content to rely entirely on friends in the veterans' movement to find employment, in mid-July

Elliot persuaded New York Congressman Robert S. Hale to approach Interior Secretary James Harlan about getting a position as a clerk in his department. (A native of Chelsea, Vermont, Hale had taught at the same Montpelier academy that Elliot once attended. After moving to Upstate New York, Hale became partner in Orlando Kellogg's law firm, and had just won a special election to fill the vacant seat created by his partner's death.) Gen. John Crocker also provided Elliot with a glowing letter of recommendation based on their service together in the war.[7]

Unfortunately for Elliot, Secretary Harlan was then involved in a dispute with President Johnson over the latter's Reconstruction policies and would be forced to resign before taking action on the application. The new Interior Secretary, Orville Browning, supported the President against the Radicals and opposed giving Black men the right to vote. Late summer, therefore, found Elliot cooling his heels at the home of C. B. Shaw, a Treasury auditor and friend of the Matthews family. He was still trying to arrange an interview with Browning, but realized the new Secretary of the Interior was unlikely to hire anyone with ties to the Radicals. Despite his friends' encouragement that his luck would change, he returned to Clifton empty-handed in early September.[8]

Campaigning for the fall election had begun in earnest by then and included impassioned attempts by all sides to corral veterans into their fold. In New York, the Radicals kicked off their bid for the soldier vote with a joint assembly in Syracuse on 19-20 September of the Soldiers' Union and Boys in Blue Clubs. (The latter first appeared in Abraham Lincoln's re-election campaign, and their torchlight parades and rallies became staples of future Republican campaigns.) All pretense the Soldiers' Union was apolitical had been dropped when Col. James McKean called the convention to order. Speakers then took turns pledging support for the civil rights amendment, offering protection to persecuted Southern loyalists, demanding Congressional control of Reconstruction, and vilifying President Johnson as a "willing dupe" of the un-Reconstructed Rebels. Frank Bramhall called for permanent headstones to replace wooden markers on the graves of fallen Union soldiers in cemeteries adjacent to battlefields in the South. Delegates were also chosen to attend a national veterans' convention in Pittsburgh the following week.[9]

The Soldiers' and Sailors' Convention held in Pittsburgh on 25-26 September drew as many as 15,000 veterans from across the nation and was widely judged more effective than similar rallies staged by Democrats and Johnson supporters. Organized by Radical Republicans under the motto "vote as you shot," invitations were sent to all like-minded veterans' organizations, including the Boys in Blue and the Soldiers' Union. Although the latter had shown initial success in forming sub-Unions in Washington and Upstate New York, its openly Radical affiliation and orientation towards officers had failed to find widespread support among rank-and-file soldiers, or match the phenomenal growth another veterans' group, the Grand Army of the Republic (GAR), had shown in the Midwest, since its formation six months earlier. Although it too was dominated by Republicans, the GAR was organized on a fraternal model that appealed to the common soldier.

As the throng of enlisted men and officers poured into Pittsburgh, they were welcomed with open arms,

Soldiers' and Sailors' Convention, Pittsburgh, September 1866. The raucous rally became a template for Republican courtship of veterans. (*Leslie's Illustrated*, 20 Oct 66)

in sharp contrast to the President's reception a week earlier, when the mayor refused to meet him and a jeering mob prevented him from speaking. The convention opened under the temporary chairmanship of Edwin Dudley. The founder of the national Soldiers' Union was accorded this honor when it was learned that he quit his Treasury job after being refused leave to attend the convention. The ex-private received thunderous applause as he used his ill-treatment to castigate the Johnson Administration and urge the audience to increase Republican majorities in Congress that fall. After a massive torchlight parade that night, the convention's climax was reached the next day, when the chairman of the Republican Veterans Committee, Gen. Benjamin Butler, pushed through acceptance of resolutions favoring his party's Radical agenda. Loyalists in Loudoun would have noted one plank in particular—a pledge to defend "with our lives, if necessary, those brave men [of the South] who remained true to us when all around were false and faithless." Then, after a harangue over the President's policies, Butler[10] worked the audience into a frenzy by declaring Southern states should not be allowed back into the Union until they ended their intolerance of the North and stopped desecration of Union soldiers' graves.

By all accounts, the convention achieved its Radical sponsors' goal of bringing not only those present, but a far larger audience, into the Republican fold. Afterwards, each attendee received a copy of the proceedings by mail, and the resolutions and Butler's fiery speech were widely reprinted in the national press. In the words of one historian, "it was the Pittsburgh Convention which rallied and consolidated the Union soldiers and sailors into an effective political force. More than any other single event, it signaled the entrance of the old soldier influence into post-Civil War politics."[11]

Another important outcome of the convention was to introduce the GAR into the Eastern states. Its leaders came prepared to recruit new members among the attendees, and representatives from the national Soldiers' Union readily accepted their invitation to merge their two organizations. Key inductees included Frank Bramhall and James McKean from the New York delegation, and Edwin Dudley, head of the D.C. Union, who had set the tone for the Pittsburgh Convention with his opening speech. In short order, the Soldiers' Union was absorbed into the GAR, as individual sub-Unions converted into GAR posts.[12]

While confirmation of Elliot's presence at Pittsburgh is lacking, it is hard to imagine he missed taking part in the start of a political movement that would become such an integral part of his later life. If he was there, the return ride on the B&O Railroad would have allowed him to spend the last weekend in September at Clifton before returning to Washington to resume his job search. Despite the exhilarating events of the prior few weeks, Elliot felt lonely and depressed on the train ride back to the capital. The cash-strapped veteran later confessed to Edie his shame at having to accept a lunch offered by a fellow passenger. Declaring he had led an "idle life long enough," he promised to redouble efforts to find work and thus fulfill his obligation to his fiancée and her family. With any hope of working for the Interior Department apparently gone, he resurrected plans to rejoin the military, and it was during this period that he invited Gen. Thomas Devin to accompany him on a visit to Clifton. The general already knew Edie's family from his stay in Lovettsville, and more importantly was slated to take command of the 8th U.S. Cavalry on the West Coast. Not only could he help Elliot join his command, but he might also persuade Elliot's future bride of the advantages inherent in a military career.[13][14]

Upon learning of her sweetheart's loneliness, Edie wrote to express sympathy, but at the same time counseled him to get out and mingle with people. She wondered whether he might tire of her once they were married, just as he had apparently wearied of the world around him. They might be engaged to marry, but she did not want either of them to just sit at home and pine for the other. After lecturing him on the need for positive thinking, Edie put aside her letter to accompany her sisters, cousin Ike Steer and jeweler Will Irish to a Methodist revival meeting. On her return, she took up the pen to reassure her beau she still went to the post office every day to look for his letters, before relating how she had denied a friend's charge that she had switched from "preferring to be *admired by all*, [to being] *loved by one*." Torrential rains had washed out bridges and roads, and Edie feared mail deliveries would suffer as a result. Asking Elliot to come "fight the *miserable rebels* for me," she expressed a widespread belief among Waterfordians that the county was deliberately punishing her "loyalist" town by failing to maintain its roads, a suspicion that lingered for many years.[15]

Following the merger at Pittsburgh, leaders of the D.C. Soldier's Union met on 12 October to establish the first GAR post in Washington. Edwin Dudley, now aide-de-camp to the GAR's national commander, presided over the opening ceremony and warned attendees to recruit only those who were trustworthy and known to be loyal to the country, *i.e.,* Republicans. Col. William Bramhall was elected commander of Post 1, and Elliot was chosen as his adjutant, making him the third-ranking officer in the most influential veterans' group in the capital. (Post 1 evolved into the GAR's Department of the Potomac, with jurisdiction over surrounding areas, including Virginia.)[16]

A closer look at the GAR initiation ritual provides insight into an organization that would have a major influence on Elliot's life. At the start of the induction ceremony, the candidate for "enlistment" was detained by the officer of the guard in the post anteroom, stripped of his coat and hat, and draped in an old Army blanket. The initiate was then led blindfolded into the ceremonial room by the guard, who announced he had "found him wandering near our lines, desiring to enter the encampment." After being led twice around the room to the accompaniment of "slow, solemn music," the candidate had to kneel before a coffin representing a Union soldier who had died at Andersonville Prison. Placing his hand on a Bible, the inductee swore not to reveal "any of the hidden mysteries, work or ritual of this band of comrades." He also promised to befriend the ex-soldier, to "employ him or assist him to obtain employment," and to support veterans for public and private office. This done, the officer of the guard shouted, "Attention, Guard! Shoulder arms. Ready! Aim!", while the officer of the day ripped off the blindfold with the words: "Hold! This is a soldier and a brother!" As the candidate stared at the coffin in front of him, the officer of the day told him it might have been his fate, except "for my timely intervention on your behalf," emphasizing his helplessness in the absence of aid from his comrades.

> The whole extraordinary initiation sequence of the 1866 ritual bristled with images of secrecy, conspiracy, and mystery very much of a piece with the clandestine political atmosphere surrounding the birth of the order. The blindfold, the repeated challenges, the twice repeated injunction to secrecy, the thinly veiled threat of the firing squad—all gave the recruit the impression that he was joining a great Unionist cabal at a time when nervous Republicans professed to see secret machinations in the South and treason in the White House.[17][18]

In Elliot's case, the benefits of his elevation to GAR adjutant became evident a few days later, when he secured temporary employment as a clerk in the Freedmen's Bureau. Created within the War Department in March 1865 to oversee the maintenance, education and employment of formerly enslaved persons, the Bureau was headed by Gen. Oliver O. Howard, a war hero and amputee, whose championship of Black education was later honored by naming D.C.'s Howard University after him. During the early years of Reconstruction, the Freedmen's Bureau played a prominent role in the South's rehabilitation, despite being almost universally detested by the White populace. At the time of Elliot's employment, the Bureau stood at the center of a dispute between the Radicals, who wanted to rule the South as a vanquished foe, and President Johnson's more conciliatory policies. Johnson had already vetoed several bills to expand the Bureau's powers, and its future seemed uncertain until Republican victories in November allowed Congress to prolong its existence until 1869. (Bureau programs for educating Black students continued several years longer.)[19]

Elliot was not enamored with his new job, which consisted of tabulating rations distributed to poor Black families. Although the outcome of the fall elections were still unknown, he suspected the Bureau had an uncertain future at best, and knew that working there would be viewed with disdain back in Loudoun, even by his Unionist friends. Saddled with an ineffectual agent in charge of its Leesburg office and undermined by the Secessionists' takeover of the county after the withdrawal of the last Federal troops, the Freedman's Bureau accomplished little during its first year in the county. Indeed, the Loudoun Bureau agent seemed more interested in helping former slave owners recover their plantations than in promoting education for the Black populace.[20]

Despite the disappointing start of the Freedmen's Bureau in many areas and policies promoted by the Johnson Administration which showed little concern for those formerly enslaved, the Radical Republicans' strong stand against the President renewed hope among Southern Blacks that things were about to change. In Waterford, the erection of a separate "colored" schoolhouse and church would soon help define and strengthen the Black community, but there were also signs of growing interest in politics. In a letter to Elliot that fall, Edie reported their servants had all gone to attend a "tournament." Jesse, normally in charge of Clifton's horses, left in "gay uniform, and high hopes of crowning the 'Queen of Love and Beauty'. I wish him all success yet could not help being reminded of the quaint expression, 'where ignorance is bliss 'tis folly to be wise'." This is the only known instance of the Loudoun Black community staging events similar to the White jousting tourneys, but like the latter, such a gathering would have had a political connotation and may have been organized by Radical activists in the Union League of America,[21] then promoting suffrage for Black men in the South.[22]

Given doubts about the longevity of his new job, Elliot was very interested when Dr. Jebediah Baxter, a boyhood friend and one of the Army's top medical officers, offered to assist him in becoming a military doctor. Despite her fiancé's oft-expressed interest in medical matters, Edie very much opposed this idea, pointing out Elliot would have to spend years studying medicine and building a practice. In her eyes, he was too old to start such a difficult profession, especially after he had already perfected his skills as a jeweler, a career she considered as "honorable and ennobling as any other." Expressing regret that he now believed he had mistaken his calling, she concluded it was too late for a change of heart. "You became unsettled during the war, at which I am not surprised, but now that 'tis over, you should concentrate your mind and strength upon one aim in life, let it be within bounds of your abilities, which *are very great,* and with a great, kind 'Father's' assistance, I believe success is assured you." Reminding Elliot of his earlier decision to fight for his country, she urged him to apply the same resolve to his current situation. "Decision dear Captain, in my sight, is one of the noblest, and most beautiful characteristics of true manhood." After reassuring her beau he was already a professional and a gentleman, Edie pointed out the position he was being offered was the "only one in the regular Army, without *title* or *honor,* and with very few advantages." All in all, it was an impressive performance from a girl still in her teens, but whether the advice proffered was right for Elliot is less certain. Her strong reaction reflected a life-long aversion to doctors, preferring instead to rely on her own home remedies, perhaps passed down from her grandmother Miriam Gover.[23]

Having ended her last letter by reporting the arrival of three gentlemen callers, Edie began the next with an account of a visit to the jewelry shop of the "irresistible" Will Irish, which in turn brought Elliot's situation to mind. The story seemed calculated to make him jealous, as well as demonstrate she would find him equally irresistible working as a jeweler. She concluded this account by tartly reminding her lover that he had not yet repaired her watch. Worried about news of an impending war with Mexico, she begged him not to impulsively join the Army without consulting with her. Instead, she urged him to find permanent employment as a civilian, reiterating she could never be an army doctor's wife. In early November, however, Edie had a change of heart and asked him to purge his memory of all she had previously said about a career. "Begin life anew (or the business part of it), relying entirely upon your own good judgment (without consulting mine), and believe that you have in all your undertakings, my prayers, and best wishes for your success."[24]

At the time, Elliot was rooming with William Bramhall in a Washington boarding house, where they were soon joined by General Crocker's son Irving. By early November, Elliot and Irving were both enrolled in a night course to prepare themselves for the cavalry board examination. Yet, in letters to Edie, he only mentioned taking some law courses, and apparently failed to tell her he was seriously pursuing a commission in the U.S. Cavalry. Perhaps he rationalized this omission by her recent declaration for him to choose a career on his own. (It is also possible the term "law studies" had been prearranged with her. Not only were his letters read by the rest of her family, but Edie had instructed him to address all correspondence to her father, fearing cousins working in Sam Gover's post office might intercept her mail.)[25]

On the Tuesday before Thanksgiving, Elliot wrote he would not be joining Edie's family to celebrate the holiday. The train to Leesburg was not yet fully operational, he explained, making it impossible for him to return in time for work on Friday. His real reasons for not going may not have been as stated. That same Tuesday, Elliot prepared a summary of his past military service as part of his Army application, and on Thanksgiving Day (30 November) Secretary of War Stanton signed his appointment as first lieutenant in the 8th U.S. Cavalry, effective 28 July 1866. The appointment was still contingent on Congressional approval and satisfactory results in an examination to be taken on 10 January. If he cleared both hurdles, he was expected to report without delay to his regiment on the West Coast.[26]

Elliot paid a brief visit to Clifton the weekend after Thanksgiving, surprising Edie on her way back from Fairfax Meeting. There is no indication they discussed his appointment, even though he must have known it had already been provisionally approved. Yet, Edie's choice of words when she wrote him the following weekend could suggest she knew more about Elliot's plans than she was willing to consign to writing. In this letter, she expressed disappointment "the military" had failed to intercept her on her way home from meeting. She had been ready to submit without resistance, just as she had a week earlier, when her "darling sogier" surprised her with a visit. C. B. Shaw and his son "Dickie" had accompanied Elliot on his previous visit and spent the week boarding at Clifton, prompting her to joke that the Treasury auditor was the type of "older man" she really liked. Her sister Annie had been well enough to accompany the Shaws to Leesburg—her longest outing in a year—but had to remain in bed the following day to recover. For the first time, Edie revealed her younger sister Marie was suffering from unspecified back pains.[27]

During a Literary Society meeting in early December, Edie heard Sarah Steer discuss a recent "Union Torch Light Procession" sponsored by the Sons of Temperance in Leesburg. A number of young people from Waterford were present at this event, which culminated in a gathering at the "Old Stone Church." Sarah's account left no doubt the Leesburg rally was more about politics than the evils of drinking, temperance being deliberately used to disguise a Unionist assembly. (Here in her account, Edie sarcastically interjected "Good for the *rebs* wasn't it?") Sarah had only agreed to go because the lecturer, Reverand Sykes, was "a thoroughly *loyal man*, worthy of our encouragement." After riding over to Leesburg and leaving their horses with "a very *dignified looking contraband*," the young Waterfordians entered the "Stone-Church" to find "a crowded house and a great Union demonstration, which surprised us very much indeed. A large number of *red, white and blue* transparencies decorated the hall, which was *pleasant to behold*. The lecture was *admirable*...and we were highly gratified to *think we had perseverance sufficient to go*..."[28]

Like the jousting tournament for the Black community earlier that fall, the Leesburg rally suggests some stirring among those opposed to the conservative takeover of the county. The change was inspired by the Radical Republicans' success in the fall elections, and a growing belief that their brand of Reconstruction would result in a more favorable environment for Southern Unionists. The Methodist "Old Stone Church," site of the above rally, had suffered a schism the year before, when the provost marshal had its pastor arrested for pro-Confederate rhetoric. The church's governing body in Baltimore appointed a Northerner, Rev. Joseph A. Ross, to replace him, but most of the congregation refused to support the new minister, and instead set up their own church on the other side of town. Threats against Ross increased after the departure of Northern troops, and in January 1866, while on his way to hold services in Waterford's Methodist church, Ross was accosted by three armed men and warned his life was in danger if he did not leave the county. Accompanied by Federal soldiers, the reverend returned the following month and forcibly ejected his Southern rival from the pulpit but would not remain in charge long. The historic Old Stone Church was eventually torn down, presumably to rid the county seat of any lingering taint of Yankeedom.[29]

Just a week after his most recent visit to Clifton, Elliot decided to forgo a reception in the city and sneak out to "Dixie" on the stagecoach to talk with Edie. Returning to Washington that night, he immediately wrote and reiterated his intention to hold her to their earlier agreement to marry in January. "I am really sorry that circumstances were such that I could not bring you back with me. Wait until next time and I will not return all alone...It seems a very long time to wait until J—y. I suppose I must be content. Won't it be nice when you *can come?*" The letter ended: "Good-by my own precious w—, I almost said. Never mind. Your devoted Elliot." Although he apparently had still not discussed the particulars of his cavalry appointment with his fiancée, it was certainly uppermost in his mind and gave added urgency to their wedding plans. He now had good prospects for supporting a wife, but given the timing of his appointment, Edie would have to stick to their original wedding date if she were to accompany him.[30]

Just before Christmas, Elliot agreed to contact acquaintances on the New York and Vermont Congressional delegations in an effort to win passage of a bill to reimburse "the loyal citizens of Loudoun" for damages incurred during Merritt's "Burning Raid." The original claims had been filed from General Devin's Lovettsville camp in February 1865 in the form of a petition to the 38th Congress, which adjourned without taking action on it. During the 39th Congress, the Joint Claims Committee reported the matter back in a proposed Senate bill, but it too appeared headed for failure as Congress prepared to close for the holidays. During the last days before the Christmas recess, Justin Morrill accompanied Elliot to the floor of the House of Representatives, where he was formally presented to New York Congressman Robert Hale and given a chance to press the Loudoun claims. In describing his performance, Elliot judged that he had urged passage of the measure "more emphatically than eloquently, yet I think it was of some purpose." Although Congress adjourned without taking action, Elliot planned to take the train to New York with Representative Hale that night, which might offer another "opportunity to annoy him still more with my stories of Loudoun Co. peoples."

Although intended as an open letter to "my dear friends" back in Loudoun about his efforts on their behalf, it was surprisingly flippant, and at one point Elliot even mentioned being mistaken for a congressman while seated on the floor of the House. He had originally expected Annie Matthews would be well enough to accompany him and give a first-hand account of her family's trials during the war. Although neither may have had much chance of persuading Congress to pass the bill that day, the staunchly Unionist Annie who, despite setbacks to her health, continued to teach Black students in her home, would have made an eloquent champion for the loyalist cause.[31]

Edie's letter of 27 December began "My Colonel (Bravo)," a reference to the brevet promotion Elliot received during his brief trip to the Empire State. Even though he had returned in time to spend Christmas at Clifton and only departed the day before, the "Colonel's sweetheart" was already missing him. He must have shared his long-range ambitions with her while discussing his recent speech before Congress, as she confessed to liking the idea of becoming the "lady" of one of the "honorables." Then, when he was elected to Congress, she could already picture how pleasant it would be to take long Christmas vacations in New Orleans.

Changing the subject, Edie expressed relief they were not getting married that cold winter morning. She had just come back from Lida Dutton's marriage to Capt. John William Hutchinson at the Methodist church, the usual venue for Quakers marrying outside their religion. Immediately after the ceremony, the couple left for their new "Northern Home" in New York City. The night before, Edie attended a wedding party at the Dutton home:

> There were a number there and the evening was very pleasant. [Lida] was gay and *lively* and seemed perfectly content with future prospects. She bade me say to you that you did not call as you promised, and she looked for you. Mr. D. asked me if the "Colonel" left this morning? and after *two* or *three* moments wondering *whom in the world he meant*, I answered that *he did*. Lida *looked very not pretty*, and do you know, I hope for your sake that *yours* would be a *fairer bride. Foolish wasn't I?* I wondered if her "Willie" thought her pretty, which of course he did, as love is blind.[32]

Chapter 19

MARRIED TO A "BONI FIDO" SOLDIER: 1867

As then customary, Elliot spent New Year's Day 1867 paying social calls on friends and professional contacts in Washington. At the War Department, Dr. Jebediah Baxter informed him that New York Congressman Robert Hale would soon arrange an appointment for him at the Interior Department—a possibility Elliot had long thought unlikely. He also discovered his temporary position in the Freedmen's Bureau would be made permanent, and the following week took the oath of office there to become a clerk, earning $1,200 per annum. In describing these developments to Edie, no mention was made of the Cavalry Board examination, scheduled ten days hence.[1]

Edie, meanwhile, spent the start of the year looking after her family. Her emaciated father had developed a racking cough, aggravating his weak heart. In addition to severe back pains, Marie now had a high fever and other alarming symptoms, while Annie and their mother Sarah remained in bed with fevers. Several relatives came to visit the invalids on New Year's Day, forcing Edie to entertain them. She had not seen Elliot since Christmas and wondered whether her "soldier" had found any servants willing to work at Clifton.[2] The need had become acute after Jesse gave notice of his plans to leave. It was Edie's turn to be despondent, and she complained of no longer feeling like a young girl. Her first real sorrow had been the affliction robbing Annie of her health, which blighted "our hopes and joys for the future." This malady was followed in "quick successions" by a string of disappointments and grief, the only positive result of which had been to bring her closer to God.[3]

On 4 January, Elliot came back to his apartment to find a blistering letter from Edie. A neighbor (apparently Nathan Walker) had informed her family of his previous marriage, and she demanded to know why he had kept this secret from her. Immediately, he sat down to write an equally emotional response.

> Can you mean what you have written? I must not permit myself to suffer the anguish that your words have occasioned. I must not do it. I am a man and will act the part of one. [Here he quotes from her letter, which has not been found.] "I do not think it *possible* for you to have *so badly deceived us*." I would rather have died than ever to have received such words from you Edith!! "and wish you. if you *can*, to contradict it *emphatically* to the world." *What am I charged with, what crime have I committed?* ...I am not a criminal. nor have I ever intentionally *done*, nor is it my nature to do, *any one* wrong. If it is a crime to have loved, and *buried* that love honorably (and woe to him who dare say differently), I would plead guilty. If it is honorable for a man to love, to prove himself worthy the love of woman in every respect and by no word, act, or deed ever occasion her one moment of unhappiness, then I ask in the name of justice, respect: What has Mr. Walker to do with me? Did he ever ask me if I was *ever* married and I denied it? Can't he, or anyone

else objecting to my marrying you, bring any other *charge against me* more [than] that I am a *widower*? Try and recollect conversations between us and can't you recall...the time I told you this long ago, and again more recently did I intimate this, and *God* knows that I believed you aware of this fact and who else did I care, should, or should not know it. Was it my place, to have told this fact to all unless asked?...All I can say [is] that I *have loved you and do,* more than any thing else, and were I to *lose* you, all else may go. I ask you to keep this letter to yourself alone, and should you feel that you love me less tell me of it, tho it break my heart...You ask me to answer without delay and I have done it and you alone can know the pain and anguish I shall suffer until I hear from you. My love, my life, God forgive me if I have made you unhappy.[4]

Feeling "somewhat overwhelmed" by his response, Edie had Annie reply:

...[A]fflictions, I believe, are always for good and this, I trust, may be sanctified to us all...I think sister Edith will write you very soon, then no doubt, all will be happy again...I never wished more that you were in your place in our little home circle...I feel wholly incompetent to advise in this matter, dear captain, but I do feel so deeply concerned to have you both do just what is right...Of course I think your duties equal, but captain you will remember sister Edith's extreme youth and that impulse may sometimes influence her when your greater experience would dictate cooler judgment. We were all surprised to learn what we did from your letter. Sister Edith remembers perfectly the conversation you alluded to, but did not at the time infer all it implied, and we feel there has been error on both sides. We did not avail ourselves of the opportunities you have given us to ask this question, and you did not tell us without being asked...This charge as you say is truly nothing against your character. With fond love, Good bye, Annie. [Her sister added a postscript, "Love from Edie."][5]

Edie's original letter on his first marriage must have been written on 2 January to arrive in Washington D.C. by the 4th; yet another letter from her, penned just two days later, gives no indication of being upset. This abrupt change in tone raises the possibility that Elliot had in fact told her of being a widower, but they had mutually agreed not to mention this to her family and friends. Thus, when Walker unexpectedly revealed their secret, Edie had no choice but to act shocked. In any case, Elliot clearly did not care to discuss his previous marriage with others, and neither he nor Edie mentioned it to their own children.

Another bombshell burst amidst their strained engagement a week later, when Elliot learned he had passed his cavalry examination. His short note on this subject may have been Edie's first inkling that her lover would soon enter the Army and be posted out West:

Darling, I have some news to tell you; now don't be at all discouraged. I am appointed 1st Lt. 8th US Cav. (Gen'l. Devin's regiment) and ordered to report to my Regt. at San Francisco. All my friends advise me to accept it by all means. Mr. [Justin] Morrill presented me with my appointment last evening and said take it and stay ten years and you will then be all right. Never mind precious I shall probably consult your happiness in this case. Say you will marry me and go with me. Dr. Baxter says, "Accept it, Elliot, get married and take your wife with you. It will be a very pleasant life for you both."...Tell Annie, I am a 'Boni fido' soldier again. Write to me on the receipt of this. This is not intended for a letter, only a little bit of news which you must not let trouble you the least. Good Bye Angel, from Elliot.[6]

Edie's response began with a detailed update on her family's ailments, so it was likely composed prior to receipt of what she sarcastically termed his "little memo," to which she responded as follows:

...I was really *disappointed* to find so brief a note from you. This is saying *little enough for it*...I was indeed surprised to hear the question in regard to your joining in the Army raised *again*, for I believed it *buried, dead long since*, as we had so often argued it, and you silenced it *finally, did you not?* by *promising* not to become a *soldier*. You know my *views*, and they are *unchanged*—therefore I will not *again* advance them—but will send in reply to your letter Ma's answer instead of my own—'tis this, that she *positively forbids my marrying you a soldier* in the regular Army. If, you think *'tis wise* for you to accept the *appointment*, do so, and if at the expiration of *ten years*, our *hearts* are *unchanged*, then she will offer no *objection*. I wish it was not *so easy* for you to procure these appointments—then your...*poor brain* would have more *rest*, and you would know better what to do. I wish I might read the future's life pages for you—then I would tell you just what to do. My brain is *too* young and inexperienced to advise you. Use *your own* judgment and I will hope for you...[Marie] says you shall not take me away.[7]

Although the couple suffered chronic lapses of communication, it is hard to believe Edie was so completely unaware of, or opposed to, her suitor's plans to re-enter the military. She had responded favorably to his promotion to colonel, albeit an honorary title, and had fondly called him a "sogier" in recent correspondence. Thus, some of her posturing may have been staged for her mother and sisters' benefit. Absent from this latest letter was her father's reaction, and both she and Elliot knew that the family's health and financial problems made it very difficult for him to flatly refuse to sanction their union. What the parents really wanted was for him to marry their daughter and remain at Clifton to manage the farm, a goal which Edie may not have completely shared at this time.

A more subdued Edie wrote several days later, asking why her lover had not come for a visit. Apologizing for her recent outbursts and any pain they might have caused, she explained she was impulsive by nature. Nevertheless, she still could not consent to Army life, which, she believed, entailed too many disadvantages to outweigh the benefits. Once again, she asked him not to make a final decision without first consulting her.[8]

On 21 January, Elliot was officially notified of passing the cavalry examination by being among the top twenty percent of applicants taking the test. He also received orders to report by month's end to the Army's Recruitment Center in New York, where he would assume charge of a detachment of recruits that would accompany him to the West Coast. Despite Edie's request to delay any decision until they met, he informed the Freedmen's Bureau two days later of his intention to resign, effective 30 January. At the same time, he persuaded his boss, Gen. Oliver Howard, to address a letter to the head of the Recruitment Center, Gen. Daniel Butterfield, praising Elliot's performance at the Bureau and suggesting the bearer be allowed to remain "on duty in New York" for an unspecified amount of time "for the interests of the service."[9]

At the end of January, the War Department agreed to amend his orders to give him an additional thirty days before he had to report for duty Elliot then took the revised orders and Howard's letter to New York, where he discussed his situation with General Butterfield. Afterwards, he informed Edie he could remain on the East Coast until early March and would have to make their wedding arrangements accordingly. He proposed they get married in Waterford in mid-February, which would allow time for her to meet his family and friends in New York before "their departure." Lest she doubt his resolve, he emphasized that, since arriving in the city, he had become even "more convinced...I have done well to accept my appointment and receive the hearty congratulations of all upon my good fortune."

Elliot had presumably visited Clifton in late January and overcome his fiancée's objections to marrying a soldier. Yet, he now faced a bigger hurdle in trying to convince her to accompany him. His letter from New York stressed how the Army encouraged married officers to take their wives by paying their passage, as well as the cost of shipping baggage and furniture. For advice on what she should take to their new home, Elliot planned to meet with General Devin's wife.[10]

While staying at Frank Bramhall's apartment in New York, Elliot managed to call on friends[11] and relatives in the city before taking the train to Glens Falls on 4 February. He advised Edie he would stay in the Glen only "long enough to complete my business concerning your father's expectations." It was the first indication he intended to sell his house there and give the proceeds to his future father-in-law.

(E. Y. Matthews had received notice in late January the mortgage on Clifton was due, and one can only speculate the degree this development had on the family's decision not to oppose the marriage.)[12]

On Valentine's Day, Elliot sent a message from Saratoga Springs about how pleased he was to receive Edie's tentative agreement to accompany him to his new post. "I almost wish at times, precious, that I loved you less and then I would not compel you to leave your dear home to accompany me so far from those so dear to you." He left for New York City the next day, planning to reach Waterford by 20 February. Edie's Valentine message advised her sweetheart not to arrive before Quarterly Meeting ended on the 20th. Having learned Army officers could receive up to ninety days leave before joining their regiment, she was hopeful he could get a similar extension, especially since he was so good at wrangling exceptions for himself. Her family's health seemed to be improving, and she believed she would be free to leave by springtime. In any case, she promised to give him a definite answer when he arrived.[13]

But by the time he reached Clifton, relapses in her father's and Marie's health made Edie hesitant to even set a wedding date. Disappointed she was not by his side, Elliot returned to New York at the beginning of March to find out the latest date he would have to depart. She knew he hated the thought of leaving for California without her but tried to console her "sogier" by pointing out they would be sharing the burden jointly, if fate so decreed. As to the possibility of his disobeying orders, or harming his career by asking for another extension, he should not shrink from his duty, as she wanted no stain on his spotless character. As it turned out, Elliot managed to have his orders amended a third time, allowing him to delay until the end of March before reporting. His commission as first lieutenant was signed several days later, but by then he had already rushed back to Waterford with the news about his latest delay.[14]

Their marriage finally took place on 18 March at a small ceremony performed by Reverend Perkins at the Waterford Methodist Church. Snow still covered the ground, and the wedding was far from a festive affair with most of the bride's family confined to their beds. Recording their union in her diary the next day, Rebecca Williams wrote that Marie "continues very sick & her father is in a miserable state of health, so that [Edith] could not leave them to go with [Elliot to California], a trying case for her and all of them." Still, the couple must have felt relief to put their emotionally trying courtship behind them and spent a few days together at the Shaws' home in Washington, their only honeymoon. Two days after the wedding, Elliot wrote the New York Recruiting Center to confirm his departure schedule. The response offered no reprieve for the newlyweds, directing him to report on the 27th to prepare for a 1 April departure.[15]

Unable to reconcile herself to leaving her mother and invalid sister and caring for her father and Marie, Edith left unresolved the question of when she would join her husband. Having exhausted all possibilities for further delay, Elliot reported for duty at Fort Columbus in New York's harbor on 29 March. That evening, he penned a note informing his "precious wife" of his safe arrival, and that he would sail three days later. Lamenting the circumstances forcing his spouse to remain behind, he nonetheless expected her to join him soon, and reiterated what he had heard about pleasant living conditions out West. His sister, Ellen Martin, had written that the sale of his Glens Falls house had gone smoothly, and he had already instructed her to

Edith and Elliot, at Time of March 1867 Wedding. (TCC)

send the $800 down-payment to Edith, who was to give the money to her father, "as I told him would be done." The remaining $1,000, to be paid in monthly installments, would be similarly handled, and Elliot promised to send his wife more details about the sale of "our" house.[16]

Being separated so soon after the wedding was hard for Edith, who did not have a new career and surroundings to distract her. In her first letter to her husband, she admitted to crying frequently and feeling depressed without her "lost, lost one" nearby to comfort her. To make matters worse, her mother remained bed-ridden with rheumatism, leaving Edie to shoulder responsibility for running the household. The roads had dried sufficiently to permit over thirty well-wishers to visit Clifton's ailing inmates, leaving the young hostess utterly exhausted in their wake. With the approach of Easter, Edith invoked symbols of Christ's crucifixion to describe her feelings of helplessness.

Wondering who would visit the other first, she hinted it would be "most gallant" if Elliot did, "but if you don't *hurry* I tell you, I *won't wait*." She was in touch with Col. William Bramhall and hoped to persuade him to escort her out West in a few months. Still sure she had done the right thing in remaining behind, Edith recognized, as a married woman, she could no longer just do as she pleased, and would have to join her husband, whenever he "directs it." "I don't say I *regret* [being married], of course, but of one thing I am certain—I won't do the like again ever." Despite Elliot's earlier instructions, she was surprised when documents pertaining to the sale of his house arrived for her signature, and only then did she realize she now owned a "share" in his property. (While not so unusual for that time, Elliot's reluctance to discuss business and career matters with his fiancée/wife also reflected their age difference.)[17]

Alarmed the doctor was still unsure how to treat Marie's undiagnosed malady, Edith had by mid-April begun to fear her little sister might die. Jesse had been persuaded to stay a while longer on the farm, but the strain of running the household was proving too much for the young bride, who believed only a visit from her "gay Galoot" could bring joy back into her life. Attempting to change the tone, she professed to not yet being a "settled matron," but the same "dreamy, romantic little maiden" he had first met. A postscript bravely proclaimed stains on the letter were "tears of joy."[18]

On 28 April, Edith's uncle Henry Gover undertook the sad task of informing Elliot of the twin tragedies just suffered by the Matthews family. In a letter the lieutenant would not receive until mid-June, Gover informed the lieutenant that, after having convulsions throughout 20 April, Marie "gradually grew weaker and suffering intensely, as she had been for some time, until ¼ past 6 o'clock on the morning of the 21st when her gentle and innocent spirit passed into an endless Eternity of eternal bliss." That same evening, while his daughter "lay a corpse" downstairs, E. Y. "was taken with a heavy chill, which was succeeded by a very high fever," forcing his wife to remain by his bedside and miss their daughter's burial the next afternoon at the Quaker cemetery. There, Samuel Janney delivered the eulogy to the "very large concourse of saddened and mourning friends," come to witness the girl's interment.

After appearing to rally, the father, heart-broken by Marie's death, succumbed to his various infirmities on 27 April. In advising Elliot of this second loss, Henry Gover added: "No doubt thy imagination will call up our saddened household and endeavor to bear a portion of our trials and anxieties, made more so of course by the great distance of thyself from the family." When Rachel Williams came to view his body the next day, she found Sarah and Annie Matthews "more composed" than Edith, who was suffering from neuralgia. His remains were interred that afternoon with "many from Goose Creek being here together, with apparently the whole [Waterford] neighborhood." A decent man, loving husband and beloved father, E. Y. Matthews often seemed to merge into the shadow of his female household, yet the disorientation and despair that his passing caused in his widow and surviving daughters left no doubt he had been the family's mainstay, without whom they felt lost.

After relating the sad facts, Edith's uncle tried to address what Elliot should do:

> Considering what the three have passed through within the last ten days, I think they are quite as well and cheerful as could be expected, having exhibited much fortitude and Christian support during the trying season. Edith has been suffering very much with neuralgia in her head. It has been painful during the day but is much better this evening, and she thinks she will not have it tomorrow. Annie was confined to her bed for a couple

of days after Mary's funeral, but is better now, and we think will soon recover her usual health. Indeed, she has been remarkably sustained throughout the whole of our sad bereavement.

Apart from the sadness occasioned in Sister S[arah]'s feelings, it will take some time for her to recover from the exhaustion...[caused by] the nursing and attendance of the sick. She thinks if thee had not started, she would not be willing for thee to go such a distance from them, but having given thee the information of the true existence of things here [i.e., financial situation], they all feel best satisfied to let thee exercise thy own judgment as to what course is best to pursue in the future. With much love from the saddened household...I remain thy friend, H. T. Gover.[19]

The first surviving letter from Edith after the deaths of her father and sister was started on 16 June. Reflecting her troubled emotional state, it alternated between melancholy and an odd playfulness. Spring fever, plus difficulty in sleeping, added listlessness to her depression, and she feared her husband might ask for a divorce, if he could see how lazy and sloppily dressed she had become. At times, she even regretted marrying a man who deserted her "e're the 'honeymoon' waned," and pointed out that in three months of marriage they had spent only seven days together. At least the new farmhand, Jim Mitchell, was there to pay her compliments, having recently declared he would rather "have suffered death, than gone and left behind him so *lovely* and sweet a little creature as Miss Edie." Jim was sure that Mr. Chamberlin would never find anyone "half so beautiful" in all of his travels out West.

Annie had managed to leave the house long enough to visit their father's and sister's graves, but their mother was still confined to her room and took "chloroform liniment" to relieve her joint pains. They had received several applications from prospective summer boarders, but Edith doubted they would be up to taking in guests that year. She still had not received any word from Elliot, and longed to know when he would come East for a visit or wanted her to travel to him. At least then she would have something concrete to look forward to. As it was, each time she heard a horse on the bridge in front of Clifton, she involuntarily looked to see if it was her husband. Lida Hutchinson and her sister Lizzie Dutton had recently called, and Edith found Lida the same "prepossessing appearing young lady that she has always been." Nevertheless, she was jealous when Lida revealed her husband's plans to return to Waterford and work for her father, leaving Edith to speculate whether the couple could adjust to life in the country, as Lida had liked New York City very much. As the young women discussed their marriages, Edith thought her old rival must be blind to compare her husband to "my splendid and handsome 'Lord'." Even when the visitors sympathized with her plight, Edith remained convinced no one had the "faintest glimmering of what I endure."

On 13 June, Edith attended the marriage of her cousin Edward White to Bettie Hough at the Lutheran Church in Lovettsville. A small group was invited to the bride's house after the ceremony, followed the next day by a larger reception given by the groom's mother, Sarah White. Edith commented that Bettie already called her "Cousin" and let her kiss the groom. ("Not the first time you know.") Randolph White seemed very pleased with his son's marriage, and the couple went directly to live with the groom's parents without the benefit of a honeymoon. Three days later, Edward left his bride to sell farm produce in Georgetown. Reminded of her own situation, Edith felt "real sorry for her."[20]

Two weeks later, Edith began another long letter with a recitation of how much she missed her husband. She managed, however, to include a compliment paid by a boarder identified only as Burton, who likened her eyes to "polished jet set in the fairest alabaster." Knowing she had been looking for a letter from her husband for a long time, Burton teased that her lieutenant must have taken a "squaw" by this time and forgotten all about his "*fair*" bride. She related an amusing story about Burton's "lung machine," which she called one of those "miserable, cheating 'Yankee' ingenuities, of which your heads are full." It had a blowpipe attached to a box with a wheel on it, and he instructed her to blow hard on the mouthpiece to make the wheel spin. When she did, flour hidden in the box flew back in her face. It was not the first time she had fallen for one of his practical jokes., but at least Burton provided some relief from the gloom that hung over the household, especially now that her "helpless sister" Annie was too "much confined and restricted in pursuits of pleasure" to fill the void left by Marie.

In a more serious vein, Edith hoped her husband had finally learned of the deaths in her family, as it was uncomfortable to receive letters with messages for her father and Marie. To remedy delays, she planned to send future letters by overland mail, *i.e.*, Pony Express. Although she no longer thought he should resign his commission, as she had right after her father's death, she still wanted him to come back and help decide what to do with the farm. She could not manage it by herself, but if they got someone responsible to rent Clifton, she could board with her mother and Annie in Waterford, or join him on the West Coast. Enclosing letters from Ellen Martin and William Chamberlin, Edie scolded her husband for not writing to his own family.[21]

At the end of June, Edith reported receiving a letter written by Elliot in early May, as he was about to depart San Francisco, and the delay made her realize for the first time the immense distance separating them. Taking her cue from his description of his activities, she recounted her own routine during a hot summer day:

> Will begin with my getting up this morning at quarter to eight (Oh! how do you get along rising at four? I am rejoiced army life is correcting some of your old bad habits.) after a miserably restless night—dressed myself for breakfast, which Barbara and I do alone. (Sweet Ma not able to get up.) Burton sitting at the waiter to pour the coffee, while I sat at the head [of the table] and boned the shad; over which we had good deal of merriment, then I prepared my precious Ma, and sister, breakfast.

> Then proceeded to our poultry yard with B.—fed my little chickens and ducks—set our hen, an old yellow one. Then with B's assistance worked round [the yard] and watered the verbenas, but the sun was so intensely warm that it made me sick, and dear Ma ordered me straight in the house...I then assisted Ma to dress, as she felt much better and quite like getting up again. When through with that, I went with Sister dear and Burton into the 'lot', where we remained until the bell rang for dinner. We had a real delightful time down there, as there was much besides ourselves to entertain us. Burton was out yesterday for mulberries and chanced in the way of a terrapin, through whose shell he put a string and put it in the water to swim, but the simple and unaccommodating animal would do nothing at all. Only once in a long time put its horridly ugly head out of its shell, look round, then draw it cautiously in again. Burton took down my flock of 17 ducks and put them in the mill pond, and oh! you never saw my little things so delighted, in such perfect rapture as they were, but would you believe, B tied his little ship to one of their feet, and made it tug it, and which it did so cunningly, but I made a terrible fuss about it, part for effect, you know. He said half the ducks are his and he can treat half just as he likes. It reminded me of your 'cat-story' when the little child was 'only pulling its half,' which I repeated to him, and made him laugh heartily, pronouncing it 'first rate.' Since dinner, I preserved some beautiful cherries, and will bring you some, when I come to you—in Asia or wherever else you may chance to be...

> [For supper I] dressed in purely white with a single white rose in my hair and bright cherry at my throat—(looking sweet, oh you don't know). At my supper feasted on delightful raspberries, which are just now in their prime. (Wish you were here to go into the mountain in search of them.) Then donned my little hat and beautiful "casey" [shawl?] of white and shaded scarlet worsted...thrown careless off my shoulders, as I confined it by a large scarlet cord and tassels in front and oh! I promise you might have imagined me 'sweet sixteen.' You would have thought me young again. Preparatory to riding with my dear sister and Burton, which I did most charmingly until quite a late hour.

> It was a perfect evening for riding—so sweet. As we returned through town, we were

attracted there by sweet strains of enchanting music proceeding from the keys of an accordion in the hands of our Mr. Norris—a splendid performer. There was quite a large company at Auntie's, also in at Mrs. Hollingsworth's, Lieutenant Hutchinson and Lady, cousin Eddie White and bride, with a number of others. We did not get out of the carriage, as we feel little like mingling with the 'gay and festive throng'—and take no part in anything of the kind. I was telling you of the music—which was oh! so very beautiful, for there was a sadness mingled in its tones—so congenial to our sorrowing hearts. We listened enraptured some time, then came home to Ma…[Arriving at Clifton she was abruptly reminded of the loved ones who were no longer there.]

Still in mourning, the Matthews family did not attend large parties given by the Duttons and Steers on Fourth of July eve. Still, Edith had already heard some gossip about the festivities, and did not hesitate recounting how Lida Hutchinson had announced her desire to kiss all of the gentlemen. After bussing Will Irish, Jake Walker, Ed White and Ike Atkinson, the hostess asked to do the same to the "beau of Mary Ruth Walker." Uncle Sam Gover and Mary Ruth were just then going out the gate, but Sam piped up that he was the man, and hurried back to kiss Lida. Asking if Elliot was sorry to have missed his chance, she noted Lieutenant Hutchinson had been visibly upset by his wife's behavior.[22]

Edith's cattiness aside, there is reason to believe Waterford parties were less restrained than had been the case before the war. Occupation by troops from both sides and the flight of its male population to unsavory border towns had a pernicious effect on traditional Quaker values that once characterized the village. Already in April 1865, the last issue of the *Waterford News* had decried the moral decay that had taken place. "Vice of every kind stalks abroad throughout the whole breadth and length of this *once* far-famed Christian land. The moral sensibilities of even the best of our people seem more or less blunted… The horrid effects of this bloody conflict will *long, long* be felt." For years the pillar of the community, the Quaker meeting was being hollowed out as younger members left for more promising venues in the Midwest, married "out of unity," or found other religions more compatible with their wartime experiences. An increasingly older and predominately female membership faced another crisis when the meetinghouse had to be rebuilt following a fire in the fall of 1867. Although the repaired structure remained in use for another fifty years, Waterford seemed to have lost its moral compass in the years following the war, or so the town's social columnist lamented in 1888: "Morally, there is occasion for the remark that Waterford is too near 'The Point' for its own good. In other towns of the County I hear the charge that there is a good deal of drinking in Waterford—and I am afraid the town is not in position to bring suit for slander on this score. Stop the jug tavern business."[23]

* * * * *

Departing from New York on 1 April, Lieutenant Chamberlin's ship headed for Panama, where he escorted his charge of recruits across the Isthmus to board another steamer for California. Arriving at Angel Island in San Francisco's harbor on or about 23 April, he was surprised to find no letters awaiting him, the first indication his wife was not using the faster (but more expensive) overland mail service. As a result, nearly two more months would elapse before he learned of the deaths in her family.

At Angel Island, Chamberlin was informed he would be commanding a detachment from Company D, 8th U.S. Cavalry, then based at Fort Walla Walla on the Columbia River in Oregon Territory. First, however, he had to deliver the recruits who had accompanied him to Department of the Columbia headquarters in Vancouver, Washington Territory. Chamberlin was gratified to find Gen. Thomas Devin still on Angel Island, although his new commander planned to move to the Pacific Northwest in time to begin an offensive against the Native Americans that summer. Edith need not worry about the pending action, as other officers assured him the dangers posed by the Native Americans were slight, given the capable men in the 8th Cavalry, all well-mounted and equipped with Spencer carbines. Noticeably proud to be a cavalryman again, he claimed in just a week of his arrival to have mastered the small but spirited California horses—despite an initial mishap.

After taken on a tour of the base and nearby naval yard by General Devin's brother, Chamberlin was so enchanted by the harbor's beauty that he wished it could be his permanent post. Comparing the comfortable housing provided the base's married officers to Corby Hall, a large brick home outside Waterford, he claimed to have heard living conditions at Fort Walla Walla were equally good. Venturing into downtown San Francisco to shop, the lieutenant was amazed by the city's grandeur and exorbitant prices. In true male fashion, the purchases for his tour of duty consisted mainly of a shotgun, fishing rod and enough uniforms to last two years. "All I lack is my own dear wife to make me happy," he exclaimed, noting that everyone wanted to know why she had not accompanied him. Then, remembering the difficulties Edith faced at home, he promised not to nag her on this subject anymore, although he still expected her to join him soon. Obviously worried about the financial situation at Clifton, he asked her to include details on the "family business" in her response.[24]

Assigned to court martial duty, Chamberlin did not depart San Francisco until 4 May, and was again detailed to a court martial upon arrival a week later at Fort Vancouver. In a brief letter to Edith on 14 May, he indicated his disappointment at still having received no word from her. Hastily writing on the back of a circular order listing the organizational makeup of his new department, he described having to wake every day at 4 AM and going to bed late, as he prepared to depart inland, while at the same time serving court martial duty. As a rather meager offering to his wife back home, he enclosed several items picked up during his travels: a kernel of Mexican corn, part of a coconut, a pressed rose and a fern leaf. Despite high prices and the necessity to pay for everything in gold or silver, he hoped to save money. What he did have in excess was an ever-accumulating store of love for his wife, and, vowing they should never be separated again, he reiterated his expectation for her to join him no later than that fall.[25]

Accompanied by four infantry privates, Chamberlin left Vancouver on 17 May and arrived at Fort Walla Walla before the end of the month. There, he found the first letters from his wife awaiting him, and in his response to Edith he expressed hope that Marie's life had been spared. He now fully realized what distress his departure had evoked in his young bride, and prayed God would forgive him for causing such pain. Aware his earlier exuberance and glowing descriptions of California might seem out of place back home, he stressed having forgone seeing the sights of San Francisco and volunteering for extra duty on Angel Island so married officers could spend more time with their spouses. Other than to say how busy he had been, he offered no description of his new post, which given its isolation and rustic appearance probably offered, he feared, little inducement for Edith to come.[26]

On 4 June, the Columbia Department's chief quartermaster sent Chamberlin $1,000 by Wells Fargo Express to use for traveling expenses on a march from Walla Walla to Fort Boise. He advised the lieutenant to take minimal pack animals for the journey, as he would be taking along a pair of six-mule teams, then on their way to Walla Walla by boat for delivery to Boise. Chamberlin's outgoing journey was accomplished without incident to the Snake River, where he established a temporary camp at Washoe Ferry. There, he turned over the mules to a party from Boise and received several deserters to escort back to stand trial in Vancouver. On the return march, a prisoner named George Davis managed to escape in the direction of Canada. Determined not to let this incident mar his first assignment, the lieutenant set out alone and eventually recaptured the fugitive. He would later maintain that exposure to the elements during this manhunt caused his rheumatism.[27]

Upon return to Walla Walla on 17 June, he found Henry Gover's letter describing the deaths at Clifton, and immediately began preparations to return to Virginia. Department headquarters in Portland granted him twenty days of leave on 22 June, which enabled him to travel onward to San Francisco where he received an additional sixty days of leave on 14 July, but he could not have gotten back to Waterford before mid-August at the earliest. Even though his children would later recall their father went out West right after the Civil War to fight Native Americans, and only missed the Battle of the Little Big Horn because of the onset of rheumatism, the lieutenant was actually at his post less than a month, and probably never encountered a hostile Native American during that time. Curiously, both Edith and Elliot also led their children to believe they only married after his return from the West, perhaps finding this simplification of the facts less painful to relate to young ears.[28]

During his absence, as her mother and Annie recovered from grief and prolonged illnesses, Edith bore the brunt of managing a household still deep in mourning. Yet soon after her helpmate's arrival, Elliot, too, was laid low by a rheumatic attack that left him bedridden and required a doctor's attention. Although nursed back to health by his wife, he would be plagued by recurrent bouts of this malady for the remainder of his life. Of more immediate impact, his illness would hinder efforts to rehabilitate the war-ravaged farm, then being run on shares by a single Black tenant.[29]

Fortunately, the War Department granted Elliot a thirty-day leave extension in early September to settle his affairs, allowing him and Edith to ponder their options. His recent rheumatoid attack had dampened his desire to remain in the inclement Northwest and, with Edith no more ready to abandon her widowed mother, Elliot tendered his resignation from the Army on 7 October. His covering letter explained having vacated his post at Walla Walla due to the death of his father-in-law, who had left "his estate in an unsettled condition and myself the only male representative of the family," which, besides his wife, consisted of her "aged" mother and "invalid" sister. (Failure to cite his own health problems would complicate later efforts to obtain a disability pension.)[30]

Elliot and Edith were then staying in Washington—their first time alone since the brief honeymoon. Her mother was upset the couple had not remained at Clifton to observe a proper period of mourning, as well as concerned over her son-in-law having left while still "crippled." Despite professing satisfaction they were at least enjoying themselves, she cautioned, "you cannot flee from yourselves...Do my darling Edith enter into no frivolous, or what might now be for thee *unlawful* pleasures...Indulgences of this kind would take much from thy character and would wound thy poor heart-stricken Mother." Sarah also included a more subtle warning that Edith was in danger of losing her plain Quaker roots by seeking material and social pleasures. Recognizing that her daughter had innate "good sense and discretion," she still worried about her lack of experience, and, echoing her own mother Miriam Gover, begged her daughter "not to let an inordinate desire for the empty and unsatisfying things of the world get the mastery over thy feelings." Warning that "first impressions are the most lasting," she urged Edith to ensure the respect of her husband's friends by being "lady-like in thy deportment."[31]

Sarah's allusion to "unlawful" activities may have reflected concern about her son-in-law's renewed involvement in political activities, which could jeopardize his military career. (She was unaware of his pending resignation.) The fall of 1867 witnessed political turmoil in the nation's capital, put in motion by Andrew Johnson's attempt to dismiss Secretary of War Stanton and culminating the following spring in the President's impeachment trial. Members of Elliot's old GAR post were in the thick of this controversy—threatening to use force to block the President's initiative by stationing guards outside Stanton's office to prevent his removal. Local GAR members were also active publishing *The Great Republic,* the official mouthpiece of both the GAR and the Union League of America (ULA). Started the year before by veterans known to Elliot, including Edwin Dudley, the paper had become one of the most outspoken critics of the President and the Democrat Party.[32]

Elliot made sure to be back in Loudoun to vote in the late October election to select delegates to draft a new constitution for Virginia. The Old Dominion was now under military rule under the terms of the Reconstruction Act passed earlier in the year, and for the first time, Black men would be allowed to vote. The Freedmen's Bureau and ULA had been actively involved in mobilizing formerly enslaved persons to exercise their new political rights, and their vote proved decisive in electing a constitutional convention that would lay the groundwork for Radical Republicans to control the state for the next two years. In Loudoun, however, local Republicans once again failed to elect a single delegate.

Soon afterwards, the couple left for Philadelphia, where Elliot was again stricken by rheumatism. A thirty-day guest pass to Philadelphia's Union League Club[33] indicates his stay in that city had a political aspect, perhaps attendance at a committee then debating the relationship between the GAR and ULA. (It was ultimately decided that unexpected Democratic gains in Northern off-year elections made it advisable for the GAR to distance itself from the ultra-Radical ULA.) Afterwards, Elliot and Edith visited New York, where he was finally able to introduce her to his family in Glens Falls.[34]

PART III
"My Old Carpetbagger"

Chapter 20

A BUREAUCRATIC FARMER: 1868-1875

His political ardor temporarily cooled by Loudoun Republicans' poor showing in the October 1867 election (but not in the state as a whole) Elliot and Edith returned to Clifton that winter determined to place the farm on a profitable footing. She was glad to be back home; his feelings about abandoning a military career for the uncertainties of farming were mixed. Although he came to love Clifton as much as his wife did, his temperament and bouts of rheumatism made him ill-suited for the life of a farmer. Fortunately for them both, the old homestead proved an ideal spot to start a family during the turbulent years ahead.

E. Y. Matthews left an estate burdened with debt, including a large mortgage. While Elliot was on the West Coast and Henry Gover living in Baltimore, Sarah Matthews persuaded younger brother Sam to serve as administrator of her husband's estate. After an August 1867 inventory valued the decedent's personal property at $1,100, Sam arranged for the sale of these assets during an auction held at Clifton later that fall while the Chamberlins were in Philadelphia and New York. Edith would later claim she could not bear to watch her father's possessions being sold, and Elliot may have deliberately avoided involvement in his in-laws' affairs; but their failure to take an active part in the initial phases of the estate settlement would exacerbate misunderstandings with Sam Gover. The auction itself grossed $1,800, and almost everything moveable sold: furniture, farm equipment, livestock and unharvested crops, the last two categories bringing the highest prices. Yet, despite exceeding the appraised value of the items sold, the sale failed to solve the family's financial problems, and an accounting submitted the following year showed the estate still owing $1,555, not including Clifton's mortgage.[1]

The farm to which Elliot and Edith returned had been stripped bare—first by soldiers and then to satisfy creditors. Their first step was to replace equipment and animals sold at auction. Supplies and groceries were purchased on credit from local merchants, in particular from Sam Gover. A running account with blacksmith Reuben Schooley was typical of Elliot's financial agreements. Begun in 1868, it shows numerous entries for repairs and parts for carriages, wagons and other equipment that were partially offset by credits for corn in late 1868 and potatoes in 1870. Schooley closed the account in 1872 and demanded full payment, but the bill was not paid off until 1874. Similarly, bills with other merchants were settled in exchange for wheat and corn.

In January 1868, Elliot paid twenty dollars to Samuel Means for used plows, harness, a harrow, and other equipment. The war had not been kind to the Loudoun Ranger captain, who two years earlier had been forced to transfer ownership of his mill and residence to his Baltimore mortgage holder. Means was allowed to occupy the premises until 1868 when creditors, including secessionists who had slapped liens on his property in 1861, forced him to declare bankruptcy. After an unsuccessful attempt to establish another mill outside Waterford failed in 1876, Means moved to Washington where his wife ran a boarding house.²

Elliot's approach to farming is best illustrated by his role in founding the Catoctin Farmers' Club (CFC), said to be "Virginia's oldest ongoing agricultural organization." Using his experience organizing veterans and with proposed by-laws already drafted, he invited a group of local farmers to Clifton in April 1868 to broach plans for a club. His ideas were accepted, and the first regular CFC meeting was held a week later at Talbott, where owner James Walker was elected president. (The other officers were also mostly Quakers with ties to the Matthews family.) As a novice farmer, Elliot took a back seat during the club's first year, content to head the Farm Machinery Committee. For him, the CFC was not only a way to overcome his inexperience, but also a possible springboard for his political aspirations. (In his history of the CFC, Eugene Scheel aptly describes its founder as having an "urban soul.")³

With the CFC slow to get off the mark that first summer, Elliot turned his attention to the Potomac Fruit Growers Association, attending its inaugural September meeting at the residence of Judge John Bramhall in Falls Church. The judge's brother Charles was elected president of the association and Elliot's good friend from the GAR, Col. Frank J. Bramhall (Charles's son), was made secretary. Elliot was placed on the executive committee and remained active in this group for many years. Like the CFC, it had a Republican cast, being composed of former Unionists from northern Virginia and Washington, many of whom were transplanted Yankees. The following month, Elliot reported to the CFC about the formation of the orchardmen's association and urged greater fruit production in Loudoun.⁴

CFC minutes record Elliot's quest for advice from other members. One of his first questions concerned how to get laborers to comply with their contracts, an indication Clifton had yet to overcome the loss of free Black workers after the war. That first year he was instrumental in getting Elisha Walker to set aside space for a club library in the schoolhouse on his father's farm (Talbott) and afterwards did more than anyone to promote use of this resource. A persistent theme at meetings centered on how to improve the road between Waterford and Clarke's Gap, the nearest stop on the Alexandria, Loudoun and Hampshire Railroad. (The AL&H line had just been extended westward from Leesburg through the Catoctin Mountain at Clarke's Gap to Hamilton.) After a motion to assess members for funds to start a turnpike association was defeated, voluntary contributions were sought. Even though he had no realistic means of paying, Elliot made one of the top pledges. He later spoke at an open meeting at Elisha Hunt's Waterford Academy in favor of selling stock to finance a new road and agreed to obtain a cost estimate from an engineer. Nothing came of this venture, however, and the road in front of Clifton remained in poor shape for another thirty years.⁵ ⁶

After succeeding Walker as CFC president in 1869, Elliot initiated correspondence about club activities with USDA Commissioner Horace Capron. The CFC was soon placed on the department's mailing list for publications and seed packets. As hosts of the club's May meeting, he and Edith treated members to tea in their yard, as well as a "liberal distribution of plants" from her garden. Throughout his term, Elliot advocated modernizing local agricultural practices. He failed, however, to win approval for purchase of a steam thresher on a cooperative basis, as a majority favored having a single member buy the equipment and rent it out to others. In this and other instances, he was ahead of his conservative Quaker neighbors in wanting to promote agrarian reform and co-ops.

Turning the presidency back to James Walker in 1870, Elliot assumed the duties of treasurer and chair of a committee to investigate forming a "Society for Protection" to combat theft in the neighborhood. As in the case of the turnpike proposal, the Quaker penchant for setting up committees to solve problems met with little success in the face of financial and political realities in postwar Loudoun. Two years earlier, Waterford citizens had tried to establish a vigilance committee to curb horse theft, and they apparently still chafed at Sheriff Elijah White's failure to protect the former Unionist stronghold.

That spring, Elliot got the club to publicize its activities in the local press but had less luck persuading members to take advantage of the club library, which he had stocked with USDA publications. He had more success handing out the department's seed packets, and once read aloud a letter from Commissioner Capron urging recipients to record and send back their results from planting the seeds. During a July meeting at Clifton, members toured its cornfield and flower garden before sitting

Steam Threshing Machine in Front of Talbot Farm. Elliot tried unsuccessfully to have the Catoctin Farmers Club purchase one. (John Souders)

down to a delicious supper. (Both Edith and Elliot excelled at gardening, a trait passed to their daughter Eleanor, who would win many awards in local and state garden shows.)

Throughout the spring and summer of 1870, Elliot tried to persuade the CFC to host a joint agricultural fair with the Loudoun Valley Farmers Club. The fair would have been held on the eve of county elections that fall and, he hoped, would provide an opportunity to promote his campaign to become county clerk. Other members failed to share his enthusiasm, and in August he was unable to pass a motion to make annual CFC fairs obligatory. The following month plans for a joint fair were completely abandoned after it was learned the Loudoun Agricultural Society would resume countywide fairs for the first time since before the war. (The Society was still controlled by the old planter class, who evidently had no intention of letting former Unionists control this highly visible event.)[7]

During 1871, Elliot served as CFC secretary, although his attendance waned after he started work at the Agriculture Department in April. At the first meeting that year, he argued for a switch from wheat to dairy production as a main source of farm income. He also continued to push for a cooperative approach to farming, urging members to hire an agent in Washington to market their produce. Elliot himself was already acting as an agent for Yardley Taylor's son Richard, then manufacturing brooms from "broom corn" grown on his farm in Lincoln. Always on the lookout for outside income, Elliot agreed to resell 200 brooms to contacts in Washington.[8]

Due to his employment in the capital, he did not hold CFC office in 1872, although he occasionally attended meetings and headed the "Fertilizer Committee." His advocacy for change bore fruit that spring, when the CFC agreed to work with the Lincoln Farmers' Club (Goose Creek changed its name to Lincoln after the war) to organize a dairymen's association. Although Loudoun's first agricultural cooperative had to overcome difficulties in securing agents and getting the railroad to commit to consistent schedules necessary for milk deliveries to the Washington market, it paved the way for the rapid growth of the county's dairy industry during the following decade.[9]

The analytic approach to farming that prompted him to establish the club in the first place, also led him to pepper its more experienced members with questions that must have amused the old-timers. His queries ranged from how to keep daisies from spreading and when to cut fence rails, to whether it was profitable to raise more hogs than needed for personal consumption, or if one could over-fertilize a garden. When his fellow members did not know the answers, he sought out experts in other clubs, visited the Agriculture Department, or corresponded with farmers outside the state. He also researched specific topics on his own, once calculating that twelve pounds of ammonia per acre fall in rain each year. Unfettered by prior experience, he routinely questioned established methods and more importantly, suggested changes. Although he was better at raising new ideas than in executing them, this did not diminish his contributions to the CFC, or to the modernization of Loudoun's agriculture. Unfortunately, these accomplishments did not always translate into success on his own farm.

* * * * *

As described in the next chapter, Elliot unsuccessfully ran for public office in November 1870, and later served briefly as postmaster at Clarke's Gap. These endeavors to supplement income from the farm were prompted in part by their growing family's needs. Their first child, Edward Chamberlin, was born in May 1868 but died nine months later and was interred in the Fairfax Meeting burial ground. (Edith had successfully petitioned for reinstatement to the Meeting after her marriage to a non-Quaker.) A daughter, Mary Matthews, arrived on 20 November 1869, an event Elliot celebrated by composing a poem for distribution to his friends.[10] Another son, Justin Morrill, was born on 26 December 1872 and named after his godfather who had become a Vermont Senator in 1867. A second daughter, Eleanor ("Nellie," later "Bidie"), arrived on 17 February 1874.

Realizing well before the 1870 election that his chances of becoming county clerk were slim, Elliot wrote Justin Morrill about getting an appointment in the Agriculture Department. His letter prompted a response that the Senator had already placed one Vermonter there and could not ask any further favors of Commissioner Horace Capron at that time. Morrill did agree to write a note outlining Elliot's "merits and qualifications," but cautioned there were many applicants for the few openings. A longtime advocate of progressive agriculture and education for farmers, Morrill was one of the department's principal supporters in Congress, and it was not long before he succeeded in obtaining a position as clerk for his protégé. In March 1871, Elliot wrote to thank Morrill for his assistance, adding he had already notified Capron of his intention to start work on 3 April.[11]

While no record of his actual duties has survived, he was initially listed as the lowest-ranked (in terms of seniority and pay) of twenty-one clerks in the department, earning $1,200 annually. (By comparison, the Chief Clerk and the Commissioner made $2,000 and $3,000 respectively.) Among Elliot's personal papers were found thirty-five letters addressed to Capron during 1870 and early 1871. Most are routine acknowledgments from governmental chiefs and politicians for receipt of seed packets and copies of the Commissioner's annual report. The only significant letter, dated 23 May 1871, was from the Japanese Legation, thanking Capron for a complete set of annual reports. More than diplomatic courtesy was involved, as Capron submitted his resignation to President Grant the following month in order to serve as an advisor in Japan. Taking with him the department's librarian and chemist, Capron is credited with modernizing Japanese agriculture in what was one of that country's first attempts to obtain Western technology.[12]

Although the North's manufacturing superiority is frequently cited for its success in the Civil War, much of the credit belongs to its agricultural base, which by the mid-nineteenth century employed far more productive methods than those used in the South. The fledgling Republican Party understood the need for keeping farmers solidly behind Lincoln's Administration and during a few weeks in 1862 Congress passed three bills that still form the cornerstone of U.S. agricultural policy. The Department of Agriculture was created in May, and even though its commissioner would not achieve cabinet status until 1889, the new agency filled a long-felt need. The following month, Justin Morrill was able to pass his Land Grant College Act, which provided public lands for each state to establish an agricultural college, and a short time later, the Homestead Law was enacted. For the remainder of the war, the agricultural sector's political support was never in doubt, and its influence grew even stronger in later years with the emergence of the "Grange movement," of which the CFC was a small part.[13]

Throughout his military and civilian career Elliot was drawn to interesting and innovative jobs, but often had problems with his supervisors, particularly if he thought them incompetent or venal. He enjoyed a good relationship with Capron, perhaps because both had followed similar paths since leaving New England. By all accounts, Capron was a capable and effective administrator who oversaw the department's transfer from the Patent Office's basement to a building of its own. His sudden departure only three months after Elliot started work was unfortunate for the agency and its employees. The new Commissioner, Frederick Watts, was seventy when he assumed office in August 1871 and had little support outside his native Pennsylvania. From the beginning, Watts allowed his son William, a clerk making $1,800 a year, to assume most of his duties. William, in turn, relied on Chief Clerk James M. Swank, a journalist by trade, to oversee the day-to-day running of the department. Senator Morrill had little use for the new Commissioner, and relied on Elliot to keep him abreast of what went on inside the department. There is evidence this information was passed to President Grant in an unsuccessful effort to remove Watts in early 1872.[14]

On 24 September 1871, scarcely a month after Watts's arrival, an article appeared in a Washington D.C. newspaper laying out Elliot's contention that the 25th N.Y. Cavalry played the decisive role in keeping Jubal Early's troops out of the capital during the Battle of Fort Stevens. The account (see Appendix A) went on to exaggerate Chamberlin's role, describing how the "plucky" captain deployed his "gallant little band" so as to deceive the Rebels into thinking reinforcements from the VI Corps had already arrived. The timing of this laudatory account suggests Elliot may have had concerns about his job security under the new commissioner or hoped it would enhance chances for a promotion. Keystone Staters such as Watts and Swank, however, may not have been pleased by his depiction of the New Yorkers as Washington's "saviors," a title claimed by Pennsylvania regiments in the VI Corps.[15]

In any case, Elliot's relations with his supervisors took a turn for the worse during the National Agricultural Convention, held in Washington on 15-17 February 1872 and attended by representatives from state agricultural societies and colleges, as well as some politicians. Topics for discussion included whether the department should be given responsibility for administering the Land Grant College Act. Senator Morrill, the bill's author, was present at the opening ceremonies, but departed after being snubbed by Commissioner Watts, who nominated another individual to chair the convention. The list of accredited delegates from Washington D.C. included Potomac Fruit Growers Association representatives Chalkley Gillingham and "E. H. Chamberlain" (*sic*, although perhaps deliberately misspelled to protect Elliot's identity). In all likelihood, Virginia's Conservative leaders excluded the predominantly Republican association from the state delegation, prompting Elliot to accredit it from Washington D.C.[16]

But the matter did not end there. An account appearing in a Republican-oriented Alexandria newspaper, most likely at Elliot's instigation, began with a description of Commissioner Watts "as a genial old gentleman...who has lived out the period in which he can successfully manage such an institution," and who therefore has "delegated the main portion of his duties to his chief clerk," and depicted him as incompetent. The account then shifted to "Colonel Chamberlin," described as a member of Virginia's GOP State Committee who had been "elected to represent our [Virginia] State Board of Agriculture" at the on-going convention. When Swank learned Elliot had been called to attend the opening session by his fellow delegates, the chief clerk summoned him to his office and reminded his subordinate that his "time belonged to the United States" and in a "galling refinement of petty tyranny" ordered him to remain at his desk all day.[17]

A Washington D.C. newspaper continued the story in a satirical article that compared Swank to the Greek despot Dionysius. Since every tyrant faced the threat of assassination by a Brutus, or a Charlotte Corday, the article warned that Swank stood in grave danger of being "perforated" by the steel pen of an irate clerk, here naming "Col. Chamberlin." In an apparent lampoon of Elliot's article of the year before, the writer described how Chamberlin used his single regiment to fool "Old Jube" into thinking the city was defended by a half-million men, resulting in the colonel being rewarded with an office under Swank, paying $1,600 annually. (If the amount is correct, Elliot's earlier article did earn him a promotion.) Here, the reporter dryly noted past governmental generosity to former generals was evidently being extended to colonels and captains.

The newspaper writer then went on to describe how Chamberlin had been made a delegate to the convention by some "inconsiderate friends," who later came to his office after the colonel, in obedience to Swank's orders, failed to appear at the assembly. The chief clerk soon found out about the visitors and burst into the office, demanding to know why Chamberlin had broken a standing edict against entertaining guests in department offices. When the accused tried to explain these were not personal friends, but "delegates...come to see me, a delegate, on business," Swank only repeated, "your time belongs to the Government, the room belongs to the Government. Put 'em out, sir; put 'em out." Here, the reporter lamented Chamberlin's failure to point out that Commissioner Watts' entire family lived on the department's top floor. But to have done so would have cost him his job, and instead Chamberlin "tumbled" the visitors out of the building. The article ended with a call for Swank's resignation.[18]

While Watts and Swank may have suspected Elliot's hand in these unflattering portrayals of the department, they took no further disciplinary action, perhaps deterred by his role in Virginia politics and recent publicity about his service at Fort Stevens. Press reports that should have gotten back to Swank show Elliot defiantly continuing his extracurricular actives with the Potomac Fruit Growers and in April he addressed a large gathering called by the Loudoun Farmers' Cooperative to discuss ways to improve transport of produce to the Washington D.C. market.[19]

Elliot finally exhausted Swank's patience, when he failed to obtain permission to attend a Soldiers and Sailors Convention in Pittsburgh on 17-19 September. The assemblage was organized by the Republican Party to shore up support for Grant's reelection among veterans, who had become disappointed by their failure to reap the anticipated benefits of their old commander's first term. As an experienced organizer of such rallies, Elliot anticipated praise for pitching in to help the Presidential campaign.[20]

Instead, when he returned to work on Monday the 23rd, he was unprepared to find his desk occupied by another clerk. A heated argument broke out when Swank informed him that he would remain temporarily suspended for unexcused absence until Commissioner Watts returned to decide his permanent fate. According to one account that made the front page of a Washington D.C. paper, a scuffle broke out when Swank unsuccessfully tried to eject the irate clerk, who allegedly challenged his supervisor to meet him outside the city to settle the matter. Calm was restored only after the police were called and escorted Chamberlin from the building. According to this account, the other clerks sided with their colleague against the "tyrannical" chief clerk. Another version, however, noted the ejected employee had often given his bosses "cause of complaint for inattention to his duties." In any case, Commissioner Watts sustained Swank's decision to fire Elliot, citing his abusive language and threats against a supervisor.[21]

After he had time to cool off, Elliot likely regretted his failure to control his temper and the impact losing his job would have on his family. He could take some solace in events later that year when Watts bowed to pressure and let Swank go, prompting one paper to comment, "No more will the gallant Chamberlain wince at the sound of [Swank's] voice." Watts proved more resilient, even if his decision to replace Swank with another son, Frederick Watts, Jr., did nothing to improve his image.[22]

Modern historians of the USDA have dismissed Watts as a petty bureaucrat, more interested in saving twine used to secure seed packages than addressing major issues. Senator Morrill shared this opinion and from early 1872 had been gathering derogatory information on the Commissioner from Chamberlin and other disgruntled employees for use in his ouster. After several earlier attempts failed, Morrill thought he had finally convinced Grant to let Watts go, as shown in the following "strictly private" letter sent to Elliot in 1874:

> I thought it might gratify you...to know that I have again waited upon the President and now I do feel confident that the Mikado of the Ag. Dept. will be made to return to the enjoyment of raising "Penn. Yellow" [corn] at a very early day. His successor will be found somewhere in the North West. I can't tell who but anything will be an improvement... Please swing your hat around and sing hosanna! But it will take perhaps a couple of weeks before we shall see the 'glory of the Lord.'[23]

Despite Morrill's optimism, Grant was never persuaded to get rid of Watts who remained in office until 1877. In an administration marked by scandals and corruption, Watts' shortcomings and nepotism may have seemed inconsequential. The consequences for Elliot, however, were severe indeed. Not only did he lose employment on the eve of the 1873 economic crisis, but he missed a chance to combine his bureaucratic skills with a love of agriculture and scientific inquiry and thereby make a career for which he was seemingly well-suited. Clearly wanting to forget the entire episode, Elliot kept no record of his tenure at the department, aside from a single clipping and the aforementioned Capron letters. In the only known instance where he referred to working there, he cited "insufficient pay" as his reason for leaving. In later years, however, Elliot was a frequent visitor to his old workplace, gathering information to aid his work in the Treasury Department and at Clifton.

* * * * *

When participation in Grant's reelection campaign failed to secure a new appointment, Elliot returned to farming at the end of 1872, only to be confronted with falling agricultural prices brought on by the 1873 financial panic. With debts mounting and a third child on the way, he asked Justin Morrill in February 1874 to contact Commissioner Asa Aldis about filling a vacancy for special agent in the Southern Claims Commission (SCC). The Senator forwarded his letter to fellow Vermonter Aldis with a favorable endorsement, pointing out the judge's colleagues already knew the applicant. (SCC Commissioner Orange Ferriss of New York had endorsed Elliot's application for an I.R.S. position in 1869.)[24]

Congress established the SCC in 1871 to consider claims by Southern loyalists for stores and supplies taken by, or furnished to, Union troops during the war. The three judges who headed the Commission would oversee 22,000 claims totaling $60 million during a filing period that ended in 1873. To handle the unexpected case load, the commissioners hired special agents who served as traveling investigators to verify individual claims. Most claimants found it difficult to substantiate their losses and loyalty during the war, and only 7,000 individuals received a total of $4.6 million by the time the SCC disbanded in 1880.[25] [26]

As a former Union officer living in the South, Elliot was well qualified for this work. Ever since his days as provost marshal at Point of Rocks, he had fielded queries from Loudouners seeking reimbursement for wartime losses and after moving to Clifton he had a chance to observe the claims process at close hand. Thus, while finding employment was uppermost in his mind, he also looked forward to a chance to rectify perceived injustices to his Unionist neighbors.

The entire household must have breathed a sigh of relief when Elliot learned in April 1874 that he would be working on an "as-needed basis" as an SCC special agent, earning six dollars per day plus expenses. To provide for his immediate needs until his salary began, Justin Morrill lent him $250, a portion of which was to be repaid by boarding the Senator's horses at Clifton that summer. In making a partial repayment that July, Elliot apologized to Morrill for the delay, which "I fear impaired your confidence in me. I tried hard to be prompt but fate seemed to be against me…We have finished harvesting a fair crop, corn looks fine, but the weather is dry, and unless we have rain soon, we will have a short crop… Little Morrill is a trump…and I would like very much to have you see him." Although he promised to remit the balance due "in a few days," his final loan payment, which included fifty dollars in interest, was not made for over a year.[27]

Elliot's first SCC assignments took him into the Shenandoah Valley in late April, and then to Charlottesville, where he finished his last investigations in early June. SCC field agents typically had a difficult time establishing a claimant's loyalty, as wartime records were often missing, witnesses had moved or died, and memories faded. Elliot found the claims process to be an invitation for fraud "in order to make a dollar," and he seldom interviewed references provided by claimants, preferring instead to talk to neighbors and other informants. (Whenever available, records of the 1861 referendum on secession were an invaluable way to confirm whether an individual had actually voted to stay in the Union.) He discovered that speculators had gone through the Valley buying up receipts for crops and animals taken by federal troops. The profiteers paid twenty-five cents on the dollar but had connections in the government enabling them to get full reimbursement. Elliot concluded it was mostly disloyal citizens who had sold their notes to speculators.[28]

Aside from a few cases in Loudoun, he did not resume work until early fall when he returned to the Valley before taking on more Loudoun cases in October and November. Aided by personal knowledge of the individuals involved, he won approval for several disputed claims. In some cases, staunch Unionists had been falsely accused of disloyalty by jealous Secessionists who did not want to see them reimbursed. In others, he questioned earlier statements attesting to a claimant's loyalty, often resulting in its disallowance. Doubting an earlier finding that Waterford widow Virginia Virts was loyal, Elliot received permission to reopen the case and, on a hunch, reinterviewed William Parmes, who formerly had been enslaved on the Virts farm. Revealing he had not been asked about Mrs. Virts's loyalty before, Parmes candidly replied: "When rebels were about she would talk rebel, and when Yankees were about she would talk yankee. To tell the truth, she was most rebel." Evidently feeling more compassion for the hard-pressed widow than their special agent, the SCC awarded her a partial payment.[29]

That fall, Elliot interjected himself into one of Loudoun's largest and most complex claims, that of the estate of Horatio Trundle, the deceased owner of Exeter Plantation outside Leesburg. His widow and executor, Elizabeth Trundle, asked for over $8,000 in losses to Union troops, and the case appeared on track for a positive settlement under the guidance of her Washington D.C. lawyer, at least until Elliot sent an unsolicited report to the SCC questioning Horatio's loyalty. To back up his charge, he enclosed a signed statement by a witness attesting to the plantation owner's support for the Confederacy. A month later, the special agent sent another report reiterating his suspicions about the Trundles, this time backed by affidavits from four more witnesses. On learning of these challenges to his client's case, the lawyer conducted a special hearing in Leesburg the following year that included cross-examination of Elliot's witnesses. But the real bombshell occurred when Horatio's son inadvertently revealed his father had voted for secession in 1861, usually an automatic disqualifier for a claim. (The SCC had a list of every Loudouner's vote, probably purloined from the courthouse by Elliot, but their index to the list had misspelled Trundle's name.) In a last-ditch effort to save the case, three former Confederate officers, including John S. Mosby, appeared before the SCC commissioners in Washington to vouch for the Trundles' loyalty to the Union cause.[30] In the end, the SCC rejected Mrs. Trundle's entire claim, but Elliot's role in denying compensation to one of Leesburg's most prominent families did little to win him friends among former secessionists.[31]

Another case that fall showed an instance when Elliot's license as an attorney (obtained several years earlier, as discussed in the next chapter) was put to use. In 1871, he had assisted Eli Pierpoint, an elderly Hillsboro farmer, file a claim that listed himself as the claimant's attorney. When Elliot received the same case to investigate for the SCC, he had to explain it was one of several claims "on which I acted as attorney…without compensation." All took place before he started work for the SCC and involved "personal acquaintances [who] were thoroughly Union and deserving in every respect." Pierpoint ended up receiving $185 of his original $245 claim, a better percentage than most.[32]

Surprisingly, no claim was filed on behalf of the Matthews estate before the 1873 deadline. Losses from the "Burning Raid" had to be handled by direct petition to Congress, but there were certainly other instances when E. Y. never received compensation for hay and other items supplied to the federals. One of the very first claims to be heard by the commissioners (number twenty-one out of 22,000 cases) netted James Walker $303 of $754 that the Clifton neighbor claimed. Had Elliot not learned of the program in time, or did he simply fail to complete the necessary forms, as would later occur with his pension? The only close relative to file an SCC claim, Henry Gover, did so from Baltimore, receiving sixty dollars for a $283 claim for damage to fences on his Waterford farmland.[33]

In advising the SCC in early December that he had completed his assigned cases, Elliot added, "I trust that I may be continued on further work." When more investigations were not forthcoming, he contacted Justin Morrill for aid in gaining a position as special agent for the Post Office Department, reminding the Senator to make sure Postmaster General Marshall Jewell was informed of his status as a veteran, and of his in-laws' wartime losses, which had made them entirely dependent on his earnings. The latter situation had grown particularly dire when Annie Matthews lost her Treasury job in 1872, just two years after Morrill had helped arrange for her to be hired. Here, Elliot suggested that Annie's termination was linked to his high-profile participation in Virginia's Republican Party. Morrill, perhaps miffed at Elliot's slow repayment of his loan, waited over a month to forward the letter to Jewell, along with a bland comment that the applicant was "a first class man."[34]

In January 1875, SCC Commissioners Aldis and Ferriss provided a more satisfactory introduction to the Postmaster General in a letter describing Elliot as an exemplary employee who had only been let go because all current cases were in the Deep South. With no Republican congressman from his Virginia district to aid him, Elliot turned to New York Rep. Robert Hale, the Glens Falls Congressman who had aided him in the past. Realizing Hale had less obligation towards a Virginia resident, Elliot asked his friend and political colleague, Clinton Lloyd, to intervene with Hale on his behalf. (Lloyd was chief clerk for the House of Representatives, but lived in Loudoun when Congress was not in session and had served with Elliot on the county's GOP Committee.) In asking Hale to nominate Elliot to a Post Office position, Lloyd added a personal touch, describing the applicant as "wonderfully versatile—an accurate accountant, an *Artist*...with a pen, and moreover possessed of wonderful Mechanical ingenuity, a Staunch Republican of great value politically to us in Virginia by reason of his good sense and discretion which make him respected by his political enemies." Hale forwarded Lloyd's letter to the Postmaster General, along with his own endorsement that Elliot receive an appointment. Then, when Hale's influence by itself proved insufficient to secure a position, Elliot had several Virginia GOP leaders sign a petition attesting to his role as "an earnest and zealous party worker." Despite everything, he did not get the Post Office job, although he would reuse these endorsements later that year in applying to the Treasury.[35]

Elliot resumed work for the SCC between May and July 1875, investigating cases in Loudoun and the Shenandoah Valley. Once again, he became involved in a particularly sensitive case, this time with troublesome roots in his hometown. As was evident in Elliot's notes on his interview with claimant Joshua Everhart, there was no doubt about the Lovettsville farmer's loyalty, or honesty. (Elliot detailed Everhart's horrific treatment by Loudoun's home-grown guerrilla, John Mobberly, who once left him tied to a tree on the mountain to die, and another time beat the farmer with a stick.) Of greater concern was the involvement of Sam Means and Waterford justice of the peace Edwin A. Atlee in submitting the original claim. The two had grossly inflated the losses claimed by the illiterate Everhart, intending to pocket the difference themselves. It is not known whether Elliot was the first to detect problems with cases filed by the former Ranger captain and Atlee, a postwar transplant from Maryland, but at a hearing in April 1875, the SCC Commissioners sent the claim of Griffith W. Paxson of Waterford back for further investigation, along with the comment that Means, the main witness, was "said not to be truthful [and]...to have [a financial] interest in claims in that vicinity." Two years later, both Means and Atlee were under investigation by the Secret Service for submitting fraudulent claims to the U.S. Government. About that time Atlee abandoned his family and moved to Indiana.[36]

After his employment with the SCC officially ended on 31 July, the Commissioners provided Elliot with a glowing letter of recommendation, stating that they had "been greatly pleased with the honest, straightforward and impartial manner in which you have acted...You have not only rendered the government efficient service...but...have secured the respect and good-will of all those persons...brought into contact with you...Such results are evidence of sound and valuable qualities in a public officer, and the Commissioners, officially and personally, will always be ready to testify to your possession of them." Elliot clearly enjoyed and excelled at the investigatory duties of a special agent—a natural outgrowth of his earlier provost and court martial duties in the Army—and soon began to look for similar work in the Treasury Department.[37][38]

* * * * *

Despite disappointment at the Catoctin Farmers Club's failure to take an active role in the revival of Loudoun's annual agricultural fairs, both Elliot and his wife took part in these popular affairs when circumstances permitted. At the 1871 Fair, Edith helped judge the "household fabrics division," which would have showcased the handiwork of Waterford's skilled weavers and quilt-makers and the following year, Elliot's exhibit of fruits and vegetables drew favorable mention in the press. A visit to the 1873 Fair by Ulysses S. Grant and his cabinet was one of the most publicized events in Loudoun's postwar history. The President's role in the readmission of Virginia to the nation contributed to his warm reception at the fairgrounds, although one reporter overheard some *sotto voce* reservations against any and all Republicans. Disenchantment with the Grant Administration apparently caused Elliot to boycott this affair, despite the CFC's receipt of complimentary tickets and the inclusion of his friend Clinton Lloyd on the list of speakers that day. He would, however, play a minor part in the 1876 Fair, serving on the reception committee and helping guide Washington newspaper writers around the exhibits.[39]

Elliot's intention to expand Clifton's orchard was already evident from his participation in the 1871 joint convention of the American and Virginia Pomological Societies, the first such meeting held in the South. His exhibit at the Richmond show featured the "Loudoun pippin," an apple variety yielding up to eighty bushels per tree. After his dismissal from the Agriculture Department, he assumed a more active role in the Potomac Fruit Growers Association, serving on its executive committee, drafting new by-laws, delivering talks, and displaying his apples, pears, grapes and nuts at meetings. In the spring of 1873, Elliot purchased 250 apple, 300 peach and 115 pear trees from Chalkley Gillingham, the association's president and owner of the Mt. Vernon Nursery. (Late autumn would have been a safer time to plant so many saplings, something Elliot later admitted after losing many of them.) That fall, the CFC thanked Elliot "for making so successful a display" at the Philadelphia Horticultural Show and allocated twenty dollars to defray his expenses. While awaiting his freshly planted trees to mature, Elliot tried to supplement his income by advertising his exclusive rights to sell Excelsior Oat seed, "the most valuable kind."[40]

After becoming vice-president of the Potomac Fruit Growers in 1874, Elliot used his position to urge members to "work more earnestly for the advancement of...the interests of fruit growers generally." During his travels for the SCC, he found many fruit growers across the state looking to their association "for light and instruction," and he urged the membership to find ways to share their knowledge. That summer, he advertised in Loudoun and Washington papers for growers to send him their finest fruit specimens for display at the Biennial Exhibition of the American Pomological Society in Chicago. There, his display of 118 varieties of Virginia apples won top prize in its division and drew favorable comment in the *Chicago Tribune*, which described him as owning an "extensive" orchard in Virginia. (On their way back home, he and Edith attended an Army of the Cumberland reunion in Utica, New York.)[41]

An early 1876 letter dunning Elliot for failure to pay tolls on the Leesburg and Snickers Gap Turnpike stands as evidence that neither the switch to fruit production nor sporadic employment with the SCC had solved the family's financial problems. In presenting the bill, the turnpike commission explained that the toll collector had initially assumed he would make good on the debt, but his prolonged failure to pay had made it necessary to add a ten dollar fine for each infraction. In reluctantly forwarding the letter to her husband, Edith urged him not do "anything rash, or ungentlemanly...I know you have been aggrieved in this subject, but now you have an explanation...and I hope the matter will end here." While Elliot certainly did not have "change" to spare, Edith's plea suggests he had a more specific grievance, perhaps anger over the Conservatives' willingness to fund turnpikes used by them, but not for improving roads to Waterford.[42]

Figure 1 provides an overview of farming at Clifton based on the four decennial U.S. agricultural censuses conducted between 1850 and 1880. One should not read too much into these snapshots (each only covered agricultural production for the previous year) but they do disclose some significant trends. Dairy production, as shown by pounds of butter and number of "milch cows," steadily increased throughout the thirty-year period, while other livestock remained stable or declined. The most important cash crops remained corn and wheat, despite Elliot's efforts to improve the orchard. (Of the 665 fruit trees Elliot purchased in 1873, only 206 survived by 1880, many apparently having fallen victim to unusually cold winters during this period.)

The most revealing statistics concern values assigned to the farm and its products. The net worth of the land and buildings almost doubled between 1850 and 1870, only to abruptly lose two-thirds of their value by 1880. Some of this decline was due to deflation and decreased agricultural prices after the 1873 depression began. Despite this trend, Obediah Pierpoint, who began renting Clifton in 1878, claimed significantly higher production values in 1880 than Elliot did ten years earlier. Pierpoint was evidently a more efficient farmer. There is also reason to believe Elliot deliberately inflated the farm's value and its production figures in the 1870 census, since equity in the farm was all that he and the Matthews family had to stave off creditors. This value manipulation is further substantiated by an abrupt increase in insurance coverage between 1870 and 1871. In the former year, the farm was insured with the Loudoun Mutual Insurance Co. for $2,500, while coverage was increased a year later to $3,800 with the Buffalo Fire Insurance Co., in a policy issued by W. L. Bramhall & Co.[43] But this strategy could only work for a while, until the 1873 crisis heralded an extended period of financial difficulty that would force the family to give up farming for over twenty years.[44]

Figure 1. Agricultural Production at Clifton, 1850 - 1880

Census Category	1850	1860	1870	1880
Name of Owner [renter]	E.Y. Matthews	E.Y. Matthews	S.E. Chamberlin	Obediah Pierpoint
Acres (improved)	120	135	135	150
Acres (unimproved)	30	25	25	21
Cash Value of Farm	$7,000	$9,000	$12,500	$4,520
Value of Farm Equipment	$250	$500	$300	$100
Wages and Board Paid	—	—	$400	$400
Value of Animals Slaughtered	$80	$114	$40	—
Value of Livestock	$1,000	$500	$300	$100
Value of Orchard Produce	$10	0	0	$100
Total Value of Agricultural Products	—	—	$1,903	$2,389
Number of Horses	5	5	5	5
Number of Milch Cows	4	5	5	5
Number of Other Cattle	16	28	4	11
Number of Swine	30	9	4	0
Number of Chickens	—	—	—	30

Wheat (bushels)	750	400	600	647
Rye (bushels)	0	50	0	0
Indian Corn (bushels)	800	1,500	620	1,000
Peas & Beans (bushels)	0	1	0	0
Irish Potatoes (bushels)	100	40	300	10
Number of Apple Trees	—	—	—	56
Number of Peach Trees	—	—	—	150
Lbs. of Butter	400	300	600	900
Tons of Hay	15	8	18	4
Bu. of Clover Seed	0	5	0	0
Bu. of Other Grass Seed	0	4	0	0
Lbs. of Hops	0	3	0	0
Lbs. of Honey	40	0	50	0

(Source: U. S. Agriculture Censuses for 1850, 1860, 1870 and 1880. The originals in the Virginia State Library in Richmond proved more legible than microfilm versions. A dash indicates that the category was not part of the census for that particular year.)

Chapter 21

AND A VIRGINIA REPUBLICAN: 1868-1875

Despite having shown considerable skill organizing veterans into a potent lobbying force, Elliot abandoned the political arena in late 1866 to join the U.S. Cavalry. By then, Virginia's "Old Guard" had regained much of their antebellum clout under President Andrew Johnson's lenient treatment of the South, which seemingly closed the door on any aspirations for elected office Elliot might have in his adopted state. This political landscape abruptly changed in March 1867, when Congress overrode Johnson's veto to pass a harsh Reconstruction Act, thereby profoundly altering the course of Southern history for the next decade. Thus, when Elliot returned from the west later that year, he found a climate more favorable to his ambitions, a factor which must have influenced his decision to quit the Army.

The bill that Pennsylvania's Thaddeus Stevens guided through his Reconstruction Committee divided the South into five military districts, each headed by a Northern general. Individual states were to remain under martial rule until they could comply with terms stipulated by Congress for readmission to the Union, including enfranchisement of Black men, barring former Confederate leaders from office, and adopting state constitutions that conformed with Congressional guidelines. Soon after the Reconstruction Act was proposed, Loudoun Commonwealth Attorney William Downey, who knew Stevens through his father, wrote the Congressman to offer support for his bill including, if needed, a petition signed by local loyalists. The writer reminded Stevens that, even though his county was a hotbed "of treason and malignancy towards the Government," it was also one where the government "has more staunch friends than in any like portion of the State." Having canvassed Loudoun's loyal segment, he found "almost universal" acceptance of Stevens's bill. "There is some...squirming about the privileges extended to the recent Slaves, but time will overcome all this, as there is no Union man who does not infinitely more fear...the domination of the recent Rebels than that of the recent Slaves." As to the county's "rebellious portion," Downey predicted it would submit, since "being in the majority will be of sufficient protection to them."[1]

The passage of the Reconstruction Act enfranchised 100,000 Black voters in Virginia alone, a bloc expected to vote Republican. Their first chance to exercise this privilege came in October 1867, when elections were held to approve drafting a new constitution and to select delegates for that purpose. Demoralized by its sudden reversal of fortune, Virginia's "Old Guard" mounted only a desultory campaign, and many Whites stayed away from the polls. The large concentration of Black voters in Virginia's Southside, combined with White voter apathy, resulted in Republicans securing sixty-eight of the 104 seats in the constitutional assembly. Radicals predominated among the GOP delegation, which consisted of twenty-four Black individuals, twenty-three "carpetbaggers," and twenty-one "scalawags."[2][3]

In the period leading up to the election, Radicals concentrated on registering former slaves in

Black-majority Southside counties and in urban Alexandria, Norfolk and Petersburg, but relatively little attention to White-majority counties in the Piedmont, Shenandoah Valley and Appalachian Southwest. Moderate Republicans should have found support among wartime Unionists in these more western counties, but many there were repelled by the party's alignment with Radicals and the Black populace. This perception undoubtedly contributed to the Republicans' failure to extend their victory into Loudoun, where the proposal for a new constitution lost by one hundred votes, and two "unreconstructed" Whites defeated William Williams of Waterford, and a former Union captain to represent the county at the convention. Thus, even with the addition of the county's Black voters, local Republicans narrowly failed to overcome a unified conservative bloc. In the old Unionist strongholds of Lovettsville, Lincoln and Waterford, there was widespread dismay over their inability to elect a single delegate at the height of Reconstruction, an outcome which boded ill for their future.[4]

Judge John Underwood presided over the constitutional assembly in Richmond, and the former abolitionist from Clarke County quickly demonstrated that his reformist zeal had not mellowed. Borrowing heavily from its 1864 Alexandria predecessor, the "Underwood Constitution" showed little sympathy for Virginia's former ruling class. In addition to enfranchising Black voters, it mandated the state's first public education system, diluted established power bases centered in county seats by setting up townships with elected officials and, of special interest to Clifton inhabitants, exempted "homesteads" of up to 150 acres from repossession for debts. The most controversial provisions, the so-called "test-oath" and "disenfranchisement" clauses, barred former Confederate officials from voting or holding office. Nevertheless, the Old Dominion had passed a major hurdle for readmission to the Union and had only to ratify its new constitution and elect state officials who could qualify for office and were willing to approve the Fourteenth Amendment, which guaranteed the civil rights of all citizens, regardless of race.

The Radicals were further heartened after Virginia's military governor, Gen. John Schofield, removed Francis Pierpont in April 1868 and replaced him with Henry H. Wells, a former Union officer from Michigan. Pierpont's willingness to compromise with the "Old Guard" had cost him support among the Black populace and former Unionists but failed to significantly enhance his image among the former Secessionists. Governor Wells quickly allied himself with the Radicals and was dubbed the "prince of carpetbaggers" by detractors. Little, however, was accomplished towards regaining statehood for over a year, partly because General Schofield proved more moderate than the new governor, and because Northern Republicans were reluctant to admit any Southern state before the 1868 presidential election, lest this increase Democratic votes.

Writing to Representative Stevens in July 1868, Commonwealth Attorney Downey also recommended that any constitutional referendum be postponed until Grant was elected, which he considered "of more vital interest" to Loudoun Republicans. In addition, the state GOP needed time to organize itself and, Downey believed, to give "the lower classes" a chance to "see the practical effect of Reconstruction...[and] go against the Slave aristocracy." In the meantime, he added, Stevens should have Congress pressure military authorities to remove all disloyal officeholders in Virginia and replace them with loyalists. "Genl. Schofield always has taken the rebel view—that there are not... qualified Union men to fill the offices & no one has done more than he to make his prophesies come true." Stevens was quite right that the party needed time to organize and expand its base, but his solution—depending on the military to keep the ex-Rebels in check—would prove illusionary.[5]

An unintended effect of the delay was to allow time for a strong opposition party to develop. Galvanized by their defeat in October 1867, a large assembly of resisters met in Richmond two months later to form Virginia's Conservative Party. Drawing mainly from antebellum Democrats, with some former Whigs and Unionists, the new party sought to unite everyone opposed to Radical Reconstruction and Black rule. By early 1868, the Conservatives were well established in Loudoun.[6]

Yet, despite the Conservative resurgence, a carpetbagger such as Elliot could still harbor hope of winning an appointed office, or even an elected one, if the restrictive clauses in the proposed constitution remained in place. His base of support, primarily in the loyalist towns of north Loudoun, had

"This Is a White Man's Government," quote attributed to Grant's opponent, former N. Y. Governor Horatio Seymour. In this Thomas Nast cartoon, a Black veteran reaches for a ballot box, while being crushed by a trio representing the Democratic Party: an Irish thug, notorious CSA cavalryman and KKK member Nathan Bedford Forrest, brandishing a "Lost Cause" dagger, and a corrupt N.Y. politician. (*Harpers Weekly*, 5Sep68, LC)

failed to win in 1867 by only one hundred votes, a margin which could be overcome if, as expected, a number of Conservatives were barred from voting.

The first part of 1868 saw the nation's attention focused on President Johnson's impeachment. The crisis began the previous fall when Secretary of War Edwin Stanton refused to resign after clashing with Johnson, forcing the exasperated President to try to remove him, despite a ban against replacing cabinet members without congressional consent. The GAR, including its Washington D.C. post, mobilized veterans to defend Stanton, with arms if necessary, and the country seemed on the verge of civil strife until the President backed down and agreed to retain the incumbent. Nevertheless, the House voted to impeach Johnson in February, setting in motion a prolonged trial in the Senate.[7]

Elliot's involvement in these GAR machinations was apparently minimal, although he was present in the Senate gallery to watch the impeachment proceedings in April. At the beginning of May, Senator Justin Morrill declined an invitation to visit Clifton, citing the press of business connected with Johnson's trial, but he did offer to get Elliot a seat for the actual impeachment vote later that month. The Radicals' failure to remove the President on that occasion (by just one vote) marked the high tide of Reconstruction, which would recede until home rule was restored throughout the South nine years later.[8]

Despite disappointment over the outcome in the Senate, Elliot's commitment to Virginia's Republican Party did not waver. Serving as secretary and Loudoun's representative at a June 1868 caucus in Alexandria, he helped select a candidate for state senator. An invitation from the state Central Committee to attend a mass rally in Richmond that summer provides further evidence of his growing status within the party. Even though Virginians could not vote in national elections, the rally was staged to endorse the presidential candidacy of Gen. Ulysses S. Grant, then running against New York's former Democratic governor, Horatio Seymour, whom diehard ex-Conservatives hoped would dismantle Reconstruction if he won. The invitation was signed by Elliot's old comrade in the veterans' movement, Edwin Dudley, who became chairman of Virginia's GOP after being fired from the Post Office Department for his outspoken opposition to Johnson's policies.[9]

After Grant's victory in November ensured an incoming Republican administration, Elliot initiated a campaign to promote his appointment to a Federal position. To keep his name before the public, he arranged to be interviewed by a Washington reporter in early 1869. The resulting bit of puffery began with the now familiar description of Waterford's wartime Quakers and favorably mentioned a bill then before the Senate to compensate them for losses during the Burning Raid. But the village's hardships had not ended, the newspaperman explained, as local Unionists now had to contend with the "notorious" Col. Elijah White as their sheriff, "a man of neither social nor public standing, and...only noted for having hung many a Union soldier and plundered many a Union family." Lamenting that Virginia's new military commander was following his predecessor's policy of leaving ex-Confederates in office on the grounds there were no suitable replacements, the reporter cited Colonel Chamberlin as just the person to replace men like White. After fighting in the Northern army, Chamberlin had "surrendered" to a local lady and settled down to farming. Although considered for "an important local office in the

County,"[10] his prior military service was deemed too much of an impediment to overcome. In closing, the reporter hoped the colonel's story would persuade authorities that there were capable, loyal men to fill local offices without resorting to "guerillas, bushwhackers and rebels."[11]

Because of his wartime experience and burgeoning political access, some, such as former Loudoun Ranger Cpl. Henry C. Hough, turned to Elliot for assistance. During the war, Hough had accepted a horse brought to Point of Rocks for safe-keeping by George Rinker, a Loudoun livestock dealer. But because it had a "U.S." brand, the Rangers' captain ordered the animal turned over to the Army without Hough receiving any compensation. In late 1868, after Rinker successfully sued him in Leesburg's "Rebel court" for recovery of the horse's value, Hough wrote Elliot, asking for help in finding a way to avoid paying the "unjust debt." (He attached a statement corroborating his account from his brother-in-law, former Ranger QM Sgt. Edward White.) In forwarding Hough's letter to the district military commander in Alexandria in January 1869, Elliot vouchsafed for the writer having been a "good and true soldier," adding he knew of similar cases "where Union soldiers have been compelled to submit to injustices, either by the…prejudiced Court or by intimidation." Elliot and Hough were therefore disappointed by the military's refusal to take any action until all means of obtaining justice in the court system had been exhausted. Hoping to provide more concrete assistance in such cases, Elliot would obtain his own law license later that year.[12]

As Grant's inauguration drew near, Elliot began gathering endorsements for appointment as IRS collector for the 7th District, which included Loudoun and Fairfax Counties. An undated petition addressed to the new IRS Commissioner, Columbus Delano, included laudatory comments from Senators Morrill (Vermont) and Waitman Willey (West Virginia), Representative Robert S. Hale (New York), future Southern Claims Commissioner Orange Ferriss, Judge Charles Bramhall, and George Lincoln, head of New York City's Board of Health. Although a number of leading Republicans from the 7th District also signed, the only recognizable Loudoun name was that of noted Quaker educator and author Samuel Janney. Noticeably absent was Loudoun's Radical leader, William Downey, although three prominent Virginia Radicals did sign, including party chairman Edwin Dudley and Central Committee member H. G. Bond.[13]

In mid-March, Judge Bramhall warned Elliot that his bid for the IRS post was being threatened. A Treasury employee had recently purchased a home in Falls Church to qualify for the position and was rumored to be using "all the instrumentalities he can control" to gain the appointment. Bramhall had been unable to convince his political colleagues in the 7th District that their policy of only awarding Federal jobs to Alexandria and Fairfax residents would inevitably cripple the GOP in Loudoun. The judge therefore advised Elliot to come to the capital to defend his interests and possibly persuade his rival to seek another position.[14]

Elliot, however, had little time for lobbying that spring. Besides attending to planting season, he and Edith were still grieving the loss of their first child, Edward, in February, followed by the death of his mother in April. Instead, he turned to Justin Morrill, and twice that spring the Senator met with the IRS Commissioner to discuss his possible appointment. Although Delano assured Morrill that his nominee would get the job by mid-summer, nothing materialized. This incident showed the limits of Morrill's influence within the Grant Administration, as well as Elliot's failure to develop access to the White House—a problem that would plague him for the next eight years. As Judge Bramhall pointed out, it also highlighted the party's failure to cultivate support in the rural western counties.[15]

A split within the state GOP that spring further hampered Elliot's chances of getting any appointment. The Republican gubernatorial convention that met in a Black Petersburg church in March began with a heated squabble between moderates ("True" Republicans) backed by Virginia railroad magnate William Mahone, and the Radicals. The latter prevailed and succeeded in picking incumbent governor Wells as their candidate but before the moderates walked out, they saddled Wells with a Black physician as his running mate, a serious impediment in any statewide election. The following day, True Republicans met separately to nominate Gilbert C. Walker, a Norfolk businessman and Mahone associate, whose stance against the test-oath and disenfranchisement clauses gave him broader appeal to White

Virginians, despite his also being a carpetbagger.¹⁶

Dropping their own gubernatorial candidate, the Conservatives joined with True Republicans to mount an intense lobbying campaign to convince President Grant to authorize separate votes on the exclusionary clauses as part of the long-delayed constitutional referendum, arguing once again that otherwise there were not enough qualified males to run the state. On the other hand, Governor Wells and the Radicals maintained, correctly as it turned out, that stripping these restrictions from the constitution would return the "Old Guard" to power and quickly nullify reforms imposed during Reconstruction. After two months of suspense, Grant set 6 July for both the referendum and gubernatorial elections. More importantly, he ordered separate votes on the restrictive clauses.¹⁷

The campaign that followed was one of the most heated in state history and the political atmosphere in Loudoun was equally inflamed by divisions existing since before the war. Even though most of the county's former Unionists were ideologically closer to the moderate True Republicans, their experiences during and after the war precluded any alliance with the Conservatives and most threw their support behind Wells' reelection. Since the county's two papers were controlled by Conservatives who effectively blocked coverage of their political opponents, a group of Quakers launched the *Loudoun Republican* in early 1869 to disseminate their views during the upcoming campaign. (Unfortunately, few copies have survived, making it all but impossible to document local GOP activities during this period.)¹⁸

Reflecting the Radicals' orientation towards Black-majority and urban areas, Wells never campaigned in Loudoun. His opponent Walker, however, addressed a large rally from Leesburg's courthouse steps in June. Even though he was running on a True Republican slate, local GOP leaders were conspicuously absent on the podium. Instead, Conservatives delivered the introductions and secondary speeches, followed by Walker who showed complete identification with his new allies. His exhortation openly urged voters to reject the restrictive clauses so that Virginia could elect a Conservative-dominated legislature, which could dismantle other objectionable parts of the Underwood Constitution, including a provision allowing Black men to serve on juries. Four days before the election, Leesburg's *Washingtonian* reiterated Walker's instructions on how "to redeem the state from Radical and negro rule." Failure to reject the restrictive clauses would "turn all the offices over to the negroes and Radicals, and disfranchise…a large number of the white people." Failure to adopt the remainder of the Constitution would leave Virginia "under the rule of Wells, and at the mercy of a vindictive Congress."¹⁹

The election provided a resounding victory for the Conservative coalition, which won fifty-four percent of the gubernatorial vote. The new constitution was ratified by an overwhelming margin, while the two disenfranchising clauses were rejected handily. The results were more pronounced in Loudoun, where Walker's ticket garnered fifty-eight percent of the vote. Local Conservative-backed candidates defeated their Republican opponents by similar margins in races for state senator and delegates. A total of 3,717 Loudouners voted, of whom 971 were classified as "colored." Since most Black men would have voted for the losing Republican candidates who consistently received about 1,525 votes, fewer than 700 White voters, mostly in the Quaker and German communities, cast ballots for local Republicans.²⁰

Loudoun as a whole celebrated the outcome in a series of victory parades, including one in Waterford that came off "pleasantly," according to a Conservative paper. A report

"The Great Turnout of the 6th of July [1869]." A Virginia woman sweeps Republican carpetbaggers and scalawags out of her state after the Conservatives Party's decisive victory. Among those fleeing is State Chairman L. Edwin Dudley, shown declaring "Now, I'll try Mississippi and Texas." (1869 lithograph, VaSL)

in the *Loudoun Republican,* however, indicated the Unionist village was still unwilling to embrace old antagonists. The event began with speeches by the winning candidates, delivered from a wagon festooned with a banner proclaiming "No Room for Scalawags or Carpetbaggers." State senator-elect Thomas E. Taylor tried to convince Black individuals in the audience he would protect their rights while in Richmond, but "the negroes of this section [were] too well posted to be honey-fuggled." In a possible reference to Elliot, Taylor "alluded, in a very ungracious manner, to the carpet-baggers who sought to obtain offices through the military." According to this report, only eleven men participated in the parade that followed, and they quickly dispersed after being subjected to pointed comments from "a number of sable gentlemen."[21]

Despite the Conservatives' lackluster reception in Waterford, Elliot recognized a banner denouncing carpetbaggers in his hometown only underscored the fragility of his political base. Moving quickly to take advantage of Republican allies still in office, he obtained a certificate from county clerk Charles Janney confirming he had been a resident in good standing for over a year. With this in hand, he persuaded Judge Charles Bramhall and Lysander Hill of the 7th Circuit Court to issue an attorney's license, entitling him "to practice in and before the Courts…of Virginia." There is little evidence he intended to become a full-time lawyer, but he did represent some clients in claims against the government and more importantly, the license boosted his credentials to fill Janney's position in the county court the following year.[22]

In September, Gen. Edward Canby removed Governor Wells short of term, and installed Walker at the helm in Richmond. The General Assembly convened the following month to ratify the Fourteenth and Fifteenth Amendments, resulting in the Old Dominion's formal readmission to the Union in January 1870. Reconstruction had come to an end sooner and with less disruption than in other Southern states but its rapid demise dealt an ultimately fatal blow to the state GOP. Even though True Republicans technically won the 1869 election, the cost of their alliance with the larger Conservative Party was high. Their campaign for Walker alienated Black voters without bringing significant numbers of White voters into the moderate camp. On the other hand, had the Radicals been willing to broaden their base and appeal to both Black and moderate White voters, they might have been able to achieve the success of the Readjuster Party a decade later.

Little is known about Elliot's only bid for public office in 1870. That spring he took out a two-year subscription to the *Loudoun Republican,* presumably the principal vehicle for publicizing his campaign. (By then, William Downey had purchased the paper to aid his own run for reelection as Commonwealth Attorney.) After the Conservative victory the year before, Republican candidates faced an uphill fight in counties without a sizable Black presence, an obstacle particularly high in Loudoun, where Radicals had never even briefly exercised control. The locally popular railroad owner, Lewis McKenzie of Alexandria, had won a seat in the U.S. Congress the year before, but was being forced on a technicality to run again, this time against a strong Conservative opponent. As the election neared, McKenzie wrote Elliot to express concern over the demoralized state of Loudoun Republicans and urge him to ensure a heavy turnout.[23]

Elliot received some needed publicity by being elected treasurer of the Virginia chapter of the Society for the Prevention of Cruelty to Animals, which met in Waterford two weeks before the election.

"The Custom House Mill." This Richmond lithograph illustrates fears Virginians had about Republicans using Customs appointments to churn out Black voters for their party. (1869 C. L. Ludwig print, VaSL)

(Elisha Walker was named secretary.) His selection was probably arranged by political allies to boost his image, as there is no subsequent indication of his involvement in the Society, although he certainly supported its goals. Like the temperance and agrarian movements, the SPCA offered one of the few platforms available for Loudoun Republicans to make their progressive views known to the electorate.

A large turnout that November failed to help Elliot, who was defeated by 600 votes in his bid to become county clerk. (The winner, George Fox, was a well-known leader in the local Conservative Party.) As expected, Elliot carried the Waterford, Lucketts and Lovettsville precincts, and won strong support from Black voters in Leesburg and Middleburg as well as Quakers around Lincoln. Most other Republican candidates were also defeated, including Downey, who lost his bid for reelection. The sheriff's office remained in the hands of the Confederate cavalry when William F. Barrett replaced his old commander "Lige" White. The only upsets were races for treasurer, won by a Republican running as an independent and for U.S. Representative, which McKenzie carried by a slim margin, although he lost his district as a whole. These two deviations caused the *Washingtonian* to fulminate about the Conservatives' failure to make a clean sweep. Corrective measures would be taken and Republican victories at the county level would be almost unknown for over a century.[24]

The electoral outcome came as no surprise to Elliot, who had already initiated correspondence with Senator Morrill about getting a job at the Agriculture Department. When an opening was not immediately forthcoming, he sought lame-duck Congressman McKenzie's help in securing appointment as postmaster at Clarkes Gap,[25] a tiny train-stop south of Waterford, which Elliot may have hoped would elevate his political image as well as match the status that Sam Gover enjoyed as Waterford's postmaster. Financial remuneration could hardly have been a factor—the commission he signed in November specified a twelve-dollar annual salary unless the volume of mail justified more. When he resigned in April 1871 to work in Washington, the total postal revenue collected was eight dollars and ninety-four cents.[26]

Employment in the Agricultural Department kept Elliot from playing an active role in local township elections in May 1871. By then, Waterford had been placed in the gerrymandered Jefferson Township, where its influence was neutralized by Conservative strongholds in Purcellville, Hillsboro and Wood Grove. He did attend the Republican state convention in Richmond that fall which, in addition to formulating a platform for the coming state elections, appointed a new Central Committee that included Elliot and McKenzie. Shortly afterwards, both men attended a district meeting in Leesburg to belatedly select candidates for the November election. A sarcastic article about the gathering, entitled "For Ways that are Dark," began, "There is a screw loose somewhere in the Radical machine." Comparing the meeting to a secret conclave to elect a pope, the Conservative newspaper reporter deliberately garbled names of the resulting Republican candidates for delegate and clerk of the circuit court before ridiculing the attendees' failure to come up with a candidate for state senator. This omission was finally remedied at an Alexandria meeting Elliot chaired later in October. There, attendees adopted a moderate platform that called for: amnesty and conciliation towards their opponents; tolerance of political and religious beliefs; punishment for civil rights violations; direct election of school boards; enforcement of the homestead law; and reduction of taxes. As acting chairman, Elliot helped win approval of this rejection of earlier radicalism, but the bid to broaden the party's appeal was "too little, too late," and all Republican candidates were defeated in Loudoun by even greater margins than the year before.[27]

Elliot's support for Grant's reelection in 1872 was lukewarm at best, and he did not attend the GOP National Convention in Philadelphia that June. At some point, however, he began working for the Republican Congressional Committee, which expanded its staff in election years to churn out campaign materials and otherwise support the party ticket. One might assume he began this campaign work after being dismissed from the Agriculture Department in September, but his purchase of a three-month rail pass in July suggests that he was already receiving party funding by then. Having an official role in the campaign is further indicated by his attendance in mid-September at the GOP-sponsored National Veterans Convention in Pittsburgh, where he was confirmed as Virginia's representative on the party's Veterans National Committee. Once he lost his Agriculture job, Elliot must have expected campaigning in Virginia and among veterans would result in a reappointment once the President won a second term.

Yet, compared to his participation in Hayes' election four years later, he was never an enthusiastic Grant supporter, in part because of the President's role in helping Conservatives regain power in Virginia. A reformer at heart, Elliot also disapproved of corruption and influence-peddling that plagued the current administration.[28]

One aspect of Grant's campaign that adversely affected Elliot's career aspirations stemmed from an introduction between the President and Col. John S. Mosby that Senator John F. Lewis (Virginia) brokered at the White House in May. The two veterans immediately took a liking to each other—the start of a friendship that endured until Grant's death. During this meeting, the former partisan indicated a willingness to assist the President's campaign in the South if, as appeared likely, the Democratic candidate was Horace Greeley, whose wartime editorials in the *New York Tribune* had earned the Gray Ghost's undying enmity. Mosby had also not forgotten Grant's role in granting him a parole after the war, or in securing an arrest exemption when Federal authorities tried to harass him in Leesburg. At the close of their meeting, Mosby pressed the President to provide a sign of his readiness to adopt a more conciliatory policy towards the South. Several days later, Representative Benjamin Butler (Massachusetts) introduced an amnesty measure which sailed through Congress and was signed by Grant, with the result that most of the South's former leaders were free to run for office.[29]

After Greeley's nomination was confirmed, Mosby, true to his word, stumped for Grant, including a well-publicized debate with Gen. Eppa Hunton who championed the Democrat. (Despite their opposing views on this occasion, Mosby helped secure Hunton's election to Congress that fall.) Although Grant's margin of victory was slim (less than 2,000 votes in the entire state and but thirty-three in Loudoun) the President credited the former Rebel with making Virginia the only Southern state to support his reelection. When the two met afterwards, Mosby turned down his "payoff"—a Federal attorneyship, which Grant presumed was expected. This act further ingratiated Mosby with the President, who began to view him as the Administration's "expert on the Southern question." From this point on, Mosby used his influence to secure the appointment of Virginians to a variety of lucrative Federal positions, many of which went to relatives and former members of his old command. His backing of the President did not, however, extend to support for Virginia Republicans in general, or carpetbaggers in particular. Instead, the colonel used his clout to replace, or bar, non-native Virginians from Federal appointment for the remainder of Grant's term.[30]

Initially buoyed by Grant's victory in their state, Republicans began preparations for the 1873 gubernatorial election. In July, Waterford's John Dutton and Elisha Walker presided over a meeting of Loudoun Republicans that selected Elliot and three other delegates to attend the state GOP convention in Lynchburg. This assemblage was marred by a factional dispute once again orchestrated by railroad magnate William Mahone, who would soon launch his own competing party. In the end, the convention chose as its candidate for governor, Robert W. Hughes, a moderate whom Grant had picked to fill the judicial vacancy left when John Underwood died in 1872. The platform adopted at Lynchburg contained a call for election reform and universal male suffrage, an indication of Republican concern over unfair treatment at the polls, particularly directed against Black voters. At the end of the convention, a new Central Committee was chosen, which again included Elliot as a representative from his Congressional district. He was also placed on the eleven-member Executive Committee that would oversee running the state GOP for the next four years.[31]

As the campaign heated up that fall, Elliot was appointed one of two Loudouners responsible for canvassing the 1st Senatorial District to drum up support for the Republican ticket. Unfortunately, Hughes proved a disappointing candidate who alienated Black voters without capitalizing on White disenchantment with Conservative rule. Whatever hopes the Republicans had were dashed when Mosby refused to support Hughes and campaigned instead for his opponent, Gen. James Kemper. Accusing Mosby of breaking his promise to Grant, the Republican press urged the President to bring the Virginian into line by expelling his federal appointees. The accusations occasioned an open letter to Grant, in which Mosby denied the charge, maintaining that, while he had agreed to overcome antagonism to the President's reelection, "I never deemed it practicable to do so through the radical [Republican] organization in Virginia...[nor did I] intend to identify myself with the negro party of Virginia, for I could not do so without social degradation." If Grant thought otherwise, Mosby urged him to replace his appointees with "Mr. Hughes' friends." The President took no action on the matter.[32]

That fall, national attention remained focused on the prolonged financial panic that began in September, and consequently paid little heed to the election of a Confederate general to the Virginia governorship. Later, Elliot spoke at informal gatherings of Republican state leaders in Washington and Richmond to discuss their recent defeat. The consensus among these party faithful was that, "notwithstanding many thousand colored men were prevented from voting by intimidation and other means," the vote for Hughes was 15,000 greater than Grant received the previous year, and included a gain of 12,000 White voters. Bolstered by these figures, attendees proclaimed the party had "come out of the fire of the campaign stronger and more united than ever."[33]

But even though GOP leaders tried to depict the 1873 election as a moral victory, their loss marked an end to their party's relevance in statewide races. Kemper was but the first of seven ex-Confederate officers to occupy the governor's mansion, and it would remain for William Mahone, also a Confederate general, to pick up the fragments of Republicanism in the late 1870s to form his Readjuster Party. As would occur elsewhere in the South, Virginia Republicans were too dependent on Federal patronage, which only accentuated their failure to develop a home-grown leadership to replace the carpetbaggers who held most key party positions. One historian has described the party's decline thusly:

> Battered by gerrymanders, social ostracism, and election fraud, [Virginia] Republicans retreated into a handful of predominantly Negro counties. Radical strength in the General Assembly slumped from fifty-six members in 1870 to only fourteen in 1878, and its demoralized State Central Committee practically ceased to exist...Deprived of adequate organization and leadership, thousands of Republican Blacks either lost interest in politics or drifted into the Readjuster camp...A small ring of influential Whites, mostly northern-born 'grip-sackers,' scooped up the choicest patronage plums...and by the end of the decade personal feuds and racial animosities had reduced the party to a shambles.[34]

As overblown as the above picture might seem, it accurately describes the problems confronting Elliot, just as he attained the state party's upper echelons. Many Republicans did abandon the party after Hughes's defeat, and little of importance occurred within the party until the onset of the 1876 election. But by that time, the Conservatives' control of the legislature and governor's mansion had succeeded in undoing Reconstruction. Black suffrage was sharply limited by imposition of poll taxes and other stratagems, while redistricting produced a sharp decline in local GOP office-holders. One partial exception was in the old Unionist communities of north Loudoun, where residents stayed true to the party of Lincoln well into the twentieth century.[35]

Like his neighbors, Elliot too remained stubbornly loyal to the Republican cause throughout this trying period. His perseverance was rewarded in April 1876 with the chairmanship of the state Executive Committee. Apparently, his GOP colleagues recognized the administrative skills he had shown in the Army and in organizing veterans. In accepting this latest position, Elliot reached the pinnacle of the party's bureaucracy, even as the GOP was becoming increasingly irrelevant in Virginia. One might well ask why he accepted such an impotent post when, as described in the next chapter, he should have been devoting his energies to succeeding in a new career. In part, he considered it his duty "as a Union soldier in a southern state" to oppose the Conservative resurgence. It was also a concrete way to honor the loyalty his wife's family and other Loudouners had shown during the war. And, as his oldest son Justin later pointed out, his father was just too stubborn to abandon his political ambitions at this point.[36]

Particularly galling to Virginia Republicans was the concurrent rise in their state of a movement which sought to glorify the "Lost Cause" of the Confederacy. Its growth was aided by the favorable political climate under Conservative rule at a time when the Deep South remained under federal control. Another catalyst was the death of Robert E. Lee in 1870, which prompted the creation of memorial associations to honor Virginia's greatest war hero. Jubal Early and other "proponents of the Lost Cause...

brooded over defeat, railed against the North, and offered the image of the Confederacy as an antidote to postwar change...[T]he leaders of this movement came from the prewar southern elite and...wrote much history that influenced the South's interpretation of the war." Union veterans living in the South found the movement particularly galling.[37]

Virginia's Confederate revival had even earlier antecedents when, shortly after the war, Southern widows and mothers initiated the practice of decorating loved ones' graves in late spring. Veterans' groups in the North adopted the custom, and in 1868, the GAR called for a national Decoration Day (now Memorial Day) to commemorate fallen comrades. By then, Quakers and other Unionists were already honoring the fallen at the Balls Bluff National Cemetery, the only official resting place for Union soldiers in Loudoun. After his return from the west, Elliot took a lead in these ceremonies, as confirmed by the following account, probably written by the same reporter who favorably contrasted him to Sheriff White:

> On the 29th of May [1869], as in the two previous years, a few carriages toiled over the rocky hillsides from the Quaker village of Waterford, and drew up at the little cemetery where sleep some fifty-six of the heroes who fell in that desperate encounter [at Balls Bluff]. After brief but appropriate remarks by Colonel S. E. Chamberlin, the ladies decked the modest graves with...spring flowers of red, white and blue, and wreathes of evergreen. No gaily dressed crowd was there, no formal procession, no martial music...no cannon thunders reverberated...but not less grand or beautiful...was the simple spectacle of those noble women, whose religion bears out the divine injunction of "Peace on earth; good Will to men," doing homage to the memories of these "unknown" men...[38]

Union memorial services in the South were fraught with emotion but, as a Winchester reporter pointed out, they had a political aspect as well. Not only did such ceremonies show "who was who," but they brought participants "closer together for the furtherance of the Union cause." Almost everything Elliot did during this period had a political component, and his participation in Decoration Day was no exception, as when he and another local Republican spoke at Balls Bluff in 1872.

Yet, his commitment to honoring Union veterans, alive or dead, was no less genuine. This was evident in his assumption of responsibility for oversight of the Balls Bluff Cemetery, and it was to him that the caretaker turned for guidance in preparing for the 1876 ceremony. When Elliot and his companions arrived that year to honor the dead, they discovered that the local Confederate Memorial Association had left flowers on the Union graves. Touched, Elliot asked his wife to prepare wreaths for Leesburg's Confederate ceremony, which prompted an exchange of letters between Edith and Confederate Association President J. W. Foster. In his reply, Captain Hatcher expressed confidence that, since her "husband was a *soldier*," they both desired to "revere the memory of our late comrades in arms...Yet, I would to God that the issues of the dead past...were allowed to slumber where they were put to rest by the *soldiers* of the late war! instead of being harrowed up by politicians desiring selfish ends." Foster closed by expressing hope "this flora offering" would prove an "augury of substantial reconciliation and a bright future." The entire incident hints at a further reduction of tension between Loudoun's two factions, much as Grant's favorable reception at Leesburg had shown three years earlier. However, Foster's letter, which appeared in the press, can also be read as a warning for his Union counterpart to stop using veterans for political purposes. If so, it fell on deaf ears that pivotal election year.[39]

Chapter 22

POLITICS DERAIL DEBUT AS TREASURY SPECIAL AGENT: 1876

Annie Matthews began working for the Treasury Department in early 1870, and her experience there foreshadowed hurdles her brother-in-law would face. Like Elliot, she relied on Justin Morrill to get her foot in the door. They met during the Senator's first visit to Clifton in 1868 and afterwards, when she accompanied him to the train station, Morrill was so impressed with her desire to seek financial independence, he offered to help her win a Federal appointment. The following year, Annie was sufficiently recovered from her riding accident for Morrill to raise her case with Treasury Secretary George S. Boutwell, who favored adding her to the limited number of "ladies" in his Department. Armed with an introduction from Morrill, Annie had a successful interview with IRS Commissioner Columbus Delano, who agreed to employ her on a temporary basis as a revenue clerk, starting January 1870. (Delano may have felt an obligation to the Senator after his failure to hire Elliot the year before.) By mid-March, Annie was able to send fifty-five dollars to Sam Gover, with instructions that her father's executor use it to pay debts stemming from her education during the war. "*Would it were enough to pay every dollar we owe*! But...it *does* make me very happy...to do *even* this much from *my own earnings*." Still, her financial security was far from certain, and just two weeks later, Morrill had to intervene to have her employment extended.[1]

The Federal work force in the capital, which numbered less than 1,300 at the start of the war, had grown to 6,000 by 1870 and would surpass 25,000 at the century's end, figures which included a growing number of females. The Treasury began hiring women during the war, and other departments followed suit after they were found to be better than men at certain tasks, thus making the government "the first large, sexually integrated white-collar bureaucracy in America." The situation facing these early female employees was fraught with threats to their social status and Victorian respectability, and most of them only took this step "when unforeseen problems created economic need within their families." But even established households could not escape the ravages of war and subsequent economic crises, which forced "thousands of middle-class women" like Annie into wage-earning jobs.[2]

Men had their own reasons to question working for the government. Prior to 1860, America's middle-class was chiefly composed of professionals, farmers and businessmen, while women were mostly limited to teaching. Virtually all these occupations were characterized by the independence they afforded, and even clerks generally aspired to owning their own businesses. Thus, it was with trepidation that middle-class men eyed the prospect of surrendering their autonomy to a large bureaucracy. (Elliot, after laboring hard to establish himself as a jeweler, chafed at restrictions imposed by military and government supervisors, which may account for his reluctance to completely abandon a political career.)

Both sexes, once they made the decision to work for Uncle Sam, faced hurdles to being hired and then retaining their positions. Since Andrew Jackson's time, even menial Federal jobs were governed by the patronage system, under which every state was allotted a "quota" of positions based on its Congressional representation. (By the 1880s each congressman from the incumbent party could fill 250 positions from the 1,700 applications he might typically receive.) All job-seekers had first to secure the support of their congressman in an arduous process called "acquiring influence." Yet, winning a position was no guarantee of keeping it, since before Civil Service reform, employees could be summarily fired and appointments were usually limited to a President's term in office. All of this was particularly difficult for women who could not vote, or list their accomplishments in the masculine political arena, and therefore had to cite the accomplishments of their families. (Annie could point to her extended Quaker family, whose wartime saga was well known in Washington, while Elliot made use of the press to burnish his credentials for holding office. Lacking support in their Conservative-dominated district, both relied on outside politicians to win and keep appointments.)[3]

During the summer of 1872, Annie contracted typhoid fever and, while still on sick leave, was dismissed after a reduction in Treasury funding. Rallying to her cause, IRS colleagues and Congressional supporters called for her reinstatement. Citing her Unionist background, one advocate argued that rehiring her provided a perfect way to honor "all those loyal ladies of Virginia, so that they may present as brilliant a contrast to their rebel sisters as they did during the war." Yet, despite the outpouring of support, Annie was not brought back.[4][5]

After over a year had passed, Annie wrote the Treasury Secretary to explain the circumstances of her dismissal and ask for reappointment, but her application was again denied. Only the installation of a new Treasury Secretary in 1874 brought changes that ultimately favored both her and Elliot. Benjamin Bristow came to the Department with a reputation as a reformer, and his selection was in direct response to concerns raised by Republican leaders worried about Democratic gains in the wake of the country's financial crisis and persistent scandals involving Treasury employees. The new Secretary took his mandate to clean house seriously, and soon began to rid his Department of corrupt employees.

As a Kentucky native, Bristow knew well the difficulties facing Unionists from Border States, and soon established procedures for hiring and job retention that favored Northern veterans and Southern loyalists.[6] The new Secretary was also close to the same reform-minded congressmen who were pushing for Annie and Elliot's reinstatement, and in May 1875, with help from Senator Morrill, Annie secured temporary employment in the IRS Redemption Division. However, without a strong patron in her home state, her job security remained tenuous and she almost lost this job during another round of personnel cuts before being saved by the timely intervention of Morrill and Dr. Christopher Cox, her landlord and head of the D.C. Board of Health.[7]

Finally, as America neared its Centennial, Elliot (now forty-one) and Edith (twenty-eight) too, found an apparent answer to their financial woes. Benefiting from a new regime in the Treasury and years of "acquiring influence," Elliot was sworn into the Special Agents' Division (SAD) of the Customs Service on 3 December 1875. His five-dollar per day salary, plus traveling expenses, was less than the SCC paid, but he would be working full-time during a depression that left many jobless. To preclude interference from Mosby's camp, Elliot had recycled Representative Robert Hale's recommendation to the Post Office Department, and his Treasury records consequently listed

Benjamin H. Bristow, Secretary of the Treasury, 1874-76. Grant would fire the reform-minded Cabinet member. (Treas. Dept. engraving)

him as appointed "from New York." His new supervisor, Crawford C. Adams, specifically requested Elliot's assignment to his division. They knew each other from the veterans' movement and would enjoy close personal and professional ties for many years.[8]

Elliot entered the Treasury as it was expanding its role in the nation's troubled economy. Between 1873 and 1900, the Department grew from 4,000 to 24,000 employees, a number exceeded only by the Post Office. Moreover, the Treasury Secretary had become the leading officer in the Cabinet, a status not challenged until the Spanish-American War. The Treasury was also the predominant source of political patronage, largely due to most Federal revenue being collected by its Customs and Internal Revenue Services. Both were large, quasi-independent bureaus, headed by commissioners reporting directly to the Secretary. Their size and influence had increased dramatically since the start of the Civil War but reforms introduced by Benjamin Bristow in 1874 reduced their autonomy, bringing the new Secretary into conflict with politicians whose appointees handled revenue collection.[9]

The Customs Service had grown apace with the Treasury as a whole, and in 1873 there were 136 customhouses spread along the nation's coastal and land borders. Large ports like Boston, Philadelphia and Baltimore had 200-400 employees. The largest, New York City, where two-thirds of all imports landed and over eighty percent of all tariffs were collected, employed 1,500. Its customs house offered the most remunerative positions in the Federal government and its collector,[10] Chester Arthur, earned more that President Grant.[11]

Customs special agents, America's first Federal investigators, trace their origin to 1799, when Congress empowered the Treasury Secretary to appoint clerks on a part-time basis to inspect the books of collectors of duty for the Customs Service, created ten year earlier. Beginning in 1846, these part-time auditors were replaced by full-time agents hired at eight dollars per day plus expenses, to oversee Customs operations and revenue collection. The Civil War, funded on the Union side by Justin Morrill's Tariff Act of 1861, significantly amplified the role of the Customs Service. The war also increased opportunities for fraud and smuggling. (Morrill's bill only passed after Southern Democrats left Congress to join the Confederacy, and the South depended on blockade runners for much of their wartime needs.) Nor did peace significantly alter this trend, as the Tariff Act of 1866 increased the government's reliance on import duties. By 1869, Secretary Boutwell counted sixty-four special agents in the Customs Service, although he declined to give Congress their names, lest it interfere with their secret work. (Under Grant's administration, some agents were co-opted by the White House to carry out sensitive missions unrelated to their regular duties.) Democrats in particular chaffed at the growth, cost and constitutionality of this body, which was only formally recognized in 1870 when Congress approved hiring a maximum of fifty-three special agents,[12] to be employed under the direct supervision of the Treasury Secretary for the purpose of preventing revenue fraud.

To re-emphasize SAD's role as an independent watchdog, Secretary Bristow removed it from the Customs Commissioner's control and placed it under the Treasury's Solicitor General. He also halved the number of special agents and inspectors, which had grown to ninety. With the exception of a small cadre in Washington, special agents and inspectors (subordinate to agents) were permanently assigned to the field. The following description of a special agent's duties is derived from a Baltimore newspaper account, for which Elliot was likely the source: Working in coordination with the Treasury Secretary, agents were primarily responsible for ensuring all Customs activities were conducted "properly and in accordance with...the law." In carrying out investigations, agents could demand the records of Customs officials and recommend changes based on their findings. To prevent the government from being defrauded, agents routinely verified valuations placed on imports. They were also responsible for inspecting ports of entry and instructing officers in charge of these installations on their duties. Their sundry duties required agents be "well posted in the custom laws."[13]

Elliot received no formal training when he joined SAD but past experience in the military and SCC prepared him to conduct adversarial interviews and debrief informants. He also had some legal expertise and understood basic accounting principles. On the other hand, he never mastered the complex auditing skills needed to discover and prove fiscal fraud, skills not easily learned on one's own. Instead, he relied on informants and other leads to detect wrongdoing. A major component of an agent's work were reports sent back to the Treasury. Despite excellent penmanship and a sound command of English, his longer reports show poor organization, with important findings often buried in the text.

By the time Elliot was hired, Secretary Bristow was absorbed in the "Whiskey Ring" investigation, the most serious scandal to beset the Grant Administration to that point. Worried about the prospect of Democratic gains in the coming elections, the President had reluctantly agreed to bring Bristow into his Cabinet to help relieve the country's financial woes and curb corruption within the Treasury Department. In turning to the capable and highly principled Kentuckian, then serving as the country's first Solicitor General, Grant got more than he bargained for. In his new post, Bristow soon discovered that whiskey distillers and distributors were routinely defrauding the government of millions of dollars by bribing IRS agents to ignore undersized bottles and furnish tax stamps at reduced rates. Grant seemingly supported Bristow's inquiry until mid-1875, when it led straight to the President's personal advisor, Orville Babcock and by implication to members of Grant's family.

The President had to personally intervene in Babcock's trial to secure his acquittal and brief return to the White House. By then, Bristow had become the darling of the Republican reformers and a strong contender for the Presidential nomination in 1876. Yet, even while the trial and investigation were unfolding, Grant's inner circle conspired against the Secretary, convincing the President that Bristow's real goal was to replace him in the White House. Only fear of creating a martyr kept Grant from dismissing him prior to the GOP Convention.[14]

Bristow planned a similar investigation of the Customs Service when he appointed fellow reformer Crawford Adams to head SAD in October 1875. Adams had been captain in a Kentucky regiment, and later served as librarian in the Interior Department. Elliot was among a small group of agents and inspectors, untainted by prior exposure in the Customs Service, whom Adams hired to staff his division. But by 1876, Bristow and his allies were too occupied with the IRS investigation to undertake a similar, politically risky probe of the Customs Service, and this preoccupation elsewhere contributed to a lack of direction from above during Elliot's initial posting.

Elliot was quite pleased when Adams assigned him to Norfolk, a city he knew from the war, and close enough to facilitate visits home. This important maritime center fell within the jurisdiction of the 5th Special Agency District, which had responsibility for seventeen ports in Maryland, Virginia, North Carolina and West Virginia. The district was headed by Col. Ira Ayer, Jr., a former commander of a Pennsylvania regiment, who worked for the Freedmen's Bureau before joining the Treasury. In November 1875, Ayer moved his headquarters from Norfolk to Richmond to be near his wife's family. This allowed Elliot to occupy Ayer's old office in the Norfolk customhouse, with responsibility for overseeing maritime operations in the busy Hampton Roads area.

A diary, begun 1 January 1876 to record his business expenses and schedule, found Elliot making customary New Year's calls on influential acquaintances in the capital, before spending the evening with sister-in-law Annie. Next morning, he caught the train to Richmond, where he took time to canvass legislators about the fall election. Such a survey by a Central Committee member was not unusual and helped him gauge support for Secretary Bristow's candidacy. What he found, however, thoroughly "disheartened" him, as most delegates seemed primarily concerned with "providing artificial limbs for ex-Confederate soldiers, filling the capitol grounds with monuments of ex-generals, [and] keeping awake...love for those who [have] done so much to destroy...Va." This attitude would, he lamented, "injure prosperity and bar immigration so much desired. When will our people cast the scales from their eyes?" On reading this, Edith urged her husband to "do everything in your power to...save the party. Would [Virginia] do herself the favor of electing a Republican President."[15]

The second leg of Elliot's journey, via steamer down the James River, awakened vivid memories of wartime. Arriving at his destination, he was more impressed by the splendid ships in the harbor than Norfolk's "quaint appearance," and his diary fails to mention his office in the customhouse or its collector, Luther S. Lee. The latter's omission is particularly odd, as he and Elliot seemingly had much in common. Not only had Lee been a captain in the 20th N.Y. Cavalry, but he later married a widow living on a farm outside Norfolk. He had sufficient political support in the area to represent Norfolk at the 1867 Constitutional Convention, and his affiliation with the Radicals led to his appointment as collector in 1870. But, as related in the next chapter, authorities would soon discover that Lee had been falsifying his books for years, which may account for the cool relationship between him and the novice agent assigned to look over his shoulder.[16]

Elliot's departure left his wife to spend a melancholy New Year's Day at Clifton, recalling happier times when her father and little sister were alive. She fretted the years now seemed to just glide by, yielding "so little in a moral point of view." Adding to her gloom, Mamie (Mary, then age five), Morrill (three) and Nellie (almost two) had chicken pox, and her mother Sarah was too ill to even visit great-aunt Nancy on her deathbed. Still, Edith was prepared to be the "gladdest little wife in all this gay glad town," if she could be assured her husband was happy in his new job, and life no longer just a burden to him.[17]

Subsequent letters were more upbeat and show Edith already counting on Elliot's anticipated salary to make long-delayed improvements at Clifton. A new maid was hired to do laundry and cleaning, as well as an additional farmhand. To provide meat that winter, Edith purchased and slaughtered five pigs. Most importantly, a carpenter enclosed the back porch to accommodate a kitchen and laundry, previously located in an outbuilding. The new room was warmed by a modern cook stove, which also helped heat the laundry water and the rest of the house. She could not imagine how they had survived cold winters before and was convinced her husband's rheumatism would no longer bother him at home.[18]

Her mood changed upon learning the Catoctin Farmers Club was scheduled to meet at Clifton in February, despite her husband's absence. "Bankrupt" and with no means of entertaining the group, she chastised Elliot for "being easy about leaving me [without money], as it subjects me to annoyance frequently and is always an embarrassment." She warned him, however, not to come back for the meeting (later canceled) or do anything which might jeopardize his career, as she was "ambitious" for him to succeed, and had even sent a barrel of apples to his boss's wife, Ada Adams.

Elliot's twin sister, Ellen Martin, had sent word of Duncan Cameron's death in Saratoga Springs of complications from his war wounds. Edith offered to send condolences to Louisa Cameron but warned her husband against offering to assist his widowed sister financially, as he already had more burdens than he could handle "satisfactorily." In early February, Elliot received his first salary payment—$258, of which he sent fifty dollars to his wife. Much of the remainder was probably used to pay off loans, but the small remittance home did little to ease Edith's financial difficulties.[19]

On his first Sunday in Norfolk, Elliot attended church services, a practice he observed regularly while traveling, and later that day moved into a boarding house to reduce expenses. His first assignment involved an arduous winter trip by steamer, skiff, and wagon to Urbanna, a small port on the Rappahannock River. Returning to White House Landing to catch the Richmond train, he found the region still showing the ravages of war, something he doubted would change any time soon given Virginia's current leadership. He arrived at the state capital on 18 January in time to attend a Central Committee meeting before catching an overnight train to Washington. The remainder of the month was spent investigating an anonymous tip that members of the Alexandria customhouse engaged in smuggling.

Finding no evidence of criminal activity, he returned to Norfolk in early February. His free time was spent studying official regulations, although he found himself "somewhat slow to get a plain insight into the laws that govern customs." A week-long inspection of lighthouses and Coast Guard facilities along the Chesapeake Bay was marred by bad weather and a tooth he had to extract himself. He returned to Alexandria after the department received a second letter repeating earlier charges of misconduct at that port. (One wonders whether it originated with the corrupt Norfolk collector, anxious to get rid of his watchdog.)

Finding bachelor life lonely, Elliot invited his wife to spend a week with him in Norfolk, but she wanted to save money to attend the Centennial Exposition that summer and suggested they delay her visit until fall. When he tried to persuade her to join him in Alexandria she again declined, although she feigned regret at having to forgo meeting the "nice young naval officers" described in his letters. In her mind, they could not afford a hotel room, and she ruled out staying with friends, as her present wardrobe was inadequate for socializing. Declaring "scarcity of money" their only source of disagreement, she suggested he visit her instead. Bowing to her wishes, Elliot spent the next weekend at Clifton, and that Sunday took the two oldest children to Meeting, prompting a neighbor to later tell Edith how proud he looked sitting beside them.[20]

Back in Norfolk, Elliot boarded the cargo ship *Southern Rights*, and cited its owners for failure to show the vessel's registration number and tonnage on the hull. His action on this minor infraction, probably prompted by the vessel's provocative name, highlighted his limited authority, as he later learned the "unreconstructed" owners had ignored the citation. The South as a whole opposed high tariffs and the Federals who enforced them. With far fewer industries to protect than the North and heavily dependent on imported goods since Colonial times, opposition to any attempt to limit shipping only increased during the Civil War, when smugglers and privateers who ran the Union blockade were considered heroes.[21]

On 10 March, Elliot crossed Hampton Roads to inspect Customs facilities at Old Point Comfort and nearby Hampton. It was his first substantive investigation in the area, and he carried an introduction from the Norfolk collector to the governor of the Soldiers' Home in Hampton. In it, Luther Lee requested that Elliot be provided transport and unspecified "creature comforts," whenever he visited that area. Clearly, Lee wanted to encourage the special agent to spend as much time as possible on the far side of Hampton Roads. He did not announce his presence in Hampton, preferring to discreetly observe operations at the port. He soon learned the customs officer at Old Point Comfort had, during his frequent absences and against orders, delegated his principal duty, that of boarding all vessels as they entered Hampton Roads, to boatmen on the government's revenue cutter.[22] The cutter's crew, however, was more preoccupied with illegally charging fees to take passengers out to the incoming ships than with inspecting them. Elliot's findings were well received by Colonel Ayer, who sent him to Suffolk, another town familiar to him from the war. On his return, he proudly recorded in his diary that his supervisor had "complimented my success and thinks I am doing splendidly."[23]

The Chamberlins' lengthy separation put strains on them both. Not having heard from him since his February visit, Edith asked if she were being punished for not joining him in Alexandria. Then, after two pages of carping, she revealed she had changed her mind and would accompany her sister to Norfolk. (Her husband had already sent Annie a steamer ticket.) With Edith's oldest child Mary in tow, the sisters were met by Elliot at Old Point Comfort on 21 March, and taken to nearby Hotel Hygeia, a popular resort overlooking Hampton Roads on a site next to Fort Monroe that is today occupied by the Hotel Chamberlin. Later, Elliot took his guests on a tour of Norfolk's Navy Yard, and in the evenings they dined with his friends in the area.

Worried about her two children back home and against her husband's wishes, Edith persuaded her sister to leave a day early. Before catching the steamer to Baltimore, Annie, still interested in the education of Black individuals, took Edith and Mary to the Hampton Institute, a Black college established in 1868. Quite moved by the experience, Edith wrote her husband not to visit the Institute until she could accompany him. Despite this entreaty, her first letter suggested that she had not enjoyed her visit as much as Elliot, who years later fondly recalled their time together at the Hygeia. Back in the confines of Clifton, she worried that he might be liking life without her too much. She was also peeved to discover that Elliot had discussed the sale of her horse "Pet"

Hotel Hygeia and Fort Monroe, Old Point Comfort, Va. (hotel stationery, TCC)

to an acquaintance without informing her first. Still, she was the first to admit they "needed money more than horses," especially now that Sam Gover, also alleging a shortage of funds, was pressing them to use Elliot's salary to repay their store debts. (In 1869, her uncle had married Temperance Matthews, a niece of Edith's father, and the couple now had two children, with another on the way.)[24]

That spring, Elliot and Colonel Ayer were involved in an attempt to salvage the USS *Merrimack,* a U.S. Navy ship scuttled deliberately when the Norfolk Navy Yard was abandoned in 1861. The Confederates refloated the vessel and converted it into an ironclad ram, renamed the CSS *Virginia.* Its historic encounter with the USS *Monitor,* the first battle between ironclads, took place in Hampton Roads in 1862. Two months later the Confederates, in turn, scuttled the *Virginia* before abandoning Norfolk, and the hull had languished in the harbor until early 1876, when a salvage operator approached the Treasury Department with a proposal to buy the wreck for $500. After Ayer recommended approval, this amount was turned over to Elliot for deposit in the customhouse. Sometime after Elliot's departure from Norfolk that summer, the money was retrieved on the grounds that the government had never finalized the sale. The Treasury later learned the salvage company had stripped the wreck of everything of value before demanding its money back. (Most likely, the company's intent all along had been to only retrieve small pieces to sell as souvenirs. Given problems at the customhouse, Lee's "return" of the money may not have been accidental.)[25]

* * * * *

The 1876 presidential campaign impinged upon Elliot's budding career from the start. At the January meeting he attended in Richmond, the Central Committee set April as the date for a state convention to choose delegates for the Republican National Convention two months later. Although the Central Committee did not endorse a candidate, most members favored Grant for a third term, with Representative James G. Blaine (Maine) as their second choice. Despite Congress having passed a resolution calling on the President to respect George Washington's two-term precedent, most party leaders in Virginia occupied Federal positions, giving them a vested interest in Grant's reelection. Moreover, he was seen as the only Republican with a chance of carrying the state. (John Mosby was credited with engineering the "third term" movement, which emerged in Virginia that winter. Like the carpetbaggers he professed to despise, Mosby had his own reasons for wanting the President to remain in office.)[26]

Veterans' groups had played a relatively minor role in Grant's 1872 campaign, as his war record was deemed sufficient to hold their vote. However, his Administration's failure to fulfill campaign promises to increase their benefits, coupled with the GOP's poor showing in the 1874 elections, underscored a need to aggressively woo the soldier vote in '76. To stem defections to the Democratic camp, GOP strategists relied on a negative campaign that branded their rivals as traitors to the Union cause. The tone was set in January, when Blaine kicked off his presidential bid with an emotional speech before Congress, in which the former Speaker of the House (then minority leader) denounced Confederate influence in the Democratic Party and reminded his audience of the mistreatment of Northern prisoners of war. (Particularly effective was Blaine's recital of an order Jefferson Davis gave to the Andersonville Prison commander to shoot prisoners before they could be freed by Sherman's army.) A day later, Ohio Congressman James A. Garfield delivered a similar speech in the House. At first, moderates questioned resurrecting old hatreds, but quickly realized Blaine's charges were causing significant discomfiture to Democrats by diverting attention from the floundering economy and scandals in the Administration. "Waving the bloody shirt," as the strategy was known, became a key element in a campaign that made Blaine a favorite of Northern veterans.[27]

Even though most veterans associations, including the GAR, tended to favor the Republican Party, they had in recent years discarded overt partisanship for an outward semblance of neutrality. As a result, both parties had created their own standing veterans committees to rally support during election years. The Republican version, Union Veterans National Committee (hereafter Veterans Committee), was established in 1868 by L. Edwin Dudley. While Gen. John Dix served as its titular head in 1876, the actual running of the Committee fell to a nine-member executive board chaired by James Garfield, with Dudley and Drake DeKay as permanent and recording secretaries. Much of the Committee's effectiveness derived from its ability to mobilize "Boys in Blue" clubs to march in their blue uniforms and sing patriotic songs during parades and rallies.

As Virginia's representative on the Veterans Committee since 1872, Elliot received an invitation from Dudley to attend the February executive committee meeting. The customs agent had no difficulty arranging his second Alexandria investigation to coincide with the Washington meeting, where, in addition to having his position as Virginia's representative reaffirmed, he was added to the executive board, subject to confirmation in Indianapolis that fall at the GOP Veterans National Convention. During the intervening months, board members were charged with organizing veterans in their area to ensure a large turnout at this event. Taking its cue from Blaine, the board also called on survivors of Southern prisons to publicly refute the "lies" of Jefferson Davis and others that they had been well treated.[28]

During his stay in Washington, Elliot joined the National Council of the Order of the Stars and Stripes (OSS), an obscure veterans association organized in the capital two years earlier. Crawford Adams was one of its founders and sponsored Elliot's induction. According to its constitution, the OSS was a charitable organization devoted to improving the lot of disabled veterans, war widows and orphans. In fact, under Adams's leadership, it had become a covert arm of the Republican reform wing, focused on promoting Benjamin Bristow's presidential bid.[29]

Involvement in the OSS carried a distinct risk as long as Grant remained in office, although any realistic chance the President might win a third term had ended in early March, when Secretary of War William Belknap resigned rather than face impeachment in the Senate over charges that his socially ambitious wife "Puss" had sold rights to lucrative trading posts in the West. When Elliot learned of the scandal on his way back to Norfolk, he wrote in his diary that Belknap's disgrace was a "terrible blow," which would be "keenly felt" by Republicans. Nonetheless, he predicted the party faithful would rally and ultimately prevail, because "the soldiers of this country are never going to let it go into the hands of the rebels." The scandal resonated with Edith as well, particularly in the widespread belief that the spendthrift "Puss" had ruined her husband's career. In a letter after the story broke, she invoked Divine assistance to keep her husband from being led astray in his new job, and to help her be a "stronger, and truer, and wiser" guide for him. (One senses Edith had more on her mind than the Belknap scandal. Earlier, she had applauded Elliot's decision to discuss an unspecified problem in Norfolk with Adams, cryptically adding "our conscience is our best guide, if only one would heed its whisperings.")[30]

A card issued in Norfolk later that month, identifying Elliot as an executive committee member of the Order of the American Union (OAU), provides further evidence of his involvement in political intrigue. The OAU was a secretive branch of the American Alliance, which in turn was heir to the anti-Catholic, anti-immigrant "Know-Nothing" Party of the 1850s. Reportedly, the OAU was then organizing working men in the Hampton Roads area on behalf of the Republican Party by playing on fears they would be supplanted by Irish immigrants.[31]

At the end of March, Elliot and Colonel Ayer traveled to Washington for a ten-day stay that allowed them to discuss strategy with Adams before attending the state GOP convention. With Grant no longer in contention, Adams hoped his subordinates could influence Virginia's delegation to back Bristow at the national convention. Yet, even though Elliot sympathized with the reform cause and could expect to benefit if the Treasury Secretary won, he was keenly aware Bristow had little support among Virginia party leaders, or with veterans in general. Moreover, as long as Blaine had Grant's endorsement, any overt action on Bristow's behalf placed his special agent's job in jeopardy.

After managing to spend two weekends at Clifton, Elliot joined Ayer on the overnight train to Lynchburg, arriving a day before the convention opened on 12 April. After a heated fight over who would preside, the delegates adopted a noncontroversial platform in support of civil rights, free schools, punishment of corrupt officials, honest elections and return to specie payments. More importantly, the convention agreed to send an uncommitted delegation to Cincinnati, although a nonbinding resolution favoring Blaine was also passed. It was a partial victory for the reform wing, although an opponent of Bristow's candidacy was elected chairman of the state Central Committee.

As a Federal employee, Elliot was barred from serving as a delegate at the national convention, nor was he reelected to the Central Committee at Lynchburg, probably a reflection of his ties to Bristow. He was, however, confirmed as chairman of the Executive Committee, a position theoretically giving him control over the state party's day-to-day activities, which assumed more importance during an election year. His selection implied satisfaction with his past service on the Central and Executive Committees, although as a Federal employee he was not supposed to hold any political office. Such technicalities, however, were frequently ignored in Virginia, where Federal appointees "had become not only the dominating leaders in the Republican party but almost the party itself."[32]

Afterwards, Elliot returned briefly to Norfolk before being called to Washington to discuss the Lynchburg convention and his elevation to executive chairman. Secretary Bristow and his advisors wanted to garner as much support as possible within Virginia's uncommitted delegates, and it was likely Elliot who identified a delegate willing to vote for the Secretary in return for the award of a Treasury position to one of his constituents. To make room for the new clerk required the removal of William S. Ball, whose appointment had been arranged by Colonel Mosby shortly after Grant's reelection. (Mosby personally escorted the Confederate veteran into the Treasury Department on his first day.) Shocked to learn he was being fired, Ball lost no time in contacting Mosby, who provided him with a letter to the President. After hearing his case, Grant addressed the following terse card to Bristow: "Unless there be reasons for the removal of W.S. Ball, other than political, I would be pleased if he could be restored to his late position." The clerk was soon back at work, Grant having made clear to all his determination to block Bristow's nomination.[33]

Elliot paid a short visit home during his latest stay in the capital but heeded his wife's warning not to interfere with her annual spring housecleaning. She knew he had "no special love for such business," but was glad to show off the newly repaired fireplace and chimney. The corn crop was in the ground, and the apple trees had blossomed, promising a good harvest. Unfortunately, heavy rains destroyed the few peach and pear buds to survive a late frost. Sam Gover, apparently not as financially strapped as previously claimed, planned to take his family to the Centennial Exhibit in May. He had also purchased new carpet and wallpaper for his Waterford home, prompting an envious Edith to admit she had only managed to weave five yards of carpet for Clifton.[34]

Meanwhile, Annie, in a late April complaint to her sister, blamed the "horrid rebels" in Congress for investigating her landlord, Dr. Christopher Cox, on trumped-up charges related to his management of the D.C. Board of Health. The Democrats reportedly viewed the doctor as too "liberal" after he placed a "colored man and a homeopath" on the board. (Modern historians credit Cox with making significant improvements to unsanitary conditions in the capital.) Annie had found a cook willing to prepare meals for summer boarders at Clifton, but worried Edith might move their mother out of her bedroom to accommodate more guests. Instead, she suggested they create space by placing a tent over the foundation of the old kitchen to serve as an outdoor dining room.[35]

Grant's reaction to Bristow's attempted firing of a Mosby appointee convinced reformers that stronger action was needed to undermine the President's support for Blaine. Believing Grant's relationship with Mosby represented a weakness which could be exploited, OSS member Samuel B. Crew queried Elliot for ammunition for use in a possible exposé. In a 4 May letter to his Norfolk office, Crew explained that he had been asked to chair a committee "to ascertain the *secret*" of Mosby's influence over the President. Informed by Crawford Adams the special agent had "valuable information...on Mosby's career and his present status with the Administration," the writer asked for specific details about the Congressman who had introduced Mosby to Grant, identification of Federal appointments made on Mosby's behalf, and about his wartime operations and later pardon for same. Crew stressed Elliot's participation would remain confidential, but he also wanted him to know that, since the former Rebel's influence over the President was clearly "prejudicial to the Government and detrimental to the interests of the late Union soldier, we consider it not only a lawful but an important matter for investigation." No response has been found, but Elliot probably chose to meet directly with Crew, a fellow Treasury employee in person rather than commit anything to writing.[36]

In mid-May, Elliot went horseback riding with Edith before heading back to Norfolk, but there is no evidence he conducted any significant business there, before returning to Loudoun to oversee Decoration Day ceremonies at Balls Bluff. In early June, Adams arranged official business for him in West Virginia to facilitate his attendance at the National Convention in Cincinnati. He left Washington by train on the 7th and stopped along the way to discuss smuggling through the mails with postmasters in Martinsburg, Cumberland, Grafton, Wheeling and Parkersburg. His main interest, however, was to canvass these political appointees about the presidential race, finding most supported Blaine. He also visited the Wheeling customhouse and inspected several ships in Parkersburg, but this too was mainly "cover business" to justify the use of public funds for his onward travel.[37]

Arriving two days before the Convention began, Elliot did not stay in the same hotel with the Virginia delegation, since his official status for being in Cincinnati was to attend an executive meeting of the Veterans Committee, scheduled during the Convention's first day. Theoretically at least, members of the Committee were not supposed to participate in the nominating process, since they were expected to support whomever won. Their executive chairman, James Garfield, was not present, having decided to remain in Washington with his close friend, James Blaine, who had suffered a mild stroke several days earlier. Without Garfield, the Veterans Committee played less a role at Cincinnati than might have been expected, which in turn may have hurt Blaine's chances. Although Maine's "plumed knight" was favored to win the nomination, his image had recently suffered from doubts about his health and charges of conflict of interest leveled by Congressional Democrats.[38]

Crawford Adams was also at Cincinnati, and his enemies would later accuse the civil servant of illegally working on behalf of Bristow's nomination. Since Elliot deliberately omitted his stay in Cincinnati from his diary, his role after the Veterans Committee meeting ended is not known, but it is unlikely he merely remained on the sidelines during the raucous assembly that followed. Through the early rounds of voting, Bristow received enough support from the reform wing to prevent Blaine from getting a majority. Finally, on the seventh ballot, the Treasury Secretary released his delegates to throw the nomination to Ohio's "favorite son," Gov. Rutherford B. Hayes, a former Union general who was well regarded by both reformers and veterans.

After stopping at Clifton on the way back from Ohio, Elliot arrived in Washington on 23 June. Adams asked him to remain at the Department for a day to discuss the consequences of the Treasury Secretary's forced resignation two days earlier. Furious that Bristow's supporters had succeeded in blocking his candidate and throwing the nomination to Hayes, Grant replaced Bristow[39] with Senator Lott Morrill (Maine). Blaine, in turn, was rewarded by being appointed to fill Morrill's vacant Senate seat, a maneuver which blocked a corruption investigation of Blaine that Democrats had opened in the House.

After nearly a month's absence, Elliot reached Norfolk on 25 June, only to return home in time to celebrate the Centennial Fourth of July with his family. He was accompanied by Crawford Adams, and the group that went into Waterford after dinner to admire the fireworks display included the wife and child of Elliot's friend Myron Baxter, boarders at Clifton that summer. The following morning, Elliot left for Norfolk, but again remained there only briefly before taking a steamer up the James to attend a Central Committee meeting and campaign rally in Richmond on 10-11 July. The last entry in his 1876 diary recorded travel to Washington on 14 July to discuss a shipping dispute between the inland ports of Richmond and Petersburg.[40]

He did not return to Norfolk, and it was then that he learned of his pending removal from the Treasury. As a Bristow appointee, the news could hardly have come as a surprise, especially after being told of Adams's demotion to a subordinate position in the Solicitor's Office. Elliot's termination, however, was not officially announced until late August as part of a reduction-in-force by the new Secretary, and even then he was allowed to remain on paid leave until mid-October. Although ties to the reformers were certainly factors in his removal, his meager accomplishments at Norfolk did not aid his cause. Fortunately for him, political operatives routinely received paid leave from the government to work on campaigns. Thus, while he did not resume special agent duties, his position in the Veterans Committee and state party were deemed important enough to keep him working on the Hayes campaign for another three months.

Not all of that summer was devoted to politics, as Elliot found time in mid-August to take the family to the Centennial Exposition. To defray expenses, they stayed with Edith's relatives in Philadelphia, and Elliot arranged to have himself appointed manager of an exhibit sponsored by the National Pomological Society. (He had advertised earlier in Loudoun for orchardmen to contact him about showing their produce at the Exposition.)[41]

Returning to Washington in late August, Elliot made a last-ditch effort to save his job. Alonzo Bell, the Interior Department's chief clerk, sent a thirteen-page letter to Treasury Secretary Morrill pleading for his reinstatement. Claiming his friend was unaware of this action and too modest anyway to advertise his achievements, Bell could only assume the Secretary was unacquainted with Elliot's accomplishments when he signed the order to let him go. After describing how they met while working on Grant's 1872 campaign, Bell included a detailed account of Captain Chamberlin's role in saving the capital at Fort Stevens. As to his record as a Treasury agent, the writer suggested his friend was not given suitable work to perform. (Ayer and Adams did encourage Elliot's political activities to the detriment of his regular duties.) He then recounted having attended a Decoration Day ceremony organized by Elliot at Balls Bluff, where members of the audience confirmed his friend's leadership among Loudoun's former Unionists. That Elliot was a Northerner made all the more remarkable his decision to reside in the South and "live out by his daily actions his faith in the Republican Party, of which he was now Chairman."[42]

Despite its Victorian grandiloquence, Bell's letter failed to sway Secretary Morrill, and on 31 August, Elliot wrote Amory Tingle, Adams's replacement as SAD chief, to acknowledge receipt of his termination notice. Since he was being paid through 10 October, he expressed willingness "to perform any service that you may need of me as Special Treasury Agent." With an eye to his future, Elliot made sure to also remain on good terms with Adams, staying with his former boss during visits to Washington. In a warm letter of recommendation, the former C/SAD expressed regret that his subordinate had been let go "through no fault of [his] own." Adams further certified his agent had performed every assignment "with promptness, fidelity and ability...that should commend itself to every officer in the service." Then, in an apparent reference to Elliot's extracurricular political activities: "You have my thanks...for the valuable aid rendered me in the discharge of my duties...I hope you may receive something more tangible...for your faithfulness as an officer and a citizen."[43]

The family received another blow that summer, when Annie, too, lost her IRS position. Concern she might be let go was already evident in late 1875, when Elliot got Crawford Adams to send a memorandum on her behalf to the Treasury's Personnel Office, pointing out Senator Justin Morrill's special interest in her case. Despite Adams's intervention, Annie confided to her sister a few months later of her constant fear of being dismissed. Even so, the family's double loss came as a shock, and Alonzo Bell was pressed into service to help her as well. Citing the now familiar themes of her family's background in a letter to the Treasury appointments clerk, he proclaimed Annie's whole family "to be true grit on the old flag. If she has been misjudged because of her location [in Virginia], let me say that she is like her mother, who would endure anything before she would turn against the Union." Justin Morrill also sprang to her defense in a missive to the Acting Secretary, explaining she had "no Virginia Senator to look after her, by no guilt of her brother-in-law." Citing her family's staunch stand for the Union, he added "it looks a little cruel to see two sisters of Mosby employed in one of the Executive Departments, and then to see Miss Matthews, whose father's buildings were burned and stock raided by Mosby's troopers,[44] turned out of another." Despite these and other pleas, Annie was not rehired at that time.[45]

* * * * *

As noted earlier, Virginia Republicans kicked off their campaign for Hayes and running mate William Wheeler with a Central Committee meeting and mass rally in Richmond on 10-11 July. The party's new executive secretary, Portsmouth businessman James D. Brady, discussed campaign strategy with Elliot on their way up the James River to attend these events, and much of the subsequent Committee meeting was devoted to the need to reorganize the state party before the fall election. As executive chairman, Elliot presented a nine-point program calling for a state-wide canvass of voters and specifying the duties of local party officials during the campaign. At the end of the meeting, he and Brady were tasked with presenting the proposal to Interior Secretary Zachariah Chandler, the Republican National Chairman.[46]

The Richmond meeting ended with a public rally, which Elliot termed a "grand success." He was one of the speakers, but the orator who attracted the most attention was M. D. Ball, a former Whig and current owner of the *Alexandria Sentinel*. When the ex-Confederate colonel tried to explain how disenchantment with Conservative rule had led him to support Hayes, he was interrupted by hisses from "a little crowd of stay-at-home loafers." According to the Republican press, Ball silenced his hecklers with a "withering rebuke," but Hayes supporters could expect similar incidents during the remainder of the campaign.[47]

Ball's speech was part of a wider strategy to woo former Whigs and others dissatisfied with conservative leadership throughout the South. Mosby proposed this course of action during a meeting with Grant in late June, and Hayes endorsed it early in the campaign. The basic premise was summarized in an article entitled "Colonel Mosby and the Old-Line Whigs," which appeared in the Republican press right after the Richmond rally. (Datelined "Fauquier County, 12 July 1876" and signed "C," it was probably drafted by Elliot.) After reiterating the same complaints about Conservative mismanagement raised by Ball, it ended with a reminder that Mosby had carried the Old Dominion for Grant in 1872.[48]

Elliot kept a copy of this article, but did not fully embrace its optimistic message, and his participation in the Richmond rally marked his most visible role in Virginia's presidential election. Once he and Brady failed to secure Chandler's support and funding for a more intensive campaign in Virginia, Elliot concluded he could do more for the party by working with the Veterans Committee in the North. Other reasons for his low profile in Virginia that fall included differences with Mosby and ties to the reform wing not shared by other state party leaders.

But far from uninterested in the outcome that fall—a Democratic victory would dash any hope for reinstatement in the Treasury—Elliot hurried to New York City to spend the rest of July and early August organizing fifty-five Boys in Blue companies to campaign for Hayes. During his stay, he received temporary membership and lodging in the Union League and Army-Navy Clubs on the recommendation of Drake DeKay, who had replaced Edwin Dudley as executive secretary of the Veterans Committee. Elliot's role in this aspect of the campaign made a lasting impression on his son Morrill, who vividly recalled "wearing a Hayes and Wheeler button, which [my father] gave me...and on which was printed 'Vote for the Boys in Blue'."[49]

Things were not going well for Mosby. After failing to establish the close rapport with Hayes he enjoyed with Grant, the colonel watched nervously as Republicans abandoned his "Southern strategy" in favor of "waving the bloody shirt." With his political bridges already burnt through past association with Grant and determined to retain his role as Virginia's "patronage broker," he decided bold steps were needed to keep himself in the campaign's forefront. On 12 August, the colonel published a lengthy letter in the *N. Y. Herald* announcing his decision to join the Republican Party and, more surprising, to endorse "the political equality of the races." Up to that point, the ex-Rebel had sidestepped both issues, and one senses a note of desperation in taking a course that would make him a "pariah" to most White Southerners.[50]

Far more than his alliance with Grant four years earlier, Mosby's decision to join the GOP and campaign for Hayes aroused scorn throughout the South. In a rebuke to a former comrade-in-arms, who urged him to support the Democrats because "they are the candidates of the Southern peoples," Mosby shot back: "I thought you knew that I ceased to be a Confederate soldier about eleven years ago, and became a citizen of the United States." The "sectional unity of the Southern people" was, he reiterated, the cause for "most of the evils they have suffered." As long as this misplaced unity persists, "the war will be a controlling element of politics, for any cry in the South that unites the Confederacy re-echoes through the North and rekindles the war fires there." But Mosby's advice went unheeded in the South, nor did his gambit change the direction of Hayes' campaign. Instead, he, along with other Southern Republicans, watched impotently as the national party's strategy of wooing Northern veterans undermined efforts to broaden their base in the Southland.[51]

Aware their chances in Virginia were slipping away and wishing to throw a sop to their state chairman, the Republican National Committee offered in mid-September to make New York's former lieutenant governor available to speak at a Richmond rally. Elliot, then preoccupied with the upcoming Veterans Convention, apparently rejected the offer, probably concluding the proposed speaker would have little impact. A short time later, Mosby came up with a better suggestion, when he asked Hayes to arrange for Carl Schurz to speak in Virginia. As head of the party's reform wing, Schurz could counter the adverse effect that corruption in Grant's Administration was having on moderate voters. But by then the national GOP was resigned to writing off the Southern states, and the request was ignored.[52]

The Union Soldiers' and Sailors' Convention, which the GOP sponsored in Indianapolis on 20-21 September, provided the setting for Elliot's most significant participation in the national campaign. There, he and Drake DeKay were given the honorary rank of "generals" in the Boys in Blue and served as aides-de-camp to "major general" James Garfield, who was in charge of the convention. By all accounts, it was a glorious success for the Republicans. "For two days, while brass bands and drum corps 'made the air quiver with martial music,' the veterans paraded, sang, and cheered the invectives which their leaders hurled against the South. All the speeches had but one object, the revival of war hatreds." By skillfully manipulating the soldiers into equating Democrats with the Southern cause, a significant bloc of votes was guaranteed for Hayes. On the last day, Garfield put Elliot and DeKay in charge of organizing the state delegations into a final grand parade. Dressed in their uniforms and accompanied by bands and banners, the line of marchers stretched three miles through the city. That evening, Garfield met with his executive committee to discuss plans for the remainder of the campaign. Elliot may have left by then, as DeKay subsequently informed him of being unanimously confirmed as Virginia's representative on the Veterans Committee for the next four years.[53]

In late October, the Veterans Committee published a letter with the ambiguous title "The Lost Cause in Virginia." Addressed to DeKay from Loudoun County and again only signed "C," it was almost certainly composed by Elliot. Using Virginia to illustrate the consequences of letting Democrats return to power, the author outlined his state's political history since the war. When the Old Dominion was readmitted to the Union in 1870, it had a constitution containing the "best features" of those governing Northern states, including free schools, the secret ballot, a ban on dueling, and township organization. However, after Governor Gilbert Walker, a Northerner, betrayed the party that elected him, "the Democratic party commenced their struggle for the supremacy of power" through such tactics as gerrymandering and intimidation. Once the Conservatives consolidated control by electing a Confederate general to succeed Gilbert, they began to dismantle the "Yankee Constitution" by eliminating townships and other provisions, including proposals to suppress Black voters and relegalize dueling. While "acts of violence" against Republican voters could be expected in November, even more prevalent would be "acts of ballot box stuffing and election frauds." Adding a personal touch, the author lamented: "To-day, a man who served in the Union army...is more disenfranchised...than he could be made by Legislative acts." Instead of dying out, "hatred for the North" was intensifying and could only "be checked...[by electing] Hayes and Wheeler....Today Virginia has placed men who were lately in rebellion against our flag in every office throughout the State...Unless the men of the North...stay this onward march, all they fought for will be lost...and the rebels of the South will have accomplished by the ballot what they failed to do by the bayonet." Clearly, Elliot relished this chance to vent frustrations long in building, and the letter's apparent admission that the future of Virginia's GOP was itself "a lost cause" serves as a poignant epitaph to his own political aspirations in that state.[54]

On 7 November, Democratic presidential candidate Samuel J. Tilden carried Virginia by over 40,000 votes and the Conservatives' constitutional amendments won by similar margins. The outcome was no different in Loudoun, where Tilden prevailed by 1,000 votes, with only Waterford, Lovetts-

Left: Elliot's Pass, 1876 Republican National Convention. (TCC); Center: Republican Veterans Committee logo on correspondence to Elliot about the Hayes campaign. (TCC); Right: 1876 Veterans' Convention Medal, reverse engraved by Elliot: "Maj. General S. E. Chamberlin, National Veterans Committee, ADC to General [James] Garfield, Commander in Chief, Boys in Blue." (JCC)

ville and Quakers around Lincoln backing Hayes. On a national level, Tilden appeared to have easily prevailed with a plurality of almost 250,000 votes, and Hayes was ready to concede, when an operative at GOP headquarters in New York (reputedly Gen. Daniel Sickles) detected a slim possibility for him to win on the basis of electoral votes. Ironically, this observation confirmed Mosby's advice about the importance of the South in securing a Hayes victory. In this case, the key lay in the results of voting in three states still governed by Republicans under the Reconstruction Act: Florida, Louisiana and South Carolina. What no one expected was that four tumultuous months would pass before the election was finally decided.[55]

Chapter 23

FIGHTING THE MOSBY BROTHERS FOR A JOB: 1877

In the aftermath of the 1876 election, when Rutherford B. Hayes' chances seemed remote, Republican appointees throughout the South despaired for their futures. Mosby, now a widower, moved his family to Washington after receiving threats in Virginia; on one occasion, he came close to fighting a duel when a man took exception to his small son's cheers for Hayes. By December, the Grey Ghost had regained some of his old aplomb, telling a New York reporter he was willing to resort to arms if Democrats tried to deny Hayes the presidency. With exile from Virginia fresh in his mind, he reminded his interviewer that "social ostracism" in the South was "a terrible weapon used against republicanism. You will not see it or feel it...but it exists, and even...brave men cannot stand against it." He blamed this attitude for the continued reliance on carpetbaggers to fill Federal appointments, which long since should have gone to Southerners. But, he lamented, while Southerners tolerate Northerners, they shun fellow natives who accept such jobs. From this and similar statements, it was plain that Mosby's eye remained on men like Elliot.[1]

With no winner declared by year's end, the nation seemed close to civil strife as Democrats and Republicans threatened to take to the streets to guarantee victory for their candidates. (Although there is no evidence Elliot was involved, the Order of Stars and Stripes was then organizing a military wing to assure Hayes' victory.) To break the deadlock, Congress passed a bill in January 1877, giving itself authority to decide the dispute. Many assumed this measure would permit a Democratic majority in the House to declare Samuel Tilden the winner. Hayes' advisors, however, did not believe this a foregone conclusion, and so began cultivating Southern Congressmen with promises to place a Southerner in the Cabinet, appoint more Southerners to Federal positions, and return home rule to states still governed under the Reconstruction Acts. (Overlooked were guarantees to protect rights gained by the Black populace during Reconstruction.) The uncertainty surrounding the election's outcome left Elliot out on a limb. If Tilden won, he would have no chance of returning to the Treasury, but Hayes' overtures to the South cast a cloud over his future as well, since carpetbaggers were likely to be penalized if the Republicans prevailed. He therefore concluded his best chance lay in getting rehired before Grant left office.[2]

Prospects brightened in the New Year when, improbably, Elliot's future became linked to that of William H. Mosby, John's younger brother. Although the colonel had already used his influence with Grant to secure positions for numerous friends and relatives, William's appointment as a Treasury special agent was certain to generate controversy, since as a lieutenant in his brother's command he had participated in many of its most publicized guerrilla operations. (Grant's commitment to hire William was likely tied to Colonel Mosby's agreement to broker Congressional support for Hayes.) To minimize political fallout, William's appointment was to take place during the last days of Grant's term and be offset by rehiring Elliot.³

Grant tentatively approved both appointments, but statutory limitations on the number of agents dictated other personnel changes take place. To carry out this task, the President turned to his most trusted operative in the Treasury, Customs special agent William B. Moore, who reported back to the White House on 18 January that the Treasury Secretary had agreed to rehire Colonel Chamberlin to his former position in the Customs Service's SAD, and an additional space could be made there, if another agent became a customs appraiser. Moore was particularly anxious to have this space filled by Joseph H. Maddox, an IRS agent who had "done some valuable service under my direction." All that remained, Moore concluded, was for the President to have the IRS Commissioner approve hiring William Mosby to fill Maddox's old slot. "This will provide for the two Gentlemen [Chamberlin and Mosby] you have named for appointment and also place Maddox satisfactorily."⁴

Despite the President's endorsement of this scenario, Elliot's future remained uncertain, and Moore's involvement was especially worrisome. As special agent, Moore had a long history of carrying out unsavory tasks for Grant's inner circle, including secretly keeping the President apprised of Secretary Bristow's efforts to eradicate the "Whiskey Ring." He was now maneuvering to take control of the Customs Special Agents Division before Grant's term ended, but was opposed by Crawford Adams, who had temporarily regained his old position as C/SAD, while Treasury Secretary Lott Morrill was on leave. The President had a vested interest in the outcome, as he wanted Moore, not Bristow's ally, to head SAD under any new administration to prevent embarrassing revelations that might otherwise come to light.

Some last-minute maneuvering must have taken place before Grant summoned Elliot to the White House on 1 February and informed him that he was being appointed to the IRS Special Agency, not to his old billet in Customs which was now being held open for William Mosby. Worried that something more was afoot, Elliot was careful to obtain additional endorsements before reporting to IRS Commissioner Green B. Raum two days later. Among those who wrote Raum were Senator Justin Morrill, Alonzo Bell, and J. C. O'Neal, the unsuccessful Republican candidate from Elliot's Virginia district, now working for the IRS Surprised or not by the latest turn of events, Elliot still must have been relieved when Raum signed papers making him an IRS agent earning six dollars per day.⁵

After celebrating with his family, Elliot began work at the Treasury the following week. Several days later, he traveled to Cumberland, Maryland, and then Baltimore, where he stayed with Henry Gover while making official calls on distilleries and other businesses. Meanwhile, Crawford Adams arranged with Acting Secretary Charles F. Conant to have Elliot transferred back to the Customs SAD. Upon receipt of this welcome news, Elliot rushed back to Washington and hastily filled out an application for employment as a Customs agent with a raise to eight dollars per day. He resigned from the IRS on 19 February, and Conant signed his new commission the following day.⁶

An abrupt break in Elliot's diary indicates his satisfaction about returning to work under his old boss was premature. Adams may have thought bringing Elliot into his office would prevent William Mosby from occupying a slot there, and thus weaken William Moore's chances of taking over. The strategy backfired, and Adams was forced to resign on 24 February, apparently after Moore brought his insubordination to Grant's attention. (Adams claimed Moore refused to specify why Grant ordered his dismissal, other than his having been too close to Bristow and writing letters that accused Moore of misconduct.)⁷

Elliot's ties to Adams and his status as a Virginia carpetbagger were now significant liabilities. On 28 February, President Grant asked Acting Secretary Conant to "place Chamberlin back in the Rev. bureau and...appt. W. H. Mosby to [Elliot's] present place as Spl. Agt. of Customs." With only three days left in Grant's term, it is unclear whether there was time for Elliot to resign his current position and be reinstated in the IRS where, in any case, he would have few allies to safeguard him. At the time, the entire Federal government was at a standstill, awaiting the outcome of the electoral crisis. Unlike Adams, and emboldened by the turmoil, Elliot did not obey Grant's order.⁸

Even while lining up support for Hayes, John Mosby continued to pursue his own agenda of procuring appointments for his followers. An anonymous letter to the *N. Y. Tribune* in late February, which was brought to Hayes' attention, contained a litany of charges against the ex-Rebel, which could easily have originated with Elliot. In it, the writer complained bitterly that Mosby had in recent months done "irreparable injury" to Virginia Republicans by using his "control over Gen. Grant" to make it "impossible for a Federal soldier to get an appointment." Earlier, the colonel had encouraged Grant to run again, fully expecting to play a prominent role in the "Third Term." When this failed, Mosby sought to get as many of his candidates appointed to office as possible, "so that when Mr. Hayes was inaugurated he could call upon them to go with him in a body and endorse him…thereby continuing his dynasty." Here followed a lengthy denunciation of his wartime actions, ending with an assertion the former partisan had lost all political or social standing in Virginia by the time he allied himself with Grant in 1872. Yet since then he had, with the President's help, placed his followers in "every department under the Government," and now boasted "his influence will be greater with President Hayes… Union soldiers hang their heads in shame."[9]

Meanwhile, Congress was in the midst of certifying election returns for each state in alphabetical order. With his career hanging in the balance, Elliot attended the final electoral count in the House on 26 and 28 February. Only when ballots from Florida, Louisiana and South Carolina were added to Hayes' column did the Republicans appear to have victory within their grasp. House Democrats, however, still refused to certify the results and mounted a filibuster which threatened a constitutional crisis if it did not end before Grant's term expired on 4 March. During these last hectic days, Hayes and his advisors reached a final agreement with Southern Democrats that resulted in the Ohio governor being declared the winner on 2 March. Not wanting to risk further delay, Hayes took the oath of office in a private ceremony at the White House the following day. His public inauguration took place on 5 March, closing one of the most bizarre and turbulent episodes in American politics. (Although Elliot is not known to have participated with the "Hayes Guards" in protecting the President-elect before and during the inauguration, it was later revealed that this secretive group of veterans was a militant branch of the OSS.)[10]

Once in office, Hayes' selection of John Sherman as Treasury Secretary proved beneficial to the country and the department he ran. Not as well remembered as his brother, Gen. William T. Sherman, John enjoyed a long and distinguished career as a cabinet member and Ohio politician. He had worked closely with Justin Morrill on the Senate Finance Committee and was well qualified for his new post, which he viewed as a steppingstone to succeeding Hayes. His two Assistant Secretaries were equally competent and favorably viewed by those who worked for them. Henry French came from a prominent Boston family and shared mutual friends with Elliot in the Massachusetts Horticultural Society. Assistant Secretary Richard C. McCormick had served on the Republican National Committee and was well acquainted with Elliot's past political activities.

Department of the Treasury, c. 1877. This massive neo-classical edifice projected dominance the department enjoyed in postwar America. (engraved vignette, Elliot's un-surrendered commission, TCC)

On the negative side, Hayes came to office deeply indebted to the Southern politicians who helped declare him the victor. One of his first significant actions in office was to remove the last Federal troops from the South, causing Republican governments in South Carolina and Louisiana to topple. Less dramatic, but of more importance to carpetbaggers like Elliot, was the Administration's commitment to fill Federal positions with native Southerners, which, according to one historian, had "devastating long-term results for...the southern Republican party." This preference for southern Democrats "even at the expense of able, honest southern Republicans...meant that the southern [GOP] would be deprived of its workers. Hayes and the civil service reformers either did not understand, or chose to ignore, the fact that...the southern party's fragile organization depended on patronage. Only the security of a federal position provided the freedom to be active in the party."[11]

It took some time before the new Secretary's team could turn its attention to personnel issues such as the dispute between Elliot and William Mosby over whom should occupy a place in the Customs SAD. Although Mosby had taken an oath of office on Grant's last day (3rd), his appointment was nullified when it was discovered Elliot still occupied the position. But until a hearing could be held to determine who should get the job, Elliot was allowed to continue working. About this time, his cause was advanced by an article trumpeting his alleged exploits during Jubal Early's raid on the capital. This laudatory account appeared anonymously in the March issue of *The Republic*, a GOP-oriented magazine published in Washington. Actually written by Assistant Interior Secretary Alonzo Bell with considerable input from Elliot, the lengthy "sketch" combined portions of Bell's long endorsement of the year before with Elliot's 1871 newspaper account of the Fort Stevens battle and some new material. As can be seen in Appendix B, its flowery language sounds overwrought to modern ears, but was typical of publicity needed to "gain influence" in that era.[12]

Elliot took an important step towards ensuring a favorable outcome to his feud with the Mosbys by meeting with the new Treasury Secretary on 20 March. He came armed with a letter of introduction from Justin Morrill, describing the bearer as Virginia's Republican executive chairman and "alternate elector" in the last election. The Senator also attached a press account of Grant's assurance that Elliot would get the Customs position. Favorably impressed with the interviewee, Sherman wrote on the back of Morrill's letter that Elliot "alleged that he was removed by misapprehension and Mosby put in his place—supposed on recommendation of W. B. Moore—Enter for consideration when Special agents considered."[13]

In a memo to Secretary Sherman a week later, Elliot included information obtained from Lynchburg's former mayor that William Mosby had recently boasted of coming out of the war with $5,000 left over from his share of "greenbacks" obtained from raids conducted by his brother on U.S. paymasters and passengers on a B&O train. Here, Elliot interjected, "I served faithfully in the Union Army... and was honestly discharged...and came out with scarcely money enough to buy me citizens clothing." Throwing modesty aside, Elliot then launched into a summary of his entire family's past military service:

> Of the five members of my family capable of serving this country when needed, one died from the effects of wounds received at the 1st battle of Bull Run, one losing his arm at 2nd Bull Run and mustered out when the war ended Major of cavalry, [and] another dying of fever at New Orleans...My father was a soldier of war of 1812, my mother had three brothers in same service. My Grandfather was a soldier of the Revolution and myself had courage enough though living South...to go North, enter the Union Army, and do my duty. My wife's family lived in Virginia and were loyal to the Union...suffering every abuse from Mosby's command...and were burnt out by our own troops...to prevent Mosby's command subsisting in their country...and made poor with myself the only male member left to provide for them. I cannot conceive any greater injustice being done me than that of being succeeded in a position under government by said W. H. Mosby.[14]

Active on his own behalf, Colonel Mosby lost no time trying to improve his access to the new

Administration and, less than a week after the inauguration, called on the White House to "give his respects." He and the President reminisced about their respective roles during Sheridan's Valley Campaign, where Hayes had been a brigade commander, and at the end of their meeting, Mosby optimistically predicted the "solid South" would soon dissolve, as Southerners came to realize how much they benefited from the new President. Even if Mosby did not raise his brother's appointment at this time, he would certainly have encouraged Hayes' decision to favor native Southerners over carpetbaggers.[15]

Several days later, the *Alexandria Gazette* reported on Mosby's campaign to have a Colonel Gordon appointed postmaster in Richmond to replace Miss Elizabeth Van Lew. (Van Lew had served as a Union spy during the siege of the Confederate capital, and out of gratitude, Grant had her appointed postmistress in 1869. Despite hostility from local inhabitants, this stalwart woman remained at her post, and now sought reappointment under Hayes.) The *Gazette*, which had assumed a visceral dislike for Mosby since his switch to the Republican side, reported the people of Richmond would prefer the nomination of the unsuccessful GOP gubernatorial candidate Robert Hughes to anyone backed by Mosby. Undeterred, Mosby came up with a new candidate to replace Van Lew, and proposed the appointment of James D. Brady as IRS collector in Petersburg to replace the incumbent, whom he described as "a Maine carpetbagger." Mosby hoped to make Brady's selection "a test case as between native Southern applicants and carpet baggers."[16]

Like Mosby, Elliot knew the value of early exposure to the President in playing the influence game. That spring, he accompanied James Brady and forty other prominent Virginia Republicans to the White House, and while the press account gave no indication of what was discussed, the group certainly tried to change Hayes' mind on Southern appointments. About the same time, Waterford's John Dutton took part in a delegation of Friends that called on Hayes. Something the President said that day prompted Dutton to write and warn Hayes not to place "too much confidence in *Col. Mosby.*" By way of explanation, the Waterford shopkeeper described his own experiences during the war, including imprisonment for refusing to support the Confederacy and his loss of $7,000 in merchandise during Mosby's raid on Point of Rocks. In his opinion, the loyal inhabitants of Loudoun had always considered Mosby an outlaw and were dismayed to hear reports "he has more influence with *our President* than anyone else in Virginia—which is certainly cause for regret (if true)." Dutton closed with an admonition not to give the former guerrilla any "*more confidence* than a repentant sinner is entitled to." In fact, Hayes heeded such advice and never relied on Mosby to the extent his predecessor had.[17]

Like the Mosby brothers, Special Agent William Moore worried about his standing in the new Administration, even though he was said to be the only Treasury employee whom Grant had specifically named to be kept in place. Adding to his concerns was the firing of IRS agent Joseph Maddox, allegedly for involvement in a last-minute attempt to switch Louisiana electoral votes from Hayes to Tilden. Maddox had worked closely with Moore on sensitive operations for the White House, which was one reason why Moore had tried to shield his friend by converting him into a Customs special agent as part of the Mosby-Chamberlin exchange.[18] In any case, Moore took advantage of Grant's continued presence in the capital after the inauguration to ask the ex-President to intervene on his own behalf with Secretary Sherman. Knowing what would irritate Grant most, the special agent explained that he was being accused of misconduct against Treasury officers who had favored Bristow's nomination at Cincinnati, a pointed reference to Adams and Chamberlin. Moore's plea may have gained him a reprieve from suffering Maddox's fate, but not for long.[19]

All this while Edith, now pregnant, had remained at Clifton anxiously awaiting the outcome of her husband's hearing at the Treasury Department. By late March she fretted over having seen nothing in the press of William Mosby's removal and was equally concerned her husband might be assigned to New York, where a crisis involving sugar imports was brewing. ("I would as soon quit, as leave my house" and go north to live.) Instead, she prayed for him to remain in Washington, which she considered their "second home." She also reminded her husband to send sufficient funds to pay off their current maid and break in a replacement before her "season of retirement from the kitchen" arrived. (Their fourth child, Edward Matthews Chamberlin, was born on 10 May.)[20]

Finally in early April a board of inquiry headed by Assistant Secretary French ruled that Elliot, not William Mosby, rightfully occupied the SAD position, since the former had neither resigned, nor been officially removed. For once, Elliot's refusal to obey orders he considered unjust had paid off. His insubordination was judged to have been mitigated by his alleged inability to transfer back to the IRS before Grant left office. His impudence could not be completely ignored, however, and he was ordered to leave the Treasury to make room for the reinstatement of Crawford Adams. Yet, even this blow was softened by allowing him to remain on the payroll until the end of April, plus assurances he would be re-hired at the first opportunity. Elliot's final report concerned inspections at Hampton Roads and along Virginia's Eastern Shore during the last half of April. By then, neither Adams nor Moore was in charge of SAD, this position instead going to Amory K. Tingle, who would hold it for the next fifteen years.[21]

Shortly after surrendering his commission, Elliot received reassurances from Justin Morrill that he would be "taken care of some way." Assistant Secretary McCormick had promised the Senator his protégé would be allowed to return to the Treasury, either to his old job, or to some other position. Morrill added a note of caution by revealing that McCormick had checked on Elliot's performance and found that in terms of "character you were held to be the salt of the earth, but for special agent you were reported as not quite aggressive enough, or not as efficient as some others." After passing this information, the Senator confirmed receipt of Elliot's recent telegram asking whether he should look for work in some other government department. It arrived too late to discuss during his last Cabinet meeting with the President, but Morrill counseled that it would be "safer to cling to the Treasury." (Today, it seems incredible that the President, Cabinet members and Congressmen would devote so much time to mid-level appointments, but contemporary accounts show this was indeed the case.)[22]

Morrill's efforts paid off in early July when McCormick advised Elliot that he would be returning to his old job in a few days. Greatly relieved, he immediately penned a note of thanks to his mentor: "You know the joy it brings to the *household*, and to you we are indebted for all. I shall enter upon my duties fully determined to do my very best." (He did not mention he would be filling the slot created by the removal of William Moore, although he must have surmised that Grant's version of a "Watergate plumber" would not bow out quietly.) On 12 July, Acting Secretary McCormick signed his commission as special agent (second class) earning eight dollars per day.[23]

He was particularly pleased to be reassigned to the 5th Special Agency District, where he would again work "under the protection" of Col. Ira Ayer. His old boss planned to move his district headquarters from Richmond to Baltimore at the end of the year, and asked Elliot to proceed there directly. Edith was delighted her husband would be closer to home, working in a city where she had numerous relatives and acquaintances. In her first letter after his departure, she began with some wifely advice to cultivate old friends and avoid making new enemies. She then mentioned their obligation to help the "needy and depressed," as prelude to reminding him that Henry Gover was out of work in Baltimore. Hopeful her husband could arrange a job for her uncle, she added, "none more than you and I—my darling—can appreciate this condition of affairs [unemployment]"—a different stance than the one taken when his sister became a widow.

In Edith's opinion, her husband's new job came at a critical juncture. With three children and a newborn to care for, she found it impossible to oversee the house, farm and gardens, yet there was no money to hire additional help. For the first time in many years, she and her mother did not plan to take in summer boarders, presumably due to lack of space and servants to accommodate them. Fortunately, Senator Morrill had sent her fifty dollars to tide the family over until Elliot's salary resumed. Even so, she was forced to sell their best milk cow to the butcher, who kept ten dollars to pay off an outstanding debt. The remainder was used to hire men to cut and stack wheat and hay.

Despite optimism that an end to their problems was at hand, she and her husband still had plenty to worry about. Perhaps at the suggestion of Grant, before he and his family departed upon an around-the-world tour, William Moore was dispatched to Norfolk in June to investigate frauds carried out by that port's former customs collector, the by then deceased Luther Lee. In the midst of this investigation, Moore was abruptly recalled to Washington and summarily fired, thus making room for Elliot's reinstatement. After his dismissal, Moore went ahead anyway and wrote up his preliminary findings in a deposition, which threatened to implicate Elliot in the Norfolk frauds. Learning of this development from her husband, Edith exasperatedly wondered if there would ever be an end to problems in the special agency force, even though she was positive her husband would have discovered the fraud himself, had he only been allowed to remain there longer. Fearful Elliot might lose his job, she warned him to avoid confronting Moore, even if the latter was "twice and thrice an agent," as long as he "*lets you alone.*"[24]

Even more improbably, Elliot was sent to Norfolk later in July to continue Moore's investigation. It could not have been a pleasant assignment—not only was he being asked to verify the existence of wrongdoing at a post where he had previously served, but the new Customs collector was predisposed against him. John S. Braxton had taken over the Norfolk customhouse shortly after Luther Lee's death in early 1877, much to the displeasure of local Republicans, who wanted to replace Lee with another Union veteran. But in what was said to have been the last appointment Grant made for Mosby, the former Confederate officer was picked instead. Soon after assuming his position as collector, Braxton discovered his predecessor had been embezzling funds from the customhouse for years, which resulted in Moore's being dispatched to conduct an investigation. Braxton, who owed his job to Mosby, was therefore less than pleased to see Moore replaced by the man who had kept his benefactor's brother from working for the Treasury.[25]

While her husband was in Norfolk, Edith began feeling ill, and feared she was again pregnant. If so, she confided to her husband that she might take "poison" to end it. Worried someone else might read his response, she warned him to omit any mention of her "fears" in his letters. (Apparently her concerns were groundless, or the home remedy worked, as their next child was not born until 1879.) And she had one more thing to worry about. That summer, labor strikes and rioting broke out across the nation after several railroad companies tried to reduce wages. The Democratic-controlled House had adjourned without funding a military appropriations bill, and some questioned whether the unpaid soldiers could be relied upon to quell the unrest. Describing the situation in the country as "terrible," Edith wished a speedy end to the "fearful excitement." Knowing her husband's impulsive nature, she added: "I pray of you, if volunteers are called for, don't you go—but of course you will not." She realized others must be in the same situation, but as he had only just gotten his job "after a long struggle…your first duty is to your family rather than your country." (State and Federal authorities would quell the violence a short time later.)[26]

The Norfolk scandal, which had been simmering for over a month, did not go away so easily. When the story of corruption at the customhouse finally broke into the open in early August and threatened to pull Elliot down again, it revealed the cutthroat nature of obtaining and keeping a Federal position before reforms were enacted. On 6 August, Washington's *National Republican* reprinted a long letter from William Moore to Secretary Sherman, in which the ex-agent described how he had been sent to Norfolk to investigate fraud uncovered by the new collector. During his stay, Moore confirmed that former collector Lee had swindled the government out of more than $60,000. He then asserted that:

> Mr. S. E. Chamberlin was stationed at Norfolk…during a large portion of the time that these frauds were going on, and there are numerous reports from him representing that he was habitually examining the office, and the records were properly kept and receipts accounted for. The facts are that there never was a day during the time that Mr. Chamberlin was making these reports of the condition of the Norfolk custom-house that the cash on hand corresponded with the amount that appeared by the cash-book…Collector Braxton informed me that…much of the confusion in the records of the office arises from the irresponsible action of Mr. Chamberlin in withdrawing so many important papers without properly accounting for them. The facts show that Mr. Chamberlin connived with the officers of the custom-house in the frauds, or was totally incompetent to cope with the conspirators, while the latter were stealing the entire duties on whole ship-loads of dutiable cargoes…

Moore then indignantly described his surprise on learning Chamberlin had been selected to finish his investigation. Only when he had returned to Washington on 8 July and tried to present his findings (the deposition to which Edith previously referred) did he learn that President Hayes had ordered his dismissal. His firing, Moore claimed, was based on the contents of sensitive correspondence between himself and Grant, which had been stolen from his office by the brother-in-law of C/SAD Tingle. These documents were later passed to Gen. Henry V. Boynton, a well-known investigative reporter for the *Cincinnati Gazette*, who allegedly contacted Moore and demanded money not to publish them. When he refused to pay, the reporter began to publish information from these papers. Claiming to be the only Treasury employee whom Grant wanted kept in place, Moore feigned outrage that some saw this preferment as proof he had engaged in illegal activities for the former President. He further alleged that Tingle had tried to persuade him to omit any reference to Chamberlin in his deposition, which he attributed to the C/SAD's role in hiring his replacement. Moore ended his epistle with a plea, supposedly backed by U.S. District Judge Robert Hughes, that the Norfolk investigation be taken from Chamberlin and given to a disinterested party.[27]

Unlike earlier difficulties at the Agriculture and Treasury Departments, Elliot's employers rallied to his defense. On the day Moore's story broke, Secretary Sherman told reporters, "no attention should be paid to the collection of lies laid before him by W. B. Moore," which he termed "false from beginning to end." Sherman pointed out that Moore did not discover the "defalcation" at Norfolk, and that "Special Agent Chamberlin…was not the inspector of that Custom House." Furthermore, Moore was "ignorant of the real reasons" for his dismissal and would be "astonished when he sees them in print. He has a record which ought to have sent him to the penitentiary." (Elliot's 1876 diary and official files confirm Sherman's statement that he was never directed to examine Norfolk's customhouse. However, the Treasury's failure to authorize a thorough inspection of such an important facility suggests that Lee enjoyed protection at a high level.)[28]

The case did not die with Sherman's rebuttal, and a day later the *National Republican* published a letter from Judge Hughes, arguing that Colonel Ayer should also be held responsible for not uncovering the fraud. During the following days, Elliot wisely refrained from challenges in the press to defend himself in print. Soon, his name and that of Ayer disappeared from the papers as attention shifted to a series of articles by Boynton describing Moore's past activities. The special agent was said to have worked secretly for Grant inside the Treasury to undermine Secretary Bristow's anticorruption campaign. To that end, Moore manufactured evidence used in the "Whiskey Ring" trial to discredit a key witness who had testified against Grant's personal secretary, Orville Babcock. This deception in turn led to Babcock's acquittal and probably saved the President from impeachment. Other revelations included Moore's role in an unsuccessful attempt to annex the Dominican Republic in 1870. At the time, Moore was involved in a plan to abduct the former American consul in Santo Domingo, Raymond H. Perry, and hold him in Texas on trumped-up charges to prevent his testifying before the Senate about Babcock and Grant's private interests on the island. The plan failed, however, and Perry's testimony proved critical to the Senate's rejection of the annexation request. According to Boynton, it was Moore's part in this affair that convinced Hayes to order his dismissal.[29]

Because of the flap, Elliot returned to Baltimore without finishing the Norfolk investigation, which was turned over to Ayer. After completion of his fieldwork in mid-August, Ayer assured Elliot his findings would hold him "entirely free from any censure whatsoever. If anybody is to blame, aside from the foul perpetrators of the frauds, it is myself, as Agent in Charge." Ayer's gallantry in shouldering responsibility for the problems at Norfolk almost cost him his job. Mosby jumped into the fray in September, demanding Ayer's "immediate removal from office." In response, the beleaguered supervising agent submitted a stack of letters from friends and professional contacts attesting to his character and professional ability.[30]

The following month, Ayer penned a lengthy defense which convinced the commission appointed to hear the case that neither he nor Elliot should be considered negligent in not having discovered the defalcation. Ayer emphasized that the deception had been "deeply covered" and of a sophistication "not before known in the...Custom Service." Since the perpetrators had excellent reputations in the local community, and lacking other outward indications of wrongdoing, no suspicion, Ayer admitted, "ever crossed my mind." He did find the Department partly at fault, since prior to Secretary Sherman's arrival, "no instructions were ever issued...relative to proper methods of examination. Had such instructions been issued four years ago, they would have been obeyed most faithfully by me, and the frauds at Norfolk would have been prevented."[31]

The new procedures to detect fraud included a lengthy questionnaire for special agents to fill out whenever they inspected customhouses and other facilities. The discovery at Norfolk had even wider repercussions, however, and were a factor in Hayes' decision to have Secretary Sherman undertake a systematic investigation to root out misconduct throughout the Customs Service. This quest inevitably led to the notoriously corrupt New York customhouse and would present the President with his biggest challenge in office.

Hayes' commitment to reform was not limited to the Treasury, but extended to the entire Civil Service. A presidential directive issued in June protected Federal employees from compulsory political contributions and dismissals on purely political grounds. Hayes' order also imposed stricter regulations against government employees holding outside political office. In August, Elliot received a letter from Veterans Committee secretary Drake DeKay, informing him that other Federal workers on the executive board were sending in their resignations in compliance with the President's directive, and DeKay asked if he wanted to do the same. Elliot apparently ignored the suggestion, as his name still appeared as Virginia's representative on the Committee in 1880. (Hayes' directive lacked statutory authority, and its provisions were not formally adopted into law until passage of the Pendleton Civil Service Act in 1883. Still, Elliot's decision to keep a seat on the Veterans Committee, as well as his executive chairmanship in Virginia's GOP, show a stubborn unwillingness to abandon politics altogether.)[32]

By late summer, Elliot was primarily occupied with uncovering fraud in sugar imports, the subject of the next chapter. However, with Ayer still tied up with the Norfolk inquiry, he went to Richmond to investigate charges that customs collector Charles S. Mills was covering up embezzlement of official funds by his nephew. In his wrap-up report, Elliot recommended leniency towards Mills, who had immediately dismissed his nephew once the discrepancy was found and had already repaid the missing funds. (The young man had a gambling problem.) Elliot noted that Mills' efforts to make good on the loss and find a new deputy had interfered with his ability to give speeches for the local GOP. In making his recommendation to Sherman to keep Mills, Elliot took the opportunity to include a letter from a Richmond lawyer, whose blunt criticism of Hayes' appointments policy mirrored his own feelings. In it, Mills was portrayed as being "so much Superior...to the miserable, hypocritical, vulgar, lying, whoring, drunken, gambling, robbing horde from which President Hayes has thus far made his Virginia appointments." Replacing Mills, the lawyer contended, would only "give place to some Rebel Renegade, or miserable, worthless, pretentious Republican cormorant who would sink the party...to still lower depths."[33]

In November, Col. James Brady approached Elliot for help in getting the position of IRS collector in Petersburg. Final approval had been held up in Justin Morrill's Finance Committee, which Brady attributed to his earlier endorsement by Mosby. Six months before, Elliot had almost lost his job to Mosby's brother, yet he now found himself in the agreeable position of being asked to aid an office-seeker, who had discovered the old partisan warrior no longer had any significant influence in Washington. In response to Brady's request, Elliot drafted a letter explaining to Morrill that he had already recommended the applicant to Assistant Secretary McCormick on the basis of their work together on the GOP state executive committee. Furthermore, even though a native Virginian, Brady had proven his loyalty by serving in a New York regiment during the war.[34]

With the exception of the attack against Ayer, Mosby was uncharacteristically quiet during the latter half of 1877, a reflection of his failure to form a Southern coalition to support Hayes, as well as the Republicans' inability to field a candidate for Virginia's gubernatorial race that year. The President recognized, however, that he owed Mosby a favor, if only out of deference to Grant, and in early 1878

Hayes assigned James Garfield the task of finding a suitable position for the colonel. Overestimating his support within the Administration, Mosby turned down an initial offer to work in the Treasury Department. He had not entirely stopped trying to influence the appointments process either, because in April 1878, Elliot received a warning from a Norfolk visitor that Mosby and Moore continued to wage "war" against him and Colonel Ayer. Most likely, this concerned Ayer's refusal to create a new slot in the Norfolk customhouse for one of Mosby's adherents, but by then Elliot was too well situated to feel seriously threatened. That summer, Hayes tried to get Mosby to accept a consular position in China, but the ex-Rebel again refused the offer. During a visit the two men made in October to Montpelier, the home of James Madison, Hayes apparently used the opportunity to impress upon his companion the political realities of his situation, because when the President next offered Mosby a consulship in Hong Kong, the latter reluctantly accepted. As the *City of Peking* steamed out of San Francisco in December 1878 with the "Grey Ghost" on board, there must have been audible sighs of relief, not only in Virginia and Washington, but also at Baltimore's SAD office. Mosby would not be given official leave to return to the U.S. for seven long years.[35]

Chapter 24

SUGAR FRAUDS AND CUSTOMHOUSE CORRUPTION: 1877-1881

Soon after his July 1877 arrival in Baltimore, Elliot made a discovery that would dramatically affect his career. The port was a major entry point for sugar, and on entering the customhouse Appraisers' office, as he later recounted, "my attention was called to the peculiar color and appearance of the sugars being largely imported there...Taking a sample with me to my office, and submitting the same to simple tests, I became convinced that the sugars were...artificially colored and this was done for the purpose of evading a higher rate of duty." On submitting his findings to the Treasury Department, he received permission to pursue the matter further. "The result was a confirmation of my suspicions and I found that some 92% of all the importations into the U.S. were sugars below No. 10 Dutch Standard in color," and thus subject to the lowest duty under the 1875 Tariff Act.[1]

Since the Civil War, import duties on sugar were calculated on the basis of the Dutch Standard (DS) which presumed darker sugars had lower saccharine content and were therefore assessed at lower rates than fully processed white sugar. In addition, American sugar refiners received drawbacks from duties collected on dark sugar to offset the cost of converting it into white sugar for re-export. Once a luxury item, sugar consumption rose dramatically after the war, spurred by the introduction of manufactured candies, drinks and other consumables. Yet by 1877 total revenues collected on sugar had significantly declined, despite a twenty-five percent increase in the tariff two years earlier. Since sugar accounted for almost half of all revenue gathered by the Customs Service, or a quarter of the Treasury receipts, this downward trend was viewed with alarm. After a cursory review of the data revealed that importation of lighter sugar had declined in inverse proportion to that of dark, Elliot was convinced foreign exporters were adding color to refined sugar to pay a lower tariff. He further hypothesized that this colorant could be reconverted to a high-quality product at a fraction of the cost of refining naturally dark sugar. In August, Treasury Secretary John Sherman authorized him to continue his investigation, and ordered C/SAD Armory Tingle to form a commission to oversee this effort.

Elliot now faced the task of substantiating his theory, which would require development of reliable tests to verify the presence of added color and measure saccharine content. Moreover, before there could be any realistic hope of getting a Democrat-controlled Congress to change existing regulations, he needed to prove his case in court. Arrayed against him were powerful sugar producers, importers and corrupt Customs officials, all of whom benefited from the existing system. He also faced opposition from Democratic politicians who generally favored lowing tariffs on all imports. While not always successful in overcoming these obstacles, his decade-long quest to establish a rational basis for assessing sugar imports would remain his most enduring achievement at the Treasury and his diaries for this period confirm his complete absorption in this task.²

A break came in late September, when he established contact with George Wilson, a disgruntled sea captain, who until recently had commanded ships for Baltimore's top sugar importer, William H. Perot. During visits to plantations owned by the Perot family in British Guyana, Wilson claimed to have observed the artificial coloring process. He also warned Elliot that the American Vice Consul there was on Perot's payroll, frequently traveling free of charge on company ships. Perot, however, soon learned his operations had been compromised, and took steps to remove colored sugar from his Baltimore warehouses. About this time, the captain also broke contact with Elliot and would later deny in court what he had told the special agent. Fearing the leak may have originated in the customhouse, Elliot hired Henry Gover as an assistant so that he would not have to use other Customs employees in his investigation.³

Baltimore Customhouse. Designed by Benjamin Latrobe and once the largest domed structure in the U.S., such imposing Federal outposts stood in 177 ports, collecting over half the revenue and second only to the Post Office in number of employees. (*Picture of Baltimore*: Baltimore, F. Lucas, Jr., [1842]. Garrett Library, Johns Hopkins Univ.)

Based on Captain Wilson's initial debriefing, Elliot was convinced one of Perot's ships, the *Mississippi*, would unload artificially colored sugar when it docked in November. After obtaining the U.S. District Attorney's concurrence that sufficient evidence existed to justify a seizure, he wired the Treasury for approval to proceed. Despite reluctance by Baltimore's Customs Collector to take any action, an affirmative response from Washington allowed Elliot to supervise seizure of 712 bags of sugar from the *Mississippi* on 30 November.⁴

Perot was subsequently charged with importation of artificially colored sugar to evade payment of proper duties, setting the stage for a lengthy trial the following year. In reality, Elliot had acted on little more than a hunch and information from a source who was no longer cooperating with the government. The success of the case therefore depended on his ability to prove the sugar was artificially colored (with intent to deceive) and demonstrate how it was done. To this end, Elliot and Henry Gover took a deposition in December from Henry J. Abbott, a technician who had installed equipment in Cuban and South American refineries. Because of Abbot's familiarity with the process, Elliot placed him under contract to assist in the trial, and later hired him as a special inspector.⁵

In January 1878, Elliot forwarded a provocative report to C/SAD Tingle, with instructions it be brought to Secretary Sherman's attention. In it, he described the discovery of a pipe at a Baltimore sugar refinery that had been secretly installed between the chemist's lab and a vat used to process dark sugar. Elliot managed to obtain a sample of the chemical passing through the pipe, which he sent to the Department of Agriculture for analysis. (It turned out to be sulfuric acid, which he concluded was the reagent used to bleach colored sugar.) He also learned Perot was allegedly being kept informed of the government's plans by an official in the Justice Department, identified only as Colonel Ashby. Receiving no reply to his latest revelations, Elliot hastened to Washington, where Tingle tried to convince him of Ashby's innocence. The special agent remained skeptical, however, especially after the colonel arrived in Baltimore the following month to work with the District Attorney on the Perot case. (This was not the only time he recorded suspicions in his diary that elements within the government were hindering his investigations.)⁶

* * * * *

When Elliot arrived in Baltimore the previous summer, he initially stayed at Henry Gover's home on Carrollton Avenue, a neighborhood of row houses on the city's west end noted today for its white marble front steps. In November, Elliot rented a nearby townhouse at 212 Carrollton Avenue to accommodate his whole family, including Sarah and Annie Matthews, as well as his supervisor, Ira Ayer, whose family chose to remain in Richmond.

Though it pained Edith to leave her beloved Clifton, she was somewhat mollified to be going to a city she knew and liked quite well. Her two oldest children, however, would find the transition to urban life more difficult and always looked back fondly on their early years on the farm. Thirteen months Morrill's senior, Mary had been his constant companion and protector there, once rescuing him after a fall into the springhouse and constantly retrieving his "most prized possession," a pink sunbonnet that was always getting lost. Nor could Morrill ever forget "grandma Sarah" in her "black, or gray silk dresses, starched & folded 'under chiefs' and stiff Quaker bonnets...& who would never consent to get into the family carriage to go to meeting, if there happened to be a cake of mud on any part of the running gear." He also retained a vivid picture of "the ease & grace with which she would remain still for a moment while walking in the flower garden & then from the depth of her flowing gown which was evidently safely spread by a hoop skirt there proceed to water from within [!], the zinnias or coarser blooms that grew along the paths." Also standing out among his childhood memories were the old meetinghouse, especially the side where the men sat, and the adjoining cemetery, full of stones marking the resting place of ancestors.

While Clifton was a paradise for young children, Waterford held its own attractions and figured prominently among Mary's early memories: "How wonderful...to go to 'town' to visit some of the Quaker relations, for the village was full of them in those days." Three great aunts lived on Main Street alone, as did her great uncle Sam Gover, whose store held "many delightful things," especially peppermint and lemon sticks. "We and our cousins found the mill-race [behind the store] a fascinating place to play and fall into...On the opposite side of the street, there was a great tannery full of tan bark & mysterious vats, filled with hides that looked black and terrible." For her too, the old meetinghouse figured "very prominently" in her memory, as the place where she used to go with her "beautiful and stately grandmother, who was dressed always (as were all...elders attending meeting) in plain Quaker garb with kerchief and bonnet."

So it was with great sadness that the children bade farewell on a chilly autumn morning to the only home they had ever known. Morrill was only four at the time, but many years later could recall the sorrow of saying good-bye to his pet calf and the other animals. Only the bare essentials were loaded into a wagon for the ride to Clarkes Gap, where they caught a train that took them to a new life in the city. (Their country origins were evident when little Nellie Chamberlin, alighting from the horse car that brought them from the Baltimore station, pointed to the pretty "branch" flowing in front of their new home, only to learn it was an open sewer.) Sarah Matthews remained behind to help her brother, Sam Gover, auction off the family's remaining possessions at the end of November. Afterwards, Clifton was turned over to Obediah Pierpoint, who rented the farm for the next five years. Sarah and her daughter Annie then joined the rest of the family in Baltimore. (A disastrous fire earlier that fall at the Treasury Department would delay Annie's reappointment until mid-1878.)[7]

* * * * *

Meanwhile, events were taking place in New York that would shape both the direction of the Hayes Administration and Elliot's career. After working his way up through that city's customhouse, Irish-born immigrant William H. Grace was assigned in February 1877 to inspect the port's principal landing facility for imported sugar. He soon discovered that the Customs weigher at the Brooklyn site was not using a government-issued scale as specified by law, but one belonging to the refiners, located in an enclosure inspector Grace could not access. He also learned from several ship captains that weights being recorded at the dock were far lower than what had been recorded at embarkation. When Grace complained to the weigher's foreman, he was dismissed with a vulgar oath, and when he raised the matter with a deputy Surveyor, he was assured his findings would be passed to the chief Surveyor, Maj. Gen. George H. Sharpe, then out of town.

During March, Grace continued to complain about irregularities at the dock, but never received any response from Sharpe who, it turned out, was conspiring with refiners to bring trumped-up charges of drunkenness and blackmail against the inspector. Then, in an effort to further intimidate him, Grace was suspended without pay pending resolution of these allegation. Sharpe, however, refused to hold an inquiry, even after a refiner withdrew the charges. Finally on 10 July, Grace met the Jay Commission which, as described below, had been sent to New York to investigate corruption and mismanagement in the customhouse. The commissioners encouraged him to send a full report of his findings and consequent travails to Secretary Sherman, but unfortunately for the inspector, Sharpe's spies saw him leave this meeting. The next day, the Surveyor confronted Grace on the street and provoked a fight by cursing and spitting on him. The inspector was then promptly arrested for assault and battery, the goal being to have grounds for his immediate dismissal and undermine anything he might have told the Jay Commission. With the help of a pliant District Attorney and judge, who barred any testimony on the reasons behind the fight, i.e. corruption in the customhouse, Grace was sentenced to four months in prison, although New York's Republican Governor cut this time in half after receiving petitions for his release. In December, Grade went to Washington to meet with President Hayes and Secretary Sherman, who arranged for the receipt of his withheld pay to the time of his dismissal and assured him he would be rehired when Theodore Roosevelt Sr. took over the customhouse. (Roosevelt died before he could assume this position and, since Grace by then was still seeking to become a special agent in 1879, he apparently suffered the fate of most whistle-blowers.)[8]

Grace's revelations on corruption in the sugar trade, which would ultimately be found to exceed revenue losses due to the "Whiskey Ring," provided Hayes with ammunition for the most contentious issue to confront his Administration, the battle to establish control over New York's customhouse. A feud between the Empire State's most powerful politician, Senator Roscoe Conkling, and the President had been brewing since the 1876 convention, when the Senator adamantly refused to support anyone backed by the GOP's reform wing, even after Hayes won the nomination. Conkling feared any attempt to reform the Civil Service would threaten the hold his political machine exercised over the customhouse, whose 1,500 employees were the primary source of patronage and funding that kept the state GOP in power. (Revenue collected on goods entering New York's harbor exceeded those from all other U.S. ports combined.) As already noted, Hayes initiated Civil Service reform in June 1877 with an executive order prohibiting "obligatory" political contributions by Federal employees and also barring them from holding outside political office. Later that summer, the President had the Treasury Secretary appoint aristocratic reformer John Jay to head an investigation of the customhouse in his home city. To no one's surprise, the Jay Commission found it to be over-staffed and poorly managed. In addition, evidence gathered from Grace and others confirmed Customs employees frequently accepted bribes, in part to offset losses caused by political skimming of their salaries.

Hayes and Sherman reacted to Jay's findings with caution, asking only that the two top Customs officials in New York, Chester A. Arthur and Alonzo Cornell, make minor changes in their operations. When both ignored Sherman's request, and Cornell refused to resign his position on the Republican National Committee, Hayes felt he had no recourse but to ask for their resignations. Conkling responded with a violent attack on the Administration in the Senate, which rejected Hayes' nominees (one of whom was Theodore Roosevelt's father) and left Arthur and Cornell in place. (The President did get approval for Edwin A. Merritt to replace the thoroughly discredited Sharpe as Surveyor.) This setback made the President more determined than ever to establish the Executive Branch's primacy over Congress in the management of the Federal workforce. In July 1878, while Congress was in recess, Hayes ordered Arthur's and Cornell's removal, and replaced them with Merritt, who was moved up from Survey to Collector, and Silas W. Burt. (Both proved to be capable and honest administrators, although the initial joy of the reformers might have been tempered had they foreseen that Hayes' actions would result in Arthur becoming President, and Cornell the next governor of New York.)[9]

Elliot's growing expertise on sugar inevitably drew him into this contentious issue. Expanding his investigations to include Boston, Philadelphia and New York, he found the first two ports relatively free of problems, but he quickly corroborated Grace's earlier allegations about the "Sugar Ring" when he visited New York in April 1878. Upon boarding one vessel, he found Customs weighers and samplers being bribed to undervalue a cargo of Cuban sugar. (Samplers selected random specimens from a ship's cargo to send back to the Appraisers for an evaluation.) Elliot did manage one pleasurable excursion that spring, when he took a special train to Chester, Pennsylvania, to attend the launch of a U.S. & Brazil Steamship Line vessel, as part of a delegation that included President Hayes, Senator Justin Morrill and Assistant Treasury Secretary Henry French.[10]

That summer, the Chamberlin family celebrated the 4th of July by attending a baseball game in Baltimore, after which Edith and her mother took the children to Loudoun, where they spent the rest of the season at a boarding house near Waterford. Before joining them there, Elliot accompanied Annie Matthews to Washington, where she resumed work for the Treasury, after both he and Senator Morrill helped secure her reappointment.[11]

After only a few days with his family, Elliot left to be present for Edwin Merritt's takeover of the New York customhouse, where he spent the next two months helping the new Collector identify corrupt employees and initiate long-needed reforms. To preserve his cover, the special agent worked out of a room in the Metropolitan Hotel where he was later joined by Colonel Ayer. Despite their precautions, a local paper broadcast their presence in mid-August, and averred that their investigations had induced Merritt to order "the entire stock of raw sugar in this city be resampled...to detect any discrepancies between the samples now...and when the cargoes...were originally assessed." Chamberlin and Ayer were further reported to have turned to experts at the Columbia School of Mines to help analyze sugar and syrup samples.[12]

Working with a team of police detectives, Elliot succeeded in catching three samplers undervaluing sugar imports, thereby convincing their supervisor of the extent of fraud in his department. In early September, he sent two preliminary reports to Secretary Sherman, which optimistically concluded: "The frauds on sugar I am bringing to light are immense. I hope soon to report complete success in breaking up the Sugar Ring of N.Y. and bringing guilty parties to justice." In a note to Elliot's supervisor on the back of one report, Sherman wrote: "a well-established case of this kind should be rigidly prosecuted without fear or favor." Reacting to the Secretary's comment, C/SAD Tingle traveled to New York several days later, but seemed mainly interested in getting his agent to return home to recuperate from a rheumatic attack and write up his findings. (His boss's lack of enthusiasm for pursuing the fraud cases probably reflected nothing more than a better appreciation of political realities in New York, although later in his career Tingle was accused of accepting bribes.) Elliot did convince his supervisor to let him stay a few more days to check progress on the development of a new method for testing sugar samples, which he had contracted out to a local chemist.[13]

When Elliot finally checked in at Washington in mid-September, he was given time off to visit his family in Loudoun. Frequently neglecting his health while on an important case, it took him a week to recover before he and Edith returned to Baltimore with Mamie, leaving Sarah behind to bring the other children later. His lenghty report was submitted on 27 September and contained recommendations to reduce fraud and improve the accuracy of sampling by New York Customs officials. Little mention was made of prosecuting corrupt employees whom he had identified, he evidently having bowed to Tingle's advice on this subject.[14]

After a quick trip to New York and Boston to line up witnesses and take depositions, Elliot returned to Baltimore for the opening of the Perot trial on 9 October. He was the first person to testify and attended most sessions of the seven-week hearing. (Other prosecution witnesses included Henry Gover and Henry Abbott.) The local press covered the trial on a daily basis, and the judge once censured Elliot for providing information to a reporter. After the defense took the stand, there were indications in Elliot's diary that things were not going well. He did not have a high opinion of the District Attorney and came to suspect that someone on the prosecution team had been co-opted by Perot's lawyers. (The sugar magnate reportedly spent $30,000 on his defense.) In the trial's final days, Elliot and other government witnesses were subjected to heavy cross-examination, although the experience was not as bad as the special agent had feared. Seeking inspiration and strength during this period, he and Edith twice attended sermons by the noted evangelist Dwight L. Moody. On 20 November, the jury sustained the government's charge that the sugar in question had been fraudulently colored but found Perot innocent on the grounds that it had not been proven he was aware of this when he imported it. Although Elliot and his colleagues professed satisfaction their basic premise had been upheld, the press and local business community viewed Perot's acquittal as a defeat for the government, and predicted the trial's only effect would be to reduce Baltimore's share of the sugar trade.[15]

Meanwhile, the 1877 discoveries of frauds by inspector Grace and special agent Chamberlin had, by the following year, morphed into a national debate on the sugar question. Americans today find it difficult to comprehend how such a dry subject as tariffs dominated the body politic during the latter part of the nineteenth century, when it pitted Democrat against Republican, North against South, and workers in industries protected by the tariff against consumers of imported products. During the Hayes Administration, the debate became focused on a single import—sugar. Soaring demand for cheap sweeteners, fear of harmful adulterants, recent discoveries of fraud, concentration of the industry into the hands of a few domestic refiners and falling tax revenues all contributed to widespread calls for change in the 1875 sugar tariff. Favoring retention of the current system were large refiners, who had mastered the "secret" of manipulating the current laws to avoid paying high duties, and at the same time stifle completion from small refiners and importers.

As chairman of the House Ways and Means Committee, Fernando Wood took the lead in Congress on sugar matters. No friend of the Administration, Wood had gone so far as mayor of New York during the war to suggest the city secede from the Union so its merchants could continue to trade with the South. By May 1878, the Chairman was pushing a bill he claimed would eliminate fraud and reverse declining revenue by use of the polariscope to test saccharine levels in sugar, plus some other minor changes to the 1875 law. In fact, the Wood Bill had been drafted by one of the large refiners, most likely Theodore Havermeyer, reputed head of New York's Sugar Ring. When a group of small refiners and importers called on Wood to complain that his bill would put them out of business or force them to adopt the fraudulent practices of the Sugar Ring, the Chairman refused to hear them, saying he had already made up his mind on the subject. (Critics of the Woods Bill favored instead reducing the number of different tariffs on sugar from four to two, and argued against use of the polariscope, which they believed would only increase the likelihood of fraud by the poorly paid, and therefore easily bribable, Customs personnel who collected samples at the dock for testing by that instrument.)[16]

It should be noted here that Elliot's empirical approach to his job and continued interest in science also led him to explore use of the polariscope. Since at least August 1878, he worked with Professor P. Ricketts to develop a device employing a beam of polarized light to test for purity and saccharine content of sugar in a dissolved state. After perfecting his apparatus later that year, Ricketts received $300 for his efforts and a contract to analyze future samples. Elliot later purchased a polariscope for his Baltimore office to test samples collected by Customs officers around the country. Although Secretary Sherman advocated its use in his 1878 Annual Report, importers challenged its accuracy and successfully blocked legislation that would have mandated its use in place of the Dutch Standard for fixing import duties.[17] Nevertheless, special agents continued to employ the polariscope as a means of checking the accuracy of Samplers and Appraisers.[18]

During September 1878 hearings held by Wood in his native New York, the Sugar Ring made sure its supporters, termed "loafers" by the press, filled the chamber, to the point where Collector Merritt could not even find a seat. When New York's chief Appraiser was summoned to testify, Wood pointedly asked whether he had been "annoyed by the interference of Special Treasury Agents." The witness replied that his office had not been directly affected, and furthermore, he "was not bound to follow the directions of these officers." The problem of fraud, if it existed, was at the docks, or so the Appraiser claimed. Theodore Havermeyer testified on behalf of the large refiners, who specialized in importing dark sugar taxed at the lowest duty, which he maintained was the only way to provide an affordable product for the working class. Defending the current tariff system, Havermeyer denied charges the government was losing $5 million annually, as some claimed, and went on to assert he did not believe sugar frauds had exceeded a total of $10,000 in the past five years. Furthermore, changing the current system would destroy an industry built up over years at the cost of millions of dollars and drive thousands of men out of work. Why, he asked, would the government want to throw refining to Cuba, when U.S. refiners can take low grade sugar and refine it here. There had been no complaint until centrifugal-processed sugar with a high saccharine level began to arrive from Demerara (Guyana) that was "undoubtedly colored," a problem he felt could be eliminated by use of the polariscope, as already done in France and England. (At one point an argument broke out between Havermeyer and a witness, claiming to have proof of fraud, who shouted: "I tell you that fraud on the revenue is the father; adulteration is the mother; and the polariscope is the child.")[19]

In January 1879, a deputation from Baltimore, including William Perot, presented a petition to the Wood Committee, signed by leading importers in that city and New York, which requested "a competent expert in the manufacture of sugar" be sent to Demerara to see whether sugar there was being artificially colored as the government alleged. That same day, a representative for Boston refiners argued for combining a simplified version of the Dutch Standard with use of the polariscope to assess duties. In advancing the so-called "Boston Plan," he did not think the polariscope too complicated for Customs officers to use, but admitted women might be better suited for this task.[20]

Hoping to influence the latest round of Congressional hearings and concerned about the growing influence of the Sugar Ring in their city, New York's civic leaders planned a public debate on 6 January to discuss changes to the tariff and protest adulteration of sweeteners sold to the public. Forewarned refiners planned to pack the hall beforehand to prevent moderates from being seated and to intimidate speakers, organizers arranged for police to guard the entrance. Thus, when "a large body of rough-looking men" showed up early, they were sent across the street, where they remained until told to go home by refinery owner Havemeyer, already well known for his earlier denials of fraud before the Wood Committee. Among the notables who made it inside were special agents Chamberlin and Crawford Adams, described in the press as having "charge of the alleged sugar frauds." Unfortunately for those expecting a civil discourse of the issues, the refiners, unwilling to countenance any further airing of their activities, managed to slip enough supporters inside to disrupt proceedings. In the forefront was Havermeyer's personal secretary, who forced his way onto the podium to argue with scheduled speakers. In the heated oratory that followed, one speaker compared the conviction of Customs Inspector Grace for exposing corruption to the hanging of John Brown. As the refiners planned, the meeting finally adjourned without being able to pass any resolutions calling for reform, an outcome that further undermined several cases Elliot was pursuing in the city.[21]

While occupied that fall with the Perot trial, Elliot had arranged for Crawford Adams, then acting as Tingle's deputy, to take over his investigations in New York. After the jury rendered its verdict in Baltimore, Elliot hurried north to confer with Adams but was disappointed to learn little had been accomplished during his absence. (In his diary, he now admitted it would be very hard to prosecute the corrupt inspectors and samplers already identified, although he was still determined to do his best.) After a quick trip to Washington to confirm Secretary Sherman still supported an aggressive approach towards the culprits, he returned with Tingle in December to pursue the cases. One press account linked their presence to confessions of wrongdoing by several samplers, resulting in their suspension from the customhouse, with more expected to follow. While Elliot managed to spend a brief Christmas holiday with his family in Baltimore, his investigations were not completed until mid-January. Despite everything, he was unable to persuade the New York District Attorney to bring any sampler to trial. Many years later, he bitterly recalled that, while several were temporarily removed, or transferred to other duties, most returned to their old jobs.[22]

In the end, his Baltimore and New York investigations resulted in only partial victories for the government. He had begun both with the zeal of a crusader, but political and administrative realities prevented him from gaining a conviction in court. Nevertheless, he accomplished more than he may have realized, especially in New York, where his actions reduced the level of corruption in the customhouse, and ultimately weakened the hold that Conkling's machine held over it. (In his monthly report for March 1879, Elliot estimated that changes to the way sugar was evaluated in New York had resulted in an additional $5,000 per day in revenue.) Moreover, the broader modifications he helped Merritt institute became a model for Civil Service reform elsewhere. The Baltimore trial also sent a clear signal to the sugar industry, with the result that importation of colored sugar began to decline, and revenue from the sugar tariff increased nationwide.[23]

* * * * *

During February and March 1879, Elliot pursued a case involving "bay oil," an extract made from leaves of the tropical bay plant for use in medicinal remedies. Henry Gover came to New York to assist in the investigation, which resulted in a seizure of bay oil and the smuggler's capture. Crawford Adams congratulated Elliot on his success and reminded him to keep the matter out of the press until he was assured of receiving his bounty. (Customs officers earned a percentage, or moiety, of assets recovered for the government, a system that augmented their salaries considerably.)[24]

To Edith's annoyance, her husband was still in New York when Adams's wife, Ada, paid an unexpected visit. Feeling the effects of another pregnancy, she remained at home, while Ayer and her mother escorted Ada around Baltimore. The guest shared a bed with Edith and the two stayed up until 3:30 one night discussing their husbands, although she assured Elliot she had "told no secrets." He had forgotten their wedding anniversary the day before and her only consolation was praise Ada lavished on their household. Still, she was pleased to think her husband was doing his part to "purify that corrupt place" (New York).[25]

A trip to gather information on the manufacture of centrifugal-processed sugar in Cuba occupied Elliot and Henry Abbott, now employed as a special inspector, throughout April and May. Prior to their departure, Elliot went to Washington to pick up essentials for the voyage: a $1,000 travel advance, passport,[26] portfolio, pocket inkstand and stationery. After obtaining visas from the Spanish Consulate in New York, the two embarked on 10 April. In a letter to Edith after reaching Havana, he boasted of eating five meals a day on board ship, despite rough weather that made most passengers seasick. From his hotel room overlooking the harbor, he watched the "natives" loading cargo on the docks, his view framed in the distance by parched hillsides that reminded him of Loudoun in August. He was finding everything "new and strange" in this, his first exposure to a foreign culture. Exploring the narrow streets, he encountered typical Spanish architecture with heavy doors and barred windows on the outside, shielding living quarters that opened onto interior courtyards. Streets were deserted during mid-day siesta, but the night before he found cafes and saloons teeming with people "drinking wine and jabbering Spanish…I saw but a few ladies and those all bare-headed and painted. I see no [real] ladies on the streets, or anywhere else, but suppose there are some somewhere…" Puffing on his own "pure Havana" as he wrote, he related to his wife how everyone smoked cigars, including priests and women.

A call on the American Consul General went "nicely," and he planned to visit some nearby plantations before proceeding to the main sugar-growing area around Cardenas. "Everybody talks of sugar and all do not deny that it is colored." To his dismay, he found "N.Y. sugarmen here and, notwithstanding all my Care, our arrival was known." Viewing this trip and a similar one the following year as covert activities, he had even developed a code for use in communications with the Treasury Department.

Anxious to get out into the countryside, he got "rid of [his] flannels," in favor of native cotton garb, and was sure his wife would enjoy Havana, which he found safe ("soldiers are to be seen everywhere") and quite healthy in the dry season. Once he had seen the interior and picked up enough Spanish "to get along," he promised to tell her more about "Cosas de Cuba." Then, after advising Edith to "try and get along without me, and I expect you will very comfortably," he added in a postscript what was probably foremost on her mind—that he had arranged to have $120 sent to her from Washington.[27]

"Cuba, The Great Sugar Industry." Satirical reference to exploitation of slave labor on Cuban cane fields, where slavery remained until 1886. (*Leslie's Illustrated*, 21Feb80)

Abbott and Elliot left Havana on 17 April for the eastern end of the island, where they toured twenty sugar plantations to observe the manufacturing process and gather samples for analysis back home. Various interviewees confirmed sugar was colored for the American market, but they never actually witnessed it being done. In Cardenas, they were joined by Peter French, an examiner from the New York customhouse—apparently sent to provide an independent check on their findings.

By the time they reached Cardenas, Elliot was markedly less enthusiastic about "Cuban things," even though the rainy season had arrived to ameliorate the heat and quench fires raging through the countryside. (He was apparently unaware that fields were customarily burned off in the tropics.) Despite occasional amenities, such as a champagne breakfast at one plantation, Elliot was homesick and hoped to return in time for Mamie's school exhibition. In one letter, he declared he could never be "induced to live here...The fleas and mosquitoes would be sufficient to drive me away." He dismissed Cardenas as having been settled by pirates and surrounded by a marsh, its growth into one the island's principal cities due solely to its railroad connections, which allowed vessels from all over the world to come and load sugar. It was the area's only export "of any importance," and he could not even find anything "interesting" to take back as a souvenir. While people on the plantations had been "very kind," what he saw of life on them was troubling: "There are no schools, no road system, no nothing that seems familiar. Sundays are the same as any other day...I wish I was home again." (He apparently assumes Edith is already aware that most workers in Cuban cane fields and refineries were slaves, the practice not being abolished until 1886.)

Continuing, he wrote that Colonel French was proving a pleasant addition to the group and would agree with their finding "before we get through with him." When they left Cardenas on the 29th, Elliot was outraged at their hotel bill. After his protests resulted in a substantial reduction, leading him to exclaim to his wife, "they have more respect for me than ever. These kind of men won't color sugar?... [In] my opinion they have done it and will keep at it, if they thought they would not be detected." They left Havana in early May aboard the *Niagara* and arrived in New York on the 13th. Elliot and Abbott's report was finished in June and published by the Treasury under the title *Report on Method of Manufacturing Sugar in Cuba*.[28] It begins with a lengthy description of samples obtained on the island, including one with dark color, as determined by the DS scale, and high saccharine content, as calculated by the polariscope. Also included are statements by owners and refinery workers, many of whom freely admitted to darkening high-quality sugar for the U.S. market. A variety of methods were employed, including molasses, and Elliot could end his report by stating with confidence that "iodine, aniline dies, and caramel...have been applied to the crystals of sugar after their completion, to give them a darker color than obtained in the natural process of manufacture."[29]

Upon receiving twenty days of sick leave to recuperate from the rigors of his trip, Elliot took Mamie (nine) to visit his family in upstate New York, where he could also treat his rheumatism in the baths at

Saratoga Springs. Edith, still pregnant, remained behind with their youngest child, Edward, while the other two children went to Loudoun with Grandmother Sarah. Once everyone left, Edith felt quite alone and fretted over Mamie's appearance. She had forgotten to pack her daughter's fan, an important adjunct to any young lady's wardrobe, and asked Elliot to buy one. "I so hope she will behave like a little queen, so that Papa will feel so proud of her." She then added that their boarder, Colonel Ayer, had taken her to a concert the night before.[30]

On their way north, Elliot and Mamie stopped in Albany to attend a GAR National Encampment, before proceeding to Saratoga, where they stayed with his uncle, George Chamberlin, and visited other relatives in the area. They arrived at Glens Falls on 26 June and spent the next five days with his twin sister, Ellen Martin. She seemed little changed from when he and Edith had visited her several years before, but Ellen's adopted son Frank had grown into a "fine young man" and worked in a local store. Elliot was impressed with the town's commercial development, which featured lumber mills extending six miles along its canal, and a large shirt and collar factory. Mamie, an avid angler, was ecstatic when her father took her fishing along the Hudson River. He in turn was pleased she was enjoying the trip, although her appetite had caused her to outgrow most of her underwear, or else Nellie's had been packed by mistake. On their return, they stopped again at Saratoga so Elliot could resume treatment at the baths. He had abstained from smoking for over a week but did not feel much better for the effort. Despite claims to have put business out of his mind, he worried the government would again be outmaneuvered by New York lawyers in a pending sugar case and asked his wife to relay some messages about this to Ayer.[31]

In September 1879, Secretary Sherman followed Elliot's advice and issued a controversial directive for Customs inspectors to ignore color and only assess sugar at its "true" value. Even with the aid of the polariscope, the order proved difficult to enforce and resulted in several lawsuits, which kept the "sugar question" alive for many years to come. That fall, Senator Morrill wrote to acknowledge receipt of Elliot's Cuba report and express hope it would be "properly appreciated at the Treasury Dept. Strange that all the Dem[ocratic] papers are down on the Government whenever I attempt to correct abuse and furnish the evidence of the Revenue Laws! But so it is, and in Congress I expect to find all the [illegible word] assailing all that you and others have done touching sugar, silk, marble or anything else where national leaks have existed in the Revenue." (Elliot was particularly proud of a system he and Henry Gover had developed for assessing imported marble, and silk was then widely smuggled into the country to satisfy the demand for women's fashion.)[32]

In January 1880, Elliot began preparations to visit sugar plantations and refineries in the British West Indies and Guyana. This time, he and inspector Henry Abbott would be accompanied by Frederick M. Endlich, a chemist from the Smithsonian Institution. Abbott's inclusion is puzzling, as he had already exhibited signs of being a management problem the previous fall, while working with Customs samplers in New York. At that time, he twice threatened his colleagues and refused to take orders, claiming to have "a private letter" from Secretary Sherman directing him to only "report to Mr. Chamberlin." Then, just two weeks before they were to depart, a charge appeared in the press that government witnesses "of notoriously bad character" in the earlier Perot trial had been rewarded with positions in the Baltimore customhouse. This pointed reference to Elliot's role in hiring Abbott indicated that his latest foray into the "sugar question" was being watched closely by his opponents. An additional cause for concern stemmed from Elliot's tendency to blur personal and business finances, repeatedly borrowing and lending money to colleagues at work. Shortly before they left for the West Indies, he lent Abbott $120 to sustain the inspector's family until his February salary arrived. Complications arose when Elliot, apparently learning of Abbott's earlier misbehavior, balked at certifying work the inspector had performed in New York, thus holding up his salary.[33]

As in the earlier trip, Elliot's team expected to gather evidence growers were shipping artificially colored sugar to the U.S., of particular importance now that a recent "English commission" claimed to have found no such sugar being manufactured in Demerara—British Guyana's sugar-growing region. (Assistant Secretary French sent a strong protest to the British Government on this point.) To assist the "American commission," the Secretary of State provided Elliot with a letter of introduction to U.S.

Consular officers in the region, asking them to render all necessary assistance. Eager to avoid the heat that had hampered their stay in Cuba, and with $3,500 in travel funds in his pocket, Elliot and his companions left New York on 5 February. Stopping at St. Thomas in the Danish West Indies a week later, he posted a short note to inform Edith of his onward travel.[34]

The only other letter to survive from this trip was sent from Roseau, the capital of Dominica, a small volcanic island in the British West Indies. Although the first four pages are missing, what remains makes clear that Elliot was thoroughly enjoying himself, in part due to the attention paid him by William Steadman, a leading merchant and plantation owner. The surviving account starts with a vivid description of Roseau's Sunday (22 February) market, filled with tropical fruits and vegetables brought into town on the heads of local women. After attending a Church of England service with Steadman and lunching at the latter's home, the businessman provided horses and his nephew as guide for Elliot and Abbott to see "Wotten Waven," a region filled with hot springs and geysers. They followed a treacherous path into the mountains, fording many streams along the way. Elliot marveled at the lush vegetation, which included tree ferns the size of peach trees. Smelling of brimstone and filled with jets of steam and pools of boiling water, their destination brought to Elliot's mind the "unformed regions" before creation. Abbott had turned back earlier, but, racing down the mountain at breakneck speed, they caught up with him on the edge of town. Although Elliot expressed great respect for their small, sure-footed horses, he admitted the ride down the rocky slopes had made him "fearful, and I am no coward of a rider."

Dominica only produced Muscavado (dark) sugars, and during visits with Abbott to plantations over the next two days Elliot found their output to be entirely different from the "artificially darkened" Demerara sugars. At one plantation he "bought out the right to run the mill" to his own specifications in order to leave in all the impurities, i.e., natural color. The results of his sampling more than satisfied him that his theories were correct and gave "the lie to the Demerara evidence" compiled by the British Commission. He then turned his attention to getting signed depositions before a magistrate to document his findings, "no easy matter" when the witnesses were all hard at work in the sugar mills. Elliot's ebullience was tempered by a lack of news from home, and by his growing impatience with Endlich, who was then on a two-day tour of "Boiling Lake," a tourist landmark near the volcano. "He has not as yet settled down to work and is all geology...Confound these strictly scientific fellows. He must do better or I will make a row."

But once satisfied he had accomplished all he could, and not wanting to miss the island's principal attraction himself, Elliot determined to reach "Boiling Lake" in one day, an outing normally requiring three. On the way, he was dumbfounded by the force of a recent eruption, which had shattered trees around the crater "into atoms." The thermal lake that normally covered several square miles with hot water and steam, had partially drained after the eruption to form a vast and colorful abyss more awe-inspiring than anything he could have imagined. Getting back to town by nightfall, Elliot gloated that an American had set "a record" in doing the round-trip in just one day.

The day before, a British naval vessel had brought the two teenaged sons of the Prince of Wales to view the aftermath of the recent eruption, and the town was decorated with banners for the occasion. On the evening he returned from the crater, Elliot found an invitation from the "President [*sic*] of the Island" to attend a dinner in honor of the royal guests. Hastily donning formal wear, he arrived at the Governor's House only a few minutes late. Afterwards, proud to have dined with the future George V, Elliot sketched a seating chart of the event for his wife, identifying himself on it as "your humble servant."[35]

On 28 February, Elliot's party left for Martinique, where they hoped to observe sugar production on the French island before proceeding to their next extended port of call on Barbados in early March. During this period, Elliot began a detailed log to record difficulties he was experiencing with his companions. On the first sheet, written on 8 March and marked "strictly confidential," he wrote that Abbott had become inexplicably surly and disrespectful. The inspector had openly questioned Elliot's expertise and termed their investigations on Dominica a waste of time, since almost all sugar grown there was for the British market. He had even challenged Elliot's authority to direct his actions, claiming this time to be working solely for Secretary Sherman. Despite a desire to abandon his subordinate and continue on his own, Elliot decided to ignore the man's "cussedness" for the time being. Endlich was described as "a good fellow," but interested in "*drink* more than anything else."[36]

In mid-March, Elliot and Abbott, now termed a "blackheart," almost came to blows, while Endlich continued to drink and spend his time gambling, all of which led their leader to conclude both men wanted to return home at once. These problems notwithstanding, the special agent was pleased with depositions collected on Barbados, and vowed: "Alone I can succeed and will." Some of the tension may have been the natural outcome of three men forced to live together for two months in unfamiliar surroundings but as team leader, Elliot should have headed off dissension before it reached the boiling point. With little supervisory experience outside of his years as a military officer, he reverted to this model during what he considered a covert mission demanding strict obedience to orders. Illness contributed to his difficulties, as his "record-breaking" climb on Dominica precipitated a crippling rheumatoid attack.[37]

On 24 March, the "commissioners" finally reached Georgetown, British Guyana's capital. By then, Elliot was too lame to visit plantations alone, but had trouble getting his colleagues to accompany him. The U.S. Consul arranged guest passes at a British club, where Endlich in particular made himself at home. Once, Elliot had to reprimand Abbott for using racial slurs against a Black sugar processor. They did get to visit one planation where they had been invited to observe the production of darkened sugar, although the actual method was not employed that day, perhaps to protect trade secrets, as Demerara sugar was far ahead of its competitors in producing dark sugar with very high saccharine level for the U.S. market. The strangest episode occurred when the team visited a plantation in the company of W. Yates Perot, son of the Baltimore importer, who had apparently been assigned to monitor their activities. The group departed for home soon afterwards and reached New York in late April. Their *Report on the Methods of Manufacturing Sugar in West India Islands and British Guiana* was published that summer under all three of their names. Highly technical and repeating many findings of the earlier Cuban report, it nevertheless made a useful contribution to the Treasury's campaign to change the manner in which sugar was graded. Elliot seemed particularly proud that his findings on Dominica had given the lie to Perot's assertion during his trial that the dark color in sugar seized from his ship was due to natural impurities. Above all, the Guyanese success in producing dark sugar with high saccharine content proved the futility of relying solely on the Dutch Standard to assess duties. Pleased by a favorable review of his latest report in the *Baltimore Sun*, Elliot ordered fifty copies for himself.[38]

During the remainder of 1880, he devoted greater attention to frauds associated with drawbacks claimed by American sugar processors. (One such practice involved the addition of domestic corn syrup to refined cane sugar to qualify for higher rebates.) He also met with the U.S. Consul assigned to Cardenas, Cuba, in an apparently successful effort to persuade the State Department to collect intelligence on overseas sugar production. The most contentious issue during this period concerned Secretary Sherman's earlier directive allowing Customs officers to use the polariscope to assess duties on sugar. Meant to stem abuses that Elliot and his colleagues had documented over the past three years, the order ran counter to existing tariff laws, which specified the Dutch Standard as the sole means for setting duties. Efforts by the Treasury Department to change the law were repeatedly stymied by Congressional Democrats and the sugar lobby. As a result, sugar importers in New York filed suit against Customs Collector Edwin Merritt to reclaim "excess" duties that had been "illegally" levied on them. That fall, Elliot made several trips to help the New York District Attorney prepare for the trial.

Since domestic sugar growers and refiners were thought to be adversely affected by the current tariff system, Elliot and Assistant Secretary French visited Louisiana at the end of the year, in a last-ditch effort to secure support from producers in that state for changes in the tariff law. Travelling by train, they spent two days in Charleston, South Carolina, to take in the sights, including visits to Fort Sumter. On Christmas Day, they boarded a train to Savannah, only to run off the tracks passing through "a swamp away from anywhere." The car carrying Elliot and French remained upright, but the engine completely overturned, and the first few passenger cars lay on their side. Quickly responding to the accident in a manner that earned praise from French, Elliot proudly related his actions to Edith: "Well, somehow I was cool and went to work, although raining hard. I broke in the door of the car next and helped the frightened people out, and then to the rescue of the engineer, who was jammed under the wreck of his engine, covered with debris." Standing in water over his waist and surrounded by steam from the hot engine, "I held the poor fellows head above the water, and directed the men to go to work...to rescue him. They obeyed every instruction, and he was taken out...not dangerously injured." After being stranded for nine hours, they finally reached Savannah that night. The next day was spent sightseeing, including a visit to the city's haunting cemetery filled with live oaks and hanging moss, before continuing their journey via a revenue cutter to Jacksonville, Florida.[39]

The remainder of their trip was apparently disaster-free, although their objective of securing the backing of Louisiana sugar growers failed to gain enough support in Congress to change the laws. After their return in January, Secretary Sherman, now very much a lame duck, made a final plea to the New York Chamber of Commerce to back new legislation. The Chamber, largely made up of Democrats, fired back a testy response demanding the Secretary rescind his earlier directive and refund all duties collected under it. Sherman had no chance of resolving the issue before he left office in March.[40]

Elliot returned to New York City to help the District Attorney defend Merritt in court. The President and his cabinet would be gone from office before the trial ended on 19 April. Once again, the government's position on sugar being artificially colored was sustained by the court, but the judge also ruled that the Treasury Secretary had exceeded his authority in sanctioning any tests besides the Dutch Standard mandated in the Tariff Act. According to one press account, the judge declared that he had never seen a case "more unprofessionally" presented by a federal attorney, and the verdict was widely viewed as a slap at Sherman's sugar policy. Despite the outcome, Elliot informed C/SAD Tingle that he was "satisfied that we have fully done our duty and fully sustained the order of the Secretary." Despite his prediction the case would be overturned on appeal, the New York Supreme Court upheld the lower court's decision, forcing the government to refund almost a million dollars. In a summary of his involvement in this entire episode several years later, Elliot tried to distance himself from the decision to use the polariscope, even though he had personally promoted its use.[41]

Despite such disappointments, his work on sugar during the Hayes Administration was probably the most professionally and personally satisfying period of his career as special agent. Unfortunately for him, Hayes had pledged not to seek a second term when he was nominated, and the country was set back for him keeping his word. Few other American Presidents have started their terms under such adverse circumstances and faced so many problems in their first year of office, all the while having to contend with a Congress controlled by forces opposed to them. While not charismatic, Hayes was a strong and principled leader who stuck by his beliefs, and in the end triumphed to an extent few thought possible. A good deal of his success must be credited to his cabinet members, Treasury Secretary Sherman in particular. Under the latter's stewardship, the nation emerged from years of economic doldrums into a booming economy. Despite a reputation as a colorless "technocrat," Sherman did not shrink from taking on his enemies, and often got a hostile Congress to back his programs. When it did not, as in the case of the New York customhouse and the sugar tariff, he was not above exceeding his prerogatives and taking action anyway. Sherman had been Hayes' heir designate, and Elliot was greatly disappointed when his boss failed to win the Republican nomination.

* * * * *

If there was one group of erstwhile supporters who were bitterly disillusioned with Hayes, it was southern Republicans, both Black and White. In the case of Virginia, the state party was so demoralized by his policies, it failed to field a candidate in the 1877 gubernatorial election. Adding to their woes that year was the emergence of the Readjuster Party under the leadership of Gen. William Mahone, a civil engineer who had commanded the Confederate defenses of Petersburg at the end of the Civil War. The entrepreneurial spirit and progressive economic views that would make him one of the state's leading railroad magnates also brought him into conflict with the ruling Conservative Party. Searching for a political base of his own, he had already tried at least twice to gain control of the Republican Party by the time of the 1877 elections. That year in Loudoun, two former Conservatives, Charles P. McCabe and John R. Carter, ran as independents for the state legislature and beat their Conservative opponents with help from Republicans, who had no one running from their party.[42] The winners later announced their intention to join Mahone's movement, and, as further defections occurred throughout the state, Conservatives and Republicans belatedly realized the Readjusters were a force to be reckoned with.[43]

During the next two years, Mahone and his allies fashioned a party composed of individuals whose interests were not being represented by the Conservatives in Richmond. They included Black residents in Virginia's Tidewater and Southside region, Whites from the Shenandoah Valley and Appalachia, and a growing urban working-class. Ironically, it was the same coalition radical Republicans tried to fashion during Reconstruction but let slip from their grasp. Readjusters took their name from their position that the state's enormous debt needed to be "readjusted" downward to prevent further increases to the already onerous taxes being paid by middle-class and poor citizens. They were bitterly opposed by "Funders," who believed Virginia had an obligation to honor debts incurred before the war. For the most part, Funders were supported by the Conservatives, or "Bourbons" as they were derisively called. Their position was hardly surprising, since the gentry class had the most to lose if the state devalued, or defaulted on, its obligations.

Virginia's 1879 election turned into a contest between Readjusters and Funders, with Republicans sitting on the sidelines. Lack of organization within the GOP was evident when, just days before the election, remaining executive committee members met in Richmond. Unlike at least two other committee members, Elliot had not resigned his position as chairman in accordance with Hayes' directive against holding outside political office. Nevertheless, he did not attend this meeting, likely due to the press of work, or the pending birth of his third son (Paul Chamberlin) on 31 October. In his absence, B. W. Hoxsey presided and called for a Central Committee meeting in January to ratify a party makeover in time for the 1880 presidential election. To aid this effort, Hoxsey asked former committee members to turn over any records in their possession. The party's disarray was further indicated by his plea for the general membership to identify party officers in each district, and if none existed, submit names of two party leaders in each county, as well as locate any Central Committee members, who had "not died, resigned, or moved out of the State."[44]

While Republicans remained mostly inactive that fall, Mahone and his supporters campaigned extensively throughout the Old Dominion, including a rally in Loudoun in late October. Unlike the rest of the South, where Republicans held power through the end of Reconstruction, Conservatives had ruled Virginia since 1870, and thus caught the blame for the economic slowdown that began in 1873. This and other consequences of their attempt to turn back the clock contributed to their defeat that fall, when the Readjusters captured fifty-six of one hundred seats in the House of Delegates and twenty-four of forty in the Senate, figures which included a few Republicans expected to vote with them.

Only in the Piedmont did the Funders/Conservatives retain their dominance, including in Loudoun, where Conservatives ousted their Readjuster opponents, McCabe and Carter, by narrow margins. (The year before, the Conservative legislature had sharply reduced the number of delegate and senate seats, which forced Loudoun Readjusters to campaign in the more hostile county of Fauquier.) The recent imposition of a "capitation tax" on voters also reduced, as its sponsors intended, turnout of Black and other working-class voters who might otherwise have backed the Readjusters. In addition, Loudoun Conservatives were helped by local Republicans, who ran no candidates in 1879. While this omission may have been intended to help the Readjusters, it further reduced turnout in north Loudoun, especially in Waterford, where many Quakers could not reconcile themselves to the fact that Charles McCabe had once been Loudoun's principal slave dealer, or that the Readjusters were led by a former Confederate general.[45]

One way the Conservatives retained control in counties like Loudoun was to relentlessly target the

Black population. A letter written in early 1880 by a Lovettsville resident, who himself was concerned by the threat of Black "equality with the Whites" under Readjuster rule, provides a stark picture of this oppression. "The Blacks are still getting worse. One is to be hung in Leesburg the 9th of April, and another broke out of jail at Leesburg, but they re-caught him near Hagerstown and have him in jail there. I guess he will be lynched. They watch very closely for him. One was lynched near Point of Rocks and one in Charles Town a few days ago. It is getting very common to hear of the honorable Negroes (so called by some of our colored white folks) being lynched."[46]

Aside from the backlash against the Black community described above, Mahone's stunning overall victory brought immediate suggestions from inside and outside the state for his party to merge with the remnants of Virginia's Republicans. In early November, John Tyler Jr., son of the former President, addressed a letter to President Hayes and Treasury Secretary Sherman, urging them to seize the moment and promote a union of the two parties. Tyler warned the fiscally conservative Hayes not to be misled by Bourbon propaganda, which had painted Mahone as a "repudiator" of government debt in general. Instead, the writer maintained that the important issue was Mahone's advocacy of a "policy...of progressive advancement in accordance with the spirit of the age and the Nation, and the Bourbons struggling in antagonism to both." But as Southern Republicans discovered to their dismay, their party's reform wing was focused on changing the North, not Dixie.[47]

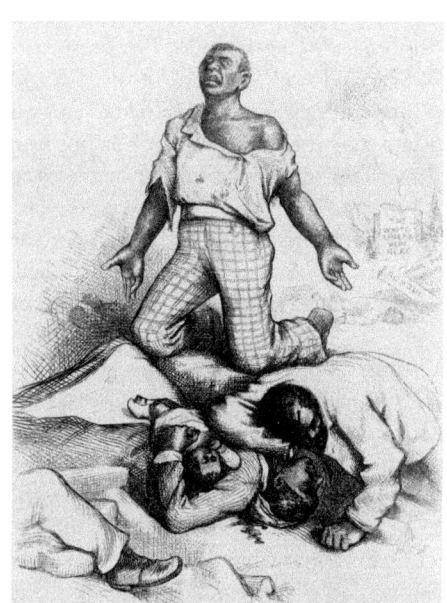

"Is *This* a Republican Form of Government?" Violence against the formerly enslaved dramatically increased as Federal troops withdrew from the South. (*Harpers Weekly*, 2Sep76)

Soon after the election, "Chairman" Hoxsey issued a statement implying his party favored a merger with the Readjusters. Learning that he had never been officially elected to that position, a reporter from a Conservative newspaper sought out Elliot, then in Richmond on business. "While not desiring notoriety and not wishing to have his name spread out before the public," Elliot refused to endorse Hoxsey's statements and pointed out the party was still governed by the platform adopted in 1876. His response reflected the position of most national Republican leaders, who were slow to grasp the significance of the Readjusters' victory and still viewed Mahone as a political maverick. (Elliot was also reflecting the opposition of most Waterford Quakers to any union of the two parties.) The following month, Mahone was elected by the legislature to the U.S. Senate, where he served six years as an independent, although usually aligned with the Republicans. (His influence grew in 1881, when Democrats and Republicans were tied in that body.)[48]

Elliot's interview was his last known public statement as a GOP state official. He had done little as executive chairman since Hayes' inauguration and was absent when the Central Committee confirmed Hoxsey as his replacement in January. At the state convention that spring in Staunton, the "Straight-Outs" resisted Readjuster efforts to take control of their party. Gen. (CSA) Williams C. Wickham, Mahone's rival in the railroad industry, presided over the stormy session and did more than anyone to prevent a merger of the two parties. (Wickham's allies reportedly resorted to setting off a fire alarm to delay a vote, when it appeared the Readjusters might prevail.) Whether this outcome was in the Republicans' best interests is open to debate. As to the pending presidential election, the convention followed Wickham's lead by endorsing Grant for a third term, an action revealing how out-of-step Virginia's GOP had become.[49]

During the ensuing decade, the "Bourbons" discarded their independent Conservative Party in favor of the national Democrats, and eventually wrested control of the Commonwealth back from the

Readjusters and pro-Mahone Republicans. In choosing to remain independent, the "Straight-Outs" failed to capitalize on the last serious opportunity for their party to exert significant influence in the state for more than a century. Of more immediate consequence to Elliot's Republican colleagues was Mahone's aggressive use of his leverage in the Senate to secure federal appointments for his followers. Those who opposed him, Conservatives and "Straight-Outs" alike, were targeted for removal from office. How this impacted Waterford postmaster Sam Gover and Treasury employee Annie Matthews is described in later chapters.

William Mahone, Confederate General, Railroad Magnate and Political Maverick. His Readjuster Party briefly united Black and disgruntled White voters. (VaSL)

Despite their leader's reversion to old-style patronage practices, the Readjusters proved to be much more than the "party of Repudiators composed of ignorant negroes and rascally whites" their enemies depicted. At a time when Bourbon "honor wouldn't buy a breakfast," they renegotiated the debt and restored the state's creditworthiness. The Readjusters deserve particular credit for championing public schools, which had languished under Conservatives who apparently preferred to deny free education to all rather than promote a system that included schooling Black students. (The number of public schools doubled under the Readjusters' four-year reign in Richmond.) Citing their progressive legislation in a variety of social and business fields, one historian declared that the Readjuster-controlled legislatures of the 1880s provided the most efficient and fiscally responsible administration Virginia would know until well into the twentieth century.[50]

Chapter 25

CLIFTON IS SAVED—AT A PRICE: 1878-1887

Edith Chamberlin's father, E. Y. Matthews, left an estate saddled with debt when he died in 1867. His creditors included in-laws Ann, Sam and Henry Gover, who held notes totaling more than $1,000, but the largest lien was the original $2,400 mortgage on Clifton. Like many Virginians, E. Y. stopped payment during the war, a practice that had the support of lenders who did not want to be paid in Confederate currency. The interest on such notes continued to mount, however, and by war's end, few debtors had sufficient greenbacks to pay off their loans. The Virginia legislature attempted to relieve this situation by passing legislation during Reconstruction that canceled pre-war debts, but these so-called Stay Laws were found unconstitutional in 1869. Similar laws to prevent repossession of "homesteads" were overturned by the courts in 1872. Much of the hatred towards carpetbaggers arose during this period, as Northern investors took advantage of the situation to purchase old family estates for far less than their pre-war value.[1]

With her older brother Henry living in Baltimore, Sarah Matthews persuaded a reluctant Sam Gover to serve as administrator for her husband's estate, although both would have been better served had she found someone who was not also a creditor. In his capacity as executor, Sam conducted an auction at Clifton in the fall of 1867, the proceeds of which ($1,800) went mostly to cover unpaid interest on the original mortgage, now held by Miss Eliza Worsley. In May 1870, Sarah Matthews arranged for Charles L. Wood, a prominent Winchester Quaker, to lend the family $1,500 at ten percent interest to pay off other pressing debts. The Wood note was secured by a second mortgage on the farm, and was signed by Sarah and Annie Matthews, as well as Edith and Elliot.

Complicating Sam's relationship with the Matthews heirs was a sense of obligation he felt towards his sister Ann Gover, who had also loaned Sarah's family money, and more recently had left her brother in charge of her affairs while she went out west to teach on a reservation. In culmination of a life-long interest in the welfare of Black and Native Americans, Samuel Janney accepted an invitation by President Grant in 1869 to become Superintendent of Indian Affairs in Omaha, Nebraska, a position he held until resigning for health reasons two years later. Ann was among several Quaker women who accompanied Janney to Nebraska, where she taught sewing to young Native American girls at a vocational school on the Pawnee Reservation.[2]

Despite his interest in agronomy, Elliot was ill-suited for the rigors of farming, and income from Clifton failed to halt the family's growing indebtedness between 1868 and 1877. Bad weather, the need to restock the farm and lack of a barn contributed to his difficulties before the 1873 economic depression ended all hope of turning the farm into a profitable dairy and orchard business. In January 1871, Elliot signed a promissory note for $507 to cover purchases made by the family at Sam Gover's store since his father-in-law's death. Yet, despite holding several outside jobs during the coming years, Elliot

Ann Gover and her Pawnee students. (C. 1871 photographs, TCC)

and his family continued to live beyond their means and owed Sam an additional $485 by the time they moved to Baltimore in 1877. Even the estate's receipt in 1873 of $683 from the U.S. Treasury to compensate for the loss of livestock during the Burning Raid did not keep Elliot from having to borrow $250 from Senator Justin Morrill a year later.

This decline in creditworthiness was documented by the R. G. Dun Company, the predecessor of today's Dun and Bradstreet. At the beginning of the decade, the company estimated Elliot owed only $150, and in 1873-74 he was described as "a man of means and responsibility with good standing and credit worth $10,000." The credit investigator obviously failed to discover the extent of the family's indebtedness, which was mostly held within the tightly-knit Quaker community. As noted earlier, Elliot also boosted his credit rating by overstating farm revenue and property value in the 1870 agricultural census, and in a new insurance policy obtained the following year. This situation changed dramatically in early 1875, when Dun reported that he only had "some little personal property, but very much [financially] embarrassed and caution advised." Later the same year, he was described as "very clever but involved. Is trying to get along and is now employed as a claims agent by the US Govt."[3]

Despite their financial difficulties, Elliot and Edith enjoyed a comfortable, if modest, lifestyle at Clifton, at least until the Panic of 1873 dried up sources for loans and forced creditors to recall their notes. The accompanying deflation placed an additional burden on debtors, who had to repay in dollars worth more than what they had borrowed. The family made no payment on the Wood note in 1873, prompting a demand for its retirement, plus an immediate payment of $500. In August 1874, Elliot finally sent a hundred dollar partial payment to Wood, explaining that rain had prevented threshing the wheat crop.[4]

In 1875, Eliza Worsley hired Powell Harrison, a prominent Leesburg attorney, to collect her mortgage, by then past due with $545 in unpaid interest. Elliot ignored the letter, and the matter lay dormant until the summer of 1877, when Sam Gover visited Harrison's office with an offer by the Matthews heirs to pay just the interest owed by the end of the year. Countering, Worsley demanded half of the interest within thirty days, and the balance by October. When no payment was received, Harrison entered Worsley's claim before the county court, which ordered an appraisal of Clifton done that fall. One appraiser described the property as having a good dwelling with piped-in water (possibly utilizing a system that stored rainwater), a horse and corn crib, little standing timber, and a sizable peach and apple orchard. He placed its total value at $7,100 and estimated the farm could be rented for $425 annually. James Walker, however, appraised its value at $6,000 and calculated potential rent at $375.[5]

By then, Elliot had moved to Baltimore and was probably aware that residency in another state would delay efforts by creditors to collect from the heirs. Edith and the children joined him a short time later, and Sarah Matthews remained at Clifton only long enough to help Sam Gover sell off the farm equipment, animals, crops, and remaining household effects. The November auction netted a disappointing $900, half the amount realized a decade earlier in the 1867 sale. Just as then, neither Edith nor Elliot was present. Once again, she did not want to watch the family's possessions sold, while he cited the press of work; but their absence only exacerbated differences with Sam. At the end of the year, the farm and dwelling were rented to Obediah Pierpoint for $400 per year.[6]

In January 1878, Sam wrote a chatty letter to his sister Sarah, informing her of developments since the sale. He had already used some of the proceeds to take care of small bills and had also authorized Pierpoint to make needed repairs at Clifton. All businesses in Waterford had been adversely affected by the depression, and Sam prayed his own store would survive to see better times. Fortunately, his post office now received mail on a daily basis, bringing customers into the store more frequently. In April, Sam forwarded the final auction receipts and expenses to Elliot, with the unwelcome news that all proceeds had been used to pay outstanding estate bills. Having heard his nephew-in-law was not satisfied with the sale, Sam wanted Elliot to know he had not charged for his services and "had never worked harder to make things bring their value." (Auction receipts confirm Sam bought a number of items at the sale.) As for Elliot's displeasure over a bill John Dutton presented for assistance rendered during the auction, Sam explained that his sisters, Ann and Sarah, had both agreed to Dutton's conditions beforehand. On the verge of bankruptcy himself, Sam hinted he might resort to legal action to collect what Elliot and his family still owed him. On other matters, he advised that James Walker and his son had filed suit to relocate the road in front of Clifton. Obediah Pierpoint favored the proposed alignment, which would move the road close to the stream and allow him to fence in the field on the farm's west side.[7]

After starting work in Elliot's office, Henry Gover was pressured into writing all correspondence pertaining to the Matthews estate. Elliot had more than a passing knowledge of the law, and his use of Henry may have been a ploy to legally distance himself from the case. In March 1878, Winchester lawyer Marshall McCormick wrote Henry about the necessity of paying off the Wood note. Meanwhile, Elliot and the other defendants in the Worsley case failed to appear in the Loudoun court twice that spring, later claiming their summonses were improperly served at their Maryland address.[8]

In June, Henry Heaton, a Loudoun attorney and member of the Virginia legislature, took over the Worsley suit after Powell Harrison died. Receiving no response to his first inquiry to Henry Gover, Heaton reiterated his client's demands in a second letter, which hinted Worsley was prepared to proceed no faster than necessary and might show "some indulgence" in allowing the defendants time to obtain alternative financing. Puzzled at not yet hearing from any of the heirs, Heaton asked Henry why all their correspondence passed through him. Favorably impressed by Heaton's conciliatory approach, Elliot arranged in late June to meet him in Washington and came away from their talk more convinced than ever the court could not order Clifton's sale any time soon. Consequently, the family continued to ignore orders to appear in court.[9]

Matters came to a head in early 1879, when Wood's lawyer (McCormick) filed a petition to have his client's note included in any settlement of the Worsley suit. Possibly aware that Heaton continued to correspond with Henry Gover about the possibility of settling with Worsley out of court, McCormick initiated legal action in February requiring the sale of the farm to pay off the Wood note, which now included over $1,000 in unpaid interest. After attempts to reach a compromise failed, Sam warned his brother Henry in April that an order for the sale of Clifton was imminent.[10]

Having exhausted all delaying tactics, the heirs hired Ed Nichols, a Quaker lawyer in Leesburg, to represent their interests. In April, Henry Gover informed Nichols that the interest on the Wood note was proving ruinous to the Chamberlins and should be renegotiated downward. Explaining the heirs had no source of income besides Elliot's salary and the farm rent, Henry added "in confidence" that any chance of his nephew coming up with additional funds was "just impossible." Since Elliot's marriage, the family's debts had "greatly increased," and "from his habits there is *no probability* of his doing better and his friends do not want to assist with this debt." Pointing out the farm was likely to bring less than $5,000 in the current market, or less than the liens on it, Henry suggested Wood would do better to reach a compromise.[11]

As a first step to ordering the farm's sale, the court gave creditors until July to file liens against the estate. In addition to the Wood note and Worsley mortgage, the decree specifically mentioned debts owed Sam Gover. Since the estate had been completely exhausted except for the farm, Sam now openly advocated its sale as the only way he and his sister Ann could recover loans made to E. Y. Matthews, plus $400 in out-of-pocket expenses he had incurred as executor, all of which further exacerbated his relationship with the heirs.[12]

One of the most bizarre aspects of their escalating dispute were extracts that Elliot surreptitiously copied from Sam's diary for August-September 1879. How or when he got access to the diary is not known, but Sam's unvarnished comments about Elliot and Edith did little to smooth over relations between the two parties. As in the previous summer, the Chamberlins arranged to board with Sydnor Barrett outside of Waterford to escape Baltimore's heat. Sam had the following to say about their visit, written in the form of a dialogue with God:

> 8.7.79...I have known for a long time E[lliot] did not like me, but that made no difference to me as thee knows he has but very little common sense and I have tried for a long time not to get angry at what he said or done, or at least show it. I have always endeavored to show no appearance to sister S[arah] or Edie. I have felt for them for a long time and have known that although they wanted to make the best showing they could, it was not altogether as pleasant as they would like. But I am and always have been at a loss to know what I have done that is objectionable to him...I have always thought it was all put on because he would not pay me anything, and he had a little shame for that...I only fear that I have not all of his first accounts [to show what I am owed]...but for the last several years I have, and would be glad to have one or two good men look over it, such as Col Ayer. They would very soon see that I had not only furnished supplies for the family, but paid bonds and furnished money for the family, and sometimes suppose for him to travel on, as he would be at home until Edie would come in and borrow a few dollars...I shall endeavor to lose no more in fortune to them than I can help. His note [for $507], if he goes on in this way, I shall secure on his interest in the farm...

> 8.19 Edie was very distant last 7th day, the 1st time we have met. I *don't expect* it to make any difference in my actions or treatments with them, but as to Elliot I never want to come in contact with him again. There are things I don't wish to write.

> 9th first 79 Sister S[arah] and Annie [Matthews] did not get to see us as they kept sending word they would. Elliot and Edie came down to R[achel] Steer's yesterday to dine and went from there to Clifton saying they were coming to my house to tea, but I did not look for them and was not disappointed. I am a little [angry?] at Sister S. & Annie, but I guess it will all come right in time...[I]f they don't pay some of the Wood debt soon, the place will be sold, and...I have about come to the time that I would about have what is coming to me as not and that is the only way I can get it...

> 9-10-79 Sister S and Annie have been with us since 1st day. Went back home yesterday. A very short visit. I think E & E had everything to do with it. They made the arrangements for Edith to come for them yesterday and soon after dinner Morrill came in and said his father was waiting for them at Aunt Sallie's. I don't think they were pleased...their stay was so short. I intended to have some talk with them but did not until just before they left...I told [Sarah [I did not expect to go to his house. She said that was best and would hurt him more than anything else. I want a chance with Sister S. and Edith some time.[13]

On 7 October, the court finally ordered the defendants to sell the farm to pay their debts. Elliot was in Leesburg that day and gave Wood's attorney a $600 payment on the note in return for an agreement not to foreclose on Clifton before April 1880. By then, both sides had worked out a satisfactory repayment schedule, enabling the heirs to retire the Wood note in May 1881. The saga was not over, however, as the Matthews estate could not be settled until the Worsley mortgage and debts claimed by Sam and Ann Gover were paid.[14]

Sam was initially content to allow the family to pay off Wood's note before pressing his own claim. The situation changed in April 1881, when he learned the Readjusters were trying to replace him as Waterford's postmaster. He had no intention of seeking assistance from Loudoun's Readjuster leader, Charles McCabe, and doubted it would help anyway. Instead, he wrote Edith to see if her husband could use his contacts to help him keep the position. She encouraged Elliot to see what he could do, pointing out he would be blessed for his good deed, since "the greater the cross, the more glorious the crown."[15]

Whether Elliot took any action is unknown, but the following month the Readjusters announced Aaron Beans would be replacing Sam as postmaster. According to the local press, "Samuel hied himself away to the P.O.D. and on returning stated that he had been represented there by somebody, to be a Democrat, and that he had set that matter right." He was congratulated on the streets of Leesburg about his apparent victory over the locally unpopular Readjusters. Suspecting this reprieve would not last, Sam offered a week later to reduce his claims against the Matthews estate by $200, in return for an agreement to refund the rest owed him in a timely manner, but once again his offer to negotiate was ignored.[16]

In November 1881, Sam wrote Elliot to thank him for a $200 draft, which Sarah had delivered while he was in Baltimore to attend Yearly Meeting. Since the money had been given without instruction as to what it was for, or so he claimed, Sam credited it against the $507 personal note his nephew signed in 1871. This action infuriated Elliot, who expected the money would be used to reduce Sam's claims against the estate, not his personal debt to Sam. Sam's letter, however, left little doubt the author knew what Elliot's reaction would be beforehand, since he had hoped to discuss the matter with him while in Baltimore, "and should have gone to thy office, had I not met thee on the street and thy refusing to acknowledge friendship."[17]

The following month, Sam complained to Henry about receiving two abusive letters from Elliot about his disposition of the $200 and handling of the estate. Up until that point, Sam claimed to have had no idea the heirs doubted the accuracy of his accountings, but as executor he promised to resolve this matter as soon as they returned estate records he had lent them several years earlier. Aware that Heaton had recently written Elliot about retiring the Worsley mortgage, Sam saw no reason why his claims could not be paid at the same time. Furthermore, after extending credit to family and friend alike for many years, he now had four young children to care for and was left with no choice but to demand repayment.[18]

That winter, Nichols repeatedly reminded Elliot of the need to find investors to replace the old mortgage but emphasized no one would lend money until the dispute with Sam was resolved. Elliot's lawyer also asked him to return Sam's accountings, which were the property of the court. In a carefully-worded reply, Elliot urged Nichols to arrange financing for a new mortgage on Clifton, but hedged about turning over the accounts, and repeated his position that the $200 had been delivered to Sam with the understanding of all parties it would be used to pay off debts against the estate. For the first time, Elliot hinted Sam's claims were no longer legally enforceable, the statute of limitations having expired.[19]

A few days later, Nichols read Elliot's letter aloud to Sam, who fired off an angry response to his sister Sarah. Offended over being called a liar, he was also bitter his sister did not even bother to answer his letters. Despite abhorrence at the thought of having to go to court to claim what was justly due him, "if that is the only way, then let it come, for a settlement we must have." He, too, warned no one would lend money until Sarah's family had settled its debts, and also let it be known he had obtained legal advice refuting Elliot's assertion the notes were no longer enforceable. In March, Nichols informed the heirs that Sam had initiated a legal suit to reclaim what was owed him, in part because Elliot had challenged him to do so. As to potential investors, Nichols informed them the primary candidate had gotten tired of waiting and put his money elsewhere.[20]

At this point, Henry wrote three letters pleading with Sam and Ann Gover to drop their claims against the estate in return for assurances the heirs would make good on the outstanding notes, and to credit the $200 to the estate. While Sam ignored the latter request, he and Ann advised the court they no longer had outstanding claims against the Matthews estate. As a result, the Worsley mortgage was finally retired in April 1882, and Elliot, Edith, Annie and Sarah signed a new six percent lien on Clifton for $2,500 that was co-signed by Ed Nichols and Robert Walker as trustees. Despite making annual payments of $150 until this note was rolled over in 1906, the family never succeeded in reducing the principal.[21]

Matters appeared settled until early 1883, when Nichols wrote that Sam was still angry at not having received the money the family had promised to pay in return for not attaching these debts to the estate. (By then, the political winds had further shifted against Loudoun Republicans like Sam, who not only lost his position as postmaster to a Readjuster in 1882, but also as town alderman and board member of the Loudoun Mutual Insurance Company.) In the exchange of letters that followed, Elliot pointed to the court's earlier declaration that the estate no longer had any outstanding debts, and claimed not to know to what Nichols and Sam were referring. In May, Sam arranged for Nichols to reopen his suit against Elliot by placing a lien against Edith's share of the farm. When Elliot ignored Nichol's advice to reach an agreement with his client to avoid an embarrassing court fight, Sam tried to get Henry to help adjudicate the dispute, but his brother instead quit Elliot's office and moved to Philadelphia to escape further entanglement in the feud.[22]

In October, Sam wrote Sarah to explain his side of the story. He had thought the matter settled and was shocked to learn that she and the other heirs now claimed to owe him nothing. Deeply regretful at having let the family talk him into serving as executor, he nevertheless had tried to get Elliot to attend the auction that had ignited their dispute. If absolutely necessary, he was still determined to go to court, but hoped Sarah could persuade her son-in-law to settle, suggesting they let Nichols mediate. It would be the "mistake of our life" to let the suit go forward, he emphasized, as the family would never be the same. "The older ones of us here will soon pass away, but the younger ones of the families will never get over it."[23]

Days before the January 1884 trial began in Leesburg, Sam wrote a final, bitter letter to Sarah stating that, unless a settlement was reached, he could no longer consider himself related to her and the Chamberlins and would henceforth communicate with them only through Henry. He disagreed that one of his letters to Elliot had precipitated the current crisis and was deeply hurt his own sister and nieces had branded him a cheat and a liar through their "agent" (Elliot). Convinced his "sainted mother and father" would have sided with him, he predicted his accusers' behavior would come back to haunt them, just as had happened to the descendants of Elijah James after he took the Govers' pigs.[24][25]

Several days later, the court ruled in Elliot's favor on the grounds the statute of limitations had run out. Sam then began a lengthy appeal, arguing the limitation period restarted once Elliot made the $200 payment, and citing evidence Henry Gover had been acting within the last five years as Elliot's agent during negotiations concerning the 1871 note. In November 1885, Henry complained to Elliot from Philadelphia over receipt of a summons in connection with his brother's appeal. Exasperated, he asked, "Is there no way to settle this vexed question without dragging me into it again? Thee is certainly aware of my repugnance...Can you not settle by some means without going into a vexatious law court, as it will only be settled by *men* wherever it is tried."[26]

The case dragged on until April 1887, when the appeals court in Richmond upheld the lower court's decision by refusing to grant a new trial. Elliot's lawyer had successfully argued that, when Sam improperly credited the $200 to the 1871 note, he had brought the total value under dispute below the $500 minimum required for a case to be heard at the state level. From the vantage point of over a century, the whole episode was a "tempest in a teapot," which should have been settled out of court. The protagonists, however, felt otherwise. Not only was their honor at stake, but the amount involved represented a significant sum to two men with large families. In his successful fight to hold on to Clifton and

Sam Gover and Temperance Matthews. (1869 Wedding pictures, courtesy of descendant Mary Ellen McFann)

minimize what was owed, Elliot showed a resourcefulness and legal cunning that served his side of the family well. When these talents were turned against another family member, they appear less admirable. Unfortunately, the particulars which led Elliot and the heirs to believe Sam had deliberately falsified his accounts have not survived, although on several occasions Sam agreed mistakes had been made. His prediction the dispute would have a lasting effect on the family was borne out, and until beginning research on this book, the author was unaware of even having Gover ancestors.

Even though Sam was reinstated as Waterford's postmaster after the Republicans returned to the White House in 1887, this time he failed to bounce back from the combined effects of two economic depressions, loss of business when the post office was in a rival store, and costly legal fights with Elliot and others. As a lifelong Republican, Sam found little support in the county courthouse, and as late as 1890 was still engaged in mostly futile suits to collect unpaid store bills. Later that year, Sam finally had had enough; he sold his business to seek a more favorable setting for his family in Washington. His sister Ann's death in 1896 left Waterford without any Govers for the first time in more than a century, and the Fairfax Meeting, already in a state of decline, would sorely miss the family, which had proved mainstays in so many ways.[27]

One of Sam's first endeavors after the move was to represent claimants still seeking compensation for losses suffered during Sheridan's Burning Raid. Congress approved a bill in 1873 to reimburse claimants for $60,000 in livestock seized during the raid, but efforts to recover $200,000 in destroyed property had not met with success. In the fall of 1890, Sam Gover collected signatures from representatives of the original claimants (Sarah Matthews signed on behalf of her husband's estate) on a petition designating him their "sole Agent and Attorney in fact" in pursuing the property claims. He also received small amounts from claimants to cover his expenses, although Elliot and Edith's names were notably absent from a list of contributors. In return for his services, Sam would receive ten percent of any amounts granted by Congress. Teaming up with lobbyist Clinton A. Rice, Sam succeeded in bringing a bill before the House in 1891, but it did not pass, and a similar effort failed the following year.[28] After Rice returned to New York, Sam retained the legal services of Charles P. Janney of Leesburg and Jonas H. McGowan of D.C. to push the claims. When another bill failed to pass Congress in 1895, and without funds to pay further legal and lobbying fees, Sam turned over his rights to any settlement to Janney and McGowan. The two lawyers were able to get bills introduced into Congress in 1899 and 1901, but neither passed, and the project was eventually abandoned.[29]

In 1891, Sam tried to obtain employment at the Treasury Department as a "watchman, messenger, or laborer." Now sixty-nine years old, he listed himself as much younger in the application, which was endorsed by numerous friends, including a petition signed by prominent Loudoun Republicans. Unsuccessful in getting hired, Sam and his son, Henry Taylor Gover, opened a small grocery store in Washington D.C., where he worked until shortly before his death in 1907. By then he had, according to his son, hardly a penny to his name, although among his papers was found a $1,000 note owed him by Colonel Chamberlin "on which not a penny had been paid." Perhaps the saddest aspect of Sam's later life was the continued ostracism by Elliot's family. In 1897, Sam wrote his sister Sarah: "Some time ago I wrote thee, & asking for an answer. I think common politeness & respect if nothing else would have guaranteed it. I now ask thee to please let me hear from you. Affectionately, S. A. Gover." At the time, they lived only blocks apart, yet they probably never saw each other before she died three years later.[30]

* * * * *

As might be expected, Clifton did not always fare well during its extended period of absentee ownership. The exception may have been the tenancy of Obediah Pierpoint, a respected member of Fairfax Meeting, who rented the farm and dwelling from 1878 until the end of 1883. As previously noted, the 1880 census showed him running the farm on a profitable basis for the first time in years, although how well he maintained it is not known. With claims against the Matthews estate seemingly settled, Elliot felt free in March 1884 to draw up an agreement with John W. Mullen to run the farm on shares for the next two years. (Mullen's brother, Michael, was Sam Means' orderly sergeant in the Loudoun Rangers.) Share-cropping became common during Reconstruction as a way for Southern plantation owners to rent out land to cash-poor formerly enslaved persons. By the late 1870s, declines in agricultural prices caused by deflation, restrictive fiscal policy and economic depression made it harder to find traditional renters in areas beyond the Deep South, and led to the spread of crop-sharing as a way to spread the risk of an uncertain market between owner and tenant.

The complex arrangement Elliot drafted required Mullen to deliver half of any wheat grown on the farm to the Clarkes Gap train station, apparently for sale in D.C. He was also required to leave two-fifths of the corn in the crib and the same amount of the hay crop in a stack, presumably for consumption by the owners' animals. The cost of seed and fertilizer was split evenly, while all labor and hauling would be provided by the tenant. Mullen had the right to graze four horses and four cattle of his own. Additional cattle would be purchased with capital provided by the owner, with the proceeds split evenly when sold, although Mullen would also have to deduct interest on funds thus provided. Aside from maintaining the farm and fences in good order, he was to keep the orchard trimmed and deliver one-third of harvested "winter fruit" to the owner, plus any other fruit the owner might require. Elliot agreed to pay for necessary repairs to farm buildings and reserved the right to use "part of the dwelling during the summer months." That summer, Edith and the children stayed at Clifton for the first time in seven years.[31]

After that agreement expired, the family arranged for former Loudoun Ranger private Charles T. Moreland to reside at Clifton as a caretaker, while much of the cropland was leased to neighbors. After the breakup with Sam Gover, Elliot and his family switched their business to a competing store in Waterford run by Flavius J. Beans and Lemuel P. Smith, both of whom were married to distant cousins of Edith. (Flavius's uncle, the Readjuster/Democrat Aaron Beans, set up his post office in this store during the two periods he replaced Sam Gover as postmaster.) An account kept by the Beans & Smith store during 1886-87 documents that Moreland was allowed to run up purchases of groceries and other supplies during months the family was not using Clifton, presumably part of his compensation as caretaker. This arrangement lasted at least into 1891, when Elliot wrote Moreland with specific instructions for getting the house and grounds ready for the family's arrival that summer.[32]

Chapter 26

SPECIAL-AGENT-IN-CHARGE, BALTIMORE: 1880-1885

Despite Rutherford Hayes' longstanding promise not to seek reelection, there was still no consensus over who should replace him by the time Republicans convened in Chicago in June 1880. The "Stalwart" faction, led by New York Senator Roscoe Conkling, favored running Ulysses Grant for a third term. The other principal contenders were Senator James Blaine of Maine and the reform wing favorite, Treasury Secretary John Sherman. Grant held the lead through thirty-five ballots, at which point Blaine threw his support to Ohio's Representative James A. Garfield, who up to that point had been Sherman's campaign manager. With the combined delegates of Blaine and Sherman, Garfield easily won the next ballot. To appease the Stalwarts, Garfield offered the vice-presidency to Chester A. Arthur, the "Gentleman Boss" whom Hayes had removed from the New York customhouse two years earlier. At the time, reformers rationalized that Arthur's "powers of mischief" would be minimal, given the slight chances of Garfield's dying in office. Having learned a lesson from the last two elections, the Democrats selected a Civil War general of their own, Winfield Scott Hancock, as their standard-bearer.[1]

Elliot had worked closely with Garfield to organize veterans for Hayes, but preparation of his report on West Indies sugar precluded participation in the early stages of the present campaign, and even then was largely confined to serving as Virginia's representative to the "National Union of the Army of the Boys in Blue," as the Republican Veterans' Committee was now called. On 1 October, Drake DeKay and General Grant signed his commission as the Union's vice-president with the rank of "general," and the following week, Elliot attended the "Boys in Blue" national convention in Indianapolis, which featured the same "bloody shirt" rhetoric that had characterized Hayes' campaign. His apparent failure to take an active part in the final weeks of electioneering suggests an unwillingness to jeopardize his career in the event of a Democratic victory. In the end, Garfield won by the smallest plurality in American history, a mere 9,000 votes. (The Republicans lost Virginia by a wide margin, however, and the results were similar in Loudoun, where only a few towns, including Waterford, voted for Garfield.) Despite these losses in his home state, Elliot was elated by the overall outcome, and his expectations of increased access to the White House were further bolstered when he received a special invitation to attend events connected with Garfield's inauguration in March 1881. Still, concerns over the new vice-president must have lingered in his mind, and he could only hope Arthur might overlook his role in getting him removed as Customs Collector.[2]

Hayes lobbied with his successor to keep Sherman as Treasury Secretary, but Garfield feared his retention would further alienate the Stalwarts and chose Minnesota Senator William Windom instead.

Invitation to March 1881 Inaugural Ball for James Garfield and Chester Arthur at the National Museum [Smithsonian "Castle"]. (TCC)

Although sorry to see Sherman go, Elliot was heartened by early indications the new administration planned to continue reforms in the Customs Service. As it turned out, the defining event of Garfield's four-month presidency was his decision to fight for the appointment of William Robertson to head the New York customhouse after the Senate's initial refusal to confirm his nominee. Robertson was opposed by the Conkling machine, which hoped to regain control of civil service appointments in New York once Hayes left office. In an ill-advised move, Conkling persuaded fellow New York Senator Thomas ("Me Too") Platt to join him and resign their seats in protest. Both expected the state legislature to return them to office and thereby deliver a rebuke to Garfield. When the legislators failed to reinstate either man, the U.S. Senate quickly ratified Robertson's appointment. Like his predecessor, Garfield viewed control of New York's customhouse as the key to determining whether the President was merely "a registering clerk of the Senate, or the Executive of the United States."[3]

Garfield's term was cut short by an assassin's bullet on 2 July 1881, and while he clung to life until September the nation was without an effective leader. The man who fired the shot had connections to New York's political bosses, and publicly declared he shot the President after being rejected for an appointment in the new administration. The tragedy had the positive effect of focusing attention on the Byzantine appointments system, which led to renewed calls for reform. In January 1883, Congress passed the Pendleton Act, thereby laying the foundation for the country's first truly professional federal workforce. Amplifying Hayes' earlier executive order, the bill prohibited forced political contributions, established competitive tests for hiring and promotion, and restricted dismissals on political grounds. Initially, the regulations only covered twelve percent of government personnel and excluded many categories of workers, including Treasury special agents and most employees outside Washington.

Garfield considered Hayes' policy on the appointment of Southerners to federal positions a dismal failure, and in the months before his assassination tried to place control of southern patronage back in the hands of the traditional Republican state parties, even though they were still mostly dominated by Black persons and "carpetbaggers." Upon assuming office, President Arthur reversed this initiative, opting instead to rely on defectors from the Southern Democratic Party. Chief among them was Senator William Mahone of Virginia who, according to a contemporary critic, informed all federal officeholders in the state they must cooperate with his Readjuster Party or lose their jobs. "A few obstinate ones were actually removed, and their places filled with Readjusters. It did not take many lessons of this sort to teach the new political faith…All semblance of organized Republican opposition to the Readjusters disappeared, and the [latter] swallowed the Republican party of Virginia, body and bones, at one gulp."[4]

During the early 1880s, the Readjuster Party controlled over 2,000 federal jobs in the state, including 200 Treasury positions and 1,700 post office employees. The only federal positions in Loudoun County were postmasters and their assistants, of whom over half ended up being replaced during 1881-82. But as these Readjuster replacements often lacked support in their communities and were widely viewed as incompetent, their tenure was short-lived. The county's relatively small Black and urban populations had much to do with the Readjusters' failure to take root there, as did the resiliency of "Straight Out" Republicans like Sam Gover, who shared a long and proud tradition that had sustained them during the war. Just as their opposition to the GOP's radical faction had helped Conservatives regain control of Loudoun during Reconstruction, their opposition to Mahone enabled the Democrats to retain a firm grip over the county during the height of the Readjuster movement in the early 1880s. In their loyalty to the past, Loudoun's "Straight Outs" shared something in common with their Democrat rivals, as both seemingly preferred continuance of "Bourbon" rule to the progressive alternatives offered by the Readjusters.[5]

Annie Matthews came close to losing her Treasury job at the same time her uncle was ousted as postmaster. In March 1882, Mahone sent a form letter to George W. Hoge, the Readjuster delegate for Mt. Gilead, asking for information about Annie, including identification of her family's political affiliation, *i.e.* whether they were "Bourbon Democrat, or Bourbon Republican." Fortunately, Hoge, a Goose Creek Meeting member, was favorably disposed towards her in his response: "Miss A. E. Matthews is the daughter of an old Quaker lady of Waterford. Her family have always been Republican, but there are no male members living. Her removal would not be politic." The Senator heeded the advice, and Annie kept her job.[6]

While Elliot's career would prosper under the Garfield/Arthur Administrations, the Treasury Department lacked the vigor and sense of direction it enjoyed during Secretary Sherman's tenure. Shortly after taking office, Arthur replaced Windom with Charles J. Folger, former Chief Justice of the New York Supreme Court. Like his predecessors, Folger believed in high tariffs and conservative fiscal measures, but his efforts to formulate economic policy were hampered when the President insisted he run for governor of New York. Folger retained his position as Treasury Secretary during the messy gubernatorial campaign that followed, and his loss to Buffalo's mayor, Grover A. Cleveland, did little to enhance his prestige before he died in 1884. Although Folger is usually credited with introducing civil service reform into the Treasury, these changes were actually mandated by Congress. Arthur's record on reform was equally mixed. He angered his old Stalwart colleagues by sustaining Garfield's selection of Robertson to head the New York customhouse, but later incurred the reformers' wrath when he fired Silas Burt, the second-ranking Customs officer in New York, for refusing to turn over a list of his employees to Republican bosses who wanted to use it to levy political assessments.

* * * * *

At the time of Garfield's inauguration, Elliot was still in New York City helping the District Attorney's defense of Customs Collector Edwin Merritt, but he managed to get away long enough to take his wife and older children to the early March inaugural festivities in Washington, including a special reception, promenade concert, and a gala at the National Museum. The New York trial marked the end of his aggressive pursuit of sugar frauds committed by importers, as he turned to more "winnable" cases involving domestic refiners. Although the Treasury did not abandon its quest for revisions of the tariff law, the "sugar question" became part of a larger national debate over whether to lower duties on all imports. Justin Morrill had guided the 1861 Tariff Act through Congress as a stopgap measure to fund the war. But now, as head of the Senate Finance Committee, Morrill remained deeply committed to high tariffs, which he and other Republicans believed were the primary reason why the government enjoyed a surplus by 1880. Veterans' groups, notably the GAR, also favored high tariffs as a means to fund their pension demands. Those who wanted lower tariffs, including most Democrats, felt a reduction would stimulate trade and make more money available to the domestic economy, which would enter another period of decline during Arthur's administration.

The importance of sugar in these debates kept Elliot busy throughout most of the decade. As the Treasury's "sugar expert," he prepared an annual report which charted trends in sugar imports and revenue derived therefrom. In addition, Customs inspectors sent samples to his Baltimore office for polariscope analysis. (Lacking any statutory basis for determining the duty on sugar, the instrument continued in use as an internal means of verification.) Elliot was also called on to teach Customs Appraisers and Samplers how to grade sugar under existing laws and maintained a stock of testing equipment for use by other customhouses.

In June 1881, he was elevated to Special-Agent-in-Charge (SAIC) of the 5th District, after Ira Ayer left Baltimore to head the district office in New York City. The promotion brought additional administrative responsibilities with fewer opportunities for the lengthy investigations that had marked his first four years in Baltimore. In the wake of the discovery of fraud at the Norfolk customhouse, the Special Agency Office developed a detailed questionnaire for agents to fill out during inspections of Customs facilities. Without Ayer to share this chore, Elliot spent much of his time on these routine reports. His new position as district chief did not include a pay raise, but he was able to avail himself of other prerogatives. For example, later that summer he arranged to be sent to Boston on official business, allowing him afterwards to take Edith and the children on a three-week sojourn with his relatives on Cape Cod.

One of his first actions as SAIC was to send a report to Secretary Windom offering to renew his investigation of adulteration by domestic refiners of sugar for re-export; but the bullet fired at President Garfield the next day delayed consideration of his proposal. Chester Arthur's assumption of the presidency that fall deeply worried Elliot, who feared the former head of the New York customhouse still bridled at his role in uncovering fraud there. He therefore made sure his next annual sugar report, completed in November 1881, implicitly drew attention to his success in raising revenue from sugar duties which, after declining for many years, had started to rise in 1879 and showed a gain of more than $2,000,000 in the latest fiscal year. (His 1882 report showed a cumulative gain of almost $5,000,000.) Arthur's replacement of Windom as Treasury Secretary with another New Yorker, Charles Folger, was further cause for concern. With this transition in mind, Elliot had friends write Folger in January 1882 to ask that he be retained in the event of an anticipated shake-up in the Special Agency Division. Fortunately, Arthur and Folger made few personnel changes in the Treasury and Elliot survived this potential crisis.[7]

As he took measure of the new Administration during late 1881 and early 1882, Elliot confined his reporting to less controversial topics, such as his discovery of false bottoms in gin barrels, and inequities in fees collected by American consular officers. In one instance, he recommended cosmetic improvements to the customhouse in Yorktown, Virginia, to improve its appearance in time for the hundredth anniversary of the Battle of Yorktown. After the festivities were over, he proposed the underutilized installation be closed.

In May 1882, he finally completed his report on sugar drawbacks, later published as *Allowances on Drawback on Sugars*. By then the export of domestically refined sugar had doubled, as the industry looked for ways to compensate for losses stemming from the Customs Service's greater scrutiny on imports. His report pointed out that domestic refiners received more money in the form of drawbacks than had originally been collected on the imported "raw" product, which he attributed to the continued importation of artificially colored sugar, which could easily be bleached and mixed with domestic corn sugar for re-export. His covering letter to Secretary Folger reiterated recommendations to amend existing tariff laws to permit testing for saccharine content and color additives, exactly what he and Secretary Sherman had advocated in 1879. The publication coincided with efforts by Republican Congressmen to revise the sugar tariff. John Sherman, now an Ohio Senator, led the fight on the Senate floor, citing Elliot's latest annual report as justification for the proposed changes. Later, referring to the special agent's publication on drawbacks, Sherman cited its author as "one of the ablest officers of the Department." Elliot took advantage of his enhanced status as sugar "czar" to hire another assistant.[8]

In the spring of 1882, Louis G. Martin replaced Amory Tingle as C/SAD, probably for no other reason than Secretary Folger's wanting a fellow New Yorker in this key position. Tingle became a "special agent-at-large" until he won back his old job in 1888, whereupon Martin returned to the regular agent ranks. (Jobs were too scarce for civil servants to consider quitting just because they lost a supervisory role.) Elliot enjoyed a closer personal relationship with Martin, and his reports to his new boss were invariably addressed "Dear Lou." Their friendship also reflected the high *esprit de corps* that permeated SAD at that time.

In his new "at-large" role, Tingle helped Elliot inspect customhouses in Richmond, Norfolk and Petersburg during the spring of 1882. Elliot returned to Virginia that fall to oversee establishment of a customhouse at Newport News, recently designated a port of entry. Located several miles northwest of Hampton, Newport News served as the terminus of the C&O Railroad. Docks were being constructed to permit offloading coal trains onto waiting vessels, and Elliot complained to Washington that debris dredged from around these piers was being dumped into the main channel, threatening navigation in the area. The new collector at Newport News was completely unprepared to begin operations, and Elliot had to order the transfer of supplies from the defunct office in Yorktown to help get the new customhouse started. He was particularly exasperated to discover the boarding station at Old Point Comfort had not improved since his inspection in 1876, and again recommended this facility have sole authority for boarding foreign vessels as they entered Hampton Roads. This arrangement would permit a preliminary inspection before a ship reached its final port of call and allow health authorities to determine if a vessel needed to be quarantined. As it was, ships coming from countries where disease was prevalent often arrived at ports as far inland as Richmond before any American official boarded them.

The following year, Elliot investigated a complaint of misconduct lodged against a "weigher" in the Baltimore customhouse. After reviewing the evidence, he concluded the charges were unfounded and recommended the man's reinstatement. The case was reopened after another complaint was received, but Elliot stuck by his original verdict and allowed the twenty-five-year veteran to keep his job. The special agent's earlier zeal to pursue wrongdoers had mellowed, and he seemed more willing to heed Edith's advice not to make new enemies.[9]

Boston special agent Norman Bingham informed him in March 1883 that they had been selected to investigate the importation of Hawaiian sugar. (In 1875, King Kalakua signed a reciprocal free trade agreement with the U.S. which was designed to stimulate sugar imports from the islands and was now up for renewal. According to press reports, Congress wanted an investigation of alleged sugar fraud on the West Coast before deciding on this issue.) Bingham was excited about their proposed trip and had already asked Secretary Folger to add a third agent to their group to provide technical expertise. This must have irritated Elliot, who considered himself the Treasury's authority on this subject, so it is unlikely he honored Bingham's request to raise the issue of a third man with Folger. Several days later, Bingham wrote that illness on his part would delay their departure, and that he no longer believed they needed to visit Hawaii.[10]

At the same time, Senator Morrill advised Elliot of an anonymous letter he had received, attacking the proposed commission on Hawaiian sugar. Its author acknowledged Elliot's expertise on the subject, but predicted Bingham would control the group and overrule anything the Baltimore agent might propose. In the end, another individual would dictate the commission's findings to Bingham, who would sign off on them. All of these machinations were allegedly being orchestrated by a ring within the Treasury that had been covering up sugar frauds for years. For his part, Morrill did not believe Bingham, a fellow Vermonter, could be bought off so easily, and was equally confident Elliot would not be influenced by anyone in drawing his own conclusions. However, when Morrill visited the Treasury several days later to determine the status of Elliot's trip, he was unable to find anyone who could give a definitive answer. The Senator therefore cautioned: "I think in the end you will go—[Assistant Secretary] French I judge favors you—but there is some hitch somewhere. Most probably a New Yorker will be put on and not any other [special agent]." As it turned out, Elliot did not go. To end competition from Hawaiian sugar, New York importers desired a commission that would recommend against the treaty's renewal, and they well-remembered Elliot's earlier hostility towards them. The Hawaii treaty was therefore not renewed for a defined period, but extended on a yearly basis until 1887, when it was allowed to expire. The cancellation of Elliot's participation on the commission was but one of several unsavory episodes inside the Treasury during the Arthur Administration.[11]

In March 1884, Edith and their young son Edward accompanied Elliot via steamship on a business trip to Norfolk and Richmond. Afterwards, Elliot recommended installation of a telephone at the Norfolk customhouse, another indication of his openness to using technology to improve the Customs Service. His earlier recommendations for improvements to the boarding station at Old Point Comfort had still not been implemented, and he was particularly concerned about the possible spread of yellow fever, unless health officers were allowed to board foreign ships entering Hampton Roads. To rectify this situation, he suggested that the "colored Inspector of Customs" there be replaced by an officer with greater authority to enforce existing regulations. Despite his support for racial equality, Elliot was finally forced to recognize that prejudice against a Black official had been responsible for the repeated failure to carry out his earlier recommendations.[12]

The approach of the 1884 election brought renewed worries about his future. The Democrats had nearly won the last two presidential elections, and there was good reason to believe they could no longer be denied. Elliot's personal sympathies probably lay with the "Mugwumps," a group of independents who unsuccessfully tried to have a reform slate chosen at the Republican National Convention in June. The party instead nominated their old warhorse, Senator James Blaine, for President, and picked Senator John "Black Jack" Logan of Illinois as his running mate. (Logan was a founder and past president of the GAR.) Displeased with this outcome, many Mugwumps deserted to the Democratic side, where they played a role in the nomination of Grover Cleveland and worked to secure his victory in November. As one historian described their defection: "Unhappy with many features of the political and social scene in the Gilded Age, these men were particularly unhappy with what they saw as the corruption of the political system by moneyed parvenus, patronage-hungry politicians and boss-led machines...and they saw James G. Blaine as the very emblem of all they found distasteful...The Mugwumps were very sure of their enemies, the corrupt spoilsmen." Why they believed Cleveland would be more sympathetic to their goals is less clear.[13]

Unwilling to support the Blaine/Logan ticket, and fearful of the consequences of a Democratic victory, Elliot avoided an active role in the presidential campaign, which has been described as one of the "dirtiest" in American history. (The Republican press devoted considerable space to Cleveland's having fathered a child during his bachelor days.) Right after Blaine's nomination, Elliot sought Senator Morrill's help in transferring to a position as a Customs Appraiser. Not only would this represent an increase in pay, but it would remove him from the special agent ranks, which were likely to be targeted for reduction under a Democratic administration. During a visit to the Treasury, Morrill learned Assistant Secretary French favored Elliot's transfer, but Secretary Folger thought he was too much a specialist for the new job. Morrill, therefore, urged him to stay put, as "your present position in any future hurly-burly [is likely] to be more permanent than would be the position of General Appraiser."[14]

Elliot heeded the advice and kept a low profile during the lead-up to the November election, which Cleveland narrowly won after carrying the key state of New York by 1,100 votes. As in the previous two elections, Virginia and Loudoun County voted in the Democratic ticket, although Blaine lost the state by only 6,000 votes, an indication of the hard fight that Mahone supporters waged on the Republicans' behalf.[15]

Faced with the uncomfortable prospect of having few, if any, allies in the incoming administration, Elliot wrote Crawford Adams to express satisfaction over Blaine's defeat. Adams was then head of Philadelphia's special agency district, and as a long-time member of the GOP reform wing, might prove a valuable helpmate. His old friend was glad to learn that Elliot agreed "demagogues and bad men cannot always win." He had opposed Blaine from the start and was convinced the Republicans could have "swept everything before [them]," had they nominated a reform slate. During a trip to New York the previous week, Adams had talked with his Mugwump acquaintances, who played a decisive role in securing the state for Cleveland and were now "very, very happy." Adams assured his colleague they would both fare much better under Cleveland and predicted a mass exodus of corrupt "scamps" from the government, which in itself would provide adequate "compensation, even if we never see anything else." (Elliot undoubtedly hoped for something more tangible.) Adams had also talked with Ira Ayer in New York and found he too accepted "the will of the people," even though he had been more "wedded" to Blaine. Whatever Adams thought, Elliot had no choice but anxiously wait out the next four months until Cleveland took office.[16]

* * * * *

Only snippets survive to document other aspects of the Chamberlins' stay in Baltimore. After the initial shock of leaving their country home, Edith and the children seemingly adapted to city life, a transition aided by relatives and acquaintances in the local Quaker community. Predictably, Elliot used his ties in the veterans movement to make contacts in his new surroundings. Soon after Colonel Ayer's arrival in February 1878, both men visited the office of Col. George Vernon, who as second-in-command of Cole's Cavalry had served along Loudoun's border during the war. Now a pension agent, Vernon headed Maryland's GAR and arranged for the two men's induction into Wilson Post No. 1, the most prestigious in Baltimore. Camaraderie with fellow veterans would play an important part in Elliot's life, and he and his family frequently attended concerts and other events at the GAR auditorium. In 1879, he was placed in charge of arrangements for Maryland GAR members to attend the unveiling of Gen. George Thomas's statue in Washington (now the centerpiece of Thomas Circle).[17]

While Elliot was in the West Indies during early 1880, Colonel Ayer wrote a surprisingly intimate letter to Edith's mother. Their boarder had been bed-ridden in New York for six weeks prior and was replying to a get-well letter from Sarah Matthews. After promising to take her to the Walters Art Gallery when he returned, Ayer asked "grandma" to tell Edith how jealous he was of the attention she was reportedly paying to "other gentlemen in my absence." Despite having already received three *very kind* letters from Edith while in New York, Ayer wondered if their content might have been different, if he were a "brunette" (like Elliot). Although Ayer's interest in the ladies was presumably platonic, a year earlier, when writing to her husband while their boarder was reading in an adjacent room, Edith had pointedly included that her door was locked.[18]

A visit by the census-taker in June 1880 provides a snapshot of the household. After their fifth child, Paul Elliott Chamberlin, was born the previous year, the family moved into a larger townhouse at 139 Edmondson Avenue. Elliot, who turned forty-six three days before the census was taken, gave his age as forty-two, and Edith shaved two years off of her age to list herself as thirty. Mary (listed as ten, but actually eleven) and Morrill (eight) attended school, while Nellie (six), Edward (three) and Paul (six months) remained at home.[19] The rest of the household consisted of Sarah Matthews (sixty-three), Mary Jones (a thirty-four-year-old Black domestic worker), and Ira Ayer (forty-six).[20]

The festivities surrounding Baltimore's Sesquicentennial Celebration in October 1880 provided a welcome respite from the presidential campaign that fall. Although the family was delighted with the Republicans' subsequent victory, all were disappointed when Elliot left with Assistant Secretary French on an extended trip to Louisiana in mid-December that kept him away for the holidays. In a warm letter written to her husband on New Year's Day, Edith described her relief at learning he had escaped unharmed from the train wreck outside Savannah. Annie had come for Christmas and ended up staying a week, after a blizzard closed the government in Washington. The two attended a performance by the celebrated French actress, Sarah Bernhardt, an event Edith proclaimed *"the first extravagant thing of my life."* Despite the bad weather, they managed to visit many friends over the holidays, and the snow allowed the children to go sledding at a nearby park, while Edith wistfully watched elegant sleighs pass, reminding her of similar rides during her youth. Nevertheless, she agreed with the children that this Christmas would have been perfect, if only "papa" could have been there to share it. This and subsequent letters reveal a deep satisfaction with her domestic life, in contrast to the frustration evident in those written from Clifton when Elliot was in Norfolk.[21]

After his return from Louisiana, Elliot spent the first part of 1881 in New York helping with the Merritt trial. While he was there, Edith urged him to attend the services of the noted clergyman and reform advocate Henry Ward Beecher, whom she felt would provide inspiration for his challenging assignment. Aware of his tendency to forgo eating and sleeping while working on a case, she repeatedly counseled him to take care of himself and was glad when Colonel Ayer went to assist him. Recalling Elliot's promises during their courtship never to leave her, she could now jokingly exclaim, "gracious, what a fraud." She openly longed for his physical presence so she could caress him but was willing to "bet her *bottom dollar*" that at that moment he "was happy as a lark" in some Broadway theater. (Here she feigned shock at her use of slang.) Were it not for the children, she was ready to pack her bag and join "my old carpet-bagger."[22]

After he returned to New York from attending Garfield's inauguration, Edith took advantage of his absence to repaper the walls of their new home, although she worried her husband might not like the dark Victorian patterns her decorator had selected. She actually preferred bright, sunny rooms, but was determined to have at least the parlor and dining room decorated in the latest fashion. She had also taken the liberty of removing some of his many pictures, hanging all over the house. (Elliot was a lifelong collector of memorabilia, and it is likely much of it ended up on their walls, along with his own drawings, certificates, and family pictures.) While her redecoration project was only undertaken after Garfield's victory seemingly ensured their future for another four years, the retirement that spring of the Wood note on Clifton also gave the family some much needed breathing room. Edith's mood reflected this improved situation, even though she readily admitted to her husband's charge that the more money she got, the more she wanted.[23]

Baltimore Studio Portraits of Elliot and Edith Reflect More Prosperous Times. Both dressed up for the photographer, but their age difference (he, late 40's; she, mid-30's) has become apparent. (C. 1880 photos, TCC)

She was particularly grateful the children's health had improved since they left the farm. Edward, whom she described as "cunning" and a "chip off the old block," could now hold his own in conversations with the older children. On Palm Sunday, she took him for the first time to the Lombard Street meetinghouse and was amused by his disappointment at finding "no male preacher," as only a female cousin and another woman had "favored" them by speaking aloud. Nellie, never an avid student, had at least passed her exams to enter the next grade, although the girl confessed to her mother that the teacher considered her very lazy. The older children, Mamie and Morrill, loved the roller skates they received for Christmas, and Edith was sure her husband would no longer think them too extravagant if he could see them in use. Mamie, who usually had to be dragged out of bed, was up at dawn every day to try them out, and neither she nor Morrill seemed to mind having to wear worn-out mittens for another few months to help pay for the skates. In fact, both had declared themselves ready to start working to help pay for their clothes. Paul, the youngest, was said to be the handsomest of the children, and Edith thought he looked just like his father.

In later life, Morrill Chamberlin provided an amusing description of what it was like for a young country boy growing up in Baltimore. As for school, he recalled continually having to ask his teacher how to spell his last name before handing in written assignments, and when his father asked how he was doing, responding he was second in his class. It would be some time before "the colonel" learned there were only two in the class. To save money to pay the Clifton mortgage, Morrill had to transfer from a private Quaker school to a public one, where whipping with a "rat-tan" was the norm. Once, Morrill got off by showing a note from his mother, certifying that Friends opposed corporal punishment.

Musical instruction was an important part of family life. Mary played the piano, and Morrill the violin, while the younger children sang songs after dinner, such as "Hold the Fort for I Am Coming" and "Rock of Ages." Sometimes the children would all be taken to "play & sing for someone father knew & after that was over the entertainers would be stood proudly in line like steps. Father's popularity waned."

At that time Baltimore was also celebrated for being the habitat of the Plug-Uglies [street ruffians] and there was not a boy who didn't "go for" some fire engine. No. 15 was Morrill's favorite. When boys were met by other boys on the street after a fire—and they didn't dare travel singly—the question would be asked: "what engine do you go for?" And oh, if you didn't happen to "go" for the same one they did! But Quaker proclivities were generally a refuge. His father had given him a new cap pistol which disappeared. When informed that a boy had taken it away from him, his father exclaimed, "Do you mean to say that you let a boy take your pistol away without fighting him?" The reply was, "It was Sunday." One day his sweet mother seeing from the window of the house on Carrollton Ave. that her son was on the ground where he was being held down, and for a long time had been so held, by a larger & much, oh much, heavier boy, called, "Morrill, throw that boy off and come in the house at once."

Bull ring with marbles, was a popular game in those days and it was played "for good," which was the same as "keeps." One day his sweet mother gave him 15 cents to buy marbles & so he got another boy, not wisely chosen, to go with him down on Baltimore Street, where they bought as many marbles, or "alleys" as they could for the 15 cents. They were all the white kind too, with green & blue & pink stripes. No common, cheap clay alleys...would be accepted in a game by any boy & all were examined closely. On the return home several bull rings were drawn on smooth spots, but later explanations were in order at least at the home of one boy for the poor showing of 15 cents worth of marbles. However, the lessons [of city life] were valuable.[24]

Due in part to the feud with Sam Gover, the family did not spend the summer of 1881 in Loudoun, but instead accompanied Elliot to Cape Cod. Little is known about their activities during the next twelve months, except that their last child, Leroy ("Boy," and later "Roy") Chamberlin, was born in Baltimore on 21 April 1882, a month overdue. His mother later claimed his delayed arrival accounted for his being able to walk and talk when he was only nine months old. Annie wrote to apologize for not visiting her sister during the last stages of her pregnancy, but she had been having difficulties at the Treasury Department. (This was when the Readjusters were asking about her status there.) In addition, the recent death of her landlord and close friend, Dr. Christopher Cox, had left her lonely and depressed. The doctor's widow had converted their home into a boarding house, a development that displeased Annie, who then had to share the place with other renters.[25]

Both Elliot and Edith helped prepare for the Sixteenth National GAR Encampment, held in Baltimore on 21-23 June 1882, and he went so far as to have special business cards with the GAR logo printed for this occasion. (Government employees in Washington and Baltimore were granted official leave to help arrange the encampment and attend the ceremonies.) Afterwards, Grandmother Sarah took the older children to Waterford, where they boarded with Edith's old beau, Will Irish, while their parents remained in Baltimore with Roy to avoid any unpleasant encounter with Sam Gover. Later that summer, they attended an opera with Henry Gover, and Edith and the baby accompanied Elliot on a business trip to Norfolk.[26]

In early 1883, Annie became involved in the women's suffrage movement after a friend took her to a rally featuring speeches on female rights, interspersed with singing. The opening speaker struck a responsive chord among the audience when she lamented having, until recently, been too tied down by domestic chores to have time for the movement. The keynote speech was delivered by Susan B. Anthony, the Quaker pioneer of the campaign to win women the right to vote. Despite looking a bit frail at age sixty-three, Annie found her oratory as "bright and charming" as ever. Afterwards, Annie asked her mother to get Edith to come stay with her in Washington for a week to help recruit for the suffragettes and was disappointed when her sister failed to appear, as she had told everyone to expect her. Edith pleaded illness for not going, but there is little evidence she shared Annie's enthusiasm for the movement. Annie resigned from Quaker meeting the following year, another indication of her changing personal views since leaving Waterford to become a federal employee.[27]

Elliot kept a ticket for the May 1883 ribbon-cutting for the Brooklyn Bridge, and presumably managed to attend the ceremonies honoring this iconic symbol of America's industrial might. In September, he lost a valuable ally in his office, when Henry Gover resigned to open a business in Philadelphia. After requesting permission to hire a replacement, Elliot joined his family in Waterford for the last two weeks of their summer vacation. While there, he took them to the Loudoun Agricultural Fair, and later attended a GAR function in, of all places, Richmond. (He kept the menu for the closing banquet, which was printed on the back of a Confederate one-dollar bill.)[28]

During the summer of 1884, Edith and the children returned to stay at Clifton for the first time in seven years. (The farm lease signed earlier that year stipulated that the tenants had to vacate part of the house during summertime.) At first, Edith had difficulty adjusting to dark, quiet nights in the country, but soon felt at home again. The children were overjoyed to return and spent much of their time swimming and fishing in the Catoctin Creek, where Mamie usually caught the most fish. When Morrill asked his mother whether they would return the following summer, she answered affirmatively, but secretly wondered whether the farm would still be theirs by then. Like the spouses of many Republican office-holders, she worried about a Democratic victory that fall, and threatened to flee the country if "Bull" (Thomas A. Hendricks) was elected president. (Edith was thinking of the pending Democratic Convention, which ended up selecting the perennial candidate Hendricks as Cleveland's running mate.) On a more practical note, Edith asked her husband to send canning jars for the fruit crop, and cheap calico so she could make curtains to brighten up the house. She also requested funds to buy an inexpensive carriage to take them on visits and run errands into Waterford.[29]

Edith was happiest when presiding over a large household, and so invited friends and relatives to stay at Clifton that summer. By early September, however, the guests had gone, and she began to miss the excitement of the city. Mamie and Morrill had returned with their father to attend school, leaving their mother to wonder if he could manage having to cook for the two children. Paul and Nellie were also ready to go back, but their mother decided to wait for a break in the heat, since the children could at least keep cool by swimming in the creek. Sam and Temperance Gover paid a call, having waited until Elliot had gone. We can presume Edith felt conflicted as she prepared to take the smaller children back to Baltimore. Clearly, they all enjoyed their stay at the old homestead, but she must have felt somewhat out of place in Waterford's aging Quaker community.[30]

Chapter 27

ON THE MOVE: 1885-1892

By the time of his inauguration in March 1885, Grover Cleveland had picked his campaign manager, Daniel Manning, to be Secretary of the Treasury. Republicans could expect little sympathy from this New York politico, and many would soon be removed from his Department. While failing to craft a coherent economic policy of his own, Manning was a superb administrator, who completely revamped departmental procedures during his two years in office. Past experience had taught Elliot the necessity of getting friends to put in a good word for him with each new Secretary, and this was even more critical under the present circumstances. Assistant Secretary French had agreed to remain at his post for several weeks to assist during the transition period and Elliot had him write a glowing endorsement that was forwarded for use by Senator Morrill. In it, French described having known Elliot "long and intimately," and termed him "one of the most honest and efficient of the Force." Citing the agent's expertise on sugar, he was "sure the new Administration will do well to retain him." As a Republican, Morrill no longer had *carte blanche* to discuss personnel matters with the new Secretary, and instead delivered French's letter to Maryland's Democratic Senator, Arthur Gorman, who promised to discuss the special agent's fate with Manning the following day. Morrill assured Elliot that: "You can feel entirely safe, at least for the present."[1]

Morrill may have overestimated his influence, but his actions undoubtedly kept his friend from being fired outright. On 1 May, Manning signed orders dismissing Elliot as special agent, but four days later, softened the blow by appointing him a special inspector at half (four dollars per day) his old salary. Reflective of the new procedures introduced by Manning, C/SAD Louis Martin forwarded Elliot's new appointment to Baltimore, along with an oath of office to sign and return, monthly accounting forms, and blanks for him to record his "daily employment." In the past, Elliot would have taken a train to Washington to handle such matters, but under a new, more efficient bureaucracy, he had to write and ask when and where he should report for his new assignment. Although he was originally slated to serve in Norfolk, Martin replied that he should remain in Baltimore until notified otherwise.[2]

His removal and replacement as special agent by a Baltimore councilman caused widespread comment in the press, not only in that city, but as far away as New York and Minnesota. Reformers were upset a senior civil servant had been removed to make room for a ward chief with no previous experience. The press generally credited Senator Gorman with having engineered the switch, while a Treasury spokesman speculated Elliot's removal was due to his peculiar background—born in Vermont, appointed from Virginia, and voting in Maryland. Also noted was Morrill's sponsorship of Elliot, and by implication, the Senator's inability to protect his protégé under a Democratic administration. The articles generally praised Elliot's performance in Baltimore, where he and his family were said to have made many friends. The *Baltimore Sun*, however, recalled his role in the Perot trial and enforcement of Secretary Sherman's policies, which had resulted in the demise of the city's sugar trade. The story of his initial dismissal was even relayed to Loudoun, where the *Telephone* expressed hope the Chamberlins would return to their farm. Whether or not the initial press play influenced Manning's decision to reappoint him is unclear, although it certainly did not hurt. (The reaction in the veterans movement to his and other firings is discussed later in this chapter.) Both the Democratic *Baltimore Daily News* and the Republican *N. Y. Daily Tribune* covered his reinstatement. Expressing satisfaction a "most dutiful and competent officer," who had not been an "active or virulent partisan," had been reinstated, the Baltimore paper cited this action as evidence of the Administration's commitment to Civil Service reform.[3]

The dismissal and reappointment to a lesser position were bitter draughts for Elliot and his family to swallow. He was not alone—of the twenty-eight special customs agents at that time, at least sixteen were fired and three resigned. He was actually fortunate to receive a position as inspector, since their number had been cut from forty-three to twenty-six. During his first year in office, Secretary Manning gave serious consideration to following the wishes of the New York business community and abolish the Customs SAD altogether. Special agents Amory Tingle and George Tichenor were directed to undertake a thorough review of the functions and statutory basis for the Special Agency force, which was later published as a lengthy supplement to the Treasury's Annual Report. In it, Manning conceded that SAD contained "useful servants of the revenue whose intelligence, zeal and fidelity cannot be…called in question. Their work is incessant, responsible, delicate in character, and at times most vexing. The best among them are invaluable aids to the [Treasury Secretary], whose services…it would be an injury…to lose." Likewise, he acknowledged the inherent "danger" in "a force of men, so near the Secretary, if not… most watchfully supervised."[4]

Manning had given SAD a reprieve but repeated his warning the following year. Both times, the Secretary emphasized that overzealous investigations of the New York customhouse had prompted suggestions to do away with the special agent force. The New York Customs Collector was paid more, at that time, than any other official in the government besides the President, and should, Manning emphasized, have authority to police his own operations. Essentially, he had concluded special agents were too valuable to eliminate entirely, but he also made it clear he did not want a group of predominantly Republican zealots hindering the Democrats' turn to control the lucrative Customs Service.[5]

Elliot viewed his demotion to inspector as an unjust political act, but his accomplishments as SAIC up to then appear less noteworthy than those of special agents allowed to remain in their old jobs. In part, his lower profile was due to the success of his regular inspections, which apparently forestalled any significant malfeasance in his district. However, not being assigned any major investigations during this period only highlighted his failure to develop leads of his own, a reflection of a more cautious approach to his work after earlier setbacks on sugar frauds. Many of the recommendations coming out of his inspections, such as those dealing with shipping in Hampton Roads, appear sound but were often ignored by his superiors, who preferred he stick to specific allegations of wrongdoing rather than generalities not directly tied to revenue collection.[6]

The Chamberlins moved to Washington in June 1885, a month after Elliot's reduction in rank. He would remain administratively attached to the 5th District's head office in Baltimore for the next eighteen months but had no desire to remain at the scene of his humiliating demotion, or to share offices with the inexperienced politician who replaced him. The family's new home at 1228 13th Street was within easy walking distance of the Treasury and after Annie Matthews joined them later that summer her contribution for room and board helped make up for Elliot's salary loss.[7]

His father's demotion and abrupt transfer to Washington were events Morrill Chamberlin vividly recalled years later:

> [Our father] was the first Republican to lose his office in Baltimore after Cleveland was inaugurated. The children were pupils at Cousin Eli Lamb's Friends School when the sad event happened. On one of the first spring days in 1885, the papers stated that gudgeon fishing was particularly good on the Patapsco…His [Morrill's?] parents reluctantly admitting that even the children were getting older, still thought that he could travel to the

fishing grounds on a half fare ticket by rail...At the station, being tall, he was asked his age [and told] "Nothing doing on half fare." ...but the fisherman went...[and returned home] about 8 o'clock after the walk of some 10 miles...After supper that had been kept hot, the *Baltimore American* was eagerly sought to ascertain what Billie Barnie's Orioles had done that day, when his eye was glued by the heading, "Col. Chamberlin Removed—Democratic axe falls on first Republican." The family moved to Washington, D.C....Oh, what a noble mother there was during those dark days.[8]

While his family remained in Washington, Elliot's career underwent a drastic change, which sent him up and down the East Coast for the next six years. One of his first assignments was to Philadelphia, where SAIC Crawford Adams dispatched him to Oswego, New York, to verify drawbacks paid on lumber. He then spent several weeks in Philadelphia writing up his findings, taking advantage of a two-week guest pass Adams arranged for him at the prestigious Union League Club. Fortunately, he was able to spend much of that winter with his family, while he prepared the annual sugar report and investigated jewelry smuggling at the port of Georgetown, in Washington D.C. (The Treasury Department had belatedly discovered there was no one else capable of producing the sugar report.) During the spring of 1886, he spent twenty days of leave at Clifton getting the farm and gardens ready for the family's summer pilgrimage to the country. Afterwards, he conducted inspections in the 5th District, including customhouses at Georgetown, Richmond, and Onancock (on Virginia's Eastern Shore), before returning to Washington in the fall to prepare the next sugar report. Throughout this period, he studiously avoided contact with his replacement in Baltimore, even though the latter was technically his immediate supervisor. In one instance, Elliot had Senator Morrill provide a letter of introduction to Baltimore's Customs Collector rather than go through his old office.[9]

One can imagine his frustration at performing the same duties he had carried out earlier, only now at half pay. Therefore, he felt particularly vindicated when C/SAD Louis Martin informed him in January 1887 of his promotion to a special-agent-at-large, with a welcome raise to six dollars per day. At the time, he was in Charleston, South Carolina, conducting an inspection tour along the Carolina coast. He had spent that Sunday in church before visiting Forts Johnson and Sumter in the city harbor. Writing that evening to inform his wife of the good news, he confessed to not feeling entirely secure until he had the commission safely in his pocket. Nevertheless, he was eager to resume duties as an agent, and had never turned in his old badge. Asking his wife to inform Annie of their good fortune, he quoted Daniel Webster: "I still live, and am back as ever." His inspection of the Charleston customhouse completed, he took a revenue cutter to Georgetown and Beaufort before heading home.[10]

As special-agent-at-large, Elliot continued to traverse the East Coast for the next two years, whenever possible timing his inspections with the seasons to minimize recurrent bouts of rheumatism. That summer, he visited ports in Maine and Massachusetts, while trips to South Carolina, Georgia and Florida were made the following winter. A January 1888 letter from the Customs Collector in Georgetown, South Carolina, revealed that they had recently enjoyed a hunting expedition together, bagging fat deer and wildfowl, which Elliot dressed and took back with him. The Collector promised to ship a fox pelt they shot and invited the agent to return for another hunt. Such diversions aside, Elliot's peripatetic career limited time with his family, which had moved across the street into more comfortable quarters at 1211 13th Street, where they would remain until 1891. (The house, which no longer stands, was located near Thomas Circle and rented for eighty-five dollars per month, to which Annie contributed thirty dollars.)[11]

Although Edith and the children soon made friends in Washington, the disruption to their lives after being forced to leave Baltimore served to strengthen their ties to Clifton, a sentiment reinforced by uncertainties about Elliot's career. Few details about this period are known, outside of Morrill's third person account of his schooling:

[In Washington, Morrill became a] pupil for two years at Franklin School...& then to Washington [later Central] High School in the Fall of 1887. He recalls how madly in love were all the boys with Frances Folsom, who had just become the bride of President Cleveland. She was a picture, truly, as she drove about the shaded streets in an open carriage.

Frequently upon returning to class after the noon recess, some boy at the head of the line would pass the word back…"Chamberlin, there's your brother!" Sure enough, there would be Paul, seated on the platform at the foot of the principal's desk. Just down, poor scamp, from…the 1st or 2nd grade & always looking so pitiful sitting there. But the thing that was most maddening was the discovery upon return to class rooms that some ornery son of a gun had erased the last syllable from my last name in written work on the black-board & had substituted the short & ugly word "pot." Invariably a rush to the black-board and the original signature was restored. Had the alteration been allowed to remain unnoticed, the annoyance probably would have ceased. [The teacher] didn't carry a rat-tan, but he had a strong right when it became enmeshed in a boy's collar and there are recollections of buttons on the floor. He was very much of a man & a splendid tutor. But the thrill of being in High School in the uniform of a cadet. [He participated as a lieutenant in the cadet corps and its "Hungry Dozen" drill team.][12]

Despite the itinerant nature of his work, Elliot did not escape the notice of his adversaries for long. In March 1888, Representative William H. F. Lee[13] (Virginia) asked the Assistant Treasury Secretary to verify whether "S. E. Chamberlin of Loudoun Co." was currently employed by the Customs Service in Baltimore, and if so, on whose recommendation had he been hired, his term of office, and whether he was protected by the Civil Service Act. Apparently one of Lee's Democratic constituents was interested in Elliot's job, and the Assistant Secretary's response that the position was *not* covered by the Civil Service Act was definite cause for concern. It was an election year, however, and the Administration was anxious to avoid further alienation of veterans working in the government, who had formed a union to protect their interests in the aftermath of wholesale dismissals at the beginning of Cleveland's term. As a result, Elliot kept his job, and his new supervisor, C/SAD James A. Jewell, sent him on a variety of assignments during the remainder of the year.[14]

That summer, the Republicans nominated former Indiana Senator Benjamin Harrison to run against Cleveland. Many businessmen, alarmed at a Democratic platform favoring free trade and low tariffs, contributed heavily to the Republican cause. Although Harrison's war record had not been particularly noteworthy, he held the brevet rank of general and enjoyed strong support among Northern veterans, especially after he successfully sponsored several military pension bills in the Senate, only to have them vetoed by Cleveland. (Even after the President made belated attempts to curry favor among this constituency, the ex-soldiers never forgave these vetoes, nor the wholesale dismissals during the first part of his Administration.) Although pleased with the prospect of an avowed champion of the Union soldier in the White House, Elliot could not openly campaign for the GOP ticket while working for a Democratic Administration. On the other hand, he was freer to reject pressure to actively support the incumbent's re-election than would have been the case earlier. In their haste to implement the Pendleton Civil Service Act, Democrats had failed to appreciate how their own chances of remaining in office might be adversely affected if federal workers no longer had to "contribute" time and money to an incumbent's reelection.[15]

In the end, Harrison handed Cleveland a surprisingly large defeat in most states outside of the South. While Loudoun County remained solidly in the Democratic camp, Harrison lost Virginia by only 1,500 votes. It was a last gasp from the coalition of Readjusters and "Straight-out" Republicans, who ceased to be significant factors in Virginia politics, outside of a few districts with large Black populations.[16] Its driving force, William Mahone, had lost control of patronage in the state when he failed to win re-election to the U.S. Senate in 1885. He made a half-hearted attempt to run for governor in 1889, but by then the Democrats were too entrenched to permit a meaningful challenge to their hegemony.[17]

Politics in the Old Dominion entered a prolonged period of stagnation after the Readjusters' disappearance. The following frank assessment of his party's failure to provide innovative and principled leadership was furnished by a member of Virginia's Democratic hierarchy shortly after the turn of the century:

> The White people carried the election [in 1883] and came into control of both bodies of the Legislature. They thereupon determined that they would never run the risk of falling under negro domination again, and they accordingly amended the election laws so that the officers of the election...could stuff the ballot boxes...to make any returns that were desired. Under these statutes the elections in Virginia became a farce. We got rid of negro government, but we got in place of it a government resting upon fraud and chicanery...[18]

The strain of traveling and long absences from home had taken their toll by February 1889, when Elliot asked C/SAD Jewell to assign him to a permanent station, preferably back in his old position as chief of the Baltimore office. Not receiving an answer, he changed tactics after Harrison's inauguration, and requested a permanent assignment to Washington as the Treasury's first official "sugar czar." The Treasury's Bureau of Statistics provided a statement attesting to the value of his annual reports, which he gave to Senator Morrill, along with a résumé of his military and government career. Adding his own recommendation, Morrill took the package to a meeting in early March with the new Treasury Secretary, William Windom, who had held the same office under Garfield.[19]

Several days later, Elliot followed up with his own letter to Windom, in which he pointed out that, even though duties on sugar constituted over one quarter of the entire revenue collected by Customs, individual customhouses were still permitted to set their own criteria to assess the tariff. Only by direct control of someone in Washington, he argued, could "uniformity be attained...in governing the action of appraising officers in sampling, testing by polariscope, and classification by Dutch standard." To accomplish this goal required the supervision of a "competent official," who could also compile statistics on sugar, monitor drawbacks, and oversee all complaints and investigations related to sugar. "From my long experience and familiarity with all matters relating to this subject, I most respectfully ask that I may be placed as Special Agent in charge of sugar matters."[20]

Despite its apparent merits, his proposal was not accepted. Complaints and suits filed against the government by importers of many different products had increased in recent years, and Windom preferred to establish procedures for standardizing Customs evaluations in general, not just on sugar, and the following year the Secretary authorized the creation of a nine-man Board of General Appraisers to resolve such disputes. Instead of getting the Washington position, Elliot was administratively assigned to Baltimore in a subordinate capacity, although he spent little time there. Several months later, he was put in charge of the 8th District office in Savannah, Georgia, a promotion that included a return to his old salary of eight dollars per day. After spending twenty-five days of leave in late summer with Edith and the children at Clifton, he departed for his new assignment. Once again, his family remained behind to prevent disruption to the children's education, and the resulting separation would prove particularly hard on their father.[21]

Two months after taking over the Savannah office, Elliot received a tip that contraband liquor was being sold at the Brighton Saloon in Tampa, Florida. Without checking the accuracy of the information, or conferring with Washington, he headed south and personally raided the bar. The proprietor of the saloon later complained to his Democratic Congressman that the SAIC had entered the saloon without a warrant and "proceeded to turn everything upside down in the most uproarious manner, he burst open every case of liquor in the place...even barrels of beer were opened and after strewing the goods about and finding nothing, refused to put them back or nail up the cases." After allegedly threatening to arrest the owner in an "abusive and threatening" manner, Elliot departed, only to return later in the day and repeat the procedure—after the owner had just put everything back in place. In his letter, the proprietor reiterated having run a law-abiding establishment for years and demanded the government open an inquiry into the matter. Unable to confirm the liquor in question had been purchased through illicit channels, Elliot received a formal reprimand from his superiors in Washington. It was not an auspicious start to his new assignment.[22]

With the exception of leave taken in May and August, Elliot returned to Washington infrequently during 1890. In November of that year, Morrill Chamberlin addressed a letter to "dear old dad" expressing hope his father would soon return to work in Washington. Morrill, now almost eighteen, had just graduated from high school and proudly announced having accepted a position as clerk in a Washington D.C. bank. The young man viewed it as a first step towards securing his future and claimed not to mind having to forgo a college education, which probably would have consisted mostly of "football, baseball, rowing and fraternities." (Morrill inherited his father's athletic ability and remained an avid sports fan in later life.) Despite his son's professed satisfaction at starting work, Elliot knew the family's finances had left little choice, and could only hope Morrill would eventually be able to earn a college degree on his own. Continuing his letter, Morrill informed his father that he planned to use part of his first paycheck for a train ticket to go and personally "investigate" what was happening at Clifton.[23]

Increasingly lonely and worried about his family, Elliot sought Senator Morrill's assistance in obtaining a transfer back to Washington to work with the IRS on issues related to sugar. In his reply, the Senator promised to meet with the IRS Commissioner and Treasury Secretary as soon as he returned from Vermont, but wondered whether Elliot might find the new position less "remunerative than the one you now hold, and your absence from home greater." Despite his mentor's misgivings, Elliot persisted with the application and received notification in early 1891 that he would be temporarily assigned to the IRS "to assist on work required under that portion of the new Tariff Law relating to bounties on sugars." The job did not begin until 1 July, however, and Elliot ended up spending almost two years in Savannah where, mindful of the Tampa incident, he confined himself to routine inspections and investigations. (The only clipping he saved from this assignment concerned seizure of sixty violins smuggled into the country as undeclared clothing.)[24]

Soon after his arrival in Washington D.C., the family moved into a large townhouse with a mansard roof and walk-in English basement that still stands at 1202 Q Street, which then rented for fifty dollars a month. Annie and her mother were no longer living with the Chamberlins, having decided the year before to rent their own place nearby so they would not have to contend with six active youngsters. (To help defray her expenses, Annie sublet rooms in their four-story townhouse.)[25]

Little is known about Elliot's twelve-month assignment to the IRS's Sugar Bounty Division, which was established to implement provisions contained in the McKinley Tariff Act of 1890. (This bill increased most tariffs but had a reciprocity clause providing for the remission of duties on products imported from countries that reduced duties on American exports. The new law proved unpopular and contributed to the Republicans' defeat in 1892, before it was repealed two years later.) The only IRS directive Elliot saved was an August 1891 request to prepare a list of articles to be included in a government exhibit at the Columbian Exhibition, which opened two years later in Chicago. After his assignment ended in June 1892, the IRS Commissioner sent C/SAD Tingle a memorandum, expressing appreciation for the fine work Elliot had performed over the past year. The following month, Elliot left for his new post as SAIC at Newport News, where he would spend the next year under the direction of Louis Martin, who now headed the 5th District in Baltimore.[26]

Although he had a pass to attend the Republican National Convention in Minneapolis as an "alternate elector," it appears unused, and there is no other evidence that Elliot participated in the 1892 election, other than hastily returning to Washington that fall to vote, even though by then he recognized the Republicans' chances for victory were slim. Harrison had campaigned as a civil service reformer in 1888, but soon found himself besieged by office seekers demanding he remove all Democrats Cleveland had installed and replace them with Republicans. The President agonized over the patronage process and became increasingly isolated in the White House after several of his early appointees proved embarrassments. Even though the Republican-dominated Congress during Harrison's first two years was noted for the significant legislation it passed, including the Sherman Antitrust and McKinley Tariff Acts, the Democrats won the mid-term elections, and Harrison found himself a lame-duck from then on. The untimely death of the capable Windom in January 1891 was another blow to the Administration, and his replacement as head of the Treasury, Charles Foster, did little to distinguish himself during the remainder of Harrison's term.[27]

Cleveland's victory in 1892, by the largest plurality of the previous twenty years, was widely anticipated. Harrison was the last Civil War general to hold the presidency, and his defeat signaled the start of a transition away from a period dominated by veterans and politicians whose outlooks had been shaped by their wartime experiences. The campaign, which featured the anomaly of two candidates who had already held the office, was a low-key affair, without the "bloody shirt" rhetoric which had characterized recent elections. Despite Harrison's poor record, Cleveland's victory inspired little enthusiasm and seemed a return to a bygone era. In Washington, however, the Democratic triumph caused great anxiety among Republican office-holders, who feared (with justification) a repetition of the massive upheavals of 1885. (Civil service laws still protected only a limited number of federal workers and were often ignored.)

* * * * *

The 1880s witnessed a marked resurgence in the veterans movement. If the years had dampened their ardor for politics, it was replaced by a desire for the fellowship provided by reunions and post activities. As they grew older, ex-soldiers also became more vocal about the need to liberalize pension laws. Their most influential organization, the Grand Army of Republic (GAR), grew from 49,000 members in 1879 to 409,000 by 1890. Much of this expansion occurred after an alliance was formed in 1881 with the *National Tribune*, a veterans' newspaper published by George E. Lemon in Washington, D.C. Started as a monthly newsletter in 1877 to promote Lemon's services as a pension agent, it was upgraded in 1881 to a weekly paper which, in addition to championing pension reform, carried detailed coverage of veterans' activities across the country. Circulation rose dramatically and facilitated the GAR's conversion from a Republican club into the most potent lobby for veterans in America.[28]

While Elliot had helped expand the GAR into Washington in 1866, he let his membership lapse after joining the U.S. Cavalry. Later, as Virginia's representative on the GOP's Veterans Committee, he organized "Boys in Blue" clubs for presidential campaigns between 1872 and 1880, but avoided affiliation with any particular group until rejoining the GAR after moving to Baltimore in 1878. Once again, the veterans movement became an integral part of his life, and he even took his young daughter to the 1880 National GAR Encampment in Albany. Two years later, he and Edith were actively involved in making arrangements for a similar encampment in Baltimore. Concurrently, he belonged to the Society of the Army of the Potomac, later attaining the presidency of its cavalry corps with the honorary rank of general. In throwing himself into these activities, he found a way to relive the army career he had abandon in 1867.[29]

Thus, by the time Cleveland assumed office in 1885, Elliot's relationship with the veterans movement had morphed from that of a political organizer to a personal search for camaraderie, better benefits, and fulfillment in ways his Treasury job no longer provided. But, while many veterans in the government naively believed assurances from their bosses that their jobs were secure, as well as Cleveland's campaign rhetoric to uphold civil service reform, Elliot remained wary. He came from a politically hostile Southern state, had already lost several federal positions, and knew better than to proclaim his Republican sentiments in a race the Democrats seemed destined to win. Yet, despite enlisting the aid of two Senators and an Assistant Treasury Secretary to argue for his retention, he and his family had the shock of discovering in the evening papers of 1 May that he was the first Republican in Maryland to be fired.

These developments coincided with the Sixteenth Annual Reunion of the Army of the Potomac (SAP), held in Baltimore on 6-7 May 1885. As members of the local reception committee, he and Edith helped prepare for this event, and his well-publicized dismissal—a harbinger of more removals to come—provided a case study for a subject that dominated discussions during the first day of this influential gathering of ex-soldiers. With the GAR seemingly powerless to stop the exodus of veterans from the government, attendees looked to the Veterans' Rights Union (VRU) to guard their interests.

Army of the Potomac Society Program Cover for 1885 Reunion. Elliot and Edith helped plan this event. (TCC)

(Launched two years earlier in New York to protect Republican veterans holding government jobs, the union expanded after the Baltimore reunion to include chapters in Washington and Maryland.) A resolution was approved to send a delegation of SAP and VRU leaders to call on Cleveland and present the ex-soldiers' demands for preferences in federal hiring, as well as protection from dismissal. The SAP reunion's second day was given over to a steamship ride to Point Lookout (site of a camp for Confederate prisoners in the Chesapeake Bay) on which Edith accompanied her husband, and a farewell banquet. The next day, a delegation of high-ranking former military officers presented the reunion's concerns to the President, who signaled willingness to adhere to existing regulations giving preferences to *disabled* (a caveat frequently overlooked) veterans over civilians in filling and replacing federal positions. The likelihood that Democratic veterans would prevail over their Republican counterparts was glossed over but would soon dampen the initial enthusiasm coming out of this meeting. In any case, it was too late for Elliot, who could only console himself that he still had a job, albeit a less remunerative one.[30]

Somewhat surprisingly, Elliot did not transfer his Grand Army membership when he moved to Washington the following month. In all likelihood, he knew the GAR post in the capital would be inundated with Democratic officeholders, a prospect he did not relish, particularly in a post he had helped found as a bastion of radical Republicanism. While talking with fellow officers at the Baltimore reunion, he would have learned that the western chapters of the Military Order of the Loyal Legion of the United States (MOLLUS) were accepting new members in this heretofore exclusive group, and he submitted an application to join its California Commandery right after his move to Washington D.C.

MOLLUS was founded only days after Lincoln's assassination by a group of Philadelphia officers who had served as honor guards for the President's funeral cortege and pledged themselves to form an organization that would "help thwart future threats to the national government." For many years thereafter, the Loyal Legion was confined to a few commanderies along the East Coast, but in 1885 it began an aggressive expansion campaign in the west. Despite limiting membership to officers who had served in the Civil War, the Loyal Legion was so successful during this period it began taking followers from the GAR, which promptly denounced its rival as "an aristocracy of officers." In July 1885, Elliot received an ornate certificate designating him a "companion of the first class" in the California Commandery. While on business in Philadelphia that fall, he availed himself of his privileges as a member to attend a lavish banquet at the Union League Club, put on by the Pennsylvania Commandery. Several years later, he transferred his membership to the Washington D.C. Com-

Chamberlin Family and Friends, 13th St. Home, D.C., c. 1887. George Lucky (friend) and Elliot stand at top; 2nd row: two more friends and Edith; 3rd row: Morrill, Eleanor, female friend and Annie Matthews; 4th row: Sarah Matthews, unidentified boy, Paul, female friend and Mary: and lowest: Edward and Roy. (TCC)

mandery, in which he remained active for the rest of his life.[31]

Expansion of the veterans movement was accompanied by increased demands for compensation from the ex-soldiers. Benjamin Harrison campaigned on this issue, and his appointment of James Tanner as Pension Commissioner promised to fulfill Republican pledges to improve the veterans' benefits. A paraplegic, who lost both legs at Bull Run, Tanner was the darling of the GAR, and an outspoken advocate of "service" pensions—payments to everyone who had served in the U.S. military. Boasting he would "drain the Treasury," Tanner went about awarding benefits with a vengeance. But he proved a poor administrator and general embarrassment to the President, the first of several ill-advised appointments that ultimately limited Harrison to one term. During the six months Tanner held office, confusion and fraud reigned at the Pension Bureau, resulting in his replacement in September 1889 by Green B. Raum, the former IRS Commissioner for whom Elliot had briefly worked. While continuing the liberal dispensation of pensions, Raum kept better reins on his bureau, until he too was ousted in 1893, when it was discovered that pension agent (and *National Tribune* editor) George Lemon was lending Raum large sums of money in return for favorable decisions for his clients.

Despite the Bureau's liberality under existing laws, the GAR and its allies continued to press for service pensions, warning that veterans would desert the Republicans in the 1890 mid-term elections if GOP lawmakers did not comply with their demands. While the administration opposed a general dispensation to all veterans on fiscal grounds, the Pension Bill that Harrison signed in June 1890 "fell short of being a 'service' measure in just one respect, applicants must show some disability, regardless of origin." In fact, they had only to demonstrate they were incapable of performing manual labor to receive twelve dollars per month for life, and a widow no longer had to prove her husband's death was service-related. Predictably, claims multiplied and were generally filled quickly by the bureau. Unfortunately for Harrison, veterans quickly forgot his largesse and renewed their clamor for service pensions.[32]

Republican 1888 Campaign Poster Asks Who Should Represent America at the Centennial [of Washington's First Inauguration]: Gen. Benjamin Harrison, "the man who risked his life," or Cleveland, "the man who sent a substitute." (Harrison papers, LC)

The timing of Elliot's initial application for a disability pension in September 1872 was dictated by the terms of the 1868 Pension Act, which gave soldiers five years from the time of their discharge to file a claim. Thus, his application had to be based on having contracted rheumatism five years earlier during his brief stint in 1867 with the U.S. Cavalry, rather than on his extensive Civil War service. Finding witnesses who remembered him at Fort Walla Walla proved difficult, and when the Pension Bureau asked for substantiation of his claim, he let the matter drop until 1876, when it looked like he might lose his Treasury position. At that time, he had Senator Justin Morrill ask Interior Secretary Zachariah Chandler, whose department had jurisdiction over the Pension Bureau, to check on his claim. To avoid paying an agent to handle his case, as most veterans did, Elliot had once again reverted to using his mentor to overcome an obstacle, but not even a U.S. Senator had much influence inside the byzantine Pension Bureau, and his application would lie dormant for more than a decade. After passage of the Arrears Act of 1879 eliminated the five-year window for filing claims, Elliot acted as agent for his widowed sister, Louisa Cameron, whose husband died of complications (gangrene) to his amputated arm. In 1882 the Pension Commissioner informed Elliot that Louisa's claim had been denied for failure to substantiate the gangrene was service-related, an outcome that use of a professional agent would almost certainly have precluded.[33]

Influenced by Tanner's far-flung promises to help ex-soldiers, Elliot took time in March 1889 to research his father's service in the War of 1812 to see if it entitled his descendants to receive remuneration in the form of bounty land, something he had tentatively started for his sister a decade earlier. Eventually, he received word from the Pension Bureau that Samuel Chamberlin had been fully compensated at the time of his discharge, although a modern day search of War of 1812 pension records suggests otherwise. Elliot next looked into the possibility of obtaining a pension based on his grandfather's Revolutionary War service. (Unfortunately, he was unaware that it was his great-grandfather Ichabod Chamberlin, who had served in that war, not his grandfather Samuel Newell Chamberlin.) In January 1891, the Pension Bureau reported its failure to locate any records confirming that a Samuel N. Chamberlain from Dudley had served in the Revolution. Despite a suggestion that he contact the Massachusetts government for further information, this claim was also dropped.[34]

In March 1891, Elliot suffered a rheumatoid attack while inspecting the customhouse in Wilmington, North Carolina, that left him bedridden and required the attention of a local physician. This latest relapse prompted him to reopen his disability claim under the terms of the 1890 Pension Act. Informing Edith of his illness, he asked her to send the necessary forms to refile a claim. Concerned he had no one to comfort him "except Dr. Pinkham" (the maker of a popular liniment), she offered to come down if he so desired. She had also discussed his situation with her cousin Edward Dawson, an Interior Department employee, who helped her obtain the necessary forms and offered to assist with the claim.[35]

After Elliot returned the documents, Edith filed his application, along with a statement from a Wilmington doctor confirming swelling in his knee and shoulders that rendered him incapable of performing manual labor. Unwisely, Elliot and his wife opted to follow her cousin's advice and once more pursue the claim on their own. This decision may have saved money but claims agents handled the vast majority of these cases and had the necessary contacts within the bureaucracy to "grease the skids" and obtain favorable outcomes for their clients. Three years later, Elliot had still not qualified for a pension. (The official explanation was his failure to locate anyone to corroborate his having contracted rheumatism while posted at Fort Walla Walla.)[36]

* * * * *

Despite sustained involvement with the veterans movement at large and its individual components, Elliot had surprisingly little contact with the men he had once served with. A partial exception were the Loudoun Rangers, with whom he had necessarily been in contact whenever staying at Clifton. Since their days together at the Point, he had helped former members with claims, pension applications, and employed an ex-Ranger as caretaker. It was therefore quite natural for him to attend the first Loudoun Ranger reunion in August 1890 while he was back home on leave from his duties in Savannah. In fact, it is likely he helped plan and host this affair. Described in a local (Republican) paper as "one of the most impressive gatherings ever witnessed in this vicinity," the gathering was attended by almost sixty surviving members of the command. It opened in particularly moving fashion, as "the original roll of the two companies was called by the surviving sergeant, [and] the solemn answer 'dead,' 'dead.' followed three-fourths of the names." Lt. Luther Slater, by then a War Department employee and fellow MOLLUS member in Elliot's Washington D.C. Commandery, gave the opening address, followed by Pvt. Briscoe Goodhart, who six years later would memorialize his companions in a stirring history of the Rangers. As he would in his book, Goodhart that day paid special homage to the hardships, and frequent deaths, that these Virginia Yankees suffered if unlucky enough to be cast into a Confederate prison. The last speaker was "Col. S. E. Chamberlin," who produced an order regarding the Rangers that he had received while stationed at the Point, and which engendered much discussion among the audience. Elliot then dismissed the assembly to partake of "a superfluity of 'rations' served on the grounds," while the Tankerville Band "rendered appropriate selections." The high point came that evening around a campfire, "where reminiscences of their past services were discussed, stories of individual exploits related, old war songs and general good feeling prevailed."[37]

The following summer, Elliot attended the first reunion of the 25th N.Y. Cavalry, held in Washington on 10-11 July 1891 to coincide with the Twenty-Seventh Anniversary of the Battle of Fort Stevens. He had just returned to Washington to work for the IRS and was among fifteen veterans who gathered at the Howard House, Gen. Oliver Howard's vacant home at Howard University. Credit for organizing the reunion belonged to Washington D.C. resident John H. Wolf, who assumed the onerous task of locating surviving members of the regiment after over a quarter century had passed. A few days before the event, Wolf provided the press with a brief history of the Twenty-Fifth, including its role during Early's 1864 raid when, in the presence of Abraham Lincoln, the dismounted New Yorkers held off the Confederates during six hours of fighting that cost "many" killed and "hundreds" wounded before the VI Corps arrived. To emphasize this point, Wolf quoted from a letter Captain Chamberlin had sent from Savannah, crediting their "gallant command...[with] saving the Capital."[38]

During the reunion's first day, attendees approved creation of a permanent body to be called the [Daniel] Sickles's 25th N.Y. Veteran Cavalry Association and adopted the "Custer badge" as its official insignia. The sobriquet "Sickles Cavalry" had been dropped shortly after the Twenty-Fifth was organized, but the veterans were aware the former general headed the New York State Monuments Commission and currying his favor might result in a memorial of their own at Fort Stevens. The "Custer badge" was inspired by medals that Gen. George A. Custer distributed to regiment commanders in his brigade during the Valley Campaign.

Henry M. Nevius, a New Jersey judge, and Chamberlin, the only officers in attendance, were elected president and vice-president of the Association, while I. Warren Bullins was chosen secretary, and John Wolf agreed to serve as treasurer and recording secretary. Presumably on the basis of his earlier published accounts of their participation at Fort Stevens, Chamberlin was appointed to chair a committee to compile a history of the regiment, to which all members were urged to contribute their reminiscences. Attendees deferred adoption of by-laws and setting dues until their next meeting, planned to coincide with the G.A.R. national encampment in Washington D.C. the following year.[39]

A number of guests, including Edith and daughter Mary, dropped by the reunion to honor the veterans and recall the dark hours when the capital almost fell into Rebel hands. A *Washington Post* reporter was particularly impressed by remarks delivered by association president Nevius, dubbing the one-armed amputee "the hero of the little reunion." Only a sergeant at the time, Nevius recounted how he had assumed command of his company that fateful first day of the battle. The audience listened raptly as he described how Lincoln's words of encouragement had strengthened their resolve to die before letting the enemy get within reach of the capital, or the President. Following a dramatic account of how the regiment drove the Rebel skirmishers back towards Silver Spring, Nevius told of continuing to lead his men after being shot, and his encounter with the President when taken back to have his wound dressed.

It was a story the association's vice president could not hope to top, especially in front of this audience, so Chamberlin limited himself to reiterating his long-held contention that it was the Twenty-Fifth's determined advance from the earthworks that fooled Early into thinking reinforcements from Grant's VI Corps had arrived. Leaving no doubt he expected his audience to share his belief that Fort Stevens had been the high point of their military service, he challenged anyone to name an "especial deed performed during the war" more important than "to have saved the Capital." His opinion was shared by Association members such as Nevius and Wolf, who would spend the next two decades in a campaign to ensure the Twenty-Fifth's role at Fort Stevens was properly memorialized.[40]

On the second day, association members toured the battlefield and cemetery where they encountered veterans of the 98th Pa. Infantry, there to celebrate the erection of a monument honoring their part at Fort Stevens, and thus uphold their claim to have "saved" the capital. Several heated arguments broke out between the two groups, but when Nevius returned the next day to witness the actual dedication of the Pennsylvania monument, he was allowed to address the assembled crowd. According to a press account, he was able to get the Keystone Staters to admit they did not arrive at the fort before 6 PM on the first day, by which time they could plainly see evidence of earlier fighting, including several buildings still smoldering. Pressing his case, Nevius cited records of the adjacent cemetery, which held five members of his regiment killed that day, and challenged them to check with the Medical Museum, where his arm was on display, to confirm he had been wounded before the VI Corp arrived. "We do not claim to have whipped Early here...We only claim to have driven back his skirmishers and have held him in check until you arrived." Here he ended with Elliot's argument that it was the Twenty-Fifth's "Providential" presence which convinced Early that Grant's "old soldiers" had already disembarked.

A reporter caught up with Nevius afterwards and asked about a complaint his paper had received about its earlier article on the Twenty-Fifth's reunion. In addition to Nevius's failure to mention the Veterans Reserve Corps contribution to manning the defenses on 11 July, the critic questioned his claim to have been promoted on the spot by Lincoln and cast doubt on the claimed number of casualties suffered by the Twenty-Fifth. In response, Nevius acknowledged Veteran Reserve members were already in the fort when they arrived, but that it was the New Yorkers' rush out of the earthworks that drove the enemy back. Likewise, while he was not actually promoted on the spot, the President promised he would be, and later notified the governor of New York to make him a lieutenant. As to the number of casualties, Nevius revealed having located another grave at the Soldiers' Home and fourteen more from his regiment at Arlington Cemetery.[41]

On arrival in New Jersey, Nevius wrote Elliot to give his version of his encounter with the "Germans" from the 98th Pennsylvania and impress upon his vice president the importance of compiling an accurate regimental history to document their accomplishments. While attending the Keystone State "blow out," he had pointed out errors in the date and number of casualties on the Ninety-Eighth's new monument. Then, after listening to speeches indicating "they had done [it] all," Nevius attempted to "show them the ridiculous light in which they were placed," and finally got them to admit others were involved in the fighting before their arrival, "but there stands the monument—a falsifier."[42]

In closing, Nevius assured Elliot that comrade Wolf would turn over information received from other veterans for inclusion in the proposed history of the regiment. A few veterans would send their recollections directly to Elliot, the most significant being that of Dr. Richard Coutant. There is no evidence, however, that Elliot ever began to organize this material, other than some notes reflecting his continued interest in Fort Stevens. Perhaps more than most, he realized a full account of the Twenty-Fifth would resurrect events better left untold. As association secretary, Wolf continued to keep in touch with his old comrades, but rather than turn their letters over to Elliot, he had the most interesting ones published in Washington D.C. papers, including the lengthy account of Sgt. Harry Lane that is extensively quoted in Chapter 6.[43]

Despite taking place during the GAR's September 1882 National encampment in Washington D.C., attendance at the Twenty-Fifth's second reunion was light and garnered minimal coverage in the press. Capt. James M. Smith succeeded Nevius as president of the Sickles Cavalry Association, while other offices remained unchanged. Vice President Chamberlin did not leave Newport News to attend, perhaps to avoid questions about progress on the regimental history.[44]

A third reunion was held in New York City's Grand Opera House on 20 September 1893, but its published proceedings confirm that Chamberlin, dogged with problems of his own, failed to attend and was replaced as vice president by Capt. John Keegan. Even though this reunion was held in the regiment's home state, only twenty-six veterans were present out of 271 surviving members identified in a directory included with the proceeding. Chamberlin may have been amused to learn that Capt. James Smith's earlier courts-martial had not prevented his re-election as president. The indispensable John Wolf remained corresponding secretary and treasurer, although his move to Ohio that year helps explain the absence of further events and press items related to the Twenty-Fifth until his return to Washington D.C. at the end of the decade. In other business, attendees voted to pay Wolf fifty dollars to cover his expenses in setting up the association after first setting annual dues at two dollars and fifty cents. Dr. Coutant read a history of the Twenty-Fifth, presumably based on what he sent Elliot two years earlier, which the association voted to make part of the record. The printed proceedings, however, devote little space to this subject beyond a list of engagements and a Roll of Honor listing thirty-nine men who died as a result of wartime service. (It was headed by Lt. Col. Aaron Seeley, listed as "died of wounds" in San Francisco.) A letter from General Sickles was read, in which he promised to attend the next reunion, scheduled to be held in New York a year thence, although no record of another gathering before 1902 has come to light.[45]

Chapter 28

DOMESTIC AND PROFESSIONAL TURMOIL: 1892-1894

Grover Cleveland's election in November 1892 and installation of his Democratic administration four months later overshadowed much of Elliot's Newport News assignment (1892-93). In addition to heightened fears about job security, this period was further marred by problems at home that tested his marriage and self-esteem. That he and Edith overcame these obstacles attests to the underlying strength of their relationship and a mutual determination to put their family ahead of personal considerations. Most of what is known about this period comes from letters, the most extensive collection of correspondence to survive since their courtship. The Chamberlins' ages at the end of 1892 were: Elliot (fifty-eight), Edith (forty-five), Mary (twenty-three), Morrill (twenty), Nellie (eighteen), Edward (fifteen), Paul (thirteen) and Roy (ten). In addition to a daily maid, the household also included Elizabeth ("Lizzie") Hayden, a close friend of Mary. At this point, Annie Matthews (forty-eight) and her mother Sarah (seventy-five) still rented a townhouse which they shared with several boarders.

The first indication of Elliot's concerns about their marriage appeared in a letter shortly before Thanksgiving 1892, when he asked Edith if she remembered their stay at Old Point Comfort in 1876, adding: "Were some things as they were then, I would rejoice." The circumstances leading to his suspicions about her are not known but probably over Thanksgiving, Edith at least partially confirmed a fleeting infatuation with another, even though she may not have revealed his identity, and apparently convinced her husband that he had since died (at least metaphorically). The most likely time frame for this liaison was during Elliot's 1889-91 posting in Savannah, although he came to suspect it lasted even longer.[1]

Edith only made oblique references to this affair in surviving letters, and only one sheds any light on the identity of the other party:

> I went out G street [at the corner of 15th] and thought of you [Elliot] so much my darling in passing my old haunts, but the place looks so changed with the various signs and posters, which almost cover its exteriors, that it fails to grieve me to look upon it, as it did so short a time past. For a long time it was with a deep down sigh and positive sorrow that I came within sight of it. I could not help it, my own best love, and 'tis gone—the fancy—and 'tis well, for I could not be true to my noble husband with this second interest in my heart. Why it ever came, dearest, will always be a mystery, as it was so accidental, and with the party, whom I'd known so long, without ever the least germ of affection within my being for him. 'Tis dead tho mine only—with the object of the daydream, and I love you—and live only for you.[2]

Edith's letter suggests that her "second interest" lived or worked on G Street and was someone she had known long before it turned romantic. While the object of her affection will likely never be known, she frequently visited the Special Agency office to attend to her husband's affairs while he was in Savannah, and at times members of that office stopped by her house with news about Elliot. A brief note Assistant Treasury Secretary George C. Tichenor sent her on 3 July 1890 raises some questions. He had been a rising star in SAD during the 1880s and was rewarded by being made assistant secretary when William Windom took over the Treasury in 1889. Edith had just written Tichenor to congratulate him on his appointment to head the newly created Board of General Appraisers, which would involve a transfer to New York. He replied: "Be assured of my high appreciation of the very cordial and graceful words of congratulations contained in your most welcome note of this morning. Amongst the vast number of congratulatory greetings with which my friends have favored me today, none, my 'Sister Edith,' were [more] highly appreciated than yours. Let me assure you that your every kind thought and wish were heartily reciprocated." What is odd about this innocuous note, other than the fact that it was deemed important enough to keep, was that a senior official took the time to answer Edith immediately, and then personally mail it that same evening on his way to the hotel on H Street where he resided alone.[3]

After spending Thanksgiving in Washington, Elliot returned to Newport News determined to put the matter behind him. His positive attitude was expressed in a poem clipped from a newspaper and sent to Edith soon after his arrival. Composed by Harry Smith in the popular vernacular style of the time, it denounced the hypocrisy of a society that encouraged a husband to abandon an unfaithful wife. Excerpts from it follow:

The Estray

Wot's that you're askin? "Will I take her back?"
You bet! an smooth things over ef I kin.
"Ungrateful" an "o' no 'count," you say?
Wall, mebbe; I can't judge another's sin.
But sunshine'll come back when she gits home—
Sence she's been gone, there ain't been much in life—
The sunshine'll come back and stay this time.
O' course I'll take her back. Ain't she my wife?
"Wot'll the folks in town say 'bout the 'fair?"
Consarn 'em! Let 'em gabble ef they will....
An Annie was so purty an so young;
She allers wuz a heap too good for me.
Wot's more, she made some 'lowances for me,
Jes' 'cause I loved her, when she took me, sir;...
I'll take her back, make her fergit it all,
An I'll fergit she ever—went away...[4]

Yet, it was not so easy to forget, or forgive. Alone in his room in the Barnes Hotel in Hampton, Elliot was reminded of incidents that demanded an explanation, and which soon led him to conclude Edith's affair had overlapped times when he had been in Washington. (In one letter, he recalled a time when her wet feet suggested an unexplained absence from home, and another when she returned with the smell of a stranger's cologne.) A visit back home in early December failed to dispel his conviction she was withholding pertinent details. The following week he attended a popular melodrama, "The Planter's Wife," at the Soldiers' Home in Hampton. The wife in the play was named Edith and the planter was a colonel. With the exception that the husband killed the villain, Elliot felt that "the rest of the story I could have told" and was unable to sleep that night.[5]

In contrast, Edith's letters portray her absorption in preparations for the holidays, with little inclination to dwell on the past. The two youngest children, Roy and Paul, were looking forward to school vacation and receiving presents. Mary had just returned from an extended stay at the home of her friend Katherine Jewell on Cape Cod, a trip she had financed by selling magazine subscriptions. The week before Christmas, Edith took her daughters shopping. They could not afford much but enjoyed the gaily decorated store windows and mingling with the smartly dressed crowd.[6]

One evening, Paul returned from his paper route with the family tomcat who had been missing since October. "Pickie" appeared to have been well fed in the interim, and Edith expressed concern to her husband he might run away again. At this point, she caught herself, "but I am getting on dangerous ground when I discourse upon people and things that go astray." In his reply, Elliot (a cat fancier) wryly commented: "A cat does not ever show much affection. It may be best to look after him somewhat more carefully. I have thought of you a good deal...and wonder if you are to be strictly depended upon." Informing her that he would be back on Christmas Eve, he pointedly added, "I suppose it is right that I announce my intended arrival."[7]

His holiday stay with his family went well enough for him to try (unsuccessfully) to have C/SAD Amory Tingle extend his leave. Despite this happy interlude, his return to Newport News after the New Year marked an extended low point in his life. Not only was he worried about his wife, but he had to face the likelihood of losing his job once Cleveland took office. To make matters worse, an unusually cold winter shut down shipping in Hampton Roads, leaving him with little to occupy his time. (He had one harrowing experience aboard a revenue cutter that went out to a ship in distress, only to get trapped in the ice for several hours.) Even the Barnes Hotel, normally a popular honeymoon and tourist destination, was empty, denying him the opportunity to play whist and euchre with fellow guests. Every night he would retire early to a cold, barren room that he only paid extra to heat on the most frigid evenings. His only diversion was to pore over letters he forced Edith to write on a daily basis. His life revolved around these missives, which, even so, failed to lift his depression, or answer questions that continued to haunt him.

Not long after his return to work, he let Edith know that "I...really think that I am in love with you. What do you think about it?" He repeated this conviction several days later, emphasizing "there was a great deal for us both to live for...I shall endeavor to do my part." Nevertheless, he still could not avoid "the depressed moments...They come to me at unexpected times and I do now want to forget some things I know, but there is that longing to know more." In a "confidential" addendum to his next letter, he bemoaned being left alone to "struggle with my thoughts." Right after proclaiming he had "nothing against you but forgiveness and love," he admitted not being able to fathom why she had done it, "but you did and nothing either of us can do will change the fact now. No matter how far you have gone or what you have done." Like many in this situation, he both wanted her to admit all and at the same time, did not want to "push beyond recovery" their chances for reconciliation. He could proclaim "the future is ours," but still feel it was largely up to her to make it so, with his "help." Writing the latter prompted him to wonder, if "except for my pecuniary aid, you would do almost as well if I was away." Then referencing her recent exhortation for him to "believe in me darling and some day you will know," he expressed confidence his "uncertainty and doubt will be removed, as it partially has been." Yet, he still begged her not to lie: "I can bear everything else."

Several days later, Elliot was less charitable. He had gone out the previous evening "to hear a humbug on spiritualist manifestations...for want of something better to do." He found the medium to be a fraud, as he had expected, but admitted, "I would have been glad to have communicated with some departed spirit that I thought of. I wanted answers to some questions I could have asked him." He was also irritated by a metaphor his wife had used, comparing their marriage to a piece of broken china that could be restored to its original appearance and made even stronger:

> Yes, I know it can be mended...and no one knows of the damage done, but the owner and the person doing the damage and the one repairing it. Still they know that it is likely to break again very easy in the same place. I think it best to repair in the best manner that it can be and then use carefully. This is better than throwing it away and getting new to

replace it. They are hard to mend. I know this by experience. It must be done thoroughly and not a single crack left. Every one should be searched for, found out, then you can repair so it will last a life time.[8]

A short time later, he took strong exception to her suggestion she be allowed to write every other day and was even more upset to learn that she did not feel she could leave the children to visit him. He also chided her failure to call on Justin Morrill and his wife, pointing out that the Senator was their best protection against losing his job. The couple's health was failing, and "we won't have them long to see anyway." (The repetition of this theme in other letters suggests Edith did not share her husband's fondness for the Morrills.) Although his next letter reiterated a willingness to believe her "fully determined to take [him] for better or worse," he would still need his wife's help to remain "good," even though he had never been unfaithful—at least up to that point. In agreeing to take better care of himself, he admitted to not yet being "fully prepared to meet some one I know in the other world," and then tried to dismiss his tendency to brood on having a large head like President-elect Cleveland. In response to his wife's request for a "small check" to cover household expenses, he enclosed ten dollars, all he claimed to have after paying off debts. (He used control of the family's purse strings to get back at Edith, who had to borrow money from her oldest son Morrill to tide her over between remittances from her husband.)[9]

Failing to convince Elliot's supervisor to have him recalled to Washington, Edith bowed to his wishes and joined him for several days in mid-February. Letters written after her return indicate the romantic interlude helped bring about a reconciliation. She called it a "restful, joyful time" to be long remembered, while he was glad his perennially thin wife had gained weight after dining on local delicacies such as oysters. The pleasure was soon cut short by the discovery she might be pregnant, leaving her "so scared, and so mad, I can't see straight. To think one can't have one drop of sweet without some bitter dregs. I did so fully enjoy my nice visit to you and did not for one moment fear so serious a result." It was her turn to feel depressed, and she begged him to understand her situation and provide the name of a doctor in Baltimore who could resolve her predicament. Although Elliot thought a pregnancy at her age unlikely, he was adamantly opposed to an abortion. Fortunately, the crisis resolved itself a few days later, which Edith credited to having heavily imbibed "Aunt Bettie's tea." Now overjoyed, she admitted to not having told him how thoroughly upset she had been.[10]

Elliot's reaction to the news was muted, and the whole incident reawakened his jealousy. In expressing doubt about whether her use of a home remedy had had any effect on her condition, he failed to show sympathy for her earlier anxiety. His insensitivity was also evident in his closing remarks. "I am glad to hear that you are not off seeing some one. I have to take your word that such is the case." He still could not fathom the "mystery" of why she had been unfaithful and admitted needing more time to put it behind him. Despite the coldness in this, his last surviving letter to his wife, she would only a week later signify her confidence that their relationship was on the mend.[11]

In late March, Edith responded to a query from her husband about whether she had received his latest remittance. After duly acknowledging receipt of the stipend and apologizing for forgetting to inform him of this, she added with somewhat pointed humor: "I...always make a note of credit for your great punctuality in responding to my requests...I do thoroughly appreciate your goodness—in every respect—and have such an exalted opinion of men—with you dear for my standard." Changing the subject, she worried his chilly hotel room might provoke another bout of rheumatism. In turning down his invitation to join him in early April to witness the Naval Review (described later), Edith feared she "might not be the joyful companion you might like." Musing about her past indiscretion, which now seemed like a "dream," which she now found "difficult to realize as something I was involved in. I wonder how ever I could have done it, and yet when I recall the inducements, and warm allurement, I don't know how I resisted so long." When with Elliot, she felt reassured all was in the past; when apart, she feared he "might grow hard and unforgiving, and I get excited and feel unsafe. Still I have every assurance of your love and trust, and I will be comforted, for it does seem that my great love for you might overcome everything." That he had been able in his last letter (not found) to treat their "serious" problems in a "humorous, almost witty" way had given her hope their estrangement was coming to an end. "I am so happy my own true dear that you do love me, so forgive me. Ah, what shadows arise when I think what might have been my fate, had you not loved me truly."[12]

Although their marriage had been saved, plans to transform Clifton into a means of livelihood for the family had suffered during this period of domestic turmoil, even as the advent of a Democratic administration put Elliot's employment at risk. At the time, Henry and Bettie Holland, an older Black couple, were living in the house in return for looking after the property and tending to a small dairy herd. Edith worried about what would happen to them if the family had to move back to the farm and suggested that her mother could sell them her "old house" in Waterford, letting Henry pay off the mortgage through work on the farm. The Hollands were assisted by Arch Wellington, a Black farmhand, who had been out of work since his previous employer, William Williams, died the year before. Elliot, however, suspected Arch was staying at Clifton without permission, and was not well disposed towards him. Arch, in turn, was upset over not being paid for his labor and wanted to remain on a permanent basis at fifteen dollars a month. Edith liked Arch and eventually persuaded her husband to let him stay.[13]

That winter, Edith served as an intermediary between Elliot and Henry Holland, despite having told her husband his instructions would "have more weight," if he wrote Henry directly. This arrangement, reminiscent of Henry Gover's role during disputes over the Matthews estate, reflected Elliot's doubts about their marriage and inability to concentrate on much else. He appeared a bit more focused in early 1893, declaring a desire to get "a great deal done…this season…Plans should be made to farm in good style…[and] make it pleasant to do so should we have to resort to it." In addition to this vague statement, he wanted Henry to prepare the hillside behind Clifton for corn and potatoes and string a wire fence around the orchard to increase pastureland. In relaying the message to Henry, Edith asked him to cut lumber for mending fences and rebuilding the barn.[14]

Finances were a frequent source of irritation that winter, but Edith was reluctant to ask her husband for additional funding for the farm at a time when she was having difficulty getting him to send enough to support the family in Washington D.C. He ignored her suggestion to stock the farm with pigs and turkeys, which could be purchased in the city at lower prices than in the country. Another time, Henry was told to purchase a horse for plowing but was not given sufficient funds and had to borrow the remainder from Robert Walker, owner of nearby Huntley farm. At one point, Morrill Chamberlin had to lend his mother money to pay Henry and Arch, who had not received their salaries from Elliot. Fearful Clifton might have to be sold if it could not be made profitable, Morrill tried to convince his father to invest in improvements and "do systematic managing." He also wanted to repair the bridge and fence at the front entrance to make the place more presentable when guests arrived. Matters took a turn for the worse after a prolonged cold snap brought the unexpected expense of having to purchase more fodder to feed the cows. Frustrated by her husband's inaction, and remembering a friend who made $300 painting china, Edith lamented not having a comparable skill to help pay for farm improvements. Finally with the arrival of spring, she had to face the reality that no major changes to Clifton could occur until the following year.[15]

While her husband remained in Newport News, Edith and her mother took the children to Clifton in time to celebrate the Fourth of July with a fireworks display on the lawn. Determined to "make a good *fight*" and armed with detailed instructions from Elliot, they set about reclaiming the property from years of neglect. Paul, Edward and Roy used corn knives to attack thistles and daisies that had taken over the pasture, while their mother's arm became so sore wielding a sickle to clear weeds around the house she could scarcely hold a pen at night. The boys helped repair fences and strung wire around the orchard, as their father had failed to remit sufficient funds for Henry to undertake this task. (The cows benefited from the additional pasture but ate most of the apples that fall.) Edith and the girls took charge of milking and churning butter, although a shortage of containers hindered shipment to Washington. The whole family pitched in to help when a steam thresher came to harvest wheat, but even so, part of the resulting 116 bushels went to the thresher's owner, as well as Arch and Henry. The arrival of rain in mid-July interrupted efforts to cut and stack hay but provided welcome relief from a drought that had threatened the corn and vegetable crops. In the end, Edith and the children were only marginally successful in making the farm more productive, but their commitment to keeping it from being sold was quite evident.

Sarah's sister, Ann Gover, had grown so feeble she had to be moved to Clifton so that Edith and her mother could care for her. Despite her infirmity, "Auntie" insisted that Edward and his mother accompany her to First-day services in mid-July. It was Edith's first Quaker meeting in some time and she found it "extremely small and uninteresting." Afterwards, she talked with a cousin who had attended the Columbian Exposition in Chicago, and came away convinced the boys at least should go, as its educational value would more than compensate for the expense. (Elliot attended a GAR Encampment in Indianapolis later that summer and may have used this opportunity to take the family to Chicago.) That same July weekend, Morrill brought out Mary's suitor, Hume Clendenin, and another friend, who recorded their Clifton visit with his camera.[16]

Family Gathering at Clifton, July 1893. From left: Eleanor, Mary, Paul, Elizabeth Hayden, Roy, Edith, Hume Clendenin(?), Morrill, Lucy Hewes and Edward. (TCC)

* * * * *

Edith's correspondence during her husband's posting in southern Virginia reveals the daily bustle of a home filled with young people. In addition to providing for them and checking on Annie and her mother, she found time to entertain friends and other visitors. Undoubtedly this upbeat patter was meant to cheer her husband, but it also expressed her positive approach to life. (On the other hand, she had never lived alone, and was probably incapable of doing so, as her husband once pointed out.) In recounting their son Morrill's disappointment over not receiving a promotion at the bank, his mother turned it into an example of the impossibility for a parent, or a spouse, to shield loved ones from life's trials. "Well they don't *kill,* and the best way is to pick up courage again—and march on with renewed effort. We have had to do a lot of this my precious—haven't we together?—but perhaps the good of it all will be seen some day—and we will be made to rejoice our trials, and crosses."[17]

A frequent visitor to the Chamberlin household was Mary's suitor, William Hume Clendenin. "Hume," a twenty-two-year-old clerk in a Washington law office, lived with his widowed mother, Alice Campbell Clendenin. He was a good friend of Mary's brother Morrill, and the two played baseball whenever the weather permitted. On one occasion, the unflappable Edith calmly wrote to her husband, while the two young men engaged in a wrestling match, her only concern being that they might ruin their clothes. A visit to Washington that spring by Hume's "millionaire aunt" was a matter of more than passing curiosity to Edith, since the widow had no children and was rumored to have included her nephew in her will. In closely following the aunt's stay, Edith admitted to having "a personal interest in [Hume's] future, as he is talking of sharing it with Mary."[18]

Either because of a lack of funds, or a preference for home remedies, Edith seldom sent the children to a physician for treatment. After Morrill suffered a severe injury to his leg that refused to heal, Hume was called on to change the bandages. Another time, when Paul cut his hand, Edith coolly told her husband, "if it had been done with swords, I'd not mind so much—but that he would fence with a boy with a carving knife—I'm certainly provoked. 'Tis his right hand, and he misses it sadly. I'll do my best with it, but would like your advice [on possible treatment]." As for herself, Edith relied on self-medication, and only went to a dentist when the pain became unbearable. Despite this casual attitude, she constantly advised her husband to guard against illness. If money was to be spent on doctors and medicine, the family breadwinner had first priority.[19]

The most serious medical problem involved Edward's eyesight. In January 1893, Edith reported, "his eyes are inflamed again—and have been too painful to use in school, tho he has gone on pretty regularly." A short time later, she lamented that the illness had prevented their son from becoming a Congressional page, which would have enabled him to earn "sufficient money to have gotten a musical education. Even those slightly gifted in this way—make a good deal of money and certainly he has more than usual talent." By February, Edward had stopped school and spent most of his time at home, helping his mother with cooking and household chores. (Perhaps as a result, Edward became closer to her than to his father, who seldom mentioned him in his letters.) Even though her son could barely read a score, Edith still hoped he might become a professional musician and arranged piano lessons for him with two sisters who once taught Mary. (Edward's eyesight continued to deteriorate to the point he was completely blind, ending a promising operatic career. Since the cause of his blindness is not known, it is unclear whether early medical attention might have saved his sight.) Despite his disability, Edward inherited his mother's cheery disposition and was frequently sought as an escort by ladies young and old.[20]

An avid reader and competent writer, Edith nevertheless had a low regard for her own scholastic skills and left supervision of schoolwork to the older children, or her husband when home. Roy was doing well in grade school, and Paul, who hated to study, had finally resolved to exert himself in order to enter high school the following year and eventually pursue a military career like his father, whom he idolized. Edith had less confidence than her husband in the academic abilities of their "little scamp," but she did not doubt Paul's newfound industriousness when, after losing his paper route for being two minutes late to pick up the early morning edition, immediately went out and found a replacement route. Nellie, too, had recently decided to finish high school, although her life revolved around friends and social activities. (Her life-long interest in the Far East was sparked by the return of a friend that spring from Japan.)

The children adored their mother, who had the ability to love each one without being overly possessive, and even when she was busy writing to Elliot they invariably gathered around her. After one lengthy "bull session" in which they discussed their futures in Edith's bedroom, Edward summarized their conclusions: Paul would go to the Naval Academy, Roy would become a Supreme Court judge, Mary a leading artist, Nellie would marry a wealthy man, Morrill would be promoted to bank president, and Edward would become a second Paderewski (a famous Polish pianist and composer). Only Paul achieved the specific goal set forth that evening, but they all were unafraid to aim high.[21]

Like her sister Annie, Edith discontinued attendance at Quaker meeting after leaving Baltimore, but her letters continued to reveal an innate spirituality. The family was now nominally Episcopalian, but she never pressured the children on religious issues, maintaining many paths lead to "the same great throne." As a result, the family was quite eclectic in its religious practices. Nellie and Edward were confirmed that winter in an Episcopalian church near their home, while Mary and her friend Lizzie regularly attended a different one. Paul and Morrill rarely went to church; Roy only occasionally attended afternoon Sunday school. When she did go, Edith favored a nearby Episcopal chapel, but admitted her spotty attendance set a poor example for the children. Like her reliance on home remedies, Edith's personal beliefs reflected a mixture of Quaker mysticism and rural superstition that sprang from her childhood in Waterford—views which often contrasted with the more rational outlook of her husband. He, on the other hand, regularly attended church wherever he might be and urged his wife to do the same, yet his letters contain few clues to his actual spiritual beliefs.

In early March, Elliot returned home briefly to attend Cleveland's second inauguration. Two of Mary and Morrill's former classmates, Lucy Hewes and John Black, arrived from out-of-town to witness the event, and ended up staying several weeks with the family. John sang Irish songs to his own guitar accompaniment and was very popular with the ladies. Along with Mary and Edward, he provided musical entertainment for the many young people who visited the house. On Inauguration Day, Edward took Lucy to stand in front of the White House where they got to shake Cleveland's "big fat hand" and catch sight of the President's baby, Ruth (for whom the candy bar is named). Edith loved the excitement, and missed the crowded streets after the inauguration was over. Before their two houseguests departed, she and Morrill threw a St. Patrick's Day party for forty guests. Many attendees were children of Congressmen, and Edith declared the gathering "as nice a set of handsome young people as you'd ever see." Morrill proved a genial and capable host, and the gathering was declared a grand success. To break the ice, every male guest had to converse with each female on a specified subject for ten minutes. Edith filled in for someone who could not attend and felt like a young girl again with the attention shown her. The party, full of music, song and dance, did not break up until after 2 AM.[22]

For the first time in their lives, Elliot and Edith had begun to save some money and could even entertain the possibility of purchasing their own house in the city. Annie and Sarah Matthews favored this idea, as it would permit the whole family to live under one roof again. Annie was doing well financially with her boarders and Treasury salary but found housekeeping difficult and threatened to move into an "old ladies' home...for the rest of her life." Chronic health issues, marked by recurrent neuralgia and rheumatism, lay at the core of her problems, but she was also unwilling to live completely on her own. When ill, she would insist Edith sleep over at her house, or else she would move in with her sister. (Their seventy-five-year-old mother was far more stoic.)

Commenting on their improved finances, Edith declared, "my only wish in all these years is [that] we had lived as in the past two—then we'd have had a nice bank account, and not feared loss of office. Still, we have done much, and are still strong and willing, and surely the Lord is on our side, if only we do our part." Although any final decision on whether to purchase a town house would have to await Elliot's fate in the new administration, he wanted to reunite the family regardless of what happened. (Not only did he enjoy the role of *pater familias* to a large household, but he may have felt better having Annie and her mother there to keep an eye on his wife.) To accomplish this in the event they continued to rent their present residence, he favored moving the dining room into the basement to create more space. Edith was less sanguine about this idea, particularly with regard to having her sister live with them. She did not want to force Lizzie Hayden to leave, and feared Annie might insist on one of her boarders joining them.[23]

When warm weather made its appearance in April, Edith was sorry to see winter go, it having brought so many "positive" things to the family—a sentiment Elliot might not have shared. Now her thoughts turned to the farm and prospects for a good growing season. Aware they might be living there soon, she twice raised the possibility of getting a horse so she could ride again, although she suspected her husband no longer shared her enthusiasm for this activity. "Do they have any more fox hunts? Think of me, for I should love to join it. I'd like to be on a wild frolic of some sort tonight. I hate frozen life. Am not built for it."[24]

Spring also brought some excitement into Elliot's life, as preparations got under way in Hampton Roads for the International Naval Review. Scheduled to coincide with the 400th anniversary of Columbus's discovery of the New World, this highly anticipated event would feature the most modern warships from the British, French, Russian, Spanish and Italian navies. As they began to assemble, lavish parties were held for the foreign visitors, and many came from Washington to join the festivities. The Review would have its grand finale at the end of April, when the combined U.S. and international fleet left Norfolk and steamed up the East Coast to another reception in New York. (Neglected after the Civil War, the U.S. Navy began its transformation into a modern service by century's end under President Harrison's Secretary of the Navy, Benjamin Tracy, who initiated a massive shipbuilding program and planned the Naval Review to awaken the American public to foreign naval superiority. The isolationist Cleveland Administration tried to reduce the naval budget, but the 1893 depression forced Democrats to continue building warships to stimulate the economy.)

Roy and especially Paul were eager to join their father and watch the spectacle presented by the most modern warships in the world. When their mother tried to argue they could not afford the trip, Paul wrote directly to his father for permission. He had saved two dollars for his steamship fare and was willing to "sit up all night" in the passenger lounge to avoid the cost of a room. Elliot agreed to let his sons come down with their sister Nellie, and together they witnessed a turning point in American history as the international fleet steamed past Old Point Comfort on its way to the open sea. Not only did the Review demonstrate the growing might of the U.S. Navy, but it also symbolized a significant departure from the isolationism that had characterized American foreign policy for decades. Five years later, this commitment to international expansion would lead to the Spanish-American War and ultimately culminate in America's global reach in the next century. After the ships departed, Elliot took a week off to take the children back to Washington.[25]

* * * * *

Within weeks of Cleveland's Inauguration, Edith's letters began to show heightened concern over her husband's future, as rumors spread about the long-feared purge of Republican officeholders. By late March, the father of Morrill's girlfriend, a deputy in the Pension Bureau, was forced to retire, and the younger children reported their classmates voiced "much uncertainty" about their futures. Belatedly moved to call on Senator Morrill, Edith only managed to speak with his secretary, Louise Sophie Swann, and her fears were not assuaged when Swann dismissed the Democrats' "great show of economy and [fiscal] reduction," as no more than a ploy "to make room for their friends." Frightened "thousands" might be let go, Edith was left to wonder "whose heads are going off now. I fear they are a cruel set in authority now."

On a visit to the Treasury, Edith encountered "little knots of men all about in the corridors talking in subdued tones, and not the comfortable appearance of security that has been evinced so long." Her husband's immediate boss, Louis Martin, provided little solace when he told her that he and Elliot were alike in that they would "die," if they did not have regular employment. C/SAD Tingle confided that he expected to receive notice of his own dismissal any day. An ex-Confederate colonel had appeared without warning at his home, and Tingle's first thought was that the man was there to take his job, or that of another special agent. When he learned the colonel only wanted to become an inspector, he hired him on the spot. Edith shared Tingle's apprehension, writing her husband, "I don't fear the democrats so much, but the ex-confederates I can't trust entirely. Still perhaps 'tis the dawning of a new era, and there will be changing for the good."

Elliot remained guardedly optimistic Senator Morrill would again save him, especially since Treasury Secretary John Carlisle had served on Morrill's Finance Committee. Morrill Chamberlin visited his godfather's house and spoke with the latter's son, James Morrill, who assured him that the Senator had already discussed Elliot's fate with Carlisle. While the Secretary had made no promises, he took down Elliot's name and gave Morrill the impression the special agent would not be removed any time soon. Towards the end of March, Edith paid another call on the Senator, but again only spoke with Miss Swann, who confirmed her husband's job seemed secure for the present. Despite these assurances, Edith wished he were at a busier post and thereby appear more indispensable.[26]

A review of his case file confirms he had been assigned little of significance since the beginning of the year. Some of this was due to bad weather and a deliberate stand down on investigations until the new Treasury Secretary took office. Finally in April, he was asked to find out why the Norfolk customhouse needed to rent a sailboat every year. He apparently considered it a frivolous request and did not respond until a second query prompted him to point out that the rental charge was not excessive, and the boat was used exclusively for official business—probably not what his new bosses wanted to hear. In another report, Elliot resurrected his old complaints about the boarding station at Hampton, a situation he had been trying to correct for over fifteen years, again not the best way to advertise his utility.[27]

By mid-April, Edith was routinely scrutinizing newspaper listings of civil service removals for clues about her husband's fate. Through Annie and friends in the Treasury, she kept abreast of the latest rumors and relayed them to Newport News. Learning from the papers that Senator Morrill was celebrating his eighty-third birthday, she dispatched her son Morrill to pay their respects. During increased visits to the Treasury, what she encountered there was hardly encouraging, and Amory Tingle could only advise her to build up Clifton's dairy herd as insurance against her husband's probable loss of a job.

After that visit, she told Elliot she was praying for his future. "Do you think He will hear my voice? He didn't about the pension, so it makes me doubt again—still He is good and does take care of us all."[28]

Later that month, a story broke in the New York press focusing unwanted attention on the Special Agency office. The allegations concerned frauds perpetrated during Harrison's administration by a ring in New York, allegedly linked to C/SAD Tingle, Assistant Secretary O. L. Spaulding and General Appraiser George Tichenor. (Spaulding, also a former special agent, had replaced Tichenor after the latter became head of the Appraisers Board.) From the start, Edith believed the charges were concocted by persons hoping to replace Tingle and the others, although she considered the accusations against Tichenor particularly unjust because of his long record of public service and recent poor health. In early May, the Treasury issued a report exonerating Tingle and his colleagues, but Democratic congressmen kept the issue alive by creating a special board of inquiry. During this period, the press published a list of special agents left over from the previous administration, identifying each by political affiliation, salary and length of service. (Nineteen of twenty-three were Republican, and Tingle and Elliot were tied for longevity in the government with twenty-three years apiece, a figure that included military service. Tingle's salary of ten dollars per was only two dollars more than Elliot's.) In the end, the C/SAD came under the heaviest fire from the press, while Elliot was never named in connection with the New York ring, and Ira Ayer, who had been in charge of the New York district office for many years, was only mentioned as being well-regarded by merchants in that city. When Edith visited her husband's home office on the day Assistant Secretary Spaulding's removal was announced, she found Tingle looking twenty years older and barely able to speak. Frightened, she anxiously inquired whether her husband had also been fired and was relieved to learn this was not yet the case. (Tingle would be removed from office that summer, amid speculation about the source of his apparent wealth, which included a new home.)[29]

Before being forced to leave office, Spaulding was able to take advantage of Secretary Carlisle's absence to send Elliot on his first meaningful assignment in months, giving him a chance to demonstrate his effectiveness. Consequently, he spent part of April in Edenton, North Carolina, investigating irregularities in the salt trade, the results of which he sent directly to Carlisle. The following month, he launched an operation he hoped would further polish his image. Having learned a vessel anchored in Hampton Roads was trying to off-load an illegal shipment of bay rum, wine and cigars from the West Indies, he personally mounted surveillance on the ship. (Edith, who was now keeping close tabs on his activities, warned him not to "get into any trouble" trying to apprehend the smugglers.) Luck was not on his side, and not only did he fail to catch the suspects in the act, but also suffered a severe rheumatic attack while working outdoors. It was hardly the image of a vigorous investigator he had hoped to portray, especially when Edith had to come down and nurse him back to health.[30]

Elliot's fate was decided on 22 July, when Secretary Carlisle removed him as special agent in Newport News and reappointed him a Customs inspector in Norfolk, a change that cut his pay in half to four dollars per day. It was essentially a repeat of what befell him in 1885, but this time the family was better prepared, both psychologically and financially. Fortunately, he would remain in the 5th Special Agency District working for his old friend Louis Martin, who arranged for him to be "temporarily" posted to the port of Georgetown, in the District of Columbia, and even though remaining officially assigned to Norfolk, Elliot managed to work out of Washington for the next twelve months. Plans to purchase a townhouse were abandoned, as Annie and her mother rejoined the Chamberlins at their Q Street home to help share expenses.[31]

That fall, Elliot drew on his background as a jeweler to evaluate gold and silver samples. A financial panic that year had driven up the price of gold, and threatened to deplete the Treasury's reserves, setting in motion a national campaign to switch to a silver, or bi-metal, standard. Soaring gold prices touched off a wave of prospecting, and several mines opened in Virginia at this time. Elliot caught the fever, and in early 1894 sent several rock samples from Clifton to a commercial chemist. Unfortunately, his latest scheme to make money off the farm came to naught, as the analysis revealed insufficient gold to justify commercial exploitation.[32]

His work as an inspector seemed to be proceeding smoothly until early August 1894, when he received notice his employment with the Treasury would end in two weeks. The circumstances surrounding his abrupt dismissal are not clear, but he later claimed it was done simply to make room for a Virginia Democrat. His termination came as a complete surprise and he was not even allowed to use up accumulated leave. His removal, preceded by a year at half his former pay, was a severe blow to the family. Moreover, his job prospects were not good at age sixty, so it is not surprising he and Edith decided to return to farming while awaiting the outcome of the next election.[33]

Annie's position was no less tenuous. The first sign of trouble came at the end of 1893, when she was denied a promotion despite having passed the necessary examination. At that time, Charles F. Chamberlayne, one of Elliot's distant relatives in Boston, wrote Secretary Carlisle to complain about Annie's treatment and stress the importance of giving her a raise now that her brother-in-law's salary had been reduced. Annie did not get the promotion; moreover, just after Elliot learned of his dismissal, she too was notified her job would end in a few weeks. Various friends rallied to her side, including Justin Morrill, who wrote Carlisle directly from his home in Vermont. The Senator complained that he had just learned of Elliot's removal, despite the Secretary's assurances he would be retained, and emphasized dismissing Annie as well would impose an insurmountable burden on their family. However, the Republicans' long-time champion of high tariffs had little influence in the current Treasury Department, and Carlisle declined to rescind his order.[34]

Chapter 29

HAPPIER TIMES: 1894-1900

After demotion to inspector in August 1893, Elliot returned from Newport News to the family's home on Q Street, where he was joined by Annie Matthews. Edith and the children arrived from the farm in September to start the school year, while Sarah Matthews remained at Clifton to take care of her sister. To use up accumulated leave, Elliot joined them on the farm for three weeks in October. It was a welcome chance to unwind in the county after the harrowing past year, and he took the opportunity at a Catoctin Farmers Club (CFC) meeting to voice his pleasure at being back in Loudoun "with its good roads, good schools, and good churches, even the air should be bottled."[1]

After Elliot and Annie lost their Treasury jobs the following summer, the family rented smaller quarters near Rock Creek Park. Lack of space forced the two girls and Edward to spend much of the next years at Clifton, first with their grandmother, and then their parents. Later that year, Morrill left his bank job to accept a position as cashier with the D.C. Collector of Taxes. His annual salary of $1,800, a princely sum in that era, was close to the most his father ever made as special agent and allowed him to take law courses at night as well as extend loans to his parents.[2]

Early the following year, help for Annie to regain her job came from an unexpected source. Nathan H. Chamberlain was a cousin whom Elliot knew as a boy and had since become a successful author. In support of the Democrats' position on lowering tariffs during the 1892 presidential campaign, he had published *What's the Matter? or Our Tariff and Its Taxes*. The popular primer branded Republican support for protectionism as "anti-American, anti-republican, aristocratic and the tool of tyranny." During a trip to Washington in February 1895, Nathan called on Elliot's family and was shocked to learn of the circumstances surrounding Annie's dismissal. Having become acquainted with Carlisle during the campaign, he offered to meet with the Treasury Secretary to press for her reinstatement. But, unable to arrange an appointment before his return to Massachusetts, Nathan wrote to Carlisle about Annie, whom he described as a distant relative, who had been unjustly fired. Alluding to their mutual acquaintances, Nathan reminded Carlisle of a letter the President had written, thanking the author for his support in the campaign. Now, in what he described as the "first, and only, favor" he intended to ask, Nathan requested the Secretary "personally inquire" into Annie's case, and "according to her record, restore her to her place." Worried the well-known reformer might make Annie a *cause célèbre*, Carlisle ordered her reinstated as a clerk in the Comptroller of the Currency's office. Although she received notice of this action in May 1895, over a half year would elapse before Annie returned to work at $900 per year, which did not include the raise she had earlier qualified for.[3]

At the end of that summer, Elliot and Edith decided to economize by remaining at Clifton with their two daughters and Edward, while Paul and Roy returned to Washington to continue their education, staying with Annie and Morrill at the Rock Creek apartment. (Paul was then a sophomore at

Western High School; Roy was in eighth grade.) Their aunt, however, did not enjoy having responsibility for two teenagers, and the family decided to give up its Washington *pied-à-terre* the following year, leaving Morrill and Annie to rent separate apartments, and forcing the boys to put their education on hold and join their parents in the country for a year.[4]

After attending several CFC meetings as a guest, Elliot was reinstated as a full member in August 1895. That fall, he exhibited produce from his garden and presented an essay on Virginia homes and farms. On being elected CFC president in December for the coming year, he joked in his acceptance speech that they had chosen a farmer whose corn crop consisted of the "most perfect nubbins he had ever seen." As president, he continued to promote dairy farming and fruit production. Edith had to serve as hostess for two consecutive CFC meetings that spring—first at Huntley farm, when Robert Walker and his wife could not be present, and then at the first meeting held at Clifton in nineteen years. Elliot consistently brought the best garden produce to exhibit, including an enormous cabbage and the first cauliflower the membership had ever seen. Yet, yields from his cash crops, primarily corn and wheat, were the lowest in the club. Still determined to make a go in the orchard business, he planted one hundred more apple trees.[5]

A letter from Mary's fiancé, Hume Clendenin, reached Clifton after she had gone back to Washington in mid-November 1895. She had complained to Hume about the work she was expected to do on the farm, and an injury to her arm while churning butter. In a rather unsympathetic reply, Hume told her he would expect her to do even more cooking and laundry once they got married. In thanking her for a shipment of apples and walnuts from the farm, he still let her know one of the apples was spoiled. Part of his pique was due to someone having told his mother that he had hurt Mary's feelings. At the time, Hume was auditing the books of important companies in Boston, and hoped to use what he was learning to make some investments of his own.[6]

Later that month, Edith described to her mother having to cook for five hungry men on the farm, including Elliot, the Hogans (probably carpenters) and a hired hand named Cornel. The children had all left, but the myriad chores she had to perform left no time to feel lonely or afraid, and even after the "Colonel" went to bed at night she was kept occupied by reading and sewing. Aside from working in the dairy, cooking and cleaning, she had put up beans and apples until running out of jars. The warm weather delayed butchering, but the Walkers had brought over fresh pork and sausage, which her husband declared the best he ever ate. "He seems so well and enjoys his meals, and his whole heart and soul are in his work." A small new dairy shed was nearly ready except for whitewashing and a few finishing touches. In addition, "they have gotten on famously with [rebuilding] the barn, and it shows from a distance now." (She was overly optimistic about the barn, which was not finished until 1903.) A new cistern had been installed, providing clear, cold water, probably obtained from rainwater. Part of Clifton was still being rented out, as she and the "Colonel" were living in just the two south rooms, prompting her perennial complaint: "If only the money was not so tight, how wonderful everything would be. I do hope...wealth will come to some member of the family." Edith also commiserated with her mother over her sister Annie who, despite having her reinstatement at the Treasury announced back in May, had yet to start work.[7]

The election over and expecting employment under the incoming Republican administration, Elliot declined CFC office for 1897, and his participation further waned after he moved back to Washington that summer, causing the club secretary to lament the resulting loss of exhibits he regularly brought to meetings. Nevertheless, he and Edith continued to host a meeting every spring when Clifton's gardens were at their peak. In a September 1898 talk to mark the CFC's Thirtieth anniversary, Cornelius Shawen paid tribute to Elliot's "many practical experiments...[and] how exactly he has demonstrated to us just how we were benefited" by keeping precise records. His continued interest in agricultural research was evident later that year when Elliot published an essay on apple diseases in a local newspaper. He also advocated opening the club to younger members and encouraged discussion on how to stem the exodus of young people from Loudoun farms. Prompted by Paul and Roy's experience during their stay at Clifton, he dropped earlier praise of the county's educational system and urged the CFC to press for improvements to local high schools. He brought Edward as a guest to an 1899 meeting, and the following year his son began to attend in his father's absences.[8]

* * * * *

The Panic of 1893 ushered in a four-year depression that hit farmers particularly hard and doomed any chance the Chamberlins might live comfortably off their farm. It also did enormous damage to the incumbent Democratic Party, which became linked in the public mind with hard times. That winter, Democrats tried to reduce costs for hard-hit consumers by replacing duties on imports with an income tax. But this came to naught when the Senate, allegedly influenced by bribes from the sugar cartel, gutted Cleveland's replacement for the unpopular McKinley Tariff Act, and the Supreme Court ruled taxes on income unconstitutional. The 1894 elections, held in the midst of the depression, saw Republicans pick up 117 seats in the House, ending the relative parity that had prevailed between the two parties since Grant's second term.[9]

With the economy still on the skids and splinter groups such as the Populist Party syphoning off votes from the Democrats, Republicans seemed assured of recapturing the White House in 1896. Their candidate, William McKinley, had entered the Civil War as a private and left with the brevet rank of major. After studying law in his native Ohio, he successfully ran for Congress in 1876 and held the seat until 1890. He later became Governor of Ohio before resigning to campaign for the presidency. The Democrats nominated William Jennings Bryan to oppose McKinley, but their candidate's oratorical skills on behalf of the free-silver issue failed to persuade a nation reluctant to try fiscal experimentation in the midst of an economic downturn. Veterans in particular worried a switch to a silver standard might devalue their hard-won pensions and lined up behind the GOP Veterans Committee (led by Edwin Dudley and Gen. Daniel Sickles) to support the Republican ticket. McKinley's margin of victory in November was the largest since Grant's re-election, and former federal employees turned out of office under Cleveland now assumed this clear mandate would ensure winning back their old jobs. Unnoticed in their celebration was Cleveland's expansion of the 1883 Civil Service Act, which had the effect of protecting Democratic officeholders appointed during the four years prior. Furthermore, McKinley was himself a reform advocate who refused to condone the mass firings that had characterized earlier changes in administration.[10]

Not having to worry about losing a job allowed Elliot to openly campaign for McKinley, although lack of an official position on the Veterans Committee and advanced age limited such activity. He did play a prominent part in the Inaugural Parade on 4 March 1897, riding at the head of the Veterans' Division as aide to its commander, Gen. Oliver Howard. In addition to his Loyal Legion uniform, Elliot outfitted himself with a black hat trimmed with gold cord, blue sash and saddle cloth, buff gauntlets and bridle rosettes, and new spurs. The day was clear and crisp, and one can sense the pride the old soldier felt as he rode down Pennsylvania Avenue beside his former boss at the Freedmen's Bureau.[11]

The inauguration, however, was but a pleasant prelude to the now familiar struggle to win reinstatement. McKinley had selected Lyman P. Gage as Treasury Secretary—a particularly apt choice—who became the most influential holder of that office since John Sherman. (Sherman was McKinley's Secretary of State, but his mental powers had slipped, and he was eased out of office a year later.) A month after the inauguration, Elliot crafted a short letter to Secretary Gage, asking to be returned to his old position as special agent. He included an outline of his military service but omitted any description of his earlier work for the Treasury, except to note he had been let go to make room for a Virginia Democrat. To this, he added letters of endorsement from Senator Justin Morrill and New York Representative Richard C. Shannon, citing his integrity, war record and "unjust" removal.[12]

Informed that at age sixty-three he was too old to become a special agent, he reapplied for a clerk's position, and in June persuaded Assistant Secretary William B. Howell to send the following recommendation to the Treasury's Chief of Appointments: "Mr. Chamberlin was formerly a Special Agent, and I believe he would make a good clerk. The Senator [Morrill] is very desirous of having him appointed to a position paying about $1,400, and has been to see me personally about it, and during his recent illness sent his son to renew the request." Howell's note was mailed from Paeonian Springs, indicating he must have been visiting Clifton at the time and knew Elliot from earlier work in the Customs Service. (By this time, Clifton used a Paeonian Springs address.) Despite such high-powered support, the application was delayed by new procedures governing appointments, which now included competitive testing for most applicants. Fearful he could not successfully contend against younger candidates, Elliot hoped his status as a veteran would exempt him from this requirement but found the application system already clogged by office-seekers.[13]

After passage of the liberal (and costly) 1890 Pension Act, most veterans realized they were unlikely to receive further direct monetary benefits and turned their attention towards obtaining preferences for being hired by the government. This issue was of vital concern to Elliot and prompted him to rejoin the Grand Army of the Republic (GAR) during the early 1890s, although he still retained membership in the Loyal Legion. While Cleveland remained "unwilling to strangle the floundering civil service-reform movement by granting unlimited veterans' preferences," McKinley's candidacy breathed new life into this cause. Having risen through the ranks during the war, the new President was justly viewed as favorable to former soldiers' demands, and soon after his inauguration, a delegation from the GAR's Department of the Potomac went to the White House to brief McKinley on his predecessor's "unjust" dismissals and call for more generous treatment in the future. The delegates also complained about civil service regulations requiring aging and crippled veterans to pass examinations to hold even minor posts, to which McKinley reportedly "listened courteously and promised action." That summer, while awaiting word on his application, Elliot attended the GAR national encampment in Buffalo and was undoubtedly pleased when attendees demanded Congress prescribe a penalty for disregard of earlier preference statutes. Although no additional legislation was forthcoming, McKinley signed several executive orders giving greater protection and pay to old soldiers in the Civil Service.[14]

Despite these encouraging developments, the Civil Service Commission waited until October to inform the Treasury it could hire Elliot as an entry-level clerk at $800 annually. The stated justification for his reinstatement without an examination was his prior military service and prior separation from the Customs Service "without delinquency or misconduct." Ironically, his first assignment was to serve on a task force assigned to help the Civil Service Commission process the large number of applications filed since McKinley assumed office. Afterwards, he was placed in the Office of the Auditor of the Navy, Treasury employees then being regularly assigned to oversee finances in other departments.[15]

Concurrent with his return to the Treasury, Elliot joined his son Morrill and sister-in-law Annie in renting a townhouse near Dupont Circle, which the family kept until 1902. Paul and Roy also lived there during the school year, while Edith and her mother stayed at Clifton with the other children. In February 1898, Elliot and his wife attended a reception at the White House, an indication of their reentry into Washington society under a Republican administration. Further cause for celebration that year was Morrill's receipt of a law degree from Columbia College (now George Washington University). A short time later, the young man proudly informed his mother of having earned his first legal fee (two dollars) after winning a case in small claims court. Morrill, however, prudently kept his position with the D.C. Collections Department while building up his own law practice.[16]

In March 1898, Elliot transferred to the Office of the Auditor of the Post Office Department, where he earned $1,000 a year overseeing money order statements submitted by postmasters across the country. His new supervisor, Henry A. Castle, was a fellow member in the Loyal Legion and would prove a valuable ally in the years that followed. That May, Castle submitted Elliot's name for promotion to class one clerk earning $1,200, which was approved, provided the applicant passed a test to qualify for the new position. Despite Castle's encouragement, Elliot resisted taking the examination, worried he could not pass. His supervisor resubmitted his name, along with a request that Secretary Gage waive the testing requirement. Describing his subordinate's past work for the Treasury, Castle emphasized that Elliot's reports on sugar had been the "standard in the Department and in Congress for many years...He has fully earned this promotion, but his mental characteristics are such that he seems to shrink from the formalities of an examination." This time, the Appointments Division promoted him on a provisional basis, subject to passing an exam at a later date. While awaiting this ruling, Elliot started a letter to Justin Morrill, asking the Senator to meet with Gage and reinforce his supervisor's request that he be given an exemption, and pointing out he was performing the same duties as clerks making $1,800.[17]

He never finished the letter, most likely because he learned the Senator's health had taken a turn for the worse. The eighty-eight-year-old Morrill, whose wife had died earlier that year, had developed the "grippe," which soon turned into pneumonia. Elliot was at his mentor's bedside when he passed away at 1:25 AM on 28 December 1898. The only other persons present were Morrill's son James, his sister-in-law and private secretary Louise Swann, and a colleague from the Senate Finance Committee. Described in the press as an "intimate friend," Elliot's inclusion in this small group underscores the bond that linked these two men for over thirty years. Indeed, he had made few important decisions without first seeking Morrill's advice and, more often than not, assistance. While the explanation for this close relationship remains elusive, the Chamberlin family owed him a debt that could never be repaid.[18]

Elliot's provisional promotion allowed him in March 1899 to become a section chief, charged with maintaining "proper decorum," recording time and attendance, and otherwise overseeing the work of inspectors in his office, as well as assisting the Chief of the Inspecting Division "in every way possible." That summer, he finally agreed to take the six-hour examination to confirm his managerial position. Although he scored eighty-five percent on office procedures, he failed the part on academic knowledge with a grade of sixty-seven, and his average score of seventy-six was not enough to keep his promotion. His poor performance in advanced mathematics and general knowledge showed the disadvantage a sixty-five-year-old had competing against applicants fresh out of high school and college. Spelling also caused him problems and reflected the somewhat outdated English usage seen in his letters. His highest scores, both ninety percent, were in simple addition and accounting. Although his penmanship and writing speed had deteriorated due to rheumatism, his score of only eighty in this category reflected the high standards of the day.[19]

1899 *Puck* Magazine Cover References Endless Demands for Veterans' Benefits. A shark-like pension agent lures GAR member with promise of "pensions for everyone, apply early, war record immaterial." Puck in turn warns the veteran his organization will remain in "bad odor just as long as you let this fellow wear your uniform and manipulate you." (LC)

Failure to pass resulted in his return to overseeing P.O. money-order accounts, where he remained until early 1901, when his supervisor again put him up for promotion. In doing so, Henry Castle described the candidate as the "best entitled to promotion among all the clerks of his grade." The request was reviewed by the Treasury's new Personnel Division, which in replacing the Appointments Division reflected a further shift away from political patronage in determining personnel matters. In the end, a panel reluctantly agreed to make an exception because of the "exceptional circumstances" involved, and a backlog of ungraded examinations that made retesting Elliot impossible any time soon. His promotion to first class clerk was signed later that spring.[20]

The federal government did not have a retirement system until 1920, forcing most civil servants to cling to their jobs as long as possible. It also motivated veterans in the government to pursue disability pensions to provide some security when they could no longer work. As already noted, Elliot had still not been approved for a pension by the end of 1891, despite renewed efforts after passage of the 1890 Pension Act. There is no reason to doubt his rheumatism was service related, but his insistence on tying it to the brief stint in the west proved difficult to substantiate and, under the new pension laws, no longer necessary. These problems almost certainly would have been quickly overcome by a pension agent, yet as late as 1893, Elliot turned down his wife's suggestion to hire one on the ground they were "doing so well" on their own. After losing his Treasury job the following year, he redoubled efforts to win a full pension, but once again failed to obtain professional help. Finally, at the end of 1896, Edith's cousin in the Interior Department, Edward Dawson, wrote the Pension Bureau to explain the difficulty of finding anyone who had known the claimant at Fort Walla Walla, pointing out that lack of a witness was no longer critical, now that the new law had relaxed requirements regarding "proof of origin."[21]

When this plea failed to elicit a favorable response, Elliot turned to Justin Morrill, who sent his son to the Pension Bureau in early 1897. James Morrill, then chief clerk on his father's Finance Committee, quickly discovered Elliot was eligible for two different pensions. Although the larger one still required proof of origin, a partial pension could be awarded with only a doctor's statement confirming current physical disability. James recommended Elliot apply for the smaller one first and pursue a full pension later. In offering to do everything possible to help his father's friend, James seemed perplexed by Elliot's failure to get the medical exam the Bureau had requested a year earlier.[22]

Within days, Elliot submitted the results of a physical, confirming rheumatism in his shoulders, back, hips, knees and ankles that made manual labor impossible. The examiner, however, considered an enlarged heart and resultant murmur more serious, even though his weight remained a trim 171 pounds. Based on these findings, the Pension Bureau notified Elliot it was suspending his original claim pending receipt of additional information, but would process his request for a partial pension, which resulted in his beginning to receive eighteen dollars a month that fall.[23]

It would be difficult to count the number of societies and clubs to which Elliot either belonged or helped found. Most involved politics, veterans or agriculture, but research into obtaining pensions based on his forebears' service in the Revolution and War of 1812 sparked a desire to learn more about his family history, and led to his helping found the Chamberlain Association of America (CAA) in 1898. Stimulated by nostalgia for the past after the 1876 Centennial, Americans were increasingly drawn to tracing their ancestry, and many of the major genealogical associations, including the Daughters of the American Revolution (DAR), Society of Mayflower Descendants and Colonial Dames, were founded during the last part of the nineteenth century. Along with the concurrent explosion of veterans, fraternal and similar associations, membership in these groups helped substitute for the extended family networks that were being disrupted by a more industrialized society.

Even before the CAA was organized, Elliot was able to call on relatives in the Boston area to use their ties with the Cleveland Administration to assist Annie Matthews regain her Treasury position. Given his expertise in establishing similar associations, it is likely Elliot helped draft the CAA by-laws, and in his capacity as one of its first vice-presidents, he was present at the CAA's initial reunion in Boston, although his attendance had to be cut short so he could be present for his son Paul's return from service in Cuba. He would continue to participate in CAA functions and correspond with members on genealogical matters. Eleanor Chamberlin shared her father's interest in the past, but her initial application to join the DAR was turned down. Like her father, she mistakenly used Samuel N. Chamberlin as the basis for admission, and only through correspondence with the CAA discovered it was

Family Coat of Arms. Elliot probably obtained this while serving as Chamberlain Association of American Vice President and later had it reproduced in color and as signet rings for his children. (TCC)

Samuel's father Ichabod who had served in the Revolution. Eleanor jointed the DAR in 1900, but her father failed to interest his other children in joining veterans auxiliaries, such as the Sons and Daughters of the GAR.[24]

After years of courting distant, but more successful, relatives in the Boston area, Elliot's correspondence and entries he made in the family Bible suggest renewed contact with his more immediate family. His oldest brother, Elijah Chamberlin, died in 1895 at age seventy-two in Vermont, never having remarried or leaving any heirs than the one son Frank, who was raised by Elliot's twin sister. Elliot's oldest sister Lucia moved to Wisconsin after the Civil War, remarried, and was living in Kansas with her only surviving child, Charles Crawford, when she died in 1911. Elliot's sister Louisa Cameron never remarried and lived on a widow's pension with in-laws near Glens Falls until she passed in 1899. His twin sister Ellen, who visited Clifton on at least one occasion, remained in Glens Falls after her husband, Frank Martin, died in 1897. She would die in 1917 at age eighty-two and be buried in the Bay Street Cemetery beside her husband and mother, in the same plot with Elliot's first wife and children.[25]

Except for his marriage in the late 1880s to Nellie Mae Walden in Santa Monica, California, little is known of the youngest brother, William Chamberlin, until he sent Elliot a letter in 1896. Addressed only to Washington, D.C., it eventually found its way to Clifton, and began with a query whether his older brother was still working for the government and "amongst the land of the living." William had been working in Los Angles for nearly eight months and bragged of having cleared $2,000 in several real estate transactions. Elliot, who was unemployed and nearly bald, must have been particularly envious when the family's "prodigal son" boasted of continued good health in the warm California climate and not even having any gray hair. Yet, Elliot would outlive his little brother, who died in Los Angeles in 1901.[26]

* * * * *

Growing tensions between the U.S. and Spain over Cuba overshadowed all other events during McKinley's first term. A large segment of the island's population had been in revolt against their colonial masters since 1895, and the draconian measures used by the Spaniards to put down the insurrection aroused sympathy for the rebels among the American public and in Congress. In January 1898, the USS *Maine* anchored in Havana's harbor to monitor the situation and provide possible assistance to Americans on the island. Matters came to a head on 15 February, when a massive explosion destroyed the battleship, killing 252 crewmembers. Although the exact cause of the blast was never established, war hysteria swept the U.S. to the rallying cry of "Remember the Maine! To hell with Spain!" McKinley, who was then in the midst of discreet negotiations with Spain over Cuba's future, tried to defuse the situation, but when the preliminary board of inquiry concluded that a mine, rather than an internal explosion, had sunk the ship, the President was forced to demand Spain immediately withdraw its forces from Cuba. With no face-saving alternative, Spain responded by declaring war on the United States on 24 April. A week later, Comm. George Dewey attacked and destroyed Spain's entire Pacific Fleet in Manila Bay. This victory was repeated on 3 July, when the U.S. Navy defeated the Spanish Atlantic Fleet as it tried to slip out of the harbor at Santiago de Cuba, ending any possibility Spain could continue the war. A preliminary cease-fire was signed in August.

Although these two victories highlighted the successful modernization of the Navy begun under the Harrison Administration, the war brought out weaknesses in America's ground forces. The U.S. Army had been neglected since the Civil War, to the point that its 25,000 officers and men were prepared for little more than putting down periodic Native American uprisings by the time McKinley took office. At the outbreak of hostilities with Spain, the President issued a call for 125,000 volunteers, but it soon became apparent the Army was not ready to accept such numbers. The first American soldiers did not land in Cuba until 22 June, almost two months after the war had begun. An 18,000-man Expeditionary Force was finally assembled on the island under the command of Gen. William Shafter, who undertook a siege of the city of Santiago, where the Spanish still maintained a defensive position after their naval forces had been destroyed. The city fell in mid-July, marking the effective end of the war. The most memorable battle of this campaign was the assault on San Juan Hill, in which Theodore Roosevelt's Rough Riders ably participated.[27]

The war had an immediate impact on the Chamberlin family, with both Paul and Mary's fiancé, Hume Clendenin, seeing service in Cuba. Paul cut short his junior year at Western High to enlist as a private in Company G of the 1st D.C. Volunteer Infantry. He was just eighteen but told the recruiter he was a year older. Soon after he began basic training, Army doctors ordered him back home for a two-month furlough to recover from intermittent fevers. Not wanting to miss the chance to go to the front, Paul reported back for duty in less than a month and joined his regiment in Cuba just as the fighting ended. Shorn of war's romantic side, the following letter, written to his father on 3 August from a camp on San Juan Heights, gives an idea of the deplorable sanitary conditions that proved to be the American soldier's worst enemy:

Pvt. Paul Chamberlin, 1st D.C. Inf., Ready to Go to Cuba. (1898, photo, TCC)

...I am extremely lucky as about 30 or 50 in every company are down with the mountain fever...When I say I am well, I mean physically well, but I am afraid I am a little homesick. I long for Clifton and after all think there are some things worse than farming. It is said that we are going to Long Island and go into Camp...before the 20th of the month. There may be some truth in this...but I am afraid it is a cute scheme of the doctors to get the fellows in better spirits as they are rather down-hearted. An entire regiment landed yesterday and it is said that another is on the way and that these are to garrison the town of Santiago and relieve the entire 5th Corp. I hope this is the case, but I am a little inclined to believe it a "rubber" as the fellows call it. There has been a society organized here the S.A.S., or Society of the Army of Santiago. We are all members and are to be given medals made from the captured cannon...I think the badges are to be made in the form of the 5th Corp badge [here he drew a pentagon]...I must say I am proud to belong to this Corps. I have been working very hard lately as only a few of us have been doing the company work, the rest being sick. I was acting corporal the other day and I had a detail of 12 men putting up hospital tents. We put up eighteen between us. There was no other details to help us...We changed camp the other day and have company mess again. I like this better than the other way of every man cooking for himself. It saves a lot of time and trouble. If we could only get good water I believe we would be in better health. We are drink[ing] water right out of the creek and a stream that drains a battle field...Tell Roy that he can be very thankful that he did not enlist...it takes all there is in a fellow to stand it. Tell him to be contented and work on the farm contentedly as that is a perfect heaven to the sights and hardships one suffers here...We are camping in an extremely dirty place and the men are ragged and dirty in consequence thereof. The newness is all gone from everything connected with the regiment. The fellows have cut the heavy lining off the bottom of their trousers as it was very hot and now they are ragged nearly to the knees. Our shoes are fixed with wire and rope. The canteens have lost their straps and are replaced with string. Most of us use a length of bamboo for a canteen. Hats are battered and torn. Cups and mess kits are blackened and dented. Our blankets are the worse for wear too. Everything looks worse for the 3 months of use and all together we are a very ragged and soiled crowd. The pay master is to be around soon and we will be paid off. I am sorry for this, as there is absolutely no use for the money here and it will just be a bother for us to take care of. We get about $35.00 each...[28]

Paul's parents could hardly fail to notice their "little scamp" had matured into a responsible soldier. Elliot knew first-hand the rigors of life in the field and had witnessed Cuba's poor sanitary conditions, so he must have worried greatly about his son's ability to keep well. As it turned out, Paul contracted malaria and typhoid fever less than a week later, and was sent back to a military hospital in the U.S. His experience was typical of thousands of American soldiers who came down with tropical diseases that summer. The Army's inability to provide adequate sanitary conditions and provisions for its men on the island resulted in the entire Expeditionary Force being brought home before the end of August. A reception center was established at Camp Wickoff on Long Island to house the returnees, serving both to keep the men from spreading tropical disease and isolate them from the press. (By this time the public was outraged to learn the Army's logistical problems, not enemy bullets, had accounted for most of the casualties.)

In mid-September, Paul was granted a two-month furlough to recuperate at home and was mustered out with the rest of his regiment shortly thereafter. Yet, the Cuban experience failed to extinguish his childhood dream of becoming a professional soldier. In January 1900, his former commanders recommended him for officer training based on his performance in Cuba, a view seconded by his high school principal. Admitted to the Naval Academy, Paul graduated as a second lieutenant in the Marine Corps. Over the next decade he saw extensive action in the Caribbean and Pacific, as the U.S. sought to consolidate its new role as a world power, a legacy of victory in the Spanish-American War.[29]

Hume had been working in the Boston area for several years when he too answered the call for volunteers when war broke out. He had been trying to establish a career that would enable him to marry and support a family but seized the opportunity to leave the dull life of an accountant to enlist as a corporal in the 8th Mass. Volunteers. He also showed a natural aptitude for military life, and served as acting sergeant while his regiment was being formed. The unit was among the last to arrive in Cuba that summer, replacing part of the original landing force. Like Paul and so many others, Hume contracted malaria soon after landing, and was furloughed back to the U.S. He spent two months recuperating at Clifton, where his mother Alice Clendenin was then living. By the time he rejoined his regiment in Matanzas, Cuba, Hume had been commissioned a second lieutenant. He was mustered out in April 1899 and, like Paul, yearned to return to military life.[30]

Mary and Lieutenant Clendenin were married at Clifton on 19 June 1899, a festive affair that presaged the family's entry into a new century.

> The ceremony was performed by the Rev. John D. La Mothe of [St. Paul's Episcopal Church in] Hamilton, in the presence of only the immediate relatives. The bride was gowned in white swiss over white taffeta, with elaborate lace trimmings, and carried a bouquet of her favorite flowers, American Beauty roses. The maid of honor, the bride's only sister, Miss Eleanor Matthews Chamberlin, wore white organdie over pink taffeta and carried La France roses. Two little cousins of the bride, Cornelia Needles Walker and Frances Almer Wright, led the bridal procession into the drawing room [to the tune of the wedding march played on the piano], making an aisle with white ribbons leading to a bower of ferns, daisies and Virginia creeper, where the bride, on the arm of her father, was waited by the groom with his best man, Mr. Justin Morrill Chamberlin. [The house and veranda were elaborately decorated in green and white.] Following the ceremony a large reception was held for the numerous friends under the old trees on the lawn.[31]

Despite the above assertion that only a few family members were present, Clifton's guest book shows almost one hundred guests in attendance, including many friends from Washington. A poem left by one attests to the good time enjoyed by all that afternoon. After the reception, Mary and Hume went to New York for a short honeymoon before spending the remainder of the summer on the Massachusetts coast. That fall Mary stayed with Hume as he began training to become an Army officer but returned to Clifton to await the birth of their first child before her husband shipped out for duty in the Philippines. She recorded her arrival back home with the following lines: "The hills are dearest//Which our childhood feet//Have climbed earliest." Even though Hume's career took her far away, Mary's heart would remain close to her home in the Virginia hills.[32]

Chapter 30

OLD SOLDIERS IN A NEW CENTURY: 1900-1909

Edward Hume Clendenin's birth on 8 March 1900, the first at Clifton in twenty-three years, ushered in a new era at the old homestead. Although the baby's father was then with the 46th U.S. Infantry in Manila, Mary's mother was there to help her care for the infant. Edith's joy over her first grandchild would be tempered a month later by the death of her mother Sarah. When the family matriarch died at home at age eighty-two, she had the satisfaction of knowing that the baby's arrival increased the likelihood the family would continue on the farm she and E. Y. Matthews had struggled to preserve for almost sixty years. She was laid to rest in the Fairfax Meeting burial ground beside her husband and daughters, Marie and Miriam. Even though her passing brought an end to the family's active participation in the Meeting, Quaker values and traditions continued to influence succeeding generations, and some descendants have returned to this faith in recent years.

The June 1900 census found Edith, her son Edward, daughter Mary, grandson Edward Hume and a Black housemaid living at Clifton. Edward, whose poor eyesight confined him to work around the house and gardens, gave his profession as "florist," a wry reference to bouquets he and his mother sold to the public. Edith divided her time between the farm and Washington and was present later that summer when the census-taker visited their townhouse at 1309 20th Street. Also listed at this address were Elliot, Annie, Morrill, and two female servants. Roy and "Bidie" (as Eleanor was called) were listed as students, while Paul had already left for the Naval Academy. (As in the past, Elliot subtracted four years from his actual age of sixty-six, while Edith unaccountably added one or two years, depending on the census, to her fifty-three years.)[1]

Later that year, Mary's mother-in-law, Alice Clendenin, moved into Clifton to help care for Edward Hume. Letters to his father record the baby's progress, including a marked attraction to horses. "You never saw anything to equal [it]! He will sit on the stile directly under Rex's nose, and hold up both little arms to pull his great head down close. His grandfather took him on his first horseback ride...and they were both *perfectly charmed*. This morning

Mary Clendenin and Infant Son, Edward Hume, 1900. (TCC)

Edward Hume turned his back directly on the threshing engine, which we thought he would like so much, and all because he saw Clyde coming along and wanted to go to him."[2]

Now comfortably situated in the Treasury, Elliot could again devote more time to veterans and civic affairs. He was particularly active in the Fort Stevens-Lincoln National Military Park Association, formed in 1900 to preserve land around the fort and mark with a statue the spot where Abraham Lincoln had stood. Louis Cass White, a veteran of the fighting during Early's raid, was the driving force behind the Association, which included two other former members of the 25th N.Y. Cavalry, Henry Nevius and John Wolf. In May 1900, Elliot helped organize Memorial Day ceremonies at nearby Battleground National Cemetery, resting place of Union soldiers killed in the battle. To mark this occasion, Elliot arranged for Judge Nevius, past president of the Sickles's Cavalry Association, to speak on behalf of the Twenty-Fifth's veterans. Two weeks later, Elliot participated in another ceremony nearby to commemorate Flag Day.[3]

Through participation in activities at Fort Stevens, Elliot became acquainted with William V. Cox, who in April 1900, presented an address before the D.C. Historical Association entitled "The Defenses of Washington—General Early's Raid on the Capital and the Battle of Fort Stevens," which two years later would be printed and sold to raise funds to preserve the battle site. Elliot probably attended Cox's original address, since soon afterwards he lent Cox a copy of his 1877 article on the Twenty-Fifth's role in the battle. (It is unclear whether Cox included any of Elliot's material in the published version, although annotations in Elliot's copy of the address suggest that he would have liked his regiment's participation to have been featured more prominently.) Cox was also secretary of the Citizens' Committee for the National Capital Centennial, and that fall enlisted Elliot's aid in organizing a parade to commemorate the one hundredth anniversary of Congress's first session in the District of Columbia.[4]

In February 1901, Gen. Daniel Sickles invited Elliot to be his aide-de-camp during William McKinley's second inaugural parade. (This prestigious assignment was likely arranged by Elliot's supervisor, Henry Castle, who served as Sickles's assistant adjutant general on this occasion.) Sickles and his aides expected to ride at the head of the Civil War Veterans Division, which in the past had always escorted the President along Pennsylvania Avenue. Shortly after he accepted the position, Sickles learned the War Department had placed them behind representatives of the regular Army, Navy and National Guard. Never one to suffer a slight, Sickles stormed into the War Department, accompanied by "Col. Chamberlain... and Auditor Castle," to complain. Still unsatisfied with a proposed compromise, the general tendered his resignation on 27 February. Unwilling to alienate the veterans, who played so prominently in his re-election, McKinley directed Secretary of War Elihu Root to countermand the order and put the Veterans Division back in its accustomed place, with Sickles in command. On 4 March, for the second time in four years, Elliot rode proudly beside the head of the Presidential escort, although this time a driving rainstorm marred the occasion.[5]

McKinley was felled by an anarchist's bullet six months later while attending the Pan-American Exposition in Buffalo. This blow to the body poli-

Gen. Daniel Sickles (r.) and Aide-de-camp Chamberlin (2nd from l.) Lead Civil War Veterans Division during McKinley's 1901 Inaugural Parade. Inset shows Elliot with GAR, 1876 Veterans Convention, Army of the Potomac, and MOLLUS medals. (group photo and tintype, TCC)

tic also signaled an end to the predominance the Civil War played in the nation's affairs, a shift already noticeable in a decline in GAR membership by 1900. McKinley's successor, Theodore Roosevelt, rose to national prominence during the Spanish-American War, and the new administration looked forward into the twentieth century, not back to a war that took place four decades earlier. Nevertheless, many former soldiers continued to turn out for national encampments and other ceremonial functions, often propelled by a belief these observances still played an important role in promoting patriotism. Such was true for Elliot, who held the honorary position of aide-de-camp during GAR encampments in 1901, 1903 and 1904; and as a founder of D.C. Post #1, the oldest continually operating GAR group in the country, he took pride in being feted at its anniversary dinners every October.[6]

The year 1902 saw an upsurge in activity by the Fort Stevens Association, including publication of Cox's *Defenses of Washington*. Disappointed the booklet's author failed to highlight the part played by his regiment, Elliot arranged to be interviewed by Smith D. Fry, a well-known correspondent whose columns appeared in the *N.Y. Tribune* and many other papers. Entitled "SAVED THE CAPITAL—Gallant Work Done by Twenty-sixth [*sic*] Cavalry//True Story of the Battle of Fort Stevens..." it included a picture of "Col. S. E. Chamberlain" and a crude sketch of dismounted troopers leaping out of the fort's earthworks. The column is a reprise of Elliot's 1877 *Republic* article, including the same excerpts from his diary to substantiate the argument that the "old soldiers," whose appearance convinced Jubal Early the VI Corps had arrived, were actually from the Twenty-Fifth. "I was senior captain that day and in command of the regiment," Elliot told Fry, "and as the years have passed away I have grown to regard it as an act of Providence that there should have been sent there, at that important moment, our veteran regiment, which deceived Early and stopped his whole army." Fry concluded with a description of his interviewee: "The veteran commander of that regiment of heroes is a quiet, elderly man, wholly unobtrusive and unpretentious. He is employed in a subordinate capacity in the treasury department. He never speaks of the achievement that day unless in reply to inquiries by his friends, and then always with modesty, giving credit to Divine Providence." In this, his last known public pronouncement on his old regiment, Elliot strayed little from what he had first published in 1871.[7]

At a preparatory meeting for the GAR National Encampment scheduled to begin in Washington on 6 October 1902, it was announced that Colonel Chamberlin would be vice-chairman of a committee overseeing an auxiliary reunion for cavalrymen. A decade earlier, a similar reunion of the Army of the Potomac Cavalry Corps had been "one of the most attractive features" of the last GAR encampment in Washington, and Elliot's committee promised this year's reunion would "excel all of its predecessors." As had occurred in 1892, an "annual reunion" of the 25th N.Y. Cavalry took place at the Howard House in conjunction with the October encampment. The only press notice of this meeting noted the New York veterans now called themselves the "Fort Stevens Heroes" (a reference to Fry's column?) and that John Wolf was elected president. We do not know if the "Heroes" continued to meet in the years that followed, but their president worked tirelessly with the Fort Stevens Association and the press to increase recognition of the battle's importance and of the role played by his regiment. A measure of success was attained in 1904, when President Roosevelt attended a fortieth anniversary commemoration of the battle and dedicated the "Lincoln stone" on the spot where the late President had stood.[8]

* * * * *

In early 1901, Elliot and Edith arranged for Washington T. Shugars, a local Black farmer, to move into small tenant quarters behind Clifton and take over management of the farm. Aware of difficulties his predecessors had over compensation, Shugars was quite specific about what he wanted in return:

> I will write to you in regard to my wages—you furnish me house, garden and firewood, furnish me a cow, 13 bu. of corn meal, 225 lbs. meat, one barrel of flour, good time to plow and work my garden, 500 fish in spring fresh and pasture my horse if I have one, and $15.00 in money and the right to reserve August [as vacation] if I...get everything in good shape and there are not much doing in August. My wife thinks she cannot be of any

service to your mother [Edith] in the early spring [as she is] now away.[9]

After Mary Clendenin and her son left Clifton in June 1902 to join Hume at an Army base on the west coast, the family's center of gravity shifted back to Washington, where Elliot, Annie and Morrill pooled resources to rent an apartment at the Marlborough, a new apartment building on 18th Street. By this time, Morrill had quit his Washington government job to devote himself entirely to his law practice. Roy, who probably lived elsewhere, was working as a private secretary to Thomas Nelson Page, a noted Virginia author, and would later try his hand at newspaper reporting. Only Edith, Edward and Bidie spent much time at the farm, although Elliot frequently joined them on weekends. Despite blindness, Edward began to show what would become a life-long interest in antiques, and on one occasion when his mother gave him money to buy a sorely needed winter overcoat, he used it instead to purchase some antiquity that caught his fancy. (His heightened sense of touch enabled him to spot fakes and alterations, and even differentiate between colors.)

During the winter of 1902-03, Shugars reported sending a barrel of garden produce for the family's use in Washington. Unfortunately, several cows had gone dry, and dogs had gotten into the pork cracklings. Worse news followed about the corn and wheat harvest, as only a dollar was left after selling the cornmeal and wheat to pay bills, and Shugars had to remind the family to remit five dollars for his wife's services. Despite disappointing results under a new manager, Elliot decided the following summer to finish rebuilding the barn Union troops had burned forty years earlier. He was confident it would provide sufficient space for milking and storage to finally achieve his dream of starting a successful dairy business. Edith had doubts about their ability to pay for it but knew how much this oft-delayed project meant to her husband. The barn was completed in 1903 and insured that year for $500. Values on the house ($1,000), furnishings ($500), corn and wagon house ($150) and feed/silage ($200) remained the same as on a policy written in 1892.[10]

Back in 1901, Elliot had brought specimens of asbestos found at Clifton to a CFC meeting. The discovery revived his interest in mining, and he later contacted an acquaintance about having some unidentified samples analyzed. The following year Mary, with perhaps a touch of irony, wrote her parents that she was anxious "to hear of developments in the mine, and trust[ed] our 'future' may be near at hand." It is unclear whether this newest scheme involved asbestos, or his earlier search for gold, but it too failed to materialize.[11]

Reviving participation in the CFC, Elliot served as its president in 1902 and 1904. At one meeting, his son Edward spoke about Loudoun's inadequate transportation system, with emphasis on long-sought improvements to the road connecting Waterford with the train station at Paeonian Springs. A better means of conveyance was critical to ensure timely milk deliveries in bad weather, and the county's continued failure to address the problem refueled suspicion Waterford still suffered discrimination because of its Republican/Unionist background. During his second term as president, Elliot arranged for an inspector from the Agriculture Department to come and review the situation. Whether or not this served as the catalyst, the road in front of the farm was upgraded five years later. Paul was guest speaker at a CFC meeting held at Clifton in May 1903, and entertained members with stories about his experiences in Guam and the Philippines. Not everything went as well as his sons' presentations. Right after Elliot helped form a CFC committee to look into problems caused by stray cattle, neighbor Edward Myers threatened to sue him over damages from livestock that had gotten out of Clifton pastures.[12]

Elliot Reads on Clifton Porch. (TCC)

When Edith wrote Bidie in April 1903, her daughter had been living in New York all winter. At the time, she and Elliot resided in the Marlborough apartment with their son Edward and her sister Annie. She was just back from an overnight stay at Clifton, where she had counted forty-two baby chicks, and found favorable prospects for the wheat, hay and apple crops, although the peach trees had suffered from frost. Edward had recently entertained his mother's guests at a tea party, after which "everyone pronounced his voice *grand* and wondered *why* he does not cultivate it, and realize large sums from it. I think it is strange too." Morrill and Roy shared an apartment elsewhere in Washington D.C. with Paul, then back in town with his pet bulldog. (Edith liked the animal, but her sister feared Paul might leave it with them to raise.) Roy was planning to compete in a horse show at Chevy Chase the following weekend. "Hope he will win a prize, although he says there are lots of fine horses there."[13]

Eleanor ("Bidie") M. Chamberlin, c. 1905. (TCC)

After Mary and her two-year-old son joined Hume at Fort Wright outside Spokane in the summer of 1902, her letters home provided a lively account of life on an Army post in the Pacific Northwest. To make ends meet on her husband's salary as a second lieutenant, Mary provided meals for the bachelor officers until pregnancy restricted her activities. Soon after their second and last child, Edith Campbell Clendenin, was born in 1903, Hume received word that the 17th U.S. Infantry would be sent to the Philippines to help quell the "Moro Rebellion," named after Muslim inhabitants of the country's southern islands. For several months, Mary debated whether to risk taking her two young children to face unknown dangers in the tropics or return with them to Clifton. In the end, she opted to accompany Hume, a decision made easier when Bidie volunteered to accompany her sister and help care for the children.

On 1 July 1903, the party steamed out of San Francisco on a military transport, which deposited them a month later on Siasi, an island at the southwestern tip of the Philippine archipelago in the center of the insurrection. Hume was post quartermaster and established his family in the relative safety of an old Spanish fort. Soon afterwards, Mary wrote home that life in their new surroundings was not as bad as she had feared, although she still missed Clifton, "the best place in the world." At the beginning of 1904, the family was transferred to the nearby island of Jolo, which Mary hoped would become their permanent quarters, as they occupied a small house overlooking the sea.

Bidie's decision to accompany her sister was not entirely altruistic, as she had a romantic interest in a young American officer stationed in the Philippines whom she had met through her brother Paul. On one memorable occasion, while riding with her beau in the jungle, their horses became mired in quicksand. Fortunately, locals witnessed the mishap and rescued the couple by tossing them a rope. The horses sank out of sight, however, and Bidie's boyfriend later got into trouble for having lost two government saddles.

In the spring of 1904, the Clendenins moved once more, this time to Zamboanga, a city at the western tip of Mindanao. After the rebels killed several of their friends, it was decided Bidie should take four-year-old Edward back to the U.S. Following a voyage through the Suez Canal, they arrived safely in Virginia in mid-1904. Hume remained with his wife and baby daughter in the Philippines for another year, winning a promotion to first lieutenant. (By then, American forces had established control over population centers in the southern islands, although the guerrillas held out in the jungle for another decade.)[14]

* * * * *

Elliot's employment as a Treasury auditor in the Post Office Department proceeded without incident after his reinstatement as section chief in 1901. The work was neither as interesting, nor as remunerative, as that of a special agent but it kept the family financially afloat. By now, the principal threat to his job security was his health, which took a turn for the worse in 1903 when he spent seventy-nine days on sick leave. In August 1904, he managed to attend a GAR encampment in Boston that coincided with a Chamberlain Association reunion in the same city, but the exertion of the trip resulted in a bout of rheumatism that confined him to Clifton after his return. In early October, Morrill visited the Treasury to find out why his father's pay had stopped and learned his sick leave had been used up. Letters of sympathy from a co-worker and supervisor Henry Castle confirm Elliot's inability to return to work that year, nor could he participate in Teddy Roosevelt's Inauguration the following March, despite an invitation to march with the Civic Grand Division. In August 1905, he was formally separated from the Treasury after Castle exhausted all efforts to keep his position open. The directive stated, however, that he would remain on a preferred list for reinstatement "should his health be restored within a reasonable amount of time." The seventy-one-year-old had served the U.S. Government under ten Presidents since joining the Army in 1862.[15]

The quest for a full military pension, now more important than ever, became a point of honor involving the whole family. A witness, Sgt. John Lee, reappeared in 1902 to provide a sworn deposition which corroborated Elliot's version of the manhunt along the Canadian border that led to his first rheumatic attack. Despite this new testimony, the Pension Bureau again rejected the claim, this time citing Elliot's failure to list illness as a reason for his 1867 resignation from the Army. After an unsuccessful appeal before a court in December 1905, Elliot turned to the Congress for relief, and finally succeeded in having a special bill passed in 1907 that raised his pension to forty dollars per month. The legislation described the claimant as bedridden for the past two years with "acute articular rheumatism affecting the heart, joints of the hands and feet, the nervous systems, kidneys and bladder." Agreeing with the claimant's assertion about the origin of his illness, the bill's authors urged approval in view of Elliot's "long and faithful service, his grievous condition, and his straitened financial circumstances."[16]

* * * * *

After Bidie's return with the Clendenin boy and Elliot's confinement to home several months later, Clifton again became the hub of family activities, with only Annie and Morrill remaining at the Marlborough apartment. In August of that year, Morrill announced his engagement to Priscilla Alden Nicolsen, daughter of a former Navy lieutenant and direct descendant of the Priscilla Alden who arrived on the *Mayflower*. When Paul heard the news, he exclaimed, "Lord, how the mighty have fallen." Priscilla and Morrill were married at St. Margaret's Church in Washington on 2 April 1905, and moved into their own apartment. Their first child, Priscilla Alden Chamberlin, was born in 1907.[17]

After his father became bedridden, Roy returned to Clifton to help run the farm. Starting in December 1904, he took Elliot's place in the CFC and was elected secretary the following year. One of his first duties was to write a sympathy letter expressing the members' appreciation for all his father had done for the club and wishing him a speedy recovery. That spring, members gathered at Clifton so that Elliot could attend his last CFC meeting. Roy was reelected secretary at year's end, but resigned in January 1907, explaining he was about to start a new career in Chicago.[18]

During the two years that Roy lived at Clifton, his attention was diverted by a budding romance with Rose Charlton Wellman, whom he had met in high school. Charlton's father, Walter Wellman, was then the Washington correspondent for the *Chicago Herald,* but two attempts to reach the North Pole overland in the 1890s had whetted his taste for exploration. When Roy wrote Charlton in January 1906, she was staying at the Ritz Hotel in Paris during a visit with her father, then overseeing construction of a dirigible that he hoped would carry him to the Pole.[19] In his letter, Roy expressed how much he missed her and vented his suspicion her mother had sent her to Europe to break up their courtship. He need not have worried, as the couple resumed their relationship after Charlton returned to Washington

Edward M. Chamberlin, c. 1906. Despite tinted *pince nez*, he was already quite blind. (TCC)

later that year. In a letter to Charlton in the fall of 1906, Edith explained Roy would be unable to visit her until the harvest was over, suggesting instead she come stay with them at Clifton.[20]

After two years of managing the farm, Roy concluded he could not make enough to support a wife and persuaded his parents to let him go to Chicago at the end of 1906 to work for the Armour meat-packing company. He must have found the training program difficult and life lonely in the "Windy City," as a letter from his mother soon after his arrival there was devoted to giving her son encouragement. Convinced he was up to any task, she urged him not to doubt his abilities. Worried, however, that he shared the family's lack of "shrewdness" in financial matters, she strongly warned her son not to marry until he accumulated enough resources to comfortably support a family. In particular, she cautioned against quitting his job as long as he was earning a good salary. Despite her reservations, Edith expressed disappointment that Charlton had not come to visit them that winter.[21]

Roy did not heed his mother's advice, returning east to marry Charlton on 6 April 1907. The wedding took place in her parents' Washington home with only family members in attendance, and was officiated by the Rev. Roger Tyler, rector of St. Paul's Episcopal Church in Hamilton, which had become the Chamberlins' primary place of worship in Loudoun. Afterwards, Roy returned to Chicago with his bride but later that year, the couple moved to New Jersey where he tried his hand at selling bonds. Their only child, Walter Wellman Chamberlin, was born at the Women's Homeopathic Hospital in Philadelphia on 15 February 1908. Unable to hear the telephone while tending to Elliot in his closed bedroom, Edith did not learn of the birth until two days later. Despite her husband's deteriorating health, Elliot was overjoyed by the arrival of their fourth grandchild, and kept repeating, "Roy has a son."[22]

Love is contagious, and Edward met his soulmate, Vera McFarland Moses, when she came to Paeonian Springs in 1906 for an extended stay with her friend Helen Meek. Vera was from a quite different background; her father, James Moses, owned the successful Mercer Pottery Company in Trenton, New Jersey, and her mother belonged to a socially prominent New Jersey family. Vera returned to Loudoun later that year, and in the days leading up to Christmas, she and Edward enjoyed sleighing parties and other festivities, as well as relaxing moments in Clifton's parlor as he played the piano. With perhaps some "shrewdness" in her calculations, Edith encouraged their relationship, despite occasional doubt about a socialite being the right partner for her disabled son. Above all, she genuinely admired the girl's courage and optimism in planning for their future together. In what his mother termed her son's "first time away from home," Edward departed with Vera on New Year's Day to consult with eye doctors

Vera Moses Feeding Edith's Chickens, c. 1908. Pre-Civil War corn crib/shed and larger rebuilt barn stand behind her. (BCC)

and look into enrolling in a school for the blind. Later that winter, Washington's leading ophthalmologist, Dr. William Wilmer, performed surgery to restore Edward's sight, and he would remain in the hospital for over a month to let the "cataract" remains be absorbed. But when the bandages were removed, his vision was no better, and he instead took classes to learn Braille and other skills needed to overcome blindness—steps that almost certainly would not have taken place without Vera's financial and personal encouragement.[23]

After Elliot lost his Treasury position, Edith and Annie joined him in signing several short-term loans totaling $4,500, which were intended to allow him to spend his last years on the farm. The notes of trust, however, brought a renewed risk of foreclosure unless the family could meet interest payments and pay them off within five years. In February 1907, Edith revealed to Roy they might have to sell Clifton and had already received one offer. Some relief appeared the following month when Congress increased Elliot's pension, and that summer Edith and Annie sold the small log cottage in Waterford they inherited from their mother. (The sale to Richard Collins for $125 was half of what Jesse Gover paid in 1839. The sisters kept the nearby Arch House as a source of rental income, and it remained in the family for many years.)[24]

With guidance from her friend and neighbor Robert Walker, Edith took over managing the farm after Roy left. She and Bidie had considerable success selling eggs, capons and pigs in the city, leading Edith to wonder whether this income might have enabled Roy to stay on the farm, had they started sooner. On the other hand, a severe winter almost forced them to sell off the dairy cows, for lack of grain and fodder to feed them. The other children contributed what they could to relieve their parents' financial burden, and Edith was particularly touched when Hume and Mary sent a barrel of food supplies. After their return from the Philippines, the Clendenins were sent to an Army post in Ohio, and Edith knew what a sacrifice had been made to provide such a gift on a military salary. Later that winter, Hume, now a captain, and his mother brought oysters for Elliot. While giving his father-in-law a shave and haircut, Hume revealed the possibility he might soon inherit some money, which he wanted to use it to renovate Clifton, including digging out the basement to install a new furnace. Both Edith and Hume's mother were less convinced the inheritance would materialize, but it was an early indication the Clendenins wanted to make Clifton their permanent residence, as well as a place for Hume's mother to stay in her old age.[25]

In an unusually poignant letter to Mary in April 1906, Edith revealed the degree to which Elliot's health had worsened. She did not know how much longer he could "take it," and did not dare to leave home for even a day. Soon after having to be carried downstairs to attend a dinner party, he was moved into a makeshift bedroom on the ground floor and given increasingly strong opiates to ease his suffering. During a visit to Clifton, Joseph Dunlap, the 7th Indiana veteran who married Lizzie Dutton, was overcome on seeing him "racked with pain," and likened the scene to "a soldier in battle and a sweet-faced wife ministering as only faithful wives can." Learning about her twin's condition, Ellen Martin wrote on the eve of their seventy-second birthday to commiserate over his declining health and offer sisterly advice on how to improve it.[26]

The old soldier had one last victory to savor that winter. For over thirty-five years, he had pushed for a monument to honor those who had given their lives from his regiment during Early's raid on Washington. At the end of 1906, he was contacted by Capt. Robert H. Moses, a veteran of the Fort Stevens battle, who two years earlier had succeeded in placing a memorial to his own regiment, the 122nd N.Y. Infantry, at the Battlefield National Cemetery. An active member of the GAR, Moses wanted each New York regiment that took part in the fighting to be similarly honored. Having heard Elliot had published material concerning the 25th N.Y. Cavalry, Moses asked for copies for possible use in lobbying for a monument. Elliot had Bidie send the requested information, which Moses used in early 1907 to address the New York Legislature on behalf of a bill to provide $3,000 for the "erection of a suitable monument in honor of…the New York troops who were engaged in the battle of Fort Stevens." In thanks for his assistance, Moses enclosed a copy of the senate bill, which passed later that year. Although a monument to the Twenty-Fifth was not erected at the cemetery until the fiftieth anniversary of the battle in 1914,

Elliot could at least know his long quest for recognition of the Twenty-Fifth was on track.[27]

In November 1907 Elliot's former supervisor, Henry Castle, published an article on Early's Raid in a veterans magazine. Borrowing heavily from the 1877 *Republic* article, Castle lauded Chamberlin's role in saving the Capital, before providing a brief sketch of the colonel's other accomplishments before health forced his retirement from the Treasury. In closing, the author declared: "It was my privilege to be closely associated with Col. Chamberlin in official life in Washington for six years...I thus learned to appreciate his worth as a citizen as well as admire his record as a soldier. A patriot and a gentleman, he was ever distinguished by kindly feelings and a high sense of honor." It was a fitting tribute, deeply appreciated by Elliot and his family.[28]

On 20 April 1908, Elliot finally surrendered to the illnesses that had hampered his life for so many years. A funeral service was conducted at Clifton the following day by Reverend Tyler, and two days later he was buried at Arlington National Cemetery in a military ceremony that included an army chaplain and a bugler to play taps. Obituaries cited his war record and the romantic circumstances surrounding his courtship of Edith while serving as Provost Marshal at Point of Rocks. Prominently mentioned were his role as chairman of Virginia's Republican Party and long career at the Treasury Department.[29]

While not unexpected, his death was a severe blow to his family, especially the children, who would later accord their father an almost mythic status. Peeling away the legend, one encounters a man who resists easy categorization. There is little doubt he was a devoted father, faithful husband, and determined breadwinner, for which his descendants have good reason for gratitude. A brief list of his many avocations—jeweler, soldier, farmer, amateur scientist and artist, politician, special agent and bureaucrat—suggests both broad interests and failure to find a truly satisfactory calling. Time and again, he seemed on the cusp of the success and recognition he had sought since leaving Vermont, only to have it slip away. Despite knowing the key participants in many of the significant events of his time, it was often from the perspective of an outsider looking in. His upbringing in a large, impoverished family, which nevertheless had aspirations to a better life, certainly had a strong influence on his personality. Likewise, a strong sense of honor and loyalty to principles that sometimes seemed outmoded often gave him the appearance of being stubborn and headstrong. Like Don Quixote, he found himself fighting perceived wrongs, regardless of whether committed by incompetent military officers, "unreconstructed" Southerners, or corrupt politicians and bureaucrats. Sometimes, poor timing, events beyond his control and a blind eye towards his own shortcomings nullified his efforts to reform the very things he found objectionable. But in the end, it is this unique mixture of strengths and weaknesses that make him interesting.

25th N. Y. Cavalry Monument, Battlefield National Cemetery, Washington, D.C. The base is inscribed: "Dedicated to the memory of our comrades who gave their lives in defense of the National Capital, July 11, 1861." Sadly, after decades of trying to boost recognition of his regiment's role at Ft. Stevens, Elliot did not live to see the statue's 1914 dedication. (Nat. Park Service)

* * * * *

It fell to Edith to guide the children through a short, but eventful period of transition following their father's death. Financial circumstances denied her the luxury of an extended bereavement. The pension Congress awarded her husband did not include provisions for a surviving spouse, so just a month after his death, Edith and Morrill initiated a claim for a widow's military pension. Due to Elliot's failure to fill out a form certifying the deaths of his first wife and children, Edith had to get Ellen Martin to provide these details about her twin brother's past in a sworn statement for the Pension Bureau. Although Edith was eventually awarded twelve dollars per month, she and Morrill began a lengthy legal battle to have it increased. In the meantime, she and Annie borrowed $1,000 against the farm to help pay off notes taken out in 1906, which were starting to come due.[30]

After two years in Ohio, the Clendenins were sent to Cuba, although their son stayed behind at Clifton. During the 1908 Christmas holidays, the rest of the family, including Roy and Morrill with their wives, gathered at the homestead. Edith used the occasion to discuss Robert Walker's recommendation to sell the farm animals and equipment. The proceeds could be used to build a proper residence for a farm manager, who would work Clifton on shares, thus allowing the family to remain in the main house without the burden of running it themselves. Roy and Edward had suggested this course of action two years earlier, but Edith had been reluctant to pursue it while her husband was still alive. Walker, a local banker and Edith's first cousin once removed, had agreed to oversee the construction of the tenant house and the sale of the livestock and equipment. Like their father, the children now opposed giving up control of the farm, and no decision was made at that time.[31]

Leroy Chamberlin, c. 1908. Possibly taken while working in Chicago, he looks a bit pensive despite his dapper attire. (JCC)

During the holidays, Edith noticed Paul seemed to be suffering from a case of "nerves," and after returning to the Brooklyn Navy Yard at the beginning of 1909, Paul informed his mother he was getting engaged to Sophia Hendrick, a woman whom he had met in New York. Knowing his mother encouraged her children to bring prospective spouses for extended stays to see if they passed "muster" and could adapt to the family, Paul asked if "Sophie" could live at Clifton for a year so she could become "one of the family." But he then revealed the crux of his problem—Sophie was already married to someone else. Six years earlier, the Hendricks had pushed their daughter into marrying an older doctor, who seemed "a good catch" and was not expected to live long. Although she had moved back with her parents within a year, she was still legally married. Asking his mother to keep the matter secret from everyone except Bidie, Paul wanted Sophie to establish residency in Virginia, so that after a year, she could seek a discreet divorce in Richmond. Edith did not agree to Paul's proposal, and Sophie had to obtain her divorce elsewhere.[32]

Justin Morrill Chamberlin, wife Priscila and baby "Cilla,", c. 1908. (BCC)

Roy's career as a bond salesman did not meet with his expectations, and he brought Charlton and son Wellman back to Clifton that summer. Although he hoped to return to work for the Armour Company, his mother persuaded him to stay through the fall and help oversee the farm. Relying on Arch Wellington to take care of the grounds and gardens, she resumed taking on summer boarders to help meet expenses. Instead of building a tenant house, Roy convinced his mother to auction off the horses and other nonessential property to finance construction of a modern dairy barn. Edith dreaded the thought of having to watch their possessions being sold yet again, but finally agreed to the idea. The new structure was built adjacent to the recently rebuilt "bank barn," and was considered state-of-the-art for its time, with milking stanchions for forty cows. Water for the dairy was provided by a hydraulic ram placed in the stream, as electricity had yet to reach Waterford. One factor in the decision to go ahead

Vera and Edward's December 1909 Wedding Party: (l. to r.) unidentified man, Paul, flower girl, maid of honor Helen Meek, bride, groom, best man Morrill, and second flower girl. (TCC)

with Elliot's long-delayed dream of having a full-time dairy was the completion that year of a macadamized road linking the farm to the train station at Paeonian Springs.

That fall, Edith was preoccupied with the pending weddings of her two bachelor sons. Paul and Sophie had resolved the problem of her marital status, while Edward and Vera had finally convinced her family to sanction their union. The previous year, Vera's parents had sent her on an extended European tour in hopes she might lose interest in her blind suitor, whom they viewed as having no prospect of supporting their daughter in the style to which she was accustomed. The plan failed and, when Vera returned in the summer of 1909, she went to live with friends in Washington to be near her fiancé who was then attending a school for the blind. Later, Vera and Edward stayed with his brother Morrill while they finalized their wedding plans. Resigned to their daughter's decision, Vera's parents came down to supervise furnishing an apartment in the Marlborough, where the couple planned to live, and to meet their prospective in-laws in Loudoun. Any reservations Edith had about Vera had evaporated, and she now strongly favored their union.[33]

At the end of November, the family traveled to New York City, where they were lodged in the Hotel Savoy, courtesy of Vera's father, James Moses, who lived in the hotel with his wife during winters. The wedding ceremony for Vera and Edward took place in St. Thomas Church on the morning of 1 December and was followed by breakfast at the Savoy. Helen Meek served as maid of honor and Morrill Chamberlin as best man. One account in the New York press was headlined "Blind Man Marries a Beautiful Heiress//Multi-Millionaire's Daughter Rests Proudly on His Arm//He is of an Old Family." The couple managed a quick honeymoon in Atlantic City before returning to New York for Paul's wedding five days later.

Paul married Sophie on 6 December in a ceremony conducted at the home of her parents, General and Mrs. William J. Hendrick, located in the fashionable Bay Ridge section of Brooklyn. Morrill again did the honors as best man, and Edith Clendenin was one of the flower girls. The wedding was strictly a "family affair," except for a few close friends of the bride and groom. Although their honeymoon plans were not revealed, the couple stopped over at Clifton a week later on their way to Paul's next assignment in Norfolk.[34]

Edith had some difficulty walking before going to New York and was bedridden after her return, although she managed to write a note thanking the Moses family for the hospitality shown her family in New York. By this time, Roy and Charlton had returned to Washington to live, leaving Edith and Bidie in charge of putting final touches on the new dairy barn and handling the farm's account books. Roy's move back to Washington D.C. had apparently been prompted by Charlton, who did not like life in the "forlorn country." By mid-December, Edith's health improved, and she began plans for a large family gathering over the holidays. Mary had already arrived with her children, and Edith wrote to Hume at his base in Georgia to make sure he would be present, and to compliment him on his promptness in paying for a barrel of apples she had sent.[35]

Edith died suddenly at age sixty-two of a stroke on Sunday evening, 19 December, while talking in Clifton's parlor with her life-long friends, Robert and Eliza Walker. Reverend Tyler officiated at her funeral, which was held at home two days later, before her interment next to Elliot at Arlington National Cemetery the following day. A local paper proclaimed, "one of the most perfect of lives came quietly and peacefully to a close...Her life was so beautiful that her many friends and relatives feel that her place can never be filled." Mention was made of how she met Elliot and that her ancestors had come from England in 1642.[36]

Edith had little fear of death and the "great unknown" that followed. Although nominally an Episcopalian, she never found an adequate replacement for the Quaker faith she had abandoned because of its failure, at least in her mind, to keep pace with the changing world. In any case, her considerable spirituality was focused on the living, and she only worried about the disruption her passing might bring to the lives of her loved ones. After administering to her husband's needs during his last years, she devoted the end of her life to putting the family's affairs in order and was remarkably successful in doing so. The new dairy barn placed Clifton on a secure footing for the first time since the Civil War. Two of her children had the relative security of military life, another was a lawyer, and the one with the greatest challenge in his disability had achieved prosperity through marriage. Bidie's cheerful disposition could be counted on to keep her afloat, and Edith's only concern may have been her youngest son Roy. He had ignored her advice not to marry before he was financially established, and still had not settled on a career.

Edith Reads in her Living Room, c. 1909. Her work done, her family raised, she appears entirely at ease. (TCC)

Despite Edith's oft-repeated regrets about their lack of financial resources, this had actually served to bind the family closer together. If she had any other cause for remorse, aside from the untimely deaths of her sisters and father, it probably concerned frustrations her husband had suffered in his work. Whether or not she blamed herself for guiding him away from a military career, or medicine, she stood by him in the ups and downs that followed, and more than atoned for her one lapse in devotion to Elliot. This account has necessarily focused on her husband, but her transformation from teenage bride to family matriarch is no less important to this story.

Starting far removed from each other in rural communities in New England and Virginia, Elliot and Edith became part of a predominantly urban middle class that emerged in the latter half of the nineteenth century, and it is no accident they employed the frequently used paths of military and government service to attain this status. More unusual was their determination to retain ties to their rural past, as evidenced by their resolve to keep Clifton. Like the portion of Loudoun that was the family's only real home, their lives were riven by social and political issues that divided the country during this period. Those who live along a borderline often do not fit neatly into history's stereotypical categories, and their lives were marked with such incongruities as Virginia Yankees, fighting Quakers, southern Republicans, and rural bureaucrats. Yet these contradictions helped them remain true to their border heritage, even when it would have been more expedient to establish permanent residency north of the Potomac.

EPILOGUE

Final settlement of E. Y. Matthews's estate did not occur until 1941, when Clifton and its land were divided among various heirs. The house is currently owned and occupied by Bruce E. Clendenin, Elliot and Edith's great-great-grandson.

Annie Matthews remained at the Treasury until 1920, the year legislation passed providing pensions for retired federal employees. She continued living at the Marlborough in Washington, until her death years later at age seventy-nine.

After her mother's death, Mary and William Hume Clendenin began to use Clifton as their primary residence. Hume died there in 1933, two years after retiring from the Army with the rank of colonel. Mary remained on the family farm for the rest of her life, dying at home in 1959 in her ninetieth year. Her two children, Edward and Edith, and their descendants survived her.

Eleanor (Bidie) Chamberlin never married, although she played an active role in raising her many nieces and nephews. A few years after her mother's death, she and Vera's sister, Laura Moses, traveled to Japan and Korea, where they were reputedly among the first western women to visit the latter's rugged interior. Bidie spent most of her life at Clifton, where she was active in local and state garden clubs, the Episcopal Church, and the local Republican Party. Known for her wit, she died in 1969 in her ninety-fifth year, the beloved matriarch of the family.

Justin Morrill Chamberlin continued his law practice in Washington and served as president of the Washington D.C. Bar Association in 1918. After suffering a heart attack in the late 1920s, he moved with his wife and two daughters, Priscilla and Ann, to California. He died in San Francisco in 1932 at age sixty. His remains were returned to Washington for burial, although his descendants continued to live in California.

Paul Elliot Chamberlin rose to the rank of lieutenant colonel in the Marine Corps until illness forced his retirement. He died in Washington, D.C., in 1921 at age forty-one and was interred at Arlington National Cemetery. He and Sophie never had children.

Leroy and Charlton Chamberlin returned to Clifton with son Wellman to manage the farm and dairy business after Edith's death. A talented cabinetmaker and architect, he designed and built his own home, Clearfield, on a portion of the family farm across the road from Clifton. Roy died at home in 1952 at age seventy. His three grandsons, Robert, John and David, still live in Virginia.

Shortly before World War I, Edward Matthews Chamberlin Sr. and wife Vera purchased the farm next to Clifton that formerly belonged to the Steer family. The old stone farmhouse was enlarged and renamed to Greystone to provide a home for their three children, Eleanor, Edward Jr. and Laura. During World War I, Edward Sr. served as the first chairman of the Loudoun Red Cross, the first of his many civic undertakings, before his death in 1940 at age sixty-two. Both Clifton and Greystone were farmed jointly for many years under the direction of his brother Roy.

Inspired by the Rockefellers' restoration of Williamsburg, Edward and Roy turned their attention in the 1930s to Waterford's preservation. To this end, Edward and Vera purchased some eighteen buildings that were falling into disrepair, which were then restored for resale or rental under Roy's supervision. It is through their efforts and those of the Waterford Foundation, established in 1943, that the village was declared a National Historic Landmark in 1970. The town still retains its nineteenth century charm and is the site of a nationally-recognized crafts fair every October, when many of its homes and buildings are open to the public.

Appendices

APPENDIX A

Chamberlin's conviction about his regiment's critical role at Fort Stevens first appeared in a Washington D.C. newspaper article (*The Capital*, 24 Sept. 1871) and was prompted by reading Jubal Early's "The Advance on Washington, 1864," published earlier that summer in *The Southern Magazine*.

THE DEFENSE OF WASHINGTON

.......On the 13th of June, 1864, Jubal A, Early was detached from Lee's army with Ewell's corps... and two battalions of artillery, and reached Charlottesville on the 16th. Here occurred his first interruption, for he had to go to Lynchburg after Hunter...Thence he marched as rapidly as possible down the Shenandoah Valley, driving Sigel before him and turning the strong position at Harper's Ferry. On the 9th of July he reached the Monocacy junction, where General Lew Wallace met him with a little army, composed mainly of hundred-days men, invalids, reserves, &c, who fought bravely until nightfall, when General Wallace was compelled to fall back to protect panic-stricken Baltimore.

Nor was Washington less panic stricken than her sister city. True she was better fortified, but where were her garrison? All the old soldiers were with Grant, and though General Augur mustered his brave Veteran Reserves, and the citizens and Government clerks rallied to the ramparts, there were few who forgot 1812, while all day on the 10th the news rolled in of the ill success of Wallace's raw levies against Early's veterans, and the march of the latter on the capital. The rebel forces camped at Rockville on the night of the 10th, and by one o'clock on the afternoon of the 11th were in front of Fort Stevens, on the Seventh-street Road.

Early says: [[portion omitted by SEC added in brackets]

> A short time after noon, riding some distance ahead of my infantry I got in sight of the fortifications of Washington, into which a force of the enemy's cavalry had retired before mine. The works were apparently feebly manned though [they] appeared to be [very] strong in themselves. My whole column was moving by the flank along the road from the necessity of the case, as the character of the country would not permit a movement in any other way, and the trains were interspersed in the column for protection. I sent word for the leading division (Rhodes') to be brought up as rapidly as possible, and for the other divisions, except one to be left as a guard to the trains, to move out of the column to the front. This, of course, was a work of time. General Rhodes was ordered to have his division brought into line as it came up, and to move at once against the works. While his brigades were coming up, he and I were in front examining the works, and before his first brigade could be formed into line we saw a cloud of dust from the direction of Washington, and a column of infantry had filed into the trenches on the right and left, and a regiment was sent to the front as skirmishers. We saw the men deploy with precision, and Rhodes remarked, 'They are not hundred days' men; they are old soldiers!' [The guns from the nearest fort immediately opened, and the first shot was at our group of horsemen, passing just over our heads. In the meanwhile, Rodes's brigades were hurrying up and forming, and I rode to direct the movement of the other troops, after repeating to him the order to move against the works as soon as possible.] While his men were forming, he threw out skirmishers, compelling those of the enemy to retire after they had fired several houses in front of the works, and he in person proceeded to make as close an examination as possible.

The result of the examination was that General Rodes reported against any attempt to carry the works, and General Early, after making a further examination to the left for a weaker place to assault, gave orders for an assault at daybreak the next morning – that of the 12th of July. During the night, however, General Bradley Johnson sent him information that two corps from Grant's army had arrived in Washington, and Early, to use his own words, "determined to retire on the night of the 12th, after demonstrating in front during the day."

The entire credit for the defense of Washington at this critical juncture, and the repulse of the enemy, is usually claimed for the Sixth Corps, particularly by [Martin T.] McMahon in the United States Service Magazine, and by Dr. [George T.] Stevens in his admirable.... History of the Sixth corps....

Careful comparison of the narratives of Early and Stevens shows that the former arrived in front of Fort Stevens at about one o'clock. The Sixth corps reached the wharf at two, marched up Seventh Street, and deployed into the groves in the rear of Forts Slocum, Stevens, and DeRussy not long before dark. Now, what forces were these which skirmished with Early, burned the buildings before the fort, and moved out and deployed with such precision as to convince Rodes and Early that they had veterans to deal with – all in the afternoon of the 11th, before the arrival of the Sixth corps? The headstones in Fort Stevens National Cemetery, and a diary in my possession, answer that question. They were the Twenty-fifth New York Cavalry, dismounted.

In the cemetery at Fort Stevens are five headboards, bearing the names of Sergeants A. C. Starbird and Thomas Richardson, and Privates Elijah Huftelin, Jeremiah Maloney, and William Fray, all of the Twenty-fifth New York Cavalry and all killed July 11. The rest are marked as having been killed in the fight on the 12th. Silent but potent and indisputable witnesses.

[Henry] Coppée, in his "Grant and his Campaigns," [William] Swinton, in his "Army of the Potomac," and [John Eston] Cooke, in his "Life of Lee," all concur in their appreciation of the boldness of Lee's plan, and its disastrous effect on the Union cause had it been successful... Indeed, had [Early] but known the little handful that opposed him, he had time as it was, for the Sixth corps had not yet reached the wharf on the Potomac when Rodes deployed his division to charge the works. Had that charge been made at that time, of its success none can doubt. But, with admirable firmness, courage, and coolness, the plucky New York captain deployed his little "Capitolian guard" with such effect to force back the enemy and to convince Rodes that there were veterans where he thought to find raw levies. The battalion was magnified into a regiment. Early hesitated, waited, and the golden opportunity was lost to him forever.

The capital was safe, for the Sixth corps, with a prestige of a hundred fights, was an army in itself, but it is no derogation to its high honor to say that for half a day Captain Chamberlin and his gallant little band alone kept the enemy at bay, secured a delay of half a day and night, and saved Washington. Officers, high in rank and understanding the circumstances, have expressed the highest appreciation of their inestimable coolness, audacity, prudence, and crowning success.

APPENDIX B

The following anonymous "sketch" from the March 1877 issue of *The Republic* was penned by Asst. Interior Secretary Alonzo Bell with considerable input from Chamberlin. After reiteration of the 1871 article and reworking Bell's complaint to the Treasury Department over his friend's 1876 dismissal, Bell addressed the special agent's latest difficulties. The resulting attempt to burnish Chamberlin's image seems florid to modern ears, but was typical at a time when one's war record played a key role in securing public office. The lengthy opening section has been omitted.

EARLY'S RAID ON WASHINGTON//A LEAF FROM HISTORY

> ...The regiment—or rather the skeleton regiment, for it numbered less than four hundred men—that had advanced as skirmishers, and deployed with such precision as to deceive both Early and Rhodes, was the Twenty-fifth New York, dismounted cavalry, under the command of Captain S. E. Chamberlin. It had been ordered to Camp Stoneman to be

remounted, for it had seen active service, and by the casualties of battle had lost, not only in numbers, but in everything save courage and endurance. It left City Point on the 7th of July, arrived at Baltimore on the 8th, and at Camp Stoneman on the 9th. It was destined to have no rest for at midnight of the 10th it was ordered to move as quickly as possible into the defense of Washington. At daybreak it had reached Fort Stevens, and during the morning it kept up an active exchange of shots with the advance posts of the rebel army. Early's sharpshooters had taken possession of the houses within rifle range of Fort Stevens, and to dislodge them and destroy the houses became a necessity. The work might well test the courage of the oldest veterans, but Captain (afterward Colonel) Chamberlain and his gallant men were equal to the occasion. At two o'clock he received the order to advance as skirmishers. The men sprang into line as if about to go on parade instead of into the face of an army of fifteen thousand strong. To make the attempt with an army at their back to support them would have been gallant work, but to charge upon the rebel outposts with only a defenseless city to fall back upon, was an act of valor unsurpassed in the history of the war. Its very boldness deceived the enemy. The sixth corps was deemed invincible. Its presence on the field was equal to an additional corp. Early had heard of its detachment from Grant's forces; he had been advised of its approach, and when he saw this skeleton regiment deploying with precision under a severe fire, and sweeping his sharp-shooters from their hiding places, no wonder he was deceived....

We have been permitted to examine the diary of Captain Chamberlain, and the entries made at the time tell the whole story. We append the record of four days:

July 10th 1864. Received orders to move into the defenses of Washington. Marched from camp at midnight. Arrived at Fort Stevens on the morning of the 11th.

July 11th. Ordered out as skirmishers at 2 P.M. Rebs within rifle shot of Fort Stevens. Advanced and drove the enemy from houses. Sharp fighting. Burned several houses by order. Was relieved by the sixth corps. Loss, five killed and thirteen wounded. Maloney of my company killed. [This entry varies significantly from that transcribed in Chapter 6.]

July 12. Went out on a skirmish line and relieved regiment of invalids. Exchanged shots with enemy until evening, when enemy advanced strong line of skirmishers. Sharp fighting by the sixth corps; enemy driven back.

July 13th. Rebs all left. Sixth and nineteenth corps in pursuit.

How well the statement of General Early confirms the belief that to the providential movement of the Twenty-fifth New York Cavalry, dismounted, we owe the preservation of the nation's capital on the 11th of July. Early says he came in sight of the defenses "a short time after noon." He ordered the attacking columns to be brought up. He says: "This was the work of time." The work of preparation must have taken at least an hour and a half, which would have made it near two o'clock when he and Rhodes saw a regiment advance on skirmish line, and with such precision as to force the latter to say: "They are not hundred days' men; they are old soldiers."

The diary of the gallant Chamberlain says, "ordered out as skirmishers at 2 P.M." Here we have the secret of that unaccountable delay which gave us the few hours that were needed to bring to the front the sixth and nineteenth corps. The statement of Early and the diary of Chamberlain show conclusively that to the brave men who advanced in the face of the rebel army at two o'clock on the 11th day of July, belong the credit of saving the capital from rebel invasion....If the prompt obedience of a soldier at the critical moment ever saved an army or wrested victory from defeat, the prompt execution of the order to advance by Captain Chamberlain saved the capital, for if Early had known that this handful of men had nothing but empty or poorly-manned trenches behind them, he could have entered the city without firing a shot. Before he knew the truth the golden opportunity had been lost forever....

On the old battlefield in front of Fort Stevens is a national cemetery in which lie buried the brave men who died in defense of the capital. The few headboards bearing the inscription "killed July 11th" mark the graves of the gallant fellows who stood in the track of a victorious army, and, by their valor, held it in check until the long- expected relief arrived. They died without knowledge of the priceless value of the services rendered, and although their sacrifices were no greater than those who fell on the 12th, a grateful nation should inscribe their names upon granite that posterity might know the men who plucked the precious hours from the grasp of time and held them until the moment of supreme danger was passed.

The gallant officer who led this forlorn hope still lives to enjoy the fruits of his heroic service. For bravery in the field, he rose to the rank of Colonel, and until the close of the war rounded out on other fields the fame he earned in the defense of Washington. Marrying into a Quaker family, well-known through Loudon County for their loyalty during the war, the Colonel resigned from the regular army, into which he had been commissioned, and devoted his time and energies to the more peaceful and congenial pursuits of civil life. Though a Vermonter by birth he has made Virginia his home, and if the better qualities of manhood combined with a chivalric love for the Republican party can find their proper appreciation in the Old Dominion, he is sure to take rank among her most honored citizens. Modest, brave, upright, he is the good type of American gentleman – distinguished alike in peace or war for his high sense of honor and his ready response to the call of duty.

Endnotes

Chapter 1
1. Sources for SEC's ancestry: Chamberlin Family Bible; David C. Chamberlin, unpublished genealogy; Welton C. Chamberlain, Richard Chamberlaine of Braintree; Chamberlain Association of America (CAA), *Annual Reports*, 1898-1911; and The Chamberlain Chain, newsletter published after the CAA's revival in 1981.
2. Sanderson, *History of Charlestown*, 306-7; and George Olcott Chamberlin obituary, *Daily Saratogian*, 12Feb82.
3. *Ibid.*; and Abigail White genealogy compiled by SEC's aunt, Mary Chamberlin, TCC.
4. Samuel Chamberlin MSR, obtained by SEC in 1889, TCC.
5. Sanderson, *loc. cit.* Records in Bible started by SEC's parents omit Samuel Newell's second family
6. Universalism appealed to Vermont's independent early settlers. Another religious non-conformist, Mormon Church founder Joseph Smith, was born a few miles from Strafford.
7. 1850 census; marriage record, Strafford Hist. Soc.; and data provided by Sanborn descendant David Colpitts.
8. Henry's initial purchase, 5Apr21, Strafford Land Book 5:510, witnessed by brother Samuel. Later entries in Books 5-6 indicate Henry had difficulty financing the tanyard.
9. Engraving of Simon Sanborn. TCC; and 1850 census.
10. 1840 census; Sanborn's will (4Feb38) copy provided by Gwenda Smith, Strafford Hist. Soc.; and Sanderson, *loc. cit.*, records S. N. Chamberlin's death and burial in the Ashley Cemetery.
11. Chamberlin Family Bible; and 1850 census.
12. Personal history statement, 1898, SEC's TD/AR file.
13. Relatives in the area included the widow and children of Henry Chamberlin, who moved to Boston after the death of Elliot's uncle in 1851. Shortly after Lucia Crawford's husband died in 1853, Elliot's older sister married Don Stone in Lowell, Mass., and the couple was living in Boston with his twin sister Ellen when their first child was born in 1855. Elliot's oldest brother Charles also moved to the Boston suburb of Brighton after the deaths of his wife and children in the 1850s.
14. Bio sketch in 1867 U.S. Cavalry examination, SEC's MSR.
15. Samuel Chamberlin (Strafford) to SEC (place unknown), 4Nov54.
16. Records provided by Gwenda Smith from Strafford Town Meeting Book 2, 6Mar55; and Strafford Land Books 12:302, 13:335-40, and 14:34. Elijah, Lucia and eventually SEC signed quitclaims for this property in return for $100 each from their mother, while Charles, Louisa and Ellen waived their rights in return for nominal sums. There is no record William signed a quitclaim.
17. Gwenda Smith, *Town House*, and "A Walking Tour of Strafford Village."
18. Cross, *Justin Smith Morrill, Father of the Land-Grant Colleges*, 51.
19. SEC's AHS certificate.
20. Little is known about Elliot's first marriage, as he and Edith never mentioned it to their children. The author first learned of Maggie from a 1908 deposition by his twin sister in support of a widow's pension for Edith.
21. SEC's cavalry examination, *loc. cit.*; and 1850 La Porte, Ind., census.
22. 1860 Nashville census; 1860 Nashville City Directory; and jeweler's tools/scale in possession of Robert Elliot Chamberlin.
23. French, *Gazetteer of New York State for 1860*, 675.
24. Warren County, NY, land and excise commission records; and 1865 New York state census.
25. *Ibid.* By comparison, the Martins' house was valued at $800 and the Camerons' at $1500.

Chapter 2
1. Charles tried to re-enlist the following year, but committed suicide at his home in Cambridge before he could rejoin his old regiment. Elliot attributed his death to wounds received at Bull Run.
2. Charles Chamberlin's MSR.
3. Maggie and the children were buried in a plot belonging to Duncan Cameron (Bay St. Cem. Records). The plot also contains graves of SEC's mother and sister.
4. John Cunningham, *Adirondack Regiment*, 12-20; and Phisterer, *New York in the War of the Rebellion*, 3384-97. The NYDMNA database is another invaluable resources on the 118th and its personnel.
5. Faust, *Illustrated Encyclopedia of the Civil War*, various entries.
6. Appointment 2nd Lt., N.Y. Adj. Gen. S.O. #82, 17Jul62; and SEC's obituary, CAA *Annual Report for 1908-10*.

7 *Republican* (Glens Falls), 5Aug62.
8 *Ibid.*, 9&12Aug62; and SEC MSR. Gov. Edwin Morgan signed commission on 10Sep62.
9 Cunningham, *op. cit.*, 17-8.
10 General McClellan banished Wool to this administrative post after the latter acted on his own initiative to prevent Fortress Monroe from falling to the Confederates and recapturing the city of Norfolk.
11 Sgt. Garrett to wife, c. 17Sep62, reprinted *Glens Falls Times*, 26Dec1917.
12 Early in the war, most prisoners were paroled to camps run by their own sides, as neither had adequate facilities to house them. These prisoners were later "exchanged" and allowed to return to the front. The parole system was gradually abandoned after the North realized it prolonged the war and favored the South's smaller population.
13 Cunningham, *op. cit.*, 27.
14 Three undated clippings, scrapbook, Crandall Library, Glens Falls.
15 OR 19(2): 474; Cunningham, *op. cit.*, 29-31; and Lt. David Dobie (H) to friend, 7Nov62, Dobie papers.
16 Capt. Jacob Parmerter (B) to wife, 1Nov62, papers in possession of descendant Robert Parmerter.
17 OR 51: 692; and Pvt. Carlos Brainerd (A) to friend, 1Nov62, Brainerd Papers.
18 *Republican* (Glens Falls), 25Nov62
19 Cunningham, *op. cit.*, 41.
20 Gen. Benjamin F. Butler began referring to ex-slaves as "contrabands of war" to justify not having to return them to their Southern masters, as U.S. law still required.
21 Lt. D. F. Dobie to friend, 7Dec62, Dobie papers.
22 SEC diary; Co. A muster rolls. Date of rank as 1st Lt., 9Dec62; commission signed by governor, 13Feb63.
23 Pvt. Oakley H. Smith (F) to family, 1Jan63, USAMHI.
24 SEC diary; and photograph taken at Walden's DC studio, USAMHI. Others had pictures taken at Matthew Brady's more prestigious studio, where they met the President (Cunningham, *op. cit.*, 51-4).
25 SEC diary; and Cunningham, *op. cit.*, 33.
26 Lt. Garret to wife, 3Feb63, reprinted *Glens Falls Times*, 26Dec1917.
27 Garrett's dream of rapid advancement was not that far-fetched. After Riggs left Co. A to become captain of Co. D, a vacancy occurred in the latter when 1st Lt. John H. Smith was "discharged for disability." The hapless Smith had only been promoted four days earlier, and after learning of his dismissal, he vented his anger on the men in his company, who, according to Chamberlin's diary, then hung him in effigy.
28 Garret to wife, 3Feb63, reprinted in *Glens Falls Times*, 27Dec1917; and SEC diary, 18Jan62.
29 SEC diary, Jan-Apr63.
30 SEC's *cartes de visite*.
31 Cunningham, *op. cit.*, 41-59; OR 51:985; and extract of Garrett's orders, 15Feb63, TCC.
32 Orders signed by Capt. E. M. Camp, "AADC," (Soldiers Rest, D.C.), 15Feb63, TCC.
33 William S. Chamberlin wrote Justin Morrill a month earlier about obtaining a government job and likely was in D.C. to pursue this goal. Other evidence suggests that he was a recent deserter, which may explain his failure to secure Federal employment, as well as the subsequent lack of contact between the two brothers. (William Chamberlin to JSM, Jan63, Morrill papers, LC. A William S. Chamberlin deserted from an Albany regiment, but his identity as Elliot's brother has not been confirmed.)
34 SEC diary; and G.O. #44, 20Feb63, TCC.
35 SEC diary.
36 Cunningham, *op. cit.*, 48-51.
37 OR 51:1003; and *Plattsburgh Express & Sentinel*, 6Jun63.

Chapter 3

1 After service in the War of 1812, Dix had a distinguished career as a U.S. Senator, railroad magnate and Treasury Secretary, before Lincoln appointed him the highest-ranking officer in the Volunteer Army.
2 Cunningham, *Adirondack Regiment*, 39; *Plattsburgh Express & Sentinel* (PE&S), 9May63; and SEC diary.
3 "Charges and Specifications against 1st Lieut. Simon E. Chamberlin," n.d., copy provided by Sharpe Swan with permission from Garrett descendant Dan Way.
4 SEC diary, 25-30Apr63; and *PE&S*, 9&23May63.
5 SEC diary.
6 *PE&S*, 14Jul63.
7 OR 27(2):819-24; Trudeau, "Gettysburg's Second Front," 16; and Hanover Co., *Survey of Civil War Sites*,

29-33.
8   Cunningham, *op. cit.*, 67.
9   SEC diary; Cunningham, *op.cit.*, 69-70; and unknown author, 13Jul63, *op. cit.*
10 Sources for this section: Col. Wardrop's 11Jul63 report, OR 27(2):842-3; Cunningham, *op. cit.*, 70-6; Watson, *Military and Civil History*, 276-7; Corell, *History of the Naval Brigade*, chap. "Second Peninsula Campaign"; *PE&S*, 25Jul63; and unknown author, 13Jul63 *op. cit.*
11 *OR* 27(2): 837-9.
12 *OR* 27(2): 858-9; Hanover County, *op. cit.*, 29-33; Hall, *Books to Bullets*, 26-7.
13 Wardrop's report, *op. cit.*
14 Getty's estimate of CSA defenses was taken from a report General Foster obtained from a civilian living in the area and a prisoner, both of whom evidently exaggerated the numbers.
15 *OR* 27(2), 818-9.
16 *OR* 27(2), 858-9, 972-3; and *Richmond Daily Dispatch*, 28Jun, 5-8Jul63.
17 Sources for this section: *OR* 27(2), 844-51; Cunningham, 72-4; *PE&S*, 25Jul63; unknown author, 13Jul63, *op. cit.*; and letters, 7&9Jul, from Edgar and George Wing (A), Halsey Wing File, Crandall Library, Glens Falls.
18 Unknown author, 13Jul63. *op. cit.*; and Norris's report, OR 27(2), 845-7.
19 *Ibid.*; and Edgar Wing letter, *op. cit.*
20 Unknown author, 13Jul63 *op. cit.*; and SEC diary. Pvt. Henry Mills (A) died of wounds on the way back and was buried at White House Landing.
21 Cunningham, *op. cit.*, 76; and *PE&S*, 25Jul63.
22 SEC diary; and Cunningham, *op. cit.*, 77.

Chapter 4

1   Mitchell, *Horatio Seymour of New York*, chaps. 13-14.
2   Nicolay quoted in Mitchell, *op. cit.*, 357; and Bernstein, *New York City Draft Riots*, 61-5.
3   *OR*, III, 3:465-6.
4   *PE&S*, 25Jul63; extract, S.O. #197, 17Jul63, TCC; and muster rolls of SEC's detachment, Nov63-Feb64, TCC.
5   SEC diary,
6   *OR*, III, 3:552-3, 633.
7   SEC diary; Larry Hart, "Tales of Old Dorp," *Schenectady Daily Gazette*, 10May1999; and OR, III, 3:677-8, 731.
8   H.R. Wing to SEC, 13Aug63, TCC. Wing wanted his son Edgar promoted to 2nd Lt. of Co. A.
9   Cunningham, *op. cit.*, 80-1.
10 See Mitchell, *op. cit.* ix, 263-7, for ties between Pruyn's family and Seymour.
11 Betsey Chamberlin to SEC, c. 2Aug63.
12 Duncan Cameron, Don Stone and Charles H. Crawford MSRs and MPAs; and *Republican* (Glens Falls), 15Sep63.
13 A respected field commander, Jackson was sent to Rikers Island to recuperate from an accident suffered in the field.
14 Extract S.O. #13, 21Aug63, TCC; and SEC diary.
15 S.O. #39, 14Sep63, TCC.
16 Leave request, 7Oct63.
17 SEC to Townsend, 10Nov63, SEC MSR.
18 Lt. Garrett to wife, 2Nov63, reprinted in *Glens Falls Times*, 4Jan1918.
19 Garrett never succeeded in taking command of Co. A; instead in early 1864, he accepted a position as 1st lieutenant in Co. B, a rank he held for the remainder of the war.
20 S.O. #115, 4Dec63, and S.O. #33, 9Dec63, TCC.
21 Detachment muster rolls, TCC; and MSRs for Detachment, NARA.
22 Photographs, TCC; and clipping, *NY Herald Tribune*, 31Dec63.
23 Sgt. A. J. Weeks to uncle, 7Dec63, *Swem Library Digital Projects*, College of William and Mary.
24 Sgt. Weeks to sister, 26Dec63, *loc. cit.*
25 Gen. Hicks to Adjutant General, *N.Y. Times*, 10Jan65. British consuls kept busy in the North and South attending to forced enlistment of their citizens (Foreman, *A World on Fire*, 503, 508-9, 600-1, 630).
26 "How Soldiers are Treated on Riker's Island," *Brooklyn Daily Union*, n.d., reprinted *Indiana State Sentinel*, 1Feb64.

27 *N.Y. Times*, 29Jan64.
28 Dix to Dewey, entry 1394, RG 393, NARA; and *N.Y. Times*, 6Feb64.
29 *N.Y. Times*, 11Feb64.
30 SEC's appointment as AAAG, S.O. # 46, 22Feb64, TCC.
31 *Republican* (Glens Falls), 28Mar64.
32 SEC to JSM, 2Apr64, SEC's MSR.
33 Phisterer, *New York in the War of the Rebellion*, 3385; and New York State, *Presentation of Flags...*, 135-6. In his copy, SEC only noted his rank and dates of service under section on the 118th, but devoted much more space to his time in the 25th.

Chapter 5

1 SEC 1864-5 diary exists only as a transcript that he made c. 1877. Other sources for the 25th include Coutant, Notes; NARA personnel files and regimental books (RLOB), Phisterer, *New York in the War of the Rebellion*, 1096-1105, and the NYDMNA database.
2 Coutant, Notes; and Clark's MSR. Special thanks are due John Charlton Chamberlin Jr., for finding BOB's letters at the N.Y. Public Library, and William B. Styple, for sharing other copies collected for possible inclusion in his *Writing and Fighting the Civil War*, an anthology of soldier letters appearing in the *N.Y. Sunday Mercury* (NYSM).
3 Muster rolls of 118th and 25th; SEC's MSR; S.O. # 125, Hqs. Draft Rendezvous, 16May64, TCC; and Col. Seeley orders, 18May64, TCC. Gov. Seymour did not sign SEC's commission until October, further indication he was not well connected with the state's Democratic administration.
4 The controversial Sickles was an apt namesake for the 25th. While serving in Congress in 1859, he gained notoriety for the first successful use of a "temporary insanity" plea after killing his wife's lover, the son of Francis Scott Key. As a soldier, Sickles was incontestably brave, but his reputation was marred by squabbles with other commanders. After the war he served as Minister to Spain and later returned to Congress. His death in 1914 was clouded by allegations he had diverted funds intended for monuments to honor New York's participation in the Civil War (Keneally, *American Scoundrel*).
5 Liebenau's MSR; and Lincoln, *Collected Works*. 8:329.
6 Phisterer, *op. cit.*, 1096; and Coutant Notes.
7 Seeley MSR; Sandford's letter to Lincoln accessed at https://repository.library.brown.edu: and Lincoln's endorsement. Lincoln, *Collected Works*, 6:452-453. BOB seldom missed a chance to promote Seeley.
8 McPherson MSR.
9 Seymour MSRs and MPR. Latter contains 1903 letter from Rep. Seymour Powers (R-Mass.) to Pension Office citing President Lincoln's endorsement.
10 *NYSM*, 15May64.
11 Correspondence between draftee Charles Lester and his mother confirm difficulties getting qualified recruits. He only enlisted in the 25th to get the bounty, and his letter of 24Apr64 indicates plans to flee back home. "I wouldn't give a shit to go in this regiment anyhow. They desert faster than they can get them" (Lester letter, USAMHI).
12 The nighttime sortie Campbell recalled was evidently meant to prevent John Mosby's partisans from freeing Rebel prisoners before they were brought in from the front.
13 *NYSM*, 29May64; Co. E Muster Roll, 30Jun64, TCC; and Campbell (Columbia, Pa) to SEC, [c. 1891.
14 Campbell letter, *op. cit.*
15 OR, 36(3):785 & 40(1):747-8.; and Philip H. Sheridan, *Personal Memoirs*, 427-50.
16 James Coutant letter, 22Jun64, Coutant Notes: and John Wolf interview, *Wash. Evening Star*, 7Jul91.
17 Sgt. Coutant letter, n.d., Coutant Notes.
18 The dismissed officers were 2nd Lts. Edward Schmidt (A) and Albert Brusle (G), brother of Adjutant William Brusle, who must remain suspect for having purchased his commission (*Wash. Evening Star*, 21Jun64).
19 S.O. #137, Draft Rendezvous, 1Jun64, TCC; Bonnell, *Sabers in the Shenandoah*, 3; and 25th RLOB,
20 Coutant Notes; Phisterer, *loc. cit.*; and John Wolf interview, *Wash. Evening Star*, 3May1914.
21 S O. #25 & 30, 30Jun & 2Jul64, signed by Col. Gates, TCC.
22 *NYSM*, 10Jul64.

Chapter 6

1 BOB 18 July letter, *NYSM*, 24Jul64, reprinted in Styple, *op. cit.*

2   See Judge, *Season of Fire*, fort account of this battle. Wallace is best known today as *Ben Hur*'s author.
3   Cooling, *The Day Lincoln Was Almost Shot*, has detailed discussion of Fort Stevens battle.
4   Judge, *op. cit.*, chaps. 11-2; and Cooling, *Jubal Early's Raid on Washington*, chap. 4.
5   After rushing back to the Capital, Asst. Sec. of War Charles Dana wired Grant about the sorry state of affairs that confronted him: "[T]here is no head to the whole, and it seems indispensable that you should at once appoint one...General Halleck will not give orders, the President will give none, and until you direct... what is to be done everything will go on in the deplorable and fatal way in which it has gone for the past week" (*OR*, 37(2):223).
6   *NYSM*, 24Jul64; and Cooling, *The Day Lincoln...*, Ch. 7.
7   Early to Lee, 14Jul64, OR, 37(2):357-9; Early, *Memoir of the Last Year of the War*, 59-60; Early, "The Advance upon Washington" 756-7; and Cooling, *The Day Lincoln...*,123-7.
8   25th veteran John Wolf letters, *National Tribune* (DC), 9Nov99 & 22Jan1914; and *NYSM*, 24Jul64.
9   Wolf to *Nat. Trib.*, 9Nov99 & 18Sep1924; Cooling, *The Day Lincoln...*, 138, 146-7, 179, 277; SEC diary; and James C. Cannon, *Record of Service of Company K*, 14-7.
10 OR, 37(2) L 197, 231; Cannon, *loc. cit.*; and Cooling, *The Day Lincoln...*, 132.
11 Sgt. Harry Lane to John Wolf, *Wash. Evening Star*, 22Jan92; Lincoln quoted in Wolf letters, *Nat. Trib.*, 9Nov99y & 2Jan1914; and Cooling, *The Day Lincoln...*, 159 (f.n. 53). See also Presidential secretary John Hay's account of Lincoln's first visit to the fort (Burlingame and Ettlinger, eds., *Inside Lincoln's White House*. 221-2).
12 Nevius quote, *Wash. Post*, 11Jul91; and Wolf interview, *Wash. Evening Star*, 3May1914.
13 McLean letter, *Nat. Tribune*, 16Jul85.
14 *Alex. Gazette*, 12Jul64; and SEC diary. The 11 July diary entry varies from a version published in 1877 (see Appendix B) that has the skirmish line deploying at 2 PM. However, SEC wrote in his copy of Cox's *Defenses of Washington* (28) that "the Regiment engaged Early's advance shortly after noon."
15 Coutant Notes.
16 *NYSM*, 24Jul64. For additional details on the battle, see Judge, *op. cit.*, and Cooling, *Jubal Early's Raid*.
17 Harry Lane to John Wolf, quoted *Wash. Evening Star*, 22Jan92.
18 Dan Dibble to *Nat. Trib.*, 16Sep1920; John Wolf to *Nat. Trib.*, 9Nov99 & 22Jan1914; and Wolf interview, *Wash. Evening Star*, 3May1914.
19 Cox, *Defenses of Washington*, 12; and Wolf and Nevius interviews, *Wash. Post*, 11Jul91 and *Wash. Evening Star*, 13Jul91.
20 McCook report, 25Jul64, OR, 37:230-4.
21 Few historians have looked at the opening hours of the fighting at Fort Stevens, or noted the participation of the 25th, and, if so, they simply accepted McCook's version of events.
22 Although for most of the war the XIII Corps referred to the Army of the Tennessee, it was later used to denote the Veteran Reserve Corps.
23 Lane letter, *op. cit.*; Cooling, *The Day...*, 130-7; Wolf to *Nat. Trib.*, 9Nov99; and Lord to *Nat. Trib.*, 31May1900
24 Early, "Advance upon Washington" 756-7.
25 Without precise times for when the 25th left the earthworks and when Rodes made his observation, it is difficult to validate Chamberlin's assertion, although the other likely candidate to have been the "old soldiers," Briggs's detachment, seemingly took the field too late to fit Early's narrative.
26 For details on President's brush with death, see Cooling, *op. cit.*, Chap. 8.
27 SEC diary; Wolf to *Nat. Trib.*, 9Nov99 & 22Jan1924; and Coutant Notes.
28 Inexplicably, BOB has the 25th lying idle on Tuesday and places the above action on Wednesday, when the battle was over. This glaring error, plus the letter's surprising failure to mention the President's visits to the fort, suggest it was changed at the *Sunday Mercury*. The paper's vehement pro-Democratic owners had just published an editorial accusing Lincoln of allowing Early to get close to Washington so that he could gain support for his re-election by foolishly coming under enemy fire (Styple, *op. cit.*, 268-9).
29 BOB's letter, *op. cit.*
30 McCook's report *op. cit.*
31 BOB letter, *NYSM*, 24Jul64; and Samuel H. Sovine to SEC, 25Feb1902. It was Sovine's third, all apparently unsuccessful, request. In this letter he mentioned their having had an altercation several months after Ft. Stevens. Wolf believed McPherson received a commendation from the President for his role in leading the 25th at Ft. Stevens (*Nat. Trib.*, 18Sep1924), but no record was found in his MSR.

32 Capt. Richard Shannon to SEC, 19Jul64; Capt. Edward Benedict to SEC, 28Jul64; and SEC diary.
33 Appendix B; *NYSM*, 24Jul64; Cox, *op. cit.*, 28-9; and Nevius interview, *Wash. Post*, 14Jul91. Although cemetery markers at Ft. Stevens show seven dead on the first day, Pvt. John Ellis of the 61st Pa. Inf. was killed the following day according to his MSR and a regimental history. The only other casualty buried there, George Marquett, 98th Pa. Inf., arrived late in the day. A picket from the 150th Ohio was also mortally wounded on the 11th.

Chapter 7

1 *NYSM*, 7Aug64.
2 *Ibid.*, 7Aug64 &18Sep64. (The latter clipping was saved by SEC and not found elsewhere.)
3 Norton, *Red Neck Ties*, 16-18.
4 Petition, James Smith CMR, case # LL 2443.
5 The lieutenants commanding Cos. B and H also signed the petition, indicating McPherson's support was mostly limited to the two captains who had remained with him inside Ft. Stevens.
6 Transcript of Eason's letter, 25th RLOB, probably dated 9Aug64 and addressed to Army's Adj. Gen.
7 Capt. Hudnut to Brig. Gen. L. Thomas, Adj. Gen., 9Aug64, copy in *ibid*.
8 Smith CMR, *op. cit.*
9 *Ibid*.
10 SEC to C. H. Raymond, AAG, Dept. of Washington, 11Aug64, SEC MSR.
11 Col. Gamble to Maj. McPherson, 15Aug64, 25th RLOB.
12 Baxter's note, SEC MSR; leave approval, 20Sep64, TCC; and muster rolls, 25th RLOB.
13 Cooling, *Jubal Early's Raid*, 221-5; and Sheridan, *Memoirs*, 254-6.
14 Sheridan, *op. cit.*, 266-7.
15 Keen and Mewborn, *43rd Battalion*, 155-9; and Wert, *Mosby's Rangers*, 189-94.
16 *OR*, 43(1): 811, 843.
17 *Ibid.*, 856, 869-70.
18 *Ibid.*, 859, 882; and Keen and Mewborn, *op. cit.*, 161.
19 Hard, *History of the Eighth Cavalry Regiment*, 311; and Janney, *Memoirs*, 218-9.
20 *OR*, 43(1): 882, 898, 909; and the *Sentinel* (Whiteside, Ill.), 8Sep64.
21 Janney, *Memoirs*, 219-21; and S. M. Janney (Harpers Ferry) to wife, 26Aug64, Janney Papers, FHL.
22 Janney, *op. cit.*, 221-3; and *Alex. Gazette*, 30Aug&1Sep64.
23 OR, 43(1):909, 942-3, 954-5, 43(2):4; Janney, *Memoirs*, 223-4; and *Alex, Gazette*, 1, 3, 5, 9, 20 & 23Sep64.
24 OR, 43(2):22, 29. For additional details, see Chamberlin and Souders, *Between Reb and Yank*, 31.
25 See Wert, *Mosby's Rangers*, Chap. 13, for account of campaign to open the railroad.
26 *Ibid.*; and OR 43(part 2): 341, 347.
27 Muster roll, Detachment 1st Brigade, 1st Div.; and Gallupe's order, 14Oct64, TCC.
28 *OR* 43(part 2): 346, 356; and Sheridan, *Memoirs*, 313.
29 "Introduction" to Sheridan, *op. cit.*, v.
30 SEC diary. Although SEC included "Cedar Creek" in a post-war list of his significant engagements, this referred to an "action" at Cedar Creek on 12 November.

Chapter 8

1 Clipping of BOB letter with SEC's marginal notes, *NYSM*, 18Sep64, TCC; and *OR* 43:861.
2 After Lazarus was released and returned to his regiment the following year, he recounted how he, Sgt. Edward Dupree (or Dupprel) and Sgt. Simpson, along with other captives, were forced to march barefoot to Staunton in three days. Those dropping out along the way were clubbed or shot to death. Simpson managed to escape by jumping out of a train near Richmond; Dupree was recognized as a deserter from the Rebel army and hanged. Lazarus ended up in the Salisbury and later Danville prisons before being exchanged (*NYSM*, 12Apr65).
3 *Ibid*.
4 *OR* 43:986; and *NYSM*, 16Oct64.
5 Col. Seeley to Adj. Gen. Thomas, 14Jan65. Seymour VSR, (S. 194 VS 1865); and McPherson MSR.
6 Sheridan, *op. cit.*, 275-80; and Worrall, *Friendly Virginians*, 433.
7 *NYSM*, 16Oct64.

8   Custer report, *OR* 43:457-9.
9   Kidd, *Personal Recollections*, 387.
10 *NYSM*, 16Oct64; and Urwin, *op. cit.*, 177-91. Recognizing Custer's role in their defeat, Confederates assigned a company of sharpshooters to target him the next time he took the field.
11 Seeley to Adj. Gen. Thomas, 14Jan65, *op. cit.*;
12 Sgt. Coutant was honored by his men as "a man insensible of fear, generous…, light-hearted in the midst of worst hardships, and one faithful to his duty as a soldier on all occasions" (Coutant "Notes").
13 Although Chamberlin never served under Custer, his copy of the "Custer Badge" is currently in the possession of descendant John C. Chamberlin. Inspiration for the badge may have been one that Custer had struck after the Winchester victory and presented to commanders of each regiment in his brigade (information provided by David Colpitts).
14 *NYSM*, 16Oct64; Coutant Notes; Devine's story from descendant David Colpitts; and Urwin, *op. cit.*, 177-91. While Phisterer (*op. cit.*, 1087) lists only seven total casualties, the veteran association of the 25th named ten men buried at Winchester Nat. Cemetery.
15 Worrall, *op.cit.*, 433-4.
16 Phisterer, *op. cit.* 1097; *NYSM*, 16Oct64; and Archibald Wilson MPA.
17 *NYSM*, 16Oct64. For detailed accounts of this affair, see Wert, *Mosby's Rangers*, 212-19, and Ramage, *Gray Ghost*, 197-200. Most historians believe Tolbert or Merritt gave the execution order.
18 Gardner to *Nat. Tribune*, 8Oct1903. Gardner apparently served under an alias, as his name does not appear on the 25th roster, but does appear on an 1893 list of veterans.
19 *NYSM*, 16Oct64.
20 *NYSM*, 23Oct64, reprinted in Styple, *op. cit.*; and Seeley CMR, case # OO 924.
21 *NYSM*, 23Oct64.
22 Myers, *Comanches*, 335-36.
23 See Krick, "Cause of all my Disasters," for assessment that Early's brave, but poorly led, cavalry contributed to defeats in the Valley. (Page 94 quotes Capt. Frank Myers that Rosser "knows no more about putting a command into a fight than a school boy.")
24 *NYSM*, 23Oct64. Phisterer, *op. cit.*, 1097, lists seven casualties that day.
25 Myers made no attempt to minimize the "shameful rout and stampede" at Woodstock (*Comanches*, 339-40).
26 According to Col. Kidd's after-action report (*OR* 43: 459-61) the 6th Mich. and the 25th N.Y. operated in the advance that day, which is probably more accurate than his later recollection that the 25th only assisted the initial charge of the 5th, 6th and 7th Michigan (*Personal Recollections*, 402).
27 Although no evidence of malingering was found, the possibility Seeley shot himself to avoid going into battle cannot be discounted. He recuperated in New York, and did not rejoin his regiment until mid-December.
28 Seeley to Adj. Gen. Thomas, *op. cit.*
29 Lt. David's accusations, 18Oct64, Seymour MSR.
30 *NYSM*, 23Oct64.
31 Lt. David's accusations, Seymour MSR.
32 Seymour to BG Stevenson (Harpers Ferry), 27Oct64, *ibid.*; and Seymour's charges against Capt. Smith, 20Oct64, Smith MSR.
33 Seymour to Stevenson, *op. cit.* and transfer notice, Seymour MSR.

Chapter 9

1   *NYSM*, 20Nov64; and daily schedule, 25th RLOB.
2   In "Mosby as a Factor in the 1864 Valley Campaign," Dennis Frye argues partisans had little effect on outcome of Sheridan's campaign.
3   25th RLOB; Wheeler order, 29Oct64, TCC; and Smith MSR.
4   SEC diary; *OR* 43(part 2): 638; *NYSM*, 20Nov64; and Keen and Mewborn, *43rd Battalion*, 209.
5   *NYSM*, 20Nov64.
6   Wearing blackface as a disguise, Brewster managed to escape from the prison and cross the Union lines near Front Royal. He was still wearing blackface when he encountered Chamberlin and his men on picket duty near Cedar Creek (Chamberlin's annotation on newspaper clipping, TCC).
7   Clipping of Brewer's account with SEC annotations, 31Oct90; and Crawford, *Mosby and his Men*, 291.
8   SEC diary; and *Supplement to OR*, 41: 719-20.
9   Krick, *op. cit.*, 105.

10 SEC diary; *OR* 43(2): 604, 611, 624; Pfisterer, *op. cit.*, 1097; and Co. A muster rolls, RLOB.
11 Williamson, *Mosby's Rangers*, 299-302, which relied heavily on Crawford, *op. cit.*, 296-8.
12 Pvt. Louis T. Powell escorted Blazer to Richmond, where the partisan's exploits at Myerstown and physique brought him to the attention of the Confederate Secret Service and John Wilkes Booth. Powell, alias "Lewis Payne," would be hanged for his role in the assassination plot against Lincoln (Roscoe, *Web of Conspiracy*, 67).
13 Williamson, *op. cit.* 304-9, Wert, *op. cit.*, chap 14; and Crawford, *op. cit.*, 300.
14 *NYSM*, 4Dec64.
15 *Ibid.*; and SEC diary.
16 Scott, *Partisan Life*, 371-3; and Bonnell, *Sabres in the Shenandoah*, 152-3.
17 *NYSM*, 4Dec64. BOB estimated there were 200 partisans with Mosby that day.
18 *OR* 43(2): 604.
19 Williamson, *Mosby's Rangers*, 263.
20 Sheridan's communiqué of 17 November was directed at Jefferson County, which had voted to secede with the rest of Virginia, before being forced to join the Unionist state of West Virginia.
21 *OR* 43(2): 639.
22 Grant to Sheridan, 9Nov64, quoted in Sheridan, *Memoirs*, 267.
23 *OR* 43(2): 602-3.
24 *Ibid.*, 671-2.
25 *Ibid.*, 679
26 Quotes from a handwritten copy kept by SEC, which differs slightly from *Ibid*.
27 Mobberly, a deserter from White's "Comanches" who appears later in this story, was widely believed to leave his captives pinned by rocks to die of starvation and exposure. This is the only account to suggest he was a primary reason for Merritt's raid into Loudoun.
28 *NYSM*, 18Dec64.
29 *Ibid*.
30 SEC diary; and *OR* 43(2): 685, 702.
31 *NYSM*, 18Dec64. Per SEC diary, the 25th returned from marching along the Blue Ridge via Upperville, Middleburg, Philomont and Unison.
32 *Ibid.*, and SEC diary.
33 *OR* 43(2): 730; and *NYSM*, 18Dec64. *NYSM*, 4Dec6.
34 Phisterer, *New York in the War*, 1097.
35 See Chamberlin and Souders, *Between Reb and Yank*, chap.33, for details on the raid's impact.

Chapter 10

1 SEC Diary; and G.O. #1, 6Dec64, 25th RLOB.
2 Birge, Wheeler and Smith CMR, case # LL 2905.
3 *NYSM*, 18Dec64 & 8Jan65.
4 *Ibid.*; and Bonnell, *Sabres in the Shenandoah*, 156-63.
5 SEC diary; Seeley invitation, 20Dec64; and SEC appointment to AAAG, 23Dec64, TCC.
6 Hannaford, "Winter Quarters near Winchester," 321; SEC diary; and *NYSM*, 8Jan65.
7 *NYSM*, 8Jan65.
8 Lt. David MSR, VSR (616-VS-1764), and CMR, case # 712. Before rejoining the 25th that fall, David served on detached duty as a recruiting officer in New York and City Point.
9 Miss Reynolds has not been identified, but was probably a relative in the Boston area. SEC only kept two other personal letters from the war—a letter from his mother and one from a female friend.
10 SEC diary; Hannaford, *op. cit.*, 329; and Taylor, *Sketchbook*, 587-90.
11 G.O. # 1, 5Jan65, 25th RLOB; and Wheeler MSR.
12 *NYSM*, 29Jan65.
13 SEC ("Captain Comdg. Regiment") to JSM, 7Feb64, SEC MSR; and JSM to SEC, 11Feb65.
14 SEC diary; and 25th RLOB.
15 *NYSM*, 5&19Feb65.
16 *Ibid.*, 12Feb65, reprinted in Styple, *Writing and Fighting the Civil War*.
17 Sheridan, *Memoirs*, 344-5. Confederates routinely used foxhunts to hone their cavalry skills.
18 *NYSM*, 26Feb65.
19 25th RLOB.

20 *NYSM*, 19Mar65, also reprinted in Styple, *op. cit.*
21 *Ibid.*; *OR* 46: 474; and SEC diary.
22 *NYSM*, 19Mar65; and *OR* 46: 484.
23 *NYSM*, 19Mar65; and SEC diary.
24 In a subsequent letter to the *Richmond Sentinel*, directors of the "Lunatic Asylum" denounced Seeley's "Northern Vandals" for taking provisions intended for the inmates, prompting BOB's rebuttal that the supplies taken by the 25th were in containers addressed to the Confederate authorities in Richmond (*NYSM*, 2Apr65).
25 *NYSM*, 19Mar65.
26 *Ibid.*; and SEC diary.
27 For Chamberlin to leave the skirmish line to rescue three damsels was in keeping with his often Quixotic nature, but he was also acting under strict orders to prevent "pillaging, and marauding," as well as drinking "intoxicating liquors" (1Mar65 orders, 25th RLOB).
28 William Gardner [aka James Sherman] to SEC, 10Aug86.
29 Union column commander John Thompson reported that the prisoners applauded his men's bravery in repulsing two attacks by Rosser's men at the ford (*OR* 46: 528). Fortunately for the Federals, Mosby's Rangers, then in Loudoun, did not arrive in time to help Rosser. BOB's account of the prisoners' reluctance to escape is accurate. Even though spies had slipped into the captives' camp to prepare them for a breakout, the "prisoners, either from indifference or despair, failed to co-operate, and though Rosser again and again attacked, all his efforts proved futile" (McDonald, *History of the Laurel Brigade*, 362-3).
30 *NYSM*, 19Mar65.
31 *NYSM*, 19Mar & 2Apr65; and SEC diary.
32 SEC diary.

Chapter 11

1 *OR* 46(3): 49; and SEC diary.
2 *NYSM*, 2Apr65.
3 Goodhart, *Loudoun Rangers*, 183; and *OR* 46(3): 95.
4 Three Seeley orders, Camp Remount, 20Mar65, 25th RLOB; and *NYSM*, 2Apr65.
5 McPherson MSR, and *NYSM*, 2Apr65.
6 *NYSM*, 2Apr65.
7 G.O. # 1, 20Mar65, 25th RLOB.
8 *NYSM*, 2Apr65; and copy of Seeley order, 21Mar65, TCC.
9 Gen. Stevenson confirmation of provost appointments, 24Mar65, TCC.
10 Nat. Park Service, "Notes on the Provost Marshal's Office"; and Moulton, *Fort Lyon to Harper's Ferry*.
11 Samuel Steer customs ledger data, Chamberlin and Peshek, *Crossing the Line*, Appendix C.
12 Louise Fisher (Boston) to SEC, 20Mar65.
13 *NYSM*, 16Apr65; and Souders and Chamberlin, *Between Reb and Yank*, 327.
14 According to Marshall Crawford (*Mosby and his Men*, 195), Mrs. Downey set up the partisans, who were captured when they returned to collect their "tithe" of bacon, several days *after* destroying her distillery. While this contradicts Briscoe Goodhart's assertion (*History of the Loudoun Rangers*, 182-2) that the still continued in operation, BOB's description of a Virginia distillery as a "small shanty" with a "five-gallon kettle and about twenty feet of copper pipe" suggests it could have easily been rebuilt.
15 *NYSM*, 16Apr65; Keen and Mewborn, *43rd Virginia Cavalry*, 255; Goodhart, *op. cit.*, 182-3; and *Waterford News*, 3Apr65. For Unionist opposition to the still, see Chamberlin and Souders, *op. cit.*, 328.
16 Stevenson's telegram, 29Mar65, TCC. Days before the border closed, Sam Means purchased a large quantity of family supplies at the Point (Steer customs ledger).
17 *NYSM*, 16Apr65; and SEC to BG Stevenson, 10Apr65, RG 393(2), entry 1169, NARA.
18 Elisha Walker journal, 2Apr65; and Mosby photograph, TCC.
19 *NYSM*, 16Apr65; and Seeley order, 9Apr65, TCC.
20 Seeley CMR, case # OO 924.
21 *NYSM*, 16Apr65; and *ibid*. On 21 April Seeley informed Harpers Ferry that the previous sutler, i.e., his brother, had disappeared and been replaced by a Berlin merchant William Bush. See Chamberlin and Peshek, *op. cit.*, 35, for Bush's involvement in scheme to remove Berlin's customs agent.
22 *NYSM*, 12Apr65.

23 *NYSM*, 16Apr65; Chamberlin and Souders, *op. cit.* 330-1; Crouch, "Rough-Riding Scout," 28-31, and Moulton, *op. cit.*, 233.
24 LR Capt. James Grubb report, 7Apr65, RG 393(3), entry 2411, NARA; *OR* 45(3): 617; Goodhart, *op. cit.*, 196; Williamson, *Mosby's Rangers*, 364; Baylor, *From Bull Run to Bull Run*, 310-16; and Chamberlin and Souders, *op. cit.*, 334-5.
25 *NYSM*, 23Apr65, reprinted in Styple, *op. cit.*, 346.
26 Stevenson's telegram to SEC (PofR), 15Apr65, TCC; and *ibid*. For the possibility that Baylor's raid on the Ranger camp was but a practice run for a special mission three days later to inset an explosive expert within Washington's defenses so John Wilkes Booth could have him explode a bomb in the War Department while Lincoln was there, see Crawford, *Mosby and His Men*, 199; and Tidwell, *Come Retribution*, and especially its sequel, *April '65*, 169-76.
27 James Walker to brother, 18Apr65, WFA.
28 Andrews (HF) to SEC, 18Apr65, TCC; and Stevenson to SEC, 24Apr65, RG 393(2), entry 1169, NARA.
29 Keene and Mewborn, *43rd Battalion*, 267-73, and Chamberlin and Souders, *op. cit.* 335-7. In *April '65*, Tidwell speculates that Mosby waited for instruction on whether to rescue Booth before disbanding.
30 SEC diary; and Steer Customs ledger.
31 *NYSM*, 14May65.
32 *Ibid*.; and printed broadside re 6Apr65 meeting, TBL.
33 SEC and Marie Matthews diaries; and Chamberlin and Peshek, *op. cit.*, Appendix C.
34 SEC diary; and 25th RLOB.
35 *Ibid*. BOB's last latter (*NYSM*, 14May65) was written on 9 May, the day before Seeley's arrest, suggesting McPherson prevented him from sending any more to the *Sunday Mercury*.
36 Seeley CMR, case # OO 924...
37 Wilson MSR.
38 James Downey to Gov. Pierpont, 12Aug64, Pierpont papers, VaSL.
39 SEC diary. Per his MSR, Seeley died of liver cirrhosis.
40 Maher CMR is filed with Seeley's, *op. cit.*
41 25th RLOB, with McPherson (Berlin) to Capt. Adams, AAAG, 19May65.
42 McConnell, *Glorious Contentment*, chap. 1.
43 S.O. #19 & 22, 28May65 and other orders, 25th RLOB; and SEC diary.
44 *NYSM*, 14May65; and printed 25th N.Y. Cav. reunion notices, 1891-3.
45 New York State, *Presentation of Flags*, not paginated.

Chapter 12
1 Ansley, "Religious Society of Friends"; and Janney, *Ye Meetg House Smal*.
2 Notes on TT's family, BCC; TT grandfather's 1723 will, DCC, and statement re TT father's estate, GP
3 Land patent records, TI#4:689-90, MdSA; and Deed Book B: 251-3, E: 814-18, F: 428-31 & G: 321-8, FCCR. Frederick separated from Prince George Co. in 1747.
4 Peden, *Quaker Records of No. Md.*, 31; Hiatt, *Early Church Records of Loudoun*, 14; Caleb Pierpont genealogy from David Nelson, current owner of Taylorstown Mill; Deed Book K:1086, FCCR; Rice, *New Facts and Old Families*, 57-59; and Tracy, *Pioneers of Old Monocacy*, 222-7. The clock (DCC) was made in 1774 by George Schmertzell of Fredericktown, Md.
5 FMM minutes quoted in Hiatt, *op. cit.*; and Will Book E: 336-7, LCCR.
6 Nichols, *Loudoun Valley Legends*, 81.
7 Marsh, "Early Loudoun Water Mills," 23; Strong, *Old Stone Houses of Loudoun*, 3; and Deed Book O: 141-4, LCCR.
8 Poland, *Frontier to Suburbia*, 15-6. Loudoun was previously part of Prince William (1730-42) and Fairfax (1742-57) Counties.
9 Janney, *op. cit.*, 13-4.
10 Hiatt, *op. cit.*, 30 *et seq.*; Barnes, *Maryland Marriages*, 1778-1800, 223; and Hinshaw, *Encyclopedia of American Quaker Genealogy*, 6: 571-2.
11 Hinshaw, *loc. cit.*; FMM "Book of Visitations," WFA; and Janney, *op. cit.*, 25.
12 Will Book E: 317-9, 336-7, G: 458-61, and H: 223-6, LCCR. TT used "plantations" in his will, a term customarily used by owners of over 400 acres.
13 Thomas Taylor was a subscriber to Oliver Evans's 1795 book, *The Young Mill-Wright and Miller's Guide*,

and Henry employed Evans's revolutionary conveyor-belt system in his new mill. The only confirmation that the author found for family lore that Henry and his father built thirteen mills along the Catoctin was a listing of "smith's tools" and "mill irons" in Henry's estate inventory (Will Book K:421-2, LCCR). The most valuable items in this inventory were two whiskey stills.

14 Scheel, *Loudoun Discovered*, 5:75-81, 93-10; and policies taken out by Henry (1803) and widow Ann (1816), Va. Mutual Assurance Society records, VaSL. The 1803 policy valued the new mill at $3500, barn $400 and house $1000. The latter already showed signs of "decay" by 1816, when it was valued at $700. Marsh, *loc. cit.*, credits TT with building the new mill in 1792, but her reference (Order Book Q: 326, LCCR) only concerns construction of a dam.

15 Janney, *op. cit.*, 60; and Henry Taylor, *From Lead Mines to Gold Fields*, chap. 1.

16 Henry Taylor, *loc. cit.* A sideboard (TCC) commissioned by Henry hints at his more lavish lifestyle.

17 *Ibid.*; 1820 census, listing six slaves at Millford; and Deed Book 3T:107, LCCR.

18 Friends, *Memorials*, 158-63.

19 In leaving home to renew her faith, Miriam was influenced by stories about her maternal great-grandmother, Ann Harbut Moore (1710-83), a Quaker missionary noted for her piety and independence. (Ann's daughter Mary married Abraham Griffith and was the mother of Ann Griffith Taylor.) An early member of Monocacy Meeting, Ann Moore moved to Baltimore with four daughters after her marriage ended in 1752. Over the next 25 years, at a time when few women dared travel alone, she journeyed throughout the Colonies and Europe doing missionary work. Her religious accomplishments and adventures, including shipwreck and capture by brigands, are described in a posthumously published diary ("Ann Moore's Journal," *Friends Miscellany* 4(1833): 249-374).

20 *Ibid.*; and Samuel A. Gover, "Jesse and Miriam Gover."

21 Family history, GP; Gover genealogy, TBL; and Jourdan, *Early Families of So. Md.*, 2:185-204.

22 Gover family papers belonging to Mary Ellen McFann, Lexington, Va.; Deed Book 2P:217-20 & Will Book N:310-1, LCCR Samuel Gover probably used proceeds from sale of slaves inherited from an aunt to finance his marriage (Mary Gover's will, probated March 1785, GP). See also MESDA files for further information on his career as a carpenter and chair maker.

23 S. A. Gover, *op. cit.*; and Hutchinson, *Apprentices, Poor Children and Bastards*, 107. Most of Jesse's siblings were dismissed from Meeting for marrying non-Quakers.

24 Wedding certificate, FMM minutes; and record of Sarah's suicide from Mary Dutton Steer's "Commonplace Book," WFA, and her father's estate records, GP. Uncomfortable in the house where his wife died, Samuel sold it to his son Anthony P. Gover, who may have rented it out as an apothecary.

25 Hutchinson, *op. cit.*, 159; and Deed Book 4B:96-7, LCCR.

26 Deed Books 2Z:507-8, 3A:9-10, 3B:407-9 & 4V:179-80 and Will Book N: 384, LCCR. The house purchased by Samuel Gover (40135 Main St.) is now called the *Hollingsworth-Lee House*.

27 Gover, *op. cit.*; Deed Boos 2Y:178-84, 2Z:139-43, 507-9, 3F:306-7 & 3T:55-6, LCCR; and *Genius of Liberty* (Leesburg), 13Dec28.

28 Martin, *Gazetteer of Virginia*, 210.

29 FMM minutes; Gover, *op. cit.*; Sarah's visitors' log, WFA; and Miriam's log, GP.

30 Crothers, *Quakers Living in the Lion's Mouth*, 143-7r.

31 *Ibid*. 170-2; Gover, *op. cit.*; and Friends, *Memorials*, 160-1.

32 FMM minutes; *Genius of Liberty*, 19Nov42; Friends, *op. cit.*, 106-9; *Friends Intelligencer*, June 1863; and Gover, *op. cit.*

33 Jesse's will and estate inventory, Will Book AA: 278, 392, and Deed Books 4F:340 4S:322, LCCR.

34 Rowberg, "Post Offices of Loudoun County," 70; Loudoun Whig ribbon. 1844 presidential campaign, TCC; Poland, *Frontier to Suburbia*, chaps. 3 and 4; and Rubin, "Between Union and Chaos."

35 Contemporary ads in Leesburg newspapers; Henry's stock ledger, WFA; Mutual Fire Insurance Co., *Century of Service*; and FMM minutes. Sam continued to operate the family saddlery (1850 census).

36 E. Y. Matthews traced his ancestry to a Quaker refugee from Oliver Cromwell's army who settled in Delaware. In the early 1700s, part of the family moved to Baltimore County, where Thomas Matthews (1725-1774) left his four eldest sons, including Mordecai (1755-1830), a tract called *Matthews Forest*. Mordecai and his wife, Ruth Hussey, raised eight children there. Their youngest (E. Y.) was born in 1805 and later educated at Westtown School in Pennsylvania.

37 Copybook, TCC; and marriage certificate, FMM minutes. Sources for EYM ancestry: Thomas Matthews's will and Matthews family Bible, WFA; Peden, *Quaker Records of No. Md.*, 32, 86; unsourced 1908 letter on

Matthews genealogy, GP; and EYM school copybook, TCC).
38 Deed Books 4T:472-4, 4V:37-8, LCCR. Joseph Wood paid $8000 for Clifton in 1816, evidence of its deterioration over the intervening years.
39 Hinshaw, *op. cit.*; and Matthews' family Bible, WFA.
40 EYM mill account, TCC; and insurance policy and early photographs, BCC.
41 1850 & 1860 ag. and pop. censuses; and receipts signed by Samuel and Noble Means, TCC.
42 Poland, *op. cit.*, 122-8.
43 Harwood, *Rails to the Blue Ridge*, 1-7; and A. L. & H. RR stock receipt, TCC.
44 For a description of *antebellum* farm life in Loudoun, see Stevenson, *Life in Black & White*.

Chapter 13

1 Court Minute Book, v. 16. LCCR; Duncan, *Loudoun County Birth Register 1853-1879*, 178; and Hutchison, *Apprentices, Poor Children and Bastards*, 159.
2 Hopewell MM minutes, Handley Lib., Winchester, Va.
3 Worrall, *Friendly Virginians*, 402-6; and FMM minutes.
4 FQM minutes, Feb60.
5 Poland, *Frontier to Suburbia*, chap. 4; and Stevenson, *Life in Black & White*, 162, 380.
6 Clinton Rice to Sec. Foster, 20Mar91, SAG TD file; and Lowe, "Republican Party in Antebellum Virginia."
7 Crofts, "Late Antebellum Virginia Reconsidered"; *Dem. Mirror*, 7&14Nov60; Poland, *op. cit.*, 176; *Loudoun Mirror*, 20Dec1923; and. Lowe, *op. cit.*, 275-9.
8 Rubin, "Between Union and Chaos"; Poland, *op. cit.*, 177-81; and Crofts, *op. cit.*, 282-6.
9 Eliza Walker (Waterford) to son Elisha, 21&26Apr61, WFA.
10 Lewis Wine, 8Jan62, PD; Anonymous, "With the Militia in North Loudoun"; and Chamberlin and Souders, *op. cit.*, 33-5.
11 *Dem. Mirror*, 8, 15 & 22May61.
12 *Ibid.*, 29May61, and Chamberlin, *Where Did They Stand?*, chaps. 1 & 2.
13 Chamberlin and Souders, *op. cit.*, 47-8.
14 HTG (Balt.) to Sec. Chase, 1Jun61 and other documents in HTG TD file. His brother-in-law, Frederick Corkran, was awarded a customs position after he narrowly escaped being lynched by anti-abolitionists.
15 Williams diary, 9Jun61.
16 Anonymous, "With the Militia in North Loudoun"; *Balt. American*, 16Jul61; Williams diary, 16Jul61; Goodhart, *Loudoun Rangers*, 19-21; *N.Y. Times*, 18Jul61&1Nov62; and Nisewaner diary.
17 *Dem. Mirror,* 8&21Aug61.
18 Amasa Hough, Jr, SCC case #21,579, RG 217, NARA.
19 Wallace, *Contributions to a History of the Richmond Howitzer Battalion*, 425-6.
20 *Ibid.* and S. A. Gover, *op. cit.*, 853.
21 Clinton Rice to Treas. Sec. Foster, 20Mar91, *op. cit.*
22 Loose document, 23Jun61, Pierpont papers, VaSL; and Divine and Souders, *To Talk Is Treason*, 28-33.
23 *Dem. Mirror*, 21Aug61.
24 *Friends' Intelligencer* (Philadelphia), 23Mar1901; and Williams diary, 18Aug61.
25 Map of 8th Va. camp, Geary Scrapbook I; Divine, *8th Virginia Infantry*, 3-4; and Williams diary, Aug-Nov61.
26 Williams diary, 11-8Aug61; Mollie Dutton to Frank Steer, quoted Divine and Souders, *op. cit.*, 35-7; and FMM, FQM and GCMM minutes, Aug-Sep61.
27 Anonymous, *Battlefields of the South*, 74, 79.
28 Hawn, *C & O Canal*, 71-2; and Grove, *History of Carrollton Manor*, 388-91.
29 Scheel, *Loudoun Discovered*, 2:60-2; Blair, *A Politician Goes to War*, 5, 12; Chamberlin and Peshek, *Crossing the Line*, 4; reports, 23Aug-17Sep61, Geary scrapbook I; and *OR*, 5:591.
30 *Washingtonian*, 24Sep58; Goodhart, *Loudoun Rangers*, 23-4; and Chamberlin, "Captain Samuel Means and the Loudoun Rangers, Part I," 25-36.
31 Goodhart, *op. cit.*, 25-7; Williams diary, 19-27Oct61; John Forsythe to *Nat. Tribune* (DC), 19Jun90; and Divine and Souders, *op. cit.*, 25.
32 Morgan, *A Little Short of Boats*, 119-23; and Loudoun Civil War Com., *Loudoun County and the Civil War*, 21-36.
33 Evans report, 31Oct61, *OR*, 5:348-52; and *Dem. Mirror*, 27Nov61.
34 Janney, *Memoirs*, 190-3; and BYM minutes, Oct61.

35 Williams diary, 10-17Nov, 3Dec61; Moore, *op. cit.*, 85-7; Hill to wife, 30Dec61, D.H. Hill papers, USAMHI; *N.Y. Times*, 3Jan61; and PD, 27Dec61, 8 &18Jan & 15Feb62.

36 Cpl. Robert Parker (Waterford) to wife, 13Dec61, and to parents, 28Dec61, copies provided by Prof. James I. Robertson, Jr., VaTech.

37 Waterford Foundation, *Waterford Perspectives*, 34.

38 FMM minutes; and Susan Walker essay, annotated by author's father, WFA. For other accounts of Miriam's eloquence, see Worrall, *Friendly Virginians*, 413-4; Janney, *Memoirs*, 193-4; and letters to *Friends' Intelligencer*, 22(1866):710-1, 57(1900):853, and 58(1901):177-8.

Chapter 14

1 Myers, *Comanches*, 18-9; Divine, *35th Battalion*, 3; Williams diary, 12Jan61; and Mary Walker to aunt, 27Jan62, WFA.

2 Myers, *op. cit.*, 10, 18-23; Eliza Walker to aunt, 27Jan62, WFA; and Worrall, *Friendly Virginians*, 414-5.

3 FMM and FMQ minutes, Feb62; Janney, *Memoirs*, 193-4; and Moore, *A Life for the Confederacy*, 102.

4 Moore, *Civil War in Song and Story*, 314; Capt. Carrick Heiskill (Winchester) to Sen. Willey, 11Feb63, Willey papers, UWVaL; OR, 5:549; SAG to Sec. of War Stanton, 18Jan64, photocopy, JDC; and Clinton Rice to Treas. Sec. Foster, 20Mar91, SAG TD file.

5 Myers, *op. cit.*, 33.

6 *Advance Guard*, 12Mar62, broadside published during Leesburg's occupation, TBL: and James Stewart, 28th Pa. Inf. (Leesburg) to family, 23Mar62, USAMHI.

7 Geary (Leesburg) to Maj. Copeland, 10Mar62, RG 393(2), entry 2098, NARA; Chamberlin and Peshek, *Crossing the Line*, 7-15; and Rowberg, "Post Offices of Loudoun County."

8 Janney, *Memoirs*, 194-5.

9 W. F. Mercer (PofR) to Gov. Pierpont (Wheeling), 3May62, Pierpont papers, VaSL; Ambler, *Francis H. Pierpont*, 165-78; and *Alex. Gazette*, 19May62.

10 FMM minutes; and Wayland, *Hopewell Friends History*, 130-131.

11 OR, 11(1):31, 12(1):636-41, 12(3):266 and 51(1):641; *N. Y. Times*, 16Jun62; and Pierpont (Wheeling) to Janney (Leesburg), 9Jun62, Janney family papers, UVaL.

12 Chamberlin, "Samuel Means..., Part I," 40-2.

13 Goodhart, *op. cit.*, 8-9, 27-8; Sam Means MSR; and roster in Stone, *Independent Loudoun Rangers*.

14 For detailed account of fight, see Chamberlin and Souders, *Between Reb and Yank*, chap. 14.

15 Eliza Walker to Elisha Hunt (Philadelphia), 4Sep62, WFP.

16 Gover vs. White, Aug66 court judgments, LCCR; Divine, *35th Battalion*, 13; and Clinton Rice to Sec. Foster, 20Mar91, SAG TD file.

17 EYM quartermaster claim, book #19, case 665, RG 92, NARA; Alpert, *History of the 45th Regiment Pa.*, 252; Capt. Richards, 45th Pa. Inf., to EYM, 1Nov62, TCC.

18 FQM minutes, Aug62; Janney, *Memoirs*, 201-3; and Thomas Russell Smith, "Account of Some Experiences during the Civil War," CW vertical files, TBL.

19 Paxson Day Book, 19Nov62; and Dutton (PofR) to Geary, 22Nov62, NAMP, M-345, roll 81.

20 Myers, *op. cit.*, 145-6; Goodhart, *Loudoun Rangers*, 79; Charlotte Nye (Alberton, Md.) to husband, 14Dec62, George H. Nye papers; and Divine, *35th Battalion.*, 19.

21 Chamberlin and Souders, *op. cit.*, chap. 15; and Crouch, *Rough Riding Scout*.

22 Waterford Foundation, *op. cit.*, 48; and FMM minutes, May63.

23 Chamberlin and Peshek, *Crossing the Line*, Part I.

24 PofR postmaster appointments, NAMP, M 841, roll 133; and *Valley Register* (Middletown), 7Nov1962.

25 FMQ minutes; Friends, *Memorials*, 162; Elizabeth Janney to Samuel Janney, 26Apr63, Janney papers, FHL; and Susan Janney (Hillsboro) to Pollock family, 22Apr63, private collection of Lewis Leigh, Jr.

26 Capt. Heiskill to Sen. Willey, *op. cit.*; Capt. Parmeter (Prov. Mar/ PofR) to Capt. Burleigh (AAG, Harpers Ferry), 13Apr64, NAMP M619, roll 316, entry W-481; and account provided by Gover descendant, WFA.

27 Chamberlin and Souders, *op. cit.*, 178-9; and flag with accompanying history provided by author's father, TCC.

28 Goodhart, *op. cit.*, 101-2; Waterford Foundation, *op. cit.*, 49-50, and Divine and Souders, *op. cit.*, 52-4.

29 Thomson, *From Philippi to Appomattox*, 169-71.

30 Myers, *op. cit.*, 210-3, 222-3; and Goodhart, *op. cit.*, 104-6.

31 J. M. Downey (Loudoun Mills) to Sen. Willey, 19Jun62, Willey papers, UWVaL.

32 Myers, *op. cit.*, 220; and J. Henshaw (Berlin) to Gov. Pierpont (Alex.), 12Sep63, Pierpont papers, VaSL.
33 Samuel Janney to Henry Janney, 7Sep63, Janney papers, FHL; Janney, *Memoirs*, 207; and Worrall, *Friendly Virginians*, 417-8.
34 Lt. John Rastall (PofR), 1st Md. E. S. Inf., to family, 27Sep53, Rastall papers, Special Coll., UMdL.
35 Copy of Unionist petition to Sec. of War, TCC; and Divine and Souders, *op. cit.*, 57-75.
36 Downey SCC case #12,461, RG 217, NARA.
37 Chamberlin and Peshek, *op. cit.*, 20-29.
38 *Journal of the House of Delegates*...; and Dutton to Pierpont, 13Oct&21Nov63, Pierpont papers, VaSL.

Chapter 15

1 Sullivan order, 11Jan64, RG 366, entry 661, NARA; Chamberlin and Peshek, *Crossing the Line*, 29-37; and *Alex. Gazette*, 6 &18Feb64.
2 Dutton (PofR) to Pierpont (Alex), 11Jan64, Pierpont papers, VaSL; W. Krantz (Berlin) to Hedenberg, 22Jan64, RG 366, entry 661, NARA; Leonard, *General Assembly of Virginia*, 498; and *Journal of the Constitutional Convention*.
3 Lowe, *Republicans and Reconstruction in Virginia*, 20-2.
4 Schooley (PofR) to Abraham Lincoln, 21Jan64, NAMP M221, roll 248, entry S-153; and Schooley to Lincoln, 19Feb64, NARG 366, entry 661; petition to Stanton, 6Feb64, "Civil War Letters" file, TBL.
5 SAG (PofR) to Stanton, 18Jan64, and MAG (Waterford) to Stanton, 19Jan64, photocopies, JDC. (NAMP M22, roll 110, entries G-32 and G-38, record their receipt and referral to Asst. Judge Advocate.) SAG named Henry Janney and J. Schofield as references in the Union League. The Govers' connection with Slough probably stemmed from his tenure as military governor of Alexandria.
6 MAG (Waterford) to Stanton, 15Mar64, with attachments and draft reply, NAMP M619, roll 316, entry W-481; and MAG to Stanton, 9May64, NAMP M221, roll 252, entry G-527.
7 Lida Dutton (Waterford) to Lincoln, 14Apr64, NAMP M221, roll 251, entry D-604.
8 Schoeberlein,"A Fair to Remember": Dutton (PofR) to Stanton, 6Apr64, NAMP, M22, roll 112, entry D-510; Schooley (PofR) to Stanton, 11Apr64, NAMP, M221, roll 255, entry S-1116; seven telegrams between PofR and HF, 18-9Apr64, RG 393(2), entry 1169, NARA; and *Balt. American*, 20&22Apr64.
9 Receipts for EM and AEM; 31Mar64 pass for EYM; and school notebook, TCC.
10 Walker (Waterford) to Pierpont, 20Mar64, and Schooley (PofR) to Pierpont, 22Mar64, Pierpont papers, VaSL; Goodhart, *op. cit.*, 119-24; Means to War Dept., 14&22Mar64, NAMP M22, roll 111, entries M-774 and M-858, and *OR* 33: 789.
11 Downey (PofR) to Pierpont, 18Apr64, Pierpont papers, VaSL.
12 Keen and Mewborn, *43rd Battalion*, 125-6; Goodhart, *op. cit.*, 126-8; Forsythe, *Guerrilla Warfare*, 8-10; *Waterford News*, 28May64; AEM testimony, Stewart MPR; morning reports, LR RLOB; and information provided by Bruce Clendenin, a Matthews descendant and current owner of Clifton.
13 *Waterford News*, 11Jun & 2Jul64; and *Phila. Daily Evening Bulletin*, 23Jun64.
14 For detailed account of the raid, see Chamberlin and Souders, *Between Reb and Yank*, chap. 30.
15 *Waterford News*, 20Aug64; and letter to *Balt. American*, 23Jul64, signed "D."
16 Divine and Souders, *To Talk Is Treason*, 84-6; *OR*, 43(1):785; and *Waterford News*, 20Aug64.
17 FQM minutes, 15Aug64; and *Waterford News*, 20Aug64.
18 BYM minutes, M548, 550 & 555, MdSA; and Janney (Phila.) to wife, 16Nov64, Janney papers, FHL.
19 Downey (PofR) to Gen. Augur (Dept. of Washington), 12Aug64, *OR* 43: 776-7.
20 *Waterford News*, 26Nov64.
21 Waterford Foundation, *op. cit.*, 81-2; Divine and Souders, *op. cit.*, 92; *Waterford News*, 28Jan65.
22 *Richmond Sentinel*, 6Dec64.
23 Chamberlin, *Where Did They Stand*, 34-48, 61-4; and Elisha Walker journal, 2-4.
24 Merritt statement, 5Dec64, TCC; and Elisha Walker journal.
25 *Sentinel, loc. cit.*; Janney, *Memoirs*, 232; Poland, *op. cit.*, 225; and Stevenson G.O. # 30, 9Dec64, TCC.
26 *Journal of the House of Delegates*, 5-8.
27 See Chamberlin, *Where Did They Stand?*, for copy of EYM claim and list of other claimants.
28 *Waterford News*, 28Jan65; and Devin order, 24Jan65, TCC.
29 Howard M. Smith papers, 168-9, LC.
30 FQM minutes, Feb65.
31 Howard Smith papers, *loc. cit.*; and Devin's *carte de visite*, TCC.

32 Gover (PofR) to wife Ellen, (Waterford), 27Feb65, copy provided by Gover descendant, WFA; Crawford, *Mosby and his Men*, 343; and Alexander, *Mosby's Men*, 155.
33 Elisha Walker's journal, 7-13Mar65; and Souders and Divine, *To Talk Is Treason*, 96-7.
34 *OR*, 46(3):279, 389; and Williamson, *Mosby's Rangers*, 360, 368, 444.
35 Elisha Walker journal, 2Apr65; and photograph found in SEC diary, TCC.
36 Divine and Souders, *op. cit.*, 96-0; *Waterford News*, 3Apr65; SEC diary; and Steer custom ledger.
37 Rebecca Williams diary, 30Apr65; Steer customs ledger; and SAG to Treas. Dept., 2&5May65, RG 366, entry 661, NARA.
38 *NYSM*, 14May65; printed broadside re 6Apr65 meeting, TBL; and SEC and Marie Matthews diaries.
39 Chamberlin and Peshek, *op. cit.*, Appendix C; and *Waterford News*, 2Jul64.

Chapter 16

1 Waterford Foundation, *Waterford Perspectives*, 82-3, as told to local historian John Divine in 1964.
2 Steer customs ledger; and SEC diary.
3 Divine and Souders, *To Talk Is Treason*, 98; and SEC diary.
4 J. Henshaw (Frederick Co., Md.) to War Dept., 22Apr65, NAMP M33, roll 120, entry H-1067.
5 *OR* 46(3):138.
6 Barbara Stahl Edwards heard the story from great-aunt Eleanor Chamberlin; and SAG to SEC, n.d.
7 Divine, *35th Battalion*, 109.
8 Burtnette MSRs and CMRs.
9 *Dem. Mirror*, 14Jun65.
10 Edward Wright CMR, case # MM 2630.
11 "Black mare" allegation, NAMP M22, roll 123, entry M-2055.
12 SEC diary; and Seeley to SEC, 7Jul65, SEC MSR.
13 Various documents, SEC MSR.
14 Broadside re 6May64 assembly, TBL; *Alex. Gazette*, 10, 13 &18May65, and *Dem. Mirror*, 14Jun65.
15 *Dem. Mirror*, 14Jun65; Poland, *Frontier to Suburbia*, 255-78; and Osburn, "Road Back."
16 Lowe, *Republicans and Reconstruction*, 29-35; Eckenrode, *Political History*, 29-31; *Alex. Gazette*, 13Jun65; and Taylor to Pierpont, 17Jun65, and Janney to Pierpont, 23Jun65, Pierpont papers, VaSL.
17 Lowe, *op. cit.*, 33-5; Eckenrode, *op. cit.*, 30; Squires, *Unleashed at Long Last*, 73; *Alex. Gazette*, 23&26Jun65; *Dem. Mirror*, 5Jul65; and *Washingtonian* (Leesburg), 7Jul65.
18 Poland, *op. cit.*, 260; and *Dem Mirror*, 19Jul65.
19 Frank Myers diary, Jun-Oct65.; and Gover vs. White, court judgments, Aug66. LCCR.
20 Myers diary, 18&22Jul, 22Oct65; and *Dem. Mirror*, 2Nov65.
21 *Dem. Mirror*, 9Aug65; and Poland, *op. cit.*, 253.
22 Wm. B. Downey (Leesburg) to Sec. Stanton, 15Aug65, NAMP M121, roll 282, D-1442; and *Dem. Mirror*, 12Jul &16Aug65.
23 *Dem. Mirror*, 9&31Aug&7Sep65; *Washingtonian*, 18Aug &1Sep65; Morefield, "The Freedman's Bureau in Loudoun County," 43-5; and Poland, *op. cit.*, 260.
24 *Dem Mirror*, 31Aug, 14&28Sep65; *Washingtonian*, 1&29Sep65; and LoCo Civil War Commission, *Loudoun County and the Civil War*, 64-6.
25 *Dem. Mirror*, 14&29Sep & 19Oct65.
26 Receipts for three horses, 21Sep65; and information author's cousin, John C. Chamberlin, learned from his father Wellman and grandfather Roy.
27 Souders, *A Rock in a Weary Land*, 44-5; and *Friends' Intelligencer*, 23Nov67.
28 Marie's diary and transcription, TCC.

Chapter 17

1 *Dem. Mirror*, 21Sep &19Oct65; and *Washingtonian*, 29Sep & 6Oct65.
2 Maddex, "Virginia: The Preference of Centrist Hegemony," 115-7.
3 SEC to "uncle" Strafford, Vt., 24Nov65, SEC MSR.
4 SEC to JSM (DC), 13Dec65, SEC MSR.
5 Jesse may have been Jesse Davis (born c. 1845) who in 1870 worked for former Loudoun Ranger Sgt. David E.B. Hough as a farm laborer. In 1860 Samuel Davis, 21, (an older brother?) worked for the Matthews family.
6 SEC (Glens Falls) to EM, 28Dec65.

7   EM to SEC (Glens Falls), 1Jan66.
8   Sadly, Maggie's wartime heroics were forgotten over time, to the point that Rachel Means was mistakenly credited with making the ride to Geary's camp to prevent Waterford's possible destruction (Divine and Souders, "*To Talk Is Treason*," 38).
9   Marie Matthews to SEC (Glens Falls), 30Dec65.
10 SEC (Glens Falls) to EM, 3-4Jan66.
11 EM to SEC (Glens Falls), n.d. and 15Jan66.
12 SEC (Glens Falls) to EM, 16Jan66.
13 EM to SEC (Glens Falls), 31Jan66.
14 EM to SEC (Glens Falls), c. 31Jan & 9Feb66.
15 *Daily Commercial* (Balto.), 14Feb66; receipt for horse and EM to SEC (Glens Falls?), n.d.
16 Probably Joseph R. Janney, a distant relative who lost a leg serving the 8th Va. Infantry and would later open a jewelry store in Purcellville (identity provided by John Souders).
17 EM to SEC (Glens Falls), 17-31Mar66; and SEC (Glens Falls) to EM, 8Apr66.
18 EM to SEC (Glens Falls), 25Mar-4Apr66.
19 SEC (Glens Falls) to EM, 8Apr66.
20 SEC (Glens Falls) to EM, 29Apr66.
21 U.S. Congress, *Report of Joint Committee on Reconstruction* (part 2): 36-9.
22 EM to SEC (Glens Falls), 10-16Apr66.
23 EM to SEC (Glens Falls), 17Mar66.
24 *Winchester Journal*, 10Aug66; Divine and Souders, *op. cit.*, 99; and *Washingtonian*, 18Sep68.
25 EM to SEC (Glens Falls), 17Mar66.
26 EM to SEC (DC), 20Oct66; *Winchester Journal*, 24Oct66; and Court judgments, Sep/Oct66, LCCR.
27 EM to SEC (DC), 24Oct66; Chamberlin and Souders, *op. cit.*, 356; and *Blue Ridge Herald*, 21Feb, 6&20Mar1924.

Chapter 18

1   Dearing, *Veterans in Politics*, is the best general work on Union soldiers' role in 19th-century politics.
2   *Ibid.*, 68-69; and Lankevich, "GAR in New York State," 40-66.
3   N.Y. Soldiers' and Sailors' Union, *Proceedings of... Convention Held in Albany*, 3-16; and undated clipping.
4   Lankevich, *op. cit.*, 42.
5   Frank J. Bramhall papers, Jun-Dec66, NYSA.
6   SEC brevet commissions; and Gov. R. E. Fenton to SEC, 8Dec66, TCC.
7   Hale (DC) to Interior Sec. Harlan, 17Jul66; and Gen. Crocker (DC) to "whom it may concern," 13Jul66, TCC. Crocker later served as head of the D.C. jail.
8   SEC (DC) to EM, 6Sep66. SEC met the Shaws while they boarded at Clifton that summer.
9   *N.Y. Tribune*, 21Sep66; and Lankevich, *op. cit.*, 47-9.
10 That fall, Butler would win a seat in Congress from Massachusetts and become one the most outspoken defenders of the Radicals' punitive policies towards the South.
11 Cashdollar, "The Pittsburgh Soldiers' and Sailors' Convention," 339-42. For additional details on Republican and Democratic efforts to woo veterans that fall, see Goldman, *One More War to Fright*, chap. 2, in which he convincingly argues that Union veterans had become the most potent group in America advocating for racial equality and other Radical reforms.
12 Lankevich, *op. cit.*, 55-8; and Dearing, *op. cit.*, 98-100.
13 SEC (DC) to EM, 7Oct66; and EM to SEC (DC), 7Oct66.
14 There is no confirmation Devin visited Clifton that fall, although Elliot took General Crocker there in November.
15 EM to SEC (DC), 12Oct66.
16 *Daily Chronicle* (DC), 13Oct66; and Beath, *History of the GAR*, 495.
17 McConnell, *Glorious Contentment*, 93-7.
18 As adjutant, Elliot would have been closely involved in the initiation of new members, and later even made Annie Matthews an honorary GAR member.
19 SEC (DC) to EM, 16Oct66, on Freedmen's Bureau stationery.
20 Morefield, "The Freedmen's Bureau in Loudoun," 68-72.
21 Commonwealth Attorney William Downey reportedly was the ULA representative in Loudoun.

22 EM to SEC (DC), 20Oct66; and Souders, *Rock in a Weary Land*, chap. 2.
23 EM to SEC (DC), 20Oct66.
24 EM to SEC (DC); 24Oct, c. 1Nov, and 6Nov66.
25 SEC (DC) to EM, 8Nov &16Dec66.
26 SEC (DC) to EM, 27Nov66; and papers re his application, TCC and SEC MSR.
27 EM to SEC (DC), 9Dec66.
28 *Ibid.; Washingtonian* (Leesburg), 14Dec66; and Steer's talk to Lit. Soc., 9Dec66, WFA.
29 Moreland, *op. cit...* 65-7.
30 SEC (DC) to EM, 11Dec66.
31 SEC (DC) to "My dear friends," 20Dec66.
32 EM to SEC (DC), 27Dec66.

Chapter 19

1 SEC (DC) to EM, 6Jan67; and Freedmen's Bureau appointment, 8Jan67, TCC.
2 Emancipation created a labor shortage throughout the South, as many former slaves and free Blacks migrated to urban centers and/or refused to do menial work for low wages.
3 EM to SEC (DC), 4, 12&16Jan67.
4 SEC (DC) to EM, 4Jan67. The previous spring, EM was shown a stereoscopic slide of Glen Falls at Nathan Walker's house, and he likely had friends in the Quaker community there.
5 AEM to SEC (DC), 6Jan67.
6 SEC (DC) to EM, 14Jan67; and cavalry appointment, TCC.
7 EM to SEC (DC), 16Jan67.
8 EM to SEC (DC), 20Jan67.
9 Cavalry examination, SEC MSR; and Gen. Howard (DC) to Gen. Butterfield (NY), 23Jan67, TCC. The test included a personal history essay that proved valuable in tracing his early life.
10 War Dept. orders, 30Jan67, TCC; and SEC (NYC) to EM, 3Feb67.
11 Elliot, who apparently did not share Edie's reservations about the Dutton girls, called on Lida and her husband while in New York City.
12 SEC (NYC) to EM, 3Feb67.
13 SEC (Saratoga Springs) to EM, 14Feb67; and EM to SEC (DC?), 14Feb67. Her letter is badly stained (by tears?) and partially illegible.
14 SEC (DC) to EM, 28Feb67; EM to SEC (NYC), 2Mar67; and amended orders, 8Mar67, TCC.
15 Frank Myers and Rebecca Williams diaries; affidavit signed by William ("Dickie") Shaw in 1909, SEC MPA; and SEC to NY Recruiting Service and response, 20&24Mar67, TCC.
16 SEC (Governor's Island, NYC) to EMC, 29Mar67.
17 EMC to SEC (San Francisco?), 4-6Apr67. EMC told her husband not to let his cabin mate have "her pillow, *feathers* would be good enough for him," and wondered if he was kept awake by SEC's snoring.
18 EMC to SEC (San Francisco?), 16Apr67.
19 HTG (Clifton) to SEC (Fort Walla Walla), 28Apr67; and Rebecca Williams diary, Apr67.
20 EMC to SEC (Fort Walla Walla), 16-8Jun67. Jim Mitchell replaced Jesse and was probably married to Laura, who appears in EMC's letters.
21 EMC to SEC (Fort Walla Walla), 26Jun67. Burton, apparently white, was the husband of the cook/housemaid (Barbara) and performed odd jobs at Clifton.
22 EMC to SEC (Fort Walla Walla), 1-4Jul67.
23 *Waterford News*, 3Apr65, and *Loudoun Telephone* (Hamilton), 24Feb88.
24 SEC (SF) to EMC, 27Apr67; Pacific Mil. Div. orders, 24-9Apr67, TCC; and SEC (SF) to EMC, 3May67.
25 SEC (Ft. Vancouver) to EMC, 14May67; and Ft. Vancouver orders, 12&6May67, TCC.
26 Receipt for commission signed Ft. Walla Walla, 2Jun67; and SEC (Fort Walla Walla) to EMC, 5Jun67.
27 QM Dept. of the Columbia, to SEC, 4Jun67; S.O. extract, 12Jun67, TCC; and documents in SEC MPA.
28 Leave orders, Jun-Jul67, TCC; and accounts provided by several family members.
29 Affidavits by SEC, EMC and SGM, 7Jun9-7Jun92 [Date needs checking—JS], SEC MPA.
30 SEC (DC) to the AAG, U.S. Army, 7Oct67, SEC MSR.
31 SGM to EMC and SEC (DC?), 7Oct67.
32 Dearing, *Veterans in Politics*, 117-23.
33 Philadelphia's Union League was founded in 1862, and its success in rallying support for the Union army and

Lincoln Administration inspired similar clubs throughout the North.
34 Testimony in SEC MPA; Dearing, *op. cit.*, 126, 131; and guest pass, 1Nov67.

Chapter 20

1 Papers in court case M622, LCCR.
2 Receipt and other documents, TCC; and Chamberlin "Captain Samuel Cornelius Means, Part 3," 1-20.
3 Original CFC by-laws drafted by SEC, TCC; minutes of subsequent CFC meetings, TBL; and Scheel, *Catoctin Farmers' Journals* vi.
4 *Records of the Columbia Historical Society* 10 (1907): 59.
5 *Washingtonian* (Leesburg), 26Feb69.
6 The main road into Waterford (Rt. 662) was impassable in bad weather due to having to climb the steep hillside on Clifton's west boundary. Despite Elliot's professed advocacy of a better road, it took a court order in the 1880s to force an agreement to allow a level roadbed passing through part of the farm. Even so, the road's overall poor condition remained a topic of CFC discussions for many years thereafter.
7 CFC minutes; and *Washingtonian*, 22Sep68.
8 CFC minutes; and Richard Taylor (Lincoln) to SEC, 25Feb71, DCC
9 Poland, *From Frontier to Suburbia*, 294, and *Dem. Mirror*, 14Feb &16Oct72.
10 Edward's approximate birth and death dates (28 May 1868 and 1 February 1869), plus the year of Mary's birth, are taken from bills presented by Dr. Thomas Bond's estate in 1873 (TCC). The family Bible erroneously lists Mary as born in 1870, but a congratulatory note from Frank Bramhall in December 1869 confirms the earlier year.
11 SEC to Capron (DC), 15Jan69, CFC papers, TBL; JSM (Strafford) to SEC, 13Oct70; and SEC to JSM (DC), 13Mar71, JSM Papers.
12 Early Ag. Dept. personnel records have not survived; SEC's position and salary from *Official Register of the U.S. Government*, published Sept. 1871. SEC arranged for EMC to collect temperature and rainfall data at Clifton for inclusion in the Department's *Monthly Report*.
13 Gaus and Wolcott, *Public Administration and US Dept. of Agriculture*, 3-7.
14 Ross, "Department of Agriculture during the Commissionership." In February 1872 Morrill invited SEC and AEM (then working at the Treas. Dept.) to dinner, adding cryptically, "I saw the President but did not obtain any decisive answer though I think he has got an impression" (JSM to SEC (DC), 1Feb72, TCC).
15 *The Capital* (DC), 24Sep71, reprinted in Appendix A.
16 *Proceedings of Nat. Ag. Convention*; and Ag. Dept. *Monthly Report* (Feb72), 59-65.
17 *Daily State Journal* (Alex.), 21Feb72.
18 Partial unsourced clipping, TCC.
19 *Nat. Republican* (DC), 6Mar72; and *Daily State Journal* (Richmond). 6Apr72.
20 Dearing, *Veterans in Politics*, 202-4.
21 *Nat'l Republican* and *Wash. Evening Star*, 25Sep72.
22 *Nat. Republican*, 31Dec72.
23 Stockberger, *Personnel Administration Development in the USDA*, 8-10; J. H. Beckwith (Parishville, NY) to JSM (DC), 13Jul72, JSM Papers and JSM (DC) to SEC, 10Mar74.
24 SEC (DC) to JSM (DC), 4Feb74, JSM Papers.
25 Introduction, NAMP M-87, roll 1.
26 For more information on the SCC, including a complete list of Loudoun claims and their outcomes, see the author's *Where Did They Stand?*
27 Canceled promissory note, TCC; SEC to JSM (Strafford), 20Jul74, JSM Papers, LC; and SEC to JSM, 4Oct75, JSM papers, VtHS.
28 SEC reports, Apr-Jun74, NAMP M87, roll 11, where most of his SCC papers can be found.
29 SEC reports, Sep-Dec74, *ibid.*; and his 24May75 report, Virginia Virts SCC case # 21,608, NARG 217.
30 This was not the only time Elliot's SCC work crossed paths with the former partisan leader. Earlier, he had successfully challenged the loyalty of a John Mosby from Albemarle County, apparently the colonel's uncle.
31 *Ibid.*; SEC's copy of rebuttal testimony, TCC; and Chamberlin, "Exeter Plantation during the Civil War."
32 SEC to SCC Commissioner, 17Oct74, Eli Pierpoint SCC case # 9497, misfiled in U.S. Court of Claims case # 703, NARG 123, includes 1873Treasury voucher for $185 made out to "S. E. Chamberlin, Esq."
33 HTG's SCC Case # 9491 (only summary available).
34 SEC to JSM (DC), 28Dec74, TCC.

35 Aldis and Ferriss to PM Gen. Jewell, 20Jan75; Lloyd to Hale, 27Jan75; Hale to Jewell, 29Jan75; and petition, SEC TD file.
36 SEC reports, May-Jul75, NAMP M87, roll 11; SEC report, 31May75, Joshua Everhart SCC case # 11,653, NARG 217; Griffith W. Paxson SCC case # 21,558, fiche 2715, NAMP M1407; and NARG 87.
37 Chief SCC Clerk Charles Benjamin to SEC, 3Dec75.
38 After Elliot left the SCC, Samuel Steer was hired as a special commissioner to take testimony involving claims in the Waterford area. ("Special commissioners" had fewer investigatory powers than special agents.)
39 *Daily State Journal* (Richmond), 1Nov72; *Washingtonian*, 8Nov73; *Virginia Press* (Hamilton), 8Nov73; Osborne, "Road Back," 72-4; and clipping and 1876 fair program, TCC.
40 *Dem. Mirror*, 12Sep71; *Daily State Journal* (Alex.), 9Jan, 6Feb &13Mar73; nursery receipt, TCC; CFC Minutes, TBL; *Washingtonian*, 8Nov73 & 28Mar74; and *Va. Press* (Hamilton), 8Nov73.
41 *Wash. Star*, early Jun74, and other clippings, TCC *Daily State Journal* (Alex.), 7Jan74; *Nat. Republican*, 5Aug74; and SEC to JSM (Strafford), 4Oct75, JSM Papers, VtHS.
42 Hatcher (Purcellville) to SEC, 4Jan76.
43 Comparison of coverages: house ($1,500 to $2,200), crops ($500, no change), household effects ($350 to $700), farm equipment ($150 to $200), and corn shed ($0 to $200). The premium cost $150 in 1870, but only $15 for expanded coverage the next year, in a policy arranged by friends in the Bramhall family.
44 U.S. agricultural censuses for Loudoun, 1840-80, TBL and VaSL; and insurance policies, TCC.

Chapter 21

1 William B. Downey (Leesburg) to Stevens (DC), 7Jan67, Thaddeus Stevens Papers, LC.
2 Lowe, *Republicans and Reconstruction*, chap. 6; and Lowe, "Virginia's Reconstruction Convention."
3 Scalawags were native Southerners who cooperated with Republicans. Many moderates, including Gov. Francis Pierpont, failed to win their districts.
4 *Winchester Journal*, 18&22Oct, 1Nov67; and Maddex, "Virginia: Persistence of a Centrist Hegemony," 120-4.
5 W. B. Downey to Stevens, 4Jul68, Thaddeus Stevens Papers, LC.
6 Lowe, *op. cit.*, 129; and *Washingtonian* (Leesburg), 21Feb68.
7 Dearing, *Veterans in Politics*, 134-47.
8 Ticket to Senate Gallery; and JSM (DC) to SEC, 1May68.
9 *Winchester Journal*, 19Jun68; and invitation to rally, TCC.
10 The "important" county office for which Elliot considered running may have been sheriff. The article's negative depiction of White, a popular war hero to many, would not have broadened Elliot's political support, if it circulated in Loudoun.
11 Clipping, *Daily Free Press* (DC?), 12Jan69.
12 H.C. Hough to SEC, 30Dec68. Former Ranger Capt. Sam Means was being similarly hounded in court.
13 Undated petition, TCC.
14 Charles H. Bramhall (Falls Church) to SEC, 15Mar69.
15 JSM (DC) to SEC, 12Apr69, and JSM (Strafford) to SEC, 20May69.
16 Lowe, *op. cit.*, 164-67.
17 Lowe, *op. cit.*, chap. 8.
18 The *Loudoun Republican* began publication after the Quakers sold it to an outside editor in April. The only complete copy the author has seen had many ads paid by Northern merchants, including one for HTG's wholesale grain business in Baltimore.
19 *Washingtonian*, 18Jun & 2Jul69; and Saffer, *Loudoun Votes*, 9-12.
20 Official Canvass Return for Loudoun Co., 8Jul69, Mss4Un312b, VaHS.
21 Transcript of article from Loudoun *Republican*, 23Jul69, provided by Asa Janney.
22 License drafted and signed by Bramhall, 2Sep69, TCC.
23 Subscription receipt; and McKenzie (Alex.) to SEC (Clifton), 12Oct70, TCC.
24 *Washingtonian*, 11Nov70, which only ran SPCA article after the election.
25 The Clarke's Gap Post Office opened in early 1869, when the station briefly served as the western terminus of the A. L. & H. rail line.
26 Appointment papers and receipts, TCC, and Postmaster Appointments files, NARG 28.
27 *Dem. Mirror*, 4, 11&18Oct &15Nov71; and Saffer, *Loudoun Votes*, 12 and appendix.
28 Alonzo Bell (Interior Dept.) to Treas. Sec. Lot Morrill, 29Aug76, SEC TD file; rail pass on A.L. & H. line,

TCC; and Curriden, *Our Soldiers and Sailors*, 53-4.
29 Ramage, *Gray Ghost*, 268-70; and Sieple, *Rebel*, 159-165.
30 Sieple, *Rebel*, 182-4.
31 *Washingtonian*, 26Jul73; *Valley Virginian* (Staunton), 7Aug73; and Hiatt, "Factionalism, Frustration and Failure," 49-57.
32 *Daily State Journal* (Alex.), 24Sep73; Sieple, *op. cit.*, 184; and Mosby (Warrenton) to Grant, 31Aug73, reprinted *Richmond Times-Dispatch*, 31Jan1904.
33 *Daily State Journal*, 6Dec73; and two clippings, n.d. & 21Dec73, TCC.
34 Moore, *Two Paths to the New South*, 69-70.
35 Pearson, *Readjuster Movement in Virginia*, 49-50.
36 SEC 1876 diary, TCC; and JMC testimony, 1Nov1909, SEC MPA.
37 Foster, *Ghosts of the Confederacy*, 5-6, and chap, 4.
38 Clipping, 21Aug69, TCC.
39 Dearing, *Veterans in Politics*, 180; *Washingtonian*, 8Jun72&10Jun76; Hiram R. Smith (Leesburg) to SEC (Norfolk), 21Apr76, BCC; and Capt. J.W. Foster (Leesburg) to EMC, 5Jun76, TCC.

Chapter 22

1 Treas. Sec. Boutwell to JSM (Strafford), 1Jun69, and AEM (DC) to "my dear uncle [SAG]," 16Mar70, TCC; and various documents, Dec69 - Mar70, AEM OPMA file.
2 Aron, *Ladies and Gentlemen of the Civil Service*, 5, 60.
3 *Ibid.*, 97-9, and Socolofsky and Spetter, *Presidency of Benjamin Harrison*, 43.
4 Mosby played no apparent part in Annie's 1872 job loss, or Elliot's dismissal from the Agriculture Department a short time later, but the Rebel colonel's influence in Grant's administration certainly contributed to difficulties both encountered trying to regain Federal employment. While Annie alone might not have drawn Mosby's attention, her brother-in-law's high profile in Virginia politics certainly did.
5 JSM (Strafford) to IRS Commissioner J. W. Douglas, 13Jul72, TCC; and IRS Assessor A. M. Crane (Staunton) to IRS Supervisor C. F. Presbrey, 15Jul72, AEM OPMA file. Other defenders included Sen. John Lewis (Va.), IRS Assessor Frank Bramhall (Harrisonburg), and two Mass. Congressmen.
6 On at least four occasions, Annie filled out Treasury forms asking what she had done "for the Union Army or Union cause during the rebellion." A typical response: "Did with my family all that a woman might..., by giving aid, comfort and encouragement to those who were fighting for it."
7 AEM to Treas. Sec. Richardson, 2Nov73, AEM to Treas. Sec. Bristow, 8May75, JSM (Strafford) to Bristow, 21Jun75, and Cox, DC Board of Health, to Asst. Sec. Conant, 25Jun75, AEM OPMA file.
8 Endorsements for P.O. job, appointment, commission and personal history statement, SEC TD file.
9 White, *Republican Era*, chap. 6, "The Treasury Department."
10 The *collector of customs*, responsible for receiving all tariff payments, occupied the top position in a customhouse, followed by the *surveyor*, who oversaw inspection and assessment of all imports, and the *naval officer*, who independently duplicated the surveyor's efforts. They were assisted by inspectors, weighers, assessors and other specialists.
11 Cohen, *Contraband*, 133-5.
12 Congress specified the following limits on agent pay: 2@$10/day; 17@$8/day; 16@$6/day; and 18@$5/day, plus necessary expenses.
13 Anonymous, "Special Agents: A History"; Corwin, "History of Special Agents' Division"; U.S. Customs Service, *History of Enforcement*, chap. 5; and *Balt. Evening News*, 11May83, TCC.
14 See McFeely, *Grant*, 405-18, for an account of the "Whiskey Ring" scandal.
15 SEC diary; AEM (DC) to SEC (Norfolk), 9Jan76; and EMC to SEC, 9Jan76.
16 SEC diary; and Lowe, "Virginia's Reconstruction Convention," 347.
17 EMC to SEC (Richmond, forwarded to Norfolk), 2Jan76.
18 EMC to SEC (Norfolk), 4-9Jan76.
19 EMC to SEC (Norfolk), 30Jan76, BCC; and SEC diary.
20 EMC to SEC (Norfolk and DC), 10, 16&23Feb76, BCC.
21 SEC (Norfolk) to Ayer (Richmond), 6Mar76, SEC's CS/SAD file.
22 The Treasury's Revenue Marine Service, the forerunner of the U.S. Coast Guard, maintained a fleet of lightly armed vessels (cutters) to patrol the nation's shores and enforce Customs regulations.
23 Lee (Norfolk) to Capt. R. Woodfin (Hampton), 10Mar76, BCC; SEC (Norfolk) to Ayer (Richmond),

23 13Mar76, SEC's CS/SAD file; and SEC diary.
24 EMC to SEC (Norfolk), 29Mar76.
25 SEC diary; and reports, 28Aug&8Sep76, Ayer CS/SAD file.
26 SEC's diary; *Valley Virginian* (Staunton), 20Jan76; and unsourced clipping, TCC.
27 Dearing, *Veterans in Politics*, 221-3; and Ridpath, *Life of Garfield*, 273-89.
28 Dearing, *op. cit.*, 223; SEC diary; other Vets' Com. docs., TCC; and *Nat. Republican* (DC), 24Feb76. Membership in the GAR declined after 1870, a trend the 1876 election helped reverse.
29 SEC diary, OSS constitution, TCC; *Natl Republican*, 6May74 & 77Jul76; and *N.Y. Herald*, 6Jul76.
30 SEC diary; and EMC to SEC (Norfolk), 6Mar76, BCC.' and McFeeley, *op. cit.*, 427-36.
31 OAU membership card, TCC; and clipping, James D. Brady scrapbook, UVaL.
32 *Mirror* (Leesburg), 20Apr76; *National Republican* (DC), 14Apr76; *Valley Virginian* (Staunton), 20Apr76; and Pearson, *Readjuster Movement in Virginia*, 50, 137.
33 William Selwyn Ball, "Reminiscences of an Old Rebel," 86-9, Mss5: B2106, VaHS.
34 EMC to SEC (Norfolk), 27Apr&7May76, last in BCC.
35 AEM (DC) to EMC, 30Apr76, BCC.
36 Crew (DC) to SEC (Norfolk), 4May76, BCC.
37 SEC diary; and reports in SEC CS/SAD file.
38 Dearing, *op. cit.*, 225, and various letters from Dudley, James Garfield papers, LC.
39 Shortly before he died, Grant summoned Bristow to apologize for his mistrust and ill treatment of his Treasury Secretary (Chernow, *Grant*, 951).
40 SEC diary.
41 *Washingtonian* (Leesburg), 5Aug76.
42 Alonzo Bell (DC) to Sec, Lott Morrill, 29Aug76, SEC TD file.
43 Various documents, including C. C. Adams (Solicitor's Office) to SEC, 5Sep76, *ibid*.
44 Elliot purposefully blurred responsibility for burning Clifton's barn, which his children also blamed on Mosby's partisans.
45 Adams to "Mr. New," 6Dec75, Alonzo Bell (DC) to J. Porter Treas. Dept., 31Aug76, and JSM to "Treasurer," 5Sep76, AEM OPMA file; AEM (DC) to EMC, 30Apr76, BCC; and JMC "Recollections."
46 *Valley Virginian* (Staunton), 20Jul76.
47 Clipping, *Nat. Republican*, c. 14Jul76, TCC.
48 Siepel, *op. cit.*, 189, quotes *N. Y. Herald*, 22Jun76, on Mosby's meeting with Grant; and clipping from *Nat. Republican*, datelined 12Jul76, TCC.
49 JMC deposition, 1909, SEC MPA; membership cards and label for rally in NYC.
50 Ramage, *Gray Ghost*, 281-3.
51 Clipping datelined 6Aug76, Warrenton, Va., John S. Mosby scrapbooks, UVaL.
52 Richard C. McCormick (NYC) to SEC (Petersburg), 14Sep76; and Siepel, *op. cit.*, 193.
53 Dearing, *op. cit.*, 226; Garfield, *op. cit.*, 3: 343, 354; copy of Garfield's orders, TCC; Drake DeKay, Sec. Vets. Com, (NY) to SEC (DC), 28Sep76, SEC TD/AR file; SEC appointment as "Major General" signed by DeKay, Garfield and Dix, TCC.
54 Letter to Sec. Vet. Com [DeKay], 26Oct76, clipping from [city unknown] *Evening Mail*, TCC.
55 Saffer, *Loudoun Votes*, 19 and appendix; and Mirror (Leesburg), 9&15Nov76.

Chapter 23
1 Siepel, *Rebel*, 193-6; and *Alex. Gazette*, 11&26Dec76.
2 *Alex. Gazette*, 11Dec76; and Woodward, *Reunion and Reaction*.
3 Keen and Mewborn, *43rd Battalion*, 351.
4 Moore to Grant, 18Jan77, William Mosby TD file (includes Grant's note cited later in chapter).
5 SEC diary; clipping re meeting with Grant, attached to JSM to TD Sec. Sherman, 19Mar77 and letters from JSM, Bell and O'Neal to Raum, 2-3Feb77, SEC TD file; and IRS appointment, TCC.
6 CS appointment, 15Feb77, and IRS resignation, 19Feb77, TCC; and commission, 20Feb77, SEC TD file.
7 Adams to Treas. Sec. Sherman, 13Mar77, Adams TD file.
8 Conant evidently showed Grant's note to SEC, who made a "correct copy" on the Secretary's stationery, TCC (original in William Mosby TD file).
9 Letter to *N.Y. Tribune*, "Hayes Scrapbook," 13:137-8, RBHPL.
10 Tickets to House of Representatives, TCC; POMG Key to Treas. Sec. Sherman, Jul77, Moore TD file; and

Nat. Republican, 23Mar77.
11 Gillette, *Retreat from Reconstruction*, 348-9.
12 SEC notes for article and his copy of *Republic* article identifying Bell as author, TCC.
13 JSM (DC) to Sherman, 19Mar77, SEC TD file, with clipping re his meeting with Grant.
14 SEC (DC) to Sherman, 30Mar77, *ibid*.
15 Sieple, *Rebel*, 198-9; and *Mirror* (Leesburg), 15Mar77.
16 *Alex. Gazette*, 17Mar & 21May77. Mosby omitted that Brady fought for the Union.
17 Clipping, n.d., TCC; and Dutton (Waterford) to Hayes, 7Apr77, RBHPL. Dutton was probably part of a Quaker group that visited Hayes in early April (*Mirror* (Leesburg), 5Apr77).
18 It is unclear whether anyone at the Treasury was aware that Maddox had been a Confederate spy. During the war, he had President Lincoln's authority to cross into Virginia from his home in southern Maryland to purchase tobacco and gather information on the South, when in fact he was a double agent working for the Confederate Intelligence Service (Tidwell, *Come Retribution*, 87).
19 Moore to Grant, 22Mar77, Moore TD file; and *Richmond Dispatch*, 2Feb77.
20 EMC to SEC (DC), 29Mar77.
21 William Mosby TD file; and SEC (DC) to Tingle, 7May77, SEC CS/SAD file.
22 JSM (DC) to SEC (Clifton), 10May77.
23 SEC (Clifton) to JSM (Strafford), 5Jul77, JSM papers, LC; and appointment and commission, TCC.
24 EMC to SEC (Balt), 14Jul77.
25 Ramage, *Gray Ghost*, 283. Although not named in his book, Ramage confirmed to the author that it was Braxton (J. S. Mosby to Sam Chapman, 12Jan1907, Thomas N. Page papers, Duke Univ. Lib.).
26 EMC to SEC (Norfolk), 25Jul77, BCC; and Hoogenboom, *Presidency of Hayes*, 79-92.
27 *Nat. Republican*, 6Aug77.
28 *Boston Herald*, 7Aug77, only clipping SEC kept on this incident.
29 *Nat. Republican*, 7-27Aug77; and McFeeley, *Grant*, chap. 21.
30 Ayer (Richmond) to SEC (Balt?); 22Aug77; and Ayer's report, 26Sep77, SEC CS/SAD file.
31 Ayer report, 13Oct77, Ayer CS/SAD file.
32 Drake DeKay (NYC) to SEC, 17Aug77.
33 SEC (Balt) to Sec. Sherman, 18Sep77, with lawyer's letter, SEC CS/SAD file.
34 Draft letter, SEC (Balt) to JSM, 14Nov77.
35 Sieple, *Rebel*, 201-2; Williams, *Hayes*, 164-6; and SEC 1878 diary.

Chapter 24
1 Summary of his sugar investigations, 25Jul88, SEC CS/SAD file.
2 EMC to SEC (Balt?), 25Sep77; *Nat. Republican*, 30Aug77; and SEC diaries, TCC.
3 SEC (Balt) to Sec. Sherman, 29Sep77, SEC SC/SAD file.
4 SEC (Balt) to Sec. Sherman, 27&30Nov77; and SEC cable to Treas. Dept., 27Nov77, *ibid*.
5 Deposition accompanying SEC (Balt) to Sec. Sherman, 10Dec77, *ibid*.
6 SEC (Balt) to Sec. Sherman and Tingle, 28Jan78, SEC SC/SAD file; and SEC 1878 diary.
7 JMC "Recollections," c. 1930, DCC; and reminiscences of Mary Chamberlin Clendenin, c. 1950, BCC.
8 Grace, *Grace's Exposure!*, 18-21, 63; and Cohen, *Contraband*, 249-50.
9 Hoogenboom, *Presidency of Hayes*, chap. 6, "Civil Service Reform."
10 SEC diary; and invitation to 6Apr78 launch.
11 AEM TD & OPMA files; and EMC (Clark's Gap) to SEC (c/o Alex. customhouse), 1Aug78, BCC.
12 *N. Y. Sun*, 18Aug78, reprinted in Charles Rabello, *Pith of the Sugar Question* (1879 pamphlet).
13 SEC (NYC) to Sec. Sherman, 5&6Sep78, SEC CS/SAD file.
14 SEC (Balt) to Sec. Sherman, 27Sep78, *ibid*.
15 SEC (Balt) to Tingle, 19Nov78, *ibid*.; SEC diary; and various articles, *Baltimore American*.
16 *N.Y. Times*, 24May78:
17 To Elliot's chagrin, former Boston special agent Henry Brown published a pamphlet in 1879 that forcefully argued against use of the polariscope, which, while accurate in a lab setting, was, he claimed, impractical for evaluating large shipments at dockside, and would make evaluators more susceptible to bribery (Brown, *Sugar Frauds and the Tariff*, 15-20).
18 Ricketts (NYC) to SEC, n.d.; Ayer to Sherman, 30Nov78; and SEC (NYC) to Sherman, 11Dec78, SEC CS/SAD file.

19 *N.Y. Times*, 17-9Sep78.
20 *N.Y. Times*, 9Jan79.
21 *N.Y. Times*, 9Jan79; and Grace, *Grace's Exposure!*, 44-6.
22 *N.Y. Sun*, 22Dec78, in Rabello, *op. cit.*; and SEC (DC) to C/SA J. Jewell, 25Jul88, SEC CS/SAD file.
23 SEC (Balt) to Sec. Sherman, 7Feb79, *ibid*.
24 SEC flimsy file of outgoing correspondence; and Adams (DC) to SEC (NYC?), 17Mar79, TCC.
25 EMC (Balt) to SEC (Astor House, NYC), n.d. & 19Mar79, BCC.
26 Elliot's passport described him as 5'11" with high forehead, hazel eyes, mustache, broad chin, dark brown hair, medium complexion, and oval face.
27 SEC (Havana) to EMC (Balt), 16Apr79; and passport, TCC.
28 French's short report is included at the end, and basically agrees with Elliot's findings. During much of his stay in Cardenas, French was accompanied only by Abbot, who was employed primarily to test sugar with a polariscope.
29 SEC (Cuba) to EMC (Balt), 27-29Apr79; SEC (Havana) to EMC, 3May79; and SEC's published report.
30 EMC (Balt) to SEC (c/o U.S. Hotel, Saratoga Springs), 18Jun79, BCC. The enormous U.S. Hotel, was partially owned by Hiram Tompkins, husband of SEC's cousin, Laurentine Chamberlin.
31 SEC (Glens Falls) to EMC (Balt), 30Jun79, BCC.
32 JSM (Strafford) to SEC (Balt), 21Sep79.
33 Various papers, Abbott CS/SAD file; and clipping, 20Jan80, TCC.
34 Sec. of State William M. Evarts to American consular officers, 22Jan80; SEC (St. Thomas) to EMC. (Balt), 14Feb80; and Col. Ira Ayer (NYC) to Sarah Matthews (Balt), 17Mar80, TCC.
35 SEC (Dominica, B.W.I.) to EMC (Balt), 27Feb80.
36 Memorandum, n.d., TCC.
37 *Ibid*.
38 Chamberlin, Abbott and Endlich, *Report....*; and *Baltimore Sun* clipping, 8Jul80, TCC.
39 SEC (Savannah) to EMC (Balto.), 26Dec80, TCC.
40 *New Orleans Democrat*, 9Jan81; *N.Y. Herald*, 12Feb81; clipping, n.d.; and *Commercial Advertiser* (NYC), 15Feb81.
41 *Journal of Commerce* (NYC), 20Apr81, TCC; SEC (NYC) to Tingle, 19Apr81; and SEC (DC) to Treas. Sec. Jewell, 25Jul88, SEC CS/SAD file.
42 Much of Carter's and McCabe's support came from former Republican stronghold in northern Loudoun, especially Lovettsville and Lucketts, as well as Black and working-class voters in Leesburg; Waterford Quakers remained markedly cool towards the Readjuster movement (Saffer, *Loudoun Votes*, appendix figures).
43 See Blake, *William Mahone*, chap. VII, for background on Readjuster Party.
44 Newspaper clipping, c. 30Oct70, TCC.
45 *Mirror* (Leesburg), 7Nov79; Poland, *Frontier to Suburbia*, 277; and Saffer, *Loudoun Votes*, 24-8.
46 John Perry Everhart letter, 12 Feb89, everhartgenealogy.com/Letters.
47 Tyler letter quoted in Blake, *op. cit.*, 156, 197-8.
48 *Richmond Chronicle* clipping, c. Nov79, TCC.
49 *Nat. Republican* (DC), 30Jan80; *Valley Virginian* (Staunton), 5Feb&29Apr80; and Pearson, *Readjuster Movement*, 136-7.
50 Blake, *op. cit.*, 189, 194-5.

Chapter 25
1 Sources for chapter include letters and papers, TCC and DCC; and legal documents in M622, LCCR.
2 Janney, *Memoires*, 251-8.
3 R. G. Dun & Co. papers, Harvard Univ. Library (courtesy of Dr. Fred Johnson).
4 SEC to Charles L. Wood (Winchester), 24Aug74, DCC.
5 Powell Harrison (Leesburg) to SEC, 1Apr75 & 6Jul77; and papers, case M622, LCCR.
6 Auction poster and prices realized, TCC.
7 SAG (Waterford) to SGM (Balt), 14Jan78 & 26Apr78, TCC.
8 Marshall McCormick (Winchester) to HTG (Balt), 12&22Mar78, M622, LCCR.
9 Henry Heaton (Leesburg) to HTG (Balt), 7&27Jun78; and SEC diary.
10 Heaton (Leesburg) to HTG (Balt), 11Jan79; SAG to HTG, 5Apr79; and other papers in M622, LCCR.
11 HTG (Balt) to Ed Nichols (Leesburg), 21&28Apr79, DCC.

12 Ed Nichols (Leesburg) to HTG (Balt), 26May79, DCC; and papers in M622, LCCR.
13 Diary extracts in SEC's handwriting on his official stationery, TCC. SEC may have accessed the diary when SAG stayed with HTG during Yearly Meeting in Baltimore.
14 Papers in M622, LCCR, including Nichols (Leesburg) to HTG (Balt), 20May81.
15 EMC (Balt) to SEC (NYC), 10Apr81.
16 SAG (Waterford) to HTG (Balt), 27May81, TCC; and *Loudoun Telephone,* 13May & 4Nov81.
17 SAG (Waterford) to SEC (Balt), 7Nov81, TCC.
18 Henry Heaton (Leesburg) to SEC (Balt), 11&30Nov81; and SAG (Waterford) to HTG (Balt), 21Dec81.
19 Ed Nichols (Leesburg) to SEC, 16&22Dec81 & 8Feb82; and SEC to Nichols, 10Feb82.
20 SAG (Waterford) to SGM, 14Feb82; and Nichols (Leesburg) to SEC, 7Mar82.
21 HTG (Balt) to SAG, 9, 17&19Mar82, cited in Gover vs. Chamberlin, Va. Appeals Court case DM 72 Q; other details in Worsley vs. Matthews estate, case M622, LCCR, and mortgage papers, TCC.
22 Nichols (Leesburg) to SEC, 29Mar, 3Apr & 28May83; and SEC to Nichols, 2Apr & 28May83.
23 SAG (Waterford) to SGM (Balt), 10Oct83.
24 In a calmer vein, Sam advised his sister of his unsuccessful attempt to sell her house in Waterford and recommendation she continue to rent it for $350 annually.
25 SAG (Waterford) to SGM (Balt), 21Jan84.
26 Printed arguments for Va. Appeals Court case DM 72), DCC; and HTG (Phila) to SEC, 27Jan85.
27 See Divine and Souders, *When Waterford & I Were Young,* 45, for anecdote by SAG's assistant, Tom McGavack, suggesting his boss was too lazy to wait on customers, but more likely reflecting bitterness towards those who refused to pay their store bills.
28 A draft speech that Sam intended to deliver before Congress argued North Loudoun had never been part of the Confederacy, and therefore the Union soldiers had destroyed property of U. S. citizens, not belligerents.
29 Gover family papers, VaHS Mss 21A.
30 Papers in SAG TD file; SAG (DC) to SGM (DC), 7Dec97; and letter from Amos Gover (Richmond) to Henry T. Gover (DC), 5Apr1955, courtesy of Gover descendent Mary Ellen Pierdon McFann.
31 Contract w/ Mullen, 20Mar84, TCC. Mullen was the grandfather of local historian John Divine.
32 SEC (Wilmington) to Moreland, 3Mar91; SEC Beans & Smith account, TCC; and info from John Souders.

Chapter 26
1 Doenecke, *Garfield & Arthur,* 21.
2 Veterans' Union circular, 27Sep80, RBHPL; Boys in Blue commission; undated clipping, and inaugural invitation, TCC; and Dearing, *Veterans in Politics,* 251-67.
3 Garfield, quoted in Doenecke, *op. cit.,* 43.
4 1882 political pamphlet, quoted in Blake, *William Mahone,* 221.
5 Various articles, *Telephone* (Hamilton); Rowberg, "Post Offices of Loudoun"; and Bake, *op. cit.,* 219-54.
6 Mahone (DC) to Hoge (Lincoln), 28Mar82, with Hoge's response, Mahone collection, Duke Univ. Lib.
7 SEC to TD Sec. Windom, 1Jul81, SEC CS/SAD file: J. Stanley Brown [formerly Garfield's personal secretary] to TD Sec. Folger, 13Jan82; and Balt. Customs Collector Thomas to SEC, 15Feb82, SEC TD file.
8 Chamberlin, *Allowances...*; SEC (Balt) to Sec. Folger, 24May82, SEC CS/SAD file; and clippings, *Congressional Record,* 25Mar & 24Jul82, SEC TD file.
9 SEC to Martin (DC), 26Feb &14May83, SEC CS/SAD file.
10 Bingham (Boston) to SEC, 12&21Mar83, TCC; and *Wash. Post,* 9Mar83.
11 JSM (DC) to SEC, 16&20Mar83.
12 Various reports, Apr-May84, SEC CS/SAD file.
13 Welch, *Cleveland,* 29-31.
14 JSM (DC) to SEC, 19&21Jun84.
15 *Telephone* (Hamilton), 7Nov84; and Blake, *op. cit.* 229-30.
16 Crawford Adams (Philadelphia) to SEC, 13Nov84, TCC.
17 SEC diary; and Sec. of War George W. McCrary to SEC (Balt), 17Nov79, TCC.
18 Ayer (NYC) to "very dear, kind friend" (SGM from context), 17Mar80.
19 The family Bible incorrectly lists Mary as born in 1870 *vice* 1869. Her parents' insistence on making themselves younger and placing their marriage after Elliot's return from the West, plus Mary's awareness she had had a deceased older brother apparently led them to shave a year off her age.
20 1880 census.

21 Programs for Baltimore celebration; and EMC to SEC (NYC), 1Jan81.
22 EMC (Balt) to SEC (NYC), 6-14Apr81 (six letters), TCC.
23 *Ibid.*; and inaugural invitations, TCC.
24 JMC's "Recollections," DCC.
25 AEM (DC) to EMC (Balt), 11&20Apr82, DCC.
26 AEM (DC) to SGM (Balt), 15Jun82, DCC; and SEC (Balt) to SGM (Waterford), 24Jul82, TCC.
27 AEM (DC) to SGM (Balt), 26Jan & 8Feb83, DCC.
28 HTG (Phila.) to SEC (Balt), 26Nov83; invitation and GAR menu, TCC; and *Telephone,* 21Sep83.
29 EMC (Clifton) to SEC (Balt?), 25Jun & 9Jul84.
30 EMC (Clifton) to SEC (Balt), 5, 10&14Sep84.

Chapter 27

1 H. F. French (DC) to JSM (DC), 13Mar85, SEC TD file; and JSM (DC) to SEC (Balt), 16Mar85.
2 Treas. Sec. Daniel Manning to SEC (Balt), 1&4May85; and L. G. Martin (DC) to SEC, 5&16May85.
3 *Baltimore Sun*, 2May85; *Telephone* (Hamilton), 8May85); *Daily News,* 7May85; and *N.Y. Daily Tribune,* 9May85, among 12 clipping kept by SEC, TCC.
4 *Annual Report of Secretary of the Treasury*, 1885, pp. xxxvii-xxxx, 274-290.
5 *Ibid.*, 1886, pp. xxxv-xxxvii.
6 Annual reports for Baltimore office, SEC CS/SAD file.
7 *Boyd's Directory of the District of Columbia*, 1886 and later editions.
8 JMC "Recollections," DCC.
9 Adams's orders and guest pass, TCC; leave request, SEC TD file; *Telephone,* 14May86; and JSM (DC) to Customs Collector Gromis (Balt), 18Mar86, TCC.
10 SEC (Charleston, SC) to EMC, 23Jan87; and orders signed by Treas. Sec. Manning, 17Jan87, with covering letter from L. G. Martin (DC) to SEC (Charleston, SC), 18Jan87, TCC.
11 Collector Levy (Georgetown, SC), 4Jan88, to SEC (DC), TCC; DC directories; and receipts relating to loan that AEM made to EMC.
12 Conclusion of JMC "Recollections," DCC.
13 The son of Robert E. Lee and a CSA major general, Lee returned to White House Landing after the war and rebuilt his home, which had been destroyed by Union troops.
14 Lee (DC) to Asst. Sec. Thompson, 24Mar88, SEC's TD file; and Dearing, *Veterans in Politics*, 312.
15 Welch, *Cleveland*, 93-8.
16 Confusion within Virginia's GOP was such that portions of both "Straight-out" and Mahone factions were seated at the 1888 Republican Convention.
17 Blake, *Mahone*, 242; and Loudoun vote totals, *Telephone,* 15Nov88.
18 William L. Royall, quoted in Pulley, *Old Virginia Restored*, 46-7.
19 JSM (DC) to Treas. Sec. Windom, 9Mar89, SEC TD file.
20 SEC (DC) to Sec. Windom, 12Mar89, *ibid.*
21 Asst. Treas. Sec. (name illegible) to SEC (Alex), 30Mar89; and Sec. Windom to SEC, 23Sep89, TCC.
22 Proprietor John Andrew (Tampa) to Rep. William Call [Dem-Fla.], 18Dec89, with notation of reprimand on back, SEC TD file; and Phila. Special Agent to SEC (Savannah?), 18Dec89, TCC.
23 JMC (DC) to SEC (Savannah), 20Nov90.
24 JSM to SEC, 10Oct90; Asst. Sec. Spaulding to SEC, 16Feb91; and *Savannah News*, 4May91, TCC.
25 Rent receipts and *Boyd's DC Directory.*
26 Memo re World's Fair, 28Aug91; order transferring SEC to Newport News, 14Jun92; SEC (DC) to Martin (Balt), 16Jun92; and IRS Commissioner to Tingle, 8Jul92, TCC.
27 GOP Convention pass for 5th day only, TCC.
28 Dearing, *Veterans in Politics*, 248, 258-75, 445-7.
29 Various GAR documents, including Post 1 QM Richardson (DC) to SEC (Balt.), 15Mar78. TCC; and *Wash. Post,* 14Jun89.
30 Dearing, *op. cit.*, 310-14; *Nat. Tribune,* 14May85; and Society of the Army of the Potomac, *Report of the 16th Annual Reunion...*, 48, 60, 103.
31 Various MOLLUS documents, TCC; and Dearing, *op. cit.*, 447.
32 Dearing, *Veterans in Politics*, 392-401; and Socolofsky and Spetter, *Harrison,* 34-37.
33 SEC MPR; JSM (DC) to SEC (Norfolk), 3May76; W.W. Dudley (DC) to SEC (Balt), 2Aug82, TCC.

34 Certified copy of Samuel Chamberlin's discharge papers, signed by Tres. Sec. Windom, 26Mar89, TCC; and Raum (DC) to SEC (Savannah), 28Jan91, DCC.
35 EMC (DC) to SEC (Wilmington, NC), 7Apr91, TCC.
36 Various documents, SEC MPA.
37 *Loudoun Telephone* (Hamilton), 5Sep90.
38 *Wash. Evening Star*, 7Jul91.
39 Two-sided printed summary of 25th NY Cav. Assn. meeting, TCC.
40 *Wash. Post*, 11Jul91; and *Columbus Journal* (Neb.), 22Jul91.
41 *Wash. Post*, 14Jul01.
42 Nevius (Red Bank, NJ) to SEC (DC), 14Jul91.
43 Coutant (Tarrytown, NY) to SEC (DC), 9Aug91, TCC; and Lane letter, *Wash. Evening Star*, 23Jan92.
44 *Wash. Evening Star*, 24Sep92; and *National Tribune*, 29Sep92.
45 *Proceedings of Third Annual Reunion of the 25th N. Y. Vet. Cavalry Assn.*, copy in NYSA.

Chapter 28

1 SEC (Newport News=NN) to EMC (DC), 20Nov92.
2 EMC (DC) to SEC (NN), 26Jan93.
3 (EMC (DC) to SEC (Wilmington), 7Apr91; and Tichenor, on official Asst. Treas. Sec. stationery, to EMC (1211 13th St., DC), 3Jul90.
4 Clipping in SEC (NN) to EMC (DC), 30Nov92.
5 SEC (NN) to EMC (DC), 29Nov, 8Dec92&15Jan93.
6 Mary Chamberlin (Cape Cod) to EMC (DC), 3Oct93, BCC. Katherine (Cousin Kitty) was the daughter of Frederick Jewell, a Chamberlin relative who owned a newspaper on the Cape.
7 EMC (DC) to SEC (NN), 17Dec92; and SEC (NN) to EMC (DC), 21Dec92.
8 EMC (DC) to SEC (NN), 22Jan93; and SEC (NN) to EMC (DC), 24Jan93.
9 SEC (NN) to EMC (DC), 29&31Jan93.
10 EMC (DC) to SEC (NN), 10, 13, 14&17Mar93, and SEC (NN) to EMC (DC), 12&14Mar93.
11 SEC (NN) to EMC (DC), 19Mar93.
12 EMC (DC) to SEC (NN), 27Mar91.
13 EMC (DC) to SEC (NN), 26Jan93, with enclosures from Arch and Henry.
14 SEC (NN) to EMC (DC), 29Jan93; and EMC (DC) to SEC (NN), 30Jan93.
15 EMC (DC) to SEC (NN), 13Mar, 9-17Apr & 2May93.
16 EMC (Clifton) to SEC (NN), 6, 11, 13&16Jul93.
17 EMC (DC) to SEC (NN), 21Jan93.
18 EMC (DC) to SEC (NN), 5&14Apr93. Mary worked part-time in Hume's law firm.
19 EMC (DC) to SEC (NN), 26Feb93.
20 Quotes from EMC (DC) to SEC (NN), 21&27Jan93.
21 EMC (DC) to SEC (NN), 3May93.
22 EMC (DC) to SEC (NN), 19Mar93.
23 EMC (DC) to SEC (NN), 27Jan, 22&25Mar & 7May93.
24 EMC (DC) to SEC (NN), 5&14Apr93.
25 EMC (DC) to SEC (NN), 15Apr (with enclosure from Paul) &2May93.
26 EMC (DC) to SEC (NN), 15, 16, 17, 20, 26 &27Mar93.
27 Documents in SEC CS/SAD file.
28 EMC (DC) to SEC (NN), 15Apr93.
29 EMC (DC) to SEC (NN), 16Apr, 6&7May93; clippings, *N.Y. Sun*, 11May93, and *Wash. Evening Star*, 6May93; *N.Y. Times*, 11May93; and Tingle TD file.
30 Asst. Sec. Spaulding (DC) to SEC (NN), 27Mar93; EMC (DC) to SEC (NN), 4May93; SGM (DC) to EMC (NN), 13May93; and reports, 12Apr&6May93, SEC CS/SAD file.
31 Tingle to SEC (NN), 22Jul93; and Martin (Balt) to SEC (DC), 1Aug93.
32 Chemist's analysis. As a boy, the author tried unsuccessfully to locate the Clifton "mine."
33 Acting Treas. Sec. (name illegible) to SEC (DC), 3Aug94; and Ass. Sec. W. Curtis to SEC, 9Aug94.
34 Chamberlayne (Boston) to Asst. Treas. Sec. Hamlin (DC), 3Jan94; JSM (Strafford) to Sec. Carlisle, 22Sep94; and other letters of support in AEM OPMA file. Chamberlayne and Elliot were both active in the CAA at the time.

Chapter 29

1. EMC (DC) to SEC (Clifton), 15Oct93; and CFC minutes, TBL.
2. *Telephone* (Hamilton), 26Oct94.
3. Nathan Chamberlain (Monument Beach, Mass.) to Carlisle, 7Mar95, *Ibid*. In the preface to his book on tariffs, Nathan gave special thanks to CAA member Charles Chamberlayne of the Boston bar.
4. Paul Chamberlin (DC) to EMC (Clifton), 23Sep95.
5. CFC minutes, TBL.
6. "Your Own Sunshine" [Hume] (Boston) to [Mary] Chamberlin, 11Nov95, E.L. Dodge Co. stationery.
7. EMC (Clifton) to SGM (DC), [late fall 1895].
8. *Ibid.*; and *Washingtonian* (Leesburg), 23Apr98.
9. Cohen, *Contraband*, 267-8.
10. Gould, *William McKinley*, chap. 1; and Dearing, *Veterans in Politics*, 455-9.
11. Veterans' Division Hqs. orders, 27Feb97, TCC.
12. SEC to Sec. Gage, 2Apr97; JSM to Gage, 5Apr97; and Rep. Shannon to Gage, 6Apr97, SEC TD file
13. Asst. Sec. Howell (Paeonian Springs, Va.) to [F.A.] Vanderlip (DC), 12Jun97, *ibid.*
14. Dearing, *Veterans in Politics*, 439-40, 466, 468.
15. Sec. CSC Doyle to Sec. Gage. 9Oct97; and CSC Examiner Steven to SEC (DC), 4Dec97.
16. JMC to EMC, 14Feb98; and JMC scrapbook given by daughter Priscilla Alden Chamberlin Ernst, DCC.
17. Docs. in SEC TD file, including Castle to Gage, 11Nov98; and unfinished SEC to JSM, 18Nov98.
18. JSM (DC) to SEC&EMC (DC), 13May98; *Wash. Post*, 28Dec98; and *Wash. Evening Star*, 28Dec98, copy provided by Coy R. Cross II, author of a recent JSM biography.
19. Instructions from C/Inspecting Div., 17Mar99; and exam results, 20Jul98, SEC TD file.
20. Various docs., Apr-May1901, *ibid*.
21. EMC to SEC, 15Oct93; and Edward Dawson to Pension Commissioner 10Nov96, SEC MPA.
22. James Morrill (DC) to SEC (Clifton), 17Feb97.
23. Physical exam, SEC MPA; and Pension Commissioner to SEC (Clifton), 26Apr97.
24. Various CAA documents and related genealogical papers.
25. Lucia Parks (Wichita, Kans.) to SEC (Clifton), 19Nov04; MPAs for Donald Stone, Charles H. Crawford and Duncan Cameron; and records of Bay St. Cemetery, Glens Falls.
26. W. S. Chamberlain to SEC, 20Jul96; SEC family Bible; and info from a William's [William Chamberlain?] descendant.
27. See Gould, *op. cit.*, chaps. 4-6, for overview of the war.
28. Paul Chamberlin (Cuba) to SEC (DC), 3Aug98.
29. Paul Chamberlin MSR ("War with Spain"); and various family papers.
30. William Hume Clendenin MSR ("War with Spain").
31. Wedding notices, *Wash. Evening Star*, 24Jun99 and *Wash. Post*, 25Jun99.
32. Clifton guest book started in 1898, BCC.

Chapter 30

1. 1900 U.S. census for LoCo. and DC.
2. Mary (Clifton) to W. H. Clendenin (Manila), 7Oct00 & [spring 1901].
3. Programs for 1900 Memorial and Flag Day ceremonies.
4. Cox to SEC, 18Jun & 27Sep00; SEC to Cox, 29Sep00; and SEC copy of Cox, *Defenses of Washington*.
5. *Nat. Tribune* (DC), 28Feb01; Gen. Sickles to SEC, 19&27Feb01; Sec. Elihu Root to Sickles, 1Mar01; and Parade Grand Marshal order, 2Mar01.
6. Dearing, *Veterans in Politics*, 497; various GAR and MOLLUS documents; and *Wash. Post*, 12Oct01.
7. SEC's copy of Fry column, cut from a one-sided, undated newspaper insert entitled "Correspondent's Page...," that may have been intended as a handout at the July 1902 anniversary of the battle. The first appearance in a paper that can be dated is in the *Philipsburg* [Ks.] *Herald*, 9Jun02.
8. *Wash. Post*, 9Sep02; *Wash. Times*, 11Oct02; and Cooling, *Day Lincoln Was Almost Shot*, 246-7.
9. Shugars (Waterford) to one of SEC's children (Edward or Mary), 6Mar01.
10. Shugars (Clifton) to EMC; SEC (DC), 30Dec02&6Jan03; and Loudoun Mutual policies.
11. CFC minutes, TBL; D. Ward (Columbus, O.) to SEC (DC), 30Sep01, TCC; and Mary Clendenin (Spokane) to EMC, 6Aug02, BCC.

12 CFC minutes, TBL; M. Dodge, Dir., Office of Public Road Inquiries, USDA, to SEC, Pres. CFC, (Clifton), 9Aug04; and Cornelius Shawen (Waterford) to SEC (DC), 29Jun03.
13 EMC (DC) to [Bidie], 31 [Apr03].
14 Various letters written by Mary to mother, Aug02-Jun04, BCC.
15 Various letters and documents, TCC; and SEC TD file.
16 Pension Bureau rejection, 27May05, TCC; and documents in SEC MPA, including Congressional Private Act, No. 2349, approved 2Mar07 and sponsored by Rep. Sulloway of New Hampshire.
17 Paul Chamberlin (USS *Takoma*, San Juan, P.R.) to JMC (DC), 7Oct04; and wedding announcement and undated clipping of wedding notice, DCC.
18 CFC minutes, TBL.
19 With funding from his newspaper, Wellman employed the airship *America* on two aerial tries to reach the Pole before being beaten to this goal by Admiral Robert Perry. A subsequent attempt in 1910 to cross the Atlantic on board the *America* resulted in its loss, and Wellman and his crew having to be rescued at sea.
20 Roy (DC) to Charlton (Paris), 15Jan06; Edith to Charlton accompanying undated letter from Roy; and material on Walter Wellman (1858-1934) provided by David Chamberlin.
21 EMC (Clifton) to Roy (Chicago), 2, 8&27Feb07.
22 EMC (Clifton) to Roy (Moorestown, N.J.), 17Feb08, DCC.
23 EMC (Clifton) to Mary (Columbus), 20Dec06&2Jan&2Mar07; and EMC (Clifton) to Roy (Chicago), 2, 8&27Feb07, DCC.
24 EMC (Clifton) to Roy (Chicago), 2, 8&27Feb07, DCC; 1906 notes of trust, DCC; and Deed Book 8G: 271, LCCR.
25 EMC (Clifton) to Roy (Chicago), 2, 8&27Feb07, DCC.
26 EMC (Clifton) to Mary (Columbus), 17Apr06; Joseph M. Dunlop (Franklin, Ind.) to SEC (Clifton), 4Mar07; and Ellen Martin (Glens Falls) to SEC (Clifton), 4Jun06.
27 Zebina Moses (DC) to SEC, 29Dec06; and Robert Moses (NYC) to SEC, 12Feb07, w/ N.Y. Senate Bill #212.
28 Castle, "Early's Raid on Washington."
29 Four unsourced newspaper obituaries, BCC. Both MOLLUS and the CAA also published memorials.
30 Documents in SEC MPA; and records of loans, DCC.
31 EMC (Clifton) to Mary Clendenin (Cuba), 5Jan09, BCC.
32 Paul (NYC) to EMC (Clifton), 28Jan09, BCC; and similar letter, postmarked 27Jan09.
33 EMC (Clifton) to Mary (Ft. McPherson, Ga.), 13Jul, 5&20Oct09, BCC.
34 Undated clippings, Loudoun and NYC newspapers.
35 EMC to Mrs. James Moses (NYC), 9Dec09; EMC to Roy (DC.), 15&19Dec09, DCC; and EMC to Lt. Hume Clendenin (Ft. McPherson), 17Dec09, BCC. Priscilla was the source for Charlton not liking country life, although Edith thought that she was wrong about Roy's wife.
36 Undated obituary, Loudoun newspaper, DCC.

Abbreviations and Bibliography

1. People

AEM	Ann (Annie) Eliza Matthews, sister of EM.
EM	Edith (Edie) Dawson Matthews, before marriage to SEC.
EMC	Edith Matthews Chamberlin, after marriage to SEC.
EYM	Edward Young (E. Y.) Matthews, father of EM.
HTG	Henry Taylor Gover, uncle of EM.
JMC	Justin Morrill Chamberlin, son of SEC and EMC.
JSM	Justin Smith Morrill, Vermont congressman.
SAG	Samuel (Sam) A. Gover, uncle of EM.
SGM	Sarah Gover Matthews, mother of EM.
SEC	Simon Elliot Chamberlin.
TT	Thomas Taylor.

2. Manuscript Collections and Other Sources.

BCC	Bruce Clendenin Collection (private).
BLCHS	*Bulletin of the Loudoun County Historical Society.*
BYM	Baltimore Yearly Meeting (microfilm records in MdSA).
CAA	Chamberlain Association of America.
CMR	Army Court-martial records, RG 153, NARA.
CFC	Catoctin Farmers Club (minutes in TBL).
CS/SAD file	Customs Service Special Agent Division case files, RG 36, Entry 13, NARA.
DCC	David Chamberlin Collection (private).
EMC	Notes compiled by author's father, Edward Matthews Chamberlin, Jr.
FCCR	Frederick County court records, Frederick, Md.
FHS	Friends' Historical Library, Swarthmore College, Swarthmore, Pa.
FMM	Fairfax Monthly Meeting, Waterford, Va. (microfilm records in TBL).
FQM	Fairfax Quarterly Meeting (microfilm records in MdSA).
GCMM	Goose Creek Monthly Meeting, Lincoln, Va. (microfilm records in TBL).
GP	"Gover Papers," Virginia Historical Society, Richmond, Va.
JDC	John Divine Collection (private).
LC	Library of Congress, Washington, D.C.
LCCR	Loudoun County court records, Leesburg, Va.
MdSA	Maryland State Archives, Annapolis, Md.
MPA	Military Pension Records, RG 15, NARA.
MSR	Military Service Records, RG 94, NARA.
NARA	National Archives and Records Administration, Washington, D.C.
NARA II	National Archives Annex, College Park, Md.
NAMP	National Archives Microfilm Publication.
M22	Registers of Letters Received by the Secretary of War.
M87	Records of the Southern Claims Commission, 1871-1880.
M221	Letters Received by the Secretary of War, Regular Series.
M619	Letters Received by the Office of the Adjutant General.

M1407	Barred and Disallowed Case Files of the Southern Claims Commission.
NARG	National Archives Records Group.
RG 15	Records of the Veterans Administration.
RG 26	Records of the Post Office Department.
RG 36	Records of the U.S. Customs Service.
	Entry 13: Case Files and Related Correspondence of Special Agents.
RG 56	General Records of the Treasury Department (NARA II).
	Entry 210: Applications and Recommendations for Treasury Department Positions in Washington, D.C., 1830-1910. (Box 95 contains SEC's personnel file.)
	Entry 286: Applications and Recommendations for Positions as Special Agents and Inspectors, 1842-1900.
RG 87	Records of the U.S. Secret Service.
RG 92	Records of the Quartermaster General.
RG 94	Records of the Adjutant General's Office.
RG 105	Records of the Bureau of Refugees, Freedmen and Abandoned Lands.
RG 123	Records of the U.S. Court of Claims.
RG 153	Records of the Army's Judge Advocate General.
RG 217	Records of the U.S. General Accounting Office (NA II).
RG 365	Treasury Department Collection of Confederate Records (NA II).
	Entry 271: Voting Lists for Virginia's Ordinance of Secession.
RG 366	Records of the Civil War Special Agencies of the Treasury Department.
	Entry 661: Correspondence Received by Supervising Special Agent Hanson A. Risley.
NYDMNA	New York State Dept. of Military Affairs, Albany, N.Y., especially on-line data base maintained by its Military Museum and Veterans Research Center.
NYSA	New York State Archives, Albany, N.Y.
NYSM	*New York Sunday Mercury.*
OPMA	Office of Personnel Management Archives, St. Louis, Mo.
OR	See U.S. War Dept., *The War of the Rebellion.*
PD	Pinkerton Debriefings of Loudoun refugees, George McClellan Papers, LC.
RBHPL	Rutherford B. Hayes Presidential Library, Fremont, Ohio.
RLOB	Regimental Letter and Order Books, RG 94, NARA.
SCC	Southern Claims Commission.
TBL	Thomas Balch Library, Leesburg, Va.
TCC	Taylor Chamberlin Collection (private).
TD file	Treasury Department appointments/personnel file, RG 56, Entry 210 (unless otherwise noted), NARA.
USAMHI	U.S. Army Military History Institute, Carlisle Barracks, Pa.
UVaL	University of Virginia Library, Charlottesville, Va.
UWVaL	University of West Virginia Library, Morgantown, W. Va.
VaHS	Virginia Historical Society Library, Richmond, Va.
VaSL	Virginia State Library, Richmond, Va.
VMHB	*The Virginia Magazine of History and Bibliography.*
VtHS	Vermont Historical Society, Montpelier, Vt.
VSR	Volunteer Service Record, RG 94, NARA.
WFA	Waterford Foundation Archives, Waterford, Va.

3. Unpublished Sources

Baltimore Yearly Meeting, minutes, microfilms M-548, 550 and 555, MdSA.
Barnard, Frank, Papers, Wisconsin Historical Society Papers.
Chamberlin Family Bible, entries begun by SEC's parents, BCC.
Chamberlin, David C., Sr., "Richard of Braintree," unpublished genealogical study provided in 1993 by its compiler, then living in Salt Lake City, UT.
Chamberlin, Simon Elliot (SEC), diaries, correspondence and other material, TCC, unless otherwise identified. His 1864-5 diary only survives as transcript in SEC's handwriting, probably prepared in 1877.
Corwin, John A., "History of Special Agents' Division," n.d., 9-page typed report, National Customs Museum Foundation Archives, Miami, Fla.
Coutant, Dr. Richard B., "Notes on the History of the Twenty-fifth New York Cavalry," 11-page manuscript mailed to SEC in 1891 and based on author's reminiscences as a medic in the 25th and letters from his relative, Sgt. James Coutant (Co. D).
Dubie, Daniel, papers, UVaL.
Fairfax Monthly Meeting, minutes, microfilm M-618, TBL and MdSA.
Fairfax Quarterly Meeting, minutes, microfilms M-614, 615 and 619, MdSA.
Goose Creek Monthly Meeting, minutes, microfilm M-623, TBL and MdSA.
Geary, John W., "Geary Scrapbook, Vol. I," RG 94, entry 159, NARA.
_____, "Geary Scrapbook. Vol. II," RG 393(2), entry 5444, NARA.
Janney, Alcinda, diary, Janney Family papers, #8409-e, UVaL.
Letcher, John, Governor Letcher Executive Papers, VaSL.
Matthews, Marie, 1865 diary, TCC.
McClellan, George B., papers, LC.
Morrill, Justin Smith, Paper, LC and VtHS.
Myers, Frank, diary (1865), copy WFA.
_____, papers, Mss 5:9 M9925:1, VHS.
Nisewaner, Christian, "Nisewaner Diary," Mss Col., TBL.
Nye, George H., papers, Nicolas P. Picerno collection.
Paxson, Charles E., "Daybook," partial transcription, WFA.
Pierpont, Francis H., Gov. Pierpont Executive Papers, VaSL.
_____, Gov. Pierpont Executive Papers, AR-1722, WVaSA.
Pinkerton, Allan, exile debriefings, see McClellan papers.
Russell, Isaac Steer, diary, partial transcription, WFA.
Steer, Mary Frances Dutton, "Commonplace Book," WFA.
Steer, Samuel, Customs Ledger kept at Point of Rocks, Md., 1864-5, WFA.
Underwood, John C., papers, LC.
Walker, Elisha H., journal, WFA.
Willey, Waitman T., Willey papers, UWVaL.
Williams, Rebecca K., "Williams Diary," FHL.

4. Published Sources

Alexander, John H., *Mosby's Men*, New York: Neale Publishing Co., 1907.
Alpert, Allen D., ed. *History of the 45th Regiment Pennsylvania Veteran Volunteer Infantry*, Williamsport, Pa.: Grit Publishing Co., 1912.
Ambler, Charles H., *Francis H. Pierpont: Union War Governor of Virginia and Father of West Virginia*,

Chapel Hill: University of North Carolina Press, 1937.

Anonymous, *Battlefields of the South from Bull Run to Fredericksburgh...by an English Combatant* (1864), reprint edition, New York: Time-Life Books Inc., 1984.

_____, "Early's Raid on Washington," *Republic Magazine*, VIII (March 1877), pp. 185-89.

_____, "Special Agents: A History," *Customs Today*, spring 1977, pp. 17-8.

_____, "With the Militia in North Loudoun in Early '61." Series of newspaper articles, c. 1900, Briscoe Goodhart scrapbook, v. 2, 49-60, TBL.

Ansley, Delight, "The Religious Society of Friends," *Encyclopedia Americana*, 1961 ed.

Aron, Cindy Sondik, *Ladies and Gentlemen of the Civil Service: Middle-Class Workers in Victorian America*, New York: Oxford University Press, 1987.

Barnes, Robert, *Maryland Marriages, 1778-1800*, Baltimore: Genealogical Pub. Co., 1979.

Bates, Samuel P., *History of Pennsylvania Volunteers, 1861-5*, Harrisburg: B. Singerly, State Printer, 1869.

Baylor, George, *From Bull Run to Bull Run*, Richmond: B. F. Johnson Co., 1900.

Beath, Robert B., *History of the Grand Army of the Republic*, New York: Bryan, Taylor & Co., 1889.

Bernstein, Iver, *The New York City Draft Riots*, Oxford University Press, 1990.

Blair, William Alan, ed., *A Politician Goes to War: The Civil War Letters of John White Geary*, University Park: Pennsylvania State University Press, 1995.

Blake, Nelson Morehouse, *William Mahone of Virginia: Soldier and Political Insurgent*, Richmond: Garrett & Massie, 1935.

Bonnell, John C., *Sabres in the Shenandoah, the 21st New York Cavalry, 1863-1866*, Shippensburg, Pa.: Burd Street Press, 1996.

Brown, Henry A., *Sugar Frauds and the Tariff*, n.p., 1879.

Burlingame, Michael, and John R. T. Ettinger, eds., *Inside Lincoln's White House: The Complete Civil War Diary of John Hay*, n.p.; Southern Illinois University Press, 1999.

Cannon, James C., *Record of Service of Company K, 150th Ohio Volunteer Infantry*, Washington, DC: n.p., 1903.

Carter, Dan T, *When the War Was Over: The Failure of Self-Reconstruction in the South, 1865-1867*, Baton Rouge: Louisiana State University Press, 1865.

Cashdollar, Charles D., "The Pittsburg Soldiers' and Sailors' Convention, September 23-26, 1866," *Western Pennsylvania Historical Magazine*, v. 48 (Oct. 1965), 331-43.

Castle, Henry A., "Early's Raid on Washington, A Leaf from History," *National Tribune Repository*, vol. 1 (Nov., 1907), pp. 34-40.

Chamberlain Association of America, *Annual Reports*, 1898-1911.

Chamberlain, Welton C., *Richard Chamberlaine of Braintree*, Pinkney, Mich.: n.p., 1991.

Chamberlin, Simon Elliot, *Report on Allowances on Drawback on Sugars*, Washington, DC: Treasury Dept. Doc. No. 283, 1883.

——— and H. J. Abbott, *Report on the Methods of Manufacturing Sugars in Cuba*, Washington, DC: GPO, 1879.

———, H. J. Abbott and F. M. Endlich, *Report on the Methods of Manufacturing Sugar in West India Islands and British Guiana*, Washington, DC: GPO, 1880.

Chamberlin, Taylor M., "Captain Samuel Means and the Loudoun Rangers," *BLCHS* (2010), 19-44; (2011), 19-50; and (2012), 1-20.

_____, "Exeter Plantation during the Civil War: Horatio Trundle's Southern Claims Commission Case File," *BLCHS* (2004), 40-75.

_____, *Where Did They Stand?: The May 1861 Vote on Secession in Loudoun County, Virginia, and Post-War Claims against the Government*, Waterford, Va.: The Waterford Foundation, 2003.

———, and James D. Peshek, *Crossing the Line: Civilian Trade and Travel between Loudoun County, Virginia, and Maryland during the Civil War*, Waterford, Va.: The Waterford Foundation, 2002.

_____, and John M. Souders, *Between Reb and Yank: A Civil War History of Northern Loudoun County, Virginia, Jefferson, NC: McFarland & Co., 2011.

———, Bronwen C. Souders, and John M. Souders, eds., *The Waterford News*, Waterford, Va.: Waterford Foundation, 1999.

Chernow, Ron, *Grant*, New York: Penguin Press, 2017.

Cohen, Andrew Wender, *Contraband: Smuggling and the Birth of the American Century*, New York: W. W. Norton & Co., 2015.

Conrow, Emma H., "Sarah, Lizzie and Lida, Three Loyal Lasses Who Edited a Union Journal in Waterford, Va.," *Baltimore American* (5 Feb.1922).

Cooling, Benjamin F., *The Day Lincoln Was Almost Shot: The Fort Stevens Story*, Lanham, Md.: The Scarecrow Press, 2013.

_____, *Jubal Early's Raid on Washington, 1864*, Baltimore: Nautical and Aviation Publication Co., 1989.

———, *Symbol, Sword and Shield: Defending Washington During the Civil War*, Hamden, Conn.: Archon Books, 1975.

Corell, Philip, *History of the Naval Brigade, 99th N. Y. Volunteers*, New York: Regimental Veteran Association, 1905.

Cox, William V., *Defenses of Washington, General Early's Advance on the Capital and the Battle of Fort Stevens, July 11 and 12, 1864*, n.p., n.d. [Pamphlet "sold for benefit of Fort Stevens Preservation Fund," originally published in *Records of Columbia Historical Society*, IV (1901), pp. 135-65.

Crawford, J. Marshall, *Mosby and his Men*, New York: G. W. Carleton & Co., 1867.

Crofts, Daniel W., "Late Antebellum Virginia Reconsidered," *VMHB*, vol. 107 (1999), pp. 253-86.

Crouch, Richard E., *"Rough-riding Scout": The Story of John W. Mobberly, Loudoun's Own Civil War Guerrilla Hero*, Arlington, Va.: Elden Editions, 1994.

Crothers, A. Glenn, *Quakers Living in the Lion's Mouth: The Society of Friends in Northern Virginia, 1730-1865*, Gainesville: University Press of Florida, 2012.

Cunningham, John L., *Three Years with the Adirondack Regiment, 118th New York Volunteers Infantry*, New York: Plimpton Press (for private circulation), 1920.

Curriden, Samuel W., *Our Soldiers and Sailors: What They Said and Did on the 10th Anniversary of Antietam*, Veterans National Committee, New York, 1872.

Dearing, Mary R., *Veterans in Politics: The Story of the GAR*, Baton Rouge: Louisiana State University Press, 1952.

Divine, John E., *35th Battalion Virginia Cavalry*, Lynchburg: H.E. Howard, Inc., 1985.

———, Bronwen C. Souders and John M. Souders, *To Talk Is Treason*, n.p., Waterford Foundation, 1996.

———, *When Waterford & I Were Young*, n.p., Waterford Foundation, 1997.

Doenecke, Justus D., *The Presidencies of James A. Garfield & Chester A. Arthur*, Lawrence: University Press of Kansas, 1981.

Duncan, Patricia B., *1860 Loudoun County, Virginia, Federal Population Census Index*, Westminster, Md.: Willow Bend Books, 2002.

_____, *1870 Loudoun County, Virginia, Federal Population Census Index*, Westminster, Md.: Willow Bend Books, 2002.

_____, *Loudoun County, Virginia, Birth Register 1853-1879*, Willow Bend Books, Westminster, MD, 1998.

Dyer, Frederick H., *A Compendium of the War of the Rebellion*, reprint edition, Dayton, Ohio: The National Historical Society, 1979.

Early, Jubal A., "The Advance upon Washington in July, 1864," The *Southern Magazine* (1871), 8:750-63.

_____, *A Memoir of the Last Year of the War for Independence*, Toronto: Lovell & Gibson, 1866.

Eckenrode, Hamilton James, *The Political History of Virginia during the Reconstruction*, Baltimore: Johns Hopkins Press, 1904.

Evans, Thomas J., "Quaker Sam: Capt. Samuel C. Means, Co., Independent Loudoun Rangers," *North South Trader*, July-August, 1982.

———, and Moyer, James M., *Mosby Vignettes*, vols. 1 and 2, privately printed, 1993.

Faust, Patricia L., *Historical Times Illustrated Encyclopedia of the Civil War*, New York: Harper Collins, 1991.

Foreman, Amanda, *A World on Fire: Britain's Crucial Role in the American Civil War*: New York: Random House, 2010.

Forsythe, John William, *Guerrilla Warfare and Life in Libby Prison* (1892), reprint edition, Annandale, Va.: Turnpike Press, 1967.

Foster, Gaines M., *Ghosts of the Confederacy: Defeat, the Lost Cause, and the Emergence of the New South*, New York: Oxford University Press, 1988.

French, J. H., *Historical and Statistical Gazetteer of New York State*, 1860.

Friends, Religious Society of, *Memorials concerning Several Ministers and Others, Deceased; of the Religious Society of Friends within the Limits of Baltimore Yearly Meeting*, Baltimore: Innes & Co., 1875.

Frye, Dennis E., "'I Resolved to Play a Bold Game', John S. Mosby as a Factor in the 1864 Valley Campaign", in Gallagher, *Struggle for the Shenandoah*.

Gallagher, Gary W., ed., *Struggle for the Shenandoah, Essays on the 1864 Valley Campaign*, Kent, Ohio: The Kent State University Press, 1991.

Garfield, James A., *The Diary of James A. Garfield*, edited by Harry J. Brown and Frederick D. Williams, 4 vols., East Lansing: Michigan State University Press, 1967-81.

Gaus, John M., and Wolcott, Leon O., *Public Administration and the United States Department of Agriculture*, Chicago, 1940.

Gillette, William, *Retreat from Reconstruction, 1869-1879*, Baton Rouge: Louisiana State University Press, 1979.

Goldman, Stephen A., *One More War to Fight: Union Veterans Battle for Equality through Reconstruction, Jim Crow, and the Lost Cause*, Lanham, Md.: Rowman & Littlefield, 2023.

Goodhart, Briscoe, *History of the Independent Loudoun Virginia Rangers* (1896), reprint edition, Gaithersburg, Md.: Butternut Press, 1985.

Gould, Lewis L., *The Presidency of William McKinley*, Lawrence: University Press of Kansas, 1980.

Gover, Samuel A., "Jesse and Miriam Gover," *Friends Intelligencer*, v. 57 (Nov. 1900), pp. 820, 835-7, 853.

Grimsley, Mark, *The Hard Hand of War: Union Policy towards Southern Civilians, 1861 - 1865*, New York: Cambridge University Press, 1995.

Grace, William H., *Grace's Exposure!, or: Unsweetened Sugars: A Compilation and Review of the Great Sugar Frauds on the Government and People*, New York: Randel & Bruno, 1879.

Grove, William J., *History of Carrollton Manor, Frederick County, Maryland*, Frederick, Md.: Marken & Bielfeld, 1928.

Hall, Charles W. L., *Books to Bullets...In Defiance of Northern Propaganda: A History of the 46th North Carolina Infantry, CSA*, n.p.: Trafford Pub., 2013.

Hall, Hillman A., Besley, W. B., and Wood, Gilbert C., eds., *History of the Sixth New York Cavalry*, Worcester, Mass.: The Blanchard Press, 1908.

Hannaford, Roger, "Winter Quarters Near Winchester, 1864-1865," *VMHB*, # 86 (1974), 320-38.

Hanover County [Va.] Department of Planning, *A Survey of Civil War Sites in Hanover County, Virginia*, n.p., n.d.

Harwood, Jr., Herbert H., *Rails to the Blue Ridge*, 2nd. ed., rev., Falls Church, Va.: Pioneer America Society, Inc., 1969.

Hawn, Thomas F., *The Chesapeake and Ohio Canal: Pathway to the Nation's Capital*, Metuchen, NJ: The Scarecrow Press, n.d.

Head, James W., *History and Comprehensive Description of Loudoun County, Virginia*, n.p.: Park View

Press, 1908.

Hiatt, Marty, *Early Church Records of Loudoun County, Virginia*, Westminister, Md.: Family Line Publications, 1995.

Hiatt, Rex Clark, "Factionalism, Frustration and Failure: Robert W. Hughes and the Republican Party in Virginia, 1870-1873," MA Thesis, University of Virginia, 1974.

Hickin, Patricia, "John C. Underwood and the Antislavery Movement in Virginia, 1847-1860," *VMHB*, Vol. 73 (1965), pp. 156-68.

Hinshaw, William Wade, *Encyclopedia of American Quaker Genealogy*, Ann Arbor, Mich.: Edwarde Brothers, 1950, particularly chapters on the Fairfax and Goose Creek Monthly Meetings in Vol. 6.

Hirshson, Stanley P., *Farewell to the Bloody Shirt: Northern Republicans and the Southern Negro, 1877-1893*, Bloomington: Indiana University Press, 1962.

Hoogenboom, Ari, *Outlawing the Spoils: A History of the Civil Service Reform Movement*, Urbana: University of Illinois Press, 1968.

———, *The Presidency of Rutherford B. Hayes*, Lawrence: The University Press of Kansas, 1988.

Horwitz, Tony, *Confederates in the Attic: Dispatches from the Unfinished Civil War*, New York: Pantheon Books, 1998.

Hutchinson, Louisa Skinner, *Apprentices, Poor Children and Bastards, Loudoun County, Virginia, 1757-1850*, Westminister, Md.: Willow Bend Books, 2000.

Janney, Werner and Asa M., *Ye Meetg Hous Smal: A Short Account of Friends in Loudoun County, Virginia, 1732-1980*, Lincoln, Va., n.p., 1980.

Janney, Samuel M., *The Memoirs of Samuel M. Janney*, Philadelphia: Philadelphia Friends Book Association, 1881.

Jourdan, Elise Greeenup, *Early Families of Southern Maryland*, 5 vols., Westminister, Md.: Family Line Publications, 1993-6.

Journal of the Constitutional Convention, which convened at Alexandria on the 13th day of February, 1864, Alexandria: D. Turner, 1864.

Journal of the House of Delegates of the State of Virginia for the Session of 1863-5, Alexandria: D. Turner, 1865.

Judge, Joseph, *Season of Fire: The Confederate Strike on Washington*, Berryville, Va.: Rockbridge Publishing Co., 1994.

Keen, Hugh C., and Mewborn, Horace, *43rd Battalion Virginia Cavalry, Mosby's Command*, Lynchburg, Va.: H.E. Howard, 1993.

Keneally, Thomas, *American Scoundrel: The Life of the Notorious Civil War General Dan Sickles*, New York: Nan A. Talese, 2002.

Kidd, James H., *Personal Recollections of a Cavalryman with Custer's Michigan Cavalry Brigade in the Civil War*, Ionia, Mich.: Sentinel Publishing Co., 1908.

Krick, Robert K., "'The Cause of all my Disasters': Jubal A. Early and the Undisciplined Valley Cavalry," in Gallagher, *Struggle for the Shenandoah*.

Lankevich, George J., "The Grand Army of the Republic in New York State, 1865-1898," Ph.D. dissertation, Columbia University, 1967.

Leonard, Cynthia Miller, *The General Assembly of Virginia: A Bicentennial Register of Members*, Richmond: Virginia State Library, 1978.

Lewis, Virgil A., ed., *How West Virginia Was Made*, Charleston, W.Va.: Nes-Mail Co., 1909.

Lincoln, Abraham, *Collected Works*, New Brunswick: Rutgers University Press, 1953.

Loudoun County Civil War Commission, *Loudoun County and the Civil War*, Leesburg, Va.: The Potomac Press, 1961.

Love, Edmund G., "The Beautiful and Anxious Maidens", *The Ladies Home Journal*, February 1962, 135-40.

Lowe, Richard, *Republicans and Reconstruction in Virginia, 1856-1870*, Charlottesville: University of Virginia Press, 1991.

———, "The Republican Party in Antebellum Virginia, 1856-1860", *VMHB*, vol. 81 (1973), pp. 259-79.

———, "Virginia's Reconstruction Convention: General Schofield Rates the Delegates", *VMHB*, vol. 80 (1972), pp. 341-60.

McConnell, Stuart, *Glorious Contentment: The Grand Army of the Republic, 1865-1900*, Chapel Hill: The University of North Carolina Press, 1992.

McDonald, William N., *A History of the Laurel Brigade*, Baltimore: Sun Job Printing, 1907.

McFeely, William S., *Grant: A Biography*, New York: W. W. Norton & Co., 1981.

Maddex, Jr., Jack P., *The Virginia Conservatives, 1867-1879: A Study in Reconstruction Politics*, Chapel Hill: The University of North Carolina Press, 1970.

_____, "Virginia: The Persistence of Centrist Hegmony," in Otto H. Olsen, *Reconstruction and Redemption in the South*, Baton Rouge, Louisiana State University Press, 1982.

Marsh, Helen Hirst, "Early Loudoun Water Mills," *BLCHS*, vol. 1 (1958), pp. 21-6.

Martin, Joseph, *A New and Comprehensive Gazetteer of Virginia and the District of Columbia*, Charlottesville, Va.: n.p., 1835.

Mendte, J. Robert, *The Union League of Philadelphia, 125 Years*, Philadelphia: 1987.

Mitchell, Stewart, *Horatio Seymour of New York*, Cambridge: Harvard University Press, 1938.

Monteiro, A[ristides], *War Reminiscences by the Surgeon of Mosby's Command*, Richmond, Va.: n.p., 1890.

Moore, Frank, *The Civil War in Song and Story*, New York: [P.F. Colkes], 1882.

Moore, Robert A., *A Life in the Confederacy*, Jackson, Tenn.: McGowan-Mercer Press, 1959.

Moore, James T., *The Two Paths to the New South: The Virginia Debt Controversy, 1870-1883*, Lexington: University of Kentucky Press, 1974.

Moore, Louis, "The Elusive Center: Virginia Politics and the General Assembly, 1869-1871," *VMHB*, vol. 103 (1995), pp. 207-236.

Morefield, Betty, "The Freedmen's Bureau in Loudoun County, Virginia, June 1865-March 1866," *BLCHS* (2007), 36-72.

Morgan III, James A., *A Little Short of Boats: The Fights at Ball's Bluff and Edwards Ferry*, Ft. Mitchell, Ky.: Ironclad Pub., 2004.

Moulton, Charles H., *Fort Lyon to Harper's Ferry*, compiled and edited by Lee C. and Karen D. Drickamer, Shippensburg, Pa.: White Mane Publishing Co., 1987.

Mutual Fire Insurance Company of Loudoun County, A *Century of Service, 1849-1949*, Waterford, Va.: n.p., [1949].

Myers, Frank M., *The Comanches: A History of White's Battalion, Virginia Cavalry* (1871), reprint edition, Marietta, Georgia: Continental Book Co., 1956.

Neff, Ray A., *Valley of the Shadow*, Terre Haute, Ind.: Ranna Pub., 1989.

Netherton, Nan, *et. al.*, *Fairfax County, Virginia: A History*, Fairfax, Va.: Fairfax County Board of Supervisors, 1978.

New York Soldiers' and Sailors' Union, *Proceedings of the Soldiers' and Sailors' State Convention Held in Albany, N.Y., April 17th and 18th, 1866*. Niagara Falls: William Pool, 1866.

New York State, *Presentation of Flags of New York Volunteer Regiments*, [Albany]: Bureau of Military Record, 1865.

Nichols, Joseph V., *Loudoun Valley Legends*, Purcellville, Va.: The Blue Ridge Herald, 1955.

Osborn, Penelope M., "The Road Back", in Loudoun County Civil War Commission, *Loudoun County and the Civil War*.

Owens, Susie Lee, "The Union League of America: Political Activities in Tennessee, the Carolinas, and Virginia, 1865-1870", Ph.D. dissertation, New York University, 1943.

Pearson, Charles Chilton, *The Readjuster Movement in Virginia*, New Haven: Yale University Press, 1917.

Peden, Henry C., *Quaker Records of Northern Maryland*, Westminster, Md.: Family Line Publications,

1994.

———, *Quaker Records of Southern Maryland*, Westminster, Md.: Family Line Publications, 1992.

Phisterer, Frederick, *New York in the War of the Rebellion, 1861 to 1865*, 3rd ed., 6 vols. Albany, NY: J. B. Lyon Co., 1912.

Poland, Jr., Charles P., *From Frontier to Suburbia*, Marceline, Mo.: Walsworth Publishing Co., 1967.

Proceedings of Third Annual Reunion of the 25th N.Y. Vet. Cavalry Ass'n, Held in New York City, Sept. 20, 1893, n.p., n.d. (Copy in Henry E. Huntington Library, San Marino, Ca.)

Pulley, Raymond H., *Old Virginia Restored: An Interpretation of the Progressive Impulse, 1870-1930*, Charlottesville: The University Press of Virginia, 1968.

Ramey, Emily G., and John K. Gott, eds., *The Years of Anguish: Fauquier County, Virginia, 1861-1865*, [Warrenton, Va.]: Fauquier Co. Civil War Centennial Committee, 1965.

Ramage, James A., *Gray Ghost: The Life of John Singleton Mosby*, Lexington: The University Press of Kentucky, 1999.

Rice, Millard Milburn, *New Facts and Old Families: From the Records of Frederick County, Maryland*, Baltimore: Genealogical Pub. Co., 1984.

Ridpath, John C., *The Life and Work of James A. Garfield*, memorial edition, Cincinnati, Ohio: Jones Brothers and Company, 1882.

Roscoe, Theodore, *The Web of Conspiracy: The Complete Story of the Men Who Murdered Abraham Lincoln*, Englewood Cliffs, N.J.: Prentice-Hall, 1959.

Ross, Earle D., "The United States Department of Agriculture during the Commissionership," *Agricultural History*, v. 20 (1946), pp. 129-143.

Rowberg, Anthony A. and Marie C., "Post Offices of Loudoun County", *BLCHS*, II, pp. 57-72.

Rubin, Anne Sarah, "Between Union and Chaos: The Political Life of John Janney," *VMHB*, vol. 102 (1994), pp. 381-416.

Saffer, Wynne C., *Loudoun Votes, 1867-1966: a Civil War Legacy*, Willow Bend Books, Westminster, Md., 2002.

Sanderson, Henry H., *The History of Charlestown, New Hampshire*, Claremont, N.H.: Claremont Manufacturing Co., 1876.

Scheel, Eugene, *The Catoctin Farmers; Journals* vol., Catoctin Farmers Club, 2022.

Schoeberlein, Robert W., "A Fair to Remember: Maryland Women in Aid of the Union," *Maryland Historical Society Magazine*, vol. 90 (winter 1995), 467-87.

Scott, John, *Partisan Life with Col. John S. Mosby* (1867), reprint edition, Gaithersburg, Md.: Butternut Press, 1985.

Sheridan, Philip. H., *The Personal Memoirs P. H. Sheridan* (1888), one-volume reprint, New York: Da Capo Press, 1992.

Siepel, Kevin H., *Rebel: The Life and Times of John Singleton Mosby*, New York: St. Martin's Press, 1983.

Smith, Gwenda, *The Town House*, Strafford: Strafford Historical Society, 1992.

———, "A Walking Tour of Strafford Village as It Was When Justin Morrill First Went to Washington," Strafford: Strafford Historical Society, 1994.

Society of the Army of the Potomac, *Report of the Sixteenth Annual Reunion at Baltimore, Md., May 6 and 7, 1885*, New York: McGowan and Slipper, 1885.

Socolofsky, Homer E., and Allan B. Spetter, *The Presidency of Benjamin Harrison*, Lawrence: University Press of Kansas, 1987.

Souders, Bronwen C. and John M., *A Rock in a Weary Land, A Shelter in a Time of Storm*, Waterford: Waterford Foundation, 2003.

Squires, W. H. T., *Unleashed at Long Last*, Portsmouth, Va.: Printcraft Press, 1939.

Steadman, Melvin Lee, Jr., *Falls Church: By Fence and Fireside*, Annandale, Va.: The Turnpike Press, 1964.

Stevenson, Brenda E., *Life in Black & White: Family and Community in the Slave South*, New York:

Oxford University Press, 1996.

Stockberger, Warner S., *Personnel Administrative Development in the US Department of Agriculture, the First 50 Years*, Washington, DC: USDA, 1947.

Stone, Lee, *The Independent Loudoun Virginia Rangers: The Roster of Virginia's Only Union Cavalry Unit*, Waterford, Va.: The Waterford Foundation, 2016.

Strong, Solange, *Old Stone Houses of Loudoun County, Virginia*, n.p., 1950.

Styple, William B., ed., *Writing and Fighting the Civil War: Soldier Correspondence to the New York Sunday Mercury*, Kearny, N.J.: Belle Grove Publishing Co., 2000.

Taylor, Henry, *From Lead Mines to Gold Fields: Memoirs of an Incredibly Long Life*, Lincoln: University of Nebraska Press, 2006.

Taylor, James E., *The James E. Taylor Sketchbook: With Sheridan Up the Shenandoah Valley in 1864*, Dayton, Ohio: The Western Reserve Historical Society, 1989.

Thompson, Margaret Susan, *The "Spider Web": Congress and Lobbying in the Age of Grant*, Ithaca, NY: Cornell University Press, 1985.

Thomson, Orville, *From Philippi to Appomattox: Narrative of the Service of the 7th Indiana Infantry*, Baltimore: Butternut and Blue, 1993 (reprint).

Tidwell, William A., *April '65, Confederate Covert Action in the American Civil War*, Kent, Ohio: Kent State University Press, 1995.

———, with Hall, James O., and Gaddy, David W., *Come Retribution: The Confederate Secret Service and the Assassination of Lincoln*, Jackson: University Press of Mississippi, 1988.

Tracey, Grace L., *Pioneers of Old Monocacy: The Early Settlement of Frederick County, Maryland*, Baltimore: Genealogical Pub. Co., 1987.

Trudeau, Noah Andre, "Gettysburg's Second Front: The 'Blackberry Raid'," *Gettysburg Magazine*, 11:16.

Tyler-McGraw, Marie, "'The Prize I Mean Is the Prize of Liberty': A Loudoun County Family in Liberia," *VMHB*, v. 97 (1989), pp. 355-71.

U.S. Agriculture Department, *Proceeding of the National Agricultural Convention, February 14-17, 1872*, Washington, D.C., Government Printing Office, 1872.

———, *Monthly Reports*, 1871-2.

U.S. Congress, *Report of the Joint Committee on Reconstruction*, Washington: GPO, 1866.

U.S. Customs Service, *A History of Enforcement in the United States Customs Service, 1789-1875*, Historical Study No. 6, San Francisco, Ca.: 1988.

U.S. Treasury Department, *Annual Report of the Secretary of the Treasury*, 1885-6.

U.S. War Department, *The War of the Rebellion: A Compilation of the Official Records of the Union and Confederate Armies*, 128 volumes, Washington, D.C.: U.S. Government Printing Office, 1880-1901. (Cited as OR in footnotes. Series 1 unless otherwise specified.)

———, *Supplement to the Official Records of the Union and Confederate Armies, Part II--Record of Events*, edited by Janet B. Hewett, Wilmington, NC: Broadfoot Pub. Co., 1997.

Urwin, Gregory J. W., *Custer Victorious: The Civil War Battles of General George Armstrong Custer*, Edison, N.J.: The Blue and Grey Press, 1983.

Wallace, Jr., Lee A., *Contributions to a History of the Richmond Howitzer Battalion*, Baltimore: Butternut and Blue, 2000.

Watson, Winslow C., *The Military and Civil History of the County of Essex, New York*, Albany: J. Munsell, 1869.

Waterford Foundation, *Waterford Perspectives*, n.p., 1983. (Reprinted articles appearing in the annual "Waterford Fair" booklets.)

Wayland, John W., *Hopewell Friends History, 1734-1934, Frederick County, Virginia*, Winchester, Va.: Joint Committee of Hopewell Friends, 1936.

Welch, Jr., Richard E., *The Presidencies of Grover Cleveland*, Lawrence: University Press of Kansas, 1988.

Wert, Jeffery D., *Mosby's Rangers*, New York: Simon and Schuster, 1990.

White, Leonard D., *The Republican Era, 1869-1906: A Study in Administrative History*, New York: The MacMillan Co., 1958.

Williams, T. Harry, ed., *Hayes: The Diary of a President, 1875-1881*, New York: David McKay Co., 1964.

Williamson, James J., *Mosby's Rangers; A Record of the Operations of the Forty-Third Battalion Virginia Cavalry* (1909), reprint of 2nd ed., New York: Time-Life Books, 1982.

Woodward, C. Vann, *Reunion and Reaction: The Compromise of 1877 and the End of Reconstruction*, Boston: Little, Brown & Co., 1951.

Worrall, Jr., Jay, *The Friendly Virginians: America's First Quakers*, Athens, Ga.: Iberian Pub. Co. 1994.

Index

A

Adams, Ada, 224
Adams, Crawford C. (C/SAD), 222-3, 227, 229-30, 231, 235, 238-9, 250, 273
Albany, New York, 15-6, 32-4, 112, 175, 178-9, 253, 284
Alden, Priscilla, 317
Aldie, Virginia, 63
Allen, Thomas E., 165
Anderson, Andrew, 115
Andersonville Prison, 43, 182, 226
Arthur, Chester A., 222, 269, 271
Ayer, Ira, 223, 226-27, 239, 241-3, 246, 248, 251, 270-1, 273-4

B

Babcock, Orville, 223, 241
Battle of Balls Bluff, 130, 134, 219, 229-30
Battle of Cedar Creek, 65, 78-9
Battle of Drewry's Bluff, 39
Battle of Fisher's Hill, 72
Battle of Monocacy, 47
Battle of Yorktown, 271
Baxter, Myron, 9, 61
Baylor, George, 103
Beauregard, Pierre, 127
Belknap, William, 227
Bell, Alonzo, 230, 235, 237, 327
Bell, John, 124
Berlin, Maryland, 99-100, 104-6, 108, 125, 127, 129, 139-40, 142, 159
Berryville, Virginia, 62, 68-69, 73, 80, 87
Black suffrage and Civil Rights during Reconstruction, 169, 172, 175, 180, 185, 210-1, 215-8, 227, 232, 259, 273
Blaine, James G., 226-9, 268, 273
BOB (Clark, Robert M.), 40-5, 47-8, 55-8, 68-9, 71-2, 75, 78-80, 82-3, 85, 89-90, 98-9, 101-5
B&O Railroad, 66, 78, 83-4, 90, 98, 135, 142
Boys in Blue (GOP Veterans Groups), 180, 227, 231-2, 268, 284
Boynton, Henry V., 241
Bramhall, Frank J., 178-80, 188, 199
Bramhall, William L., 178, 182-3, 19
Bristow, Benjamin (Treasury Secretary), 221-3, 227-9, 235, 238, 241

Burning Raid into Loudoun, 2-3, 85, 87, 102, 105, 149, 151, 158, 266
Butler, Gen. Benjamin, 144, 181, 217

C

Cameron, Duncan, 8-9, 12-3, 17, 35, 171, 174, 224
Catoctin Farmers Club (CFC), 199-201, 207, 302-3, 315, 317
Chamberlain Association of America (CAA), 307, 317
Chamberlain, Ichabod, 6-7, 287
Chamberlayne, Charles F., 301
Chamberlin, Betsey Sanborn, 7-12, 19, 34-5
Chamberlin, Charlton Wellman, 317-8, 321-2, 324
Chamberlin, Edith M., 189-95, 198-201, 223-5, 238-41, 251-3, 260-5, 271-7, 284-5, 291-303, 314-6, 318-24
Chamberlin, Edward Matthews, 238, 272, 274, 291, 295-7, 302, 304, 307, 315-6, 318, 321-2, 324
Chamberlin, Eleanor ("Nellie," "Bidie"), 201, 291, 297, 315-6
Chamberlin, Justin Morrill ("Morrill"), 201, 274-5, 285, 291, 295, 297, 299, 322, 324
Chamberlin, Leroy ("Roy," "Boy"), 276, 295, 321-4
Chamberlin, Mary Matthews, 201, 274, 288, 291, 293, 296-7, 303-9
Chamberlin, Paul Elliot, 257, 274, 291, 295, 309, 324
Chamberlin, Samuel (Elliot's father), 7, 10, 287
Chamberlin, Samuel N., 7-8, 307
Chamberlin, Simon Elliot ("Elliot," "S. E.")
Ancestors/parents, 6-8; early life in Vermont and ties to Senator Justin Morrill, 8-11; jeweler in Midwest, first marriage, death of wife and children in Glens Falls, N.Y., 11-5; lieutenant, 118th N.Y. Infantry, 15-38; assigned to Draft Rendezvous, New York City, 40-6; transfer to captain in 25th N.Y. Cavalry, 40-6; Battle of Fort Stevens, 47-57; dispute with Major McPherson leads to detached duty, 58-66; return to 25th N.Y. Cavalry in the Shenandoah Valley, 79-97; provost marshal, Point of Rocks, 98-108; prolonged stay with Edith's family in Loudoun,

155-69; return to Glens Falls and involvement in veterans affairs, 169-76; brevet promotions to Major and Lt. Colonel, 179, 185; at Freedmen's Bureau in Washington, 177-85; marriage and brief stint with 8th U.S. Cavalry on West Coast, 186-94; managing Matthews family farm (see also Catoctin Farmers Club and Potomac Fruit Growers Association), 195-204, 206-9; problems with Grant administration, 214, 216-8, 220-2, 231; employment at Department of Agriculture, 200-4; special agent, Southern Claims Commission, 204-6, 221-2; role on Central and Executive Committees, Va. Republican Party, 210-19; start as Customs special agent in Norfolk coincides with involvement in Treasury Secretary Bristow's bid to win GOP nomination, 221-30; Hayes' contested election and struggle with Mosby brothers for special agent job, 230-43; uncover sugar fraud as customs special agent in Baltimore, 244-59, 270-4, 278; helping Hayes remove Chester Arthur from New York customs house, 242-8, 270, 274; difficulties with Sam Gover and other creditors over family farm, 260-7; demoted as SAIC Baltimore by Cleveland administration and removal to Washington, 279-84; Renewed involvement in veterans organizations (see also Republican Nat. Veterans Committee, Boys in Blue, GAR, MOLLUS, Society of the Army of the Potomac, Loudoun Ranger reunion, 25th N.Y. Cav. Reunion, Fort Stevens memorial proposals and Memorial Day celebrations at Balls Bluff), 273-4, 276, 284-90, 313-4, 317; assignments as SAIC Savannah and with IRS under President Harrison, 281-4; Cleveland's re-election results in demotion followed by exit to farm, 291-301; return to Treasury Dept. under McKinley and last days on the farm, 313-20.

Chamberlin, Susan Ellen (Elliot's twin sister, married William Martin), 8-9, 12, 19, 24, 34-5, 171, 174, 189, 192, 224, 253, 308, 319, 321

Chamberlin, Wellman, 321, 324

Chandler, Zachariah, 231, 286

Clark, Robert M. See BOB

Clendenin, Alice Campbell, 296

Clendenin, Edith, 322

Clendenin, Edward Hume, 312-3

Clendenin, Hume, 296, 303, 309, 312, 324

Clendenin, Mary (see also Mary Chamberlin), 310, 312, 315, 324

Clifton (family farm), 1-2, 119-25, 129, 137, 140, 150, 152-3, 155-9, 161-75, 177-8, 189-93, 198-209, 224, 228, 246, 260-7, 274-5, 277, 282-3, 295-6, 299-310, 312-25.

Cox, Christopher, 221, 228, 276

Cox, William V., 313

Cunningham, John, 17–9, 21–2, 24–9, 34

Custer, Gen. George A., 67–77, 79–80, 83, 85, 89, 93–5, 288

Customs Service, 221-3, 235, 238, 242, 244, 269, 271, 279, 281, 301

Special Agency Division (SAD), 230-1, 235, 241, 244-5, 248, 256, 271, 278, 280-3, 293, 299-300.

D

Davis, Jefferson, 86, 124, 147, 153, 158, 169, 227

Dawson, Edward, 287, 307

Dawson, Scott, 166

Devin, Gen. Thomas C., 82, 84, 90, 93, 98, 149, 152

Devin's Brigade, 86, 150–52

Downey, James, 140-43, 146, 149, 163, 168

Dudley, L. Edwin, 178, 181-2, 195, 212-4, 226-7, 231

Dutton, John B., 128–29, 138–9, 142–43, 145–6, 148, 151–52, 175, 238

Dutton, Lida, 144, 146, 148, 150, 166, 185

Dutton, Lizzie, 128, 140, 147, 149, 191, 319

F

Fauquier County, 19, 64–66, 83–4, 89, 101, 105, 231

Fenton, Gov. Reuben E., 39, 179

Fisher's Hill, 72–73, 76

Folger, Charles J., 270–2

Folsom, Frances, 281

Fort Boise, 194

Fort Columbus, 189

Fort Delaware, 43

Fort DeRussy, 54–5

Fort Dix, 23

Fort Edward, 15

Fort Ethan Allen, 18-9, 21, 35

Fort Harrison, 39

Fort Johnson, 280

Fort Marcy, 18, 21

Fort McClellan, 23

Fort McHenry, 83

Fort Monroe, 225

Fort Slocum, 54, 327

Fort Stevens, 48–52, 54–57, 59–60, 202–3, 288–9, 313–14, 319, 326–9
Fort Stoneman, 76
Fort Sumter, 12–13, 124, 255
Fort Union, 24
Fort Vancouver, 194
Fort Walla Walla, 193–94, 286–7, 307
Fort Wright, 316
Foster, Charles, 283
Fox, George, 216
Frazee, John N., 49
Fredericksburg, Virginia, 22, 43
Free Blacks, 101, 110, 124, 129, 161
Freedmen's Bureau, 165–66, 175, 182–3, 186, 188, 195, 223
Front Royal, Virginia, 64–5, 72–3, 80–2, 89–91

G

Gage, Lyman P., 304, 306
Gallupe, George, 64–5
Gamble, William, 59–60
Garfield, James A., 226–7, 229, 232–3, 268–9, 282
Garrett, James S., 17, 20-4, 28-9, 34, 36
Geary, John W., 130, 134–6, 144
Getty, George W., 25–8
Gettysburg, 24, 27, 29, 31, 41, 140, 145
GOP. See Republican Party
Gover, Ann, 158, 166, 261, 264–5, 296
Gover, Ann Taylor, 116
Gover, Edwin R. (Loudoun Ranger), 103, 124, 136, 143, 146, 152
Gover, Henry, 118, 121, 123, 245, 251, 253, 260, 262, 276–7
Gover, Jesse, 115, 319
  death, 118
Gover, Margaret A. Parkins ("Maggie"), 122, 128, 135–6, 139, 144, 160, 171
Gover, Miriam Griffith Taylor, 114–19, 132, 136-7, 139, 183, 195
Gover, Nathan, 160
Gover, Robert, 115
Gover, Samuel, 115-6
Gover, Samuel A. ("Sam"), 127, 135, 139, 142, 144–5, 153, 198, 260–1, 266–7, 276
Grant, Ulysses S., 83, 89, 92, 108, 201–2, 207, 212, 214
Greenback Raid, 78, 83

H

Halleck, Henry, 24–5
Hayes, Rutherford B., 229–34, 236–8, 241–3, 246–7, 249, 256–8, 268–9
Heaton, Henry, 262, 264
Hough, Amasa, Jr., 127, 142, 153
Hutchinson, John, 148, 193

I

Independent Loudoun Virginia Rangers, see Loudoun Rangers
Internal Revenue Service (IRS), 221–2, 235, 239, 283, 288

J

Jackson, Gen. Nathaniel J., 21, 35-40
Janney, John, 118, 124, 136, 169
Janney, Mahlon, 115
Janney, Samuel M., 63, 117–8, 129, 131, 134, 141, 149, 151, 153
Janney, Sarah, 115
Janney's Mill, 113
Jesse (Black farm hand), 170-2, 186, 190
Jewell, James A. (C/SAD), 281-2

L

Lincoln, Abraham, 49, 61, 80, 124, 147, 177, 180
  assassination, 3, 104–5, 153, 175, 285
Loudoun County, Virginia, 17, 19, 62, 64–5, 84, 89, 269, 273
Loudoun Rangers, 2, 98, 100-4, 106–7, 134, 136–41, 145, 147, 152, 158, 287
Loudoun Valley, 1–2, 84–5, 112, 120–1, 149
Lovettsville, Virginia, 90, 93, 103, 105, 125, 127–8, 150–1, 153, 168–9

M

Maddox, Joseph H., 235, 238
Mahone, William, 213, 218, 256–9, 269–70, 273, 281
Manassas, Virginia, 13, 126–8, 130
Manning, Daniel, 278
Martin, Louis (C/SAD), 278, 280, 283, 299-300
Matthews, Annie (Edith's sister), 1, 120–1, 132, 139–40, 145-6, 152, 156, 158-9, 166-7, 170, 172-4, 184-7, 190-2, 195, 205, 220-1, 223, 225, 228, 230, 246, 248, 259-60, 263, 265, 270, 274, 276, 279-80, 283, 291, 296-307, 312, 315-21, 324
Matthews, Edith (see Chamberlin, Edith Matthews)

Matthews, Edward Young ("E. Y.," Edith's father), 1-4, 119-21, 123-5, 132, 137, 139, 145, 150-1, 169, 173, 189-90, 198, 205, 260
Matthews, Mary Ruth ("Marie," Edith's sister), 1, 120-1, 132, 155-67, 171-3, 184, 186, 188-92, 194, 312
Matthews, Sarah Harris Gover (Edith's mother), 1, 116, 118-9, 132, 139, 149, 155, 158-60, 172, 186, 190, 195, 198, 224, 246, 248, 260, 262-6, 274, 276, 291, 298, 302
McClellan, George B., 61, 67, 130, 134–35, 138, 140
McKinley, William, 10, 304–5, 308, 313
McPherson, Maj. Samuel W., 42, 48–50, 59–61, 67, 69, 76–7, 79, 99, 105–8
Means, Rachel, 141, 166
Means, Capt. Samuel C., 2, 120, 130, 134–7, 141, 153, 161, 198, 206, 267
Merritt, Edwin A., 247–48
Merritt, Wesley, 72, 75, 79, 84, 86–7, 89, 93, 149–50
Middleburg, Virginia, 85–86, 216
Mobberly, John W., 83, 85, 101, 103, 138, 141, 146, 157
MOLLUS (Military Order of the Loyal Legion of the United States), 285, 287, 313
Monocacy Meeting, 112–3
Moore, special agent William B., 235, 239–41
Morrill, Justin Smith (Vermont politician), 10–11, 201–4, 212–3, 220–1, 230, 235–7, 239, 248, 299, 306–7
Morrill, Lot (Treasury Secretary), 230, 235
Morven Park, 161
Mosby, John S., 1, 89, 98, 102, 140, 143; raid on Point of Rocks, Maryland, 143, 238; sanctuaries in Loudoun County, 62; surrender, 153
Mosby, William H., 153, 234–43
Mosby's Partisan Rangers (43rd Battalion, Va. Cav.), 19, 72, 80–1, 83–4, 91
Moses, Vera, 318-9, 322, 324
Myers, Frank M., 74, 123, 134, 164, 176

N
Nevius, Henry M., 49, 53–54, 57, 288–89, 313
Newport News, Virginia, 271–72, 283, 289, 292–3, 295, 299–300, 302
New York State, 7, 9–10, 31–35, 37, 41–42, 79–80, 178–80, 188–9, 246–53, 269–70, 273–4, 321–2
Supreme Court, 256, 270
New York City, 12, 32–33, 37, 40–42, 256, 160, 162, 178–9, 270
Customhouse, 242, 248, 252, 256, 268–71, 279
Draft Riots and Draft Rendezvous, 31-9
Nichols, George F., 14, 21, 29, 95
Norfolk, Virginia, 23, 25, 223–9, 239–42, 271–2, 274, 276, 278, 300
customhouse, 223, 240, 243, 271–2, 299

O
One Hundred and Eighteenth N.Y. Infantry Regiment ("Adirondack"), formation/early training, 14-6; service in Maryland, 16-8; Ft. Ethan Allen and Washington, 18-22; siege of Suffolk, 23-4; Expedition to the South Anna, 25-30; leadership controversy, 31-4, 38-9
Opequon Creek, 69, 71, 80
Order of the American Union (OAU), 227
Order of the Stars and Stripes (OSS), 227, 236

P
Paeonian Springs, Virginia, 305, 315, 318, 322
Pamunkey River, 25–6, 43
Parkins, Nathan, 82–83, 122, 136
Payne, Louis. See Powell, Louis T.
Pension Bureau, 286–87, 299, 307, 317, 321
Perot, William H., 245, 248–50, 253, 255, 278
Perry, Raymond H., 241
Pierpont, Gov. Francis, 136, 141–44, 146, 151, 162–3, 165, 168
Potomac Fruit Growers Association, 199, 203, 207
Powell, Louis T., 104
Purcellville, Virginia, 63, 216

R
Radical Republicans, 177, 180, 183–4, 195, 257, 285
Readjuster Party, 215, 218, 256–59, 264–5, 269–70, 276, 281
Republican Party (GOP), 213, 218, 226–8, 230–32, 237, 257, 269
Richards, Adolphus, 146

S
Seeley, Aaron (Lt. Col. 25th NY Cav), 40-3, 59–60, 71, 73–7, 79–80, 89–93, 95, 97–100, 102-8, 156, 159, 162, 169, 290

Seventh Army Corps, 25-8
Seymour, Maj. Charles J. (25th NY Cav), 42-3, 69-77, 79-90, 102
Seymour, Gov. Horatio, 21, 31-4, 38, 41, 80, 89, 205, 212
Shenandoah Valley. See Valley Campaign
Sheridan, Gen. Philip H., 1, 44, 61, 64, 68, 74, 91
Sherman, John, 236, 244, 268, 271, 304
Sherman, Gen. William T., 95, 226, 236
Sickles, Daniel, 41, 233, 288, 295, 304, 313
Sickles Brigade, 41–42, 288
Sickles Cavalry Association, 289, 313
Slater, Luther, 287
Sixth Army Corps, 48, 54-6, 65, 82, 202, 288-9, 314
Smith, Harry, 292
Smith, Howard, 151
Smith, James M., 59, 67, 71, 76, 79–80, 88, 289
Smith, Lemuel P., 267
Snickers Gap, 63, 84, 86–7
Snickersville, 84, 86–7, 150, 157
Southern Claims Commission (SCC), 204–7, 221–2
Stanton, Edwin M., 38, 42, 61, 65, 144–6, 162, 164–5, 195
Staunton, Virginia, 47, 91, 93–5, 97, 258
Steer, Rachel, 129, 137, 146, 149-50, 152
Steer, Samuel, 124, 126–7, 135–6, 147, 153, 164
Steer, Sarah, 147, 166, 172, 184
Stevenson, John D., 76, 79, 98, 148, 156
Stevenson, William, 28–29, 32
Strafford, Virginia, 7–10, 61, 169
Strasburg, Virginia, 62, 72, 76, 81–2
sugar fraud, 244–59, 270, 272, 279
sugar trade, 247–51, 255–6, 271
Sullivan, Jeremiah, 142, 144

T
Talbott (farm), 2, 119, 124, 129, 134, 138, 152–3, 199–200
Taylor, Henry, 113-4, 124
Taylor, Thomas, 3, 111–4
Taylorstown, 3, 101, 112, 114, 127, 152
Tingle, Amory K. (C/SAD), 230, 240-1, 244–5, 248, 250, 256, 271, 279, 283, 293, 299-300
Torbert, Alfred, 72, 75, 79, 89, 108
True Republicans, 213–15
Trundle, Elizabeth, 205
Twenty-Fifth New York Cavalry ("Sickles"), difficulties in formation at Saratoga and New York Draft Rendezvous, 40-3; in Virginia, 43-6; defense of Washington, (see also Fort Stevens), 47-57; dispute with Maj. McPherson, 58-61; with Sheridan and Custer in the Shenandoah Valley (see also Third Battle of Winchester), 67-77; encounters with Mosby in the Shenandoah Valley and Loudoun, 78-87; winter at Camp Russell, 88-93; advance to Staunton and return, 93-7; guarding Maryland's Potomac border, 97-105; Col. Seeley's court martial, final days, muster out, 105-8, veterans reunions, 289-90, 313-4
Tyler, John Jr., 258
Tyler, Roger, 318

U
Upperville, Virginia, 85, 87

V
Valley Campaign, 61, 64, 67, 69, 72–4, 79, 81, 106, 149
Vernon, George, 274
Virginia's Republican Party, 202, 205, 212, 232, 237, 242, 258
Virts, Virginia, 205

W
Walker, Cornelia Needles, 310
Walker, Elisha, 150, 152, 159, 171, 174, 199, 216–7
Walker, Eliza, 124–5, 134, 166, 322
Walker, Gilbert C., 213, 232
Walker, James, 134–35, 138, 141, 146, 150–2, 199, 205, 261–2
Walker, Robert, 265, 295, 303, 319, 321
Wallace, Lew, 47–48, 326
Wardrop, David, 24–28
Waterford, Virginia, 2–4, 101–5, 110–9, 121–29, 131, 134–41, 145–58, 162–4, 166–9, 171–2, 188–94, 214–6
Quakers, 110, 114, 124, 126, 132, 134, 138, 141
renamed, 113
Watts, Frederick, 201–3
Waynesboro, Virginia, 94–95, 153
Weber, Max, 144, 146, 148
Weeks, Andrew J., 36
Wellman, Walter, 317
Wells, Henry H., 211, 213–4
Wheeler, Stephen W., 49, 77, 79, 88, 91

Whig Party, 10, 118, 121, 124
White, Edward, 146, 213
White, Elijah V., 74, 83, 134, 13738, 164, 175, 212
White, Randolph, 161, 191
White, Sarah, 191
White Post, Virginia, 82
White's Cavalry (35th Battalion Va. Cav., "Comanches"), 136, 138, 140-1, 143, 157, 164, 175-6
Wickham, Williams C., 258
Williamsburg, Virginia, 30, 324
Wilson, James H., 72–73
Winchester, Virginia, 66, 69–71, 80, 83, 95–98, 122, 136, 139, 160
  Confederate evacuation, 136
  Third Battle of Winchester, 69–70

www.ingramcontent.com/pod-product-compliance
Lightning Source LLC
Chambersburg PA
CBHW081327230426
43667CB00018B/2858